Black
CHILDREN
SECOND EDITION

Black Children:
Social, Educational, and Parental Environments
is dedicated to my own Black children and grandsons,
Michael Garnett McAdoo,
John Lewis McAdoo III,
Julia BethAnn McAdoo,
David Harrison Pipes McAdoo, and
Joseph Brandon McAdoo,
William Harrison McAdoo,
John Lewis McAdoo IV,
Michael Garnett McAdoo, Jr.

Harriette Pipes McAdoo, Editor
Michigan State University

Black
CHILDREN
SECOND EDITION

Social,
Educational,
and Parental
Environments

Sage Publications
International Educational and Professional Publisher
Thousand Oaks ▪ London ▪ New Delhi

For information:

Sage Publications, Inc.
2455 Teller Road
Thousand Oaks, California 91320
E-mail: order@sagepub.com

Sage Publications Ltd.
6 Bonhill Street
London EC2A 4PU
United Kingdom

Sage Publications India Pvt. Ltd.
M-32 Market
Greater Kailash I
New Delhi 110 048 India

Printed in the United States of America

Library of Congress Cataloging-in-Publication Data

Black children: Social, educational, and parental environments /
    edited by Harriette Pipes McAdoo.— 2nd ed.
        p. cm.
    Includes bibliographical references (p.) and index.
    ISBN 0-7619-2002-1 — ISBN 0-7619-2003-X (pbk.)
    1. African American children—Social conditions.
        I. McAdoo, Harriette Pipes.
    E185.86 .B524 2001
    305.23—dc21   2001002219

        03   10   9   8   7   6   5   4   3

Acquiring Editor:	Jim Brace-Thompson
Editorial Assistant:	Karen Ehrmann
Production Editor:	Diana E. Axelsen
Editorial Assistant:	Cindy Bear
Copy Editor:	Jacqueline A. Tasch
Typesetter:	Marion Warren
Indexer:	Mary Mortensen
Cover Designer:	Michelle Lee

Contents

Part I   Perspectives on African American Parenting

Part II   Racial Messages

Part III   Educational Environments of Children

Foreword

ASA G. HILLIARD III

The history of social science and its application to African Americans and other ethnic groups who have been the victims of European domination in the world is not a good one. On the one hand, the social sciences were born and nurtured in the context of European hegemony and the companion ideology of white supremacy. There is abundant literature to document the devastating impact of these factors on the practice of the social sciences of anthropology, sociology, psychology, family studies, and other academic disciplines.

Fortunately, a growing number of social scientists are challenging old paradigms, priorities, and findings, with beneficial results. It is with a culturally responsive orientation and a politically aware perspective that *Black Children: Social, Educational, and Parental Environments* makes a major contribution to our knowledge. The authors are uniquely qualified for their task. These results are very meaningful for African American families, their children, and the community in general. In addition, the approaches presented here are models that can be followed with benefit in studies of any ethnic group.

Books such as Robert Guthrie's *Even the Rat Was White,* Alan Chase's *The Legacy of Malthus,* and Leon Kamin's *The Science and Politics of IQ* are examples of the contamination of science with politics and ideology. On the other hand, independent of hegemony and ideology, the powerful reality of cultural diversity in the world demands cultural competency of social scientists. The practice of social science must be more than culturally nonbiased; it must be culturally salient. Cultural reality is a defining aspect of human behavior. Therefore, this is not a matter of fairness, it is a matter of validity. So the political and cultural aspects of context must be taken into account if research findings are to be valid.

These authors are no strangers to the study of children of African ancestry. The book reflects a deep knowledge of the children's culture and conditions, the primary issues, and future needs. Given that all children have needs in common, it is the uniqueness of our children that propels this text.

Asa G. Hilliard III—Nana Baffour Amankwatia II
Fuller E. Callaway Professor of Urban Education
Georgia State University

Preface

This book was designed to explore in depth the unique experiences and situations that are common to Black children and their parents. The volume was developed within the framework that all children—regardless of race, ethnicity, social class, or gender—must complete similar developmental tasks if they are to become competent adults. Therefore, the book does not attempt to duplicate the information that will be found in comprehensive developmental textbooks. Instead, it documents how these developmental tasks are uniquely experienced in the environments of African American children's growth and development.

This is an exploration of the diversities of childhood experience that are confronted by children who are members of the largest American ethnic group of color. Members of this group are defined as those whose ancestors originally are from the many cultural groups of the African continent. This cultural group arrived in America in a variety of circumstances, but the majority were enslaved and continued as children and family members to live lives that were initially dominated by the ethnic group composed of former Europeans. They merged their own cultures, assimilated with their enslavers' culture, and created new and unique forms of family life that were functional for them within the situations in which they existed.

African American children often have existed within environments that have been nonsupportive of their optimum development. The wider supportive network of the African American family and Black community institutions has long attempted to provide a buffer for Black children and to shield them from the negative images that continue to be perpetuated by the wider societal environment. African American children develop a duality for their existence. To be fully functional, they must develop the skills to do well simultaneously in two different cultures, both Black and non-Black.

For this reason, this book has been developed around the themes of the significant environments within the lives of Black children. Each of the environments is viewed as presenting the potential for optimum functioning and, simultaneously, areas for negative and detrimental development. The selection of environments was based on an awareness of the developmental experiences of the majority of Black children. We do, however, attempt to avoid the all-to-common approach of presenting stereotypes of these children. In most literature, the Black child is presented in a pejorative manner. In other literature, the opposite tack has resulted in the Black child being presented in a totally positive manner. To use either approach is to perpetuate myths that shield the wider public, the developmental professionals, and, most important, the parents themselves from the complexities and diversities of the experiences of young Black American children.

There are two major assumptions made as this book is developed: One is related to the economic environment of many Black children and the other is related to the negative images that are carried about Black children by members of the wider society. The first assumption is that despite the economic mobility of some Blacks, the vast majority of Black children live within environments that put their very existence in jeopardy. The second assumption, that non-Blacks view Black children through negative lenses, is shown clearly in several of the reviews of the child development literature in chapters throughout the book. Black children have been totally ignored or, when used in empirical studies, have been treated in a negative manner that would be considered ridiculous, except that the consequences are so real and so painful for the Black child.

The environments that were selected for detailed development are:

1. Theoretical and socioeconomic environments
2. Aspects of parental environments
3. Internal environments of children's racial attitudes and racial socialization
4. Educational environments

The importance of the theoretical frameworks and the empirical environments is stressed. The dominant views presented in the professional writing of these environments are perpetuated in the child development literature by people from the majority racial ethnic groups. Variation of Blacks from the norms formed by majority race children, who often are in adequate economic environments, too often are viewed as deviancy or pathology. The research methodology used and the interpretations of data often are clouded by the continuous reinforcement of negative images in the literature, which makes it difficult for researchers to provide objective examinations and interpretations of data obtained from Black children. To offset the prevailing images in the literature, we have attempted to present empirical and conceptual studies to provide real life data-based analyses of the lives of African American children.

The parental environment is considered to be the most crucial of all. This environment shields children from the often hostile external environment and prepares them to function within their own and the wider environments. This environment often enables children to function effectively within conflicting demands, lifestyles, and value systems. The maternal and paternal roles are highlighted. Too often, the paternal role is considered to be nonexistent or, at best, ineffectual within Black family environments. More Black children are being raised by their grandparents. Part I details the adaptations that African American parents must make to raise their children.

Socioeconomic environments are examined, for these may be the most crucial predictors of the life experiences of young Black children. We feel that extended theoretical or conceptual discussions about the Black child's developmental components would be superfluous unless all developmental aspects are considered in the context of the dire economic realities of many Black children and their families. Recent reports have only demonstrated the increasing poverty in the lives of Black children.

The socioemotional environment of Black children has had differential effects on their self-esteem and their ethnic group identities, as detailed in Parts II and IV. The strains of belonging to an ethnic group that so consistently has faced economic disaster has been hypothesized to cause a lessening of feelings of self-worth. Empirical studies do not support this contention. Black children have been found to have the same distribution of self-esteem scores as those in all other populations. Some feel good about themselves, whereas others do not. Black children have been able to maintain feelings of positive self-worth through their own tenacity and through the support of their wider family network.

The sociocultural environment is seen to interact with the racial attitudes and the independently derived self-esteem of Black children. The pressures of the dominant society have tended to socialize all young children to exhibit preferences for characteristics of the majority non-Black population. In earlier studies, these out-group preferences have been found to move gradually in the direction of racially neutral preferences; finally, by middle childhood, children have adopted strong preferences for their own racial and cultural group. They are able to master the duality of their lives while maintaining positive evaluations of their own self-worth, independent of their racial preferences.

The next environment, in order of importance, is that of education, which is examined in Part III. This is the battleground for much of the negative literature and many of the experiences of Black children. The educational environment has long been felt to be the one saving factor in Black children's lives, allowing them and their families to develop the skills to provide a more secure economic environment. Education has been the source of inspiration, success, and mobility for hundreds of children. At the same time, however, it has been the place where thousands of children have been cowed into lower expectations and where they have experienced failure. Much has been written to document the failure of Black children to succeed within this environment.

Many of the empirical chapters grew out of the efforts of Black researchers who have met, presented empirical papers, and soundly critiqued one another in closed sessions of the Empirical Conference on Black Psychology. This organization has held annual meetings and has provided a fertile environment for enthusiastic junior researchers and for exhausted, overextended senior researchers.

The Empirical Conference on Black Psychology has become the key organization that encourages—in fact, requires—that statements about Black children and their families must be substantiated by hard data. Rhetoric may have its place, but Black children are considered too important to be used in the polemical exercises of professional researchers, regardless of their race.

Attendance at the Empirical Conference is invitational, after a nationwide call has been issued and scores of researchers across the country have responded. Papers are given blind reviews before an invitation is extended. It has become an increasing honor to be selected to attend and present work. It has been, and continues to be, a warm, unique experience. At least nine of the authors of the chapters in this volume have experienced this critiquing process in past years at the Empirical Conference, or are colleagues of Empirical members. Conference authors are considered to be among the best of those who are producing empirical work on Black children. Whether they are colleagues or original members, the Empirical Conference's reach has gone out in the past 20 years to touch many people.

Members of the planning committee for the Empirical Conference are Harriette Pipes McAdoo, Algea Harrison-Hale, Anderson J. Franklin, A. Wade Boykin, and earlier, William Cross. Funding for these efforts has come from the Russell Sage Foundation, the Ford Foundation, the Center for Studies of Minority Groups Mental Health Programs of the National Institute of Mental Health, the Michigan State University (MSU) Foundation, and MSU College of Human Ecology.

One earlier book has been produced from the Empirical Conference process, *Research Directions of Black Psychologists,* edited by A. Wade Boykin, James Anderson, and Frank Yates (1979). That volume was nominated as an Outstanding New Text in Psychology by the American Psychological Association in 1980. The present work will follow the direction of the earlier editing of *Black Children,* in 1985, by providing valuable information for those who are concerned about the optimal growth and development of Black children.

Black Children: Social, Educational, and Parental Environments has been designed to be useful to undergraduate and graduate courses related to human growth and development, ethnic studies, and family life education studies, as well as to professional students in social work, public health, and education. It also will be invaluable for practitioners working directly with Black children and their families. It will be helpful to parents as they attempt to negotiate the environments in which their children must develop.

Finally, I want to express my deepest appreciation for the work that B. J. Bruder, my administrative assistant, has contributed to this project.

Harriette Pipes McAdoo

Reference

Boykin, A. W., Anderson, J., & Yates, F. (Eds.). (1979). *Research directions of Black psychologists*. New York: Russell Sage Foundation.

Part I

Perspectives on
African American Parenting

1

The Dynamics of African American Fathers' Family Roles

HARRIETTE PIPES McADOO
JOHN L. McADOO

The roles of fathers have been ignored too long in the social science literature, particularly in the area of family studies. The dynamics of the roles of
fathers in all ethnic groups—especially among African Americans—have
changed dramatically over the years. The purpose of this chapter is to explore the roles that African American fathers play in families, whether they
are present or absent during the day-to-day running of the household.
These roles must be examined in relation to the many people who may be
part of today's family: mother, grandparents or other relatives, and friends.
This chapter also explores why African American men are seen as invisible
or absent players in the family dramas that take place every day.

Over the last several decades, changes have occurred in almost all
American families because of economic factors. It is increasingly difficult
for one parent to earn enough of a living wage to support an entire family.
Jobs have gone offshore, companies have been downsized, and entire industries have been mechanized. Those at the lower end of the occupational
hierarchy, particularly poor people of color, have experienced the most

AUTHOR'S NOTE: This chapter was originally published as "Fathers and Families in a Diverse and Changing World," in *Michigan Family Review*, 3(1), pp. 7-15 (1998), and is reprinted here with permission. It was written from notes made prior to the death of John L.
McAdoo.

negative effects. Most mothers of young children are now employed at some level outside the home, marriages and relationships have been truncated and changed, children are being cared for through a variety of arrangements, and parents of both genders have had to become involved in family tasks. These are patterns that have existed within the African American community for decades.

African American fathers are as different from one another as they are from other groups. They come in all shades, shapes, and types; yet, the stereotyped Black father is seen—by those who are not of color—as a visitor to his family, underemployed, marginal to his family, inattentive to his children, rather violent, and plainly not in the family picture. In reality, African American fathers are as dedicated to their children and families as are men of other racial groups; some are models of perfection, and some are deadbeats.

An important issue is why the negative image of Black males and fathers is so strongly embedded in the psyches of lay and professional family social scientists. The reasons lie in three historical circumstances: economic isolation, enslavement, and the carryover of African family forms that differ from Western forms. The contemporary portrayal of African American men in the media only adds to the negative images. The ultimate reason for this depiction is the racism that Black men face throughout their lives. This racism has isolated them from the world of work and education and is seemingly ingrained in the fabric of Western societies.

The widely held ethnocentric view is that a traditional family is an independent residential unit with two parents and a mother who is not employed. Even though we know that, historically, this has not been the pattern for all families, it is still presented as the ideal. In past times, women on the farms and in rural areas worked as hard as their husbands, families were often extended, and roomers in the home were commonplace. Yet, we are presented with a romantic version of family.

A report about child-rearing practices from the National Institute of Child Health and Human Development contradicts the traditionalist view. It concludes that young children cared for by adults other than their parents have normal cognitive, linguistic, social, and emotional development. In addition, the quality of infant care, which ranges from poor to excellent, greatly influences the development of young children; good quality day care can to some extent make up for poor parenting (Scarr, 1997). We can no longer say that children need full-time maternal care, and working parents can be more confident that quality day care can be a positive experience for their children. Indeed, children may benefit from multiple attachments, rather than an exclusive attachment to their mothers.

The roles of fathers in families are influenced by internal as well as external factors (Bowman, 1993; Hyde & Texidor, 1994; McAdoo, 1988, 1993). Research has shown that social capital networks, in the form of coping strategies and community-wide resources, help to mediate negative external influences that may interfere with the parenting role (Hanshaw & Thompson, 1996; McAdoo, 1993). Furthermore, Taylor, Chatters, Tucker, and Lewis (1990) stated that significant growth has occurred in the quality and quantity of African American family life. Fathers, however, are often overlooked by researchers, professionals, and practitioners (McComanachie, 1994).

African American fathers are away from their children for reasons linked to external factors: unemployment, imprisonment, high death rates, and the imbalance of the male-female ratio. Joblessness among Black fathers meant separation from their families so that mothers could qualify for state aid. Historically, Black males have always been incarcerated at a higher rate than White males (Ross, 1996). Black men in Michigan die prematurely at twice the rate of White men and the rest of the state's population (Bauza, 1997). Traditionally, there have been more marriageable women than men (Chapman, 1996). Therefore, some children are born to older women who do not expect to marry the fathers of their children.

The African American Family and Male Demography

The Black population of the United States in 1996 was 33.9 million, or 12.8% of the total, up from 30.4 million in 1990 (U.S. Bureau of the Census, 1996a). At present, there are 15.8 million Black men and 18.1 million Black women. Blacks are younger than Whites, with a median age of 28.4 years for Blacks compared to 36.5 years for Whites. About 31% of Blacks are married and live with their spouses, but 43.6% have never married. The respective figures for Whites are 57.8% and 23.6%.

Fathers in Families

The family structure of Black children in 1996 differed drastically from families in the White population. About 71.6% of White children under age 18 live with both parents, whereas only 38.7% of Black children do; 56.9% of Black children live with their mother. The 3.9% of Black children who live with only their fathers is similar to the White rate of 3.4%. Grandparents are parenting 5.4% of Black children, and 1.3% are in foster care (Children's Defense Fund, 1997; U.S. Bureau of the Census, 1996b).

A major difference between Black fathers and fathers in other groups at the same income level is that fewer Black fathers live in the same home as their children. Black families did not differ significantly from mainstream families until 1970, when the majority still had two parents. Modifications in the structure and orientation of Black families occurred then as the result of a series of recessions in the 1970s, which became depressions with the Black community (Hill, 1988). These changes also occurred within mainstream families in the late 1980s and began to have even greater impact in the 1990s.

Men's Health

The survival rate has been declining for Black men, whereas the rate for Black females and all White groups has been increasing. According to a Michigan study, African American Male Initiative, the percentage of men expected to live until age 65 fell from 61% in 1960 to 58% in 1993 (Bauza, 1997). Black males had the highest rate in 9 of the top 10 causes of death in Michigan, with the exception of suicide. The suicide rate is 11% lower for Black men than for White men.

The top five causes of death among Black males in Michigan (in descending order) are heart disease, cancer, homicide, AIDS, and stroke. Black males die of heart disease at a rate 46% higher than that of White males; cancer deaths are 50% higher—with the highest rates for lung, rectal, and prostate cancer. In 1990, Michigan's homicide rate was 58% among Blacks. In 1995, Black men between 25 and 34 years of age were nine times more likely to die as a result of homicide than were White men in that age group. AIDS is the second leading cause of death among Black men between ages 25 and 49, and the third-highest cause for Whites that age (Bauza, 1997).

These bleak statistics point to the fact that African American families cannot depend on a long sustained presence of the father. Even if the father lives with the family, his time there is more limited than it is in other types of families.

Education and Workforce Participation

In 1996, national education levels were lower for Blacks: 84.5% had finished high school, 32.1% had attended college, and 13.7% had college degrees. For Whites, the figures were 92%, 29.4%, and 30.6%, respectively. Blacks older than 16 years of age were in the labor force, and 67% of Whites were employed also. The unemployment rate in 1996 was 11.6% for Blacks and 4.6% for Whites. The per capita income for Blacks was $10,982, compared to $19,759 for Whites (U.S. Bureau of the Census, 1996a). In families with children under 18 years, 7.7% of the Black households had fathers who worked and mothers who remained at home (Children's Defense Fund, 1997). The income of 2.1 million Black families (26%) was below the poverty level (U.S. Bureau of the Census, 1996a). The result is that 41.3% of Black children under age 18 years live below the poverty line. Some child support was received by 14.4% of the children under age 18, usually from the father (Children's Defense Fund, 1997). The poverty levels of families, the strain of coping in families who are recognized to be different from the mainstream, and the inequities associated with education provided to African Americans have been major obstacles to educational achievement of Black children.

Perspectives on Father's Roles

The major roles that Black fathers play are marital, provider, and child-socializing roles. Ecological systems theory (Bronfenbrenner, 1979) allows exploration of the historical, political, and familial influences on African American fathers. Peters (1997) notes that this theory allows researchers and practitioners to observe paternal role functioning in the environment in which it occurs. To understand the developmental processes of parents and children of color, it is necessary to explore the intersection of social class, culture, ethnicity, and race to create integrative models for developmental competence (Coll et al., 1996).

More research is needed on the use of religion, the extended family, and community networks by men for parenting (Bowman, 1993; McAdoo, 1993). Fathers of various socioeconomic classes make choices in their efforts to support their families and to find stability. We need to explore the positive and negative roles they play and the impact on their families. Two areas in particular deserve attention.

The Child Socialization Role

Although mothers are the primary socializers of children, both parents provide nurturance and discipline. In a study across two generations, Cazenave (1981) found that fathers reported that they were more involved with their children than their own fathers had been. They took an active part in child care, changing diapers and playing with their children. This trend is similar in all racial groups and social classes.

It has been found that in two-parent, middle-class homes, the nurturance of mothers leads to positive self-esteem in their children (McAdoo, 1993). There appeared to be no direct relationship between highly nurturant fathers and self-esteem of the children. Instead, there was an indirect relationship between the fathers' nurturance of the mothers and the higher self-esteem of their children. When a nurturant environment is provided, children are often able to develop better self-esteem.

In families where the father's interaction with the children is limited because of marital status, he still has an effect on the children, but to a lesser extent. The role of father figure is assumed by male relatives, partners of the mother who live in the home, and extended-family helping networks (McAdoo, 1997).

The Marital Role

Little attention has been paid in the literature to the positive role that the husband plays in the nurturance of his wife. Some researchers have investigated the relationship between paternal happiness or subjective well-being and marital happiness (Taylor, Chatters, Tucker, & Lewis, 1990). In a study by Zollar and Williams (1987), all classes of Black men reported greater happiness than did their wives, but both spouses reported being happy. As the couples grew older, the levels of happiness increased for both partners.

Even in families in which the father is not present, the father has an important role to play. Researchers have found that more than 30% of the fathers in divorced, separated, or never-married homes do have some level of contact with their children (McAdoo, 1983, 1992). These contacts are not necessarily regular—and often financial aid is irregular—but they still are important. It should be noted that two thirds of unmarried mothers are women older than age 20, and many of them have been married previously.

Only one third of unmarried births are to adolescents (Edelman, 1987). This finding refutes many of the stereotypes about young men and women. Many of the unmarried women older than 20 years of age have been married before but were unable to maintain the marriage because of the imbalance in the gender ratio. The competition for men is often a real problem in Black communities.

Conclusions

Some African American fathers live within the home, and some live outside the home. Blacks have families of all types and have continued to exist within the supportive networks composed of kin, friends, churches, and the greater community (Hatchett, Cochran, & Jackson, 1991). These supportive networks are the mainstay of many African American families. With increasing poverty, restructuring in the marketplace, and unending racism, such networks will continue to be essential to fathers and their families. To meet the developmental needs of fathers, mothers, and their children, it is necessary to assess accurately the roles fathers play, the pressures under which they function, and who they are in reality.

Literature on African American fathers is available and should be sought out by family researchers and practitioners. It is counterproductive to use stereotypes about the roles that African American fathers play within families. As we look at the intersection of class, race, and culture, we cannot assume that all African American fathers are lower class. We must realize that fatherhood cuts across all groups; all people will want services at some point in their existence. Misconceptions will interfere with the provision of services, assistance, and support that these families need. If nonobjective approaches are used, research efforts will lead to incorrect conclusions. Social service workers, educators, researchers in the family field, and the parents themselves need more objective images that will allow for more meaningful service and support.

References

Bauza, M. (1997, July 19). Black men facing "health crisis." *Lansing State Journal,* p. 83.

Bowman, R. (1993). The impact of economic marginality among African American husbands and fathers. In H. P. McAdoo (Ed.), *Family ethnicity: Strength in diversity*. Newbury Park, CA: Sage.

Bronfenbrenner, U. (1979). *Ecology of human developmental experiments by nature and design*. Cambridge, MA: Harvard University Press.

Cazenave, N. (1981). Black men in America: The quest for "manhood." In H. P. McAdoo (Ed.), *Black families* (pp. 176-185). Beverly Hills, CA: Sage.

Chapman, A. (1996). The Black search for love and devotion: Facing the future against all odds. In H. P. McAdoo (Ed.), *Black families* (3rd ed.). Newbury Park, CA: Sage.

Children's Defense Fund. (1997). *The state of America's children yearbook 1997*. Washington, DC: Author.

Coll, C., Lamberty, G., Jenkins, R., McAdoo, H. P., Wasik, B., & Garcia, H. (1996). An integrative model for the study of developmental competencies in minority children. *Child Development, 67,* 1891-1914.

Edelman, M. (1987). *Families in peril: An agenda for social change*. Cambridge, MA: Harvard University Press.

Hanshaw, C., & Thompson, D. (1996, November). *Fathers raising children with special needs: The role of social capital*. Paper presented at the annual meeting of the National Council on Family Relations, Kansas City, KS.

Hatchett, S., Cochran, D., & Jackson, J. (1991). Family life. In J. Jackson (Ed.), *Life in Black America*. Newbury Park, CA: Sage.

Hill, R. (1988). Cash and noncash benefits among poor Black families. In H. P. McAdoo (Ed.), *Black families* (2nd ed., pp. 306-318). Beverly Hills, CA: Sage.

Hyde, B., & Texidor, M. (1994). Childbearing and parental roles. In R. Staples (Ed.), *The Black family: Essays and studies* (3rd ed., pp. 157-164). Belmont, CA: Wadsworth.

McAdoo, H. P. (1983). *Extended family support of single Black mothers: Final report* (Grant No. RO1 MH3159). Washington, DC: National Institute of Mental Health.

McAdoo, H. P. (1992). Upward mobility and parenting in middle-income Black families. In A. Burlew, C. Banks, H. P. McAdoo, & D. Azibo (Eds.), *African American psychology: Theory, research, and practice*. Newbury Park, CA: Sage.

McAdoo, H. P. (Ed.). (1997). *Black families* (3rd ed.). Thousand Oaks, CA: Sage.

McAdoo, J. L. (1988). Changing perspectives on the role of the Black father. In P. Bronstein & C. Cowan (Eds.), *Fatherhood today: Men's changing role in the family* (pp. 79-92). New York: John Wiley.

McAdoo, J. L. (1993). The role of African American fathers: An ecological perspective. *Families in Society: The Journal of Contemporary Human Services, 74*(1), 28-35.

McComanachie, H. (1994). Changes in family roles. In P. Mittler & H. Mittler (Eds.), *Innovations in family support for people with learning disabilities* (pp. 73-83). Lancashire, UK: Lisieux Hall.

Peters, M. (1997). Historic note: Parenting of the young. In H. P. McAdoo (Ed.), *Black families* (3rd ed., pp. 167-182). Thousand Oaks, CA: Sage.

Ross, M. (1996, June). The death penalty in Black and White. *Friends Journal*, pp. 10-14.

Scarr, S. (1997, August 8). New research on day care should spur scholars to reconsider old ideas. *Chronicle of Higher Education*, p. A48.

Taylor, R., Chatters, L., Tucker, M., & Lewis, E. (1990). Developments in research on Black families: A decade review. *Journal of Marriage and the Family, 542*, 993-1014.

U.S. Bureau of the Census. (1996a, March). *The Black population in the United States*. Washington, DC: Government Printing Office.

U.S. Bureau of the Census. (1996b, March). *Current population survey*. Washington, DC: Government Printing Office.

Zollar, A., & Williams, J. S. (1987). The contribution of marriage to the life satisfaction of Black adults. *Journal of Marriage and the Family, 49*, 87-92.

2

Diverse Children of Color

Research and Policy Implications

HARRIETTE PIPES McADOO

Children from families of color have become an increasing area of concern for those who conduct research and formulate social policy. Study and preparation are required if we are going to address the challenges that will come from a demographically diverse society. This chapter will explore the dynamics of the changing demography of the United States. It will examine the type of policy that would be more supportive of diverse children and their families and the programs that are most in jeopardy. Information will be given on sources of help for researchers and parents.

Contextual Diversity of Children of Color

Policy and research considerations of children of color will be discussed within the framework of an integrative model for the study of developmental competencies in children of color (Garcia Coll et al., 1996). The social position and social stratification constructs are at the core of a theoretical formulation of children's development. Variations in behavior occur in large part because children grow up in different developmental niches

AUTHOR'S NOTE: This chapter was first published in H. E. Fitzgerald, B. M. Lester, and B. S. Zuckerman (Eds.), *Children of Color: Research, Health, and Policy Issues*, 1999, pp. 205-218. Used with permission.

(MacPhee, Fritz, & Miller-Heyl, 1996). Cochran, Larner, Rile, Gunnarsson, and Henderson (1990) stated that structural forces in society constrain network membership by means of group identity, prejudice, and limited access to social capital, which varies with cultural placements. The importance of the history of oppression, prejudice, and social and economic segregation in policy formulation must not be overlooked.

The financial resources that are available to families of color are directly related to the economic isolation in which these families have been placed. For all families, national trends in available resources have changed enormously in the past half century; there have been six demographic transformations (Hernandez, 1997). The first three were the shifts to nonfarm work, smaller family size, and increased educational attainment. The second three had special significance for people of color: increased employment of mothers, the increase in families headed by a single-parent mother, and a substantial rise in childhood poverty. For families of color, these changes occurred about 10 years sooner than for families who were not of color (McAdoo, 1996b). Compared to other children, those affected by these changes live in environments that differ in many ways in social organization, economic opportunities, and behaviors (Hernandez, 1997).

As these culturally diverse families are examined within the context of the family, school, and community, both the strengths and weaknesses in the developmental process will need to be considered (Boykin & Toms, 1985; Garcia Coll & Garcia, 1995; McAdoo, 1993a, 1995). In the context of family, the cultural sustaining roles of family and kin networks are a protective resource for children of color. These inhibiting and promoting environments influence the day-to-day interactions and experiences, interacting with the children's personal characteristics. However, McLoyd (1990) found that ethnic groups consistently differed in measures of social stratification. When these differences were covaried in pooled regressions, ethnicity did not explain variance in child-rearing practices. Therefore, it is necessary to be sensitive to the conditions of the children and not to be driven by what may be conceptual error, as we formulate policies that will address the issues that confront them.

Major Increases in Multicultural Families

Few other countries have the proportion of ethnic families that the United States will soon have. As a country, the United States is moving toward a complex level of multiculturalism. The United States will need to become more pluralistic in orientation to address the multiple issues that will become of even more concern in the immediate future. A fact of family life in America today is that families are composed of differing groups of individuals who have had many diverse experiences.

In North America, family lives fall into many differing patterns of economic and social levels (Hernandez, 1997; McAdoo, 1997). The growing diversity of economic and social experience is increasing exponentially. The common element of being of a particular cultural descent does not entirely determine what the life patterns of individuals will be. Some groups of color have made major gains and are prospering; some groups are barely holding on to their gains; and some families are sliding backward into economic chaos (McAdoo, 1995).

U.S. society is becoming more multicultural and multidimensional. Growing proportions of people in U.S. society are coming from diverse families, through both natural population increases and immigration. The U.S. Bureau of the Census predicts that the current population of 281 million will more than double to 571 million by the year 2100, with the median age rising above 40 and much larger proportions of ethnic people of color (Schmid, 2000). Whites of European descent will become a new minority group by then.

The changes have been the result of legal and illegal immigration and natural increase. U.S. immigration was efficient when labor was needed for growing industrialization. However, immigration becomes less appealing during recessions and economic slowdowns, when there are fewer optimistic views of the future. Immigration is less desirable when surplus labor comes in different colors, languages, family patterns, and diverse religions (McAdoo, 1995). As a result, policies are beginning to change to prevent further entry of people who are so different.

The United States has had a major influx of immigrants, as well as births among people of non-European origin. Drastic population increases have been found in certain areas of the country. The number of people whose ancestors are from China, Japan, and the Pacific Rim countries increased by 74.3% between the 1990 and the 2000 census. During the same period, the number of people of Latino descent increased by 57.9%, whereas the number of African Americans increased by 21.1%. The number of Native Americans, Eskimos, and Aleuts increased by 14% to 2.4 million people, just less than 1% of the total population. Families belonging to non-White ethnic groups are no longer a minority in the United States (U.S. Bureau of the Census, 2000).

Immigration among people of color has come at a time when natural birthrates have also increased. People of color tend to have larger families, because of cultural patterns and, often, religious beliefs about not limiting family size. An additional factor is that families of color are younger than families of non-Hispanic White groups. Therefore, they will be in a fertile age range far longer than most families. As a result, people of color have more children per family, whereas nonethnic families have children at less than the replacement rate. More children of color are being born, and fewer are born who are not of color.

These changes have caused each new generation of Americans to be more racially and ethnically diverse than its predecessor. The use of the term *minorities* has been questioned, because of the demographic changes that are occurring in the United States. Soon, children of color will no longer be minorities; they will become the numerical majority of people in U.S. society. The United States will reflect the colors, the races, the diversities, and the languages of different groups who are now citizens.

Of the original baby boomers, 75% were non-Hispanic Whites of European descent. In 1994, fewer than 66% of newborns were of non-Hispanic European descent. These new babies differ radically from each other in race, socioeconomic class, and living arrangements. In addition, the next baby-boom generation, the children of the boomers, will be the first generation to question seriously all traditional racial categories. This is because so many of today's children are of mixed races. Owing to an increase of interracial marriages, there is one mixed-race child for every 35 babies born in their cohort (Mitchell, 1995).

The growing majority of people of color is already occurring in states such as California, New York, and Florida. These groups will increase even more in the future. Legal and informal means have forced these groups of color into a even narrower context of isolation. But, these populations are here to stay, and we must therefore begin to examine our research and policy approaches to these families (McAdoo, 1996b).

Resilience and Challenges Among Families of Color

Different social classes, divergent cultural groups, different ethnic group identities, and historical experiences in North America have resulted in family patterns and trends for people of color that may differ from those of families who are not of color. Ethnic families have been resilient and have overcome many overwhelming barriers (McAdoo, 1995; Wilkinson,

1997). These families, from all socioeconomic levels, should be viewed not only as people who need help but also as groups who collectively are becoming the dominant groups in North America.

Attempts have been made to focus on the large number of families of color who are in trouble. The tendency is to overlook the families who are coping under less than ideal conditions and are rearing their children to be competent adults despite difficult situations.

It is important to understand that the common element of being people of color does not decide exactly what the life patterns of individuals will be (McAdoo, 1995). It has, however, become more difficult to excel under the present environment.

Sociocultural Challenges of American Families and Children

The exchange of information between racial-cultural groups and the wider society is facilitated by social networks of kin and friends (Wellman, 1990). Communication between the spheres of children's lives is a crucial component of coping with differences that may exist.

When parents are in situations that may be marginal, they have difficulty responding to the developmental needs of their children. Even when sociocultural resources are more than adequate, children and families confront the damaging effects of devaluation, racism, and isolation, which can have an impact on self-efficacy (Harrison, Wilson, Pine, Chan, & Burie, 1990; Jones, 1991; McAdoo, 1995). The inability to access effectively the resources of the mainstream environment is one reason that people of color tend to rely on their extended family and friends. The social capital that is available from their social networks will play an important role in the ability of parents and children to obtain needed resources from the environment. The assistance of social networks buffers the negative effects of stress from being in a different social-cultural group in an environment in which cultural differences are not readily accepted. People of cultural groups have developmental niches that are unique to each racial-ethnic group (MacPhee et al., 1996). These niches are elements that should be taken into consideration as research is designed and policies are implemented to support people of color.

Child-rearing practices of some groups will be affected by the ecological dimensions of class, ethnicity, and educational attainment. Native Americans, for example, tend to emphasize communal values (Dehyle,

1992). Hispanic parents tend to value conformity and obedience and are more inclined to be controlling and to use punishment (Knight, Verdin, & Roosa, 1994; Martinez, 1993; Quintana, 1991). These attributes and values may put the children at a disadvantage when they enter into competition with the mainstream environment.

Researchers have recognized that factors beyond the structural makeup of the family may help to determine indirectly the disciplinary styles and practices of families (Erlanger, 1974; Portes, Dunham, & Williams, 1986). However, when the data are examined, the factors of racial diversity, lower income, and lower socioeconomic status are often confounded. The designers of research efforts will need to be more articulate in the delineation of characteristics. They should attempt to avoid the misuse of lower socioeconomic status samples for their research. Too often, low-income groups are selected because they are more accessible, compliant, and unsophisticated. To be able to make observations about people of color that accurately present generalizable data, it will be necessary to examine the wide range within each ethnic group. Middle-class, educated, urban people will often present pictures of their family life and their children that contradict many of the widely accepted beliefs or stereotypes about a particular group.

When racial or ethnic groups are analyzed for commonalities, strong similarities emerge. There are very similar family patterns in groups of color: Native American, Mexican American, African American, and Asian families. Common cultural patterns have contributed to the resilience of families of color. These include supportive social networks, flexible relationships within family units, a strong sense of religiosity, extensive use of extended-family helping arrangements, the adoption of fictive kin who become family, and strong identification with their racial group (Allen, 1993; Boyd-Franklin, 1989; McAdoo, 1993b; Stack, 1974).

The role of extended families among African Americans is practically the same as the *familism* among Mexican Americans, but the two groups are rarely discussed together or compared. The respect that is given to the elderly in Asian families is similar to the central role of the elderly in Native American families. All of these groups have culturally evolved in unique ways that reflect the country of origin, the culture, and the geographic location of their groups; yet, their family patterns are very similar. Elements of these behaviors are imbedded in a sense of obligation and are reciprocal in nature (Dodson, 1996; Keefe, Padilla, & Carlos, 1979; McAdoo, 1996a; Quintana, 1991). The sense of connectedness and respect for family members is commonly found at all socioeconomic levels, even in groups with few resources. Cochran et al. (1990) argued that structural forces in society constrain social network memberships that vary across cultures by means of prejudice, group identity, and limited access to social capital. Even when behaviors of some individuals are far from ideal, as may happen in poor urban centers, elements of care and respect for kin and fictive kin will be found.

These extended family arrangements are coupled with extensive helping arrangements that are typical social supports of many families (Aschenbrenner, 1975; Harjo, 1993; McAdoo, 1993a). These "webs of kinship" form cooperative relationships that cut across families and households (Fortes, 1949). However, extended-family helping arrangements have begun to be modified with increasingly limited family resources. These extended patterns of resilience have continued to provide protection for entire families and communities. Family members have found themselves financially stretched and are often close to the breaking point because of economic survival issues. Younger people are also growing up without the protection of wider family networks and, therefore, family patterns are changing. Extensive helping networks are slowly becoming erased because of the economic situations in which families find themselves.

Family patterns are changing in all U.S. families; the primacy of dual-parent homes may never be recovered. Younger people are growing up without the protection of wider family networks and without both parents in the home. In many groups, higher proportions of children are growing up without both parents. Economic uncertainty accounts for many of the family structures, but the overwhelming causal factor is the gender imbalance in families of color (Bennett, Bloom, & Craig, 1989; Cready & Fossett, 1997; Guttenberg & Secord, 1983; McLanahan, Garfinkle, & Watson, 1988; Tucker & Mitchell-Kernan, 1991). There are simply not enough men available who would make good husbands. This fact causes marriages not to form or, when formed, to disintegrate because of stresses and strains that are inherent within the living situations of groups of color.

Research Implications of Changes in American Families

We will need to be aware of policies and research approaches that will be more sensitive to children who come from different experiences and cultures. Design requirements, along with the race and culture of the people involved in the design process and the actual interviewing, may have to changed to reflect the group that is being studied.

A more realistic view of these diverse children and families is required, and the use of stereotypes must be avoided. Researchers need to explore the wide range of socioeconomic groups that are found in all ethnic groups. Misleading pictures are obtained when only the mean scores of groups are known. On all variables, researchers need to get the distribution of the social class groups' educational levels.

The country of origin for children is a very important but too often overlooked design element. For example, too many studies use the term *Hispanic* for anyone who speaks Spanish, regardless of the very different cultural groups and individual histories that have this characteristic. The term *Asian* is sometimes used to embrace Chinese, Japanese, East Asians, and other groups without regard for significant cultural differences. Yet, we know that there are different cultural norms, child-rearing approaches, and levels of acculturation in each of these groups.

When research projects are designed, it is necessary to be aware of the difficulties in analyzing the results of any study that uses this approach. It is impossible to have a sample of 80% to 90% children of color without discussing the contextual cultural situation of these children. But U.S. society is not open to and accepting of change. We should be aware that the growing levels of conservatism did not emerge overnight. Groups within U.S. society are afraid of change. They are well financed and organized, and they are not concerned with being supportive of families and children who may be different. These are the opinions and attitudes with which we are faced in attempts to help children.

As researchers, it is necessary to respond to new policies that are often not supportive of children. Politics plays a great part in the situation of children and families today. Family income, welfare, and resources are for the most part politically determined, especially for people of color. As many changes occur in Congress and in state capitals of the United States, it is often easy to overlook the political realities that are being played out within the lives of families.

Policy Implications of Growing Multiculturalism

Policies are often based on commonly acknowledged beliefs about different groups of people of color. However, the research on which such beliefs are based often has major faults that contradict many of the claims presented in current literature. Because of changes in demography, increases in families of color, and a growing awareness of the role of culture, family of origin, and race, better research is required on which to base policies.

Changing demographics have not been accepted with total grace by people who are in positions of authority. People of color are increasingly faced with problems, including the devaluation of their institutions, individuals, values, and artifacts related to their cultures. This devaluation is the result of insistence on the continuation of former research paradigms that are European American in orientation. The predominant cultural beliefs have been handed down for generations in the European context and have been brought to the Americas.

The use of these ideas has placed people of color into situations and institutions that are indeed inferior. As a consequence, people of all colors have found themselves isolated to an extent from the educational and economic mainstream of American life. Devaluation of cultural attributes has a profound impact on the development of people of color, as they become isolated from the mainstream of American life.

Research agendas must be developed for all areas related to children. In the health arena, for example, the House Appropriations Committee has asked for such an agenda related to health care as it affects quality and outcome measures. The Agency for Health Care Policy and Research (1997) has responded by presenting a report.

The goals of preventing or coping with poverty among children are in direct competition with policies that are currently being considered. These new policies are aimed at concentrating wealth and power among a few White males. We once held these truths to be self-evident: the rights of children, female empowerment, nondiscrimination, and the desire for a level playing field. Now, we have found that progress in this direction is tenuous and totally dependent on the whims of those who are in power at any one time.

Programs such as school lunches and welfare support are being threatened. Calls are being made for block grants instead of funding for individual programs at the state level. This is very reminiscent of earlier calls for state's rights, especially in the Southern segregationist states. Racism is entering the process even more, as cognitive abilities are assailed in the "bell curve," as affirmative action is denigrated, and, increasingly, as policymakers are becoming more conservative in orientation. Majors (1994) has stated that achieving racial justice is a long-term goal.

Research agendas for children and families of color will have to focus on specific issues. To be effective in providing programs based on empirical research, and in transferring what is known to people who are making policy and implementing programs, it will be necessary to modify the approach to working with policy makers and program administrators. Research can no longer be conducted as it has been in the past. As researchers, we may not have money, but we do have the skills to design studies and interpret data. The usual tactic of conducting studies and simply publishing the results in academic journals is no longer sufficient. Empirical research must provide succinct results. Suggested programs of implementation must be provided to the agency or department that handles such policies. Issues and monies are moving from the national to the state level. Researchers had trouble keeping abreast of federal policies; now, it will be necessary to understand 50 different state levels of policies on important issues.

There is a need to become more vigilant and politically active and to conduct research that will document the impact of new policy changes that are sure to come. Research must be made accessible to advocacy groups. There is an important need for us to translate our findings into language that is understandable to advocacy groups, policy designers, and congressional staffers. Testimony will have to be refined for congressional hearings. It has been said that research findings and interpretations of concepts should be placed on two or at most three 4-by-6-inch bibliography cards. More information than this will not be read or remembered. To be useful, it is necessary for us to become educated and to pass on our knowledge to those who are formulating policies. Individual efforts will have to be augmented with the collective voices of our professional organizations, coupled with the skillful use of multimedia tools. We will need to become more sophisticated in the uses of media and publicity to allow the research findings to be heard by those who are in position to formulate policies.

Some organizations and advocacy groups have materials that can be very helpful as we attempt to work on behalf of policies that are supportive of families of color. The National Council of Family Relations's (1994) Public Policy Committee has produced a pamphlet titled *Action Alert: Critical Legislative Developments at Federal and State Levels Affecting Poor Families*. It condenses the most recent and relevant ideas of the Children's Defense Fund, the Child Welfare League, and the Center for Law and Social Policy. Foundations are becoming increasingly important in translating existing knowledge. The Packard Foundation (Center for the Future of Children, 1995) is one example of a foundation attempting to provide objective analysis and evaluation of effective programs and policies. This book is presented to complement the technical analysis that is found in academic journals. It also attempts to supplement coverage in the popular press and to augment the efforts of special-interest groups.

Marian Wright Edelman (1996) of the Children's Defense Fund has stated that we must formulate an action agenda for our children. Edelman has provided directions for useful policies affecting African American children, but these would be relevant for all people of color and for researchers who are sympathetic to the cause of influencing policies and programs that will be appropriate in the coming years. Edelman stated that it is necessary to (a) become an active and effective advocate for ethnic and poor children; (b) become well informed about the needs of children and families in your area and nationally; (c) not accept or give excuses for doing nothing; (d) understand that no one is going to give these children anything, especially if it seems to be taking something away from mainstream children; (e) recognize that the ground rules for achieving change are different now than they were 5 or 10 years ago; (f) focus attention and energies; (g) expend energy on real issues and not on symbolic ones; (h) persist and dig in for a long fight; (i) use what you have to get what you must; and (j) confront and attack the right enemies and stand united. This action agenda for children and families focuses on specific goals to help children now and in the future. Two kinds of activities for researchers and advocacy workers are included in this agenda. Activities at the local level will need to be undertaken and often can entail the use of existing research and resources. At the state and national levels, the policies and practices will need to be changes at the institutional and governmental level. As we move into a period when more people of color will be in the labor market, and when they will form the majority of people in this country, we are all dependent on the futures of our families and children. They will need to draw even more on the traditional sources of support that have been found to be successful in the past.

Aldous (1997) has stated that in the future, emphasis will be placed on coalition building and negotiation among leaders of interested groups. A variety of agencies and programs have responsibility for the health, education, social and financial welfare, housing, and civil rights of America's children. These policies and programs will need to be monitored and changed to ensure the equitable treatment of all children. The future of all of us will be determined, to a great extent, by our ability to take action and to improve the situation of America's children.

References

Agency for Health Care Policy and Research. (1997). *Child health services: Building a research agenda.* Washington, DC: U.S. Department of Health and Human Services.

Aldous, J. (1997). Making family policy in difficult times. *Journal of Family Issues, 18*(1), 4-6.

Allen, W. (1993). Black families: Protectors of the realm. *Morehouse Research Institute Bulletin, 93*(3), 1-3.

Aschenbrenner, J. (1975). *Lifelines: Black families in Chicago.* New York: Holt, Rinehart & Winston.

Bennett, N., Bloom, D., & Craig, P. (1989). The divergence of Black and White marriage patterns. *American Journal of Sociology, 95,* 692-722.

Boyd-Franklin, N. (1989). *Black families in therapy.* New York: Guilford.

Boykin, A., & Toms, F. (1985). Black child socialization: A conceptual framework. In H. P. McAdoo & J. L. McAdoo (Eds.), *Black children: Social, educational, and parental environments* (pp. 33-52). Beverly Hills, CA: Sage.

Center for the Future of Children. (1995, Spring 1995). *The future of children, 5*(1). Los Angeles: The David and Lucille Packard Foundation.

Cochran, M., Larner, M., Rile, D., Gunnarsson, L., & Henderson, C. (1990). *Extending families: The social networks of parents and their children.* Cambridge, UK: Cambridge University Press.

Cready, C., & Fossett, M. (1997). Mate availability and African American family structure in the U.S. nonmetropolitan South, 1960-1990. *Journal of Marriage and the Family, 59,* 192-203.

Dehyle, D. (1992). Constructing failure and maintaining cultural identity: Navajo and Ute school leavers. *Journal of American Indian Education, 31,* 24-47.

Dodson, J. (1996). Conceptualizations of African American families. In H. P. McAdoo (Ed.) *Black families* (3rd ed.). Thousand Oaks, CA: Sage.

Edelman, M. (1996). An advocacy agenda for Black families and children. In H. P. McAdoo (Ed.). *Black families* (3rd ed., pp. 323-332). Thousand Oaks, CA: Sage.

Erlanger, J. (1974). Social class and corporal punishment in childrearing: A reassessment. *American Sociological Review, 39,* 68-85.

Fortes, M. (1949). *The web of kinship.* London: Oxford University Press.

Garcia Coll, C., & Garcia, H.A.V. (1995). Hispanic children and their families: On a differing track from the very beginning. In H. Fitzgerald, B. Lester, & B.

Zuckerman (Eds.), *Children of poverty: Research, health care, and policy issues* (pp. 57-83). New York: Garland.

Garcia Coll, C., Lamberty, G., Jenkins, R., McAdoo, H. P., Crnic, K., Wasik, B., & Garcia, H. (1996). An integrative model for the study of developmental competencies in minority children. *Child Development, 67,* 1891-1914.

Guttenberg, M., & Secord, P. (1983). *Too many women? The sex ratio question.* Beverly Hills, CA: Sage.

Harjo, S. (1993). The American Indian experience. In H. P. McAdoo (Ed.), *Family ethnicity: Strength in diversity.* Newbury Park, CA: Sage.

Harrison, A., Wilson, M., Pine, C., Chan, S., & Burie, R. (1990). Family ecologies of ethnic minority children. *Child Development, 61,* 347-362.

Hernandez, D. (1997). Child development and social demography of childhood. *Child Development, 68*(1), 149-169.

Jones, J. (1991). Racism: A cultural analysis of the problem. In R. Jones (Ed.), *Black psychology* (3rd ed., pp. 609-635). Berkeley, CA: Cobb & Henry.

Keefe, S., Padilla, A., & Carlos, M. (1979). The Mexican-American as an emotional support system. *Human Organization, 38,* 144-152.

Knight, G., Verdin, L., & Roosa, M. (1994). Socialization and family correlates of mental health outcomes among Hispanic and Anglo American children: Consideration of cross-ethnic scholar equivalence. *Child Development, 65,* 212-224.

MacPhee, D., Fritz, J., & Miller-Heyl, J. (1996). Ethnic variations in personal social networks. *Child Development, 67,* 3278-3295.

Majors, B. (1994, September/October). General assembly news. *World: Journal of the Unitarian Univeralist Association,* pp. 47-53.

Martinez, E. (1993). Parenting young children in Mexican American/Hispanic families. In H. P. McAdoo (Ed.), *Family ethnicity: Strength in diversity.* Newbury Park, CA: Sage.

McAdoo, H. P. (1993a). Family equality and ethnic diversity. In K. Altergott (Ed.), *One world, many families* (pp. 52-55). Minneapolis, MN: National Council on Family Relations.

McAdoo, H. P. (1993b). The social cultural contexts of ecological developmental family models. In P. Boss, W. Doherty, R. LaRossa, W. Shumm, & S. Steinmetz (Eds.), *Sourcebook of family theories and methods: A conceptual approach* (pp. 298-301). New York: Plenum.

McAdoo, H. P. (1995). African American families: Strength and realities. In H. McCubbin, E. Thompson, A. Thompson, & J. Fromer (Eds.), *Resiliency in ethnic minority families: African American families.* Madison: University of Wisconsin Press.

McAdoo, H. P. (1996a). *Black families* (3rd ed.). Thousand Oaks, CA: Sage.

McAdoo, H. P. (Ed.). (1996b). *Family ethnicity: Strength in diversity.* Newbury Park, CA: Sage.

McAdoo, H. P. (1997). African American families. In C. Mendel, R. Habenstein, & R. Wright (Eds.), *Ethnic families in America: Patterns and variations.* Englewood Cliffs, NJ: Prentice Hall.

McLanahan, S., Garfinkle, I., & Watson, D. (1988). Family structure, poverty, and the underclass. In M. McGeary & L. Lynn, Jr. (Eds.), *Urban change and poverty* (pp. 102-147). Washington, DC: National Academy Press.

McLoyd, V. C. (1990). The impact of economic hardship on Black families and children: Psychological distress, parenting, and socioemotional development. *Child Development, 61,* 311-346.

Mitchell, S. (1995, October). The next baby boom. *American Demographics,* pp. 22-31.

National Council of Family Relations. (1994). *Action alert: Critical legislative developments at federal and state levels affecting poor families.* Minneapolis, MN: National Council of Family Relations.

Portes, P., Dunham, R., & Williams, S. (1986). Assessing child-rearing styles in ecological settings: Its relations to culture, social class, early age intervention, and scholastic achievement. *Adolescence, 21,* 723-735.

Quintana, F. (1991). *Pabladores: Hispanic Americans in the Ute frontier.* Notre Dame, IN: University of Notre Dame Press.

Schmid, R. E. (2000, January 13). Twice as many Americans by 2100. *Augusta Chronicle.*

Stack, C. (1974). *All our kin: Strategies for survival in a Black community.* New York: Harper & Row.

Tucker, B., & Mitchell-Kernan, C. (Eds.). (1991). *The decline of marriage among African Americans: Causes, consequences, and policy implications.* New York: Russell Sage.

U.S. Bureau of the Census. (2000). *Overview of race and Hispanic origin: Census 2000 brief.* Washington, DC: Government Printing Office.

Wellman, B. (1990). The place of kinfolk in personal community networks. *Marriage and Family Review, 15,* 195-225.

Wilkinson, D. (1997). American families of African descent. In M. DeGenova (Ed.), *Families in cultural context: Strengths and challenges in diversity* (pp. 335-360). London: Mayfield.

3

African American Grandmothers' and Grandfathers' Influence in the Value Socialization of Grandchildren

LINDA McWRIGHT

The preponderance of literature on African American grandparents has primarily focused on grandmothers, extended-family support networks, child care, and family structures. These studies significantly added to the understanding of African American grandparenting dynamics. However, questions regarding cultural belief systems that are passed on from one generation to another are limited.

Researchers have established that grandparents are instrumental in the transmission of family values and beliefs (McAdoo & McWright, 1994; McWright, 1998). The transmission of family values is crucial to the maintenance of culture and the socialization of children within families. Several cultural relativity scientists have investigated proverbs and the values inherent in the proverbs as a viable means of transmitting values transgenerationally. Proverbs are statements that reflect the shared values, beliefs, and wisdom of the African American culture (McWright, 1998). However, most proverb research designs focus on mothers' and grandmothers' perceptions and are descriptive rather than theory-based and predictive. There is a need to empirically address the influence of African American grandmothers and grandfathers in transgenerational value transmission and its impact on the socioemotional growth and development of their grandchildren.

Based on a regional survey of African American mothers, this chapter examines the mothers' perception of the transgenerational transmission of grandparents' values and the socialization of the mothers' children through proverb use. Proverb researchers suggest several factors to consider in assessing the transgenerational transmission of values between grandparents and grandchildren: (a) the theoretical framework, (b) the nature of proverbs being transmitted, (c) the mothers' perceptions of the values inherent in the proverbs, and (d) the grandparents' contribution to the socialization of grandchildren. These factors are considered in turn.

Social Exchange Theory

Jackson (1994) established social exchange theory as an appropriate framework for considering the transmission of proverbs because it addresses the interdependence of individuals inside the family system and the rewards of cultural value transmission. Jackson asserts that social exchange involves making investments that constitute some level of commitment or obligation to the other party. In this context, proverbs are shared because they have special meaning to family members. If an individual adopts a belief in a proverb and receives a certain amount of pleasure (healthy or unhealthy) or reward (internal or external), that individual will be more inclined to share the proverb with other family members. Moreover, once there is family acceptance of a proverb, there is mutual trust among family members that the process will not end. Furthermore, such a family is less likely to consider other proverbs outside of those in which they already believe (Jackson, 1994).

African American Proverbs

During slavery, proverbs served as pearls of wisdom for the survival of the extended family and provided ingenious educational systems because children were surrounded by the lessons of their ancestors, dead or living, in such a natural way that they didn't recognize the experience as a lesson. Parents developed instructional and socializing techniques for their children that were difficult to suppress. Because parents worked long hours, the task of transmitting the culture fell to elderly grandparents, who cared for and taught small children who were too young to work. When children were old enough to work in the fields, their education into the culture continued with the singing of spirituals and work songs and the telling of stories, proverbs, and folktales (Mitchell, 1986).

Most recently, Prahlad (1996), in a social-cultural ethnographic study, examined proverb use and meaning among African Americans in a variety of settings, such as pool halls, bars, auto repair shops, retirement homes, medical offices, churches, basketball courts, and football fields, as well as folklore archives from the University of California, Berkeley, and other researchers. Prahlad found that proverbs were less likely to be used during formal church services and more likely to be used in informal conversations between men and women before and after church services. The greatest percentage of proverb interactions occurred in the home between adults and children. The proverbs were often combined with a facial expression and vocal intonations to reinforce a message.

Prahlad further asserted that proverbs are linked to the historical past as well as the personal past of the users. Users are in some way mediating between the past and present as well as mediating symbolic meaning and value each time a proverb is verbalized. Furthermore, through the process of symbolic meaning, the proverbial items become folk beliefs, truths to live by or personal mottoes. In other words, a proverb that was learned by someone whose parents used it repeatedly would have greater symbolic value for that person than a proverb overheard in a conversation among strangers. In this context, proverbs are instrumental in teaching values.

The Mothers' Perception of the Values Inherent in the Proverbs

Page and Washington (1987), using a sample of single low-income mothers, and McAdoo (1991), using a sample of working- and middle-class mothers and fathers, are credited for establishing one of the most developed conceptualizations of proverb transmission. Employing a social-cultural contextual approach, these cultural-relativity scholars created an empirical framework to (a) measure the mothers' perception of the proverbs transmitted across three generations and (b) describe the values inherent in the proverbs. Their work distinguished 15 African American church-based proverbs (see Table 3.1, p. 31, for a list).

Page and Washington (1987) examined the relationship between traditional proverbs and Rokeach's values and the disposition to receive and transmit values intergenerationally. The mothers in the study transmitted values related to equality, family security, ambition, and social control. These proverbs represent the worldviews of equality, family security, and self-control. The values of family and equality were most highly valued across the three generations. These proverbs measured the values of self-respect and sense of accomplishment. The values the single mothers seemed to embrace were those that promote family, community, and independence, whereas those least embraced were individually centered values.

McAdoo (1991), building on Page and Washington's (1987) research, studied transgenerational values and socialization outcomes for children. The working- and middle-class parents in this study stressed values that were family-oriented, that promoted self-sufficiency, self-esteem, and positive racial attitudes. McAdoo concluded that the family and work values that African Americans have cherished in the past are fundamental in the socialization of African American children today.

Page and Washington's (1987) study is significant in intrafamilial value literature, as they established normative measures for assessing and interpreting cultural norms (McWright, 1998; Prahlad, 1996). McAdoo's (1991) work supported the increasing reliability of proverbs as a viable means of transgenerational value transmission by examining gender and socioeconomic status factors. Previous researchers found it difficult to demonstrate empirically the influence of parental values on their children, with correlates ranging from the .20s to the low .30s (Whitbeck & Gecas, 1985). Page and Washington's finding revealed correlates that ranged in the .80s, and McAdoo's correlated results ranged from the .20s to the .60s. However, these studies were somewhat limited. Both of the studies examined maternal value transmission. The values that grandfathers believed in and passed on were not mentioned. This study of value transmission includes grandfathers as a unit of analysis and uses Page and Washington's and McAdoo's conceptualizations and measurement of values.

Grandparents' Influence in the Socialization of Grandchildren

Grandparents function as a family resource through intergenerational connectedness by bridging the past, present, and future, giving younger generations a sense of security, aiding in their ego development, and offering them a vision of the future (Baranowski, 1982; Kornhaber & Woodward, 1981; McAdoo & McWright, 1994; McWright, 1998). Kornhaber and Woodward (1981), in a study of grandparent-grandchild relationships, identified several modes of attachment between grandchildren and grandparents: (a) the grandparent as the essence of family bonds; (b) the grandparent as a constant object in the life of the grandchildren, who knew their grandparents through personal experience and through stories; (c) grandparents as teachers of basic skills; (d) grandparents as negotiators between children and parents, helping one to understand the other; (e) same-sexed grandparents as role models for adulthood; (f) grandparents as connections between the past and future, giving a sense of historical and cultural rootedness; (g) grandparents as determinants of how the young feel about the old in society; and (h) grandparents as great parents, providing a secure and loving adult-child relationship that is next in emotional power only to the relationship with parents. Through these emotional bonds, grandparents socialize grandchildren (McAdoo & McWright, 1994; McWright, 1998).

Additional research examining the grandchild's perspective of grandparents identified these roles: historian, mentor, role model, wizard, and nurturer/great parent. Historian grandparents provided both a cultural and familial sense of history. Mentor grandparents offered wisdom, taught grandchildren to work with the basics of life, and deepened sex-role identity. Role model grandparents served as examples for the grandchildren's future roles as grandparents, for aging, and for family relationships. The fourth role, wizard grandparents, were magical to grandchildren, telling stories and stoking the grandchildren's imagination. The fifth role, nurturer, was the most basic role that grandparents played, widening the support system for grandchildren (Kornhaber & Woodward, 1981). The love, nurturance, and acceptance that grandchildren have found in the grandparent-grandchild relationship conferred a natural form of social immunity on grandchildren, which they could not get from any other person or institution (Kornhaber & Woodward, 1981; McAdoo & McWright, 1994). A summary of Kornhaber and Woodward's research showed the significance of emotional attachments and socialization between grandparents and grandchildren to the grandchildren's socialization. However, their investigations failed to differentiate findings by race, gender, or social class (McWright, 1998).

Based on the review and assessment of the proverb and value literature, the following relationships were hypothesized, dealing with value transmission between the mothers' perception of the grandparents' values and the mothers' perception of the grandchildren's values.

1. There are positive significant relationships between the Grand-mothers' Value Index and the Grandchildren's Value Index.
2. There are positive significant relationships between the Grandfa-thers' Value Index and the Grandchildren's Value Index.
3. There will be a positive significant transgenerational effect be-tween the Grandmothers' Value Index and the Grandchildren's Value Index.
4. There will be a positive significant transgenerational effect be-tween the Grandfathers' Value Index and the Grandchildren's Value Index.

Methodology

Sample

The data for this study were drawn from the Ethnic Families Research Project (EFRP) data set (McWright, 1998). The original survey, which be-gan in 1995, involved a Midwestern sample of 259 African American and Mexican American parents. The families were recruited through commu-nity centers, public agencies, and schools in two metropolitan cities. From the targeted areas, community residents, public agencies, and school per-sonnel identified potential respondents from African American families. Potential respondents were screened by telephone, and face-to-face inter-views of 2½ hours in duration were conducted with those who qualified and who were willing to participate.

The proposed unit of analysis for this study consisted of a subset of 127 African American women who were raising learning disabled elementary or middle school-age children. Data on the grandparents and grandchil-dren were collected from the mothers who participated in the study. The majority of the respondents were biological mothers; 11% were extended-family members in the parenting role (grandparents, aunts, and sisters). The mothers ranged in age from 21 to 60 years, with a mean age of 34 years. Most of the mothers, 57%, were previously married, and 42% were never married. The mean years of education completed by the moth-

TABLE 3.1 Traditional African American Proverbs

1. What goes around comes around.
2. Blood is thicker than water.
3. Cleanliness is next to Godliness.
4. If you don't think anything of yourself, no one will.
5. Man cannot live by bread alone.
6. Don't count your chickens before they are hatched.
7. All men are created equal.
8. The darkest hour is just before the dawn.
9. The blacker the berry the sweeter the juice.
10. You can't see the valley if you don't climb the hill.
11. Don't let no one make you ugly.
12. Pretty is as pretty does.
13. Better be envied than pitied.
14. The hand that rocks the cradle rules the world.
15. It is a poor dog that won't wag his own tail.

ers was 12.4 years. Of the sample, 28% of the mothers reported being middle class, 28% were working class, and 42% were impoverished. The average number of children per household was 3.2. The mean age of the children was 9 years; 65% were males and 35% were females.

Measures

The instrument included 15 traditional proverbs (Table 3.1) that assessed the beliefs of African American adults (Page & Washington, 1987). The Southern, church-based proverbs examined the intrafamilial and transgenerational transmission of values of African Americans (McAdoo & McWright, 1994).

Page and Washington's (1987) instrument was a 45-item scale that contained three proverb indexes: (a) the proverbs the mother believed in, (b) the proverbs the grandmother believed in (perceived proverb from mother), and (c) the proverbs the mother planned to pass on to her children (perceived grandchildren proverbs). McAdoo (1991) added to the instrument by including the proverbs the grandfather believed in (perceived proverb from father). Each of the four proverb scales was presented on a 5-point Likert scale, with 1 = *never used proverb* and 5 = *believed in and used frequently.*

Principal component factor analyses were conducted on each index to determine which proverbs clustered together to ascertain the strongest values inherent in the proverbs. For the purposes of this study, coefficient loadings of .50 or greater were included in each index. The mean scores of each of the factors were summed to develop a value index (Whitbeck & Gecas, 1985). The variables rotated into five factors. The first three factors were selected. Factor loading in the fourth and fifth rotation were eliminated due to one-item loading and/or low coefficient scores. The first coefficent loading in each factor, which is the strongest coefficient, was used to determine the value labels of each factor grouping (Borg & Gall, 1983; McAdoo, 1991; McWright, 1998). The factors are listed in Tables 3.2 and 3.3. Each factor was tested for reliability. The factors appeared to measure several values, but to list them all in this discussion would be very confusing; therefore, the established rule of factor labeling was used in this study.

Dependent Variable: Mothers' Perception of Children's Socialization Values

The Grandchildren's Proverb Index, which measured the proverbs the mothers planned to pass on to their children, was used to develop the Grandchildren's Value Index. The factor-analyzed proverbs that the mothers would like to pass on to their children represent values related to family connectedness on Factor 1 (see Table 3.2). Factor 2 depicted value dimensions of spirituality, whereas positive racial attitude was measured in Factor 3. The overall reliability for the Grandchildren's Value Index was .79. The grandchildren's factor-analyzed values were family connectedness, spirituality, and positive racial attitude.

Independent Variables: Mothers' Perceptions of the Grandparents' Values

The Grandmothers' Proverb Index, which measured the proverbs the mothers received from the grandmothers, was used to develop the Grandmothers' Value Index. The grandmothers' factor-analyzed proverbs represented the value dimension of family connectedness on Factor 1 (See Table 3.3). Factor 2 reflected values of positive self-image. Factor 3 was eliminated because the Cronbach's alpha was .109. The Grandmothers' Value

TABLE 3.2 Factor Analysis of the Grandchildren's Proverbs

Grandchildren's Proverbs	Grandchildren's Factors		
	1	2	3
Family connectedness			
Blood is thicker than water.	.77		
If you don't think anything of yourself, no one will.	.72		
Cleanliness is next to Godliness.	.69		
Don't count your chickens before they are hatched.	.59		
What goes around, comes around.	.55		
Spirituality			
The darkest hour is just before the dawn.		.74	
All people are created equal.		.70	
Don't let no one make you ugly.		.65	
It's a poor dog that won't wag his own tail.		.56	
Positive racial identity			
The blacker the berry, the sweeter the juice.			.76
You can't see the valley if you don't climb the hill.			.65
Better be envied than pitied.			.52
Pretty is as pretty does.			.52

Index consisted of the values of family connectedness and positive self-image. The overall reliability of the index was .55.

The Grandfathers' Proverb Index, which measured the proverbs the mothers received from the grandfathers, was used to develop the Grandfathers' Value Index. The grandfathers' factor-analyzed proverbs on Factor 1 represent values that seem to measure family connectedness (see Table 3.4). Factor 2 denoted values related to perseverance, whereas Factor 3 depicted values related to positive self-image. The Grandfathers' Value Index represented the factor-analyzed values of family connectedness, perseverance,

TABLE 3.3 Factor Analysis of the Grandmothers' Proverbs

	Grandmothers' Factors		
Grandmothers' Proverbs	1	2	3
Family connectedness			
Blood is thicker than water.	.86		
Cleanliness is next to Godliness.	.75		
What goes around, comes around.	.72		
One cannot live by bread alone.	.68		
The blacker the berry, the sweeter the juice.	.60		
If you don't think anything of yourself no one will.	.59		
Positive self-image			
Better be envied than pitied.		.79	
It's a poor dog that won't wag his own tail.		.70	
Pretty is as pretty does.		.63	
The hand that rocks the cradle rules the world.		.63	
Perseverance			
The darkest hour is just before the dawn.			.72
You can't see the valley if you don't climb the hill.			.53

and positive self-image. The overall reliability for the index was .96. The Grandfathers' Value Index internal consistency score was the highest of the four indexes.

Analysis Plan/Strategies

Zero-order correlation was used to examine the extent of the association among the variables and the associations between the independent variables and the proverbs passed on to the grandchildren (McAdoo, 1991;

TABLE 3.4 Factor Analysis of the Grandfathers' Proverbs

Grandfathers' Proverbs	Grandfathers' Factors		
	1	2	3
Family connectedness			
Blood is thicker than water.	.87		
What goes around, comes around.	.77		
Don't count your chickens before they are hatched.	.75		
Cleanliness is next to Godliness.	.72		
The blacker the berry, the sweeter the juice.	.70		
If you don't think anything of yourself no one will.	.64		
Perseverance			
It's a poor dog that won't wag his own tail.		.83	
You can't see the valley if you don't climb the hill.		.75	
Don't let no one make you ugly.		.69	
The darkest hour is just before the dawn.		.61	
Positive self-image			
Better be envied than pitied.			.80
All people are created equal.			.66
The hand that rocks the cradle rules the world.			.65
Pretty is as pretty does.			.63
One cannot live by bread alone.			.52

Page & Washington, 1987). Regression analyses were used to determine if a relationship existed between the predictor variables and the dependent variables (Borg & Gall, 1983).

Results

Zero order correlations were conducted to examine relationships between the factor-analyzed value indices (see Table 3.5). Hypothesis 1 suggests that the grandmothers' values and the grandchildren's values have a significant positive relationship. Hypothesis 1 was not rejected. Significant bivariate correlations for the grandmothers' values and the grandchildren's socialization values range from .47 to .30. The more the grandmothers believed in the values of family connectedness, positive self-image and perseverance, the more likely the mothers passed on values to their children related to family connectedness, spirituality, and positive racial attitude. The two grandmothers' values were significantly related to all three of the grandchildren's values. These finding indicate that the mothers attempted to socialize the grandmothers' values in the grandchildren.

Hypothesis 2, which suggests that there are positive significant relationships between the Grandfathers' Value Index and the Grandchildren's Value Index, was not supported. The grandfathers' value domains of assertiveness and positive self-image did not have a statistically significant relation to the values the mothers planned to pass on to their children. However, the grandfathers' and grandchildren's variable of family connectedness had a positive significant relationship. The correlations indicated that the mothers were likely to pass on grandfathers' values of family connectedness.

Multiple regressions were conducted to determine possible transgenerational effects of the grandmothers' and grandfathers' values on the socialization of the grandchildren. Only the variables that were significant in the correlation were used in the path analyses (Borg & Gall, 1983). There were two steps in the analyses to determine the effects of the independent variables. In Step 1, the grandchildren's values of family connectedness, racial identity, and spirituality were used as the dependent variables, with the grandmothers' values of family connectedness and positive self-image as independent variables in a regression model. In Step 2, the grandchildren's values were entered as a dependent variable with the grandfathers' value of family connectedness as the independent variable. The enter method was used in the regression analyses.

Hypothesis 3 predicts a positive significant transgenerational effect between the factor-analyzed Grandmothers' Value Index and the factor-analyzed Grandchildren's Value Index. Hypothesis 3 was not rejected.

TABLE 3.5 Zero-Order Correlations of the Variables

	Children's Values		
	Family Connectedness	Spirituality	Racial Identity
Grandmothers' values			
Family connectedness	.47***	.34***	.30**
Self-image	.18*	.31**	.31**
Perseverance	.03	.03	−.13
Grandfathers' values			
Family connectedness	.24**	.16	.06
Assertiveness	.05	.15	.09
Self-image	.10	.17	.16

*$p < .05$. **$p < .01$. ***$p < .001$.

Table 3.6 shows the results of the regression analyses for the variables. The grandmothers' predictors, family connectedness and positive self-image, accounted for 43% of the variance in the grandchildren's outcome variable, positive racial identity, $F(3, 119) = 8.99$, $p = .001$. In addition, the grandmothers' predictors, family connectedness and positive self-image, were found to be significant and accounted for 41% of the variance in the grandchildren's value of spirituality, $F(3, 119) = 12.07$, $p = .000$. Also, a transgenerational positive significant relationship between the grandmothers' value of family connectedness and the grandchildren's value of family connectedness accounted for 49% of the variance. Findings suggested that grandmothers' value of family connectedness and positive self-image had a strong transgenerational influence on all three of the grandchildren's values.

Hypothesis 4 was supported. There was a positive significant transgenerational effect between the Grandfathers' Value Index and the Grandchildren's Value Index. The grandfathers' predictor values of family connectedness accounted for 32% of the variance in the grandchildren's value of family connectedness, $F(3, 113) = 4.37$, $p = .001$ (see Table 3.6). The regression analyses indicated that the grandfathers' predictor

TABLE 3.6 Stepwise Multiple Regression Analyses: Children's Values and Predictors, Grandmothers', Grandfathers', and Mothers' Values

Outcome Variable	Step	Predictor	B	t	R^2	p
Children's values		Grandmothers' values				
Family connectedess	3	Family connectedess	.47	5.58	.49	.000
Racial identity	3	Family connectedness	.28	3.20	.43	.002
	2	Self-image	.25	2.96		.004
Spirituality	3	Family connectedness	.29	3.37	.41	.001
	2	Self-image	.24	2.84		.005
		Grandfathers' values				
Family connectedness	2	Family connectedness	.51	3.36	.32	.001

pointed to a transgenerational effect on the grandchildren's values of family connectedness.

Summary of Findings

The data obtained to test the hypotheses under consideration have been presented in this chapter. Each hypothesis was restated, and the results of an analysis of the responses to the items selected to determine the validity of the hypotheses were elaborated. The findings were analyzed by using correlations and regressions at the .05 level of significance.

The results of the present study clearly indicate that the mothers' proverb transmission was influenced by the grandmothers' and grandfathers' proverb use and transgenerationally influenced the socialization of their grandchildren. These findings supported Jackson's (1994) assumption that families repeat behaviors that were rewarding in the past. Researchers have both accepted and relied on family interactions as being critical in understanding the family system and the socialization of children. The mothers' values, the grandparents' values, and the grandchildren's values encompassed socialization features in African American family systems.

Research Question

The major question of this study was whether there are relationships between the grandmothers' and grandfathers' values and the socialization values of their grandchildren. The regression model indicated that there are transgenerational linkages between the grandmother-child and the grandfather-child. Grandmothers and grandfathers who value family connectedness socialize their grandchildren to value family and to have positive racial identification. These findings were congruent with McCoy (1985); grandmothers and grandfathers played an important role in linking generations even when they didn't take an active role in the grandchildren's lives. Grandparents have been found to influence the family socialization experiences as grandchildren develop and formulate their values and beliefs (Roberto & Skoglund, 1996). The grandmothers' values of family connectedness and self-image increased the grandchildren's racial identity and spirituality.

Cultural transgenerational socialization involved the transmission of certain messages and patterns that related to personal and group identity, the relationship between and within groups, and the ethnic group's position in society (Marshall, 1995). The family socialization values seem to influence the grandchildren's group identity related to race and spirituality.

Interestingly, Rokeach (1973) found that racial identity was a value fathers passed on to their children. However, in this study, the grandmothers were passing on male-type values to their grandchildren. The majority of the mothers are single. It appeared they had assumed dual roles and had taken the responsibility of instilling male-oriented values. In addition, married mothers, as a result of current social norms, may be experiencing a diffusion of roles as they increasingly share financial responsibilities in the family.

Limitations of the Study

Several caveats need to be considered when interpreting the current results. First, because this study involved secondary analysis, the variable measures were limited to those in the earlier data collection. Second, the sample did not include fathers or children as units of analysis in the research. Thus, the generalizability of the findings to the larger population of children or fathers is unknown. Third, the results were limited based on the indirect method used to assess grandparents' and grandchildren's values. The results were based on the mothers' perception of the transgenerational values. Fourth, the study did not assess the effects of the quality of personal relationships between the groups. Researchers suggested that intergenerational value transmission was related to the quality of the parent-child relationship (Whitbeck & Gecas, 1985). The present study did not control for quality of relationship; however, the study did find a strong positive association between the mothers' values and the grandchildren's values.

Conclusion

This study has attempted to integrate a social exchange model with a family ecosystem in assessing transgenerational value transmission. Taken as a whole, the findings suggest the usefulness of incorporating propositions drawn from exchange theory into the examination of family values. To understand more fully the process of transgenerational value transmission and the socialization outcomes for children, more attention needs to be paid to the mediating factors, such as the age of respondents, the age of children, and the education and socioeconomic status of parents and grandparents.

The family values scale is a reliable instrument in assessing family socialization values. Although it is inappropriate to infer that perceptions of mothers are the sole or most important determinant of transgenerational value assessment, it seems appropriate to conclude that mothers are able to socialize their children based on proverbs that have served as coping mechanisms for African Americans since enslavement.

Implications

The results of this study are consistent with findings from earlier studies indicating that contemporary African American mothers believe in the same values that their ancestors held and that these values are being passed on to their children. Like the earlier studies, this study emphasizes the importance of considering generational value transmission in the socialization of African American children. Such considerations are necessary so that researchers and family professionals can enhance their understanding regarding African American family functioning.

In addition, this information may contribute to an understanding of grandfathers in African American families. Findings from this study tended to suggest that values affecting family connectedness and security may be contributed through the grandfathers' role in the family. These findings are inconsistent with earlier value studies of fathers that used a predominately White sample. The earlier studies indicated that fathers are conditioned to value achievement and intellectual pursuits, whereas mothers are socialized to value love, affiliation, and the family.

Conversely, the grandparenting literature suggests that grandparents function as a family resource bridging the past, present, and future for younger generations, giving them a sense of security. A possible reason for this difference is that African American grandfathers may be more likely to assume the father's role in homes where the father is not present. Therefore, those working with families may need to consider the grandfathers' role in assessing families and understanding children.

Findings from the present study illustrate the importance of ecological research design in examining African American families. The information from this study may encourage family professionals to consider other tools in assessing socialization factors related to African Americans. Cultural issues are of particular concern for family practitioners, social workers, and teachers. Professionals may find it helpful to integrate proverbs into the discussion when developing coping strategies for parents and children.

Suggestions for Future Research

The Ethnic Family Research Project (EFRP) data set affords an excellent opportunity for researchers to continue to examine factors related to value transmission and outcomes for children. Surveys of the EFRP assessed mothers over a 2-year period, providing two separate databases. Some of the variables are the same in both data sets. Therefore, future researchers may wish to examine changes over time in the subjects' value orientation.

In addition, more research is needed to fully understand how proverbs and child characteristics combine with predictor variables such as parental stress, depression, self-concept, parents' expectations and aspirations for the child, and parents' health to influence value transmission. Other contextual factors, such as neighborhood safety, housing situations, parent-child relationships, age and education of mother, family environment, and racial issues, may be included in future studies. Finally, future studies may also consider using the father, grandmother, grandfather, and child as the unit of analysis. The present study focused on the mother as the unit of analysis. The assessment of other family members may add to the information that shapes the development of African American children.

References

Baranowski, M. D. (1982). Grandparent-adolescent relations: Beyond the nuclear family. *Adolescence, 17,* 575-584.

Borg, W. G., & Gall, M. D. (1983). *Educational research: An introduction.* New York: Longman.

Jackson, V. R. (1994). Proverbs: A tool for work with older persons. In V. R. Jackson (Ed.), *Aging families and use of proverbs for values enrichment.* New York: Haworth.

Kornhaber, A., & Woodward, K. L. (1981). *Grandparent grandchildren: The vital connection.* New York: Doubleday.

Marshall, S. (1995). Ethnic socialization of African American children: Implications for parenting, identity development, and academic achievement. *Journal of Youth and Adolescence, 24*(4), 377-396.

McAdoo, H. P. (1991). Family values and outcomes for children. *Journal of Negro Education, 60,* 361-365.

McAdoo, H. P., & McWright, L. A. (1994). The roles of grandparents: The use of proverbs in value transmission. In V. R. Jackson (Ed.), *Aging families and use of proverbs for values enrichment.* New York: Haworth.

McCoy, E. (1985, March). What's great about grandparents. *Parents,* pp. 65-70.

McWright, L. A. (1998). *African American mothers' perceptions of grandparents' use of proverbs in values socialization of grandmothers.* Unpublished doctoral dissertation, Michigan State University.

Mitchell, E. P. (1986). Oral tradition: Legacy of faith for the Black church. *Religious Education, 81,* 93-112.

Page, M. H., & Washington, N. D. (1987). Family proverbs and value transmission of single Black mothers. *Journal of Social Psychology, 127,* 49-58.

Prahlad, S. A. (1996). *African American proverbs in context.* Mississippi: University Press of Mississippi.

Roberto, K., & Skoglund, R. (1996). Interactions with grandparents and great-grandparents: A comparison of activities, influences, and relationships. *International Journal of Aging and Human Development, 43*(2), 107-117.

Rokeach, M. (1973). *The nature of human values.* New York: Free Press.

Whitbeck, L., & Gecas, V. (1985). Value attributions and value transmission between parents and children. *Journal of Marriage and the Family, 50*(1), 829-840.

Part II

Racial Messages

4

The Village Talks

Racial Socialization of Our Children

HARRIETTE PIPES McADOO

African American children are the result of all of the experiences that they, their parents, and their ancestors have experienced. The concept of the village symbolizes the interrelatedness of all of the people, living and dead, who are invested in their wealth.

African American families and children can be fully understood only in relation to the interaction of their race, social class, culture, and ethnicity (Garcia Coll et al., 1996). We will look at parenting in the context of these variables. Children bring to school in the early years a chain of experiences, both positive and negative, that will lead to positive outcomes in adulthood (Luster & McAdoo, 1996; Werner & Smith, 1992). Parents influence what children bring to school and influence how well these children acquire school-related skills and other behaviors that are likely to affect achievement and attainment. Parents who place a high value on education will tend to have children with higher attainment in school and in their later careers (Eastman, 1988; Seginer, 1983). But the parents' actions while the children are at home are more important than the amount of time that the children spend in school (Luster & McAdoo, 1996).

Many African Americans want their children to reach higher educational and occupational status than they themselves obtained. The parenting approaches and higher expectations are essential, especially in the long run.

There are many issues that lie within the historical consideration of parenting by African Americans. All of these issues are within the context of experiences with discrimination and the vestiges of enslavement. These elements have had an impact on the resources that are available to these parents and on European-oriented media and environments.

Unrelenting Racism and Discrimination

Unfortunately, the one fact of life that parents of color have to face is that their children will have to contend with devaluation of their own worth and their future potential in school and in careers. At one point, it was expected that racism would lessen. But experience has shown that full integration of schools and neighborhoods has not occurred. Legal access may be available, but there are serious, deep reservoirs of devaluation for anything that is African based. There are more sophisticated ways now of handling exclusion or isolation of African Americans. Even when parents are highly educated, have sufficient resources from professional positions, and are middle class in orientation, they encounter subtle discrimination throughout their lives.

This context of parenting is difficult and will call on a full range of actions and messages from the parents. Parents must first protect their children from racism, not only outside the group but also within their ethnic group. But parents must not overprotect their children, for the youngsters must be prepared to cope with racism their entire lives. They will have to develop what Du Bois (1899) called a "double consciousness," viewing the world through Black eyes and also through White eyes. The ability to "code switch" in situations enables children to understand that certain behaviors are acceptable only in specific situations. This skill at being bicultural is essential. Only when they are able to achieve this perspective and, with wariness and caution, make the necessary adjustments, will the children be able to function effectively amid the complexities of the world.

Even if it were possible to wave a magic wand and eliminate racism, there would still be gaps between where Black families are and where they need to be for their opportunities to be equal to those of White families. Some form of "catch up" would be needed. Affirmative action plans, with all of their difficulties, were one attempt to level the playing field. Much progress was made, but now, concern among Whites that Blacks were being given priorities has brought that progress to a standstill.

The group that benefitted the most from affirmative action hiring policies was White women (Guy-Sheftall, 1993; Ladson-Billings, 2000). Also, because more Whites live in two-parent families, these women who earn incomes also support households in which other Whites live. Therefore, not only White women but also White men, women, and children benefit from these civil rights policies, thus increasing the disparities between Whites and Blacks.

Legacies of Enslavement

The historical past of many African American families is substantially different from the background of all of the other immigrant groups that have come to the United States. The enslavement experience within the Americas brought loss of control, violent uprooting, and great suffering to Black people. Those brutal experiences have shaped the ideological forces that lead to modern-day families, with their strengths and weaknesses (Wilkinson, 1997). Billingsley (1968) has stated that the legacy of enslavement and the caste-like system of segregation have left many African Americans in an inferior status, both psychologically and in reality.

To cope with enslavement and its aftermath, family members have felt the importance of maintaining communal family traditions, which means more matriarchal family systems (Prince, 1997). Many of their strengths have helped families to cope with adversities (Dodson, 1997; Sudarkasa, 1993, 1997). Among the cultural legacies that are African derived and have been transmitted and altered in the United States are the communal practices of shared child care, spirituality, and oral traditions (Boykin, 1986; Jones, 1991). The importance of coresidential extended families and their support systems has been cited as one of the major survival systems of African American families (Billingsley, 1968; Hatchett, Cochran, & Jackson, 1991; Hill, 1997; McAdoo, 1992). There are many family similarities among those in the African diaspora, among Brazilian, Caribbean, and American families with African roots (Herskovits, 1941).

Racial Socialization

One of the most important parenting tasks of African American parents is racial socialization. This socialization takes the form of the socialization messages that are passed on and the actions that are taken by the parents. They may use different racial strategies with their children (Frazier, 1963). The social context of the parenting will determine the ethnic identity that the children acquire (Murray & Mandara, 2002, this volume).

Most parents are aware of their responsibility to teach their children about race. Racial socialization is the process by which the parents shape their children's attitudes about race and show the children how they fit into the context of race in their society (Murray & Mandara, 2002; Phinney & Rotheram, 1987). Historically, African Americans have understood the importance of training their children in the race-appropriate manner of confronting a White person. There are many approaches to imparting attitudes toward race and the appropriate actions to take, or not to take.

Parents use racial socialization messages associated with the significance that parents place on issues regarding race (Boykin & Toms, 1985). Blacks have been found to perceive that race is more important than class considerations in terms of influencing their life chances and social status (Durant & Sparrow, 1997; Feagin, 1989; Myrdal, 1964).

Children overhear parents' conversations about race, they notice how parents react to people of other races, and they receive direct instructions from their parents (Murray & Mandara, 2002). They receive further messages at school from their peers. They begin to internalize stereotypes, prejudices, and racism from all of these sources.

Some parents feel that it is essential to teach their children about race, whereas others feel this issue is insignificant (Tatum, 1997). Parental action ranges from not acknowledging race at all to overemphasizing the race issue. Peters (1985) states that children should be taught an awareness of racism and learn not to expect fair play always by White children. This lesson will help them avoid being hurt and will teach them to have pride. Children should be taught that although racism is White people's problem, they will have to deal with it.

Many parents do not talk about race with their children. They feel that society will teach the child eventually. Others believe that to discuss race will make children feel inferior. Those parents do not teach anything about race. They seem to think that if the concept of race is not discussed, it will never hurt their children.

Some parents have a lower sense of closeness with the African American community. They feel that people must work hard and be good citizens; race is not discussed with children. Peters (1985) states that this type of humanistic parenting will not prepare children to negotiate effectively within their own community and the larger society.

Sometimes, negative stereotypes are accepted (Demo & Hughes, 1990). If a cautious/defensive attitude is used, parents will pass on their own prejudices, suggesting, for example, that Whites have power and should be kept at a distance. When children are raised in this atmosphere, they may become alienated as adults from their own community.

The approach that parents use depends on their own racial identity attitudes. These are defined by the degree to which they understand themselves as and identify with being African American (Martin & Hall, 1992). Attitudes are also held about the physical features of hair texture, shape and size of the lips, and skin complexion. These attitudes are communicated to children in various ways. Hatchett et al. (1991) found that 61% of Black children received socialization messages of one type or other; only 39% were told nothing about being Black. Fifty-two percent were given no messages about how to deal with Whites.

Children focus on characteristics such as skin color to place people into groups (Asher & Allen, 1969; Spencer, 1999; Williams & Morland, 1976). In the early years, children exist in a world in which membership in categories is unconditional (Murray & Mandara, 2001). The process that children go through, regardless of race, is similar for about the first 5 years of their lives. Then, there is a divergence, and it is more difficult for children of color than for those who are not of color. Whites continue as before, while Blacks must make a major adjustment in attitudes toward their own racial group. At the same time, the messages that children are given are different for the racial groups.

Race awareness occurs at 2 to 3 years of age. Children quickly achieve gender and race awareness, but no meaning is placed on being in one or another group. They just know that some people are darker and others are lighter, some people are girls and others are boys. At age 3 to 4, racial identification with a particular group begins. Children know that their mother or best friend is like them or different from them. At first, no meaning is placed on these differences. Then, almost immediately, the messages of their environment seep in, and they form a racial preference for one over the other racial group.

At first, all children prefer Whiteness over Blackness. This is not something to be overly concerned about. A subtle form of devaluation occurs with the color caste system that continues in many forms to this day. The preference for Whiteness over Blackness by the media, television, and books has caused many problems with the development of racial attitudes and preferences among African American children and adults (Cohen, 1972; Cross, 1985; McDonald, 1970). This preference for Whiteness is simply an acknowledgment of society's preferences, but when the preference is extended for years, it has been found to result in mental distress (Fulmore, Taylor, Ham, & Lyles, 1994; Guthrie, 1976). Originally, it was felt that this preference reflected a rejection of Black children's own selves; however, research has shown that children are able to discriminate between their racial preference (White-oriented) and their self-esteem (Black-oriented). Thus, their racial attitudes can be modified (McAdoo, 1985). At these early ages, there is no relationship between the children's self-esteem, how they feel about or evaluate themselves, and their racial attitudes. Although they are still out-group oriented, they may feel really good or not so good about themselves. This is obvious when we look at groups of happy Black children. If self-esteem were related to race preference at this age (5 to 8 years), all Black children would be depressive. But they are not.

Children who are White remain in this position of racial preference, which is reinforced in the media and in power situations, in the schools, and in their environments. Children of color have to change in order to develop an own-group orientation. This is done between the ages of 5 and 8 years of age. It is not until the age of 9 that Black children become totally comfortable with their own racial identification. They must overlook the Whiteness-orientation of their environments. The process of seeing their racial group in a positive manner takes a great deal of work and input from many elements.

It is as if the children say, "I know that it may be easier to be White. But I am Black and I feel good about being Black." When this happens around Grade 3 or age 9, the children are well on their way to developing strong, positive, own-group racial attitudes. It behooves us to be diligent to maintain these positive attitudes. We must protect Black children from adverse actions of others. They will have to be taught to stand up and fight, when appropriate, or to run when it is not appropriate. Parents, teachers, and others of the village will have to be diligent to protect our children.

References

Asher, S., & Allen, V. (1969). Racial preference and social comparison processes. *Journal of Social Issues, 25,* 157-165.

Billingsley, A. (1968). *Black families in White America*. Englewood Cliffs, NJ: Prentice Hall.

Boykin, W. A. (1986). The triple quandary and the schooling of Afro-American children. In U. Neisser (Ed.), *The school achievement of minority children: New perspectives*. Hillsdale, NJ: Lawrence Erlbaum.

Boykin, W. A., & Toms, F. (1985). Black child socialization: A conceptual framework. In H. P. McAdoo & J. L. McAdoo (Eds.), *Black children: Social, educational, and parental environment* (pp. 35-51). Beverly Hills, CA: Sage.

Cohen, R. (1972). *The color of man*. New York: Bantam .

Cross, W. E. (1985). Black identity: Rediscovering the distinction between personal identity and reference group orientation. In M. B. Spencer, G. K. Brookins, & W. R. Allen (Eds.), *Beginnings: The social and affective development of Black children* (pp. 152-172). Hillsdale, NJ: Lawrence Erlbaum.

Demo, D. H., & Hughes, M. (1990). Socialization and racial identity among Black Americans. *Social Psychology Quarterly, 53*(4), 364-374.

Dodson, J. E. (1997). Conceptualizations of African American families. In H. P. McAdoo (Ed.), *Black families* (3rd ed., pp. 67-82). Thousand Oaks, CA: Sage.

Du Bois, W. E. B. (1899). *The Philadelphia Negro*. New York: Schocken.

Durant, T., & Sparrow, K. (1997). Race and class consciousness among lower- and middle-class Blacks. *Journal of Black Studies, 27*(3), 334-351.

Eastman, G. (1988). *Family involvement in education*. Madison, WI: Department of Public Instruction.

Feagin, J. R. (1989). *Racial and ethnic relations* (3rd ed.). Englewood Cliffs, NJ: Prentice Hall.

Frazier, E. F. (1963). *The Negro church in America*. New York: Schocken.

Fulmore, C., Taylor, T., Ham, D., & Lyles, B. (1994). Psychological consequences of internalized racism. *Psych Discourse, 24*(10), 12-15.

Garcia Coll, C., Lamberty, G., Jenkins, R., McAdoo, H. P., Crnic, K., Wasik, B. H., & Vasquez Garcia, H. (1996). An integrative model for the study of developmental competencies in minority children. *Child Development, 67*(5), 1891-1914.

Guthrie, R. (1976). *Even the rat was White*. New York: Harper & Row.

Guy-Sheftall, B. (1993, April). *Black feminist perspectives on the academy*. Paper presented at the annual meeting of the American Educational Research Association, Atlanta, GA.

Hatchett, S. J., Cochran, D. L., & Jackson, J. S. (1991). Family life. In J. S. Jackson (Ed.), *Life in Black America* (pp. 46-83). Newbury Park, CA: Sage.

Herskovits, M. (1941). *The myth of the Negro past*. New York: Harper & Row.

Hill, R. (1997). *The strengths of African American families: Twenty-five years later*. Washington, DC: R & B.

Jones, J. (1991). Racism: A cultural analysis of the problem. In R. L. Jones (Ed.), *Black psychology* (3rd ed., pp. 609-635). Berkeley, CA: Cobb & Henry.

Ladson-Billings, G. (2000). Racialized discourses and ethnic epistemologies. In N. Denzin & Y. Lincoln (Eds.), *Handbook of qualitative research* (2nd ed., pp. 257-277). Thousand Oaks, CA: Sage.

Luster, T., & McAdoo, H. P. (1996). Family and child influences on educational attainment: A secondary analysis of the High/Scope Perry Preschool data. *Developmental Psychology, 32*(1), 26-39.

Martin, J. K., & Hall, G. C. (1992). Thinking Black, thinking internal, thinking feminist. *Journal of Counseling Psychology, 39*(4), 509-514.

McAdoo, H. P. (1992). Upward mobility and parenting in middle-income Black families. In A. Burlew, W. Banks, H. P. McAdoo, & D. Azibo (Eds.), *African American psychology: Theory, research, and practice* (pp. 63-86). Newbury Park, CA: Sage.

McAdoo, J. L. (1985). Modification of racial attitudes and preferences in young Black children. In H. P. McAdoo & J. L. McAdoo (Eds.), *Black children: Social, educational, and parental environments* (pp. 342-256.) Beverly Hills, CA: Sage.

McDonald, M. (1970). *Not by the color of their skin.* New York: International Universities Press.

Murray, C., & Mandara, J. (2002). Racial identity in African American Children: Cognitive and experimental antecedents. In H. P. McAdoo (Ed.), *Black children* (2nd ed.). Thousand Oaks, CA: Sage.

Myrdal, G. (1964). *An American dilemma.* New York: McGraw-Hill.

Peters, M. F. (1985). Racial socialization of young Black children. In H. P. McAdoo & J. L. McAdoo (Eds.), *Black children* (pp. 159-173). Beverly Hills, CA: Sage.

Phinney, J., & Rotheram, M. (1987). *Children's ethnic socialization.* Newbury Park, CA: Sage.

Prince, K. (1997). Black family and Black liberation. *Psych Discourse, 28*(91), 4-7.

Seginer, R. (1983). Parents' educational expectations and children's academic achievements: A literature review. *Merrill-Palmer Quarterly, 29,* 1-23.

Spencer, M. (1999). Social and cultural influences on school adjustments: The application of an identity-focused cultural ecological perspective. *Educational Psychologist, 34*(1), 43-57.

Sudarkasa, N. (1993). Female-headed African American households: Some neglected dimensions. In H. P. McAdoo (Ed.), *Family ethnicity: Strength in diversity* (pp. 81-89). Newbury Park, CA: Sage.

Sudarkasa, N. (1997). African American families and family values. In H. P. McAdoo (Ed.), *Black families* (3rd ed., pp. 9-40). Thousand Oaks, CA: Sage.

Tatum, B. D. (1997). Out there stranded: Black families in White communities. In H. P. McAdoo (Ed.), *Black families* (3rd ed., pp. 214-233). Thousand Oaks, CA: Sage.

Werner, E. E., & Smith, R. S. (1992). *Overcoming the odds: High risk children from birth to adulthood.* Ithaca, NY: Cornell University Press.

Wilkinson, D. (1997). American families of African descent. In M. DeGenova (Ed.), *Families in cultural context: Strengths and challenges in diversity* (pp. 335-360). London: Mayfield.

Williams, J., & Morland, J. (1976). *Race, color, and the young child.* Chapel Hill: University of North Carolina Press.

5

Racial Socialization
of Young Black Children

MARIE FERGUSON PETERS

Regardless of their particular economic circumstances, Black American families live their lives under continuous and varying degrees of oppression because of racism. Because of their racial identity, the normal, everyday life of Black people in this country encompasses a reality, both subtle and overt, of prejudice, discrimination, and devalued and depreciated status and opportunities (Pierce, 1975; Powell, 1973). Prejudice and discrimination affect jobs and income of Black heads of household as well as the standard of living of their families, including housing, neighborhood, quality of schools, and medical care. For Black families, this is a fact of life, taken for granted in the world they know. It is a 450-year-old legacy that Black parents cannot and do not ignore. Although they may hope for a better future world of fairness and racial equality, Black parents understand that they face an extraordinary challenge: to raise children who will be able to survive in a racist-oriented society.

Only Black families and certain other minority families in America live and socialize their children under conditions that are glaring contradictions of national beliefs and ideals. Keniston (1978) described children in

Black families as "the most endangered children in our society. . . . Although our national creed insists that all children should have equal chances, from the start the deck is systematically stacked against [Black children]" (pp. xiii-xiv). Many Black children must overcome obstacles caused by poverty, unemployment, and crowded ghetto living, and all Black children must learn to cope with ubiquitous deterrents and roadblocks that inhibit their access to mainstream American life.

Black families make resourceful and creative adaptations as they cope with discrimination and low income (Hill, 1972; Stack, 1974), and their supportive child-rearing strategies buffer some of the cruel and demeaning messages Black children receive from a hostile world beyond the Black community (Nobles, 1974; Richardson, 1981; Taylor, 1976; Willie, 1976). In a study of racism and child rearing, Richardson (1981) wrote,

> Historically, the survival of Black Americans depended on certain strategies which were necessary for their continuing existence in a hostile society. It has been the responsibility and the task of black parents and the black community to prepare and condition black children for such a world. *Black mothers are required to mediate the hostile external society for their children* [italics added]. (p. 99)

It is clear that this reality, racism and the response to racism, must be included in any interpretation of parental behavior in Black families. To understand the dynamics of child socialization in Black families, the racism factor must be considered. Although the classic stress theories of Hill (1963) and others (Hansen & Hill, 1964; Hansen & Johnson, 1979; McCubbin et al., 1980) do not incorporate a racism factor in their stress formulations, when research involves Black families, the theories can be modified to incorporate the influence of racial identity on both the cause and subsequent reactions to a stress/crisis event. A theoretical conceptualization for adapting Hill's classic formula for stress/crisis events in the lives of Black families has been presented in detail elsewhere (see Peters & Massey, 1983). Basically, this perspective views Black families, because of their constant exposure to overt or concealed racism, as living under mundane extreme environmental stress (Pierce, 1975) and suggests that research that examines Black family functioning must incorporate this fact.

Racial Socialization:
Definition and Inquiry

The socialization of children in Black families, then, occurs within the mundane extreme environment of real or potential racial discrimination and prejudice. The tasks Black parents share with all parents—providing for and raising children—not only are performed within the mundane extreme environmental stress of racism but include the responsibility of raising physically and emotionally healthy children who are Black in a society in which being Black has negative connotations. This is racial socialization.

What racial experiences do Black parents and their children have? What do Black parents do about it? What do they say? Through questions such as these, the impact of race on child rearing was explored in a sample of Black families who participated in a 2-year long longitudinal field study of the social development and rearing of young children. The study was entitled the Toddler Infant Experiences Study (TIES). TIES respondents talked about discipline, management, and other aspects and problems of child rearing that concern parents. As Black parents, however, they could not escape including how racism, discrimination, and prejudice affected their lives, their children's lives, and their thinking about their children's future. This chapter will describe some of the experiences parents had involving racial discrimination and prejudice and will describe how being Black affected the way the parents viewed their children, their racial identity, and their behavior as Black parents of Black children.

The Toddler Infant Experiences Study

TIES was an ecologically oriented descriptive study of the socioemotional development of young Black children and the child-rearing behaviors, attitudes, and goals of their parents. For 2 years, beginning when they were 12 months old, 30 Black children were observed and their parents interviewed once a month for 2 to 3 hours in their natural home environment. There were two different foci, the child and the parent. Children's behaviors, their transactions with the physical (home) environment, and their interactions with parents and others were examined to reveal patterns of parent-child behavior. At the same time, extensive interview data were gathered to explore in depth parents' interpretations of and inputs into their children's development. In addition, about half of the mothers (16) participated in a lengthy interview concerning the racial socialization of their children: their attitudes, behaviors, and goals as parents who were raising minority children in a majority culture.

Sample

The study population consisted primarily of two-parent working-class and middle-class Black families, each of whom had a child born between September and December of 1977. Thirty families participated; all were principally caring for their children at home. A few also had a baby-sitter or used day care on a part-time basis for less than 20 hours a week. Although the study families were self-selected, recruited from many sources, and cannot be considered representative of Black families in the city in which they live, their state, or the nation, the families can be considered viable examples of the ordinary, average-income, law-abiding, hard-working, working-class Black families that are part of the backbone of America. Like the majority of Black families, the majority of the study families were two-parent, nonwelfare families with children at home. A minority were single parents. All were urban. Although all now live in the Bay Area of California, like the majority of Black Americans, they have family roots in the South. At the beginning of the study in September 1978, the family income ranged from below $500 per month to more than $2,000 per month. Family size ranged from one to six children, although most had only one or two children. Seven families had a baby during the 2-year study.

Recruitment

Families were recruited for TIES via radio announcements, television interviews, newspaper articles, signs in supermarkets, and friends. Many people were attracted to a project on Black children. The constraints of the research design, however, which required cohorts of infants born within a specific 3-month period, at least one parent home with the child during the day, and willingness to participate monthly in a 2-year-long study, quickly narrowed the field to 30 families over the 2-year period.

Procedure

Data were gathered via monthly observations and interviews. An observer/interviewer visited each family at home once a month and spent 2 to 2½ hours observing the child, recording and videotaping the child's behavior, and interviewing the mother or other caregiver at home with the child. The parenting and race interviews, which took 4 to 5 hours, were reserved for the end of the 2-year field observations. These special interviews were conducted at the research office. Sixteen mothers volunteered to participate in these interviews.

The parenting and race interviews consisted of two sections. First, respondents were interviewed concerning how they were rearing their young children. We probed about their general worries, concerns, and problems as parents of active toddlers. These findings have been reported elsewhere (Peters & Massey, 1981). The second section of the interviews focused specifically on issues Black parents face as they socialize their Black children. We talked about their child-rearing goals and behavior as Black parents raising Black children. We explored the situations they encountered in which their Black identity created a problem, and we discussed the stress families experience that can be attributed to racism.

Rearing Black Children in a Black/White World

Raising Black children in a society in which Blackness often is devalued may seem to some to be a difficult task for Black parents, who themselves experience prejudice. The TIES parents understood that they were not simply raising American children; they also were raising African American, Black American children, whose culture, background, and present situation differ from that of other American children. As we talked to parents about the problems of parenting, many recounted experiences they had had with racism, discrimination, or prejudice. In general, parents tended not to initiate a racially oriented discussion concerning their parenting. However, in response to our probes, it became clear that racial identity was an important factor in their lives and in how they were raising their children.

To ascertain how Black parents conceptualize their roles as the first and, for the first few years, the prime socializers of their children, and to understand how they perceive the impact of racism on their children's lives, a series of open-ended questions focused on the values and attitudes Black parents hold concerning rearing Black children.

As Richardson (1981) found in her study of Black mothers, the mothers in TIES understood the nature of the mundane extreme environment in which they lived. She concluded,

> Black mothers know that their children will ultimately experience racism. They believe that racism experiences can be devastating and destructive if the child has not been prepared to recognize or develop techniques and strategies for coping with these experiences. The mothers also know that black children will ultimately have to know that they are black and understand what a black identity means in a racist society. (pp. 168-169)

The TIES sample of young Black mothers expressed similar views, and they felt strongly a responsibility not only to provide and care for their children but to teach their children how to survive the harsh world of prejudice and discrimination. Parents conceptualized survival in terms of coping. They expressed this in many ways; for example, one mother's immediate response to a question concerning what Black parents should teach their children was "to be able to cope with whatever it might be." A mother of two small boys added, "It's most important for me to teach my sons how to deal with society as it is—to let them know they're protected as long as they're at home, but when they get out there in the world, *they're not protected anymore.*" A young mother of a 2½-year-old daughter explained simply, "I have to teach her to cope."

Parents are explicit when stating why teaching children how to cope is so important. A mother of two boys put it bluntly: "I've got to teach them that in a White society they're going to get pushed around and be used." A mother of two older children and a 3-year-old daughter said that it was important for her to give her daughter a "good foundation—something to fall back on when the going gets rough so she won't have to turn to dope when she has problems." Another mother explained, "I think my sons are going to have to have a little tougher skin or a little more tolerance to be able to make it."

The Importance of Self-Respect and Pride

It is important for children to know about racism. Moreover, parents must specify qualities they encourage in the development of their children.

Parents mentioned that it is important that their children "be positive about themselves." They want a daughter to "have respect for herself" or a son to "get respect for being himself." Pride and self-respect often are seen as having practical value for Black children. As one mother pointed out, "I'd like them to have enough pride, because if you have enough pride or self-confidence in yourself, you'll let a lot of things roll off your back." Or, as another parent expressed it, "so nobody can put them down." A mother of two said that she wanted her children "to feel sure of themselves. They need this to be able to make the best of their future."

On a more subtle level, building self-respect and pride concerning their racial identity undergirds every parent's child-rearing philosophy. Parents expressed this in very direct terms:

> I want them to be proud of the fact that they are Black.

> I tell my child, "You're Black, we're all Black in this family; be proud of it!"

> I've told my daughter many times, "You're a pretty little Black girl and I'm proud of you!"

> I tell them to hold their heads up and not to be ashamed to be Black.

Parents are careful to put pride in racial identity in proper perspective so that it becomes neither an obsession nor a crutch. For example, a parent of a precocious 3½-year-old explained,

> I want her to know that she's Black, but I don't want her to put Black in front of everything she does. She's going to put herself right up there and her color isn't going to have anything to do with her success.

Understanding That Fair Play May Not Be Reciprocal

Parents encourage honesty and fair play, but at the same time, some parents warn their children that they cannot necessarily expect fair play in return. For example, a mother of a 3-year-old girl who attended nursery school part-time while her mother attended classes at the local community college stated,

> I want my daughter to be aware that there are differences between Blacks and Whites. She can't do certain things White kids can. She can do them, but she won't get away with them. She's got to understand that they'll get a break faster than she will.

A mother of two boys agreed:

> Just the fact that they are Black means that they may be treated differently sometimes and they're going to have to put up with a lot more. If your White boss calls you "nigger," he's not going to get in as much trouble as if you turn around and call him a "honky." You're likely to get fired, even if it's the other way around and you're his boss. They come down a lot heavier on you when you're Black. He's going to have to know that there are some things that he's going to have to let shine on—just for his own survival.

Parents emphasized the importance of getting along with others. They stated that children must know how to "live in this world with other people" and "fit into society"; or, as a mother of a pretty 3-year-old child with very dark skin explained,

> I have to teach her to get along with everybody because they're going to down her one way or the other, sometimes, just because she's dark. Some people—Black, White, or Mexican—are going to treat her differently because she's dark.

A Good Education: A Top Priority

Parents were asked, Are there any special coping strategies you feel that are especially important to teach a young Black child? A number of parents replied immediately, "Yes, a good education!" Like most American parents, the TIES parents felt that it was most important for their children to have a good education; but these parents shared a compelling and culture-specific reason. As a mother of three boys explained, "When you're Black, you've got to get a little more education than Whites have."

A number of parents, in addition, viewed obtaining a good education as somewhat problematic for Blacks. "I have to get her a good education," said a mother of two teenagers and a preschooler, "but I'm finding it to be a hard problem when so many teachers don't really care about little Black kids these days." Another mother of three feared her children might be discouraged from venturing into occupations outside the Black community: "I don't want them to be afraid of going into professions because only White people are in them."

But Most of All—Love

Parents were asked, What is the most important thing you do for your children? Most parents mentioned love first:

What I do is give mine love.

I try to give them love and security. I feel they need this most of all.

I love her so she'll love others. I don't want her prejudiced against any other race.

I give her a lot of love.

To me, it's love. We give them security and love. They're the same.

Love and security is the prescription these parents believe provided their children protection from potential emotional scars caused by onslaughts of bigotry and duplicity by detractors.

Do Parents Perceive Racism as Stress?

The parents in this study, like parents in every society, socialize children according to the norms of their culture and the validity of the environment in which they live. Black parents experience the American phenomenon of racism in varying degrees, and every parent has a philosophy or theory regarding how to best survive as a family now and how their children will be able to survive as adults. The interviews with these parents revealed dramatically that these Black families lived their lives in the everyday ubiquitous environment of the mundane extreme environmental stress described earlier in this chapter.

Family crises often were precipitated or exacerbated by racism on the part of an employer, institutions, or individuals. Parents cited instances of poor medical care, trouble in a job situation, problems with the law, and many minor unpleasant, more subtle incidents with racial overtones. Parents often were concerned about how these situations affected their children. Although it is difficult to prove direct linkages between a family crisis event, racism, the event's effect on the child, and the child's response, a number of parents clearly saw the connections in their particular situation. Table 5.1 illustrates five situations that linked a racially caused family event to child behavior. For each event, the table shows the racially connected cause, the effect on the child, and the child's observed coping behavior. It is interesting to note that in one of the examples, the young child does not exhibit an adverse response to the family stress situations that involved death. Two situations, the death of three cousins/playmates and the death of child's aunt, were seen as affecting the young child directly. The father's loss of a job, the mother's negligent abortion, and the mother's working although ill were believed to affect the child indirectly through the behavior of a parent. In three cases, the child's coping behavior in reaction to the family stress/crisis event placed an added strain on the parent because the child made excessive demands for attention.

Discrimination was not necessarily experienced in concrete situations, as seen in Table 5.1. Often, it was the subtle prejudice Blacks sensed in the behavior of Whites they met in the course of their daily activities. Blacks never know when a store clerk, bank teller, or a server in a restaurant is going to show overt prejudice, which is not only insulting but also difficult to ignore. An ordinary business transaction, shopping excursion, or pleasure outing suddenly can be transformed into a source of anger and emotional stress.

One mother, for example, who had taken her two little girls to their favorite ice cream shop, became "fed up" and walked out because the waitress not only ignored their table and served customers who came in after them but also was "nasty" when the mother finally requested service. "I had a difficult choice to make," this mother said, "walk out and face the kids' howling because they didn't get their ice cream, or sit there and sizzle."

Another parent described even more graphically how she felt.

> You keep sitting there, wondering when you're going to get waited on, watching everybody else being waited on, and it just makes you feel bad and then it makes you want to be violent, you're wondering if you should get up and do something. All these things go through your head.

TABLE 5.1 Examples of Racially Caused Events in Black Families and the Effect on the Children

Event	Racially Related Cause	Effect on Child	Child's Observed Coping Behavior
Father's loss of job	Being last hired, Blacks are first fired on this job	Father bored, short-tempered; leaves home to "hang," child misses father	Avoids father or demands attention from father
Surgeon's negligent handling of mother's hospital abortion	Blacks receive poor clinical/ doctor care in this hospital	Mother becomes depressed and neglects child	Amuses self when mother appears to be preoccupied or demands attention from mother
Death of three young children close to the family	Inadequate nutrition and health care—prenatal and postnatal	Coping with absence (death) of companion/ playmate	Asks a few questions; seems to accept fact that playmates are gone
Mother unable to leave job when ill	Racist attitude of employer who treated Blacks unsympathetically	Exacerbated mother's health problem, mother is tired and ill when home and has little energy or time for child	Whines for mother's attention
Death of mother's sister	Childbirth complications not properly monitored in hospital	Child must share family resources with the cousin who now resides in child's home	Accepts and enjoys having an older "sister" who was already living in the family when the child was born

A third mother talked about the more subtle attitudes of some waitresses: "They ask, 'Can I help you?' But you know they don't really want to help and you wonder about the food they bring out."

Twelve mothers, or three fourths of the interview participants, volunteered stories about discrimination in restaurants. Even more (14) had experienced discrimination by a salesperson. Typically, they mentioned that salesclerks waited on others before coming to them. A mother who had worked as a salesclerk added that White customers sometimes ignored her and waited for a White salesperson. A number of parents described incidents, such as going into a bank to transact business with an officer or shopping in a store that featured high-priced merchandise, when it was assumed they were too poor to be serious customers. Table 5.2 lists the places parents mentioned in answer to the questions, Have you ever been discriminated against? Where?

As we have seen, it is evident that racism affects important aspects of the daily lives of the Black families in our study, and these experiences influence the parents' perceptions of the external world their children someday must enter. However, parents "don't dwell on it," as one mother said.

Because mundane extreme environmental stress is a normal environment for Blacks in this country, the phenomenon of racism may not be perceived as stress by Black parents. We therefore said to each respondent during the interviews, "Some people feel that being Black places an added stress in the lives of children. What do you think about this?" Opinions were divided: A little over half (9) of the 16 parents who participated in the racism interview agreed. For example, one mother answered in the following manner:

> Yes, I certainly do agree about that, because your children have to act better, be smarter, perform better than somebody comparable who is White. Then they get the idea that they are being resented just because they're acting better, performing better, and are smarter than Whites are.

A mother whose older children attended a racially mixed school agreed:

> Because they have to learn to deal with our culture as Black people and also deal with the mainstream culture at the same time, it's hard trying to relate, trying to intermingle the two and come up with a good understanding of what life should be all about.

A parent whose oldest daughter is in second grade replied simply, "This is the problem I'm having at my daughter's school. I can't see her

TABLE 5.2 Discrimination Experienced by Parents

Where or By Whom	Number of Respondents
By a salesperson	14
In seeking a job	12
In a restaurant	12
On the job	11
In a hospital or clinic	9
In a school	8
In seeking housing	7
In a bank	6
At a recreational facility	4
At a bar or disco or night club	3
By an employee of a public utility, such as the telephone company or the electric company	1

NOTE: *N* = 16.

teachers—who are Whites—relating to her culture. So my daughter has a problem!"

On the other hand, almost half (7) disagreed. They did not feel that children were necessarily stressed by racism. One mother of two boys said, "I disagree. It depends on how you bring up the child. If parents bring up their children so that they know how to handle things, then there's no stress."

A mother of two preschoolers, considering the question in terms of her children's situation now, replied, "Kids don't know what's happening. They can't do anything about discrimination and it really doesn't bother them at this age, [un]less their parents want to carry on about it." A number of parents expressed the view that if children feel stressed, it is because their parents subject them to their own feelings of stress. As a mother of five pointed out, "When Black children feel stressed it's because they're getting it from their parents."

A mother of two daughters and a son explained that stress is avoided because children learn "about how it is." She added,

From the time you're a kid, your mother and father tell you about discrimination, brothers and sisters, aunts and uncles, they all tell you about it. So
when you grow up and put in for a position but don't get it, you'll say,
"Hey, I knew I wasn't going to get it." So you don't feel too bad about it.
You've accepted the possibility of rejection before you put in for the position. You really know you're not going to get it, but you put in for it any-
way.

When the question turned from stress on children to stress on adults,
most parents (13) felt that being Black placed an added stress in their lives.
A mother of a 3½-year-old, connecting stress of parents with stress on children (see Table 5.1), said, "If we can't deal with situations, it causes stress,
and we give that stress to our children."
Another mother commented,

I strongly agree. It's harder to get a job even when you're qualified, and
when you do get a job, you don't get the promotions that are due you. I
know, it happened to my husband, and it just happened to my sister a little
while ago.

Another mother, emphasizing the effects of the stresses of discrimination and prejudice, noted, "It makes some Blacks have a chip on their
shoulders, be mad all the time, even hate White folks."

Summary

In conclusion, the general consensus of the 16 parents was that being Black
brought a different dimension to the way they were raising their children.
They recognized that being Black brought an added stress into the lives of
children as well as into their own lives. However, there were "special
things" parents did to prepare their children for being Black in this society.
We term these special things *racial socialization*. Although a majority of the
respondents believed that their 2½- to 3-year-old children did not know the
difference between the races and did not understand their own racial identity, about half of the parents already had explained to their preschoolers
that they were Black, and the other half planned to talk about race to their
children later. Incidents of racial discrimination or prejudice had occurred
to *all* adults in the study, but most of the preschoolers had not yet experi-

enced it. Finally, although parents felt that it is important to prepare their children to "deal with racism," a number of parents felt that they were not necessarily "prepared" by their own parents for coping with the racial prejudice and discrimination they had experienced.

This study has explored in some detail the experiences of a group of Black parents raising their young children in the unpredictably hostile environment of racial discrimination and prejudice that Pierce (1975) has called both mundane and extreme. Respondents were pragmatic and unflappable in their awareness of the persistence of racism in the real world their children must experience, and they were especially concerned about the racial socialization of their children in individual yet similar ways. Although this was not a representative sample of Blacks in America, there is no reason to believe that the TIES respondents were any more thoughtful, articulate, or concerned about racism than other Black parents anywhere in this country would be discussing the various ramifications of race in their lives.

In her study of Black mothers, Richardson (1981, p. 318) suggested three propositions: (a) that racism acts as an intervening variable in the socialization process of Black children, (b) that the sociocultural/racial environments and experiences of mothers influence their perception of social reality, and (c) that parents' perception of social reality and the adaptations they make affect their child-rearing values and behavioral strategies. These three propositions were supported in the present study; in addition, parents understood these connections and influences. The socialization of Black children takes place in a unique environment. Attempts by child development experts to modify the parenting styles of Black parents must be based on an understanding of the functional value of racial socialization—the culture-specific child-rearing values, attitudes, and behaviors Black parents have developed.

References

Hansen, D. A., & Hill, R. (1964). Families under stress. In H. T. Christensen (Ed.), *Handbook of marriage and the family*. Chicago: Rand McNally.

Hansen, D. A., & Johnson, V. A. (1979). Rethinking family stress theory: Definitional aspects. In W. R. Burr, R. Hill, F. I. Ney, & I. L. Reiss (Eds.), *Contemporary theories about the family*. New York: Free Press.

Hill, R. (1963). Social stresses on the family. In M. B. Sussman (Ed.), *Sourcebook on marriage and the family* (pp. 303-314). Boston: Houghton Mifflin.

Hill, R. (1972). *The strengths of Black families*. New York: Emerson Hall.

Keniston, D. (1978). Foreword. In J. Ogbu (Ed.), *Minority education and caste*. New York: Academic Press.

McCubbin, H. I., Joy, C. B., Cauble, A. E., Comeau, J. K., Patterson, J. M., & Needle, R. H. (1980). Family stress and coping: A decade review. *Journal of Marriage and the Family, 42*(4), 855-871.

Nobles, W. (1974). Africanity: Its role in Black families. *Black Scholar, 5*, 10-17.

Peters, M. F., & Massey, G. C. (1981). *Black beginnings: Childrearing patterns in a sample of Black parents and children age 1 to 3*. Paper presented at the annual meeting of the Society for Research in Child Development, Boston.

Peters, M. F., & Massey, G. C. (1983). Mundane extreme environmental stress in family stress theories: The case of Black families in White America. In H. L. McCubbin, M. B. Sussman, & J. M. Patterson (Eds.), *Advances and developments in family stress theory and research*. Binghamton, NY: Haworth.

Pierce, D. (1975). The mundane extreme environment and its effect on learning. In S. G. Brainard (Ed.), *Learning disabilities: Issues and recommendations for research*. Washington, DC: National Institute of Education.

Powell, G. (1973). *Black Monday's children: A study of the effects of school desegregation on self-concepts of Southern children*. New York: Appleton-Century-Crofts.

Richardson, B. B. (1981). Racism and child-rearing: A study of Black mothers. *Dissertation Abstracts, 42*(1), 125-A.

Stack, C. (1974). *All our kin: Strategies for survival in a Black community*. New York: Harper & Row.

Taylor, R. (1976). Black youth and psychological development. *Journal of Black Studies, 6*, 353-372.

Willie, C. V. (1976). *A new look at Black families*. Bayside, NY: General Hall.

6

Racial Identity Development in African American Children

Cognitive and Experiential Antecedents

CAROLYN BENNETT MURRAY
JELANI MANDARA

Developmental readiness, parental society.

Most research on African Americans focuses on self-concept and/or racial identity but too often ignores developmental readiness, parental racial socialization, and societal and historical traditions that stress racial membership as a determinant of group and individual treatment. Recent studies indicate that intraindividual variability correlates with abrupt changes in cognitive development (McAdoo, 1985). The findings reveal that both Black and White children between the ages of 3 and 6 display White-biased choice behavior, whereas older Black children (age 9) display Black preference, and their White counterparts remain Eurocentric. Only minimally has the role of the family and the societal context been integrated with this recent emphasis on the cognitive readiness of the child. It is paramount to examine racial identity development within a larger societal framework if we are to understand how children come to view themselves and their world. This chapter considers the cognitive maturation of the child within the context of family racial socialization and of societal and historical traditions (e.g., media, education system, and language) that stress racial membership as a determinant of group and individual treatment.

Defining Race

To understand racial identity, one must first understand the concepts of race, ethnicity, and identity. In current usage, *racial group* designations refer mainly to a person's phenotype (such as skin color, hair texture, and facial shape), whereas *ethnic group* designations refer mainly to a person's sociocultural heritage (country of origin, religion, language, and manners). Although race has a genetic base, it is in part socially and politically defined due to the phenotype overlap between groups (Jones, 1998). People commonly think of races and sometimes ethnic groups as sharply distinguishable biological entities, but their boundaries are set by social agreement. Whatever sharpness racial boundaries may have springs in part from the fact that people react to the members of these socially recognized groups in quite different and important ways. Therefore, a person's legally recognized race may depend as much on the social context and political ramifications as on phenotype. Also, the race with which people identify may be more an issue of social context and wishes and desires than their phenotype.

Identity or self-concept is essentially an organized system of schemas or particular beliefs about the self (e.g., I am shy, I am tall, I am Black, I am good at sports) that characterize the individual's behavior in salient social settings (Markus & Kunda, 1986). *Racial identity* is a schema or mental representation of the racial aspect of the self, including perceived attributes and the feelings associated with them (e.g., I am Black, Black people do X, I like X). The issue here is how African American children decode and understand the complex and often abstract concept of race when they begin to form a racial identity.

How humans develop a social identity in general is a critical issue. Children do not enter the world with a conception of self. Rather, this cognitive notion develops as they mature (Bandura, 1986). Infants need to become aware that they are unique, independent, and separate from other individuals and can have an influence on their surroundings (Bandura, 1986; Bertenthal & Fisher, 1978). By age 2, children can recognize themselves in a mirror (Amsterdam, 1972; Harter, 1988; Lewis & Brooks-Gunn, 1979).

By age 2½, children see themselves as separate and autonomous from others (Neisser, 1988).

Although many factors affect identity development, it occurs in two general ways. First, people begin to view themselves as seen by significant others (Cook & Douglas, 1998), who usually are family members, peers, and macrosystem forces (such as teachers and media images). Second, people gain increased self-knowledge or insight into their true beliefs and attributes. In racial identity development, individuals move toward higher states of understanding race, membership in a racial group, and the consequences of that membership. This chapter examines certain factors (cognitive readiness, family racial socialization, and societal and historical traditions) that affect the development of racial identity in African American children.

Cognitive Readiness

The content of the self-concept and the way children process and convey information about themselves is linked with cognitive maturation (Branch & Newcombe, 1986; Semaj, 1985; Spencer, 1985). According to Piaget (1952), cognitive development proceeds through a sequence of invariant stages for all human beings. The stages are innately determined by the biological sequence of growth. Each stage is qualitatively different from the others as the child's cognitive abilities become more sophisticated. Social knowledge is constructed by children from their interactions with other people. More specifically, social awareness development is shaped by children's adaptation to their environment. For Piaget, this adaptation involves two interlocking processes: assimilation and accommodation. Assimilation in a cognitive sense refers to the incorporation of environmental experiences (such as skin color) into a meaningful form to fit existing mental structures. Assimilation allows people to respond to new environmental experiences and situations with their present mental abilities. Accommodation is a reciprocal process in which changes occur in a person's mental structure to fit new experiences or stimuli.

In Piaget's theory, the cognitive level during the first 2 years of life is *sensorimotor;* children understand and deal with the world mainly through the sensory messages received and the motor behavior used to react to them. The *preoperational stage* starts about age 2 and ends about age 7. Thought processes begin to involve symbols (such as skin color) that represent objects in the environment. The *concrete operational stage* occurs between ages 7 and 11. Children are concerned only with objects that are concrete—present, tangible, or real (such as racial awareness)—and are not yet able to visualize ideal, hypothetical, or theoretical concepts or objects. The term *operation* refers to some action that is reversible and that can be internalized by the individual (e.g., racial constancy). Another characteristic of this stage is the ability to classify, owing to an understanding of part-whole relationships, which enables children to classify objects, people (e.g., racial groups), and so on. The *formal operational stage* is the last stage, occurring about age 11, and it involves abstract logical thinking (e.g., social and political ramifications of race). The literature indicates that not until adolescence does the individual become aware of the full complexity of human thoughts, feelings, and intentions or realize that behavior may vary with situations, internal states, or transitory factors (Marcia, 1983).

If cognitive readiness were the only antecedent for racial awareness and identity at the preschool age, all children would have an egocentric racial identity, that is, they would view race from their own perspective. Given the variation within non-White racial groups (Holmes, 1995) and the Eurocentric tendency of many non-Whites, it is clear that children's experiences within the family and wider society have a significant influence. Direct learning from parents often accounts for racial preference, but the process is more complex. Children's assumptions are influenced by several mechanisms other than direct learning (Katz, 1975), including various reinforcements relevant to racial attitude formation. Within Western culture, the color white and White people are highly valued. Black children are placed in a conflictive situation because their human need to value their color and their group is negated by societal reinforcements and communications that inform them of white's value and black's negative character (Hodge, Struckmann, & Trost, 1975). Similarly with respect to gender, males are more valued than females, which results in most boys being egocentric about being boys, and a sizable number of girls being tomboys—they want to be like boys, prefer male playmates, and participate in such masculine activities as climbing trees and playing baseball (Hyde, 1983).

In sum, although cognitive readiness determines when children are capable of developing racial and/or ethnic identity, the social context determines the identity they acquire. Thus, a comprehensive model of identity development must take into consideration both the age of the child and the societal context.

Racial Awareness
and Identity Development

Racial awareness refers to a knowledge of the differences in racial categories. Children possess racial awareness when they can recognize, identify, and make distinctions among racial categories. In the preschool years, children describe themselves in terms of membership in certain groups as defined by physical characteristics: "I have brown skin" (Burns, 1979; Harter, 1983); possessions: "I have a fire truck" (Damon & Hart, 1982); and gender: "I am a boy" (Damon & Hart, 1988). Emphasis is placed on material (concrete) and salient qualities rather than symbolic or affective qualities. Children become aware of their skin color before they come to learn that skin color ultimately determines racial or ethnic membership (Semaj, 1985; Spencer, 1988). For instance, a young child's statement that she has "brown skin" is not linked with the fact that she will be socially labeled in our society as African American (Spencer, 1988).

The ability to apply a racial label correctly or to identify which person goes with what racial label is usually measured by showing children pictures of people or dolls of different hues and hair textures. Preschoolers are keenly aware of phenotypic qualities such as skin color, which serve as standards of comparison to differentiate themselves from others (Butler, 1989; Ramsey, 1987; Spencer, 1988). One mother recounted that her daughter, at age 3, despite the mother's objections, thought her mother was White even though her skin is light brown. The child did not have a category for light brown, the mother's skin color was closer to White than Black, so in her mind her mother was "White." Most cognitive theorists believe that children aged 3 to 7 rely on concrete information rather than abstract knowledge and possess no complex ideas about racial identity (see Wardle, 1992). It is proposed that by the middle school years children begin describing themselves in reference to others (Butler, 1989; Ruble, 1987), following the acquisition of racial constancy—the knowledge that race is a permanent part of the self or identity.

Other researchers expand developmental theory to include the role of the sociocultural context. This approach does not reject mainstream theories but argues for greater attention to collective, interpretive reproduction (Coarser, 1992). For instance, Vygotsky (1962) places children in a social world in which interactions are the source of mental functioning (Peterson & McCabe, 1994) and of meanings for social concepts.

Knowledge about self and others grows simultaneously (Lewis & Brooks-Gunn, 1979, Spencer, 1985). Neither can exist alone, because the two develop in response to social situations. Thus, the degree of contact or interaction that the child has with different racial groups is important to the development of racial identity (Amir, 1969).

The importance of both cognitive readiness and the societal context is revealed by research that finds White-based choice behavior in both Blacks and Whites between ages 3 and 6 but an abrupt change in racial attitudes and preferences after the preoperational stage only for Black children (Spencer, 1982). There appears to be a definite link between cognitive readiness and sociocultural messages and practices so that changes in group identity can be expected, given variations in the child's developing cognitive construction of the world. Although some of these sociocultural messages are consistent in the wider society, the immediate family and surrounding community often mediate their effect. Therefore, children show a variation in terms of the age at which racial awareness and identity occur, the evaluation of racial categories, and the degree to which they identify with their own racial group. We will focus on the most salient sociocultural racial socializers.

The Role of Symbols

Children in general are influenced by the language and symbols of a society. In our society, black is bad, and white is good. If a Black child gleans from fairy tales that only bad people and witches wear black and that heroes and princesses are always dressed in white, the child may reject other things that are black and dark (Russell, Wilson, & Hall, 1992). A girl of 7, who was so dark she was Black, was asked by Clark and Clark (1947) to take the coloring test generally given along with the doll test; she picked a flesh color, pink, to color herself. In an ethnographic study by Holmes (1995), Black children often used peach or pink to color themselves, although they stated that they knew they were not that color. One little girl with very dark skin said, "I am Black on the outside, but my heart is peach." It is clear that both the child's skin color and the skin color of people in the child's immediate sociocultural environment, including related language and symbols, must be considered in understanding a child's racial awareness and preference.

Misunderstanding of the use of color may threaten the developing self-conception of which racial identity and awareness are important aspects (Phinney, 1989; Phinney & Rotheram, 1987; Semaj, 1985; Spencer, 1985). Specifically, when presented colors to select, children often do not like the color black, especially in terms of representing their skin color. Several parents in our longitudinal study reported that during the preschool and early elementary years, their children refused to be called Black: "I am brown, mommie." At this age, skin color is absolute, not symbolic of ethnicity or race. Skin color is not simply an overt and recognizable characteristic. It helps the child develop a sense of self and group identity (e.g., Cross, 1985; Semaj, 1985; Spencer, 1982, 1984, 1985).

Initial studies of racial awareness and identity asked Black and White children to choose between a very dark and very light doll. Black children identified the White doll as having positive traits, and they preferred to play with it significantly more often than White children selected the Black doll. Furthermore, a sizable number of the Black preschoolers selected the White doll as looking like them. Most of the children who chose the White doll had brown to light brown skin. Studies during the 1970s found that the addition of a tan doll eliminated the selection of the White doll by light-skinned Black children (Brand, Ruiz, & Padilla, 1974). When given a doll in a color category closer to their concrete perception of their skin color, they selected that doll and not the White one.

The Role of Skin Color

In American culture, racial and ethnic categories are immutable, and membership is determined by skin color or ethnic heritage. Young children acquire this knowledge at an early age. For African American children, the attribute of skin color may be a more important expression of their self-conceptions than are details about their personal experiences (Harter, 1983; Spencer, 1988). Social comparison emerges in the early school years, at which time children begin to describe themselves in reference to others (Butler, 1989; Ruble, 1987). They focus on salient characteristics, such as skin color, in making this comparison (Asher & Allen, 1969; Burns, 1979; Harter, 1983; Ramsey, 1987; Spencer, 1985) and in systematically classifying people into groups (Aboud, 1988; Tajfel, 1981; Wilder, 1986; Williams & Morland, 1976). Because a child's world is absolute, membership in a category is unconditional, and members are believed to be homogeneous; a person either belongs or does not belong to a particular category.

With regard to Black children's racial awareness, an often overlooked aspect is that skin color varies considerably within the African American population, from white to coal black and everything in between (Bianchi, 1998; Coard, 1997; Draper, 1999). We contend that children's skin color, as it contrasts to other members of their family, is an extremely important factor in determining their racial awareness (Jackson, McCullough, & Gurin, 1997). The degree of variation in a child's immediate family should affect the development of racial awareness. The greater the variation, the less likely is the child to see group differences, as opposed to individual differences, and the later racial awareness or identity will develop. This is exemplified by the personal experience of one of the authors (Carolyn B. Murray):

> In my preschool, skin color was like height or weight. People came in different colors just as they came in different sizes and weights and had different faces and gaits. My father was "dark as a hundred midnights," and my mother and her sister, although "Black," looked "White." People were a rainbow of different hues, all beautiful. I was especially fascinated by dark skin, perhaps because mine was light brown or perhaps because my dad, whom I loved beyond a fault, had dark skin.

If the child's family is homogeneous (e.g., dark) in skin color, but the surrounding community exhibits variation or a salient difference (e.g., White), the child is more likely to notice the contrast. For instance, Japanese preschoolers who live in Japan do not develop racial awareness, but those who live in the United States do (McGuire, McGuire, Child, & Fujioka, 1978). Phinney (1991) found that White adolescents do not normally think in terms of racial identity, but when they are in the minority, their racial identity is very salient for them. In sum, through maturation, children develop self-awareness and group awareness, but their personal characteristics and the surrounding environment give meaning to what is perceived.

The Role of the Media

The media are sociocultural agents and a source of stereotypical information about African Americans (Hamilton, Stroessner, Driscoll, & Denise, 1994). The media teach and reinforce negative attitudes about Blacks (Dixon, 2000). African Americans are disproportionately portrayed as criminal, aggressive, less competent than Whites, "flashy," irresponsible, comic, and so on (Dixon, 2000; Oliver, 1994). Hamilton and Trolier (1986) argue that beliefs about Blacks develop from media exposure. This is especially relevant to discussions about racial identity because African American children are reported to view twice as much television as White children (Tangney & Feshbach, 1988), independent of parental level of education, child's sex or age, and family composition.

One reason for the disproportionate use of television by Black children is that Black families are comparatively poorer than Whites; less mobile and less able to afford alternative forms of entertainment and baby-sitters, they rely more heavily on television (Anderson & Williams, 1983). More important, a number of studies indicate that the usage of television by Blacks differs from that of Whites. For example, Blacks much more than Whites view television as a source of information and news (Anderson & Williams, 1983; Tan & Tan, 1979). African American adolescents report using television to learn dating behavior (Gerson, 1968) and occupations (Greenberg & Atkin, 1982). When television is used as a baby-sitter and as a source of information and cheap entertainment, it has powerful potential as a socializer and an influencer on the self-esteem of Black children (Stroman, 1991).

Research also indicates that television viewing is negatively correlated with numerous indices of adjustment for Blacks and Whites (Tangney & Feshbach, 1988). Various writers (Graves, 1982; Janis, 1980; Rosser, 1978) have speculated about the effect of television on the self-concept of African American children, and the prevailing conclusion is that the influence is negative. Several studies point out that the absence of Blacks from prime-time programming is harmful to Black children's self-concept because it minimizes the importance of their existence (Anderson, 1982, cited in Anderson and Williams, 1983; Powell, 1982). Another effect may be children's overidentification with non-Black heroes. Others suggest that the television roles in which Blacks are cast communicate to Black children the negative value society places on them (Barnes, 1980). For some children, a growing awareness of the intensity and universality of such denigration can frustrate the formation of a positive racial identity (Comer, 1989).

The Role of the Public School Curriculum

After the family, the major socializing agent of Black children's identity is the schools.

If an African American child attends two years of preschool, nine years of elementary, four years each at high-school and college, it will total nine-teen years. If we multiply this with the average six-hour day, thirty-hour week, or twelve-hundred-hour year, we derive a sum of 22,800 hours. (Kunjufu, 1984, p. 31)

Furthermore, the time spent in school is when children are most alert and focused. The messages communicated there and the type of education offered are designed to perpetuate the sociopolitical-economic context. In American society, the curriculum, practices, and policies of the educational system support racism, oppression, and domination of minority groups in general and of Blacks in particular (Hilliard, 1997). Children are rewarded tangibly (such as grades) and intangibly (such as being liked by the teacher) for internalizing the lessons communicated. Moreover, those in charge of indoctrinating children (teachers) are legitimized by parents (Do what your teacher tells you; Education is the only way you're going to be successful; The teacher is the authority) and the society-at-large.

School performance is a by-product of self-esteem and stems from expectations. Most Black children, from the time they enter school until they leave, receive overt and covert messages that they and all African Americans are intellectually deficient (Murray & Fairchild, 1989). Teachers evaluate the probability of future academic success by the degree to which children are similar in essential characteristics to their parent population. For African Americans, this biased cognitive process is extremely detrimental because of the plethora of stereotypes—both lay and "pseudo-scientific" (for instance, Herrnstein & Murray, 1994)—regarding skin color. A large segment of society uses these stereotypes to explain and predict African American behavior (Murray & Jackson, 1999). Consequently, teachers hold significantly lower expectations for Blacks than for Whites (Murray & Jackson, 1999). The teacher's biased beliefs negatively influence the child's self-concept and group identity. Teachers' fulfill their own expectations by labeling children with words such as *slow, deficit,* and so on and by assigning them to the low ability track, where an inadequate curriculum limits their scholastic achievement. Ultimately, too many children internalize these racist beliefs about themselves and their group (Murray & Fairchild, 1989; Murray & Jackson, 1999), as illustrated by the experience of one of the authors (Carolyn B. Murray) and her husband:

All our daughter's life, my husband and I communicated to her that she was smart and beautiful. At the beginning of each year, from first grade though eighth grade, I visited her school and asked to have her moved from the lower ability to the upper ability track. Each teacher arbitrarily made the decision to put her in the lower ability track despite the fact that the previous year she had been assigned to the upper track, her grades were As and Bs, and her achievement test scores were above average. When she was 14, she shared with me that all those years, she believed all the other Black children who remained in the lower academic track were dumb, that she also was dumb, and that the only reason she was in the upper track was because of me. She said, "Mother, now I see it's by design, and not due to the unfortunate circumstance of being born Black."

Before they acquire abstract thinking, children evaluate their environment based on concrete reality. Thus, if Black children are in low ability tracks, it must be because they are dumb. If more Blacks go to jail, it must be because they are more criminal; and so on. Teachers do not overtly say that Blacks are dumb; children know who is in the slow track. Moreover, the curriculum communicates that Whites are honest (George Washington could not tell a lie), emancipators (Abraham Lincoln freed the slaves), and people who civilized and Christianized the world (European conquests). God gave them the right to other people's land and labor (manifest destiny). White people must be smarter, their privilege must be legitimate, and therefore, teachers must be right in their placement decisions. Adolescents have the cognitive maturity to understand the political and other motivations for differential status between Blacks and Whites as well as the mythology surrounding White domination, but if parents or significant others do not communicate positive countermessages, children will continue to assume Blacks are dumb, or criminal, or somehow less than Whites.

Racial Socialization

Racial socialization is the process by which the family shapes attitudes and beliefs about race and explains how the child fits within this context. It is the "processes by which children acquire the behaviors, perceptions, values, and attitudes of an ethnic group, and come to see themselves and other members of such groups" (Phinney & Rotheram, 1987, p. 11). Although the family is the origin of the child's awareness (McAdoo, 1997; see Stevenson, 1999), it is often ignored in studies of racial identity (Murray, Strokes, & Peacock, 1999). Recent literature suggests, however, that racial socialization within the family takes many forms. When children overhear parents talking about race, observe their reactions to people of other races, or receive direct instructions from them regarding other races, their racial awareness and identity are being developed. As children mature and are influenced by external agents, such as peers and school curriculum (Murray et al., 1999), they begin to learn and internalize notions of group stereotypes and prejudices (Devine, 1989; Miller, 1982; Quattrone, 1986), but the family maintains an interpretive role (Jackson et al., 1997).

The African American family is directly and indirectly affected by negative conceptions and treatment of Blacks (Thornton, 1997). Messages are received through the media; the political, economic, educational systems; even the church (e.g., White Jesus) and other value-laden institutions and subsystems within American society (Allen & Hatchett, 1986). The family serves at least two important functions in the African American child's early development. First, it fosters the development of a personal frame of reference for self-identity, self-worth, achievement, group identity, and other behaviors in society. Second, it provides comfort and affection, which lessen the negative and often deleterious consequences of racism (Murray & Mandara, in press; Murray et al., 1999).

A review of the literature indicates that about two thirds of African American parents consciously race-socialize their children, and the remainder do not (Marshall, 1995; see Murray et al., 1999 for a review; Parham & Williams, 1993; Spencer, 1983; Whitty, 1994). A void still remains in terms of empirical research on the relationship between race socialization and racial identity development, but the theoretical link is the subject of ongoing debate. There is confusion due to differences between the two predominant theories. The most noted is the Nigrescene model, which posits that racial identity is individualistic or intrapersonal, based primarily on the individual's perception of, attitude toward, or response to racial treatment (Cross, 1991). It assumes that racial identity is formed in reaction to racism. In contrast, Nobles (1973) and Semaj (1985) propose an African-centered view, that the maturing identity includes a sense of self in terms of *we* or the extended self, which "is dependent on the corporate definition of one's people" (p. 300). This interpersonal view of self-identity necessitates an investigation of key socializing institutions or situations likely to shape, damage, and/or protect people's identity. This theory proposes a more interactive understanding of racial identity development (Burke, 1980). Specifically, identity development can be buttressed, supported, and/or alienated by messages and interactions that children experience in the first socializing agency, the family, and that are either confirmed or disconfirmed by other surrounding socializing agencies (such as peers, clergy, the media, and teachers).

Because of historical within-group variance among African Americans in United States, there are individual differences in the experiences with and perceptions of opportunity. Moreover, the variability in parents' life experiences influences perceptions of their racial group and of the broader society (Thornton, 1997). Thus, measures of group identity should reflect significant differences in family "backgrounds, economic and social situations, and degree of acculturation to mainstream norms" (Spencer & Markstrom-Adams, 1990, p. 293). The available evidence indicates that marital status, age, gender, socioeconomic status (Spencer, 1983), and geographic factors (Jackson et al., 1997; Tatum, 1987; Thornton, 1997) relate to variations in racial socialization (Spencer, 1983; Thornton, Chatters, Taylor, & Allen, 1990).

Concern about variations in socialization strategies was voiced by Greene (1992), who argues,

> African American parents must find ways of warning their children about racial dangers and disappointments without overwhelming them or being overly protective. Either extreme will facilitate the development of defensive styles that leave the child inadequately prepared to negotiate the world with a realistic perspective. (p. 64)

To a great extent, racial socialization by African American parents ultimately prepares children to function either effectively or ineffectively in the world in which they live.

Ideally, parental socialization values should reflect and complement those of other major socializing agents (e.g., teachers, clergy, and police) and vice versa (Thornton et al., 1990). For African American families, however, "socialization occurs within a broader societal environment that is frequently incompatible with attaining positive mental health"

(Thornton et al., 1990, p. 401). The process of racial socialization is one means by which African American parents address this problem.

Types and Effects of Race Socialization Messages

Black parents communicate a range of race socialization messages to their children: (a) mainstream prescriptions (e.g., individualism) or ethnic group values (e.g., "we-ness"), (b) participation in mainstream institutions or in ethnic group activities, and/or (c) a group blame perspective or a system blame perspective (see Murray et al., 1999, for a review). These and others can be readily identified. There is no monolithic African American experience (Boykin & Toms, 1985). Empirical evidence also suggests that certain identified behaviors (e.g., treat everyone with respect, no matter what their race) tend to be overtly and consistently displayed and taught to Black children (Boykin & Toms, 1985). Furthermore, it has been documented that parents communicate specific racial socialization messages designed to instill an understanding of children's racial group (Bowman & Howard, 1985; Smith, Fogle, & Jacobs, in press).

The literature indicates that African American parents may behave proactively (teach their children strategies to deal with race issues), actively (openly discuss race and discrimination), reactively (take a defensive stance on racial issues), or passively (never talk about racial issues) (Bowman & Howard, 1985; Boykin & Toms, 1985; Murray & Mandara, in press; Parham & Williams, 1993; Spencer, 1983; Stevenson, 1994, 1995). The latter strategy provides little or no active socialization regarding racial issues (see Stevenson, 1998, for a discussion; Spencer, 1983). A logical assumption is that a more positive self-concept and higher self-esteem will be acquired through a recognition of unity and responsibility toward African American communities. Yet, consistently across studies, at least a third of Black parents believe race is not important and that opportunities in America are open to all. Clearly, without knowledge of the race messages children receive within the primary rearing unit (the family), one cannot understand racial identity development.

For years, many researchers maintained that African Americans suffered from poorer self-concepts and consequently lower self-esteem compared to majority group members (Coopersmith, 1967; Gordon, 1980; Porter & Washington, 1979). Aside from easily biased clinical studies (Kardiner & Oversey, 1951), however, no significant self-concept studies were conducted between 1939 and 1960 (Cross, 1991). During this period, findings were based almost entirely on racial group orientation (Banks, 1976). A number of recent works provide evidence to the contrary, indicating that both the personal and the racial self-images of African Americans are often positive, especially their self-concepts (Holmes, 1995; Porter & Washington, 1989; Spencer, 1999). The conclusions from earlier research about the negative nature of personal identity were based on myth, not empirical documentation (Cross, 1991). The apparent inconsistency between the earlier and current findings can be more clearly understood if one considers how race socialization affects the group identity and self-esteem of African Americans.

Recent studies indicate that youth who are socialized to be cognizant of racial barriers and cautioned about interracial protocol (Murray & Mandara, in press; Thornton et al., 1990) show more positive behavioral and psychological outcomes than youth who are taught nothing about race or who receive negative in-group messages (Bowman & Howard, 1985; Rotheram-Borus, 1990). It also has been reported that African American children who are racially socialized appear to be farther along in identity development than those who are not (Marshall, 1995). In particular, youth who receive proactive in-group messages (i.e., ethnic pride and strategies to deal with the broader society), in contrast to those who do not, attain higher grades (Sanders, 1998; Whitty, 1994) and have more personal efficacy (Bowman & Howard, 1985), fewer behavior problems (Rotheram-Borus, 1990), and higher in-group racial preference (Spencer, 1983).

A few researchers reported that a strong inculcation of Black pride and a sense of common fate with other Blacks negatively relate to self-esteem (Rasheed, 1981) and grades (Marshall, 1995). These inconsistent findings are difficult to interpret, given that the studies did not investigate thoroughly the content of the messages communicated or whether youth who received certain socialization internalized those messages, resulting in predictable behavioral outcomes (e.g., grades) and/or psychological outcomes (e.g., self-esteem). This situation is especially disconcerting given that for African American youth, the societal (e.g., media, education institution, and so on) racial socialization messages are often counter to those of the parent (Thornton et al., 1990).

A study by Murray and Mandara (in press) suggests that both ethnic pride and strategies to deal with the broader society's messages (i.e., a proactive strategy) are necessary. The longitudinal/cross-sectional study investigated socialization and personality development among 116 African American youth (54.3% of them female) ranging in age from 14 to 16 years. The socialization strategies investigated were racial empowerment, racial awareness, race defensiveness, and race naivete. *Racial empowerment* reflects a proactive approach that stresses racial identity and the ability to overcome obstacles in life despite racial barriers (e.g., the power to change things at school). *Racial awareness* reflects an active strategy in teaching children to be proud of their racial group. *Race-defensiveness* teaches a dislike for other racial groups but the usefulness of imitating European American behavior (e.g., think it is best to act like Whites). Race naivete is a strategy that minimizes modern race issues (e.g., racism is a thing of the past).

The findings revealed that African Americans exposed to race empowerment strategies were significantly higher in racial identity and self-concept, whereas the reverse was found for those exposed to a race-defensive strategy. A logical conclusion is that positive self-esteem is acquired through a recognition of Black achievements, strategies to deal effectively with racism, and responsibility toward African American communities. The racial awareness and race naivete approaches were not found to be significant predictors of self-esteem, and they only moderately predicted racial identity. These findings emphasize that message content is as important as whether a parent race-socializes or not. The study also helps explain why some research does not find a positive relationship between race socialization and child outcomes.

There are many views in the African American community about how children should be educated about race and racism, if at all. Moreover, some parents are ill-equipped to instill a positive racial identity in their children. They do not give their children the needed protection from the deleterious influences that hamper the development of constructive group identity and positive mental health (Semaj, 1985). In sum, the absence or ineffectiveness of racial socialization agendas in a substantial number of African American families underscores the need to understand the effects of various strategies, including a lack of strategy, as well as the need to educate parents about the most effective approach.

Conclusion

An examination of racial identity development out of context (i.e., American society) is like studying plant growth without considering carbon dioxide. Clearly, children's racial identity is intimately tied to their social knowledge, which is influenced by their minority group status. Some researchers conclude that although awareness of race as a sociobiological phenomenon is related to developing cognitive structures, knowledge of racial stereotypes is not related to social cognition. Instead, children's Eurocentric values concerning race appear to reflect unchallenged exposure to racial epithets or stereotypes (Spencer, 1999). Therefore, the socialization of African Americans in a Europeanized context and its implications for identity development are important issues. Thus, a proactive racial socialization agenda buffers and prepares African American children to face the challenges of racial discrimination. Whitty (1994) notes, however, that such a strategy is "the exception rather than the rule" (p. 13).

References

Aboud, F. (1988). *Children and prejudice.* Cambridge, MA: Basil Blackwell.

Allen, R., & Hatchett, S. (1986). The media and social reality effects: Self and system orientations of Blacks. *Communications Research, 13*(1), 97-113.

Amir, Y. (1969). Contact hypothesis in ethnic relations. *Psychological Bulletin, 11,* 319-342.

Amsterdam, B. (1972). Mirror self-image reactions before age two. *Developmental Psychology, 5,* 297-305.

Anderson, W. H., & Williams, B. M. (1983). TV and the Black child: What Black children say about the shows they watch. *Journal of Black Psychology, 9*(2), 27-42.

Asher, S. C., & Allen, V. L. (1969). Racial preference and social comparison processes. *Journal of Social Issues, 25,* 157-165.

Bandura, A. (1986). *Social foundation of thought and action: A social cognitive theory.* Englewood Cliffs, NJ: Prentice Hall.

Banks, W. C. (1976). White preference in Blacks: A paradigm in search of a phenomenon. *Psychological Bulletin, 83*(6), 1179-1186.

Barnes, E. J. (1980). The Black community as the source of positive self-concept for Black children: A theoretical perspective. In R. L. Jones (Ed.), *Black psychology* (pp. 106-130). New York: Harper & Row.

Bertenthal, B., & Fisher, K. (1978). Development of self recognition in the infant. *Developmental Psychology, 14,* 44-50.

Bianchi, F. T. (1998). The relationships among racial identity attitudes, collective self-esteem, awareness of racism, individual self-esteem, and optimism among

Afro-Brazilian males. *Dissertation Abstracts International: Section B: The Science and Engineering, 58*(8-B), 4437.

Bowman, P., & Howard, C. (1985). Race-related socialization, motivation, and academic achievement: A study of Black youth in three-generational families. *Journal of the American Academy of Child Psychology, 24,* 134-141.

Boykin, A. W., & Toms, F. D. (1985). Black child socialization: A conceptual framework. In H. P. McAdoo & J. L. McAdoo (Eds.), *Black children: Social, educational, and parental environments* (pp. 33-51). Beverly Hills, CA: Sage.

Branch, C. W., & Newcombe, N. (1986). Racial attitude development among young Black children as a function of parental attitudes: A longitudinal and cross-sectional study. *Child Development, 57*(3), 712-721.

Brand, E., Ruiz, R., & Padilla, A. (1974). Ethnic identification and preferences: A review. *Psychological Bulletin, 81,* 860-890.

Burke, P. J. (1980). The self: Measurement requirements from an interactionist perspective. *Social Psychology Quarterly, 43,* 18-29.

Burns, R. (1979). *The self-concept: Theory, measurement, development, and behavior.* New York: Longman.

Butler, R. (1989). Mastery versus ability appraisal: A developmental study of children's observations of peer's work. *Child Development, 60,* 1350-1361.

Clark, K. B., & Clark, M. B. (1947). Racial identification of Negro preschool children. In K. Russell, M. Wilson, & R. Hall (Eds.), *The color complex: The politics of skin color among African Americans.* New York: Harcourt Brace Jovanovich.

Coard, S. I. (1997). Perceptions of and preferences for skin color, Black racial identity, and self-esteem among African Americans. *Dissertation Abstracts International: Section B: The Science and Engineering, 58*(3-B), p. 1523.

Coarser, W. A. (1992). Interpretive reproduction in children's peer cultures. *Social Psychology Quarterly, 55*(2), 160-177.

Comer, J. P. (1989). Racism and the education of the young children. *Teachers College Record, 90*(3), 352-361.

Cook, W., & Douglas, E. (1998). A looking-glass self in family context: A social analysis. *Journal of Family Psychology, 12*(3), 299-309.

Coopersmith, S. (1967). *The antecedents of self-esteem.* San Francisco: W. H. Freeman.

Cross, W. (1985). Black identity: Rediscovering the distinction between personal identity and reference group orientation. In M. Spencer, G. Brookins, & W. Allen (Eds.), *Beginnings: The social and affective development of Black children* (pp. 155-171). Hillsdale, NJ: Lawrence Erlbaum.

Cross, W. E. (1991). *Shades of Blacks: Diversity on African American identity.* Philadelphia: Temple University Press.

Damon, W., & Hart, D. (1982). The development of self-understanding from infancy through adolescence. *Child Development, 52,* 841-864.

Damon W., & Hart, D. (1988). *Self-understanding on childhood and adolescence.* New York: Cambridge University Press.

Devine, P. (1989). Stereotypes and prejudice: Their automatic and controlled components. *Journal of Personality and Social Psychology, 56,* 5-18.

Dixon, T. L. (2000). A social cognitive approach to studying racial stereotyping in the mass media. *African American Research Perspectives, 6*(1), 60-68.

Draper, C. V. (1999). Intrafamilial skin color socialization, racial identity attitude, and psychological well-being in African American women. *Dissertation Abstracts International: Section B: The Science and Engineering, 60*(1-B), p. 0363.

Gerson, W. M. (1968). Mass media socialization behavior: Negro-White differences. *Social Forces, 45,* 40-50.

Gordon, V. V. (1980). *The self-concept of Black Americans.* Lanham, MD: University Press of America.

Graves, S. B. (1982). The impact of television on the cognitive and affective development of minority children. In G. L. Berry & C. Mitchell-Kernan (Eds.), *Television and the socialization of the minority child* (pp. 37-67). New York: Academic Press.

Greenberg, B. S., & Atkin, C. K. (1982). Learning about minorities from television: A research agenda. In G. L. Berry & C. Mitchell-Kernan (Eds.), *Television and the socialization of the minority child* (pp. 215-243). New York: Academic Press.

Greene, B. A. (1992). Racial socialization as a tool in psychotherapy with African American children. In L. A. Vargas & J. D. Koss-Chioino (Eds.), *Working with culture: Psychotherapeutic intervention with ethnic minority children and adolescents* (pp. 63-81). San Francisco: Jossey-Bass.

Hamilton, D. L., Stroessner, S. J., Driscoll, D. M., & Denise, M. (1994). Social cognition and the study of stereotyping. In P. G. Devine & D. L. Hamilton (Eds.), *Social cognition: Impact on social psychology* (pp. 291-321). San Diego, CA: Academic Press.

Hamilton, D. L., & Trolier, T. K. (1986). Stereotypes and stereotyping: An overview of the cognitive approach. In J. F. Dovidio & S. L. Gaertner (Eds.), *Prejudice, discrimination, and racism.* Orlando FL: Academic Press.

Harter, S. (1983). Development perspectives on the self-system. In P. Mussen & E. Hetherington (Eds.), *Handbook of child psychology: Vol. 4. Socialization, personality, and social development* (pp. 275-385). New York: John Wiley.

Harter, S. (1988). Development processes in the construction of the self. In T. D. Yawkey & J. E. Johnson (Eds.), *Integrative processes and socialization: Early to middle childhood* (pp. 45-78). Hillsdale, NJ: Lawrence Erlbaum.

Herrnstein, R. J., & Murray, C. (1994). *The bell curve: Intelligence and class structure in America.* New York: Free Press.

Hilliard, A. G. (1997). *SBA: The reawakening of the African mind.* Gainesville, FL: Makare.

Hodge, J. L., Struckmann, D. K., & Trost, L. D. (1975). *Cultural bases of racism and group oppression.* Berkeley, CA: Two Rider Press.

Holmes, R. M. (1995). *How young children perceive race* (Race and Ethnic Relations, Vol. 12). Thousand Oaks, CA: Sage.

Hyde, J. S. (1983). *Half the human experience: The psychology of women* (4th ed.). Lexington, MA: D. C. Health.

Jackson, J. S., McCullough, W. R., & Gurin, G. (1997). Family, socialization environment, and identity development in Black Americans. In H. P. McAdoo (Ed.), *Black families.* Thousand Oaks, CA: Sage.

Janis, I. (1980). The influence of television on personal decision-making. In S. B. Withey & R. P. Abeles (Eds.), *Television and social behavior: Beyond violence and children* (pp. 161-189). Hillsdale, NJ: Lawrence Erlbaum.

Jones, J. (1998). Psychological knowledge and the new American dilemma of race. *Journal of Social Issues, 54*(4), 641-662.

Kardiner, A., & Oversey, L. (1951). *The mark of oppression.* New York: Norton.

Katz, P. (1975). *Toward the elimination of racism.* Elmsford, NY: Pergamon.

Kunjufu, J. (1984). *Developing positive self-images and discipline in Black children.* Chicago: African American Images.

Lewis, M., & Brooks-Gunn, J. (1979). *Social cognition and the acquisition of self.* New York: Plenum.

Marcia, J. E. (1983). Some directions for the investigation of ego development in early adolescence. *Journal of Early Adolescence, 3*(3), 215-223.

Markus, H., & Kunda, Z. (1986). Stability and malleability of the self-concept. *Journal of Personality and Social Psychology, 51*(4), 858-866.

Marshall, S. (1995). Ethnic socialization of African American children: Implications for parenting, identity development, and academic achievement. *Journal of Youth and Adolescence, 24*(4), 377-396.

McAdoo, H. P. (1985). Racial attitudes and self-concept of young Black children over time. In H. P. McAdoo (Ed.), *Black families.* Thousand Oaks, CA: Sage.

McAdoo, J. L. (1997). The roles of African American fathers in the socialization of their children. In H. P. McAdoo (Ed.), *Black families.* Thousand Oaks, CA: Sage.

McGuire, W. J., McGuire, C. V., Child, P., & Fujioka, T. (1978). Salence of ethnicity in the spontaneous self concept as a function of one's ethnic distinctions in the social environment. *Journal of Personality and Social Psychology, 36*(5), 511-529.

Miller, A. (1982). *In the eye of the beholder: Contemporary issues in stereotyping.* New York: Praeger.

Murray, C. B., & Fairchild, H. H. (1989). Models of Black adolescent academic underachievement. In R. L. Jones (Ed.), *Black adolescents.* Berkeley: University of California at Berkeley.

Murray, C. B., & Jackson, J. S. (1999). The conditioned failure model revisited. In R. L. Jones (Ed.), *African American children, youth, and parenting.* Hampton, VA: Cobb & Henry.

Murray, C. B., & Mandara, J. (2001). An assessment of racial socialization and ethnic identity as predictors of self-esteem. Unpublished manuscript.

Murray, C. B., Strokes, J. E., & Peacock, M. J. (1999). Racial socialization of African American children: A review. In R. L. Jones (Ed.), *African American children, youth, and parenting* (pp. 209-229). Hampton, VA: Cobb & Henry.

Neisser, U. (1988). Five kinds of self knowledge. *Philosophical Psychology, 1,* 35-59.

Nobles, W. W. (1973). Psychological research and the Black self-concept: A critical review. *Journal Social Issues, 29*(1), 11-31.

Oliver, M. B. (1994). Portrayals of crime race and aggression in "reality-based" police shows: A content analysis. *Journal of Broadcasting and Electronic Media, 38*(2), 179-192.

Parham, T. A., & Williams, P. T. (1993). The relationship of demographic and background factors to racial identity attitudes. *Journal of Black Psychology, 19*(1), 7-24.

Peterson, C., & McCabe, A. (1994). A social interactionist account of developing decontextualized narrative skill. *Developmental Psychology, 30*(6), 937-948.

Phinney, J. S. (1989). Stages of ethnic identity development in minority group adolescents. *Journal of Early Adolescence, 9,* 34-49.

Phinney, J. S. (1991). Ethnic identity and self-esteem: A review and integration. *Hispanic Journal of Behavioral Science, 13,* 193-208.

Phinney, J. S., & Rotheram, M. (1987). *Children's ethnic socialization.* Newbury Park, CA: Sage.

Piaget, J. S. (1952). *The child's conception of the world.* London: Routledge & Kegan Paul.

Porter, J. R., & Washington, R. E. (1979). Black identity and self-esteem: A review of studies of Black self-concept. *Annual Review of Sociology, 5,* 53-74.

Porter, J. R., & Washington, R. E. (1989). Developments in research on Black identity and self-esteem: 1979-1988. *Revue Internationale de Psychologie Sociale, 2*(3), 339-353.

Powell, G. J. (1982). The impact of television on the self-concept development of minority group children. In G. L. Berry & C. Mitchell-Kernan (Eds.), *Tele-*

vision and the socialization of the minority child (pp. 105-131). New York: Academic Press.

Quattrone, G. (1986). On the perception of a group's variability. In S. Worchel & W. Austin (Eds.), *Psychology of intergroup relations* (pp. 25-48). Chicago: Nelson-Hall.

Ramsey, P. (1987). Young children and thinking about ethnic difference. In J. S. Phinney & M. Rotheram (Eds.), *Children's ethnic socialization* (pp. 56-72). Newbury Park, CA: Sage.

Rasheed, S. Y. (1981). Self-esteem and ethic identity in African American third grade children (Doctoral dissertation, University of Michigan). *Dissertation Abstracts International, 42*(6B), 2604.

Rosser, P. L. (1978). The child: Young, gifted, and Black. In L. E. Gary (Ed.), *Mental health: A challenge to the Black community* (pp. 95-113). Philadelphia: Dorrance.

Rotheram-Borus, M. J. (1990). Adolescent's reference-group choices, self-esteem, and adjustment. *Journal of Personality and Social Psychology, 59*(5), 1075-1081.

Ruble, D. (1987). The acquisition of self-knowledge: A self-socialization process. In N. Eisenberg (Ed.), *Contemporary topics in developmental psychology* (pp. 243-270). New York: John Wiley.

Russell, K., Wilson, M., & Hall, R. (1992). *The color complex: The politics of skin color among African Americans.* New York: Harcourt Brace Jovanovich.

Sanders, M. (1998). Overcoming obstacles: Academic achievement as a response to racism and discrimination. *Journal of Negro Education, 66*(1), 83-93.

Semaj, L. T. (1985). Afrikananity, cognition, and external self-identity. In M. Spencer, G. Brookin, & W. Allen (Eds.), *Beginnings: The social and affective development* (pp. 59-72). Hillsdale, NJ: Lawrence Erlbaum.

Smith, E. P., Fogle, V., & Jacobs, J. (in press). Assessing parental ethnic socialization: Issues and implementation. In D. Johnson (Ed.), *Racial socialization.* Hampton VA: Cobb & Henry.

Spencer, M. B. (1982). Personal and group identity of Black children: An alternative synthesis. *Genetic Psychology Monographs, 183,* 59-84.

Spencer, M. B. (1983). Children's cultural values and parental child rearing strategies. *Developmental Review, 3*(4), 351-370.

Spencer, M. B. (1984). Black children's race awareness, racial attitudes, and self-concept. An interpretation. *Journal of Child Psychology and Psychiatry, 25,* 433-441.

Spencer, M. B. (1985). Cultural cognition and social cognition as identity factors in Black children's personal growth. In M. Spencer, G. Brookins, & W. Allen (Eds.), *Beginnings: The social and affective development of Black children* (pp. 215-230). Hillsdale, NJ: Lawrence Erlbaum.

Spencer, M. B. (1988). Self-concept development. *New Directions for Child Development, 42, 59-72.*

Spencer, M. B. (1999). Social and cultural influences on school adjustment: The application of an identity-focused cultural ecological perspective. *Educational Psychologist, 34*(1), 43-57.

Spencer, M. B., & Markstrom-Adams, C. (1990). Identity processes among racial and ethnic minority children in America. *Developmental Review, 61*(2), 290-310.

Stevenson, H. C. (1994). Validation of the Scale of Racial Socialization for African American adolescents: Steps toward multidimensionality. *Journal of Black Psychology 20*(4), 445-468.

Stevenson, H. C. (1995). Relationship of adolescent perceptions of racial socialization to racial identity. *Journal of Black Psychology, 21*(1), 49-70.

Stevenson, H.C. (1998). Theoretical considerations in measuring racial identity and socialization: Extending the self further. In R. L. Jones (Ed.), *African American identity development* (pp. 217-255). Hampton, VA: Cobb & Henry.

Stevenson, H. C. (1999). Theoretical considerations in measuring racial identity and socialization: Extending the self further. In R. L. Jones (Ed.), *African American identity development* (pp. 217-255). Hampton, VA: Cobb & Henry.

Stroman, C. A. (1991). Television's role in the socialization of African American children and adolescents. *Journal of Negro Education, 60*(3), 314-327.

Tajfel, H. (1981). *Human groups and social categories.* New York: Cambridge University Press.

Tan, A. S., & Tan, G. (1979). Television use and self-esteem of Blacks. *Journal of Communication, 29,* 129-135.

Tangney, J. P., & Feshbach, S. (1988). Children's television-viewing frequency: Individual differences and demographic correlates. *Personality and Social Psychology Bulletin, 14*(1), 145-158.

Tatum, B. (1987). *Assimilation blues.* Westport, CT: Greenwood.

Thornton, M. C. (1997). Strategies of racial socialization among Black parents: Mainstream, minority, and cultural messages. In R. J. Taylor, J. S. Jackson, & L. M. Chatters (Eds.), *Family life in Black America* (pp. 216-248). Thousand Oaks, CA: Sage.

Thornton, M. C., Chatters, L. M., Taylor, R. J., & Allen, W. R. (1990). Sociodemographic and environmental correlates of racial socialization by Black parents. *Child Development, 61,* 401-409.

Vygotsky, L. S. (1962). *Thought and speech.* Cambridge: MIT Press.

Wardle, F. (1992). Supporting biracial children in the school setting. *Education and Treatment of children, 15*(2), 163-172.

Whitty, J. P. (1994). "Ethnic socialization: The case of African American adolescent males." At *The significance of ethnic identity and socialization for African*

American youth: Findings from pre-to-late adolescence, a symposium conducted at the Fifth Biennial Meeting of the Society of Research on Adolescence,
California.

Wilder, D. (1986). Social categorization: Implications for creation and reduction of
intergroup bias. In L. Berkowitz (Ed.), *Advances on experimental social psychology* (Vol. 19, pp. 293-255). New York: Academic Press.

Williams, J., & Morland, J. (1976). *Race, color, and the young child.* Chapel Hill:
University of North Carolina Press.

7

Racial Socialization Processes in Single-Mother Families

Linking Maternal Racial Identity, Parenting, and Racial Socialization in Rural, Single-Mother Families With Child Self-Worth and Self-Regulation

VELMA McBRIDE MURRY
GENE H. BRODY

Parenting traditionally is defined as the fostering of children's growth through nurture, protection, and guidance. These tasks are continuous and interactive. In addition, unlike parents in mainstream society, Black parents have the responsibility of preparing their children to live in a society in which they frequently are devalued (Murry, 2000; Peters, 1985). To understand fully the growth and development of African American children, it is

AUTHORS' NOTE: This study is part of a larger research project, Rural African American Program for the Study of Competence in Children and Single-Mother Families, Gene H. Brody, principal investigator. The project is supported by a grant from the National Institutes of Health. Correspondence concerning this chapter should be addressed to Velma McBride Murry, Department of Child and Family Development, University of Georgia, Athens, GA 30602, vmurry@arches.uga.edu. This chapter was presented at the annual conference of the National Council on Family Relations, Irvine, California, November 1999.

important to know what their parents teach them about race and ethnicity and how these lessons are imparted (Bowman & Howard, 1985; Peters, 1985; Thornton, Chatters, Taylor, & Allen, 1990). Race-related socialization, defined by Smith and Walker (1999) as "processes employed by Black parents which focus on race, as well as other relevant dimensions that may be important to, or related to race" (p. 4), is an important aspect to consider in studying Black families (Tatum, 1992; Thornton et al., 1990).

Few studies have examined how social class, racism, and discrimination affect Black children's development. Even less is known about Black parents' experiences with racism, their racial self-perceptions, and the ways in which these experiences and perceptions are incorporated into child rearing. This study is a preliminary effort to investigate the linkage of maternal racial self-perception, race-related socialization approaches, other parenting processes, and maternal psychological resources with child outcomes in economically stressed rural Black families. The purpose is to understand how economic deprivation, minority status, and stigmatization due to oppression and racism affect child development. Because race-comparative models are criticized for perpetuating an image of abnormality and incompetence in Black families when compared to White families, we use an intragroup design.

Conceptual Framework

The Competence Model

The competence model of family functioning (Waters & Lawrence, 1993) was selected as the conceptual framework because it describes many of the processes used by Black parents to rear competent children. The model assumes that parenting behaviors represent adaptive responses to environmental challenges. These behaviors "make their world work, grow, and change" (Waters & Lawrence, 1993, p. 7). We view them as manifestations of the drive for mastery of the environment. Rather than regard families in which parenting problems arise as dysfunctional, we see them as attempting to adapt to an environment over which parents have little control. The competence model also assumes that parents may have strengths that can explain variations in competence among children living in high-risk environments (Murry & Brody, 1999).

The Mundane Extreme Environmental Stress (MEES) model also provides a framework for this study. It assumes that racism is a major, ubiquitous, constant, and daily contextual variable in African American life (Peters & Massey, 1983). A realistic portrayal of Black families, therefore, must include experiences of racism and discrimination, as well as the processes by which family members absorb, deflect, combat, succumb to, or overcome these experiences.

Also relevant to this study is how parenting affects children's development, specifically self-regulatory behavior and sense of self-worth. *Self-regulation,* defined as the ability to control one's attention, emotions, and behavior, is linked to resiliency and control (Baldwin, Baldwin, & Cole, 1990). Children's inability to organize behavior and to manage anger and aggression is associated with lower levels of social competence (Rothbart & Bates, 1998), a heightened risk of antisocial behavior, and academic problems (Hinshaw, Zupan, Simmel, Nigg, & Milnick, 1997; Zahn-Waxler, Cole, Welsh, & Fox, 1995). Self-worth is linked to children's resiliency (Compas, 1987; Rutter, 1987; Werner & Smith, 1982). Rutter (1987) notes that loving, secure personal relationships with significant adults and accomplishment in school, social groups, and sports increase the likelihood that children will develop a positive sense of self. This gives children the confidence necessary to negotiate difficult life circumstances and unstable environments.

Protective factors are defined as behaviors and circumstances that decrease the likelihood of negative or undesirable outcomes. They include the resources, skills, and abilities of parents and other family members; personal or social control (e.g., religious beliefs, parental monitoring); involvement in extracurricular activities (e.g., family, church, or youth groups); and commitment to conventional institutions (e.g., academic aspirations). Protective factors may exert a direct effect on child development outcomes by insulating children against risk, or they may act as moderators by determining the strength of the association between risks and developmental outcomes.

Parenting and Race-Related Socialization

Unlike mainstream parents, African American parents must foster in their children skills that will enable them to be productive citizens in a society that frequently devalues them and their families. Racial socialization, or race-related socialization, involves balancing tactics for survival in the majority culture with pride in the Black culture (McLoyd, 1991; Peters, 1985). Peters (1985) describes racial socialization as the "process of raising physically and emotionally healthy children who are Black in a society in which being Black has negative connotations" (p. 161). Stevenson, Reed, Bodison, and Bishop (1997) describe the challenge facing African American parents as the rearing of children in a "hope lost" society that expects and sees the worst in them. Psychological well-being among Black children, therefore, largely depends on the racial socialization they receive from their families.

The literature linking social context with parenting practices indicates that the socialization of Black children is based on cultural and political assumptions that their parents derive from their own experiences. For example, the daily child-rearing approaches used by many Black parents are, directly or indirectly, powerful lessons of resistance that were scripted by the parents' childhood experiences of being marginalized. Some parents openly discuss racism and discrimination with their children and attempt to protect them by encouraging children to value their Black identity and take pride in their heritage (Bowman & Howard, 1985; Demo & Hughes, 1990; Peters & Massey, 1983). Others adopt fewer proactive strategies, especially if they are concerned about inducing fear and distrust in their children (Marshall, 1995; Peters & Massey, 1983). They deemphasize the significance of race, despite the fact that they "fully expect their children to encounter racial discrimination or prejudice some day, [but] not talking about it is a way of avoiding this brutal experience as long as possible" (Peters & Massey, 1983, p. 106).

Ward (1996) describes the parenting of Black children as a political act because it includes messages about the world and the children's place in it. These messages are derived from the parents' experiences. Moreover, racial socialization transmits values and attitudes not only about racial issues but also about rules for conduct and moral values. Many Black parents emphasize the importance of hard work, education, and self-pride in preparing their children for potential racial bias (Peters, 1985; Thornton et al., 1990).

Racial Socialization and Child Psychosocial Development

Racial socialization in African American families may serve as a protective factor. For example, Black children who are exposed to explicit messages about race relations are more likely to reject stereotypic images of their race, exhibit high self-esteem, and experience academic success. Racially informed children also can cope more effectively with challenging life circumstances (Smith & Brookins, 1997; Stevenson et al., 1997; Taylor, 1976). The extent to which racial socialization buffers children from the deleterious effects of racism appears to be linked to the content of the messages that parents convey. Taylor, Chatters, Tucker, and Lewis (1990) found that when messages focused on barriers to Blacks' success, children were less likely to believe that education is linked to greater life opportunities. Exposure to messages about the victimization of Blacks may lead to a sense of helplessness and hopelessness.

Black children are less likely to develop a negative self-image if their parents skillfully weave messages about self-esteem and self-worth into moments of intimacy. This cultivates resistance against beliefs, attitudes, and practices that can erode children's confidence and impair positive identity development (Kofkin, Katz, & Downey, 1995). Resilient Black children and families, therefore, are those who can determine when, where, and how to resist oppression as well as know when, where, and how to accommodate to it (Ward, 1996).

Racial Socialization and Parents' Racial Identity

Most studies of race-related socialization focus on racial identity and developmental outcomes among children and adolescents. The linkage between Black parents' racial attitudes and their child-rearing practices has not been examined. This issue is important because parents' racial self-perceptions may explain what and how they teach their children about race, and that information would be help us understand Black children's growth and development (Bowman & Howard, 1985; Peters, 1985; Thornton et al., 1990). McLoyd (1998) points out that research models dealing with Black children should incorporate the unique history of the oppression experienced by their parents and ancestors. To understand the development of African American children and the challenges confronting their families, researchers should consider the linkages among parental perceptions of race, economic deprivation, stigmatization, discrimination, prejudice, oppression, and racism.

The studies reviewed here suggest the need to identify family processes associated with race-related socialization and the extent to which the latter affect children's social and emotional development. Our research explores the linkage of Black mothers' racial self-perception, psychological resources, and parenting processes with their children's self-regulatory behavior and feelings of self-worth. We sought to examine how single mothers living in rural areas view themselves with regard to race as well as the extent to which their attitudes are linked to parenting practices, including racial socialization. We also investigated the extent to which specific aspects of family and parenting processes, as well as child personality traits, are linked to psychosocial development among economically stressed rural Black children. We hypothesized that children whose mothers emphasize racial pride will exhibit more positive prosocial development than those whose mothers emphasize separatism or avoid teaching about race altogether. In addition, we predicted that mothers who emphasize racial pride will report greater psychological well-being, social support, and parenting efficacy than would those who promote separatist views. Finally, we hypothesized that greater self-regulatory behaviors and feelings of self-worth among Black children are linked to maternal racial socialization strategies that emphasize ethnic pride.

Method

The Data

The data from the present study were gathered as part of a longitudinal project, Rural African American Program for the Study of Competence in Children and Single-Mother Families, whose purpose is to examine the links among family processes, parenting, and psychosocial competence of children who live in economically stressed families.

The Participants

The participants in our study were 156 Black single mothers who had a 6- to 9-year-old firstborn child and who lived in rural Georgia. Only counties in which at least 25% of the population is African American were sampled to ensure that a viable Black community existed. Each family was paid $100 for participation. In 86% of the families, the mother had never married; in 11%, the mothers were divorced; and in 3%, the mothers were widowed. In 50% of the households, the mother was the only adult residing;

25% included the single mother and her own mother; and 25% had three to four adults (the mother's romantic partner, adult relatives, or both). Annual per capita income in 75% of the households was reported as $3,300 or less ($M = \$2,358$), that is, in the U.S. Bureau of the Census's (1992) first quintile, which indicates poverty status. Only 41% of the mothers were employed. In terms of education, 47% of the mothers had not finished high school; 34% had a high school diploma; 18% had some college or vocational training or an associate's degree; and 1% had a bachelor's degree.

Procedure

Field researchers made two home visits to each family as close to a week apart as the families' schedules allowed. Self-reported and observational data were collected during the visits, each of which lasted about 2 hours. Black students and community members served as field researchers, and they received 1 month of training in administering the self-report instruments and in observational procedures. During the first visit, the mother gave informed consent to her own and her child's participation in the study, and the child consented to his or her own participation.

At both home visits, mothers and children were videotaped in three activity contexts. One involved playing the board game *Trouble* (Gilbert Industries), in which players' pegs are moved around a board in accordance with numbers rolled on a die; the first player with all pegs in the "finish lane" wins. In another task, the mother told her child a story from a picture book, which served as a stimulus for parent-child interaction. Finally, the mother and child constructed a model from an assortment of Legos that the field researchers provided. Each observational task lasted at least 10 minutes. Similar observational tasks have been used in previous studies involving rural Black families with children in the same age groups as in our study (Brody et al., 1994). The families found the activities enjoyable, interesting, and understandable.

Black student research assistants received at least 10 hours of training in observational coding, which included study and discussion of coding category definitions and observation of videotaped family interactions. The research assistants worked in teams of two, viewing the videotapes and independently rating the mother-child interactions on a conflict-harmony dimension. The scale ranged from 1 (*very conflicted*; the relationship between mother and child was hostile and tense, with frequent displays of negative verbal and nonverbal behavior) to 7 (*very harmonious*; the relationship was warmly supportive, dialogue was relaxed, the mother and child clearly worked together to resolve issues, the tone was friendly). Because family interactions took place in three task settings, the scores were averaged across tasks to increase the reliability of the assessments (Epstein, 1979). Coders who also worked as field researchers did not rate any families whose home they visited. Reliability was calculated using split-half, Spearman-Brown coefficients computed for each possible pair of observers. Mean agreement scores were calculated across subjects for each pair and across all pairs of observers. Interrater reliability was estimated at .86.

At each home visit, self-report questionnaires were administered to the mother and the target child in an interview format. Each was interviewed privately, without other family members present or able to overhear the conversation. At no time during the presentation of the instruments did the field researchers assume that a family member could read. This literacy concern was one reason for adopting an interview format. When responses to a Likert scale were required, participants were shown a card with a series of graduated dots whose size corresponded to the range in magnitude of responses from which to choose, and they were asked to indicate their feelings using the dots on the card.

Measures

Maternal Personal Resources

Three resources were examined. First, religiosity was measured using a scale developed by Faulkner and DeJong (1966) that includes subscales to assess ideology ($\alpha = .75$), intelligence ($\alpha = .71$), rituals ($\alpha = .71$), experiential ($\alpha = .73$), and church importance ($\alpha = .72$). Second, marital history was measured by an item asking whether the mother had ever been married. Third, years of formal education were indicated by five choices: some high school, high school diploma, some college, vocational training or associate's degree, and college degree.

Maternal Psychological Resources

Three variables were examined. First, parental satisfaction was measured by a single item on which mothers indicated their satisfaction as parents. Second, optimism about the family's economic status was measured by a single item. Third, racial self-perception was assessed by a scale on which mothers reported how they felt that Black people and members of other races should be treated. The following attitudes were assessed: negative (three items, α =.58), positive (seven items, α =.76), and unidimensional (four items, α =.74).

Parenting Processes and Family Behavior

Six variables covered this dimension. First, developmental goals for children were indicated by how important mothers thought it was for their children to be respectful, independent, well-educated, happy, self-respecting, well-behaved, responsible, cooperative, motivated to do their best, and strongly oriented to moral values. Second, maternal involvement was measured by level of participation in the child's school activities. Third, mothers' self-perception of racial identity was measured using the Black Ethnocentrism Scale (Berry, Trimble, & Olmedo, 1986) to assess these orientations: Black pride (α = .78), separatist (α = .75), and integrationist (α = .56). Fourth, attitudes about racial socialization were assessed with the three subscales of the Parental Racial Attitude Scale, which measure limited focus on Black culture (α = .63), primary focus on Black culture (α = .74), and bicultural focus (α = .81). Fifth, home environment was assessed using the Family Routines Inventory (Jensen, James, Boyce, & Hartnett, 1983) as well as items from the revised HOME scale (Bradley & Caldwell, 1984), which measure the degree to which the home is intellectually stimulating.

Child Characteristics

Two factors were examined, personality traits and cognitive competence. Personality traits included two temperament dimensions that are linked to lower levels of self-regulation in children (Rothbart & Bates, 1998), emotionality and activity level. These were assessed using the Temperament Assessment Battery (Martin, 1984). Cronbach's alphas were .50 for emotionality and .72 for activity level. Cognitive competence was assessed using Harter's (1982) six-item scholastic competency subscale. Cronbach's alpha was .76.

Neighborhood and Community Support

Four items from the Neighborhood Support Scale (Greenberger, Goldberg, & Hamil, 1989) were used to measure the mothers' perceptions of specific neighborhood support for parenting (Cronbach's $\alpha = .75$). Using a Likert scale ranging from 1 = *strongly disagree* to 6 = *strongly agree,* mothers responded to such items as "You do not have a regular plan worked out for exchanging child care with any of your neighbors" and "Your neighbors help you out by looking after your child if you want to run a brief errand." Also, seven items from the Neighborhood Support Scale (Greenberger et al., 1989) assessed overall perception of neighborhood support such as "You are part of a close-knit neighborhood where people are friendly and help each other out" and "You can call on your neighbors to lend a hand without feeling that you are imposing on them." Cronbach's alpha was .63.

Children's Developmental Outcomes

Variables examined were self-regulating behavior and feelings of self-worth. Self-regulation was assessed by responses of mothers to Humphrey's (1982) five-item Children's Self-Control Scale. On a 5-point scale, mothers indicated how often their children think ahead of time about the consequences of actions, plan ahead before acting, pay attention to what they are doing, work toward goals, and stick to what they are doing until it is finished, even on a long, unpleasant task. The alpha coefficient for self-regulation was .72. Self-worth was measured by maternal ratings of the Global Self-Worth subscale from Harter's (1982) Ratings of Competence for Children. Cronbach's alpha for self-worth was .74.

Analytical Procedures

Pearson's *r* was used to examine the bivariate correlations of each study variable with the selected outcome variables. Hierarchical multiple regression was used to test the study hypotheses. This procedure eliminated the problem of collinearity because it ensured the exclusion of redundant variables (Diekhoff, 1992; Tacq, 1997). Analyses indicated the extent to which demographic characteristics, maternal psychological resources,

TABLE 7.1 Intercorrelations of Race-Related Issues, Mother's
Education, and Child Outcomes ($N = 157$)

	1	2	3	4	5	6	7	8
1. Black pride	–	.622**	.407**	.249**	–.200*	.052	.056	–.092
2. Separatist		–	.192*	.120	–.321**	–.066	–.082	.029
3. Integrationist			–	.285**	–.084	.111	.056	.073
4. Race-related socialization				–	.122	.046	.177*	.002
5. Mother's education					–	.100	.123	.004
6. Religiosity						–	–.052	.088
7. Self-worth							–	.121
8. Self-regulation								–

*$p < .05$. **$p < .01$.

racial socialization, child personality traits, and community support contributed unique variance to child self-worth.

Results

Descriptive Statistics and Bivariate Correlations

Univariate statistics revealed that more mothers perceived their racial
identity as Black pride (40%) or separatist (37.1%) rather than integrationist (22.9%). Intercorrelations among race-related issues, maternal
characteristics, and child outcomes are presented in Table 7.1. The relation
between maternal racial identity and racial socialization was significant.
Mothers who identified with Black pride and separatist views were likely to
believe that their children should be given explicit messages about race ($r =$
.25 and .29 respectively, $p < .01$). Mothers with more education were significantly less likely to identify with Black pride and separatist orientations
($r = -.200$ and $r = -.321$, respectively). Exposure to messages that focus on
Black culture was associated with increased self-worth among children.

Furthermore, maternal education also related positively to children's feelings of self-worth ($p < .05$).

Hierarchical Regression Analyses and Child Outcomes

Two hierarchical regression analyses were executed; the results are presented in Tables 7.2 and 7.3. The variables remaining in the model (Table 7.2) explained 28% of the variance in child self-worth. Entering racial socialization in Step 1 accounted for 2.4% of the variance in self-worth (see Table 7.2). With the entry of maternal resources at Steps 2 and 3, R^2 increased to .057 and .111, respectively. Home environment factors, entered at Step 4, resulted in a significant increment of .013 ($p < .01$). When developmental goals were entered at Step 5, R^2 increased to .197. Child characteristic factors entered at Step 6 resulted in an increment of 6.5% over and above the contributions of parenting and maternal resources variables. The entrance of social support from neighbors in Step 7 resulted in a change in R^2 of .081 ($p < .01$).

The β coefficients reveal that, for economically stressed, rural Black children, a positive sense of self was linked to positive race-related messages from mothers, more financial resources, greater maternal satisfaction, and developmental goals that encourage children to be well-behaved and well-mannered and to do their best. Less positive feelings about self emerged among children whose mothers attend church frequently and focus on respect, independence, and happiness as developmental goals for them. Self-worth also was negatively associated with high parental expectations regarding mathematics performance and anxious personality in the child. Maternal racial identity did not contribute significantly to children's feelings of self-worth.

The results presented in Table 7.3 indicate that the predictors of children's self-worth differed somewhat from the predictors of self-regulation. For example, two maternal racial identity domains contributed 1.4% of the variance in child self-regulation. The β coefficients reveal that a maternal racial identity with Black pride was negatively associated with child self-regulation, whereas a separatist view was positively associated with it. Entering maternal resources at Steps 2 and 3 increased R^2 to .211 ($p < .01$), and entering home environment factors in Step 4 increased it to .267. Variables concerning parents' developmental goals and involvement in child's education, entered at Step 5, explained 18.3% of the variance and in-

TABLE 7.2 Hierarchical Regression Analysis of Race-Related Issues, Maternal Resources, Parenting Processes, Child Factors, and Community Support With Child Self-Worth

Outcome	Block	F Test	Total R^2	Variables in Final Model	β at Final Step
Self-worth	1. Race-related socialization	4.14*	.024	Race-related socialization	.149*
	2. Maternal personal resources	5.08**	.057	Family financial resources	.142*
	3. Maternal psychological resources	4.65**	.064	Church attendance	-.142**
		5.15**	.111	Parental satisfaction	.170*
	4. Home environment	3.83**	.124	Intellectually stimulating	-.189‡
				General environment	.241**
	5. Parental expectations	3.53**	.197	Goal 1: be respectful	-.257**
				Goal 2: be independent	-.226**
				Goal 4: be happy	-.136‡
				Goal 6: be well-behaved, well-mannered	.202**
				Goal 9: do his/her best	.214**
				Mathematics	-.226**
	6. Child characteristic	4.25**	.262	Anxious	-.183
				Manageability	.134‡
	7. Social support	4.13**	.280	Neighborhood support	.145*

‡$p < .10.$ *$p < .05.$ **$p < .01.$

109

TABLE 7.3 Hierarchical Regression Analysis of Maternal Resources, Racial Identity, Home Environment, Parenting Processes, Child Temperament, and Community Support With Child Self-Regulation

Outcome	Block	F Test	Total R^2	Variables in Final Model	β at Final Step
Self-regulation	1. Maternal ethnic identity	1.19	.014	Separatist	.218**
				Black Pride	-.230**
	2. Maternal personal resources	2.96*	.070	Employment	.206**
				Education	-.099
	3. Maternal psychological resources	5.39**	.211	Religious ideology	.334**
				Religious intent	-.252**
				Church attendance	.123*
				Parental satisfaction	.082‡
	4. Home environment	5.77**	.267	Family routines	.220**
				Intellectually stimulating	-.094‡
	5. Parental expectations	7.83**	.450	Conduct	-.202**
				Parental Involvement	.263**
				Goal 2: be independent	-.186*
				Goal 6: be well-behaved	-.268**
				Goal 8: get along with others	.090‡
				Goal 10: have strong moral values	.233**
	6. Child characteristic	9.47**	.530	Cognitive competence	.160*
				Activity level	-.209**
	7. Social support	9.92**	.560	Neighborhood support	.176*

‡ $p < .10$. * $p < .05$. ** $p < .01$.

creased R^2 to .450. Child personality traits, entered at Step 6, explained 8% of the variance in self-regulation over and above the contributions of parenting, maternal resources, and home environment. Social support, entered at the final step, accounted for 3% of the variance in child self-regulation. The final model predicted 56% of the variance in children's self-regulatory behavior.

Conclusion

This study focuses on mothers' self-perceptions of race and racial socialization as factors in child development among economically stressed rural Black families. The findings highlight the importance of contextual factors in understanding the influence of Black parents' attitudes and behavior (Gray & Cosgrove, 1985; Harrison, Wilson, Pine, Chan, & Buriel, 1990; Kofkin et al., 1995) on their children's development. Different race-related issues emerged as significant predictors of different child outcomes. For example, racial socialization was more strongly related to child self-worth than to child self-regulatory behaviors. This suggests that the parenting tasks associated with rearing African Americans not only are multidimensional but also have differential effects on child development.

The findings also highlight the significance of parental perceptions of race. Children whose parents held separatist racial views exhibited more self-regulatory behavior than the children of mothers with integrationist or Black pride attitudes. Regardless of these parental self-perceptions, however, mothers who communicated to their children positive messages about Black identity were contributing to a sense of self-worth. As Kofkin and associates (1995) note, Black children are less likely to internalize negative attitudes when their parents skillfully weave messages about self-worth into moments of intimacy. This cultivates resistance to negative beliefs, attitudes, and practices that can erode the child's self-confidence and impair identity development.

The intricacies of racial socialization by Black parents warrant future investigation, but our study points to the complexities they face. Stevenson et al. (1997) describe racial socialization as a multidimensional process in which parental guidance not only prepares children for experiences with oppression but also builds ethnic and racial pride and a sense of cultural empowerment (Peters, 1985). The process varies according to its purpose, type, and approach (Demo & Hughes, 1990). At the same time, it appears from our study that race-related issues are somewhat less important in understanding child development than are maternal psychological well-being, a supportive home environment, and clear expectations that foster social competence. These factors need to be included in models and programs developed for Black families.

Educators, practitioners, and researchers should not disregard the influence of race and culture in parenting processes. Our point is that each parent is shaped by individual experiences, and each family has a unique history of oppression (McLoyd, 1998). These, in turn, contribute to the present findings, demonstrating the importance of understanding parents' racial identity and the attitudes that parents teach their children, as well as how they teach them. We need to know more about this process to understand more fully the growth and development of African American children.

References

Baldwin, A. L., Baldwin, C., & Cole, R. E. (1990). Stress-resistant families and stress-resistant children. In J. Rolf, A. S. Master, D. Cicchett, K. H. Neuhterlein, & S. Weintraub (Eds)., *Risk and protective factors in the development of psychopathology* (pp. 257-280). New York: Cambridge University Press.

Berry, J. W., Trimble, J. E., & Olmedo, E. L. (1986). Assessment of acculturation. In W. Lonner & J. W. Berry (Eds.), *Field methods in cross cultural research* (pp. 291-324). Beverly Hills, CA: Sage.

Bowman, P. J., & Howard, C. (1985). Race-related socialization, motivation, and academic achievement: A study of Black youths in three-generation families. *Journal of the American Academy of Child Psychiatry, 24,* 134-141.

Bradley, R. H., & Caldwell, B. M. (1984). The relation of infants' home environments to achievement test performance in first grade: A follow-up study. *Child Development, 55,* 803-812.

Brody, G. H., Stoneman, Z., Flor, D., McCrary, C., Hasting, L., & Conyers, O. (1994). Financial resources, parent psychological functioning, parent co-caregiving, and early adolescent competence in rural two-parent African American families. *Child Development, 65,* 590-595.

Compas, B. (1987). Coping with stress during childhood and adolescence. *Psychological Bulletin, 101,* 393-396.

Demo, D. H., & Hughes, M. (1990). Socialization and racial identity among Black Americans. *Social Psychology Quarterly, 53,* 364-374.

Diekhoff, G. (1992). *Statistics for the behavioral sciences; univariate, bivariate, and multivariate.* Dubuque, IA: Brown.

Epstein, S. (1979). The stability of behavior: I. On predicting most of the people much of the time. *Journal of Personality and Social Psychology, 37,* 1097-1123.

Faulkner, J. E., & DeJong, G. F. (1966). Religiosity in 5-D: An empirical analysis. *Social Forces, 45,* 246-254.

Gray, E., & Cosgrove, J. (1985). Ethnocentric perception of childrearing practices in protective services. *Child Abuse and Neglect, 9,* 389-396.

Greenberger, E., Goldberg, D., & Hamil, T. (1989). Survey measures for the study of work, parenting, well-being. *Developmental Psychology, 29,* 181-197.

Harrison, A. O., Wilson, M. N., Pine, C. J., Chan, S. Q, & Buriel, R. (1990). Family ecologies of ethnic minority children. *Child Development, 61,* 347-362.

Harter, S. (1982). The perceived competence scale for children. *Child Development, 53,* 87-94.

Hinshaw, S. P., Zupan, B. A., Simmel, C., Nigg, J. T., & Milnick, S. (1997). Peer status in boys with and without attention-deficit hyperactivity disorders: Predictions from overt and covert antisocial behavior, social isolation, and authoritative parenting beliefs. *Child Development, 64,* 880-896.

Humphrey, L. L. (1982). Children's and teachers' perspectives on children's self-control: The development of two rating scales. *Journal of Consulting and Clinical Psychology, 50,* 624-633.

Jensen, E., James, S., Boyce, T., & Hartnett, S. (1983). The Family Routines Inventory: Development and validation. *Social Science Medicine, 17,* 201-211.

Kofkin, J. A., Katz, P. A., & Downey, E. P. (1995, March). *Family discourse about race and the development of children's racial attitudes.* Paper presented at the Society for Research on Child Development, Biennial Meeting, Indianapolis, IN.

Marshall, S. (1995). Ethnic socialization of African American children: Implication for parenting, identity development, and academic achievement. *Journal of Youth and Adolescence, 24,* 377-396.

Martin, R. P. (1984). *Manual for the Temperament Assessment Battery.* Unpublished monograph, University of Georgia, Athens.

McLoyd, V. C. (1991). What is the study of African American children the study of? In R. L. Jones (Ed.), *Black psychology* (3rd ed., pp. 419-440). Berkeley, CA: Cobb & Henry.

McLoyd, V. C. (1998). Socioeconomic disadvantage and child development. *American Psychologist, 53,* 185-189.

Murry, V. M. (2000). Challenges and experiences of Black-American families. In P. C. McKenry & S. J. Price (Eds.), *Families and change: Coping with stressful events* (2nd ed., pp. 333-358). Thousand Oaks, CA: Sage.

Murry, V. M., & Brody, G. H. (1999). Self-regulation and self-worth of Black children reared in economically stressed, rural, single-parent families: The contributions of risk and protective factors. *Journal of Family Issues, 20*, 458-484.

Peters, M. F. (1985). Racial socialization of young Black children. In H. P. McAdoo & J. L. McAdoo (Eds.), *Black children* (pp. 228-241). Beverly Hills, CA: Sage.

Peters, M. F., & Massey, G. (1983). Chronic vs. mundane stress in family stress theories: The case of Black families in White America. *Marriage and Family Review, 6*, 193-211.

Rothbart, M. K., & Bates, J. E. (1998). Temperament. In W. Damon (Series Ed.) & N. Eisenberg (Vol. Ed.), *Handbook of child psychology: Vol. 3. Social, emotional, and personality development* (15th ed., pp. 105-176). New York: John Wiley.

Rutter, M. (1987). Psychosocial resilience and protective mechanisms. *American Journal of Orthopsychiatry, 57*, 316-331.

Smith, E. P., & Brookins, C. C. (1997). Toward the development of an ethnic identity measure for African American youth. *Journal of Black Psychology, 23*, 358-377.

Smith, E. P., & Walker, K. (1999). Ethnic identity and its relationship to self-esteem, perceived efficacy, and prosocial attitudes. *Journal of Adolescence, 22*, 867-881.

Stevenson, H. C., Reed, J., Bodison, P., & Bishop, A. (1997). Racism stress management: Racial socialization beliefs and the experience of depression and anger in African American youth. *Youth and Society, 29*, 197-219.

Tacq, J. (1997). *Multivariate analysis techniques in social science research*. Thousand Oaks, CA: Sage.

Tatum, B. (1992). *Assimilation blues*. Northhampton, MA: Hazel-Maxwell.

Taylor, R. (1976). Black youth and psychological development. *Journal of Black Studies, 6*, 353-372.

Taylor, R. J., Chatters, L. M., Tucker, M. B., & Lewis, E. (1990). Developments in research on Black families: A decade review. *Journal of Marriage and the Family, 54*, 993-1007.

Thornton, M. C., Chatters, L. M., Taylor, R. J., & Allen, W. R. (1990). Sociodemographic and environmental correlates of racial socialization by Black parents. *Child Development, 61*, 401-410.

U.S. Bureau of the Census. (1992). *Household and family characteristics: 1991* (Current Population Reports series P-20, No. 458). Washington, DC: Government Printing Office.

Ward, J. V. (1996). Raising resisters: The role of truthtelling in the psychological development of African American girls. In B. J. Leadbeater & N. Way (Eds.), *Urban girls: Resisting stereotypes, creating identities* (pp. 85-99). New York: New York University Press.

Waters, D., & Lawrence, E. (1993). *Competence, courage, and change: An approach to therapy.* New York: Norton.

Werner, E. E., & Smith, R. S. (1982). *Vulnerable but invincible: A study of resilient children.* New York: McGraw-Hill.

Zahn-Waxler, C., Cole, P. M., Welsh, J. D., & Fox, N. A. (1995). Psychophysiological correlates of empathy and prosocial behaviors in preschool children with behavior problems. *Development and Psychopathology, 7,* 27-48.

Part III

Educational Environments of Children

8

A Psychological and Educational Perspective on Black Parenting

ANDERSON J. FRANKLIN
NANCY BOYD-FRANKLIN
CHARLENE V. DRAPER

This chapter presents a discussion of issues confronting African American parents in the psychological and educational development of their children. Much of the discussion is based on our clinical work, the supervision of psychological and psychiatric services provided to African American families, and issues presented by current practitioners in the discipline of school psychology. In the first part of this chapter, we discuss a definition of psychoeducation and the role of parenting vis-à-vis the education of children. We next present the social and historical context of parenting and a discussion of the demands faced by African American parents of children with educational and psychological difficulties. This includes delineating some of the educational tasks in parenting, reviewing strategies for coping with single parenthood and becoming an advocate for your children. We also emphasize teaching African American children about racism, and we stress the importance of parental vigilance about socially impacted educational trends. In the end, we note some pitfalls in the school system that may result in educational and clinical problems, and we offer some suggestions for intervention as well as prevention of such situations.

Overview of Parenting Issues

A psychoeducational perspective on Black parenting is the view that children's experiences contain both socioemotional (i.e., affective) and learning (i.e., cognitive) components. These two elements are always interactive in the daily transactions of children and are not mutually exclusive. *Parenting* refers to the person(s) responsible for the nurture and guidance of children through developmental periods into adulthood. In no way is this restricted to any particular family model or biological linkage. Parents are the people responsible for the care and welfare of the child. They are the people who perform the parental duties from childhood into adolescence and young adulthood. Children's psychological and educational development is enhanced when parenting combines love, commitment, and advocacy. When there is parental contempt for, rejection of, or lack of advocacy for children, their psychological and educational development suffers.

In response to daily learning experiences over time, children acquire knowledge and a wide range of feelings. Therefore, parenting is more than teaching survival skills, which in our view is a subsistence goal; rather, parenting involves a larger strategy toward the child's self-actualization. This elevates the importance of monitoring children's daily activities as a prime purpose of parenting. Fulfilling the educational tasks of parenting may take many forms, but the objective is clear: to optimize the intrinsic talents and abilities of children.

For African American people, parenting has too often been consigned to teaching kids to survive and to not submit to the inequities of racism. There is no choice in this regard. However, even this fundamental task in African American parenting is changing. Perhaps as a result of preoccupation with the oppressive socioeconomic depression in the African American community, the new generation of African American parents seems to be overwhelmed by the full responsibilities of parenting African American children. Caretaking must be accomplished in addition to nurturing Black identity and teaching the nuances of racism. Our clinical work with young Black parents has exposed a crucial difference between this generation and previous ones in the teaching of racial consciousness to children. Young Black parents have not experienced the blatant restrictions of overt public segregation and Jim Crow laws. Many do not know what Jim Crow laws were, much less their history. This generation is more a victim of the covert forms of institutional racism. Unlike their grandparents, members of the new generation must be more vigilant about how subtle social policies and practices eclipse opportunities for African American children. They must battle the seduction of pseudo access and participation in society and confront the real status of equal opportunity. Success at this is directly related to preparing African American children to develop positive self-esteem and skills in negotiating a racist society. This goal can only be achieved by parental advocacy for an effective and relevant education for African American children. Children spend fully half of their waking time within schools. African Americans view quality educational opportunity as the path toward success and upward mobility. Institutional racism (e.g., racial inequality in educational treatment, access, and resources) combined with socioeconomic inequities continues to relegate too many African American children to inadequate education, low self-esteem, and lack of self-actualization.

As Harrison-Ross and Wyden (1973) have written, Black parents want

> to bring their children up to be comfortable with their blackness, to be secure, to be proud, to be able to love, to grow up being and feeling equal, comfortable, responsible, effective, and at home in the world they live in. (pp. xx-xxi)

The education African American children receive often fails to support this perspective, placing even greater burdens on African American parents.

This task of adequately educating the African American child is at times difficult, given the hurdles of racism and oppression. In addition, Black parents must help prepare their children for bicultural existence in a Black world represented by their home, family, and community and a White world represented by school, work, and the broader reaches of American society (Comer & Poussaint, 1975). Success in raising African American children requires greater knowledge, diligence, and vigilance than are required of parents of other ethnic groups.

The Social and Historical Context of Black Parenting

To understand Black parenting today, the historical factors that influenced current child-rearing practices must be acknowledged. The influence of the African orientation on parenting and children must be considered (Sudarkasa, 1981). Most societies in Africa were primarily tribal in organization. Child rearing was a communal task, with the entire tribe sharing responsibility for raising children. The philosophy was based on a "we" focus rather than the Western individualistic or "I" focus (Mbiti, 1970; Nobles, 1980). Children were raised to believe that their primary allegiance was to the tribe. Therefore, if children did not carry out responsibilities, an adult member would provide appropriate discipline. Although caution is warranted in drawing direct parallels between African traditions and current African American practices, there are a number of similarities. It is not at all uncommon for Black children in America today to be raised in large extended families in which a number of blood and "nonblood" relatives may provide role models and accept some parenting or child-rearing responsibilities (Boyd-Franklin, 1989; Hines & Boyd-Franklin, 1982).

The key issue is that parenting may be a shared task that goes beyond the traditional "nuclear family" structure. Because parenting is a shared task, it is incumbent on the family to ensure that the child is fully understood. To be a responsible parent and advocate, one family member should consistently interact with the educational system to present an accurate profile of the child to pupil personnel within the school system. Different family members interacting with school personnel at different times may present less than fully developed profiles of children's learning needs and personalities (C. V. Draper, personal communication, December 3, 1999).

Values and Racial Identity

The task of parenting involves the transmission of social and cultural values. These include folkways, religious practices, mores, and socialization in terms of the appropriate behavior for different social situations. These tasks are implicit in psychoeducational development. On the affective level, the task of parenting is to help a child relate in an emotionally appropriate manner to family members and others. These relationships become the prototype for relationships outside the family, such as those with peers, classmates, teachers, and community authority figures. In the area of social and cultural values, African American children are often misperceived and misunderstood by White pupil personnel (Tettegah, 1996). White teachers bring their own racial identity attitudes and consciousness to the instruction of African American children. Their level of racial identity consciousness affects their perception of the "teachability" and cognitive ability of African American students. In Tettegah's (1996) research, overall, African American students were rated more negatively (less cognitive ability, less motivated, less verbal) than were Asian or White American students. Teacher concepts and expectations of African American children affect children's self-concepts, motivation, academic achievement, and future ambitions. Teacher expectations have been found to become self-fulfilling prophecies. Inconsistent home-school values may result in lower expectations, lower achievement, and negative self-concepts (Slaughter-Defoe & Carlson, 1996).

Contemporary Black Parenting

Being responsible parents is a complex task. Parents are required to understand the way children think and feel, as well as to guide their thoughts and feelings toward constructive and positive goals. To have their children achieve the goal of becoming responsible adults, parents must act in a responsible manner. The task of dutiful parents is to define the parameter of responsible parenthood. Society, through its system of values, provides one set of parental guidelines that may differ from particular ethnic traditions and values embodied in parents' community and family heritage. Parents' interpretation and reconciliation of those values and their philosophy of life provide the foundation for their own personal parental strategies. These strategies may or may not be consistent with those of the educational system within which the Black child must operate. Under special circumstances, family strategies for educating African American children may need augmenting by outside resources and a network of supportive individuals.

With the contemporary world relying more on technology, there are demands for new skills and means of survival. Computers are redefining the way people communicate and transact business. Concomitantly, the skills required to participate in the job market are changing. Increasing pressure is being placed on parents to evaluate their strategy for raising children as well as parental goals in the preparation of the child for adulthood. Whatever may come with the 21st century, child rearing will require parents to manage both the psychological and educational welfare of children in a society more governed by a global economy with global technology and global values.

Demographics and Black Families

To approach the task of Black parenting, the status of the Black family must be considered. As noted in the National Urban League's (1984) *State of Black America,* there has been a rapid growth in the number of Black families headed by women (47%). This rate has remained stable through 1996 (U.S. Bureau of the Census, 1997). The income of these families approximates only 64% of the income reported by White families in the same circumstances. Black families in general have an income that is 62.6% of that of White families. In 1996, compared to Whites, twice as many Blacks made less than $25,000 annually. More than twice as many Whites as Blacks made more than $50,000 annually. The percentage of Black families below poverty level decreased from 27.8% in 1990 to 26.4% in 1996, but 70.4% of Black babies were born to unwed mothers. In 1994, 23.2% of Black children were born to teenage mothers. Rates of completion of elementary and secondary school for African American children continue to drop, and preparation in basic, let alone marketable, skills has fallen to crisis proportions, particularly in U.S. urban areas. Unemployment for Blacks is more than double that for Whites, and the rate for Black youth is even higher (U.S. Bureau of the Census, 1997). The dilemma for the Black family is the loss of momentum toward upward mobility and the increasing noncompetitive status of the next generation of young Black adults.

The Social Context of Childrearing

Perhaps an equal if not greater concern is the demands placed on child rearing under these social circumstances. There are obviously fewer material resources to work with in a state of impoverishment. Moreover, the inability of Black men to find and maintain secure jobs has created instability in family roles and structures (Bowman, 1992). In spite of the socioeconomic direction of Black families, inferences about the consequences to Black child development can be overly pessimistic. Black families have a resiliency and strength that has withstood poor social circumstances (Franklin, 1999; Hill, 1972; McAdoo, 1981). These strengths should not be overlooked, any more than weaknesses should go unacknowledged. The task for behavioral scientists as well as Black parents is to be realistic in the appraisal of the social and educational context in which Black child development occurs (Boyd-Franklin, Franklin, & Toussaint, 2000).

Single-Parent Issues and Coping Strategies

There clearly are many ways to interpret current statistics on Black families. The classic stance taken by sociologists in the 1960s was to "blame the victim" (Moynihan, 1965; Ryan, 1971). We can blame the victim, or we can work toward the development of strategies designed to meet the needs of Black families, particularly single-parent families. First, we must be aware that statistics, particularly those gleaned from census data, often mask the support systems and coping skills developed by families specifically to manage their life circumstances. Second, researchers and service providers often lose sight of the reality that growing up in a single-parent family does not necessarily predestine children to pathology.

Some issues are unique to single parents, particularly mothers struggling to raise children alone. Some key issues are the financial pressure and the scarcity of resources. With the dwindling of fiscal support from federal, state, and local authorities, many of these single parents face a constant battle to provide the bare necessities of life for their children. This often preempts concerns about psychoeducational and socioemotional development. In turn, the educational system often unfairly attributes to these parents a lack of interest in their children's education. Coleman (1991) notes that parents need a particular concern before they will, in general, maintain contact with their children's school. Most parent-school contact centers on crisis issues.

It is not surprising that many a single parent feels overwhelmed by the demands of everyday living. This feeling is magnified for Black single parents, as more than 50% of them have incomes significantly below the national poverty line, in contrast to about 30% of White single parents (Cummings, 1983). In addition to financial support and necessities such as housing and food, there is the question of emotional support for single parents. If parents are to adequately nurture the psychoeducational development of their children, they must receive some attention to their own needs. Part of this process requires encouraging Black single parents to use available resources. First and foremost, parents can look to their own extended families for individuals who can help with the psychoeducational task of parenting and provide additional role models for their children. The fundamental task of single parents is to create an environment that will enhance the psychoeducational development of the child. There is nothing sacred about traditional or extended family structures if they do not work. Single parents who live some distance from relatives must use other available resources and networks, such as friends, churches, or community agencies, to create an environment for the psychological and educational development of their children.

Supportive Networks for Parents

For many generations, African American families also have relied on African American churches to contribute to the psychoeducational development of their children and to provide additional role models. Often, mothers struggling alone can enlist the aid of a minister and church members, as well as Sunday school and church activities, to instill values that clearly shape Black children's development. Churches in the African American community also have provided emotional support to parents overburdened with the task of parenting. Often, these churches contribute directly to the formal education of African American children and their cognitive development by providing low-cost day care and/or elementary school programs.

The task of single parents to provide an enriched, supportive, educational and social environment for children is difficult but not impossible to accomplish. A number of special programs within the urban public school system (e.g., alternative educational settings, talented and gifted classes, and charter schools) offer effective alternatives to regular public school education. These schools often require interviews, testing, and awareness of deadline dates as well as the focus and location of the programs. Single and working African American parents, already burdened, may feel they do not have the time to pursue these hopeful alternatives. Making a point to set aside time early in the school year to call the district office for this information, taking time to review the information and choosing the most feasible possibilities, may help single parents to obtain higher quality education without an added financial burden. Single parents can also obtain suggestions from pupil personnel knowledgeable about their children's strengths and weaknesses, interests, and academic ability. Making telephone calls during parents' lunch hour and writing notes directly in their children's notebook requesting information, appointments, and feedback can reduce time taken from parents' duties after work. A key initial issue here is finding appropriate day care facilities that support the parental values for the child from a very early age. In addition, single parents face alone a dilemma that confronts even two working parents—that is, how to carefully monitor children after school and give enough attention to important areas such as physical care as well as homework assistance. Many children are alone for hours after school and receive relatively little monitoring. The problem of "latchkey children" has reached epidemic proportions throughout this country. Addressing issues for working parents, Wirth (1991) enlists the school as a cooperative and flexible partner in the meeting of parents' needs: weekend parent-teacher conferences, parent-teacher association meetings in the evenings with specific goals, provision of afterschool programs, holiday and snow-day child care when parents have to work, respect for the time considerations of these parents, and the attitude that these parents do care about their children's education. These are all viable options that single parents can suggest to their particular schools to help parents maintain greater contact with their schools.

African American parents in many communities have had to band together and demand after-school services from their school programs and their churches; in some cases, they have pooled their limited resources to provide after-school baby-sitting services. Support groups that address survival, educational, and parenting issues can serve the needs of single parents. These can and should be offered in schools and through other community agencies.

Many African American single parents have expressed tremendous fear about their perceived inability to protect their children from the "dangerous" elements in their communities. These might include peer influences, drugs, and delinquent activities. Community violence may also be an issue and have particular effect on younger members of the community (Randolph, Koblinsky, & Roberts, 1996). This situation can sometimes result in parents' being overprotective and taking an overcontrolling stance, such as restricting a child from going out into the street to play with peers. It is important that parents make education about these influences an important part of their children's psychoeducational development; they should also place emphasis on learning to cope with the realities of urban life. Extreme overprotectiveness can be as detrimental as a total lack of monitoring, because it can stifle the socioemotional development of children by limiting their development of independence, good reality testing, and appropriate social judgment. If this situation is to be avoided, African American parents must be particularly conscious of the need for "unified parenting." This involves the coordination and management of parenting so that the key caretakers are all giving a single message to the child. It is important for those involved in parenting to discuss carefully and reach agreement on child-rearing practices, especially on disciplinary and socialization issues.

Another possible effect of violence on the psychoeducational development of children is parents' response to their perceived inability to protect children. Parents may "experience depression, anxiety, and reduced self-efficacy" (Randolph et al., 1996, p. 285). Violence affects the child's cognitive, socioemotional, and coping capacities. Professional or religious counseling may be enlisted to lessen these effects.

Parents and other key family members have the chief responsibility for creating the social/environmental context for children. This might include decisions about exposing children to their history, cultural heritage, and the impact of racism. It would include expectations for children's education and school performance. Although some research suggests that African American children are less motivated to achieve, Banks and McQuater (1995) found that when interest was controlled for, there was no difference in motivation between African American and White students. With this knowledge, parents can provide activities that are geared to their children's interests and also support academic achievement. Shields and Dupree's (1983) research suggests several ways to accomplish this goal. For 91% of their child participants, the giving of "tangible rewards" (p. 442) was directly related to school achievement. Books of interest as well as educational books (not encyclopedias) and mothers' visits to their children's schools were also related to better reading skills. Encouraging children to figure out how to pronounce words, helping children with reading when necessary, and encouraging extra reading at home were listed as supportive of greater reading achievement. Setting up a home environment consistent with these conditions is probably viable for many single and working parents. These activities at home also support greater bonding between parent and child.

Teenage Mothers

With the growing incidence of teenage pregnancy in the Black community, multiple caretaking families will grow, and one has to wonder what role parents play or do not play in this statistic. Adolescence is admittedly a complex period in the life span (Franklin, 1982). Social and personal development is beginning to assume adult form. On the other hand, can teenage parents be required to handle the task of equipping children with the survival skills that they themselves are still cultivating? It is not so much whether teenage parents can be successful at parenting, because there is evidence that they can. Rather, the question is whether they are ready for parenting and for giving the quality of care required by the child.

For African American teenagers, prevention of early pregnancy is often related to school achievement. Low academic functioning and early teen pregnancy coexist often with teenagers' attitude that pregnancy does not present any disadvantages to them. To help teenagers understand the long-term impact of pregnancy, a realistic presentation of its disadvantages in the light of adolescents' goals must be the gist of adolescent sex education. The relationship between pregnancy, dropping out of school, and failure to achieve life goals needs reinforcing, both at home and in school, especially for adolescents designated as limited in their ability to learn as rapidly as others (Prater, 1992).

A significant aspect of this social phenomenon is its commentary on Black female-male relationships. Whereas teenager mothers and their children frequently return to her family of origin, teenage fathers often are on the periphery, if they are included at all. Although this may be a practical solution, it may convey a subtle social message about the value of family and the structure of male-female responsibilities in parenting.

Enhancing the Learning Experience

Enhancing the social context in Black child development maximizes psychoeducational development. Children in general negotiate three major environmental settings: home, school, and community. Within each are particular experiences that nurture and direct affective and cognitive development. The settings are interdependent. Black parents in the past have been sensitive to this interdependency in the teaching of survival skills in a racist society. Parents must also be sensitive to this interdependency for educational achievement.

Many of the critical skills of Black parenthood needed in the past are needed in contemporary Black America. Black children's response to the conditions at home, in their school, and in the neighborhood is a product of their ability to understand their experiences (i.e., the cognitive domain) and their emotional reactions (i.e., the affective domain). That they are not mutually exclusive must be continually stressed. Contained in the approach to managing life experiences is the structure of personality. Achievement or failure, adaptive or maladaptive behavior, is simply a manifestation of the child's personal management style. Black parents can play a significant role in shaping that style. Children must learn the skills of survival to negotiate the social and racial conditions of society. They must acquire literacy and marketable skills to compete in the world of work. But foremost in the tasks of Black parenting is teaching the child about the nuances and impact of racism.

For African American parents to deny the existence of racism is to misguide the psychoeducational development of their children. Even if children are insulated from overt personal confrontations with racism, the vestiges of a racist society are omnipresent. Too many Black parents are abdicating their child-rearing responsibilities to instruments of institutionalized racism (Pierce, 1974). Infant and day care centers are reducing parent-child contact at critical periods in development. Moreover, to gauge their success at enrichment, these centers must be monitored as closely as primary school systems, where the quality of education for Black children remains woefully inadequate and where an alarming number of parents are failing to become involved.

Getting a "good" education for their children remains African American parents' hope for improving their children's access to better life opportunities. Monitoring school achievement is no less important today than in the past. However, the increasing dropout rate of Black students before completion of secondary school requires scrutiny of what is happening to Black youth's future. Schools are social environments, not simply repositories for knowledge. Going to school must be rewarding for both socioemotional and educational reasons. Hence, accountability becomes an important parental task. This includes monitoring children's progress in school and checking to see if the school is fulfilling its commitment to educate. For African American parents cognizant of the ravages of racism, evaluation of the formal educational process becomes uppermost in the task of guiding the psychoeducational development of their children. This obligation is more than signing end-of-term grade reports. It means that parents fully engage in the configuration of activities that contribute to the affective and cognitive experiences of their children. Hence, parent-school interactions are as important to child development as are parent-child interactions (Carlson, 1991; Coleman, 1991). Community school board decisions can be as consequential to the psychoeducational development of Black children as any parental decision. Black parents must come to terms with what Ogbu (1981) poignantly delineates as the cultural-ecological context of Black education: viewing formal education as an instrument of societal priorities.

Black parents must constantly evaluate if those priorities serve the best interests of their children and in what form. One form that has gained in national concern among professionals is standardized testing.

Psychological Testing and Special Placement

In spite of the admonitions of Black psychologists and educators about the consequences of psychological and educational testing, this pervasive product of the modern world is increasingly accepted by parents, notwithstanding its impact on the educational and career opportunities of Black children (Miller, 1980; National Association for the Advancement of Colored People [NAACP], 1974, 1983). The National Academy of Sciences, in a major report, has found that testing is not unduly biased or inherently discriminatory. This endorsement will only increase the use of standardized testing by institutions. A more ominous trend in the future is the development of personal computer software facilitating the administration and interpretation of psychological and educational tests. This capability expands the access of these tools to institutions and people professionally untrained in their use but in positions to establish social and economic policy based on test results.

The practices and social policies of these institutions must be carefully monitored by Black parents. In California, the case of Larry P. (*Larry P. v. Wilson Riles*, 1978) exemplifies the danger posed by testing (Hilliard, 1983). A disproportionate number of Black and Mexican American children were placed in special education classes, giving scientific support to adherents of stereotypical notions about Black children's abilities. This trend continues into the 21st century, as African American children are referred to and placed in special education classes significantly more often than children in other ethnic groups (Russo & Talbert-Johnson, 1997; Serwatka, Deering, & Grant, 1995). Russo and Talbert-Johnson's "resegregation" perspective in education affects African American males more often than any other group, as noted by Harry and Anderson (1994). This tendency to overrepresent African American children in special education classes coincides with an underrepresentation of African American children in classes for the gifted and talented (Ford, 1995; Lambert, 1988; Patton, 1992).

Corporal Punishment

Compared to White children, African American children, males in particular, are subjected to significantly greater instances of corporal punishment in schools by adults. According to 1992 data collected by the Office for Civil Rights of the U.S. Department of Education, an African American male was 16 times more likely than a White female to receive corporal punishment and six times more likely to be suspended from school (Gregory, 1995). The Office of Civil Rights, with a "congressionally mandated duty to monitor civil rights issues in U.S. schools nationwide," surveyed 286,539 incidents of corporal punishment in 1992, of which 44.4% were inflicted on African Americans. About 34% of these were targeted to African American males (Gregory, 1995).

Such practices begin to structure the personal life of Black children. Being retained in the same grade, being suspended from school, and dropping out of school are also more prevalent among African American students than among their White counterparts (Slaughter-Defoe & Carlson, 1996). Black parents must be vigilant about these social trends. Proactive parental involvement is often reflected in the minimization of these trends and greater student achievement.

The American Dream and the African American Reality

All African American children at some point in their development must reconcile aspirations for the "American dream" with their odds of attaining it. Psychodynamically, W.E.B. Du Bois (1965) still best represents this struggle in his *Souls of Black Folks*:

> The Negro is a sort of seventh son, born with a veil, and gifted with second-sight in the American world—a world which yields him no true self-consciousness, but only lets him see himself through the revelation of the other world. It is a peculiar sensation, this double-consciousness, this sense of always looking at one's self through the eyes of others, of measuring one's soul by the tape of a world that looks on in amused contempt and pity. One ever feels his twoness—an American, a Negro; two souls, two thoughts, two unreconciled strivings; two warring ideals in one dark body, whose dogged strength alone keeps it from being torn asunder. (p. 2)

Black children must be educated and psychologically prepared for this inevitable feeling of duality in their lives. The racial indignities of everyday racism pose a persistent challenge to Black racial identity (Franklin, 1993, 1999). Guidance through this emotional maze should come foremost from parents. The Black community, however, always has managed to provide mentors in addition to parents for this personal experience, and it must continue to do so.

Emergence of Clinical Problems: Issues of Prevention and Intervention

In our role as clinicians, we are too often confronted with the casualties of African American children and families who are unaware of the mental health implications of the issues discussed in this chapter. Casualties can manifest themselves with a variety of symptoms or presenting problems, such as learning disabilities, school failure, or behavioral and emotional problems. Although these problems may initially manifest themselves in the family, they are rapidly transmitted to the school and the community context as the child grows older. For our purposes in this chapter, we would like to present preventative strategies and parenting intervention steps for avoiding these pitfalls.

The current literature on learning disabilities, for example, addresses issues such as the role of prenatal factors and early nutrition in providing a sound basis for neurological development. Educating African American parents about the importance of a sound, well-balanced diet for children during their early years is essential. There is an ongoing debate, for example, about the impact of excessive sugar intake on the development of hyperactive conditions (Davis, 1981; Kolata, 1978). In addition, early recognition of learning problems and clear understanding of "normal" child development would greatly assist Black parents in gaining early diagnosis and remediation of learning problems. Even basic screening programs for the detection of hearing and visual defects often are overlooked in Black communities. This requires an educational program on sex and parenting health and nutrition care in general for future parents, which can begin in junior high and high school courses, before motherhood or fatherhood becomes a reality.

Once children leave the home environment and enter school, their social sphere expands considerably. This occurs at an earlier and earlier age with the tendency toward day care and nursery programs for infants and young children. Black parents need to be educated to the importance of a close working arrangement between parents and teachers. If this does not occur, children's progress cannot be adequately monitored, and problems often will become severe before teacher conferences are sought. As in the case of the diagnosis of learning disabilities, the earlier that school behavioral problems are caught, the more effective intervention strategies can be. Finally, Black parents can benefit greatly from understanding the etiology and prevention of emotional and behavioral disorders. Current child development literature stresses the importance of early bonding and attachment to parental figures. Parents, who are themselves overwhelmed by serious life and survival realities, often lose sight of these attachment needs, Many hospitals, clinics, and mental health centers now feature infant stimulation and parenting programs. Workshops on these topics are now an important part of any day care programs.

Disciplinary Practices

Although most parents love their children and work to ameliorate any emotional problems they may observe in them, at times it is possible for the children's parents or caregivers to contribute significantly to the development of emotional and behavioral problems. The key element here is the impact of inconsistent disciplinary practices. For example, some parents who discipline children state that the children must remain in their room for a period of time after disobeying a family rule. If this is not followed through and maintained, children will quickly discover this inconsistency. All children in this position begin to test their parents. If this pattern continues, it can lead to serious emotional and behavioral disorders.

It is the perception of many White mental health practitioners that Black parents resort to more physical punishment than many parents in White ethnic groups (Boyd, 1977). Many Black parents believe firmly in the philosophy that if you "spare the rod, you spoil the child." Black parents need to be helped to understand that certain forms of spanking may have a place in an overall disciplinary program but that an exclusive reliance on this form of discipline can be counterproductive. In extreme situations, such discipline can even contribute to child abuse. It is important for Black parents to be exposed to other behavioral paradigms for effective management of disturbing behaviors (Boyd-Franklin et al., 2000). Once again, mental health centers, clinics, and schools can provide a much-needed service by offering workshops and groups on effective parenting. The key here is that parents must have a clear responsibility for guiding, enhancing, and monitoring their children's psychoeducational development to avoid the development of problems.

Children With Special Needs

The psychoeducational task of parenting children designated as "special" is often an overwhelming responsibility for many African American parents. This label and classification of children is given all too often to African American children. Questions must be asked by the parents to ascertain the reason their children were identified as in need of special placement. This is true especially for behavioral referrals, in which Black males are frequently targeted. Careful review of the circumstances, situations, responses, and attitudes of pupil personnel must be considered. For some lower income parents, social security benefits for a child labeled "special" may seem alluring when money is scarce. Some parents have encouraged special education placement to receive benefits to help with the financial survival of the family. But, parents must be mindful of the negative consequences as well as the benefits of their decisions.

Both the school and the parent may request an evaluation for special education placement. But what are the tasks of parents whose children have been identified for placement in special education? Many parents are not familiar with the process or their rights as parents. Other parents disagree with the assessment that their children need special services but are unaware of ways to challenge the issue. Other parents may have little faith in the ability of standardized tests to assess their child accurately.

Another example of an assessment outcome is parental values about appropriate child behavior, such as children being told to fight back. Such a conventional practice can contribute to children being identified for special education because of their behavior. In speaking with several school psychologists, a recurrent theme was "My mama told me not to let anybody hit me so I hit him back." Too many fights, even in response to hostile confrontations from peers, can lead to a child's referral as an at-risk student and to labeling him or her as a troublemaker (C. V. Draper, personal communication, December 15, 1999).

Strategies for Helping the Identified Child

A number of practical tasks can be undertaken by parents of children viewed as at-risk for special services. Once their children have been identified as at-risk for special education evaluation, parents can contact the pupil personnel committee, which is designated to come up with interventions to prevent a child from having to be placed in special education. A major concern is what strategies have been employed to help the student and what other options are there for the child and parent. Parents need to find out if the pupil personnel committee actually exists in their children's school. Often, it does not. Agencies such as the Learning Disabilities Association of New York City will also assess children. Parent-parent interactions are particularly helpful, as parents of children already in special education can be a resource for information on out-of-school evaluations, remediation, support groups, and the specific deficit related to a child. Medical examination to rule out underlying medical causes for the targeted behaviors is a must, as is looking at possible personal issues that are remediable without special education. Loss of friends through moving or death, parental loss, home conflicts, and a host of other factors can precipitate behavior often labeled for special education remediation. Parents who do not agree with referral for special education can ask for mediation and impartial hearings.

Impartial hearings make the final binding determination on the child's need for special placement. Parents who still do not accept the decision for special education have a limited option: They can remove their child from the public school system altogether, as some parents opt to do. If children remain in the public school system and parents refuse to abide by the decision made at the impartial hearing, parents will be cited for educational neglect. This can trigger investigation by local school officials, child services authorities, or, ultimately, Family Court, if a resolution cannot be achieved. Lack of quality education is characteristic of special education programs. Parents can, however, demand appropriate placement for their children in a private school setting if they feel that the public school setting is not meeting the needs of their children. Often, this alternative is not conveyed to African American parents, and most parents are unaware of this stipulation.

Parents who agree with standardized testing can request, if necessary, test modifications (flexible scheduling, flexible setting, revised test formats, revised test directions, use of aids) to ensure as accurate an assessment as possible. Often, parents are unaware of these test modifications.

Parents have a right to a copy of the psychological evaluation, which should be written in simple lay language. Even with lay language, parents may need help understanding the diagnosis, placement, and implications for their children's future academic goals. When parents do not understand the evaluation, the evaluation should be taken to someone who can assist. The ramifications of special education placement often are not clear to parents. Once children have been placed in special education, it often takes years to have them mainstreamed again; it may never happen.

A frequent codiagnosis in high school special education students is depression. These students are often teased and stigmatized and have low self-esteem. Parents often underestimate the effects of special education placement on the academic and socioemotional development of African American children. Participating in activities of interest, cultivating skills such as dancing, singing, or playing board games, or learning something else of interest that the child can excel in, can help with feelings of low self-esteem. Monitoring the individualized education plan is a must as students often receive the same plan with the same educational goals year after year. Academic challenge may not be addressed, and students leave school with little or no functional knowledge.

In conclusion, the struggle to raise children in this world is a difficult task for any parent. This struggle is magnified considerably when parent and child are Black. Added to all of the other jobs of Black parents is the task of preparing children to feel proud of themselves and their racial identity in a racist world. If Black children are to have a chance at survival, Black parents must become even more aware of the psychoeducational process and participate in it in a meaningful way. It is only through this process that Black children can have a chance for a viable future and an opportunity to realize their potential as adults.

References

Banks, W. C., & McQuater, G. V. (1995). A deconstructive look at the myth of race and motivation. *Journal of Negro Education, 64*(3), 307-325.

Bowman, P. J. (1992). Coping with provider role strain: Adaptive cultural resources among Black husband-fathers. In A.K.H. Burlew, W. C. Banks, H. P. McAdoo, & D. A. Azibo (Eds.), *African American psychology: Theory, research, and practice* (pp. 135-151). Newbury Park, CA: Sage.

Boyd, N. (1977). *Clinicians' perception of Black families in therapy.* Unpublished doctoral dissertation, Teachers College, Columbia University, New York.

Boyd-Franklin, N. (1989). *Black families in therapy.* New York: Guilford.

Boyd-Franklin, N., Franklin, A. J., & Toussaint, P.(2000). *Boys into men: Raising our African American teenage sons.* New York: Dutton.

Carlson, C. G. (1991, November). Getting parents involved in their children's education. *Education Digest,* pp. 10-12.

Coleman, J. S. (1991, November). A federal report on parental involvement in education. *Education Digest,* pp. 3-5.

Comer, J. P., & Poussaint, A. E. (1975). *Black child care.* New York: Simon & Schuster.

Cummings, J. (1983, November 20). Breakup of Black family imperils gains of decades. *New York Times.*

Davis, A. (1981). *Let's have healthy children.* New York: New American Library.

Du Bois, W. E. B. (1965). *The souls of Black folk.* London: Longmans, Green.

Ford, D. Y. (1995). Desegregating gifted education: A need unmet. *Journal of Negro Education, 64*(1) 52-62.

Franklin, A. J. (1982). Therapeutic intervention with urban Black adolescents. In E. Jones & S. Korchin (Eds.), *Minority mental health.* New York: Praeger.

Franklin, A. J. (1993, July/August). The invisibility syndrome. *Family Therapy Networker,* pp. 32-39.

Franklin, A. J. (1999, November). Invisibility syndrome and racial identity development in psychotherapy and counseling African American men. *The Counseling Psychologist, 27*(6), 761-793.

Gregory, J. F. (1995). The crime of punishment: Racial and gender disparities in the use of corporal punishment in U.S. public schools. *Journal of Negro Education, 64*(4), 454-463.

Harrison-Ross, P., & Wyden, B. (1973). *The Black child: A parent's guide.* New York: Peter H. Wyden.

Harry, B., & Anderson, M. G. (1994). The disproportionate placement of African American males in special education programs: A critique of the process. *Journal of Negro Education, 63*(4), 602-619.

Hill, R. (1972). *The strengths of Black families.* New York: Emerson Hall.

Hilliard, A. G. (1983, August). IQ and the courts: *Larry P. vs. Wilson Riles* and *PASE vs. Hannon. Journal of Black Psychology, 10,* 1-18.

Hines, P., & Boyd-Franklin, N. (1982). Black families. In M. McGoldrick, J. Giordano, & J. K. Pearce (Eds.), *Ethnicity and family therapy* (pp. 66-84). New York: Guilford.

Kolata, D. (1978). Childhood hyperactivity: A new look at treatment and causes. *Science, 199,* 515.

Lambert, N. M. (1988). Perspectives on eligibility for and placement in special education programs. *Exceptional Children, 54*(4), 297-301.

Larry P. et al., v. Wilson Riles, et al., 495 F. Supp. 928 (9th Cir., 1979).

Mbiti, J. S. (1970). *African religions and philosophies.* New York, NY: Anchor.

McAdoo, H. P. (Ed.). (1981). *Black families.* Beverly Hills, CA: Sage.

Miller, L. (1980). Testing Black students: Implications for assessing inner-city schools. In R. L. Jones (Ed.), *Black psychology.* New York: Harper & Row.

Moynihan, D. P. (1965). *The Negro family: The case for national action.* Washington, DC: U.S. Department of Labor, Office of Policy Planning and Research.

National Association for the Advancement of Colored People (NAACP). (1974). *Task force on minority testing.* New York: Author.

National Association for the Advancement of Colored People (NAACP). (1983). *Quality of education, update.* New York: Author.

National Urban League. (1984). *The state of Black America.* New York: Author.

Nobles, W. (1980). African philosophy: Foundation for Black psychology. In R. Jones (Ed.), *Black psychology.* New York: Harper & Row.

Ogbu, J. U. (1981). Black education: A cultural-ecological perspective. In H. P. McAdoo (Ed.), *Black families.* Beverly Hills, CA: Sage.

Patton, J. M. (1992). Assessment and identification of African-American learners with gifts and talents. *Exceptional Children, 59*(2), 150-159.

Pierce, C. (1974). Psychiatric problems of the Black minority. In G. Caplan (Ed.), *American handbook of psychiatry* (Vol. 2). New York: Basic Books.

Prater, L. P. (1992). Early pregnancy and academic achievement of African American youth. *Exceptional Children, 59*(2), 141-149.

Randolph, S. M., Koblinsky, S. A., & Roberts, D. (1996). Studying the role of family and school in the development of African American preschoolers in violent neighborhoods. *Journal of Negro Education, 65*(3), 282-293.

Russo, C. J., & Talbert-Johnson, C. (1997). The overrepresentation of African American children in special education, the resegregation of educational programming? *Education and Urban Society, 29*(2), 136-148.

Ryan, W. (1971). *Blaming the victim.* New York: Pantheon.

Serwatka, T. S., Deering, S., & Grant, P. (1995). Disproportionate representation of African Americans in emotionally handicapped classes. *Journal of Black Studies, 25*(4), 492-506.

Shields, P. H., & Dupree, D. (1983). Influence of parent practices upon the reading achievement of good and poor readers. *Journal of Negro Education, 52*(4), 436-445.

Slaughter-Defoe, D. T., & Carlson, K. G. (1996). Young African American and Latino children in high-poverty urban schools: How they perceive school climate. *Journal of Negro Education, 65*(1), 60-70.

Sudarkasa, N. (1981). Interpreting the African heritage in Afro-American family organization. In H. P. McAdoo (Ed.), *Black families*. Beverly Hills, CA: Sage.

Tettegah, S. (1996). The racial consciousness attitudes of White prospective teachers and their perceptions of the teachability of students from different racial/ethnic backgrounds: Findings from a California study. *Journal of Negro Education*, *65*(2), 151-163.

U.S. Bureau of the Census. (1997). *Statistical abstract of the Unites States* (117th ed.). Washington, DC: Government Printing Office.

Wirth, E. (1991, November). Working parents work for schools. *Education Digest*, pp. 21-22.

9

Family and Child Influences on Educational Attainment

A Secondary Analysis of the High/Scope Perry Preschool Data

TOM LUSTER
HARRIETTE PIPES McADOO

Numerous studies have demonstrated a relation between educational attainment and adult outcomes such as level of income and occupational prestige. Because of the significance of educational attainment for understanding outcomes in adulthood and subsequently poverty rates for young children (National Center for Children in Poverty, 1992), this study uses longitudinal data to explore factors that contribute to individual differences in educational attainment in a low socioeconomic status (SES) African American sample.

AUTHORS' NOTE: A version of this chapter was first published as H. P. McAdoo & T. Luster, "Family and Child Influences in Educational Attainment: A Secondary Analysis of the High/Scope Perry Preschool Data," *Developmental Psychology, 32,* 26-39, 1996. Copyright © 1996 by the American Psychological Association. Adapted with permission.

Over the past two decades, the percentage of African American youth who have completed high school has increased substantially. Nevertheless, dropout rates remain high for African American adolescents from low SES families (National Academy of Sciences, 1993). According to Kids Count (2001), one out of five 16- to 19-year-olds in urban, high-poverty neighborhoods were high school dropouts in 1999. Several factors contribute to high rates of school failure in these communities, including relatively low levels of funding for schools, low expectations for students, high levels of stress in families, pressure from peers not to excel, and the belief among some adolescents that the relation between educational attainment and success in the mainstream economy is tenuous (Fordham & Ogbu, 1986; McLoyd, 1990; National Academy of Sciences, 1993; Ogbu, 1985). Despite these obstacles, many African American children from poor families succeed in school, and we know far too little about factors that contribute to this success.

The data that are used for this study were collected for the Perry Preschool Study in Ypsilanti, Michigan. Data collection began when the children were preschoolers, and the most recent data were collected when the subjects were 27 years old. Longitudinal studies of African American children are rare, and to our knowledge, this is the only study to follow African American children over such an extended period of time.

All of the children in the Perry Preschool study lived in low SES families during the early childhood period; yet, the outcomes in adulthood are quite diverse. In the area of education, the number of years of education achieved ranged from 6.5 to 18 (i.e., a master's degree). The central question addressed in this study is, What factors contributed to such diverse outcomes in the educational realm? Earlier analyses of the Perry Preschool data have shown that preschool was one factor that influenced the developmental trajectories of the children in the study. Children who attended preschool were more likely than their peers in the control group to have favorable experiences in the early elementary grades and ultimately to achieve desirable outcomes at age 19 (Berrueta-Clement, Schweinhart, Barnett, Epstein, & Weikart, 1984).

In this study, we are interested in what factors *other than preschool* contributed to success in the area of education. Both individual differences among the children at the time of school entry and characteristics of the families in the study will be examined. Of particular interest is the role that families played in the lives of these children. The positive role that African

American families play in the development of their children has been largely overlooked by researchers (Luster & McAdoo, 1994). Much of the research on African American families and children has focused on problem outcomes (e.g., school failure) and differences between African American and Caucasian families and children (e.g., achievement test scores). This focus on failure may contribute to the generation of faulty and inaccurate images of African American families in the literature and the media (McAdoo, 1990; Slaughter-Defoe, Nakagawa, Takanishi, & Johnson, 1990).

The conceptual model guiding this study was influenced by earlier longitudinal studies that have focused on childhood antecedents of adult outcomes (e.g., Werner & Smith, 1992) and case studies of several of the Perry subjects when they were 19 years of age (Berrueta-Clement et al., 1984). Consistent with past research, it is assumed that outcomes in adulthood, such as educational attainment, often represent a continuation of a chain of events in childhood and adolescence (Rutter, 1989). Positive experiences at one point in time often lead to positive experiences at later points in time.

Families in poverty who provide supportive rearing environments during the earliest years of their children's lives are likely to have children who arrive at school with the social and cognitive skills that are rewarded by teachers (Entwisle & Alexander, 1990; Slaughter & Epps, 1987; Sroufe, 1983). These relatively skillful children should also profit more from experiences in school and achieve more than their less skillful peers. Success in the early elementary grades is likely to increase the odds that a child will have positive experiences in later grades, which in turn should serve to motivate the child toward greater achievement and ultimately higher educational attainment. In contrast, poor experiences in the early grades can lead to a downward spiral of events, culminating in a decision to drop out of school before high school is completed (Ensminger & Slusarcick, 1992). The hypothesis that the characteristics that children bring to the school in kindergarten set in motion a chain of positive or negative school experiences will be explored with the available data.

Parents influence not only what children bring to the school setting when children begin school but also how well children acquire school-related skills throughout the school years (e.g., working with the child on homework). These activities can influence other behaviors, such as study habits, which are likely to affect the achievement and attainment of children and adolescents. Based on past research and the earlier case studies, we expected that those who achieved higher levels of education would have parents who were more involved in school (Eastman, 1988) and who had higher educational aspirations and expectations for their children (Seginer, 1983). Case studies of the Perry subjects at age 19 suggested that those who completed high school tended to have parents who placed a high value on educational attainment (Berrueta-Clement et al., 1984). In this study, we examine this possibility systematically, and we also assess the relation between parent's expectations and children's educational attainment when children's early achievement is controlled. With a few notable exceptions (e.g., Ensminger & Slusarcick, 1992), studies of parents' expectations of adolescents typically do not control for past achievement, which may influence how much education parents expect their children to achieve (Entwisle & Hayduk, 1978).

Another hypothesis tested in this study is that children with parents who have an authoritative style of discipline (Baumrind, 1967, 1991) achieve more years of education than other children. Several recent studies have demonstrated a relation between authoritative parenting and success in school; however, the relation has been less clear-cut for African American adolescents than for adolescents from other sociocultural groups (Dornbusch, Ritter, Leiderman, Roberts, & Fraleigh, 1987; Steinberg, Lamborn, Dornbusch, & Darling, 1992; Steinberg, Mounts, Lamborn, & Dornbusch, 1991). Although findings are not consistent across studies, there is some evidence from past research that an authoritative parenting style can have a positive influence on low income, African American children (Clark, 1983; Slaughter & Epps, 1987).

Case studies of some of the Perry subjects at age 19 suggested that role models were significant influences in the lives of relatively successful children. Although people outside the family can be positive role models for children (Werner & Smith, 1992), the hypothesis tested in this study is that the children who turn out to be most successful in the educational realm will identify one or both of their parents as their most significant role models. At the last interview, the Perry subjects (age 27) were asked to identify their most significant role model and these data were used to test this hypothesis. Although it seems reasonable that African American children who look to their parents as role models are likely to be more successful in school, to our knowledge, this possibility has never been tested systematically in earlier studies.

Another potential influence on educational attainment, particularly for females, is early childbearing. There is some debate in the literature about the effect of early childbearing on educational attainment (Hayes, 1987). Early childbearing is clearly associated with lower levels of education, but the relation may be spurious, with both low attainment and early childbearing resulting from low intellectual ability and a history of poor school performance. The hypothesis tested in this study is that there is an effect of teenage childbearing on educational attainment when IQ scores and achievement test scores are controlled.

In summary, this study focuses on the developmental pathways of African American children from low income families, with the goal of understanding factors that contribute to individual differences in educational attainment. We expected to find that successful students started school on more positive developmental trajectories and that early success in school would lead to later success. We also hoped to understand why some students who appeared to be at risk for school failure when they entered school nevertheless completed high school. We expected that in many cases, their families played a role in putting them on more positive trajectories, and we examine that possibility in this study. Other factors, such as early childbearing, may alter developmental trajectories in negative ways, causing adolescents to achieve fewer years of schooling than would be expected based on their ability and early achievement.

Method

Subjects

The Perry Preschool sample includes 123 subjects and their families. The subjects were born between 1958 and 1962 and resided in a neighborhood served by the Perry Elementary School in Ypsilanti, Michigan, when they were recruited into the study as preschoolers. Each child was randomly assigned to attend preschool or to be in a no-preschool control group. The study included five cohorts of children, who were enrolled in the study from 1962 to 1965. (Two cohorts were recruited in 1962, a group of 4-year-olds and a group of 3-year-olds.)

Background information on the children and their families is summarized in Table 9.1. All of the children in the sample were African American and came from low SES families, as indicated by parental educational level. The average levels of education of the mothers and fathers were 9.4 and 8.6

TABLE 9.1 Sample Characteristics

	Mean	SD	Percentage
Child's family of origin			
Mother's education	9.42	2.20	
Father's education	8.60	2.40	
Number of siblings at child's entry	4.13	2.51	
Number of siblings at age 15	4.93	2.59	
People/rooms at child's entry	1.30	.46	
People/rooms at age 15	.85	.32	
Father in home at child's entry			53%
Father in home at age 15			45%
On welfare at child's entry			48%
Child characteristics			
Male			59%
Preschool			47%
IQ at entry	79.02	6.45	
IQ in kindergarten	88.63	11.28	

NOTE: "At entry" refers to the time during the preschool years at which the child entered the study.

years, respectively. None of the mothers and only one of the fathers had education beyond high school.

The children had four siblings on average, and many lived in crowded conditions, with the number of people in the home typically exceeding the number of rooms at the beginning of the study. The father was present in about half the homes at the start of the study and in 45% of the homes when the children were age 15.

About 59% of the children were male, and 47% attended preschool. At entry, all of the children had Stanford-Binet IQ scores between 60 and 90. Children who attended preschool and those in the control group did not differ on the Stanford-Binet at entry, nor did they differ significantly ($p < .05$) on any of the other family background characteristics presented in Table 9.1. As has been reported elsewhere, children in the preschool group had higher IQ scores than children in the control group in the early elementary grades. In kindergarten, the average Stanford-Binet IQ score in the preschool group was 91.2; in the control group, the average was 86.3 ($t = -2.43$, $p < .05$).

As earlier studies by the primary investigators have shown, those who attended preschool differed from those who did not attend preschool on other measures assessed in adolescence and adulthood (Berrueta-Clement et al., 1984; Schweinhart, Barnes, Weikart, Barnett, & Epstein, 1993; Schweinhart & Weikart, 1980). Children who attended preschool had higher achievement test scores in eighth grade and did homework more often at age 15 than those who did not attend preschool. Females who attended preschool had fewer pregnancies by age 19. Parents of children who attended preschool had higher educational aspirations for their children at age 15. Those who attended preschool also obtained more years of education by age 27 than those in the control group (11.9 versus 11.0 years, $t = -2.46$, $p < .05$). However, this difference in educational attainment is largely due to differences between females in the two groups. Females in the preschool group completed 12.2 years of education, compared to 10.5 years for the control group females ($t = -3.06$, $p < .05$). Males in the preschool and control groups did not differ in their average level of educational attainment (11.6 and 11.4 years, respectively, $t = -.46$).

Although the preschool and control groups had different mean scores on some of the variables of interest in this study, the pattern of correlations among the variables tended to be similar for the two groups. The correlations among key variables (i.e., those presented in Table 9.2 through Table 9.5) were calculated separately for the preschool and control groups, and r to z transformations were performed to determine if the correlations of interest differed in magnitude (Snedecor & Cochran, 1980). In all cases, the differences between the correlations were not large enough to be statistically significant. Therefore, combining the two treatment groups into one sample for this study is appropriate.

Similar analyses were conducted to determine if the relations of interest varied as a function of the sex of the subject. Few differences in mean scores were found for the two gender groups; of particular interest is the fact that males and females did not differ in terms of average educational attainment by age 27 (11.5 and 11.3 years, respectively, $t = .44$). However, there were a few instances in which the relation between two variables differed for males and females. These differences are noted when the results are presented.

Attrition

Data were collected on the Perry Preschool children from the preschool years through age 27. Relative to other longitudinal studies, the attrition rate in the Perry Preschool study has been low. About 98% of the participants were interviewed at the age 19 follow-up, and 95% (117/123) were interviewed at the most recent follow-up at age 27. At this latest follow-up, Schweinhart and colleagues (Schweinhart et al., 1993; Schweinhart & Weikart, 1980) reported that the median rate of missing data across all measures was only 4.9%, and the mean was 8.7%. For this study, data are used from seven points in time. The number of subjects who provided data on the key variables used at each of these time points was (a) preschool ($N = 123$), (b) kindergarten ($N = 117$ to 120), (c) first grade ($N = 113$), (d) eighth grade ($N = 95$), (e) age 15 ($N = 95$ to 100), (f) age 19 ($N = 121$), and (g) age 27 ($N = 113$ to 117).

Of all the variables used in the analyses reported in this chapter, the largest number of missing data points are for variables related to fathers; for example, father's level of education is not known for 51 cases. The highest number of missing data points for a variable used in this study that does not involve the father is 28 (23%) for achievement test scores at the end of eighth grade. Further information on sample characteristics, recruitment, attrition, and the preschool program can be found in earlier publications by those who did the primary analyses with these data (Berrueta-Clement et al., 1984; Schweinhart et al., 1993; Schweinhart & Weikart, 1980).

Measures

The primary outcome of interest is educational attainment at age 27, which is measured in years and half years. For example, a person who attended one semester of college would receive a score of 12.5. The average level of educational attainment was 11.43, and the standard deviation was 1.89. About 37% of the sample had less than a high school education, 33% completed 12 years of schooling, and 30% had some schooling beyond high school.

Children were assessed regularly on measures of cognitive ability during the elementary years. The two measures used here are the Stanford-Binet (Terman & Merrill, 1960), assessed in kindergarten, and the California Achievement Test total score (Tiegs & Clark, 1963), assessed in first grade and eighth grade. Information on the children's adjustment was collected from teachers in kindergarten through third grade with the Pupil Behavior Inventory (Vinter, Sarri, Vorwaller, & Shafer, 1966). Two measures completed by kindergarten teachers are used in this study, academic motivation and personal behavior. The academic motivation score is the average of nine 5-point items (*very frequently* to *very infrequently*). Sample items are "motivated toward academic performance" and "uninterested in subject matter." The average score was 2.99 (*SD* = .82) with a range from 1.00 to 4.89. Cronbach's alpha for this measure was .94. The kindergarten teachers' ratings of academic motivation were positively correlated with ratings given by first-, second-, and third-grade teachers (*r* = .50 to .57). The personal behavior score is the mean of six items scored on the same 5-point scale. Sample items are "lying or cheating" or "swears or uses obscene words" (Cronbach's alpha = .69). The mean for this measure was 4.01 (*SD* = .65) with a range from 2.00 to 5. Kindergarten teachers' ratings of personal behavior were significantly correlated with ratings given by first- to third-grade teachers (*r* = .40, .37, and .54 respectively). High scores on both the academic motivation and personal behavior measures are desirable.

Kindergarten teachers also rated maternal involvement in the school on two items scored on a 7-point scale, with high scores being positive. The two items are "mother's degree of cooperation shown" and "prediction of mother's future school relationship." The average of these two items was used (*M* = 4.03, *SD* = 1.84). Kindergarten teachers' ratings of maternal involvement correlated positively with the ratings given by teachers in first through third grade (*r* = .45 to .62).

Preschool attendance is a dummy variable, with a higher score indicating that the child was in the Perry Preschool Program. Although the effects of this intervention have been discussed extensively elsewhere, preschool is included in the multiple regression analysis so that the effects of family and child characteristics can be examined while preschool experience is controlled.

The most extensive data on the family of origin were collected on the children at age 15, when both parents and children were interviewed. Parent interview information used in the analyses includes their educational aspirations (i.e., amount desired) and educational expectations (i.e., attainment actually expected of the child). Responses to the questions about aspirations and expectations were scored on a 4-point scale ranging from *less than high school* to *college.* Higher scores indicate high aspirations and expectations for their children.

Two items were used to assess parental involvement in their adolescents' schooling at the age 15 interview: "Over the years, how often have you gone to parent-teacher conferences when invited by one of youth's teachers?" and "How often have you gotten in touch with youth's teachers on your own to talk about youth's progress?" Responses regarding parent-teacher conferences were scored on a 5-point scale ranging from *never* to *always.* A three-point scale, *never* to *often,* was used for the question regarding contacting the teacher. Higher scores indicate greater contact with teachers.

The adolescents were also asked a series of seven questions on parental style at the age 15 follow-up. The constructs tapped by the items were parent-youth communication, parental fairness, and parental restraint in the use of coercion (Schweinhart & Weikart, 1980). The items were scored on a 5-point scale (*always* to *never*), and the sum of these items was used as an indicator of authoritative parenting, with higher scores indicating a more authoritative approach. Sample items are "yell, shout, or scream at you" and "talks over important decisions with you." Cronbach's alpha for this measure was .70.

One item was used to assess the adolescents' study habits at the age 15 interview: "How many days a week, on average, do you spend outside of school in preparation for classes?" The average number of days spent on homework was 1.44 with a standard deviation of 1.86. More than half of the respondents (51.5%) spent no time on homework in an average week.

Teenage childbearing was assessed at the age 19 interview. About 29% of the adolescents had a child by age 19. About 45% of the females and 18% of the males indicated that they had children.

At the age 27 interview, the subjects were asked to identify anyone inside or outside the family who had a strong influence on them. This variable was coded dichotomously, with a score of 1 indicating that participants picked one or both of their parents and a score of) given for all others. About 58% of the respondents selected a parent or both parents.

Results

A goal of this study is to explore the developmental pathways of poor African American children from kindergarten to adulthood. We expected that children's characteristics at school entry would affect their experiences in school (e.g., achievement) and eventually adult outcomes such as educational attainment. The results section is organized to follow the chain of events from early childhood to adulthood and is divided into the following sections. First, the relation between family characteristics at the start of the study and children's characteristics in kindergarten is examined. Second, the relation between children's characteristics in kindergarten and their level of scholastic success is explored. Next, we determine the extent to which achievement in the elementary grades is predictive of educational attainment by age 27. The extent to which family characteristics and other factors in adolescence (e.g., early childbearing) affect the developmental trajectories of the children is examined next. Of particular interest is why some children who appear to be at risk for school failure in kindergarten nevertheless finish high school. Next, the extent to which educational attainment is associated with occupational status and income at age 27 is assessed, and finally, a path model is presented to show linkages among variables assessed from early childhood to adulthood.

Predictors of Child Characteristics in Kindergarten

Three key child characteristics were assessed in kindergarten: IQ, academic motivation, and personal behavior. The correlations among these three child characteristics ranged from .40 (personal behavior and IQ) to .58 (personal behavior and academic motivation). The correlation between IQ and academic motivation was .49.

As the first step in the analysis, the relation between family characteristics and child characteristics in kindergarten was examined, and the results of these analyses are presented in Table 9.2. The information available on the family included background data on parent education and family structure, as well as teacher ratings of maternal involvement in kindergarten. No additional data on family processes were available from the earliest years of the study. The relations between preschool experience and kindergarten characteristics are also presented in Table 9.2.

The zero-order correlations indicated that the most consistent predictors of child characteristics were maternal involvement in kindergarten and mother's education. Children with more favorable scores had mothers with more years of education and mothers who received more positive ratings from teachers. In contrast, father's level of education was

TABLE 9.2 The Relation Between Family Characteristics and Child Characteristics in Kindergarten

	Stanford-Binet IQ		Academic Motivation		Personal Behavior	
	r	beta	r	beta	r	beta
Preschool	.22*	.20*	.11	.06	−.04	−.10
Mother's involvement, kindergarten	.43*	.38*	.52*	.45*	.61*	.52*
Mother's education	.27*	.13	.39*	.23*	.39*	.23*
Father's education	.00		.11		.23+	
People/rooms at child's entry	−.08	.01	−.04	.01	−.04	−.04
Father in home at child's entry	−.05	−.09	−.04	−.10	.18+	.11
F		7.30*		10.96*		16.92*
df		5, 110		5, 110		5, 110
R^2		.25		.33		.43*

NOTE: Standardized betas are reported in table. "Father's education" was not included in the regression equation because of the number of missing cases.
+$p < .10$. *$p < .05$.

not significantly related to children's characteristics in kindergarten. Preschool experience was associated with high IQ scores but was unrelated to academic motivation or personal behavior in kindergarten.

A multiple regression equation was computed for each of the child outcomes, with the family variables and preschool entered simultaneously. As indicated by the standardized betas in Table 9.2, maternal involvement in kindergarten was the strongest predictor of all three child characteristics. The only other significant family background variable in the model was mother's education, which was related to academic motivation and personal behavior when other family characteristics at the child's entry were controlled. Preschool was a significant predictor of IQ scores when family background characteristics were controlled. The variables in the model accounted for 25% to 43% of the variance in the three child characteristics.

The Relation Between Child Characteristics
in Kindergarten and Scholastic Attainment

One of the hypotheses in this study is that children's characteristics at the beginning of school will influence the degree to which they experience success in school and, ultimately, their overall educational attainment. To test this hypothesis, the relation between the children's characteristics in kindergarten and their achievement and attainment was examined. Achievement test scores from the beginning of the elementary grades (first grade) and from the end of the elementary years (eighth grade) and years of education completed were used as the outcome measures.

The three child characteristics were positively correlated with the achievement test scores and educational attainment. The relations between the family characteristics at the child's entry and these three outcomes are also reported in Table 9.3. The two family variables that were predictive of children's characteristics in kindergarten—teacher ratings of maternal involvement and maternal education—were also correlated with the children's achievement and attainment.

Preschool experience was positively related to the children's eighth-grade achievement and educational attainment at age 27. Preschool was only marginally related to achievement test scores in first grade.

Multiple regression was used to assess the extent to which preschool, child, and family variables predicted scholastic attainment. In these analyses, preschool, the three child characteristics, and four family characteristics were entered simultaneously. Preschool experience was unrelated to achievement test scores in first and eighth grade when child and family characteristics were controlled. However, it was predictive of educational attainment.

Of the family background characteristics, only the mother's education was predictive of the child's achievement in first grade. The presence of the father in the home at the child's school entry was associated with more favorable achievement scores in eighth grade, even though the zero-order correlation between these two variables is close to zero. Children who were more motivated and who had higher IQ scores in kindergarten scored higher on achievement tests in both first and eighth grade. IQ scores in kindergarten were also predictive of educational attainment when other factors were controlled, but academic motivation was not a significant predictor. Contrary to expectations, the sign of the coefficient for personal

TABLE 9.3 Predictors of Achievement and Educational Attainment: Bivariate and Multiple Regression Analyses

	Achievement First Grade		Achievement Eighth Grade		Years of Education	
	r	beta	r	beta	r	beta
Preschool	.16+	−.04	.34*	.13	.22*	.18*
Stanford-Binet IQ	.54*	.37*	.47*	.29*	.41*	.17*
Academic motivation	.53*	.35*	.52*	.48*	.38*	.04
Personal behavior	.28*	−.24*	.23*	−.21+	.45*	.34*
Mother's involvement, kindergarten	.38*	.10	.34*	−.02	.33*	-.01
Mother's education	.40*	.23*	.32*	.12	.30*	.08
Father's education	.06		.02		.04	
People/rooms at child's entry	−.08	−.07	−.08	−.05	−.08	−.03
Father in home at child's entry	−.05	.04	.08	.20*	.01	−.06
F		10.37*	7.64*		5.83*	
df		8, 98		8, 79		8, 107
R^2		.46		.44		.30*

NOTE: Standardized betas are reported in the table. "Father's education" was not included in the regression equation because of the number of missing cases.
+$p < .10$. *$p < .05$.

behavior was negative and statistically significant for the achievement measures in the regression equation. However consistent with expectations, the beta for personal behavior is positive and significant when educational attainment is the outcome.[1]

As an additional check on the relation between child characteristics in kindergarten and educational attainment, the children were divided into three groups (lowest third, middle third, and upper third) based on their IQ, academic motivation, and personal behavior scores. For each kindergarten measure, the percentage of children in each third of the distribution who completed high school was determined. One third of the children who received the lowest ratings on academic motivation by kindergarten teachers completed high school, compared to 55% of the children in the middle group and 68% in the group with the most favorable ratings. When the children were divided into groups based on teacher ratings of personal behavior, cross-tabulations revealed graduation rates of 32%, 52%, and 72% for the respective groups. When the children were divided on the basis of IQ scores, 41% with the lowest scores graduated from high school, compared to 49% in the middle group, and 72% in the upper group. The chi-square statistic for each cross-tabulation was significant at the .05 level. These analyses clearly show that children on a positive developmental trajectory at the beginning of school fare better than peers with less positive characteristics. It is also important to point out that the data show that many children who appear to be at risk for school failure in kindergarten nevertheless complete high school. Possible reasons for this positive turnabout will be examined later in the chapter.

The Relation Between Achievement in the Elementary Grades and Educational Attainment

It was hypothesized that children's characteristics would influence their achievement, which, in turn, would influence their educational attainment. The relation between achievement test scores in grade school and educational attainment is examined in this section.

Achievement test scores in the first grade were strongly related to achievement test scores in the eighth grade ($r = .71, p < .05$), which were, in turn, predictive of educational attainment by age 27 ($r = .45, p < .05$). The relation between achievement in first grade and educational attainment was .24 ($p < .05$).

Predictors of Educational Attainment and Study Habits During Adolescence

More successful students in the elementary grades spent more time on homework at age 15 than less successful students (see Table 9.4). Teens who spent more time on homework at age 15 also tended to achieve higher levels of education.

The relation between family characteristics in adolescence and educational attainment was also examined. Adolescents who achieved more

TABLE 9.4 Zero-Order Correlations: Later Predictors of Educational Attainment and Study Habits

	Years of Education	Days/Week Homework	Achievement Eighth Grade
Achievement test scores			
CAT, first grade	.24*	.35*	.71*
CAT, eighth grade	.45*	.39*	
Family processes, adolescence			
Parents' educational aspirations	.28*	.25*	.31*
Parents' educational expectations	.33*	.17	.30*
Authoritative parenting style	.21*	.36*	.15
Parent attends parent-teacher conferences	−.04	−.04	−.05
Parent contacts teacher on his/her own	-.15	−.11	−.14
Family structure, age 15			
Father in home	−.06	−.10	−.17
Number of siblings	−.10	.04	.00
People/rooms	−.27*	−.15	−.13
Other variables			
Days/week homework	.37*		.39*
Teenage parenthood	−.35*	−.01	−.07
Parent as role model, age 27	.30*	.14	.31*

+$p < .10$. *$p < .05$.

years of education had parents with higher educational aspirations and expectations. They also had parents who were perceived as being relatively authoritative in their parenting style. Overall, the frequency with which parents attended parent-teacher conferences or contacted the teacher on their own was not related to the years of education their children achieved. However, further analyses revealed an interesting sex difference in this area. For males, there is a significant negative correlation between how often parents contacted the teacher on their own and educational attainment by age 27 ($r = -.44, p < 05$); for females, the correlation is .20, $p > .05$). The correlations for males and females were significantly different from each other ($z = 3.21, p < .05$). Presumably, many parents who had sons contacted teachers because they were concerned about their children's progress in school. Parents of sons contacted teachers more often on their own if their sons had relatively low achievement test scores the previous year ($r = -.31, p < .05$). This was not the case for daughters ($r = .15$), and the correlations between achievement in eighth grade and parents contacting the teacher on their own differed for males and females at age 15 ($z = 1.99, p < .05$).

One possible way in which families may influence their children's scholastic attainment is by encouraging or requiring their children to spend extra time on their studies. To explore this possibility, the relations between the family variables and days per week spent on homework were examined. Adolescents spent more time on homework on average if their parents had higher educational aspirations and were authoritative in their parenting style. For sons, parents' educational expectations were positively correlated with time spent on homework ($r = .35, p < .05$); the correlation was negative but not statistically significant for females ($r = -.18$), and the correlations for males and females were different from each other ($z = 2.52, p < .05$).

Hierarchical multiple regression analysis was used to determine if family processes in adolescence were related to study habits when preschool experience, academic motivation in kindergarten, and achievement in eighth grade were controlled. The results indicated that an authoritative parenting style was related to time spent on homework when preschool, academic motivation in kindergarten, and achievement were controlled. (These results are not presented in a table.) Preschool, academic motivation, and achievement in eighth grade, which were entered at the first step, accounted for 15% of the variance in time spent on homework. The change in R^2 that resulted from adding parenting style at the second step was .08, and the F for the change in R^2 was 7.34 ($p < .05$). Of the four variables in the final equation, achievement and parenting style were significant predictors of study habits. Parents' educational aspirations were not significantly related to children's study habits when preschool, academic motivation, and achievement were controlled. Parental expectations were predictive of time spent on homework for males, when other factors were controlled; the sample of females was too small to run a regression analysis with four predictor variables. For males, achievement, preschool, and motivation accounted for 23% of the variance in time spent on homework when entered at the first step, and parental educational expectations accounted for an additional 12% of the variance at Step 2 (F for change in R^2 was 7.64, $p < .05$).

Similar analyses were conducted with educational attainment as the outcome to determine the impact of family processes in adolescence on educational attainment. Two models were tested for each of the family variables. In the first model (Model A), the family variable was entered at the second step, after controlling for kindergarten characteristics, which were predictive of educational attainment in earlier analyses (i.e., intelligence and personal behavior), and preschool. In Model B, the family variable was entered after the effect of achievement in eighth grade, intelligence, personal behavior, and preschool experience were taken into account. Given that prior achievement may influence family variables such as authoritative parenting or educational expectations, Model B allows us to determine if there is an effect of the family variables from the age 15 follow-up when achievement test scores assessed a year earlier are taken into consideration. Model B, however, may underestimate the contribution of parents to scholastic success because the family processes assessed at age 15 probably also influenced achievement at age 14 (if one assumes some stability in family variables such as educational expectations and authoritative parenting style), and this contribution may be partialled out in Model B. For this reason, we believe that both Models A and B contribute useful information.

IQ, personal behavior, and preschool experience accounted for 29% of the variance in educational attainment (see Model 1A, Table 9.5). Achievement test scores in eighth grade accounted for an additional 7% of the variance, and together, these four variables explained 36% of the variance in educational attainment (Model 1B). As noted earlier, achievement data were missing for 28 children, and this explains why there are fewer residual degrees of freedom when achievement test scores are included in the model.

Model 2 shows what happens when parents' educational expectations are added to the respective equations. Expectations account for 5% of the variance beyond that accounted for by IQ, personal behavior, and preschool, and the F for the change in R^2 (6.35) is significant (Model 2A). However, the parental expectations variable is not a significant predictor of educational attainment when achievement is added at the first step (Model 2B).[2]

TABLE 9.5 Multiple Regression Analyses: Predictors of Educational Attainment

	Model 1		Model 2		Model 3		Model 4		Model 5		Model 6	
	A	B	A	B	A	B	A	B	A	B	A	B
1. Personal behavior, kindergarten	.37*	.28*	.33*	.26*	.33*	.25*	.30*	.23*	.39*	.30*	.28*	.25*
Stanford-Binet IQ, kindergarten	.21*	.19+	.13	.12	.14	.08	.22*	.20+	.18+	.17+	.14	.13
Preschool experience	.19*	.12	.13	.09	.21*	.09	.18*	.12	.16*	.11	.12	.08
Achievement in eighth grade		.26*		.29*		.35*		.25*		.22*		.20+
2. Parents' educational expectations			.23*	.09					.18*	.10		
3. Authoritative parenting style					.18+	.12						
4. Teenage parenthood						−.29*		−.26*		−.30*	−.24*	
5. Parent as role model									.19*	.20*	.19*	.20*
Overall Model	*1A*	*1B*	*2A*	*2B*	*3A*	*3B*	*4A*	*4B*	*5A*	*5B*	*6A*	*6B*
R^2	.29	.36	.30	.34	.26	.35	.37	.42	.35	.39	.44	.43
F	15.4*	11.6*	9.9*	7.4*	7.7*	7.1*	16.6*	12.0*	14.3*	10.6*	11.3*	7.66*
df	3, 113	4, 84	4, 91	5, 72	4, 86	5, 67	4, 112	5, 83	4, 106	5, 82	6, 87	7, 70

NOTE: Standardized betas are reported. In Model A, personal behavior and IQ assessed in kindergarten were entered on the first step. In Model B, personal behavior, IQ, and eighth grade achievement were entered on the first step. The R^2, F, and degrees of freedom for the overall model are presented at the bottom of the table.
+$p < .10$. *$p < .05$.

159

When authoritative parenting style was entered at the second step following IQ, personal behavior, and preschool, it accounted for an additional 3% of the variance in educational attainment. The F for the change in R^2 was 3.78 ($p < .10$) (see Model 3A). But like educational expectations, an authoritative parenting style does not contribute uniquely to predicting educational attainment when eighth-grade achievement is included in the equation (F for change = 1.43).

In the fourth model, teenage parenthood was added at the second step. Early childbearing was a significant predictor of educational attainment when the effects of child characteristics, preschool, and achievement were partialled out. It accounted for an additional 8% of the variance in Model 3A and 6% of the variance in Model 3B.

Further analyses were conducted to explore the relation between teenage parenthood and high school completion. Thirty-six of the Perry subjects (13 males and 23 females) were parents by age 19. Overall, 36% of those who had children by 19 completed high school compared to 62% of those without children ($\chi^2 = 6.92, p < .05$). Females who did not have a child by 19 were twice as likely as early childbearers to complete high school (71% versus 35%, $\chi^2 = 6.85$, $p < .05$). About 39% of the males with children by age 19 completed high school compared to 58% of their peers. This difference, however, did not reach statistical significance.

In Model 5, the dichotomous "parent as role model" variable was added to the equation. Those who selected either parent or both parents as role models tended to achieve higher levels of education. The change in R^2 that resulted from adding the role model variable was .03 for Model 5A and .04 for Model 5B; the F for the change in R^2 was significant in each case.

As was done with teenage childbearing, the relation between the role model variable and high school completion was examined. Two thirds of those who selected their parents as role models were high school graduates, compared to 41% of those who selected someone else ($\chi^2 = 7.42, p < .05$). About 49% of those who selected their parents as role models enrolled in courses beyond high school, compared to 18% of those who selected someone else ($\chi^2 = 11.69$, $p < .05$). On average, those who selected their parents as role models completed 11.99 years of education; those who selected someone else completed 10.89 years ($t = -3.32$, $p < .05$).

In the final set of regression analyses, parental educational expectations, teenage parenthood, and parent as role model were entered together at the second step. When IQ, personal behavior, and preschool were entered at the first step, the three variables accounted for an additional

18% of the variance at the second step, and the regression coefficients for all three variables were statistically significant (Model 6A). The R^2 for the model was .44. When achievement, IQ, personal behavior, and preschool were entered at the first step, the three variables entered at the second step accounted for an additional 10% of the variance in educational attainment (Model 6B). The coefficients for teenage parenthood and parent as role model were significant at the .05 level. Together, the seven variables accounted for 43% of the variance in educational attainment.

Factors Related to High School Completion
Among Academically At-Risk Kindergarten Children

As was noted earlier, kindergarten children who were in the lowest third of the distribution for IQ, academic motivation, and personal behavior were at-risk for not completing high school. Nevertheless, many children who appeared to be at-risk for school failure based on kindergarten measures did finish high school. An important question is, What factors contributed to their success.

To pursue this question, all of the children who were in the bottom third on one or more of the three kindergarten measures were identified. Sixty-seven of the children were identified as at-risk children based on the kindergarten measures. Of those 67, 28 (42%) eventually completed high school. In comparison, 66% of children who were not in the bottom third on any of the three measures graduated from high school.

The at-risk children who graduated and those who dropped out did not differ on the IQ measure in kindergarten. Those who graduated tended to get somewhat higher scores on the achievement tests in first and eighth grades, but the differences did not reach statistical significance (see Table 9.6).

The families of those who graduated and those who did not were compared, and a number of differences were found. Mothers of those who graduated tended to receive somewhat more favorable scores on school involvement from kindergarten teachers ($p < .10$). The parents of those who graduated were viewed as being authoritative by their adolescent children and had higher educational expectations. The two groups did not differ in terms of family structure or parental education.

As was the case for the entire sample, at-risk children who graduated from high school were more likely than nongraduates to select a parent as

TABLE 9.6 A Comparison of At-Risk Children Who Graduated and Dropped Out

	Graduates Mean/ Percentage	(SD)	Nongraduates Mean/ Percentage	(SD)	t or χ^2
Child IQ and achievement					
IQ kindergarten	84.5	(11.3)	81.0	(7.0)	-1.55
CAT total, first grade	83.4	(29.7)	72.0	(36.9)	-1.32
CAT total, eighth grade	98.9	(33.4)	85.0	(26.4)	-1.63
Family processes					
Maternal involvement, kindergarten	3.79	(1.78)	2.96	(1.60)	-1.98+
Authoritative parenting style, age 15	25.12	(4.15)	22.23	(5.07)	-2.30*
Parental education aspirations	3.23	(.82)	2.90	(.90)	-1.44
Parental education expectations	2.50	(.86)	1.97	(.89)	-2.27*
Days/week homework	2.00	(2.17)	.33	(.71)	-3.99*
Parents as role models	56%		28%		5.19*
Teenage parenthood	21%		46%		4.33*

NOTE: Children were considered to be at-risk if they were in the lowest third of the distribution on one or more of the following kindergarten measures: Stanford-Binet IQ and teacher ratings of academic motivation and personal behavior.
+$p < .10$. *$p < .05$.

their most influential role model. Those who named their parent or parents as role models were twice as likely to graduate as those who named someone else (56% versus 28%).

One of the most striking differences between the groups was the number of days per week adolescents spent on homework at age 15. Those who graduated averaged 2 days of homework per week compared to .33 days per week among those who dropped out. The percentage of adolescents who reported spending 0 days per week on homework were 44% and 80% for the respective groups.

A final difference between the groups that probably influenced graduation rates was teenage parenthood. The nongraduates were twice as likely to be parents by age 19 as the graduates.

In reviewing the evidence, the impression is that the two groups did not differ markedly in academic potential, but those who eventually graduated received more support from their parents and came closer to realizing their academic potential than those who did not graduate.

Educational Attainment and Socioeconomic Status at Age 27

The relation between educational attainment and socioeconomic status of the Perry subjects at age 27 was examined. Three indicators of socioeconomic status were used: (a) respondent's work income for the previous year, (b) occupational prestige as measured by the NORC prestige scale, and (c) months unemployed in the previous 2 years. Those who attended preschool did not differ from those in the control group on these three indicators. Moreover, males and females in the sample, on average, did not differ on these three outcomes.

As expected, years of education was positively related to work income (.55) and occupational prestige (.42) and was negatively related to months unemployed (−.50). T tests were used to compare the means of those who finished high school with the means of those who did not. The average income of graduates was $16,954 versus $6,232 for nongraduates ($t = -6.35, p < .05$). Graduates had higher prestige scores than nongraduates (32 versus 23; $t = -2.86, p < .05$) and spent fewer months unemployed in the previous 2 years (9.9 versus 2.5; $t = 4.81, p < .05$). Thus, the findings from this study are consistent with those from other studies in showing that high educational attainment is associated with favorable outcomes on work-related measures in adulthood.

Additional analyses were conducted to determine if educational attainment mediates the relation between early childhood characteristics and adult socioeconomic status outcomes or if there is an effect of child characteristics on work-related outcomes when educational attainment is controlled (Baron & Kenny, 1986). Kindergarten IQ, academic motivation, and personal behavior were significant predictors of work income and unemployment in the previous 2 years when each variable was entered alone as a predictor variable. None of the three kindergarten measures was related to occupational prestige. When the kindergarten predictors were entered with educational attainment, the effect of these variables was reduced to nonsignificance with one notable exception. Personal behavior in kindergarten was a significant predictor of work income at age 27 when educational attainment was controlled and accounted for an additional 6% of the variance in income. When entered together, the standardized betas for educational attainment and personal behavior were .46 and .22, respectively.

Path Analysis

An argument has been made in this chapter that the concept of developmental trajectory is useful for understanding individual differences in educational attainment and other adult outcomes, such as work income. Children's characteristics assessed at the beginning of their school careers can influence subsequent achievement and, ultimately, years of education completed. We have also argued that subsequent experiences, such as family support and early childbearing, can alter those developmental trajectories. Path analysis was used to illustrate the linkages between assessments made in early childhood and outcomes in adulthood.

To do an analysis involving numerous data collection points with a relatively small sample, adjustments had to be made for missing data. The variable with the greatest amount of missing data was achievement test scores in eighth grade. A multiple regression equation was used to estimate achievement test scores for those who were not assessed; IQ test scores and maternal education were used to estimate achievement.[3] If kindergarten teachers' assessments were missing, the ratings on the same variables made by first-grade teachers were used, if they were available. Similarly, if an IQ test score was not available in kindergarten, the Stanford-Binet assessed at the end of preschool was used. If data were missing on the outcomes of interest (e.g., income), the cases were not included in the analyses. By taking these steps, it was possible to compute path coefficients with 110 cases.

The results of these analyses are presented in Figure 9.1. Only path coefficients that were statistically significant or approached significance ($p < .10$) are included; one variable that was included in the analyses but was not predictive of other variables when confounding factors were controlled (and therefore is not included in the path diagram) was the presence of the father in the home at the start of the study. The results support the view that what children bring to the school in terms of abilities and attitudes influences their subsequent achievement and educational attainment.[4] Early experiences in the home and the preschool setting are likely to influence these abilities and attitudes that children have when they begin school.

The results also illustrate that subsequent experiences, such as early childbearing and having a parent as a role model, also influence the life course. Given that both early childbearing and having a parent as a role model are dichotomous variables, they were not used as dependent variables in the multiple regression analyses, and no paths are shown leading to these variables. However, logistic regression was used to predict these two outcomes; all of the variables in the path model assessed prior to these two outcomes were used as predictor variables. Only one variable, maternal education, was a significant predictor of early childbearing in this sample; personal behavior in kindergarten approached significance ($p < .10$). Those who had a child before age 19 tended to have mothers with fewer years of education and to exhibit more problem behavior in kindergarten. Those who viewed their parents as role models had mothers who were rated as being more involved in school by kindergarten teachers and had higher achievement test scores in eighth grade. For reasons that are not clear, those who at age 27 selected their parents as role models had lower ratings on academic motivation in kindergarten than others, when other predictor variables were controlled. In contrast, bivariate analyses showed that those who selected their parents as role models did not differ from those who did not in terms of average level of academic motivation in kindergarten ($t = -.57$).

Although the results of the path analysis generally correspond to the results of the multiple regression analyses presented earlier, it should be

166

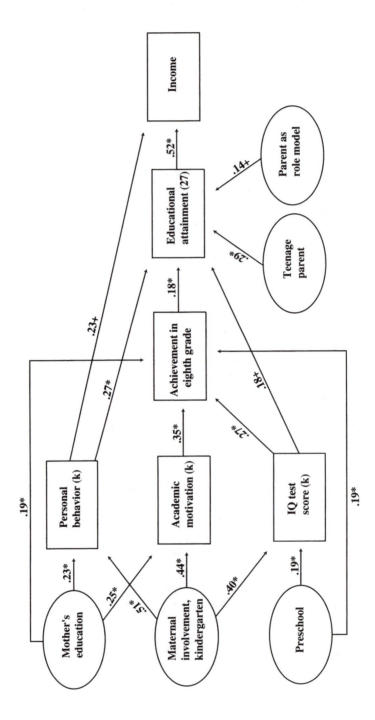

Figure 9.1. Black Children: Social, Educational, and Parental Environments

+ ≤ .10. *p < .05.

pointed out that the results may have been influenced by the steps taken to deal with missing data, particularly achievement test data. Maternal education, which was used in the estimation of achievement test scores, is significantly related to achievement in these analyses but was not a significant predictor of achievement when other factors were controlled in an earlier analysis (see Table 9.3). The presence of the father in the home, which was related to achievement in an earlier analysis, is not a significant predictor in the path analysis.

Discussion

The central question addressed in this study was, What factors contributed to individual differences in educational attainment of the Perry Preschool participants? Unlike earlier studies using this data set, this study focused on factors other than preschool, especially characteristics of the children and their families, that influenced the developmental trajectories of the children.

One of the hypotheses tested in this study was that characteristics of the children at the time of school entry would influence the degree to which they experienced success in the elementary grades, which, in turn, would influence the level of education obtained. There was considerable support for this hypothesis. Children's cognitive competence and academic motivation in kindergarten were predictive of achievement test scores in the elementary grades. The degree of success in the elementary grades, as measured by achievement tests, was related to how long children remained in school. In addition, children who were relatively well-adjusted in kindergarten ultimately attained higher levels of education. This finding is consistent with those of others (Caspi, Elder, & Bem, 1987; Ensminger & Slusarcick, 1992; Hinshaw, 1992; Martin, 1989) in showing that child characteristics other than intelligence contribute to individual differences in educational attainment.

Although the results indicate that children's characteristics at the time they enter school affect their developmental pathways, we have little information about the antecedents of those characteristics. We focused on whether or not there were relations between contextual factors (i.e., family characteristics and preschool experience) and children's characteristics in kindergarten (e.g., IQ), but it seems likely that individual differences among children also reflect genetic differences (Plomin, 1990, 1994). The design of the study did not allow us to assess the extent to which genetic differences contributed to individual differences among the children in this sample.

The way in which African American families influenced the educational attainment of their children was also of interest. One hypothesis was that families who were more involved in school would have children who were more successful students. There was some support for this hypothesis, but the evidence was mixed. Mothers who were rated by kindergarten teachers as being more involved tended to have children who were rated as being relatively competent, motivated, and well-adjusted in kindergarten. Given that teachers completed the ratings on both child characteristics and maternal involvement, it could be argued that perceptions of the child characteristics may have affected kindergarten teachers' ideas about how involved mothers were in their children's education. Although this alternative explanation cannot be ruled out, it should be noted that teacher ratings of involvement in kindergarten were positively correlated with teachers' ratings of maternal involvement over the next 3 years. In addition, teacher ratings of involvement in kindergarten were correlated with parents' reports of how often they attended parent-teacher conferences when the child was 15 years old ($r = .27$, $p < .05$).

During adolescence, parental involvement in school as measured by parent-teacher conference attendance was unrelated to years of education achieved. For males, there was a negative relation between how often parents contacted teachers on their own and level of education attained. It appears that involvement in school in some cases may be prompted by concern about poor performance or a student's seeming lack of interest in school.

Parents may affect their children's educational outcomes more by what they do in the home than by the amount of time they spend in the school. Case studies of the Perry participants at age 19 suggested that more successful students tended to have parents who placed a high value on education. To test this notion systematically, the relation between parents' educational expectations and children's attainment was examined. Parents expectations were positively correlated with children's educational attainment and were predictive of years of education, even when child characteristics in early childhood and preschool experience were controlled. However, when the effect of achievement in eighth grade was partialled out, educational expectations were not a significant predictor of attainment. Thus, we could not rule out the alternative hypothesis that parental expectations are shaped by the degree to which their children have been successful in school. It may be that there is a bidirectional relation between parents' expectations and children's performance, with each influencing the other over time. Data collected on parental expectations at both early childhood and adolescence would be needed to test that possibility. The only study that we are aware of to do this was conducted by Ensminger and Slusarcick (1992). They assessed parents' expectations and aspirations when children were in first grade and in adolescence and found that parental expectations and aspirations when the children were in first grade did not predict high school completion. In contrast, expectations and aspirations in adolescence were predictive of high school completion when grades in first grade were controlled. High expectations were particularly important for females with low grades in early childhood.

Past research has tended to document a positive relation between an authoritative parenting style and success in school, but such a relation has not always been found in African American subsamples. The relation between authoritative parenting and years of education completed, rather than test scores or grades, was examined in this study. A modest correlation was found between parenting style and educational attainment, and at-risk kindergarten students who completed high school were more likely than those who did not to have authoritative parents. However, as was the case with parents' expectations, we could not rule out the possibility that authoritative parenting results from, rather than contributes to, success in school. The relation between authoritative parenting and educational attainment was not significant when eighth-grade achievement was controlled.

Although more research is needed to document such a relationship, one way in which authoritative parents may affect their children's rate of high school completion is by influencing and monitoring their study habits. Authoritative parents had adolescents who spent more time on homework than their peers when past achievement was controlled. Males also spent more time on homework if their parents had high educational expectations. Time spent on homework at age 15 was positively related to educational attainment.

When the Perry subjects were 27 years old, they were asked to reflect on their lives and identify significant role models. Of interest to us was whether or not those who selected their parents as their most significant role models achieved higher levels of education. Those who finished high school and/or enrolled in courses beyond high school were much more likely than those who dropped out to identify their parents as role models. No doubt, children can benefit from positive role models they encounter in any setting, and these role models probably affect individual children profoundly; however, the data from this study suggest that children, on average, are better off if the people they look up to are their parents, who have an opportunity to influence their children over an extended period of time.

Given that the data on role models were collected when the Perry participants were 27 years old, long after many of them completed their formal educations, a possibility that must be entertained is that those who were more successful in terms of education and SES tended to look more favorably on their parents. According to this interpretation, parent role models had no effect on educational attainment, and the direction of effect is the opposite of what we have proposed. One way to see if the parents who were selected as role models differed from those who were not selected was to examine kindergarten teachers' ratings of maternal involvement (teachers did not rate paternal involvement). Mothers who were identified as role models at age 27 received significantly higher ratings on involvement by kindergarten teachers than mothers who were not selected by their children as role models ($t = 2.07$, $p < .05$). These results are consistent with the interpretation of the data that seems more plausible to us—namely, that positive parental role models contribute to higher levels of education.

Another factor that influenced educational attainment, especially for females, was teenage parenthood. Although this result is not surprising, we believe it is noteworthy that there is a very clear effect of teenage parenthood on educational attainment when the effect of achievement and intelligence are taken into account. Earlier studies that examined the relations among these variables using cross-sectional data produced results that were open to varied interpretations. These data provide more compelling evidence that early childbearing is a hindrance to educational attainment for females.

Although the Perry Preschool data provided a unique opportunity to explore these questions of interest, the data set also has some limitations. One limitation is that the sample size was not very large, and all of the study participants lived in one community. The sample sizes were particularly small when separate analyses were done for males and females. Although attrition was low overall, there were missing data for different participants at different points in time. To do the path analysis, scores were estimated for missing data, and this may have influenced the results that were obtained; the results of path analysis should be interpreted with that limitation in mind. A third limitation that should be considered is that these children, like any other age cohort, grew up in a unique historical context. One can only speculate about how the historical context may have influenced these children and their families in unique ways. For all of these reasons, it will be important to do further research in this area to determine if these results can be replicated.

In conclusion, several factors examined in this study were related to individual differences in the educational attainment of the Perry Preschool participants. Children's characteristics assessed as early as kindergarten were found to be predictive of educational outcomes in adulthood. The positive role that African American families play in the lives of their children was also documented. Even though all of the families in this study were low SES families, many parents helped their children to overcome obstacles associated with low SES and obtain higher levels of education than they themselves had achieved. Given that past research has tended to overlook positive aspects of family life among low SES African Americans, we believe that this is an especially important aspect of this study. We hope that research of this type will help provide greater balance in the portrayal of African American families by those who help to shape the images of American families.

Notes

1. For both achievement in first grade and achievement in eighth grade, the sign of the coefficient for personal behavior is positive if academic motivation is not included in the regression equation. These two kindergarten measures are correlated with each other ($r = .58$).

2. Because the number of cases on which the regression equation is computed depends on which variables are in the model, the amount of variance accounted for by the same variables (e.g., IQ and personal behavior) can vary slightly from model to model.

3. The correlation between achievement tests scores and educational attainment, when achievement test scores are estimated for missing cases, was .44. This is very close to the correlation obtained between achievement and educational attainment when missing cases were not included in the analyses (r = .45).

4. Achievement test scores in first grade are not used in the path analyses because they are highly correlated with achievement test scores in eighth grade (r = .71).

References

Baron, R. M., & Kenny, D. A. (1986). The moderator-mediator variable distinction in social psychological research: Conceptual, strategic, and statistical considerations. *Journal of Personality and Social Psychology, 51,* 1173-1182.

Baumrind, D. (1967). Child care practices anteceding three patterns of preschool behavior. *Genetic Psychology Monographs, 75,* 43-88.

Baumrind, D. (1991). Parenting style and adolescent development. In J. Brooks-Gunn, R. Lerner, & A. C. Peterson (Eds.), *The encyclopedia on adolescence* (pp. 746-758). New York: Garland.

Berrueta-Clement, J. R., Schweinhart, L. J., Barnett, W. S., Epstein, A. S., & Weikart, D. P. (1984). *Changed lives: The effects of the Perry Preschool program on youths through age 19.* Ypsilanti, MI: High/Scope Press.

Caspi, A., Elder, G. H., & Bem, D. J. (1987). Moving against the world: Life-course patterns of explosive children. *Developmental Psychology, 23,* 308-313.

Clark, R. (1983). *Family life and school achievement: Why poor Black children succeed or fail.* Chicago: University of Chicago Press.

Dornbusch, S., Ritter, P., Leiderman, P., Roberts, D., & Fraleigh, M. (1987). The relation of parenting style to adolescent school performance. *Child Development, 56,* 326-341.

Eastman, G. (1988). *Family involvement in education.* Madison: Wisconsin Department of Public Instruction.

Ensminger, M. E., & Slusarcick, A. L. (1992). Paths to high school graduation or dropout: A longitudinal study of a first grade cohort. *Sociology of Education, 65,* 95-113.

Entwisle, D. R., & Alexander, K. L. (1990). Beginning school math competence: Minority and majority comparison. *Child Development, 61,* 454-471.

Entwisle, D. R., & Hayduk, L. A. (1978). *Too great expectations: The academic outlook of young children.* Baltimore, MD: John Hopkins University Press.

Fordham, S., & Ogbu, J. (1986). Black students' school success: Coping with the "burden of acting White." *Urban Review, 18,* 176-206.

Hayes, C. (1987). *Risking the future* (Vol. 1). Washington, DC: National Academy Press.

Hinshaw, S. P. (1992). Externalizing behavior problems and academic under-achievement in childhood and adolescence: Causal relationships and underlying mechanisms. *Psychological Bulletin, 111,* 127-155.

Luster, T., & McAdoo, H. P. (1994). Factors related to the achievement and adjustment of African American children. *Child Development, 65,* 1080-1094.

Martin, R. P. (1989). Activity level, distractibility, and persistence: Critical characteristics in early schooling. In G. Kohnstamm, J. E. Bates, & M. K. Rothbart (Eds.), *Temperament in childhood* (pp. 451-462). Chichester, UK: John Wiley.

McAdoo, H. P. (1990). The ethics of research and intervention with ethnic minority parents and their children. In C. Fisher & W. Tryon (Eds.), *Ethics in applied developmental psychology* (pp. 273-283). Norwood, NJ: Ablex.

McLoyd, V. C. (1990). The impact of economic hardship on Black families and children: Psychological distress, parenting, and socioemotional development. *Child Development, 61,* 311-346.

National Academy of Sciences. (1993). *Losing generations: Adolescents in high-risk settings.* Washington, DC: National Academy Press.

National Center for Children in Poverty. (1992). *Five million children.* New York: Columbia University.

Ogbu, J. (1985). A cultural ecology of competence among inner-city Blacks. In M. B. Spencer, G. K. Brookins, & W. R. Allen (Eds.), *Beginnings: The social and affective development of Black children* (pp. 45-66). Hillsdale, NJ: Lawrence Erlbaum.

Plomin, R. (1990). *Nature and nurture: An introduction to human behavioral genetics.* Pacific Grove, CA: Brooks/Cole.

Plomin, R. (1994). *Genetics and experience: The interplay between nature and nurture.* Thousand Oaks, CA: Sage.

Rutter, M. (1989). Pathways from childhood to adult life. *Journal of Child Psychology and Psychiatry, 30,* 23-51.

Schweinhart, L. J., Barnes, H. V., Weikart, D. P., Barnett, W. S., & Epstein, A. S. (1993). *Significant benefits: The High/Scope Perry preschool study through age 27.* Ypsilanti, MI: High/Scope Press.

Schweinhart, L. J., & Weikart, D. P. (1980). *Young children grow up: The effects of the Perry Preschool program on youths through age 15.* Ypsilanti, MI: High/Scope Press.

Seginer, R. (1983). Parents' educational expectations and children's academic achievements: A literature review. *Merrill-Palmer Quarterly, 29,* 1-23.

Slaughter, D. T., & Epps, E. G. (1987). The home environment and academic achievement of Black American children and youth: An overview. *Journal of Negro Education, 56,* 3-20.

Slaughter-Defoe, D. T., Nakagawa, K., Takanishi, R., & Johnson, D. J. (1990). Toward cultural/ecological perspectives on schooling and achievement in African- and Asian-American children. *Child Development, 61,* 363-383.

Snedecor, G. W., & Cochran, W. G. (1980). *Statistical methods* (7th ed.). Ames: Iowa State University Press.

Sroufe, L. A. (1983). Infant-caregiver attachment and patterns of adaptation in preschool: The roots of maladaptation and competence. In M. Perlmutter (Eds.), *Minnesota symposium in child psychology* (Vol. 16, pp. 41-81). Hillsdale, NJ: Lawrence Erlbaum.

Steinberg, L., Lamborn, S. D., Dornbusch, S. M., & Darling, N. (1992). Impact of parenting practices on adolescent achievement: Authoritative parenting, school involvement, and encouragement to succeed. *Child Development, 63,* 1266-1281.

Steinberg, L., Mounts, N., Lamborn, S., & Dornbusch, S. (1991). Authoritative parenting and adolescent adjustment across various ecological niches. *Journal of Research on Adolescence, 1,* 19-36.

Terman, L. M., & Merrill, M. A. (1960). *Stanford-Binet Intelligence Scale Form L-M: Manual for the third revision.* Boston: Houghton-Mifflin.

Tiegs, E. W., & Clark, W. W. (1963). *Manual: California Achievement Test, complete battery.* Monterey Park: California Test Bureau (McGraw-Hill).

Vinter, R. D., Sarri, R. S., Vorwaller, D. J., & Shafer, W. E. (1966). *Pupil Behavior Inventory: A manual of administration and scoring.* Ann Arbor, MI: Campus Publishers.

Werner, E. E., & Smith, R. S. (1992). *Overcoming the odds: High risk children from birth to adulthood.* Ithaca, NY: Cornell University Press.

10

Sankofa Shule Spells Success for African American Children

SHARIBA W. RIVERS
FREYA A. RIVERS

African American children in the public school system have been suffering. Statistics report high attrition rates, a disproportionate number of special education students, and low success rates. Educators and researchers have attributed the problem to cultural deprivation, economic status, racism, curricular deficiencies, inadequate teaching skills, and a variety of other factors. Suggested solutions have included curriculum reform, African-centered education, and multicultural education.

In this chapter, we begin with a review of the various explanations for the failure of African American students as well as corrective strategies that have been employed. We then focus on the philosophy and curriculum of Sankofa Shule, an African-centered charter school in Lansing, Michigan. Although one particular method or ideology may not work for all, effective schools and educators tend to have certain characteristics. We examine these at Sankofa Shule, which can serve as a model for what works well when teaching the African American child.

Explanations for Failure

A common argument offered by researchers for the lack of success among Black children is that school curricula do not offer any incentives for learning. Caroline Persell (1993) and Geneva Gay (1993) maintain that tracking is used all too often for Black children. Gay reports that the number of Black children who perform below their grade level has been on the rise since 1980, and educators typically have tried to solve this problem by placing the youngsters into special categories and low-track classes. Children are not encouraged to perform because teachers believe these children are low achievers. Furthermore, Persell maintains that children in low-track classes are given work that is neither challenging nor very meaningful to them. She adds that teaching has been one of "the most effective means of denying educational equality to ethnic minority students" (p. 179). In comparison to students in high-track classes, the low-track students have less instructional time, fewer and inferior-quality resources, less motivated teachers, and work that involves basically computation rather than critical thinking or problem solving. Many African American students have come to believe that tracking is normal and that they must accept inferior education as a consequence of their supposed inferior mental capabilities.

Many researchers and educators have pointed to the dominance of the White male's history and values in the school system. Gay (1993) states that instructional materials are Eurocentric and that the curriculum has been designed to enforce White middle-class values and norms. James Banks (1993) points out that supporters of assimilation largely attribute the accomplishments of American society to its British heritage and therefore support the idea that White middle-class values are the standards by which people should live.

According to Fenwick English (1992),

> Knowledge is never neutral. The selection of knowledge to include in a school curriculum is fundamentally a political act of deciding who benefits . . .and who is excluded or diminished. Because this is never a truly open-ended process, the knowledge "selected" really has been preselected, preshaped to fit whatever the dominant cultural configuration happens to be at the time. (pp. 30-31)

M. J. Shujaa (1994) also believes that the school system accepts the European worldview as universal. These middle-class norms have distorted the perceptions and images that African American children hold of their history and culture and of themselves. "We have become ashamed of our tribal contributions. We believe that we [have] done nothing to contribute to society" (Akbar, 1984, p. 18). Such an attitude further disassociates children from the public school system.

Another problem is that African American children often cannot understand how what they are learning applies to real-life situations. For them, life is generally quite different from what they are taught is normal. The information they are forced to learn is not relevant to what they experience at home or in their neighborhood. History classes enforce the idea that African Americans have contributed little or nothing. Instruction in textbook English only alienates children from their surroundings at home. Math classes teach formulas but no reality-based concepts. The list continues.

Because African American children operate in a point of reality that is different from that of most of their teachers, they have been labeled as culturally deficient. This "deficiency" is cited as yet another reason for their lack of success in the public school system. It is claimed that poverty, socioeconomic status (Haynes & Comer, 1990), the lack of family support, and lack of self-esteem all contribute to the Black child's failure.

Although poverty creates a stressful environment, research has shown that poor children can learn if given the proper attention and education. It has also been noted that most African American families value and support education and that Black children enter school with very high self-esteem and self-perception. After being in school for a couple of years, they begin to doubt themselves (Kunjufu, 1990; Persell, 1993).

Teachers and instructional methods are consistently offered as other reasons for the failure of Black students. Persell (1993) and others point to the fact that teachers' expectations of students become self-fulfilling. When teachers believe Black children are inferior because of cultural deficiencies, they teach them less because they think the children can learn only so much material at a time. The children, as a consequence of the teachers' attitude and lack of motivation, become increasingly uninterested in school.

Gay (1993) addresses teacher education programs, which she argues do not adequately prepare teachers to deal with "cultural traits, values, and attitudes of different ethnic minority groups" (p. 182). Most teachers in the public school system are White females, and an increasing number of students are from other backgrounds. By not fully understanding the circumstances of their students, even well-intentioned teachers may approach their job from a White middle-class perspective, which further alienates the African American child.

Several other explanations are given for the lack of success among African American students:

1. Instructional materials are inadequate to support a multicultural curriculum (Boateng, 1990). Teachers continue to use the same materials that have been used over the years and, therefore, perpetuate the same ideas.

2. Linguistic chauvinism (Boateng, 1990) can be directly related to teaching methods; textbook English is consistently taught as the "norm," and Ebonics (Black English) is considered unacceptable.

3. School climate (Boateng, 1990; Kunjufu, 1990) reflects teachers' attitudes and perceptions, the type of curriculum taught, and the racial atmosphere in the school.

4. Racism is cited by many as the underlying problem. It has dictated the curriculum for many years and is part of the basic foundation of the public schools.

Suggested Solutions

Curriculum Reform

Advocates for curriculum reform argue that the main problem lies in the fact that what is taught is based on White middle-class male norms. Akbar (1984) maintains that "we must demand that the educational system produces reality" (p. 23).

This can be done by matching teaching methods to learning methods. Each student is different and will use different learning strategies to grasp different concepts. Classes may need to be restructured accordingly. More experiential techniques would use all of a child's senses and more fully engage children in the learning activity.

Another way to achieve reality in the classroom is to teach "the interdependence of the world in which Whites are a small numerical minority" (Gay, 1993, p. 187). Children should learn about the various other cultures that have been historically underrepresented in the public school curriculum. The number of African American, Asian, and Hispanic students is increasing, and "students learn best and are more highly motivated when the school curriculum reflects their culture, experiences, and perspectives" (Banks, 1993, p. 195).

As already noted, it has been suggested that children should be taught skills that are transferable to the world outside the classroom. Shujaa (1994) also suggests that we begin to deal honestly with the existing power relations in American society.

Gay (1993) points out the need to rid the schools of tracking as well as norm-referenced tests, which are used to group and evaluate children. Students should be assessed in terms of their own records and progress as opposed to records of the entire class. Gay (1993) adds that when tracking is absolutely necessary, it should involve hard work, meaningful assignments, and a commitment by teachers and students.

A large part of curriculum reform requires teacher reform. Teachers' attitudes toward African American children must change if they are to teach these students effectively and obtain positive results. Writers and educators such as Gay (1993), Kunjufu (1990), Ladson-Billings (1994), Lomotey (1994), and Shujaa (1994) argue that being able to relate to a student's cultural experiences is one characteristic of effective teachers and administrators.

Multiculturalism

All these suggestions have been put forward by advocates of multicultural education, which is an approach for educating all children equally. Boateng (1990) states that major goals of multicultural education are to help students

1. reach their potential by drawing on their cultural experiences and by helping them to view events from diverse cultural perspectives,
2. overcome their fear of diversity, which leads to cultural misunderstanding and cultural encapsulation,
3. view cultural differences in an egalitarian mode rather than in an inferior-superior mode, and
4. expand their conception of what it means to be human in a culturally diverse world and to develop cross-cultural competency—the ability to function within the range of cultures. (p. 77)

Critics claim that there are too many schools of thought in multi-cultural education, none of which offers a complete package for acceptable change within the schools. One group wants to maintain the core curriculum but diversify it by recognizing all the cultures that have contributed to the collective U.S. national identity (King & Wilson, 1994). This approach fails to address issues of racism, sexism, classism, and position with respect to politics and power.

Other groups merely want equal representation in textbooks, ignoring the context in which the texts were written and overlooking the need to revise them (McCarthy, 1993). Still others advocate cultural sensitivity programs in the schools to correct for the racism in textbooks but not to deal with the racism that exists in society (McCarthy, 1993). "The assumption that higher educational attainment and achievement *via a more sensitive curriculum* would lead to a necessary conversion into jobs for Black and minority youth is frustrated by *the existence of racial practices in the job market itself* [italics added]" (McCarthy, 1993, p. 53).

Sankofa Shule: What Works and Why

African-centered education is not new. Independent Black institutions have been in existence for more than 20 years, but they generally serve a limited number of students. Although it has been proven that African Americans respond more positively to teachers who respect, can relate to, or share their cultural traits, it is not simply this that sets African-centered schools apart from Eurocentric schools. African-centered schools are different because of the people who teach in them, the style they use, and the beliefs they hold.

Gloria Ladson-Billings (1994, pp. 33-52) lists these characteristics of effective culturally relevant teachers. They

- have high self-esteem and a high regard for others,
- see themselves as part of the community, see teaching as giving back to the community, and encourage their students to do the same,
- see teaching as an art and themselves as artists,
- believe that all students can succeed,
- help students make connections between their community, national, and global identities, and
- see teaching as "digging knowledge out" of students.

Ladson-Billings (1994, pp. 61-70) also lists the characteristics of culturally relevant teaching, focusing on the act of imparting knowledge as opposed to the person who imparts it:

- A teacher-student relationship that is fluid and "humanely equitable"
- The cultivation of the relationship beyond the boundaries of the classroom
- A demonstrated connectedness with each of the students
- A community of learners (as opposed to individual learners)
- Encouragement for students to learn collaboratively and the expectation that they will teach each other and take responsibility for each other

Sankofa Shule was founded in response to the negative effects of public school education on African American males. It quickly became a model for educating African American children in general. The teachers in Sankofa Shule "travel a different route to ensure the growth and development of their students" (Ladson-Billings, 1994, p. 15). They teach from an African-centered perspective, starting with the ancient African ideals embodied in Ma'at. Ma'at represents all that is truthful, just, righteous, harmonious, and equally balanced.

Sankofa Shule's educational philosophy also embodies reciprocity, which is an African ideal. It embraces the give and take of life. As Akoto (1994) affirms, "Afrikan-centered education seeks to restore the traditions of Afrika to prominence, to revitalize those traditions and imbue them with the liberating and progressive dynamics of nation building" (p. 47). In opposition to a culture that believes in destroying the Earth's natural resources for man's benefit, the philosophy at Sankofa Shule insists on respecting everything that has a spirit force—anything that has energy. Instructors at Sankofa Shule teach the whole child by using a multisensory approach. Children learn by employing all their senses. Teachers guide the lessons and help students learn by smelling, hearing, touching, tasting, and seeing. Students learn to use their senses and their sense to solve problems independently. They "become" (Rivers, 1998, p. 26).

The 10 Steps

The founder of Sankofa Shule, Freya Rivers, developed 10 steps to educational excellence as a guide for teachers to ensure the consistent delivery of a high-quality, fair, and challenging education. The school has begun to develop its own curriculum to deliver the quality education that African American students deserve.

Step 1: Respect. When teachers convey the real history of the mother continent and respect for all people and cultures that have evolved since the beginning of time, African American children start with a deep sense of pride in heritage and self. Students also learn that all people are worthy of respect and should be treated accordingly. No positions of superiority or inferiority are imposed. Equal value is placed on the lives, cultures, and heritage of others.

Respect works both ways. Teachers must treat students and their ideas respectfully. Teachers must be able to maintain pride in their own culture while giving equal relevance and importance to those within the class. Ladson-Billings (1994) incorporates this idea under culturally relevant teaching practices, with the phrase "fluid and 'humanely equitable' " (p. 61).

Students are taught to respect all human beings and to understand that everything in nature has a life force. The ancient Africans believed in respecting all things that contain this force. They believed in the miracle of life, recognizing that the circle of life remains constant if nurtured properly. The philosophy at Sankofa Shule is that people have begun to lose touch with nature and, as a result, with themselves. Teaching is aimed at restoring the connection not only with nature but also with the African past. Lomotey (1994) calls this learning "to see the world through the eyes of Africans" (p. 213).

Step 2: Expect. Once an atmosphere for respect is achieved, expectations can be outlined and met. Teachers in an African-centered class believe their students can do anything. They do not accept theories of social or cultural deficiency; they pay no attention to such descriptors as "at-risk" or "economically deprived." Lee (1994) points out that one characteristic of an effective teacher is to "take for granted that all children are capable of learning" (p. 305).

Step 3: Success. Success is achieved through little steps of encouragement and learning. Rivers (1998) points to the need for individualization. Teachers must recognize the different characteristics of students and what motivates each one. This knowledge can be used to help children succeed.

"The wonderful part of individualization is that an educator gets to know, understand, and respect each child as a unique individual. Education becomes reciprocal" (Rivers, 1998, p. 31).

Success in the African-centered class also requires participation of the family and the community. The more encouragement children have from family and the more opportunities presented in the community, the more motivated students become. An active interest from all people involved will help keep students moving in a positive direction.

Parents should participate in the school (Akoto, 1994). They can be teachers' aides and chaperones or coaches for extracurricular activities. Community people can act as sponsors and provide hands-on experience in the job market through internships or apprenticeships. Sankofa Shule teachers use all available resources to help motivate their students to succeed.

Step 4: RIP (Reward, Invest, Praise). Teachers should reward children for doing well. Rewards can range from making a child the teacher's assistant for the day, to reading a child's favorite story, to placing a special star beside the child's name. Teachers should also invest the time to notice a child's progress and praise children for their efforts.

Step 5: TAP (Take Away Privileges). Teachers at Sankofa Shule do not expect perfect classrooms all the time, and measures must be taken to deal with the unexpected. Children may become anxious or agitated; the first response is a warning about disrespect for other classmates or the teacher. If this does not work, privileges are revoked until the student and the teacher come to an agreement based on mutual respect. If the offense becomes serious, the teacher involves the parents. The faculty believe wholeheartedly in the proverb "It takes a village to raise a child." Children are responsible for their "brothers and sisters" within the school; teachers assume the roles of educator and parent; and parents are expected to play a significant role in their children's education, both in school and at home.

If a child egregiously violates the rules of the Sankofa family, not only are privileges such as going on a field trip lost but also the mother or father must take the day off from work and spend the day at school with the child. This type of intervention ensures parental involvement, which studies show is a positive factor in the success of African American children. It also serves as a deterrent to the misbehaving student.

Step 6: The Afrocentric perspective. African-centered education has two primary goals when addressing history: (a) put European history into perspective and teach it truthfully and (b) teach African history and its relevance to the rest of the world. Putting European history into perspective means, for example, teaching about Greek history but including the fact that many of the "great" Greeks, such as Plato and Socrates, studied in Egypt. It also addresses the other side of the Columbus story, the Native American perspective. It includes understanding why the written word became so important to Europeans as well as why they need to validate and substantiate their history while omitting and ignoring that of others.

Teaching African history means starting with the beginning of civilization, getting rid of such terms as *precivilization* and *preliterate era*, and continuing through the different African dynasties, inventions, findings, and traditions that have been passed down and exist today. Examples of African contributions are wide-ranging: the phrase "Man know thyself," Aesop's fables, metallic ores, drainage systems, the calendar, an understanding of the solar system, and mathematical and science concepts. Teachers make the importance of African contributions well-known to their students.

Step 7: Multisensory. "Since people remember 90 percent of what they say and do and only ten percent of what they read" (Rivers, 1998, p. 61), the teachers of Sankofa Shule design classroom projects that employ more than just writing or reading skills. Hopkins (1969) offers several suggestions to language teachers: Allow children to take photographs of their field trips or class experiments and then have them talk about the trips or draw pictures about the experiences instead of writing about them. Storytelling is also a good way to involve students in learning, including acting out the story. Storytelling can be used to teach lessons on grammar or punctuation. These and other methods are used at Sankofa Shule. For example, students may create raps about a history lesson. Around the school are posted pictures and other pieces of art created by the students. This artwork attests not only to the various types of learning but also to the skills unleashed in an atmosphere that fosters difference and creativity.

Another technique employed to make math computation fun is to open "bank accounts" in the class and teach students about money, loans, interest, and dividends. Students are allowed to "buy" pencils or other products with "money" deducted from their bank accounts. Good conduct "earns" a certain amount of money, and so forth. Science projects are easily multisensory projects. It only takes a teacher who is interested in the full development of a child to go the extra step to diversify classroom settings.

Step 8: Multimodal. African-centered educators realize that multisensory approaches will mean many *styles* of teaching. "Using the eclectic process a teacher takes a little of this and a little of that to make a potion for each child" (Rivers, 1998, p. 68). Lecturing may be the best way to teach a lesson one day, but encouraging experiential learning may be best another day.

Step 9: Multidimensional. The African-centered teacher understands the interdependence of health, intellectual stability, and spirituality. A complete person will not develop if one of these dimensions is neglected. Multidimensional means teaching students about exercise and good eating habits. Teachers use exercise or breathing techniques and drills to invigorate or focus a child, respectively. Also stressed is the importance of learning to do things independently, such as growing fruits and vegetables and making clothes. This type of learning helps to ensure that, regardless of what society dictates, African American students will be able to feed and clothe themselves.

This type of knowledge brings about a sense of security, which helps maintain intellectual stability. Good health promotes clear thinking. When physical and mental goals are met, the African-centered teacher helps the student achieve spirituality. Religious beliefs are not taught in Sankofa Shule, but inner peace is emphasized as an aid in coping with external stresses and pressures. Through being able to openly express themselves in a respectful manner that in turn demands respect, African-centered students also can act without a heavy conscience and learn to deal with consequences calmly and rationally.

Step 10: Hotep. Hotep means peace. Teachers help children become respectful of themselves, fellow beings, and their environment through a truthful representation of history and society, and they also help children learn to be at peace with themselves. Even though racism abounds in practically every phase of life, students will know that the problem is not rooted in their so-called intellectual inferiority or cultural and economic deprivation. Rather, they learn that racism is pervasive and is linked to the history of this country.

African-centered education does not deny the significance of other races or cultures. It reveals that each contributes to a world full of diversity and beauty. Respect for differences and the enhanced role students play in their own learning sets African-centered education apart from Eurocentric education. African traditions stress truth, honesty, justice, righteousness, and reciprocity; this makes it difficult for African American children to be taught the lies or partial truths that public schools have taught for generations, and then be expected to function normally based on what they learned in school. African-centered education respects the students; it does not reject them. It also includes all the people that play a role or will play a role in the children's lives.

African-centered education has been found to be highly effective for all children. Both Blacks and Whites benefit from it and become socially and politically adept. In an African-centered school, all children develop a serious desire to learn and become very involved in learning. Students who enter without any foundation—not knowing colors, shapes, words—leave the classroom speaking and writing in complete sentences, with problem-solving skills, critical-thinking skills, creative talents, and sometimes a beginning knowledge of several languages, such as Swahili, Japanese, and variations of Native American languages.

Conclusion

The mere use of the word *African* is usually grounds for rejecting an African-centered education in the public school system. Yet, several of the strategies employed in African-centered schools have been touted as the most effective ways to teach African American children and have been employed, in one form or another, in other programs.

The Success for All program has been implemented in 50 schools throughout the country, and its primary goals are "prevention and immediate, intensive intervention" (Slavin, Madden, Shaw, Mainzer, & Donnelly, 1993, p. 86). Teachers accomplish these goals by involving parents and using whatever classroom techniques will help students succeed. (These elements are essential in African-centered schools.) The success rate for the program has been outstanding. Among third graders in the program since first grade, only 3.9% performed below grade level, compared to 11.7% in the control group. In schools implementing the program, special education classes dropped from 22 to 6, and the retention rate (children held back in a class) was near zero (Slavin et al., 1993). These are the types of results teachers are trying to obtain. It takes having respect for children, expecting no less than the best from children, and encouraging parental and community involvement to help motivate them to succeed.

Another example of African ideals at work is a program that uses empowerment for restructuring. Ancient Africans believed in the power of the community and the child's commitment to it. In the community, everyone learns from others. Learning is a never-ending process. By being able to offer input and suggestions for their own learning, students learn responsibility and commitment. The empowerment project has been initiated in several districts across the country. Teachers are given more control over their classrooms and over what and how they teach. They get together with other teachers to plan lessons so that these will be consistent and so that students can move through the educational process with relative ease. Each teacher knows what the previous teacher accomplished and what teaching methods do or do not work with a student. The students are invited to help create the lessons for the upcoming term. The result has been highly satisfied teachers who work as a community to educate the students and a group of students who reinvest their energies and time in obtaining an education.

There is no *one* way to teach African American children effectively. A combination approach is best, such as the seven components of culturally equitable teaching proposed by Jackson (1993-1994): (a) build trust, (b) become culturally literate, (c) build a repertoire of instructional strategies, (d) use effective teaching strategies, (e) provide effective feedback, (f) analyze instructional materials, and (g) establish positive home-school relations. Other strategies have been discussed in this chapter, such as those proposed by Ladson-Billings and Rivers.

Experience at Sankofa Shule suggests the following. Teach the truth: about history and about the present. Without accurate historical information, the truth about the present can never be put into perspective and identified. Use different teaching methods. Teacher education should include classes that help develop different teaching strategies. Also, teacher education should help correct the inadequacies of textbooks.

Teachers cannot educate alone. A concerted effort is needed from the administration, the community, and families. With regard to parental involvement, Gay (1993) warns that "it is understandable [that parents] are reluctant or unable to do [participate]. The schools that are failing their children are the same ones that failed them when they were students" (p. 190). For families, success means education and, for many, reeducation. Sankofa Shule ensures that the family is at the center of the child's life; not only is education a lifelong process for the student, it is also the family's obligation.

References

Akbar, N. (1984). *From miseducation to "education."* Jersey City, NJ: New Mind Productions.

Akoto, A. (1994). Notes on an Afrikan-centered pedagogy. In M. J. Shujaa (Ed.), *Too much schooling, too little education: A paradox of Black life in White society.* Trenton, NJ: Africa World Press.

Banks, J. (1993). Approaches to multicultural curriculum reform. In J. Banks & C. Banks (Eds.), *Multicultural education: Issues and perspectives.* Needham Heights, MA: Allyn & Bacon.

Boateng, P. (1990). Combating deculturalization of the African-American child in the public school system: A multicultural approach. In K. Lomotey (Ed.), *Going to school: The African-American experience.* Albany: State University of New York Press.

English, F. (1992). *Deciding what to teach and test: Developing, aligning, and auditing the curriculum* (Vol. 4). Newbury Park, CA: Corwin Press.

Gay, G. (1993). Multicultural education: Characteristics and goals. In J. Banks & C. Banks (Eds.), *Multicultural education: Issues and perspectives.* Needham Heights, MA: Allyn & Bacon.

Haynes, N. M., & Comer, J. P. (1990). Helping Black children succeed: The significance of some social factors. In K. Lomotey (Ed.), *Going to school: The African-American experience.* Albany: State University of New York Press.

Hopkins, L. B. (1969). *Let them be themselves: Language arts enrichment for disdvantaged children in elementary schools.* New York: Citation Press.

Jackson, F. (1993-1994). Seven ways to culturally responsive pedagogy. *Journal of Reading, 37,* 298-303.

King, J. E., & Wilson, T. L. (1994). Being the soul-freeing substance: A legacy of hope in AfroHumanity. In M. J. Shujaa (Ed.), *Too much schooling, too little education: A paradox of Black life in White society.* Trenton, NJ: Africa World Press.

Kunjufu, J. (1990). *Countering the conspiracy to destroy Black boys* (Vol. 3). Chicago: African American Images.

Ladson-Billings, G. (1994). *The dreamkeepers: Successful teachers of African American children.* San Francisco, CA: Jossey-Bass.

Lee, C. D. (1994). African-centered pedagogy: Complexities and possibilities. In M. J. Shujaa (Ed.), *Too much schooling, too little education: A paradox of Black life in White society.* Trenton, NJ: Africa World Press.

Lomotey, K. (1994). African-American principals: Bureaucrat/administrators and ethno-humanists. In M. J. Shujaa (Ed.), *Too much schooling, too little education: A paradox of Black life in White society.* Trenton, NJ: Africa World Press.

McCarthy, C. (1993). Multicultural approaches to racial inequality in the United States. In L. A. Castenell, Jr., & W. F. Pinar (Eds.), *Understanding curriculum as racial text: Representations of identity and difference in education.* Albany: State University of New York Press.

Persell, C. (1993). Social class and educational equity. In J. Banks & C. Banks (Eds.), *Multicultural education: Issues and perspectives.* Needham Heights, MA: Allyn & Bacon.

Rivers, F. (1998). *Heshima to Hotep: African-centered steps to educational excellence.* Lansing, MI: Sankofa.

Shujaa, M. J. (1994). Education and schooling: You can have one without the other. In M. J. Shujaa (Ed.), *Too much schooling, too little education: A paradox of Black life in White society.* Trenton, NJ: Africa World Press.

Slavin, R., Madden, N., Shaw, A., Mainzer, K. L., & Donnelly, M. (1993). Success for all. In J. Murphy & P. Hallinger (Eds.), *Restructuring schooling: Learning from ongoing efforts.* Newbury Park, CA: Corwin.

Part IV

Conflict in African American Children

11

Conflict Resolution Styles Among African American Children and Youth

ALGEA O. HARRISON-HALE

Because of recent trends in school and community violence (Richters & Martinez, 1993), there is heightened interest in how children in America resolve conflicts. Also of interest is the role of ethnic culture in behavioral outcomes. Cultural norms for communication within relationships may differ, and ethnicity may influence behavior in situations of potential conflict (Schneider, Fonzi, Tomada, & Tani, 2000). *Ethnicity* refers to a sense of commonality transmitted over generations by the family and reinforced by the surrounding community (McGoldrick, 1982).

Ethnic groups are not monolithic. There are variations within groups due to geography, gender, social class, education, patterns of discrimination, and religion. There is a consensus, however, that regardless of other salient factors among African Americans, survival issues based on interdependence and racial oppression are commonalities that transcend individual and group differences (Hines, Garcia-Preto, McGoldrick, Almeida, & Weltman, 1992). Ethnicity is relevant to styles of conflict resolution among African Americans because it shapes and influences interpersonal communications, beliefs about causes of problems, and problem-solving approaches.

The context within which children grow and develop also is an important factor in behavioral outcomes, and ethnicity represents an important context (Harrison, Wilson, Pine, Chan, & Buriel, 1990). Thus, it is informative to review the literature for a general view of how African American children and youth resolve conflicts. Such review can illuminate the mechanisms involved and suggest the basis for intervention and policy recommendations. As background to the review, a brief examination of data on families and conflict resolution is pertinent.

Demographic Data

The African American population in the United States numbered 34.9 million as of July 1, 1999, accounting for 13% of the total (U.S. Bureau of the Census, 2000). It is projected to be 59.2 million in 2050, a 70% increase; at that time, it will represent 15% of the total population. The number of non-Hispanic Black children in the United States was 9.3 million (15%) in 1980 and 10.2 million (15%) in 1997; the projection is 12.2 million (16%) in 2020. Before 1997, non-Hispanic Blacks were the largest minority population of children in the United States, but Hispanic children are expected to be the largest group in 2020 at 17.2 million (22%) (U.S. Bureau of the Census, 1998a).

About 51% of African American children age 6 and younger are poor (U.S. Bureau of The Census, 1993). In 1996, median income for White families was $44,756 compared to $26,522 for Blacks (U.S. Bureau of the Census, 1998b). African Americans and Hispanics who are poor are more likely to live in isolated urban ghettos than are poor Whites (Wilson, 1987). Almost 19% of Black children live in very poor neighborhoods, compared to 11.3% of Hispanic children and 1.2% of White children (U.S. Department of Health and Human Services, 1998b). High levels of violence in some inner-city African American communities have been noted (Richters & Martinez, 1993). Among Black males between the ages of 10 and 19, homicide accounts for 42% of deaths (Healthy People 2000, 1991).

The children of poor African Americans and Hispanics experience severe economic deprivation and have few prospects for economic improvement as adults (Crane, 1991). Parents who are regularly employed provide a degree of financial security for their children, and parental attachment to the labor force is associated with children's escape from poverty (U.S. Department of Health and Human Services, 1998b). *Secure attachment* refers to full-time employment over the course of an entire year. In 1996, the proportion of Black children with a parent securely attached to the labor force was 56%, compared to 79% for Whites and 64% for Hispanics. In 1997, 71% of Black, 68% of White, and 54% of Hispanic children lived in families in which all resident parents were working. In 1996, 63% of Black mothers, 67% of White mothers, and 49% of Hispanic mothers were employed. Black mothers are the most likely to be employed full time (52%) (U.S. Department of Health and Human Services, 1998b). Although the data indicate that a large percentage of African American parents are working, half the population of Black children live in poverty (McLoyd, 1990).

According to both theory and empirical evidence, families and communities are important in shaping behavioral outcomes among children. Selected data can be viewed as indices of the potency of conflict resolution styles in Black families and communities. Although African Americans constituted 16% of all children under age 18 in 1995, they accounted for 27% of cases of child abuse and neglect (U.S. Department of Health and Human Services, 1998a). A high incidence of maltreatment indicates a breakdown in conflict resolution among family members.

In some African American families and communities, a combination of economic hardship, limited access to supportive services, and the psychological burden of oppression combine to disadvantage children and place significant obstacles in the way of their healthy development (Barbarin, 1993). One such barrier is the failure to resolve family conflicts in a constructive manner. Children learn adaptive coping styles from adult role models.

The abuse of alcohol or other controlled substances, carrying of weapons, physical fighting, firearm-related deaths, and youth homicides and suicides indicate social problems and suggest, among other things, difficulties in resolving conflicts. Substance abuse impairs reasoning and judgment and is often implicated in early sexual activity, fighting, and delinquency (U.S. Department of Health and Human Services, 1998b). In 1996, 13% of youngsters age 12 to 17, regardless of ethnic origin, reported binge drinking and/or use of an illicit drug during the previous month (marijuana, cocaine [including crack], heroin, hallucinogens [including PCP], inhalants, and nonmedical use of psychotherapies). Binge drinking is defined as five or more drinks on the same occasion on 1 or more days in the previous 30 days (U.S. Department of Health and Human Services, 1998b).

The carrying of weapons reduces the incentive to compromise and makes violent conflict resolution more likely (Public Health Service, 1993). A study of African American boys and girls in a predominantly low-income North Carolina school system (Cotton, et al., 1994) revealed that carrying weapons predicted aggressive behavior and fighting in school. The researchers believe that students may gain confidence and security from carrying a weapon and thus may perceive fewer risks to themselves in aggressive situations. In 1995, 22% of Black, 19% of White, and 25% of Hispanic teens reported having carried a weapon. For White and Black students, these figures are down from 1991 (when they were 25% and 33%, respectively). High school males are much more likely than females to carry a weapon, regardless of ethnic group (U.S. Department of Health and Human Services, 1998b).

In sum, there seems to be very little ethnic difference in the propensity of youth behavior with the potential to affect how conflict is resolved. To see whether that is true, a closer examination of conflict resolution among African American children and youth is needed. Two types of conflict will be investigated: parent-child and peer-peer.

Parent-Child Conflicts

Does partner/marital conflict influence the techniques used in parent-child conflicts and indirectly those used by children? The question is of interest to numerous researchers. Social learning and family system theories offer conceptual frameworks about the effect of family subsystems on other relationships. These suggest that children learn their styles of conflict resolution through the processes of modeling, observational learning, and experiences of family interactions. A small body of work concludes that there is a consistent relationship between parental styles and those children use in handling interpersonal conflicts (Dadds, Atkinson, Turner, Blums, & Lendrich, 1999; Jorgenson, 1985). For example, adolescents exposed to parental violence were likely to use similar methods (Garrett, 1997). Fincham, Grych, and Osborne (1994) argue that the techniques used to resolve conflict with partners are used with children. For example, there was a correlation between spouse and child abuse, and partners who frequently expressed hostility toward each other were more likely to respond negatively toward their children (Kerig, Cowan, & Cowan, 1993). In other words, people who tend to use aggression in conflict situations will do so whether the target is a partner or child. Also, there is evidence of a spillover of negativity and tension from partner/marital conflicts to parent-child relations (Reese-Weber & Bartle-Haring, 1998).

Reese-Weber and Bartle-Haring (1998) investigated how conflict resolution styles in one family dyad relate to other family dyads and relationships outside the family. They used a convenience sample of White middle-class first-year college students from traditional families to investigate whether marital conflict affected adolescents' romantic relationships. Path analysis revealed a direct relationship for the mother-adolescent and father-adolescent dyads and an indirect relationship for sibling and romantic couple dyads. For example, if the marital partners used compromise in settling their conflicts, then they both used that style in dealing with the adolescent. If parent and adolescent used an attacking style, then the adolescent was likely to use that in conflicts with a romantic partner.

There is contradictory evidence regarding ethnic differences in styles of resolving conflicts with romantic partners. Feldman and Gowen (1998) found that African American teens were more likely to use violence in these situations than any of the other ethnic groups (Asian American, European American, and Hispanics). The authors consider findings consistent with data from other studies, which indicate that ventilating and aggressive behaviors are a cultural pattern for resolving conflict in Black families and communities (Garrett, 1997). In contrast, Jensen-Campbell, Graziano, and Hair (1996) compared African Americans, Mexican Americans, and European Americans and found that negotiation was consistently rated the best choice by all ethnic groups and for all kinds of relationships. Results were similar in a study by Lind, Huo, and Tyler (1994), who examined ethnic differences in a task of procedural preferences in response to a hypothetical conflict as well as self-reports of a life experience in resolving conflict. There was an overall pattern of fairness for all ethnic groups in both cases. Although more empirical investigation of how African Americans resolve conflicts in a specific type of relationship is needed, it appears that children and youth are influenced by the conflicts they experience.

Furthermore, families living in poverty are more likely to have difficulty in resolving conflicts in an adaptive and healthy manner. Poor adults are more likely to report high levels of psychological distress relative to nonpoor adults (Kessler, 1982). Poor children are more likely than others to be participants in or witnesses to family and community violence. More Black children live in poverty than do White or Hispanic children, although a large percentage of African Americans are working. Psychological distress and poverty are predictors of harsh punishing techniques and low levels of parental responsiveness to children's needs (Rutter, 1990). McLeod and Shanahan (1993), using data from the 1986 National Longitudinal Survey of Youth, explored the relationship among poverty, length of time spent in poverty, maternal parenting behaviors, and children's mental health. They found that mothers in poverty tended to resolve conflict with physical punishment and were often unresponsive to the needs of their children. These parental behaviors were likely to result in poor mental health and behavioral conduct problems among children (McLoyd, 1990).

American culture accepts the idea that sometimes it is necessary and supposedly harmless to punish children physically, and spanking is widely used. More than 90% of American parents use corporal punishment on toddlers, and just over half use the practice with adolescents, hitting them an average of eight times a year (Straus & Yodanis, 1996). Among economically disadvantaged families, parenting techniques of African Americans are more restrictive, critical, controlling, and tougher than those of Whites. This style tends to limit opportunities for resolving mother-child conflicts through verbal exchanges, but it correlates positively with high achievement, good mental health, and positive social adjustment. Black children and adolescents sometimes are permitted to express their feelings and opinions in family settings, but they are not allowed to argue with adults after a final decision has been made (Hines et al., 1992). When they do, they are immediately told, "Don't talk back to me" or "Don't argue with me" or "I done told you." In short, African American families have developed child-rearing techniques that are different from those of mainstream families, but they are effective and work under disadvantaged circumstances (Rende & Plomin, 1993). Yet, there is contrary evidence that poor Blacks were likely to use harsh parenting techniques that lead to less favorable child behavioral outcomes (McLoyd, 1990).

An issue of interest to some researchers is the sources of conflict between parents and offspring. Some scholars maintain that African American mothers use harsh parenting techniques because of the threatening, hostile, racist climate in which they rear their children. In previous years, conflicts with Whites and the threat of lynching were common. From 1882 to 1968, there were 4,742 lynching of Blacks recorded by the U.S. Bureau of the Census (Lind, 1998), but countless others occurred. Today, problems of the inner city include police brutality, gang activity, and random neighborhood violence, as well as early pregnancy, which often leads to dropping out of school and limited life opportunities (Hines et al., 1992).

Sagrestano, McCormick, Paikoff, and Holmbeck (1999) examined the association between development and parent-adolescent conflict in a sample of 302 urban low-income Black youngsters (mean age 11) and their parents (mean age 35). The findings indicate that conflicts with parents were associated with the onset of puberty, and the patterns of conflict resolution differed for boys and girls. Parents reported using more verbal aggression with sons during mid-puberty than early or late puberty and having more heated discussions with sons who matured early or late as compared to those who matured on time. Sons reported having more heated discussions and discussing heated issues when they were more developed than when they were less so. In comparison, parents reported using more violent tactics with younger than with older daughters, and they discussed more heated issues and had more heated discussions with daughters who matured early versus those who matured on time or late. This research suggests that as children become more mature (including increases in physical size), parents may begin to use more aggressive techniques.

Somewhat different findings emerged from the study by Smetana and Gaines (1999) of adolescent-parent conflict in middle-class African American families. Conflicts were relatively frequent, low in intensity, and occurred over such mundane issues as the adolescent's room, chores, choice of activities, and homework. Most conflicts were resolved by adolescents' giving in to parents. Use of this technique declined with age, and it eventually evolved into a negotiation style.

Growing in maturity is accompanied by demands for autonomy and independence, which brings adolescents into more frequent conflict with family rules. Adolescents also want to spend more time with their peers as they enter the period of life when separating from parents is an important identity issue. Furthermore, arrival of puberty signals a change in parents as well (Sagrestano et al., 1999), because they are more aware of the implications of puberty than adolescents and thus begin to interpret and anticipate behaviors from a different perspective. Also, conflict may arise when adolescents believe that the advice of adults is not appropriate to the context in which they operate (Hines et al., 1992). Yet, parents living in poverty may feel that the concerns and distress of children are trivial compared with their difficult life experiences, and this insensitivity may hamper conflict resolution. Parental status is more important for boys than girls as a factor in increased conflict. Single mothers encounter more conflict than mothers in two-parent households do. Also, parents of boys report higher rates of conflict than parents of girls. To protect their sons from gang involvement, drugs, and neighborhood violence, parents may be more restrictive of males than females, which increases parent-son conflicts.

Children exposed to well-managed conflict between their parents can learn constructive problem-solving strategies for use in other relationships (Kitzmann, 2000). When there are traumas such as divorce, marital conflict, economic stress, and unemployment, the mother's behavior toward the child is affected, including handling of conflicts. There may be increased rejection and hostility, less parental warmth, less sensitive and involved parenting, and more arbitrary and controlling behavior. One empirical investigation found that marital conflict lowered the quality of parents' general conversation with their sons, although the effects were not prolonged (Jouriles & Farris, 1992). In contrast, a later study (Mahoney, Boggio, & Jouriles, 1996) found that mothers who had a conflictual marital discussion subsequently showed more empathy toward their sons than did mothers who had a nonconflictual marital discussion. As noted earlier, there is considerable evidence that resolution styles used in marital conflict have a direct relationship with mother-adolescent and father-adolescent conflict resolution styles.

In sum, parental approaches can potentially influence how offspring resolve conflicts at home and with peers. A review of how young African Americans handle peer conflict is of interest for planning intervention and prevention strategies.

Peer-Peer Conflicts

Peer relations play an important role in the developmental process. Much has been written about the extensive influence of peers on individual behavior. Conflict resolution is an important aspect of peer relations, and several styles have been identified: compromise, distraction, avoidance, overt anger, seeking of social support, and violence (Feldman & Gowen, 1998). Malloy and McMurray (1996) have defined *conflict* as a situation in which two people have incompatible goals and use a variety of prosocial and antisocial strategies to influence each other's behavior. Generally, one partner insists on a win-lose outcome. Simply separating two young children often resolves conflicts, and adults often intervene to impose this or another resolution.

Sometimes, conflicts are resolved by physical violence (Fry, 1996). A substantial amount of literature indicates that violence among inner-city youth is associated with a combination of environmental stressors, such as victimization, exposure to violence in the community, family characteristics, and personal factors (Durant, Cadenhead, Pendergrast, Slavens, & Linder, 1994; Murata, 1994). Individual characteristics also influence whether youngsters will use fighting or violence to resolve conflict. Fitzpatrick (1997) examined personal characteristics and environmental factors in a sample of nonaggressive and aggressive African American youths. He found that most differences between the groups could be attributed to varying degrees of exposure to violence, specifically as witnesses to and victims of it, and to possession of a weapon.

Consuelo, McCoy, and Craig (1999) studied the extent to which two predictors of violent behavior among adolescents—parental involvement and negative peer behavior—were correlated with ethnic identity and the use of fighting. It was found that parental involvement influenced child behavioral outcomes through direct parenting techniques that prohibit fighting and other acts of physical violence as a means of resolving conflict. Peers may directly instigate or encourage fighting. A higher level of parental involvement and lower levels of negative peer behaviors were thus associated with more peaceful means of conflict resolution. These two predictors, combined with positive feelings about the person's ethnicity, were related to self-reported attitudes and skills about resolving peer conflicts in nonviolent ways. Zimmerman, Steinman, and Rowe (1998) have similar findings. These findings are similar also to research by Mason, Cauce, Gonzales, and Hirage (1996), which revealed the importance of maternal control of problem adolescents during their involvement with problem peers (see also Griffin, Scheier, Botvin, Diaz, & Miller, 1999).

The excessive use of physical violence reflects that a tendency toward aggression is a personal characteristic of concern to educators, parents, and mental health specialists. Fighting is a contributing factor in many nonfatal and fatal intentional injuries (Healthy People 2000, 1991). Synder, Horsch, and Childs (1997) found that the amount of time children spent interacting with aggressive peers predicted changes in observed and teacher-rated aggressiveness 3 months later. According to Cotton and colleagues (1994), age (being an older adolescent), gender (being male), carrying a weapon, and attitudes toward violence were predictive of aggressive behavior and fighting at school. As aggressive youngsters develop, they become less likely to resolve conflicts peacefully, and children exposed to violence directly or indirectly were more likely to use it in conflict resolution (Garrett, 1997). Children and adolescents who have been abused physically were especially vulnerable. Evidence suggests that excessively aggressive behaviors in the early years continued into adulthood (Hudley et al., 1998).

Intervention programs to teach nonviolent means of handling conflict have potential. Social scientists, educators, and mental health workers have begun to address this issue with a moderate degree of success (Brown, 1996; Hudley & Friday, 1996). A program that combines anger management classes and conflict resolution group treatments has proved effective (Stern, 1999), as have other approaches that use both behavioral and cognitive techniques.

Conclusion

Ethnic culture is an important differentiating factor in determining styles of conflict resolution. Data indicate no ethnic differences in youth between the ages of 12 and 17 in reported binge drinking, use of illicit drugs, and carrying of weapons, all of which have the potential to affect conflict situations. The most visible evidence of ethnic differences in resolving conflicts is the rate of death by homicide, which is highest for African American males. General observations have been made by some writers about the high levels of aggression and violence in African American communities. The external environment includes poverty, poor housing, poor education, and a biased justice system. These factors compound problems for individuals and families who are trying to cope with emotional challenges, aggressive environments, and no or inappropriate role models.

According to social learning and family systems theories, children learn their styles of conflict resolution from modeling, observational learning, and family interactions. Empirical evidence supports this view. Styles parents use with partners are also used with children. Furthermore, studies show a consistent relationship between parental styles and those children use to handle conflicts. Resolution of marital conflict has a direct relationship with mother-adolescent and father-adolescent patterns and an indirect relationship with sibling and romantic couple patterns. There is contrary evidence as to whether African American teens use more violence in resolving their conflicts with a romantic partner. More research is needed on the topic to develop prevention and intervention policies.

The sources of parental conflict with children are perceived threats to well-being from the environment, the developmental phase of desire for autonomy and independence, physical maturity, and mundane household chores and demands. Conflicts are generally resolved when young children give in to parental demands, but use of this strategy decreases as children get older. The manner in which parents resolve marital conflicts, the degree of parental involvement in monitoring children's behavior, and the influence of aggressive peers influence later patterns of conflict resolution.

References

Barbarin, O. A. (1993). Coping and resilience: Exploring the inner lives of African American children. *Journal of Black Psychology, 19,* 478-492.

Brown, E. R. (1996). Effects of resource availability on children's behavior and conflict management. *Early Education & Development, 7*(2), 149-166.

Consuelo, A., McCoy, H. R., & Craig, A. B. (1999). Ethnic identity as a predictor of attitudes of adolescents toward fighting. *Journal of Early Adolescence, 19,* 323-340.

Cotton, N. U., Resnick, J., Browne, D. C., Martin, S., McCarraher, D. R., & Woods, J. (1994). Aggression and fighting behavior among African-American adolescents: Individual and family factors. *American Journal of Public Health, 84*(4), 618-622.

Crane, J. (1991). Effects of neighborhoods on dropping out of school and teenage childbearing. In C. Jencks & P. E. Peterson (Eds.), *The urban underclass* (pp. 299-320). Washington, DC: Brookings Institution.

Dadds, M. R., Atkinson, E., Turner, C., Blums, G. J., & Lendrich, B. (1999). Family conflict and child adjustment: Evidence for a cognitive-contextual model of intergenerational transmission. *Journal of Family Psychology, 13*(2), 194-208.

Durant, R. H., Cadenhead, C., Pendergrast, R. A., Slavens, G., & Linder, C. W. (1994). Factors associated with the use of violence among urban Black adolescents. *American Journal of Public Health, 84,* 612-617.

Feldman, S. S., & Gowen, G. L. (1998). Conflict negotiation tactics in romantic relationships in high school students. *Journal of Youth and Adolescence, 27*(6), 691-717.

Fincham, F. D., Grych, J. H., & Osborne, L. N. (1994). Does marital conflict cause child maladjustment? Directions and challenges for longitudinal research. *Journal of Family Psychology, 8*(2), 128-140.

Fitzpatrick, K. M. (1997). Aggression and environmental risk among low-income African-American youth. *Journal of Adolescent Health, 21*(3), 172-178.

Fry, D. (1996). *Cultural variation in conflict resolution: Alternatives to violence.* Mahwah, NJ: Lawrence Erlbaum.

Garrett, D. (1997). Conflict resolution in the African American. *Aggression & Violent Behavior, 2*(1), 25-31.

Griffin, K. W., Scheier, L. M., Botvin, G. J., Diaz, T., & Miller, N. (1999). Interpersonal aggression in urban minority youth: Mediators of perceived neighborhood, peer, and parental influences. *Journal of Community Psychology, 27*(3), 281-298.

Harrison, A. O., Wilson, M. N., Pine, C. J., Chan, S. Q., & Buriel, R. (1990). Family ecologies of ethnic minority children. *Child Development, 61,* 347-362.

Healthy People 2000. (1991). *Healthy People 2000: National health promotion and disease prevention objectives* (DHHS publication PHS 91-50213). Washington, DC: U.S. Department of Health and Human Services.

Hines, P. M., Garcia-Preto, N., McGoldrick, M., Almeida, R., & Weltman, S. (1992). Intergenerational relationships across cultures. *Families in Society: The Journal of Contemporary Human Services, 73*(6), 323-338.

Hudley, C., Britsch, B., Wakefield, W. D., Smith, T., Demorat, M., & Cho, S. (1998). An attribution retraining program to reduce aggression in elementary school students. *Psychology in the Schools, 35*(3), 271-282.

Hudley, C., & Friday, J. (1996). Attributional bias and reactive aggression. *American Journal of Preventive Medicine, 12*(Suppl. 5), 75-81.

Jensen-Campbell, L. A., Graziano, W. G., & Hair, E. C. (1996). Personality and relationships as moderators of interpersonal conflict in adolescence. *Merrill-Palmer Quarterly, 42*(1), 148-164.

Jorgenson, D. E. (1985). Transmitting methods of conflict resolution from parents to children: A replication and comparison of Blacks and Whites, males and females. *Social Behavior & Personality, 13*(2), 109-117.

Jouriles, E., & Farris, A. (1992). Effects of marital conflict on subsequent parent son interactions. *Behavior Therapist, 23,* 355-372.

Kerig, P., Cowan, P., & Cowan, A. (1993). Marital quality and gender differences in parent child interactions. *Developmental Psychology, 29,* 931-939.

Kessler, R. C. (1982). A disaggregation of the relationship between socioeconomic status and psychological distress. *American Sociological Review, 47,* 752-764.

Kitzmann, K. (2000). Effects of marital conflict on subsequent triadic family interactions and parenting. *Developmental Psychology, 36*(1), 3-13.

Lind, A. E., Huo, Y. J., & Tyler, T. R. (1994). And justice for all: Ethnicity, gender, and preference for dispute resolution procedures. *Law and Human Behavior, 18*(3), 269-290.

Lind, M. (1998, August, 16). The beige and the black. *New York Times Magazine*, p. 38.

Mahoney, A., Boggio, R., & Jouriles, E. (1996). Effects of verbal marital conflict on subsequent mother-son interactions in a child clinical sample. *Journal of Clinical Child Psychology, 25*, 262-271.

Malloy, H. L., & McMurray, P. (1996). Conflict strategies and resolutions: Peer conflict in an integrated early childhood classroom. *Early Childhood Research Quarterly, 11*, 185-206.

Mason, C. A., Cauce, A. M., Gonzales, N., & Hirage, Y. (1996). Neither too sweet nor too sour: Problem peers, maternal control, and problem behavior in African American adolescents. *Child Development, 67*(5), 2115-2130.

McGoldrick, M. (1982). Irish Americans. In M. Goldrick, J. K. Pearce, & J. Giordano (Eds.), *Ethnicity and family therapy.* New York: Guilford.

McLeod, J. D., & Shanahan, M. J. (1993, June). Poverty, parenting, and children's mental health. *American Sociological Review, 58*, 351-366.

McLoyd, V. C. (1990). The impact of economic hardship on Black families and children: Psychological distress, parenting, and socioemotional development. *Child Development, 61*, 311-346.

Murata, J. (1994). Family stress, social support, violence, and sons' behavior. *Western Journal of Nursing Research, 16*(2), 154-168.

Public Health Service. (1993). *Public health reports on high-risk adolescents* (Vol. 108, Suppl. 1). Rockville, MD: Author.

Reese-Weber, M., & Bartle-Haring, S. (1998). Conflict resolution styles in family subsystems and adolescent romantic relationships. *Journal of Youth and Adolescence, 27*(6), 735-752.

Rende, R., & Plomin, R. L. (1993). Families at risk for psychopathology: Who becomes affected and why? *Development & Psychopathology, 5*(4), 529-540.

Richters, J. E., & Martinez, P. E. (1993). Violent communities, family choices, and children's chances: An algorithm for improving odds. *Development and Psychopathology, 5*, 609-627.

Rutter, M. (1990). Psychosocial resilience and protective mechanisms. In J. Rolf, A. S. Masten, D. Cicchetti, K. H. Neuchterleiln, & S. Weintraub (Eds.), *Risk and protective factors in the development of psychopathology* (pp. 181-214). New York: Cambridge University Press.

Sagrestano, L. M., McCormick, J., Paikoff, R., & Holmbeck, G. (1999). Pubertal development and parent-child conflict in low-income, urban, African American adolescents. *Journal of Research in Adolescence, 9*, 885-107.

Schneider, B. H., Fonzi, A., Tomada, G., & Tani, F. (2000). A cross-national comparison of children's behavior with their friends in situations of potential conflict. *Journal of Cross-Cultural Psychology, 31*, 259-266.

Smetana, J., & Gaines, C. (1999). Adolescent-parent conflict in middle-class African American families. *Child Development, 70*(6), 1447-1463.

Stern, S. B. (1999). Anger management in parent-adolescent conflict. *American Journal of Family Therapy, 27*(2), 181-193.

Straus, M. A., & Yodanis, C. (1996). Corporal punishment in adolescence and physical assault on spouses in later life: What accounts for the link? *Journal of Marriage and the Family, 58,* 825-841.

Synder, J., Horsch, E., & Childs, J. (1997). Peer relationships of young children: Affiliative choices and the shaping of aggressive behavior. *Journal of Clinical Child Psychology, 26,* 145-156.

U.S. Bureau of the Census. (1993). *Statistical abstracts of the United States.* Washington, DC: Government Printing Office.

U.S. Bureau of the Census. (1998a). *Current population reports* (Series P-25, No. 1095, Table 1; and No. 1130, Table 2; also unpublished data). Washington, DC: Government Printing Office.

U.S. Bureau of the Census. (1998b). *Statistical abstracts of the United States.* Washington, DC: Government Printing Office.

U.S. Bureau of the Census. (2000). *Statistical abstract of the United States, No. 15: resident population by race, 1980 to 1999, and projections, 2000 to 2050.* Washington, DC: Government Printing Office.

U.S. Department of Health and Human Services, Children's Bureau. (1998a). *Child maltreatment 1996: Reports from the states to the National Child Abuse and Neglect Data System.* Washington, DC: Government Printing Office.

U.S. Department of Health and Human Services, Office of the Assistant Secretary for Planning and Evaluation. (1998b). *Trends in the well-being of America's children and youth* (Document HE 1.63:998). Washington, DC: Government Printing Office.

Wilson, W. J. (1987). *The truly disadvantaged: The inner city, the underclass, and public policy.* Chicago: University of Chicago Press.

Zimmerman, M. A., Steinman, K. J., & Rowe, K. (1998). Violence among urban African American adolescents: The protective effects of parental support. In *Addressing community problems: Psychological research and interventions* (pp. 78-103). Thousand Oaks, CA: Sage.

12

Violent Crime, Race, and Black Children

Parenting and the Social Contract

BILL E. LAWSON
RENÉE SANDERS-LAWSON

> When an individual is no longer a true participant, when he no
> longer feels a sense of responsibility to his society,
> the content of democracy is emptied.
> *Martin Luther King, Jr. (1991)*

In the United States, violent crime is a serious social problem, and much of it occurs in inner cities. Why? Many explanations are offered. Some conservative scholars argue that the root cause is the negative cultural values of the urban inhabitants. They consider respect for authority a basic value and argue that the failure to teach this value ultimately leads to crime. In short, the problem is due to bad parenting. More liberal scholars view most of the violence as the work of a small minority of criminals. Still others blame the basic structure of society and the conditions in inner-city neighborhoods: Although no one would deny that there are bad parents in any community, scholars who are more liberal have argued that a primary cause of violent crime is the social environment in which many poor urban residents are forced to live. These areas are often the site of dilapidated housing, bad schools, high unemployment, and questionable police protection of lives and property. Some scholars argue that the social values of residents reflect the life they are forced to live (Kirkland, 1992). The views of Myron Magnet (1992) and Joan McCord (1997) are representative of this ideological split.

Magnet, an editor at the Manhattan Institute's *City Journal*, represents the conservative position; McCord, a professor of criminal justice, takes the more liberal stance. Although they disagree about the causes of violent urban crime, both believe it undermines the social contract. This chapter examines not only the explanations for this violence but also the extent to which the social contract is undermined. Our focus is on the problems faced by Black parents in providing their children with a healthy self-concept about their status as U.S. citizens. We begin by reviewing the bad-parent argument and then examine the social environment thesis. Next, we discuss the social contract, a notion developed in the 18th century by Thomas Hobbes and John Locke, among others. Finally, we explore the relationship of Blacks to the state and the social contract.

The Bad-Parent Argument

According to Magnet (1992),

> When crime flourishes as it now does in our cities, especially crime of mindless malice, it isn't because society has so oppressed people as to bend them out of their true nature and twist them into moral deformity. It is because the criminals haven't been adequately socialized. Examine the contents of their minds and hearts and too much of what you find bears out this hypothesis: free-floating aggression, weak consciences, anarchic beliefs, detachment from the community and its highest values. They have not attained the self-respect or the coherent sense of self that underlie one's ability to respect others. (p. 158)

In Magnet's (1992) view, poor young Black women are bad parents. They lack the socialization skills needed to pass on the correct modes of social behavior to their children. It is not the environment that does this. It is the fault of the mothers and more likely than not their mothers. It is the fault of absent fathers. It is not the fault of society.

To support these claims, Magnet (1992) draws on the work of Thomas Hobbes and Sigmund Freud, among others. He notes that theories of crime make an assumption about whether men are predisposed by nature to force and violence or whether violence gets into their hearts from some outside force. One of these traditions is just wrong, he believes, the one that sees men as inherently good and as turning to crime when the society in which they live oppresses them. Exalted in the work of Michael Harrington, this perspective was the hallmark of the 1960s and influenced views about Black criminal behavior until the 1980s (Magnet, 1992). The correct position, according to Magnet, is the other tradition, which for most of history has been dominant in Western political philosophy. It takes as its starting point the irreducible reality of human aggression.

The fundamental purpose of the social order, of the civilized condition itself, is to restrain man's instinctual aggressiveness so that human life can be something higher than a war of all against all. The great 17th- and 18th-century political theorists, most notably Hobbes, imagined that restraint was accomplished by a social contract. Driven to desperation by the universal warfare that made their lives "solitary, poor, nasty, brutish, and short," in Hobbes's famous phrase, men in the early ages agreed to renounce unlimited freedom of aggression to promote the security of all (Magnet, 1992, p. 156).

Freud maintained that the taming of aggression and the replacement of the rule of force by the rule of law were significant events in the history of humankind. Magnet (1992) sees this as a stage in an individual's life history as well. In early childhood, under continual parental pressure, individuals are made to renounce the unlimited aggressiveness with which they are born. During this protracted process central to early childhood, a person's innermost being is transformed. As the civilizing demands of parents and the community that speaks through them are internalized, an entirely new mental faculty is acquired, a part of the inner self, given not by nature but by society. In Freud's term, this is the *superego,* analogous to the conscience; like conscience, it punishes people with feelings of shame and guilt, speaking with the voice not of divinity but of society. According to Magnet (1992),

It has been man's ability to make the societal voice speak as the voice of reason that has civilized man. The arts, humanities, and sciences have been made possible because man has been able to overcome his natural aggression. Accordingly, man's humanity is tied to his being socialized away from his natural aggression. The socialization of the child performs an inner transformation. (p. 157)

How do people attain this inner transformation? They are socialized by their parents. Based on these assumptions, crime is not caused by the social order, for that is the very thing that restrains it. The social order is precisely what makes life something other than a scene of constant mutual invasion, in which all live in continual fear and danger of violence (Magnet, 1992).

Central to this argument is the assumption that parents must teach their children to be loyal and obedient members of society. They must do this regardless of how they feel about the status of their group in the political order. For Blacks, this means they must agree with conservatives that the system is basically fair and just, and they must view the problems they face in the United States as of their own making. Although the system may have some social and political shortcomings, these can be overcome in time with hard work on the part of individuals. This leads to the notion that Black parents, particularly the poor, have not taken responsibility for instilling positive social values in their children. Interestingly, Magnet does not list social conditions among the variables that can contribute to criminal behavior. There is no mention of racial or class oppression. It is postulated that crime is solely the fault of bad parenting in general and of Black parenting in particular.

This view has been criticized vehemently and contrasts sharply with the liberal position that urban crime is rooted in the unequal social, economic, and political status of Blacks.

American Culture and Violence

McCord (1997) argues that "high rates of societal violence seem partially explicable as reflecting an emphasis on presumed equality in the face of a reality that is exclusionary, coupled with concern for status differentiation and a learned tolerance for the use of violence" (pp. 103-104).

It is not the lack of parenting skills among poor Black mothers that gives rise to violent urban crime, it is the social and political structure of the neighborhoods in which many Blacks are forced to live. Anderson (1997) notes that

The inclination to violence springs from the circumstances of life among the ghetto poor, the lack of jobs that pay a living wage, the stigma of race, the fallout from rampant drug use and drug trafficking, and the resulting alienation and lack of hope for the future. (p. 1)

Even urban families that want to pass on decent values to their children understand there is a "code of the street."

The code revolves around the presentation of self. Its basic requirement is the display of a certain predisposition to violence. Accordingly, one's bearing must send the unmistakable if sometimes-subtle message . . . that one is capable of violence and mayhem when the situation requires it, that one can take care of oneself. (Anderson, 1997, p. 19)

Both two-parent and single-parent families understand that a child's survival depends on being able to negotiate the streets. According to Anderson (1997), the code of the street is dominated and maintained by those in the community who are most socially alienated.

The attitudes of the wider society are deeply implicated in the codes of the street. Most people in inner-city communities are not totally invested in the code; but the significant minority of hard-core street youths who do embrace it have to maintain the code in order to establish reputation, because they have, or feel they have, few other ways to assert themselves. For these young people, the standards of the street code are the only game in town. (p. 28)

These alienated youths "experience, feel, and internalize racist rejection and contempt from mainstream society," so they tend to express contempt for society in turn. "Some youngsters will consciously invest themselves and their considerable mental resources in what amounts to oppositional culture to preserve themselves and their self-respect" (Anderson, 1997, p. 28).

Even those less alienated may assume the "street-orientated demeanor as a way of expressing their Blackness" (Anderson, 1997, p. 28). Youngsters often slip back and forth between street behavior and a more moderate way of life. Most of these young people want the same things most Americans want—an attractive and safe neighborhood to live in and a decent job. Black parents face a difficult task. They must rear their children to be street smart, yet to appreciate mainstream values, and at the same time they must instill an understanding of how racism in the United States affects life chances.

In the final analysis, the social environment contributes significantly to the acting out of violent behavior on the part of many young Blacks.

> A vicious cycle is created. The hopelessness and alienation that many young inner-city Black men and women feel, largely because of endemic joblessness and persistent racism, fuel the violence they engage in. The violence serves to confirm the negative feelings many Whites and some middle-class Blacks harbor toward the ghetto poor, further legitimating the oppositional culture and the code of the streets in the eyes of many poor young Blacks. Unless this cycle is broken, attitudes on both sides will become increasingly entrenched, and the violence, which claims as victims Black and White, poor and affluent, will only escalate. (Anderson, 1997, p. 28)

An underlying theme of Anderson's work is that if poor Blacks felt invested in the United States, they would behave differently. McCord's position is similar. Many inner-city residents feel cut off from full participation in the system, and their street-wise lifestyle gives them a respect and status they are otherwise denied. If this is true, then something is very wrong with the social contract. When members of a group feel alienated from society and unprotected by the government, two basic elements of the social contract are missing. This raises the interesting question of what Black parents in general, and the poor in particular, should teach their children about what it means to be a U.S. citizen.

The Social Contract Reconsidered

As noted at the outset, an important issue is whether urban violence undermines the social contract and, if so, how. Magnet (1992) writes,

> For all Americans, the wholesale overturning of the bars to crime and disorder has scrambled the moral order. What becomes of the sense of justice when, almost daily, people violate the fundamental principles of the social contract? What becomes of the sense of personal responsibility for the actions when people are not held accountable even for the most evil deeds?

> With the ground on which the sense of values rests giving way beneath their feet, no wonder many reel with moral vertigo. (p. 171)

Magnet (1992) thinks that the social contract requires instilling societal values that promote "good" behavior and that do not give rise to concern among fellow citizens about their safety. Because poor urban parents have not done this, we have urban violence, he says.

McCord (1997) believes the failure of government to protect Blacks has undermined the social contract. The lack of social and economic benefits for the masses of Blacks has eroded their faith in the contract, which has little meaning for them. "Some adjustments will be necessary in order to increase the benefits inner-city residents receive from the larger society or else they will not perceive that society as one with which they have a social contract" (McCord, 1997, p. 104).

Important for our discussion is how the respective arguments use the writings of Hobbes. Magnet (1992) draws on what he takes to be a Hobbesian theory of human nature; McCord (1997) draws on what she takes to be the Hobbesian understanding of protection. We see problems in both cases.

Magnet (1992) gives a very aberrant reading of Hobbes. Philosopher and Hobbes scholar Edwin Curley (1994) writes,

> First let us dispose of one common misunderstanding. When Hobbes talks about the state of nature, he is not necessarily talking about the prehistoric condition of the human race, or what life was like in the primitive societies of his day. He is talking about any situation where there is no effective government to impose order. (p. xxi)

Hobbes argues that individuals are concerned with their personal safety. If they do not feel that the state is protecting them, all bets are off. They are then forced back into what Hobbes calls the "state of nature." They can rely only on themselves for protection. In accord with this reading, people who live in crime-ridden urban areas must protect themselves. Such areas are unsafe because the state cannot or will not enforce the peace. These individuals appear to be in a state of nature (Lawson, 1990). They are indeed acting as Hobbes predicts. The role of the state is to ensure that people's lives are protected. When it does not do this, it has no value.

McCord (1997) believes with Hobbes that the state has the duty to provide physical protection. Without it, in civil society, all other rights—such as the right to property—are meaningless. This view also puts unprotected people back in the Hobbesian state of nature, but that is not what McCord wants. Her theory of the social contract postulates both physical protection and protection of property, elements found in John Locke's work (Laslett, 1988).

Locke's *Second Treatise of Government* explains how individuals come to have political obligations and discusses the extent of the state's obligations to citizens and vice versa. Before the formation of civil society, humans lived in a state of nature, which for Locke meant relative peace despite the lack of a civil authority. This presented some inconveniences, however, in the case of disputes over property and in other instances. In the absence of civil authority, each man was his own judge, jury, and executioner.

According to Locke, all persons are not equally suited to press property claims against others; some mechanism of adjudication is needed. Free, equal, and autonomous individuals come together to form a compact whereby they cede to the state certain rights they naturally possess, such as the right to be their own judge, jury, and executioner. By freely consenting to join with others in civil society, each is politically obligated to obey the dictates of the state. The state ensures protection of their property, including their lives, by providing public laws, judges, and punishment for violations. Individuals then can live peacefully, secure in the knowledge that their property rights will be respected. In this manner, their chances for a life free of the inconveniences of the state of nature are ensured.

Locke's work is not totally applicable to the situation of Blacks, particularly because Locke is basically concerned with individual rather than group protection and with the quasi-historical nature of consent (Lawson, 1990). Yet, his work has significance because of its role in the debate about what U.S. citizenship means (Mills, 1999). Antislavery advocates appealed to Locke's concept of natural rights and the role of the government in protecting them. Locke emphasized protection and property rights as essential to people's status as full members of the state. From this perspective, Locke can provide some insight into the problem of instilling in Black children a sense of full citizenship. He saw the relationship between the citizenry and the state as a trust. Those entrusted with civil authority ensure that members of the state are protected and treated justly. African Americans still maintain that they are treated unjustly.

The Social Contract and Black Americans

The social contract did not apply to American Blacks in the United States before 1865. With the end of slavery, however, they hoped they would be accorded equal protection under the law, but that did not happen (Lawson, 1999). Because governmental protection was never given, it is argued that African Americans are not parties to the contract. Blacks wanted full citizenship protection but were denied it, so they can rely only on themselves for protection. Thus, they have no obligation to obey the laws of the United States (Natanson, 1970).

This position has found support in the African American community, but we reject it. It is a misreading of Locke, African American history, and our basic understanding of citizenship. There are two immediate problems. First, if Blacks are not citizens, what is their relationship to the United States? Are they aliens? Acts of disobedience by nonmembers of the state are very different from protests by citizens. If Blacks are living in the state of nature and are aliens, their disobedience can be viewed as an act of war against the United States. We must be careful not to let theory outdistance reality.

Second, we take seriously the notion that states can decide who is and is not a citizen. If the definition is a person who pays taxes, defends the state, and expects state protection of his or her political rights, then such a person is a citizen. On passage of the Fourteenth Amendment, Blacks became citizens, and in Lockean terms, these citizens should have been protected (Lawson, 1990). Although Blacks have been forced to use all sorts of tactics to obtain government protection, not only of their lives but also of their political and economic rights, this does not mean they are in a state of nature or are not full members of the state. It means they are not receiving that to which they are entitled. In a liberal democratic state, it is possible to have laws that are not enforced and rights that are not protected. It does not follow that those who are unprotected are not citizens. It does follow, however, that they are justified in protesting the lack of protection of their rights (Lawson, 1992a).

The history of Blacks in the United States is a long struggle for respect as well as legal and political protection. The end is not in sight (Lawson, 1992b). The government has often hindered rather than helped, and many Blacks feel besieged. Many argue that the government never will have as a goal the protection of Blacks (Patterson, 1951). In view of the high rate of crime victimization, the availability of drugs, and what seems a constant attack on Black males in inner-city neighborhoods, it is understandable that many Blacks think they can depend only on themselves for protection. They despair of achieving full membership in the state. They do not trust government, and they do not trust Whites (Lawson, 1992c).

These attitudes are passed on to their children. Anderson's (1997) comments about street codes are very telling. Black parents must teach their children how to survive on the streets yet instill mainstream values. At the same time, they realize that the wider social environment hinders a positive self-image for Black children and can limit their life chances. Parenting within these constraints is not an easy task.

Parents must be truthful with children about their prospects in the society in which they find themselves. When parents feel that government is not doing its job to protect Blacks, this is communicated to their children. Parents may push children to achieve, but that is often qualified by the knowledge of their status as Black people in the United States.

All parents want their children to be safe. To many Blacks, however, it appears their lives do not have enough value to warrant protection, so the social contract has no real meaning. Racism and economic oppression thus undermine the social contract for non-White, non-propertied people in the United States. Many Blacks rightfully feel they are not equal citizens.

Equal citizenship requires each citizen to be treated with equal concern and respect (Dworkin, 1977). People must feel that they and the group to which they belong are respected by the state. This plays an important role in the formulation of self-concept.

According to Howard McGary (1992),

In this view, citizens are competitors in a game of life in which rules are not rigged in favor of any of the competitors. However, this view does not assume that people cannot be treated unfairly because of the unjust actions of individuals; it is clearly understood that the unfairness is not the result of the design of the basic structure of society. Persons who feel that they are full citizens believe that their rights are recognized and protected and that their failings can be traced to some personal shortcoming, individual act of injustice, or poor fate, but not to the design of the basic structure of society.

Belief that one has full citizenship also allows one to feel comfortable in supporting and defending what John Rawls has called the "basic struc-

ture of society." By [that he] means "the way in which the major social institutions distribute fundamental rights and duties and determine the division of advantages from social cooperation." Rawls goes on to define
major social institutions as "the political constitution and the principal
economic and social arrangements." The major institutions "define people's rights and duties and influence their life prospects." Full citizenship
certainly does not entail that one will get whatever one wants, but it does
say that one will have the opportunity to satisfy one's needs and desires.
When these things cannot be satisfied, it cannot be blamed on the basic
structure of society. (p. 60)

For many Blacks, the basic structure of U.S. society is not just. They see
the game of life as rigged in favor of White competitors, so why compete?

Although race relations in the United States have improved somewhat,
for most of this country's history, Blacks have been view negatively and
their social status has been lower than that of Whites (McGary & Lawson,
1992). A basic cause has been racist laws and public policies. McCord
(1997) is correct that adjustments must be made if Blacks are to perceive
this society as one with which they have a social contract. The role of the social contract is to explain the mutual obligations of the state and the citizenry. In the Lockean model, members of the state are to be accorded equal
respect as individuals. The treatment of members cannot be unjust (Laslett,
1988). The experiences of Blacks have been otherwise. How can they not
pass these beliefs on to their children?

Parenting and the Social Contract

Should Blacks living in crime-ridden areas believe that the political and economic system is just? Even those who are well off question the fairness of
the system (Cose, 1995). Black parents must teach their children to be on
guard in their contacts with members of the wider White society. It would
be imprudent if they did not. In addition, inner-city parents must instill
so-called mainstream values but at the same time teach their children how
to survive in violent neighborhoods. Even middle-class Black parents in af-
fluent suburbs feel ambivalent about citizenship in a country that has so often failed to fulfill the social contract. Mistrust is even greater in urban areas. Unless opportunities are made available to inner-city youth, the cycle
of violence will continue. The state has a duty to ensure that its members

feel secure. Conservatives are correct about the role of parents in transmitting values to their children, but liberals recognize how the social environment affects their understanding of what those values should be. The informal system of political education in Black families must factor in racism and how it influences life chances.

Black parents face a dilemma. They must teach their children to believe in their own abilities but at the same time must acknowledge that, in the United States, ability often is not enough. This is a challenge for middle-class Blacks as well as inner-city residents. Meanwhile, significant decreases in violent crime and an increase in positive feelings about being full members of society are very unlikely for Blacks.

References

Anderson, E. (1997). Violence and the inner-city street code. In J. McCord (Ed.), *Violence and childhood in the inner city.* New York: Cambridge University Press.

Cose, E. (1995). *The rage of a privileged class.* New York: HarperCollins Library.

Curley, E. (Ed.). (1994). *Thomas Hobbes: Leviathan.* Indianapolis, IN: Hackett.

Dworkin, R. (1977). *Taking rights seriously.* Cambridge, MA: Harvard University Press.

King, M. L., Jr. (1991). *A testament of hope: The essential writings and speeches of Martin Luther King, Jr.* (J. M. Washington, Ed.). San Francisco: Harper.

Kirkland, F. (1992). Social policy, ethical life, and the urban underclass. In B. E. Lawson (Ed.), *The underclass question* (pp. 152-187). Philadelphia: Temple University Press.

Laslett, P. (Ed.). (1988). *John Locke: Two treatises of government.* New York: Cambridge University Press.

Lawson, B. (1990). Crime, minorities, and the social contract. *Criminal Justice Ethics, 9*(2), 16-24.

Lawson, B. (1992a). Citizenship and slavery. In H. McGary & B. E. Lawson (Eds.), *Between slavery and freedom* (pp. 55-70). Indianapolis: Indiana University Press.

Lawson, B. (Ed.). (1992b). *The underclass question.* Philadelphia: Temple University Press.

Lawson, B. (1992c). Uplifting the race: Middle-class Blacks and the truly disadvantaged. In B. E. Lawson(Ed.), *The underclass question* (pp. 90-113). Philadelphia: Temple University Press.

Lawson, B. (1999). Frederick Douglass and African-American social progress: Does race matter at the bottom of the well? In B. E. Lawson & F. M. Kirkland

(Eds.), *Frederick Douglass: A critical reader* (pp. 365-399). Malden, MA: Basil Blackwell.

Magnet, M. (1992). *The dream and the nightmare: The sixties' legacy to the underclass.* New York: Encounter Books.

McCord, J. (1997). Placing American urban violence in context. In J. McCord (Ed.), *Violence and childhood in the inner city* (pp. 78-115). New York: Cambridge University Press.

McGary, H. (1992). The Black underclass and the question of values. In B. E. Lawson (Ed.), *The underclass question* (pp. 57-70). Philadelphia: Temple University Press.

McGary, H., & Lawson, B. (Eds.). (1992). *Between slavery and freedom.* Indianapolis: Indiana University Press.

Mills, C. (1999). Whose fourth of July? Frederick Douglass and "original intent." In B. E. Lawson & F. M. Kirkland (Eds.), *Frederick Douglass: A critical reader.* Malden, MA: Basil Blackwell.

Natanson, H. (1970). Locke and Hume: Bearing on the legal obligation of the Negro. *Journal of Values Inquiry, 5*(1), 35-43.

Patterson, W. (1951). *We charge genocide: The crime of government against the Negro people.* New York: International Publishers.

Index

Abuse:
    child, 195, 196
    spouse, 196
Adolescents:
    conflict resolution, 202-203
    conflicts with parents, 199-200, 203
    conflicts with peers, 201
    educational attainment, 155-161
    effects of parents' marital conflict on romantic relationships, 197
    homicide victims, 194
    racial identities, 80
    sex education, 129
    weapons, 196
    See also Teenage parents
Affirmative action, 48-49
African American Male Initiative, 6
African Americans:
    citizenship and rights, 215
    conflict resolution behaviors, 197
    education levels, 7
    employment, 195
    in inner cities, 194
    incomes, 7, 124

    marriage rates, 5
    poor, 194
    population, 5, 15, 194
    poverty, 7, 177, 194, 195, 197-198
    proverbs, 28-29, 33
    social contract and, 215-217
    unemployment rates, 7, 124
    See also Racial identity
African-centered education, 180-185, 186
AIDS, 6
Alcohol abuse, 195
Asian Americans:
    family patterns, 18
    population, 15
    use of term, 20

Bartle-Haring, S., 197
Binge drinking, 195
Black, negative connotations of color, 76, 78-79
Black Ethnocentrism Scale, 105
Blacks. *See* African Americans

221

About the Editor

Harriette Pipes McAdoo is a University Distinguished Professor at Michigan State University, Department of Family and Child Ecology. She is a Director of the Groves Conference on Marriage and the Family; was a National Adviser to the President of the White House Conference on Families; was former President and Board Member of the National Council on Family Relations; and was a member of the Governing Council of the Society for Research in Child Development. She was the first person honored by the National Council on Family Relations with the Marie Peters Award for Outstanding Scholarship, Leadership, and Service in the Area of Ethnic Minority Families. Previously, she was Professor at Howard University in the School of Social Work and Visiting Lecturer at Smith College, the University of Washington, and the University of Minnesota.

Dr. McAdoo received her B.A. and M.A. from Michigan State University and her Ph.D. from the University of Michigan, and she has done postdoctoral studies at Harvard University. She has published on racial attitudes and self-esteem in young children, Black mobility patterns, coping strategies of single mothers, and professional Kenyan women and HIV/AIDS in Zimbabwe. She is editor of *Black Families, 3rd edition* (1998, Sage) and *Family Ethnicity: Strength in Diversity, 2nd edition* (1999, Sage). She coedited *Black Children: Social, Education, and Parental Environ-*

233

ments with John L. McAdoo (Sage Focus Edition, of which this is the 2nd edition) and *Young Families, Program Review, and Policy Recommendations.* She is coauthor of *Women and Children, Alone and in Poverty.* She has four children and four grandchildren.

About the Contributors

Nancy Boyd-Franklin is an African American family therapist, psychologist, and Professor in the Graduate School of Applied and Professional Psychology at Rutgers University. She is the author of *Black Families in Therapy: A Multisystems Approach* (1989) and an editor of *Children, Families, and HIV/AIDS: Psychosocial and Psychotherapeutic Issues* (1995). Her latest book, *Boys Into Men: Raising Our African American Teenage Sons*, with A. J. Franklin and Pamela Toussaint, was published in 2000. An internationally recognized lecturer and author, she has written numerous articles on topics such as the treatment of African American families, extended family issues, spirituality and religion, home-based family therapy, group therapy for Black women, HIV and AIDS, parent and family support groups, community empowerment, and the Multisystems Model.

Gene H. Brody is Distinguished Research Professor of Child and Family Development and Director of the Center for Family Research at the University of Georgia. His research addresses the contribution of contextual influences to children's and adolescents' academic, social, and emotional development. Currently, he is examining how parenting, sibling, and neighborhood processes contribute to resilience in African American children living in rural Georgia.

235

Charlene V. Draper is a clinical and school psychologist and is Adjunct Professor of Education at the Herbert Lehman College of the City University of New York. For many years, she taught assessment and educational evaluations in the School Psychology Master's Program at the City College of the City University of New York. She has experience in early childhood education and work with youth. Over the years, she supported her education by working with the New York City Department of Parks and Recreation, where she continues part-time as assistant manager of the large historic Harlem Hansborough Recreation Center, which has thousands of community participants.

Anderson J. Franklin is Professor in the Clinical and Social Personality Psychology Program at the City College and Graduate School of the City University of New York. He is a psychotherapist in private practice working with African American males in individual, group, marital, and family therapy. He is currently president of the Society for the Psychological Study of Ethnic and Minority Issues, a division of the American Psychological Association. His numerous publications and presentations concern the mental health of African Americans. He has lectured and been a consultant on cultural diversity issues at universities and institutions throughout Europe, Africa, and the Caribbean. He is coauthor of a book with Nancy Boyd-Franklin, *Boys Into Men: Raising our African American Teenage Sons,* which was published in 2000.

Algea O. Harrison-Hale is Professor of Psychology at Oakland University in Rochester, Michigan, and is currently a leading national and international expert on ethnic minority children, youth, and families. She has been a Visiting Scholar and Professor at the University of Zimbabwe, Nanjing University, and the Free University of Amsterdam, where she collaborated with colleagues on cross-cultural research projects. With her international colleagues, she has completed empirical studies on the topics of social support, ethnic identification, and conflict resolution. Her scholarly work has been supported with awards from the Fulbright and Kellogg Foundations, among others. She has published extensively in professional journals, and is the author of numerous book chapters.

Asa G. Hilliard III is the Fuller E. Calloway Professor of Urban Education at Georgia State University. Previously, he taught in the College of Education and in the College of Arts and Sciences' Honors Program in philosophy at the University of Denver. At San Francisco State University, he was department chair for 2 years and Dean of Education for 8 years. He was also consultant to the Peace Corps, Superintendent of Schools in Monrovia, and a school psychologist in Liberia, West Africa. He has written more than 200 research reports, articles, and books on testing, ancient African history, teaching strategies, African culture, and child growth and development. His most recent books are *The Maroon Within Us: Selected Essays on African American Community Socialization* and *SBA: The Reawakening of the African Mind*.

Bill E. Lawson is Professor of Philosophy at Michigan State University. His previous professional appointments include Spelman College, West Virginia University, and the University of Delaware. His research interests include African American social and political philosophy, political obligation theory, and urban environmental philosophy. He has published articles on the urban underclass, John Locke's theory of political obligation, social contract theory and African Americans, jazz, and urban environmental philosophy. His books include *The Underclass Question* (Editor), *Between Slavery and Freedom* (with Howard McGary), and *Frederick Douglass: A Critical Reader* (edited with Frank Kirkland). He has testified before Congress on the issue of welfare reform. He is also a Vietnam veteran who served from 1968 to 1969.

Tom Luster is Professor in the Department of Family and Child Ecology at Michigan State University, where he has been a faculty member since 1985. He is currently doing research in three areas: (a) teenage pregnancy and parenthood, (b) factors related to successful outcomes in at-risk children and adolescents, and (c) influences on parenting practices. For the past 10 years, he has conducted a study of adolescent mothers and their children who participated in the Family TIES family support program at the Mott Children's Health Center in Flint, Michigan.

Jelani Mandara is a Ph.D. candidate in the Department of Psychology at the University of California, Riverside, under the guidance of Carolyn Bennett Murray. He has recently coauthored several empirical articles on the effects of family functioning and fathers on African American adolescent self-esteem, racial identity, sexual activity, and drug use. His other research interests include the synthesis of general systems and cybernetic theories with basic psychological constructs such as self-control, depth of processing, non-conscious perception, and cognitive resources.

John L. McAdoo was Professor in the Department of Family and Child Ecology at Michigan State University. He received his M.S.W and Ph.D. from the University of Michigan and completed postgraduate training at the University of Michigan Institute of Survey Research, at the Johns Hopkins University in public health, and at the Harvard Graduate School of Education. He published several articles in the areas of racial attitudes and self-esteem in Black preschool children, father-child interaction patterns in Black families, patterns of parent-child interactions and self-esteem in young children, and fear of crime and well-being of Black elderly people. He died on October 25, 1996.

Linda McWright is Assistant Professor of Sociology and Anthropology, chair of the Department of Social Sciences, and director of the Criminal Justice Program at Olivet College in Olivet, Michigan. She is a licensed family counselor and currently, in addition to her college responsibilities, is the director of a family counseling center. She is coauthor of *Role of Grandparents: The Use of Proverbs in Value Transmission* and most recently the author of *African American Mothers' Perception of Grandparents' Use of Proverbs in Value Socialization of Grandchildren*. Her current research focuses on religious counseling in African American communities.

Carolyn Bennett Murray is Associate Professor in both the Psychology and Ethnic Studies Departments at the University of California, Riverside. She was awarded a 4-year grant from the National Institute of Child Health and Human Development, National Institute of Mental Health, to conduct a longitudinal study of the socialization processes used by African American families and of personality development of African American children. Her earlier research and published work was in the area of attribution and affective consequences of negative stereotypic expectations for academic achievement. In 1999, she was awarded the Association of Black Psychologists' Distinguished Psychologist Award; she received the Distinguished Teaching Award from the University of California at Riverside in 1989-1990.

Velma McBride Murry is Associate Professor of Child and Family Development and Faculty Fellow to the Institute for Behavioral Research at the University of Georgia. She is the codirector of the Center of Family Research and Cofounder of the Study Group on Culture, Ethnicity, and Family Processes. Her research and scholarship are in the areas of stress and resiliency within rural, economically stressed single-parent families; social and environmental factors linked to African American family and children's physical and mental health; and the significance of multiple ecologies in explaining and predicting the sexual behavior patterns of African American and Hispanic adolescent and young adult women. Her publications include both theoretically and empirically based topics on ethnic minority families and children.

Marie Ferguson Peters was a member of the faculty of Human Development and Family Relations at the University of Connecticut and P.I. Toddler and Infant Experiences Studies. She was secretary of the National Council on Family Relations and director of the Groves Conference on Marriage and the Family. She conducted research on socialization, stress, and development of children in Black families. The National Council on Family Relations named a major award in her honor. She was posthumously named a member of the Academy of the Groves Conference on Marriage and the Family. She had a strong influence on the socialization of Blacks and other ethnic minorities into the professional organizations and existing networks of the family and child development fields. She died on January 8, 1984.

Freya A. Rivers has diversified experience as a teacher, educational consultant, retail business owner, and leader in government, economic, and social issues. Her educational background includes postdoctoral studies at Michigan State University in family and child ecology. She is the author and editor of several publications in education and is currently working on a language arts curriculum. She is founder and superintendent of Sankofa Shule, a college preparatory public school academy in Lansing, Michigan; founder of Sankofa Watoto, a preschool and before- and after-school program; founder and president of Sankofa Publishing Company; and cofounder and president of Sankofa Enterprises, an educational management company.

Shariba W. Rivers joined the staff of Sankofa Shule in 2000 and also serves as administrator for Sankofa Watoto. Previously, she served several years on the administration and faculty of Medgar Evers College in Brooklyn. She is currently a Ph.D. candidate in educational leadership, research and counseling at Louisiana State University. Her research interests and articles published are in the areas of independent Black institutions, urban education, and techniques for motivating and retaining students of African descent within the educational system from pre-K through college. She also is a reviewer for American Educational Research Association and is senior copy editor for Sankofa Publishing.

Renée Sanders-Lawson recently received her Ph.D. in educational administration from Michigan State University. Her dissertation was entitled *Black Women School Superintendents Leading for Social Justice*. Prior to entering the Ph.D. program, she was a school counselor, assistant principal, principal, and human resources director in North Carolina schools. Her appointment as principal of Selma Middle School made her the first Black woman to serve as principal in her school district since the schools were integrated in the late 1960s. She has presented at numerous local, state, and national conferences and has served as a consultant to various groups and organizations.

THE ETHICS OF COACHING SPORTS

THE ETHICS OF COACHING SPORTS

Moral, Social, and Legal Issues

Edited by

ROBERT L. SIMON

HAMILTON COLLEGE

WESTVIEW PRESS

A Member of the Perseus Books Group

Westview Press was founded in 1975 in Boulder, Colorado, by notable publisher and intellectual Fred Praeger. Westview Press continues to publish scholarly titles and high-quality undergraduate- and graduate-level textbooks in core social science disciplines. With books developed, written, and edited with the needs of serious nonfiction readers, professors, and students in mind, Westview Press honors its long history of publishing books that matter.

Find us on the World Wide Web at www.westviewpress.com.

Every effort has been made to secure required permissions for all text, images, maps, and other art reprinted in this volume.

Westview Press books are available at special discounts for bulk purchases in the United States by corporations, institutions, and other organizations. For more information, please contact the Special Markets Department at the Perseus Books Group, 2300 Chestnut Street, Suite 200, Philadelphia, PA 19103, or call (800) 810-4145, ext. 5000, or e-mail special.markets@perseusbooks.com.

Designed by Cynthia Young

Library of Congress Cataloging-in-Publication Data

The ethics of coaching sports : moral social and legal issues / edited by Robert L. Simon.
    p. cm.
Includes bibliographical references and index.
ISBN 978-0-8133-4608-3 (pbk. : alk. paper)—ISBN 978-0-8133-4609-0 (e-book)
1. Coaching (Athletics)—Moral and ethical aspects.   2. Sports—Moral and ethical aspects.   I. Simon, Robert L., 1941–
GV711.E82 2013
796.07'7—dc23

2012045429

10 9 8 7 6 5 4 3 2 1

To my brother David—
A great companion in sports and in life

Contents

Preface

The coach is a major figure in the sports world and even in the general culture, as shown by the success of such television series as *Coach* and *Friday Night Lights*. Legendary coaches such as Knute Rockne and Vince Lombardi are virtual icons, and giants of the coaching profession ranging from Dean Smith to Bill Belichick to Pat Summit seem better known than their star players. Moreover, thousands of coaches at different levels of sports, ranging from youth sports to high school and college to the professional level, have had a positive effect on their athletes and often are positive role models for their communities and beyond. However, there also is a less positive side to coaching represented by a win at all costs mentality, the use of bullying and intimidation, and even participation in academic fraud at some colleges and universities.

In light of the complexity of the decisions involved in coaching and the moral conundrums faced by coaches at all levels of sports, it is surprising that sports philosophers have not paid more attention to the ethical conundrums involved in coaching sports. To my knowledge, the only other volume by philosophers examining the role of the coach and the ethics of coaching (the similarly named *Ethics of Sports Coaching*) was published first in the UK and is cited in several chapters in this book. The present volume, *The Ethics of Coaching Sports*, which I believe to be the first book of its kind published in the United States, is broad in scope and examines the role and responsibility of the coach and ethical issues that arise in the practice of coaching, as well as some of the legal issues.

These chapters, which are designed to be accessible to nonspecialists, raise important questions about various aspects of the coaching role, offer a reasoned approach to arriving at answers, and attempt to add to the critical discussion of sports ethics in the existing scholarly literature. Each selection is followed by Questions for Review and Discussion, which should be useful to students using the book as a text, and a list of references for further reading (supplementing the sources cited in the notes). As editor, I hope the breadth of the topics covered and the accessibility of the discussion to nonspecialists, coaches, and students will allow the book to have a significant impact on coaching practice as well as the philosophy of sports.

There are a number of ways readers may approach this book. Let me suggest two that may be useful, especially to instructors of college and university courses but also to coaches and readers.

What I think of as the default approach is represented by the table of contents. The chapters proceed from general and perhaps abstract analysis of the role of the coach at various levels of sports to the ethical considerations that apply to specific ethical and legal issues that arise in coaching. The order presented in the table of contents encourages development of a broad conception of the role of the coach and the rights, duties, and virtues associated with coaching that can provide a foundation for assessing the chapters in Parts 2–3, which focus on specific ethical and legal issues that arise in coaching. This approach also has the virtue of introducing general issues in the ethics of coaching before confronting controversies about hot-button issues, thereby allowing for reflection on broader principles and values in a cool moment.

Alternately, readers might begin with a chapter that focuses on a problem of special interest to them, for example, John Russell's provocative chapter claiming that coaches have strong moral reasons to help correct officiating errors that significantly benefit their teams, Scott Kretchmar's discussion of coaches' obligations to benchwarmers, or Matthew Mitten's discussion of the legal responsibilities of coaches to protect the health and safety of their athletes. These chapters, like the others in this volume, lead to broader questions about the role of the coach and the ethics of coaching covered in the chapters in Part 1. Some instructors may be able to involve their classes in discussion more quickly by proceeding along this route. However, both paths will lead readers into philosophical analysis of coaching and judicious discussion of the ethical and legal ramifications of issues that arise in coaching practice.

AS THIS BOOK GOES TO PRESS, I owe a great debt to many people. My wife, Joy, remains a proofreader extraordinaire as well as my greatest (and perhaps only) golf fan. She has been a constant source of encouragement and good cheer even in the face of medical difficulties over the past few years.

I am also grateful to my colleagues in the Philosophy Department at Hamilton College for providing a friendly, supportive, and intellectually challenging atmosphere; I couldn't ask for a better teaching and writing environment. I am also grateful to Hamilton College for supporting my research over the years and for granting me a faculty research fellowship that freed me up in the spring of 2012 to complete this project.

I would be remiss if I did not thank a trio of athletic directors at Hamilton College—Tom Murphy, David Thompson, and Jon Hind. Tom Murphy encouraged me to become head coach of men's golf in 1987 and then after I retired as coach in 2001 to continue working with the team as a volunteer assistant.

I also am grateful to the coaches at Hamilton College for their goodwill and support and for their dedication to the athletic and overall educational development of our student athletes. Much of what is right in college sports goes on in Division III of the NCAA. The coaches at small liberal arts colleges such as Hamilton do at least as good a job as any coaches in practicing the ideals of ethical coaching as developed by the contributors to this book. Thanks as well to the players I coached on Hamilton's men's golf team from 1987 to 2001, when I served as head coach and since then while I have also served as a volunteer assistant coach for providing a laboratory for field research on coaching and always showing good humor while I was learning on the job. (The informal rule on one of our highly ranked teams was that I was not allowed to touch a player's clubs because if I did so, magic might take over and reverse his playing ability.)

As always, the editorial team at Westview was wonderful. My initial editor, Kelsey Mitchell, persuaded me to undertake this project after an informal discussion about it and steered me through a number of editorial decisions with tact, grace, and good judgment. When Kelsey left Westview to pursue a career in teaching, Priscilla McGeehon stepped in and, along with editorial assistant Brooke Smith, helped me complete the project without a hitch. Sandra Beris and her production team guided me through the production process with great care, good judgment, and understanding. Thanks and good wishes to everyone at Westview.

I also am indebted to the external reviewers who examined an earlier version of the manuscript. I appreciate their conscientious reading of the text. Their acute comments and suggestions helped me and the other contributors to make improvements that are far too numerous to list.

Finally, I wouldn't have embarked on this project if I did not believe in the importance of ethical coaching at all levels of sport. Of course, significant ethical issues arise in coaching, as in every other significant human endeavor. But in my view, the vast majority of coaches from youth sports to elite levels of athletic competition fulfill their duties with dignity and honor. I hope the chapters in this collection not only shed light on moral and related legal issues in coaching but also help coaches to analyze, understand, and react appropriately to the many ethical issues that arise in their coaching endeavors.

PART 1

Introduction

One

The Ethics of Coaching

ROBERT L. SIMON

The television program *Friday Night Lights* was an especially thoughtful, well-acted series that explored the role of high school football in a small Texas town while following the lives of local young people and adults over several football seasons.[1] The central character, Coach Eric Taylor (played by actor Kyle Chandler), while not without faults, was not only a good father and husband, a leading educator in the area, but a great coach and, most importantly, a role model for his players. Although he sometimes made bad decisions, both in his family life and on the field, he could be counted on by his family members and his players, who came from a variety of backgrounds and economic circumstances and often confronted major personal and social crises.

In the real world, many issues facing the coaching profession, particularly in high profile sports, raise significant ethical questions about the behavior of coaches. Joe Paterno's fall from grace at Penn State, due to the allegations of sexual abuse leveled against former assistant Jerry Sandusky, is a case in point. Some have argued that Paterno fulfilled his moral obligations by informing the university athletic director about the problem and that the scandal was external to football. However, the devastating report by former FBI director Louis Freeh alleges that Paterno contributed to the cover-up of sexual abuse of children and that fear of going up against the renowned Penn

State football program deterred some university employees from reporting the abuse. The Paterno case did not directly involve his coaching practices; by all accounts Coach Paterno ran a clean program, made sure his players graduated, and used funds raised by Penn State football to support the academic mission of the university. However, Paterno's legacy has been significantly tarnished as the Freeh report, released in July 2012, charged that Penn State officials, including Paterno, showed "total and consistent disregard by the most senior leaders at Penn State for the safety and welfare of Sandusky's child victims."[2] On July 23, 2012, the National Collegiate Athletic Association (NCAA) announced unprecedented penalties against Penn State, imposing a $60 million fine (to be used to help victims of child abuse), vacating Penn State football victories from 1998 to 2011, and reducing the number of football scholarships the program can offer.

Moreover, a significant number of NCAA Division I intercollegiate programs were involved in serious rule violations, apparently with the knowledge and even support of the coaching staff. These range from NCAA violations committed in the Ohio State football program under Coach Jim Tressel (which led to his firing) to cases of academic fraud, such as the University of Minnesota case where an NCAA investigation found that tutors did academic work for some basketball players with the knowledge of their coaches. Recently NFL investigators have charged that players on the New Orleans Saints football team were awarded bonuses for hard hits against rival players that resulted in the targets being removed from the game, all with the knowledge and possible support of some members of the coaching staff.[3]

While coaches in youth sports are mostly volunteers and high school coaches who put in enormous amounts of time for little financial reward, men's basketball and football coaches at elite high profile intercollegiate programs make huge incomes, some earning more than the presidents of their institutions. In 2011 Rick Pitino, the basketball coach at Louisville, had a total pay of well over $7 million. Mike Krzyzewski, the basketball coach at Duke, had a reported total payout of over $4 million, and John Calipari, whose teams at different institutions have been cited for violating NCAA rules, made nearly $4 million at Kentucky. Salaries for top collegiate football coaches are comparable.[4] While some argue that huge compensation packages are justifiable as the result of free market bargaining, others have raised questions about whether this reward structure is economically sustainable and whether it is appropriate to pay coaches so much more than top faculty members.

On the other hand, many coaches (perhaps most coaches) at both the collegiate and the interscholastic level not only play by the rules but, like Coach Taylor, play a positive role in the athletic development of their athletes as well as in their educational and personal growth. It is important to look past the negative publicity surrounding some high profile coaches and understand that coaching is a practice that takes place in a wide variety of contexts ranging from professional to youth sports. These good coaches often don't get the attention the media bestow on bad behavior in high profile sports.

Nonetheless, many ethical dilemmas arise among coaches who labor in youth, high school, and college sports and in various low profile clubs and leagues, perhaps *especially* in such cases. For example, is winning the coach's primary goal? Which value takes precedence when winning clashes with other goals, such as showing loyalty to experienced players who are less skilled than newcomers, allowing all the players on the roster to participate, protecting the athletes' health, and showing good sportsmanship when doing so hurts the team's chances at winning? Should coaches tolerate gamesmanship by their players and should they set rules or codes of conduct that apply to the behavior of their players off the field or during the off-season? Is it permissible for coaches to "work" officials, even to the point of intimidation, or bully players in an attempt to improve their performance? To what degree, if any, should coaches stress competition, as opposed to developing skills or just having fun, in youth sports?

The chapters in this book deal with some of the most significant ethical issues facing coaches. They also explore the role of the coach and the duties, responsibilities, and even ideals that apply to coaching behavior, in both ethics and law. In particular, they explore the reasoning that may be used to support different positions on the issues being examined and so provide an analytical as well as a moral perspective on the role of the coach and the practice of coaching.

Sports, Coaching, and Philosophical Analysis

Sports attract attention around the world. The World Cup and the Olympic Games enjoy the greatest visibility, but many sports such as basketball and golf are becoming increasingly international in scope, with Asian as well as American and European players making a major impact. Soccer (elsewhere called football) is arguably the most popular sport worldwide. Children are becoming increasingly involved in youth sports and developmental programs. In the United States, college and high school athletic competitions attract huge audiences throughout the country. Sports are the subject of major films such as the award-winning *Chariots of Fire, Hoosiers,* and *Million Dollar Baby.*

Increasingly, sports are receiving attention from various academic disciplines. Psychologists, economists, and sociologists study empirical questions, for example, investigating what mental qualities tend to contribute to success in athletic competition (sports psychology), or whether highly visible Division I college sports actually bring in revenue for their institutions rather than operate deep in the red (economics).

However, many questions about sports go beyond the ordinary parameters of the natural and social sciences. Social scientists can describe the effects of competitive sports on participants, but can they tell us whether competition is good or bad, ethically permissible, desirable, or morally reprehensible? Whether a high school coach should give significant playing time to the less skilled players on the team, what responsibilities coaches should be expected to meet in protecting the safety of their players, or how much they should involve their players in making strategic decisions (a democratic vs. authoritarian style of coaching) raises ethical issues that are beyond the scope of the natural and social sciences.

Philosophy can help us approach such evaluative issues in part by helping to clarify key concepts and assessing arguments that attempt to justify answers to questions such as, What counts as fair play in sports?

Before turning directly to coaching, however, we need to view the practice of coaching in the broader context of sports and athletic competition. Ethical issues involving such concerns as athletes' use of performance enhancing drugs, questions of gender equity in university athletic programs, and misbehavior by elite athletes are widely discussed in the media, by fans, and even by casual observers. Some behaviors, such as doping to achieve a competitive advantage, are alleged to be violations of the ethics that should govern sports. But even if that claim is true, it presupposes that we have some idea of what that ethic should be. Criticizing a practice as unethical suggests that we have some notion of what is ethical.[5] But while we all have intuitive ideas about, for example, what counts as fair play, it is not easy to articulate the principles that justify our intuitions, defend them, or apply them to hard cases where our principles may appear to conflict.

This suggests a deeper set of questions that go beyond current headlines. Is athletic competition a good thing? Are competitive sports valuable activities? If so, why? Does their value depend on circumstances or context? What circumstances are important or relevant to moral evaluation? Are sports purely recreational or do they also have an educational function, especially in youth sports but perhaps also at the interscholastic, intercollegiate, and professional levels?

In developing responses to such questions, we may ask about the role coaches do play and should play at the different levels of sports. Are coaches purely technical advisers who help their athletes develop better techniques, like a swing coach in golf? Or are they more like generals or CEOs who develop and maintain a "program" as at elite Division I colleges and in professional sports? Or are coaches more like teachers or professors, educating their players about the sport and even about the kind of character needed to play well? Should they aim at developing personal virtues among their charges? Or does that take them beyond their proper role? Does the coach's role depend on context? For example, perhaps different ethical guidelines apply to coaches in youth sports than to coaches in intercollegiate athletics. But even if that is true, are there some universal principles that apply to coaching in all contexts?

Indeed, the role and moral duties of the coach not only change significantly from one context to another (e.g., professional vs. youth sports) but arguably from one cultural context to another. At times in ancient Greece, as well as in nineteenth- and early-twentieth-century England, athletes were expected to succeed on their own; working with a coach was considered unsporting. Part of the charm and interest of the movie *Chariots of Fire,* which tells the story of two contenders for the 1924 Olympics, is that it illustrates the British aristocratic ethics of the time, which frowned on the use of a coach by one of the characters, Harold Abrahams, thereby showing how people's beliefs about sports ethics can be influenced by existing social practices and cultural norms. (Of course, whether the views are defensible depends on the soundness of justifying arguments, not merely on what people at a given time believe is ethical.)[6]

The prevailing attitude throughout most of the world today is very different, but to what extent can the attitude prevalent at a given time and place be justified? What ethical rules, principles, and ideals apply to coaching? Should coaching as we now know it be regarded as purely instrumental, designed only to promote winning, or is it a multifaceted activity subject to moral standards? If the latter, which moral standards apply? How can we *justify* the moral considerations we believe apply?

The contributors to this book attempt to clarify, explore, and in some cases resolve ethical and related legal questions about coaching, including some of those raised above. They look beyond the daily sports headlines and analyze in depth the ethical issues that arise in coaching as most of us experience it; in such contexts as youth sports, high schools, colleges and universities, clubs and other informal organizations, as well as professional and elite teams and institutions. All the contributors hope to advance our theoretical and philosophical understanding of coaching. However, just as important, they also present well-reasoned examinations of issues that coaches face in carrying out their duties and suggest recommendations for coaching practices that can be explored and debated by students, coaches, sports administrators, and fans.

Each chapter, other than the two introduction chapters, is followed by a series of review questions designed to bring the main theses and potential lines of criticism of them into focus. A short list of suggested readings also follows, which may include works cited in the footnotes if the author regards them as especially deserving of attention. Those interested in exploring the issues raised even further should consult the sources cited in the endnotes.

Two

The Coach as Moral Exemplar

JAN BOXILL

Unquestionably, sports play a significant role in our society. Just consider the enthusiasm generated by March Madness, the Olympic Games, the Super Bowl, and the World Series. But perhaps their greatest significance is the moral role sports play for both the participants and society in general. I have argued that given their nature and design, sports provide a unique model for understanding our society, for seeing who we are, our values, and our ethics.[1]

Americans recognize the potential for sports to build character and promote necessary virtues for a greater cause. As a society, Americans value sports and what they can offer. But Americans also believe that an overemphasis on winning threatens sports, possibly by motivating rule breaking and by taking the fun out of it for too many people. Role models, particularly coaches, can play an important part in maintaining the integrity and value of sports. Coaches often function as surrogate parents, bonding strongly with the people they coach. A study by the U.S. Anti-Doping Agency (USADA), in partnership with Discovery Education, concluded that coaches, more than parents, teachers, peers, religion, and school, have the greatest influence on youth sport participants.[2]

Sport can be great fun to play and entertaining to watch. However, it offers something more important. The lessons it provides—taught properly—apply directly to life. Many of those lessons are usually taught first by a good mother and father, but sports can help make them stick and add a few more.[3]

Given the results of the study, the people entrusted to teach these lessons must be the coaches. Like parents they teach skills, but they also teach life lessons, including morals, ethics, tolerance, and most of all respect, both for themselves and for others. So coaches must be good teachers as well as good role models.

A recent USADA survey showed that more than three-fifths of US adults, approximately 162 million Americans, claim some relationship to sports-related activities. Thus, given the engagement and power of sports and more importantly the power of coaches, ethics and sports must be integrated in the coaches who influence those they coach. But this cannot happen unless coaches possess character and integrity, and intentionally teach and model these values. Since sports play a significant moral role in society, coaches have a greater responsibility in how sports fulfill this role. Of course coaches are not the only ones who bear this responsibility; others, particularly well-known athletes, bear some responsibility as well. However, "coaches have an . . . unparalleled power and platform in young people's lives."[4] This is an awesome and sometimes frightening platform for transforming people's lives. What makes it so is that this is a role they have freely chosen. With that choice comes great responsibility, not just to teach what they know and how to perform and behave, but to model this behavior as well. "There are at least five million coaches with the potential to become one of the most influential adults in a young person's life. Forever."[5] This is a tremendous challenge that requires coaches to serve as moral exemplars.

Coaches are teachers, and coaching, like teaching, takes skill, art, and knowledge. It is a skill that helps young people become stronger athletes and stronger individuals. The hope is to produce excellence in those they coach. We see many examples of this, but unfortunately we see the opposite as well. Part of this has to do with professing one thing while doing another. In the survey coaches responded that teaching self-discipline, doing one's best, having fun, building self-esteem, and respecting others are among the most important values children will learn from playing sports; they ranked playing fairly and winning as the least important.

But while winning seemed least important to the coaches, study participants responded that winning was what they viewed their coach as promoting, that winning was much more important than other values. And according to a summary in *USA Today*, a new NCAA study of college athletes reveals the following:

- Only 39 percent of Division I women's basketball players said their head coach "defines success by not only winning, but winning fairly." Also, just 39 percent said their head coach can be trusted.

- Only half of all Division I men's basketball players said they felt their coaches were as interested in fairness as in winning. In baseball, it was 43 percent. Football coaches scored highest, a still modest 57 percent. The proportion of players who trusted their coaches ran much the same: 50 percent in men's basketball, 52 percent in baseball, 56 percent in football.[6]

These findings lead us to examine why so many athletes lack trust in their coaches, the people entrusted to teach fair play, sportsmanship, and winning within the structure of the rules that define and regulate the games we play. Two possible conclusions may be drawn. Either this lack of trust is a result of misperceptions among athletes or it is evidence that many coaches are deceived about their own teachings. The USADA research revealed a disconnect between what coaches profess and what the participants perceive to be the case.

Sports constitute a secular religion and coaches are its ministers. They hold the same power and we expect the same qualities in our coaches as we do our clergy—trustworthy people who exemplify dignity, empathy, integrity, respect, and virtue. Players, like parishioners, evaluate coaches and learn their values by watching how they treat their players, their opponents, and other coaches. They gauge coaches' values by observing their actions. Given the hypercompetitive atmosphere present in athletic programs at every level, plus the countless documented cases of cheating and malpractice by coaches, it is not unreasonable to conclude that many athletes have good reason not to trust their coaches.

These findings present a sad statement about college sports, which justify their nonprofit status by claiming to teach sportsmanship and character. And this carries over to youth sports as well. However, as a sports enthusiast, ex-coach, and teacher, I argue that the nature and design of sports play a significant moral role in society by *reflecting* and *affecting* changes in our society, and those involved in sports play a significant role in these changes. Sports provide the model for the changes, both positively and negatively. And if the research is correct, coaches play a significant and exalted role, and if change is to be positive, it is a role that coaches must embrace.

Though I have discussed the nature and design of a sports model elsewhere,[7] I will briefly describe it and the obstacles to its implementation here.

Nature and Design of Sports

Here I want to present a paradigm or model of sports to illumine their moral significance. (This model is normative in that it presents a morally defensible conception of sports; see especially the chapters by Simon, Russell, and Torres and Hager for fuller discussion of such normative conceptions. It also describes sports at their best.) I identify four features as essential to the model.

First, in its paradigmatic form, sports participation is a freely chosen, voluntary activity, designed with no end outside itself. Though people may participate in sports for many different reasons, sports are designed to be ends in themselves. Whatever reasons people have for engaging in sports, they are designed to have a constant result, which is sufficient to justify the sport. Even if I play for money, the excellence displayed is sufficient to justify the sport.

For example, you may play basketball for money, but basketball itself is designed to develop and display excellence even if that is not your reason for playing it. Thus in order to make money playing the game you will have to display certain excellences. Further, given human nature, you are likely to respond positively to these excellences and to make them your ends. In this way the game is an unalienated activity. Further participation in the many different sports is an expression of the individual's creativity and his or her freedom to choose which of these various excellences to develop.

Second, sports are governed by constitutive rules and regulative rules. Constitutive rules define the game and the permissible moves allowed within it. These rules define the activity and are usually designed to develop and exhibit sets of skills and talents. Some sports have more rules than others, and the rules may change over time. But whatever the constitutive rules, their existence comes from their acceptance.

Regulative rules complement the constitutive rules. These rules govern fair play, decency, and safety. Rules of fair play include penalties for infractions of the constitutive rules and for moves of strategy within the game. For example, in football the defense wants to rush the passer, but according to the constitutive rules no one can cross the line of scrimmage before the ball is snapped. Regulative rules require that a team that violates this off-sides rule be penalized to restore the competitive balance. Rules of decency reflect basic moral standards. For example, after a great tackle, the tackler should not stand over the tackled player and taunt or gyrate. Rules of safety are designed to protect the participants as they play according to the constitutive rules. For example, no one can tackle a player by grabbing his face mask. In combination, the constitutive and regulative rules impose discipline and create a safe and moral framework for self-expression and self-development. Both sets of rules are regularly evaluated and often revised to promote a competitive, safe, and moral framework.

Third, sports must be physically challenging within the designated framework and rules. This feature contrasts sports to games. Games need not be physically challenging. Again, the constitutive rules are continually evaluated to keep the sports physically challenging.

Fourth, sports involve competition as a mutual challenge to achieve or strive for excellence[8] within the framework set by the constitutive rules and the regulative rules of fair play and decency. The struggle involves both the process and the product, a desire to win, and a desire to be tested.

The mental and the physical come together in competition. Each participant must develop strategies to counter another competitor's skills and strategies. Competition can lead to respect, friendship, or combat—opponents can be viewed either as partners in the struggle or enemies to be conquered. Here coaches play a significant role as skilled strategists. They work with the athletes in practice and discuss the mental aspects of the sport in the locker room. What the athletes learn from their coaches they carry onto the playing field. They must make quick calculations and decisions based on what they have learned. So it is vital that coaches understand and promote the model.

Obviously this is a model and, like any model, is subject to deviations in practice. Nonetheless, it is the model we should use to evaluate how sports are taught, coached, and played out in society. Given the high status of sports, we need to carefully examine the issues that tear at the fabric of the model in order to ensure the integrity and value of sports and allow us to embrace the role that sports plays in our society. But this is a shared responsibility.

Obstacles

What deviations occur from the model? Here I will briefly discuss three of them: the emphasis on winning, the lack of moral courage, and relativism.

Emphasis on Winning in Competition

There are those who place winning above all else and are willing to cheat to achieve this goal. The high stakes involved in winning factor into this orientation.

The desire to win is fundamental to competition, but this does not entail winning at all costs. People desire to win for different reasons. But as noted above, sports are designed so that in order to win, participants will have their skills challenged and tested, and the results of the tests are displayed in winnings and rankings. This is not unlike the tests we give our students in classes. We challenge our students to learn new material. To meet the challenge they strive to do well on exams that require them to learn the skills. But some place winning (e.g., getting an A) above all else and are willing to cheat for the sake of this goal. It is up to the teacher to promote the desire to do well, but not at all costs. Consider a teacher who said, "Here are the rules, and here are the ways to break those rules and avoid getting caught, so that you can get an A." If everyone were given the ways to break the rules, they would become rules unto themselves and cheating would no longer be cheating. It would be cheating if we provided the information to a few who then kept it to themselves to gain an edge. Maintaining the integrity of the academic endeavor requires that while teachers may give students strategies to help them prepare for the exam, they must challenge students to strive to achieve excellence, not just an A.

Sports are no different. If we are to maintain the integrity of sports, while coaches give strategies to help participants prepare for competitions, they must abide by both the constitutive and regulative rules. They should challenge the participants to strive to achieve excellence, not just to win. In this way coaches must serve as exemplars who uphold the integrity of sports. (Critiques of overemphasis on winning are found in chapters by Reid, Simon, and Russell, among others.)

All of us, participants, spectators, administrators, parents, journalists, and coaches, share responsibility for instilling a culture of honor and integrity in sports. But given the power and influence coaches command, they bear a greater responsibility. The pressures are great, including those posed by the excessive public attention to sports and exaggerated monetary rewards at elite levels of competition, but the willingness to prioritize winning, at the sacrifice of ethics and health, erodes our trust in the inherent value of sports. As a nation, we should embrace the positive role that sports can play in our society, as well as the issues now facing sports, in order to determine how to ensure their enduring integrity and value.

Lack of Moral Courage

My colleague Kim Strom-Gottfried has pointed out, quoting Edward Kidder, that "the key to ethical action is moral courage. . . . When we uphold ethical principles, . . . we are acting with moral courage."[9]

It has been said that we all know right from wrong but lack the moral courage to do the right thing or act when we see others doing wrong. Opportunities for ethical action are plentiful, but so too are the reasons not to act. Strom-Gottfried offers five obstacles to moral courage: discomfort, futility, socialization, bystander effect or diffusion theory, and personal cost.[10] These obstacles apply to all aspects of life and are dramatized in sport. Although participants may know what the right thing to do is, they find it difficult to go against what is actually being asked of them; and if they did, they would be criticized for not being a team player or would find themselves ostracized. Participants get their cues from coaches who either reward or condemn rule breaking and unsportsmanlike behavior. So again coaches must serve as moral exemplars for the athletes they coach. However, coaches face these obstacles as well.

It is equally uncomfortable for them to go against the actual demands of the position. And although they might like to do the right thing, they may see it as a no-win situation. Perhaps no one cares or "everyone is doing it," or they believe that ethical appeals will fall on deaf ears. Moral courage may be too expensive if it costs the coach his or her position or professional standing. But those who worry about the cost of action fail to consider the cost of inaction.

"Ethical action often is not easy, but it can be practiced. It can be taught and can be reinforced when we see it in others. . . . As individuals we can support those around us who do the right thing. We can also demand that our society do the same."[11] This is the essence of fair play, sportsmanship, and following the rules for achieving excellence. In this lies the moral significance of sports, the duties of those involved, and their relationship to society. And coaches face even greater demands.

Relativism

People attack moral standards they don't find convenient by making relativistic arguments. Their argument goes something like this: since different societies or institutions in society have differing moral codes, it follows that there is no objective standard that can be used to judge the relative merits of particular codes. But is this argument *sound*? Does the conclusion logically follow from the premise? The premise is about belief systems or what people believe, while the conclusion is about what really is the case.

Because belief systems may have disagreements, does it *logically follow* that there is no objective truth in the matter? Certainly not. The fact that people once disagreed about whether the earth is flat does not mean that there was no objective truth about its shape. Further, it is a mistake to overestimate the extent of the differences. We need to consider underlying goals and principles. I do not deny that we allow some things in sports that we would not allow in society; the hits that we allow in football we would not allow on the street, for example. It does not follow, however, that society and sports do not share common goals and principles.

The constitutive and regulative rules that govern each sport are designed to challenge participants to develop their skills. But there are also descriptive and moral rules necessary for sports to even exist and must be embraced by all. Deliberate harm and cheating are two examples. These rules are in force in all sports and in all cultures. Sports may differ in what they regard as legitimate exceptions to the rules, but those differences exist against a broad background of agreement. And sports exist within a society that shares this broader agreement. So it is a mistake to overemphasize the differences at the expense of the broader background of agreement, whether in our society or in any society. As Robert Simon so aptly puts it, "Sport . . . provides an arena which illustrates a framework of universal values within which the competition takes place."[12] (But see Chapter 5 for William J. Morgan's defense of the importance of historical and social context, which might lead him to dissent from the idea of universal values.)

Given the great impact of sports on society, it is critical that they exemplify this broader moral agreement. Sports both reflect and actively affect society. This is one reason for their moral significance. Sports teach us what is acceptable and what is unacceptable, what is condoned and what is shunned.

Understanding the place of sports in our society and our role in perpetuating it requires us to understand the paradigm and how it is applied. Those who coach and administer sports bear the burden of upholding the integrity of sports. It isn't easy; there is no algorithm to plug in the variables, no simple recipe to follow. Sports display excellence and moral courage, as well the undermining of excellence and the lack of moral courage. We expect our teachers, our coaches, to promote the best displays and serve as exemplars. We cannot expect them to be perfect. Coaches are human and fallible, but in accepting the role of coach, they accept the responsibility of developing excellence in those they teach.

Conclusion

The chapters that follow discuss the moral and legal responsibilities of coaches, examine issues of coaching policy such as allocation of playing time among team members, and the proper emphasis on competition in youth sports. They also explore issues in ethical justification that investigate the logical grounds that might be offered in developing and supporting decisions by coaches. Coaching, far from being a purely technical or strategic activity, is permeated by ethical and related educational concerns. I hope this book contributes to our philosophical and intellectual understanding of the complexities of coaching and to better coaching as well.

Sports provide a unique model for understanding who we are and what we want to achieve. In this way sports serve a significant moral function and as an exemplar for public ethics. Everyone bears responsibility to uphold honor in our society and in sports, but coaches, given their power, bear a greater responsibility. Understanding this is important for all of us, because *the death of ethics is the sabotage of excellence.*

PART 2

The Coach's Role: Conceptions of Coaching

ROBERT L. SIMON

The chapters in Part 2 explore a set of related questions concerning what function coaches should play in sports. What is the best way of understanding the role of the coach? What are a coach's duties, responsibilities, and rights? By what criteria should a coach's performance be evaluated? How should coaches themselves think of their roles and functions?

A quick answer is that the coach's job is to teach the relevant physical skills, with due allowances for the age and physical development of those receiving the coaching—technical coaching about the mechanics of the sport, for example, a pure swing coach in golf who only works on making a player's physical movements as efficient and technically sound as possible.[1]

Is it the coach's job simply to win? I examine and reject this suggestion in my own contribution to this section. For now, it is perhaps enough to say, first, that winning should not be the only goal of coaches in youth and children's sports and, second, that a win in a sloppily played game against an inferior opponent is not necessarily anything to be proud of.

Indeed, a moment's reflection will suggest that in most sporting contexts, these accounts of the coach's role are simplistic. For example, we normally expect the coach to teach not just the physical skills but also the mental skills necessary for good play. Coaches should help players make smart decisions in game situations as well as understand the strategies best employed in contests. Many people also would maintain that coaches, perhaps particularly in youth sports but elsewhere as well, should teach respect for officials and opponents, promote the ideals of fair competition and being a good sport, and generate enthusiasm for the sport among the players.

Should we also expect coaches to have a positive effect on the character of the athletes? If so, what do we mean by "positive effect"? Is it reasonable or fair to expect coaches to have expertise at character building as well as teaching skills relevant to the sport? Do coaches have ethical responsibilities that go beyond building character, such as upholding standards of fair play and respecting the rights of all competitors including opponents?

The contributors to this section address issues such as these as they explore the role of the coach. Heather Reid considers the purpose of athletic competition and its implications for the role of the coach relative to its roots in ancient Greek philosophy. In particular, as Reid explains, Plato saw training in athletics as a major part of a good education designed to produce virtuous people. While many critics of intercollegiate sports regard athletics as an intrusion on the true mission of educational institutions, Reid suggests that on the contrary, when properly carried out, athletics and academics can be integrated elements of an educational process aimed at producing good citizens. The coach, on this view, is in the broadest sense a teacher of virtue.

Theorists who stress the virtues can be divided into those who regard the virtues as fundamental ethical values, not derivable from any more fundamental ones, and those who see them as derivative. For example, utilitarians, who ethically evaluate actions or general practices solely by their consequences, striving for the best ratio of good to bad effects, might regard virtues as those traits of character which incline the bearer toward actions that have good consequences.

Virtue theorists influenced by the writings of Plato and Aristotle regard the virtues as basic; right actions are the ones virtuous people would choose. Virtuous individuals exercise practical wisdom and good judgment that they develop through experience, rather than follow a set of mechanical rules. Wise coaches, on this view, make good judgments that reflect their own virtues and promote the growth of good character in their players. Thus wise coaches know which play to call at which moment, how to motivate players, and how to balance such values as competitive success and broad participation, not through the application of rigid rules but through habits of good judgment they have developed through years of experience. By exhibiting the virtues, they are excellent role models for others and help their players to develop as virtuous persons.

Critics of virtue theory raise a number of concerns. Critics can question whether what counts as a virtue changes from one historical context to another. For example, did the ancient Greeks or medieval knights value honor more than we do? Other critics ask if claims made by virtuous coaches and other sports figures based largely on their personal experience can be justified to others in public discourse. More generally, what would be the nature of justification of ethical claims in sport?

In my own contribution to this section, I explore the question of how ethical and other evaluative claims made in sports can be justified or supported by reason. I first reject what I regard as some crude ideas about sports, such as the view that they should be thought of primarily as a means of discharging aggression, and some equally crude views about the function of the coach, such as the claim that the coach's only obligation is to win. I then argue for what has been called a broad internalist or intepretivist approach to the ethics of sport. According to this approach, similar to the account of law advanced by legal theorist Ronald Dworkin and applied to sports by a number of thinkers, we best understand the value of sports, and why so many find it fascinating, by interpreting the activity in a way that makes sense of its key features and presents it in its ethically best light.[2] For example, why do sports, or at least such paradigm cases as baseball, basketball, soccer, field hockey, and golf, have rules that create artificial challenges to what otherwise would be a relatively easy task, such as simply placing a small ball in a hole compared to holing one's shot according to the established rules of golf? This feature is best explained, as I and other broad internalists argue, by the idea that sports are constructed to provide challenges and that the pursuit of challenge is fundamental to understanding sports and making moral judgments about them. Of course, other areas (e.g., doing well on the SAT exam or in a job) also involve challenges, but we do not normally take the SAT or go to work just for the challenge; we need a decent SAT score to get into college and we need a job to earn a living.[3] Of course, we play sports for other reasons too, for example, to make friends or get exercise, but we make the friends and get the exercise by trying to meet the challenge of the sport. That is what makes challenge so fundamental. (See Jan Boxill's chapter on the idea that a sports contest normally is freely chosen by all parties who wish to challenge themselves in what has been called a "mutual quest for excellence.") Of course, the pursuit of excellence through challenge does not imply an isolated morality of sports separate from more general ethical considerations; such pursuit is constrained by a number of moral considerations, including principles of fairness and respect for others.

As broad internalists and legal interpretivists have developed the idea, a theory of sports includes broad principles that sometimes must be weighed against one another, not simply rules such as "three strikes and you are out," that apply in an all-or-nothing manner. Thus J. S. Russell has suggested as a basic principle of sports that we interpret the rules of a sport "in such a manner that the excellences embodied in achieving the lusory goals of the game are not undermined but are maintained and fostered."[4] Russell cites an 1887 major league baseball game where a runner crossed home plate; according to the then rules of the game he was no longer a base runner and hence not governed by rules prohibiting interference with fielders. He then wrestled the opposing catcher to the ground, enabling a teammate to score. The umpire, however, ruled correctly that the rule about noninterference should be interpreted to prohibit such behavior. This ruling can be justified according to Russell's principle, since wrestling is not a skill baseball was designed to test.

My own version of broad internalism suggests that sports are in significant part an educative activity; we learn about ourselves and others and can develop ethically through our attempt to meet the challenges of sports, especially when carried out as broad internalism recommends. Coaches, on this view, are educators who, particularly in youth sports and educational institutions, should be charged with teaching the physical, mental, and moral skills required to meet the challenges of their sport, which often are closely related to those required for success in the classroom as well.

In my chapter, I briefly suggest, and have argued more fully elsewhere, that a broad internalist theory which survives extended criticism from diverse perspectives might achieve universal assent and might be regarded as justifiable for all reasonable people. More modestly, it would not be unreasonable to believe that the best explanation of why such a theory has survived such critical scrutiny is that it is truly the best interpretive theory applying to the areas of sports in question and accordingly ought to be accepted by all sporting communities.

In his chapter, William J. Morgan endorses many of the ethical recommendations in my chapter and adopts many of the features of interpretivism. However, he rejects the universalism implicit in my development of the approach. Rather, he suggests, any consensus about justification in sports applies to specific social and historical contexts. Thus, to take his example, the role of the coach was viewed very differently among the upper classes in nineteenth- and early-twentieth-century England. Sports were understood as gentlemanly activities characterized by amateurism and generosity, rather than in the "winning comes first" atmosphere of elite sports today. On his view, proponents of these different views would be unable to engage in discussion with one another or reach a consensus based on reason since they lack the common premises with which to argue. (I would question whether different historical and social contexts are as discrete and isolated from one another as he suggests and point to sports such as top amateur and professional golf, which combine fierce competition with respect for and generosity toward opponents as an example of how dialogue and discussion might lead to an improved blend of the two traditions.)

Be that as it may, Morgan forcefully argues that even if interpretations of sports are historically relative, they still can have critical force. We do not have to accept the superficial views of sports prominent in our own culture but through rational critique identify the deep basic principles and values that are most justified within our own cultural tradition and use them to criticize popular but shallow social understandings that cannot pass critical scrutiny.

What is the relevance or practical significance of broad internalism, and the debate over whether or not interpretations of sports are historically relative? Why does this rather abstract debate matter to coaches and those interested in the ethics of coaching?

Let me offer two suggestions. First, if the other contributors and I are correct in maintaining that coaches have ethical responsibilities, coaches need to be able to make sound ethical judgments as well as sound strategic ones. Surely a defensible overall theory of the moral aspects of sports, along with a specific account that makes sense of their own sports and views them in a morally supportable manner, is crucial to such an endeavor. As Doug Hochstetler argues in the concluding chapter of this section, coaches always have a philosophy even if it is never fully articulated. Making that philosophy explicit can help make the individual coach's judgments more consistent with one another and also allow for critical examination of and consequent improvement of it.

Second, on both Morgan's view and my own, coaches need to look beyond a shallow popular consensus on what is ethical in sports.[5] What is popular or widely accepted may not necessarily be supported by good reasons. On Morgan's view, we need to look for the deeper values implicit in our own cultural practices, while on mine, even those are subject to critical scrutiny that through discourse and debate can potentially yield a justifiable universal consensus. But either way, coaches carry out their ethical responsibilities best by being able to distance themselves from widely accepted but not necessarily well-grounded views of sports and examine them with a critical eye.

Doug Hochstetler agrees that coaches need a philosophy and implicitly suggests that coaches need not engage in abstract philosophical theorizing to the extent that my own and Morgan's conceptions of broad internalism seem to require. Hochstetler draws on his own experiences as an athlete and on the approach to pragmatism of American philosopher Henry Bugbee to stress the pragmatic function of the coach's approach to the game.

Pragmatism emphasizes that ideas are tools and are evaluated by how they help us solve specific problems. Hochstetler suggests the coach frequently functions as a problem solver. While he does not deny the need for justification and validation of the coach's approach to problems that arise in sporting contexts, Hochstetler stresses the role of sensitivity and openness to change that characterize good coaching. Coaches, on this view, draw on their experience and judgment and their sensitivity to what is at stake, rather than an elaborate philosophical theory (which still might be useful is assessing coaching decisions after they are made) in order to make good decisions under the pressure of competition. As leaders of their teams, they need to project confidence but also show humility and be open to change and growth as they learn through experience.

In spite of differences in approach, which sometimes run deep, the contributors to Part 2 agree on some main themes that are worth reviewing. First, they all agree that there is a significant moral dimension to coaching and reject the idea that the coach's main function is entirely technical (teaching mechanics of the sport) or purely strategic, let alone simply to win contests. Second, they also agree on the need for development of a moral perspective or theory that can be used not only by coaches themselves but also by those who assess or evaluate their performance. Disagreement among contributors may arise, however, over what moral perspective is most applicable to coaching: for example, whether a virtue-centered approach, a pragmatic one, or one that focuses more on the respect for the challenge of the sport and its implications for fairness and the rights and duties of participants.[6] The other contributors and I hope that the following chapters will stimulate readers to test the ideas proposed and use them to develop their own philosophy of coaching.

Three

Coaching for Virtue
in Plato's Academy*

HEATHER REID

The power to learn is present in everyone's soul [but] the instrument with which each learns is like an eye that cannot be turned around from darkness to light without turning the whole body.

—PLATO

Conventional wisdom holds that sports build character. Many social scientists contend that the opposite is true: sports actually degrade moral character. Purists shun the question entirely, believing that sports, as a form of play, require no broader justification. Sports' inclusion in schools and universities, however, does deserve some sort of justification. Recreation and health promotion are only part of the story, and out of proportion to the emphasis placed on competitive athletics. If sports can indeed function as a form of moral education, then their place in the academy would be clearly warranted—not least because classroom presentation of ethical theories has very limited potential for improving moral behavior. Because sports

*Originally published in *Sport Ethics and Philosophy* 4:1 (2010): 16–26.

involve physical activity and interpersonal interaction in a rule-governed environment, they may indeed be an excellent medium through which to habituate good moral character. This was the role of sports in ancient Greek education: the cultivation of a kind of moral and personal excellence known as *aretē*.[1]

But as suggested by some modern social science data, good moral character is not an automatic outcome of athletic participation.[2] Coaches who put character first, or at least near the top of their educational goals, need to be thoughtful and intentional about achieving it. They may have to distance themselves from the conventions and reward systems common in sports today. Since moral education is such an important social task, however, coaches who strive to achieve it are fighting the good fight. I am one of a group of scholars who believe that the cultivation of *aretē* is the highest social good that sports can bring and should therefore be the guiding principle of sports participation and promotion—an approach we call aretism.[3] A better understanding of the relationship among *aretē*, athletics, and education in ancient Greek thought may inspire the modern coach who puts character first to find creative ways to fight that good fight and to become a coach of virtue.

The History of Sports and *Aretē*

A link with *aretē* exists at the very origin of sports. The earliest evidence comes from ancient Sumerian, Egyptian, and Minoan societies in which royal displays of athleticism were offered to the populace as evidence of their leaders' divine favor and worthiness to lead. Of course these were not open competitions; most often they were uncontested displays, or even unwitnessed feats that gained legendary status in their poetic retelling. Whether Gilgamesh actually out-wrestled Enkidu, or whether the Sumerian Shulgi in fact ran the length of his kingdom (over 100 miles) and back in a single day was immaterial.[4] The point was not so much to prove the leader's worth to a skeptical public, but rather to provide comforting and inspiring tales of strength and virtue, not unlike the myths of Heracles or Theseus.[5] What remains most interesting to us is that athleticism was taken to be a sign of virtue and civic worth so many millennia ago. Somehow the link between sports and moral character has endured, despite immense changes in human life and society, up to this day. Although the nature of polities and conceptions of virtue vary with time and place, there seems to be a fundamental link between virtue and sports that transcends those differences.

We can see this variation in ancient Greek literature. Originally the *aretē* associated with athleticism was understood to be something inborn:

the product of divine ancestry or natural aristocracy. Heracles' moral and physical strength comes from his divine father, Zeus, and is displayed immediately when he saves his brother by strangling two snakes as an infant in his crib—there are no ancient stories about him training.[6] Homer's heroes Achilles and Odysseus seem naturally athletic as well. When Odysseus washes up on the island of the Phaeacians and a young man makes the insulting insinuation that he is a tradesman rather than a nobleman, Odysseus puts the matter to rest by grabbing a discus and hurling it (without training or even a practice throw) farther than all the local athletes.[7] Later, upon returning to his kingdom disguised as a beggar, he proves his *aretē* again through athletic feats—defeating even the noblemen courting his wife, Penelope.[8] In ancient Greece athleticism and virtue were thought of as gifts inherited through noble bloodlines rather than earned through training.[9]

In real athletic contests, of course, ancient Greek athletes hired coaches and trained regularly. But the lingering idea that the *aretē* associated with athleticism was inborn rather than acquired is evidenced by early efforts to hide the use of coaches and training. In early poetic and monumental celebrations Olympic victory is attributed to divine favor and the glory of one's family; coaches, instruction, and systematic training programs are almost never mentioned.[10] But as the popularity of athletics and the prestige associated with victory grew (in no small part because of its association with *aretē*), the use of coaches and the success of athletes from humble origins became impossible to hide. The evidence that athletic success could be achieved through training, combined with the traditional link between athleticism and *aretē*, generated the revolutionary idea that virtue could be trained and was not just a matter of birth.

This belief that virtue is trainable underpins the whole concept of higher education—education that goes beyond teaching skills like writing and arithmetic and actually seeks to produce excellent human beings. In the aretic context this concept implies good citizenship.[11] This idea had special appeal in the Greek west (i.e., southern Italy and Sicily), where émigrés seem to have used athletic games, especially the Olympic Games, to prove their *aretē* on the mainland. Indeed the fifth century BCE Sicilian Epicharmus of Syracuse was among the first to suggest that training or practice was more important to virtue than heredity.[12] He may have gotten the idea from Pythagoras, whose sixth century BCE school in southern Italy was among the first institutions to train virtue. It was not mere coincidence that Pythagoras recruited students in the gymnasium,[13] nor does it seem mere coincidence that Plato, after visiting the area in the fourth century BCE, opened his own school in an Athenian gymnasium called the Academy.

Plato likely included athletic exercises in the Academy's program, partly because of tradition but more precisely because he embraced the idea they could contribute to moral education.[14] In a letter describing his experiences in Italy, Plato laments his failure to transform Dionysios, the young tyrant of Syracuse, into "a man who was just and courageous and temperate and wisdom-loving [and therefore able to live] in subjection to justice combined with wisdom."[15] The educational program he outlined in Plato's *Republic*, meanwhile, uses athletic games to select and train leaders with the very qualities that Dionysios lacked: the ability to strive for excellence while resisting temptation, to subject themselves to common laws, and to toil not for individual glory but rather for the benefit of the larger community. Perhaps we can call Plato the first coach of virtue since he used sport to develop self-controlled, hardworking, law-abiding team players—much like many modern coaches. The interesting question is, How?

Winners Versus Wins

The first characteristic of coaching for virtue is that its overarching goal is *aretē*. All other athletic goals, including victories, championships, and equipment contracts, must be subordinated to that. The objective is to produce winners—people with dispositional virtues such as respect, discipline, courage, justice, and wisdom—and not necessarily wins. Although a good win-loss record may provide some evidence of a coach's ability to cultivate *aretē*, it is hardly a reliable measure in and of itself. This is because athletic victory is not a fail-safe indicator of virtue, and defeat is not always caused by the lack of virtue. Sometimes victory doesn't even indicate athletic superiority. Competitors who win by cheating, bribery, or other illicit means fail to be winners in both the moral and the athletic sense. But even in legitimate victories, virtue-irrelevant factors such as brute strength, superior equipment, good luck, or bad officiating can be the deciding factor.[16] Only in closely fought contests where athletes are challenged to bring out their best can we say that victory indicates *aretē*—but in those cases the losers likely demonstrated virtue as well. *Aretē* is not a zero-sum game, and coaches aimed at virtue cannot judge their success strictly in terms of wins and losses.

This is not to say that winning doesn't matter. Striving to win fairly in close competition is a manifestation of virtue in sport. It is victory without virtue that is worthless because it is *aretē* that gives winning its value in the first place. The athletic skills that lead to victory have little value beyond sport. It is not the ability to put a ball in a net or to overtake an adversary that is admirable in champion athletes—after all, machines and vehicles are more efficient than athletes at completing such tasks. Rather, we value these skills and the wins that go along with them because of the virtues we perceive to be embedded therein.[17] Courage is valuable not because it is needed to complete a marathon race, but because it is useful in more important human endeavors like battling disease or searching for truth. In events such as the Susan G. Komen Race for the Cure, which benefits cancer research, the efforts of all the runners, not just the winners, celebrate the kinds of virtues needed to fight disease. In this sense they resemble ancient funeral games, like those held for Patroklos described in Book 23 of Homer's *Iliad,* which celebrated the *aretē* of the deceased. The winner in such events becomes a symbol of those virtues. Without the association with *aretē*, however, he is just a guy who had the skills to make it across the finish line first; he hasn't done anything to benefit mankind.[18]

Plato artfully illustrates the distinction between skill (*technē*) and virtue (*aretē*) with the example of telling falsehoods.[19] Being a good liar certainly does not equate with being a good person, but the skill of lying may be put to good use if the liar also has *aretē*. For example, a liar may use her skill to extort money from innocent victims in a Ponzi scheme, or she may use it to protect innocent victims from injustice—perhaps by lying to Nazi soldiers about the presence of Jews in her basement. The skill of lying is morally neutral; it is a person's *aretē* that makes it potentially valuable. Likewise athletic skills are morally neutral; their value depends on *aretē*. In Plato's dialogues, Socrates is the symbol of *aretē*. He sometimes gets tripped up by the sophists, whose intellectual skills in rhetoric and *eristic* argument were designed not to discover truth, but rather to trick opponents or win over audiences. Their lives are dedicated to short-term success, whereas Socrates' is dedicated to the cultivation of *aretē,* which is the real source of happiness.[20] Athletic skill may lead to victory, but it is virtue that makes victory worthwhile.

Unfortunately, virtue is harder to measure than victory, and reward systems for coaches and athletes alike are calibrated toward the latter. This is not a problem unique to sports. In society more generally, both ancient and modern, the extrinsic rewards of fame and fortune draw people away from the intrinsic goods connected to happiness. Chastising the citizens of Athens in 399 BCE, Socrates said, "Wealth does not bring about *aretē*, but *aretē* makes wealth and everything else good for men, both individually and collectively."[21] For some reason, legions of depressed millionaires and suicidal superstars are not evidence enough to deter young people from pursuing fame and fortune at a very high cost. Athletic paths to stardom are particularly risky. Any other college program with such a low professional placement rate would be considered a failure.[22] We may decry young athletes who are motivated by money, but we have to ask ourselves what values they are supposed to learn from coaching staffs preoccupied with salaries and institutions that see athletics primarily as a means to generate revenue and court alumni donors. Coaching for virtue means not only exhorting athletes to put *aretē* first; it also requires coaches to model this priority personally in their own choices and attitudes—despite an incentive and reward structure that often works against that.

In discussing the educational value of athletics, Plato's *Republic* never mentions wins or losses. Students are to be subjected to "labors [*ponous*], pains, and contests [*agōnas*]" so that they may be tested "more thoroughly than gold is tested by fire."[23] They are to be selected for advancement based on their performance in these contests, but not necessarily by whether they win, and certainly not by whether they have the physical size and strength to achieve Olympic victory.[24] Socrates distinguishes these students from "all other athletes" on the grounds that their goal is psychic rather than muscular strength.[25] Platonic educators are therefore looking for spiritual qualities that can be developed into virtues: the willingness to confront imperfection, the desire to work hard without promise of immediate reward, the discipline to resist laziness and temptation, and the ability to subject oneself to rules as an equal with others. These, at least, are the kinds of traits that Plato describes in relation to the cardinal virtues in his ethical philosophy—virtues still widely valued today: respect (*eusebia*), courage (*andreia*), moderation (*sophrosynē*), justice (*dikaiosynē*), and wisdom (*sophia*). Let us imagine how a coach in Plato's Academy might have used sport to help develop these virtues.

Respect (*Eusebia*)

The foundation of education for *aretē* in the Platonic scheme is summed up in Socrates' famous declaration that his wisdom lies precisely in the awareness that he is not wise.[26] Not unlike a twelve-step program, in which you must admit that you have a problem before you can begin to solve it, the Socratic admission of imperfection initiates and motivates the self-improvement process. Socrates explains his avowal of ignorance as a kind of religious humility. Having been declared by the oracle at Delphi (and therefore by the god Apollo) to be the wisest of men,[27] Socrates sets out to investigate the matter by questioning poets, politicians, and craftsmen who seem to him to be wise. What he discovers is that these men *think* themselves wiser than they really are, and so he concludes that the oracle has declared Socrates wisest because he, unlike these others, admits that he doesn't have knowledge. Furthermore, he spends his days questioning others in search of the truth, as a kind of mission to the god. In other words, Socrates regards it as a kind of piety, first, to acknowledge his imperfection with respect to the gods' perfection, and, second, to work tirelessly to bring himself and others around him closer to perfection through inquiry. In short, he is exercising the virtue of respect: respect for the excellence of the gods, respect for himself in striving for improvement, and respect for others in striving to help them improve.

Long before Socrates, athletics was a milieu that symbolized this conception of respect. The gulf between perfection and imperfection was understood in terms of the contrast between gods and human beings. Respect demands that we humbly acknowledge the gods' superiority—failure to do so amounts to the vice of *hubris*, the characteristic source of dreadful consequences in Greek tragedy. Ancient athletes showed their humility partly by competing in the nude, stripped of the trappings of their worldly ties and status. Athletes were anointed with olive oil and victors were symbolically dedicated to the gods, wearing the same cloth fillets and crowns of vegetation used to adorn sacrificial animals.[28] In the *Republic,* it is likewise said that a man must be "stripped" of his worldly reputation, honors, and rewards in order to be tested for the virtue of justice.[29] Even when we compete in clothes, athletic competition symbolically strips athletes of their social rank and demands that they respect not just the rules of the games they play, but also one another as imperfect equals under those rules. Just as Socratic questioning demonstrates respect by admitting imperfection and encouraging others to improve themselves, athletic competition demands that we admit our imperfection and encourage our competitors (by challenging them) also to improve themselves.

Coaching for respect means, first, admitting one's imperfection and helping others to come to terms with their own. Sports make us aware of our limitations, but in cases of dominant athletes or lack of good competition, may need a little help. When the goal is an ideal of excellence rather than mere superiority to others, there is room for criticism even in a runaway victory. Plato recognizes that flattery, which can come in the form of easy victory as well as verbal approbation, undermines the natural desire for improvement and replaces it with the desire for—and expectation of—constant praise.[30] Coaches talk a lot about being respected, which is important, but showing respect for rules, officials, superiors, and especially inferiors, is the best way to teach respect to others.

As Socrates understood, our individual differences in excellence are negligible compared with our collective distance from the ideal of excellence, as symbolized by the gods. Individual sports have their own "gods," namely, the great athletes, coaches, and officials who have built the history of our sports, and these too deserve recognition and respect from athletes and coaches alike. Beating Jesse Owens's time in the 100 meters does not mean you have achieved the same level of excellence or made the same social impact. Clearly not everyone deserves the same level of respect, but everyone deserves a basic level of respect—even people we neither like nor admire.[31] As human beings, we all fall short of perfection, and our struggle for improvement should be shared. Opponents, officials, sponsors, and staff all contribute to an athlete's personal improvement by making sports possible in the first place. Teaching respect means giving respect, and giving respect appropriately results in earning respect.

Courage (*Andreia*)

The respectful admission of imperfection provides a basis from which the passionate pursuit of excellence can be launched. The next thing Platonic educators look to be revealed through sports is an athlete's courage, as evidenced primarily by *philoponon*, literally the love of hard work.[32] They are looking for souls that do not give up easily, even when there is little hope of immediate reward. It isn't hard to imagine how athletic competition might reveal such a quality; as the proverb says, you can learn a lot about people by watching them play a game.[33] The reason Platonic educators are looking for courageous souls in sports has nothing to do with athletic championships, however. They want to find students who will courageously pursue knowledge because, as Socrates says, "people's souls give up much more easily in hard study than in physical training."[34] In short, they are looking for future philosopher-kings, people willing to "take the longer road and put as much effort into learning as into physical training, for otherwise, as we were just saying, he will never reach the goal of the most important subject and the most appropriate one for him to learn."[35] In short, the courage a student shows in sports is expected to apply as well in academic studies.

A plausible response to this idea of selecting students through sports is that Plato has no idea what he is talking about because in the real world (or at least the modern world), athletes who train and play with outstanding effort and courage rarely employ those qualities in academic pursuits. Plato does seem to have been aware of this problem. In *Republic*, Socrates says that athletes training and competing at the highest levels have little interest in anything else but sleeping.[36] The period in which students are examined and selected on the basis of their athletic performance is accordingly limited to two years devoted strictly to physical training. The study of difficult mathematical and philosophical subjects comes after that.[37] It is never expected of individuals that they dedicate themselves to the highest levels of sport and study simultaneously. It is expected, however, that virtues like courage, which are revealed and rewarded by sports, will be applied to the more important tasks of learning and leadership. Plato's educational philosophy is not aimed at producing star athletes or even commercial titans (although both existed in his day). The goal is to create excellent individuals who apply their virtues for the benefit of the larger community—something similar to the stated aims of most modern colleges and universities.

So what would it mean to coach for courage and other virtues that will be expressed beyond athletics? First, recognize that human beings cannot perform their very best at both athletics and academics simultaneously.[38] Second, incentives and accolades should be structured (within athletic and academic programs) to reward the cultivation of virtue and especially its application in activities that benefit the larger community. In the typical high school or college, standards of excellence for participating in sports are much higher than those for academics. Student athletes are required to make only minimal academic progress toward graduation, while they must train and compete at a very high level to earn a place on a team. Community celebration and reward of top athletes, furthermore, usually outstrips that given to top students. Is it any wonder that individuals tend to "spend" their virtues on sport in this environment? As in the case of win-loss records, coaches need to swim upstream to encourage the application of virtues beyond the athletic field. They need to demand that students always put virtue first and never neglect their obligations to other worthwhile activities and relationships, not that students always put sports first in their lives.[39] Plato's dialogue *Laches* argues that courage requires not just endurance but also the wisdom to direct it toward good causes. Bravery shown only and exclusively in sport is not a virtue at all; those who coach for virtues promote their expression beyond athletics as well.

Moderation (*Sophrosynē*)

Plato's Socrates explicitly rejects the idea that physical training is primarily for the benefit of the body, while the rest of education serves the soul (*psychē*). Rather, he argues that both physical and academic training are primarily for the benefit of the soul.[40] To make sense of this, we must first understand that the Greek word *psychē* is more expansive than many modern ideas of soul. In Plato's philosophy, the soul encompasses three parts: the wisdom-loving intellect, the honor-loving spirit, and the appetitive part associated with desires for food, drink, and sex. *Aretē* on Plato's scheme is explicitly described as a harmony among these three parts of the soul, a harmony that is compared (but not equated) with physical health. Indeed, even physical health has its origin in the soul, for as Socrates says, a fit body does not produce *aretē*, but rather that the soul's virtue makes the body as good as possible.[41] In fact, Socrates says that physical training in isolation risks squelching the soul's native love of learning, creating a person who "bulls his way through every situation by force and savagery like a wild animal."[42] A person pursuing *aretē*, even through the medium of sport, explains Socrates, will not "assign first place to being strong, healthy, and beautiful, unless he happens to acquire moderation (*sophrosynē*) as a result. Rather it's clear that he will always cultivate the harmony of his body for the sake of the consonance of his soul."[43]

This virtue of moderation (*sophrosynē*) may be described in the context of modern sports as a kind of self-discipline. It combines the power to resist appetitive temptations ranging from laziness to greed, with the ability to discern and pursue noble goals with enthusiasm. In the dialogue *Phaedrus* the virtuous soul is illustrated with the metaphor of a two-horse chariot. The driver represents the intellectual part of the soul, the obedient horse represents the spirited or honor-loving part, and the disobedient horse represents the appetitive part of the soul. In order for the chariot to perform well, the spirited and appetitive parts have to be trained to obey the rational part.[44] I don't think it is just by coincidence that Plato uses an athletic metaphor here (chariot racing was an important Olympic event in ancient Greece). Even today athletes must train themselves to resist destructive appetitive desires. The temptations to indulge in unhealthy food or alcohol, to stay out late or leave practice early, must be overcome to maximize athletic potential. Because the game tends to punish those who fail to control such appetites—sometimes in the humiliating form of a poor public performance—sports can help us to follow through in action with what the intellect discerns to be right. Socrates claims that athletic training helps to harmonize the three parts of the soul; to keep appetites in check and to pursue with enthusiasm the well-chosen goals of the intellect.[45]

Coaching for moderation means letting that process take place. Athletes must develop not only the intellectual capacity to make wise choices, but also the moral capacity to follow through with those choices in action. On one level, this requires coaches to allow the space for athletes to make mistakes and suffer the consequences. For example, athletes should come to practice because they know it is the right thing to do and they are following through, as a matter of honor or pride, with what they know to be right. If they come to practice simply to avoid punishment, they will be learning to obey the appetitive fear of pain rather than the intellectual conviction of purpose. This is nothing more than doing what feels good, a habit that can lead to all kinds of troubling behaviors. If, on the other hand, the athlete learns to do what is right because she understands its importance, she will have acquired an important moral skill. As in the case of winning and losing, however, sports do not reliably reward the virtue of moderation and punish the vice of immoderation. For this reason, coaches might create rules and rewards designed to guide rather than force athletes toward virtuous behavior. For example, they might prohibit potentially dangerous supplements so that athletes may come to appreciate the joy of achieving goals without the "help" of shortcuts. Coaches might bench even top-performing players who behave immoderately as a public way of putting virtue first. But restrictions on athlete behavior should be aimed at the goal of self-regulation. Like training wheels on a bike, their purpose is to make themselves unnecessary.

Justice (*Dikaiosynē*)

In using athletics to train and select the rulers of his ideal city, Plato was looking for outstanding individuals who, despite their personal excellence, could see themselves as equal with others before the law and ultimately understood their welfare to be inextricably connected with the good of the whole community. This social virtue was called justice (*dikaiosynē*), and it was learned through sports, on a foundational level, by the simple act of following rules. In the *Republic* it is stipulated that children's games be strictly governed by rules so they could develop the habit of respecting and following laws.[46] Ultimately, the model is of guardians and rulers completely devoted to the state; they are not allowed to have private property or even private families.[47] Their decisions are expected to serve the greater good of the community, disregarding personal concerns or desires. Athletics formed part of the training and selection process through which "they must show themselves to be lovers of their city when tested by pleasure and pain and that they must hold on to their resolve through labors, fears, and all other adversities."[48] To be a just person in Plato's Academy meant not only to have the three parts of your soul in harmony with one another, but also to be in harmony with your community, understanding your particular role within it, and regarding yourself as equal with others before the law.

Obviously the sociopolitical context of Plato's Academy is different from ours today. His understanding of the social virtue of justice, however, is as relevant as ever. In fact, the (relatively) modern invention of team sports seems to be a particularly good tool for promoting the understanding of individuals' dependence on the larger group. Paradoxically, much of the selfish and immoderate behavior seen today comes from athletes in high profile team sports. Like the ancient tyrants who plagued Greece in Plato's day, some superstar athletes are driven by their appetites to regard themselves as above the rules and to disregard the deleterious effects of their selfish actions on their teams. Coaches too behave like tyrants when they use their teams to satisfy their appetite for fame and fortune. These coaches are more dangerous than tyrannical players since they generally have more power. Fortunately, most team sports are structured in ways that penalize selfish behavior. Individual superstars may command big salaries, but they can win only with the cooperation of their team.

Meanwhile, players who put team harmony before personal desire tend to be rewarded by the game.

However, sports do not reliably reward the virtue of justice and so Platonic coaches need to promote it separately. As Socrates says in the *Republic,* "It isn't the law's concern to make any one class in the city outstandingly happy but to contrive to spread happiness throughout the city by bringing the citizens into harmony with each other."[49] The same could be said for the structure of a team. The basis of justice, it will be remembered, is equality before the law. In addition to treating players equitably, coaches should set an example of respect for rules, officials, opposing players, and coaches. Just as players should be smart enough to see the connection between their own success and that of the team, coaches should be smart enough to see the connection between their own success and that of the larger athletic and academic community. Coaches who bend rules or try to manipulate the system for the competitive benefit of the team may believe they are teaching loyalty and dedication to a purpose. But in fact, they are teaching their players to selfishly indulge their own desires at the expense of the community. Furthermore, coaches should penalize players who fail to exercise the virtue of justice—even if doing so hurts the team competitively. These actions reinforce sports' ability to cultivate the virtue of justice and may spur the other players to work more closely together rather than relying on a selfish star. As Socrates says of the guardians, just people are even happier than Olympians because their victory is shared by the entire community.[50]

Wisdom (*Sophia*)

The last of the key Platonic virtues is wisdom (*sophia*). Unlike the other virtues discussed above, he dedicates none of his dialogues to it. I can think of two good reasons for this. First, wisdom is a kind of crowning virtue—the culmination of the harmonious acquisition of all the other virtues. Each virtue depends for its value on some level of wisdom: justice requires the understanding of one's relationship to the community, moderation demands the subjection of appetites and honor to a discerning intellect, courage entails not just the will to take risks, but the ability to understand which risks are worth taking, and respect is based on the wisdom of knowing that one doesn't know. This brings us to the second reason Plato never explicates wisdom: like Socrates he probably would deny that he has it. The Academy educates philosophers, lovers of wisdom who believe themselves to be in perpetual pursuit of it, rather than sophists, people who believe that they possess it.

Wisdom and the virtues that Plato connects with it are strongly intellectual. But they derive their worth precisely from our ability to act in accordance with them. Aristotle defines human happiness as activity in accordance with virtue.[51] So athletics has its place in the Academy because it is an activity, something that requires us to act. Sports, insofar as they reward virtuous action and penalize the opposite, are an important part of training for *aretē* and the wisdom that is essential to it. Coaches, insofar as they promote virtue and penalize its opposite, are accordingly educators of virtue and as such they have an important place not only in Plato's ancient Academy but in modern schools, colleges, and universities. Athletics is not merely an add-on to education; it is wrapped up in its roots, and its link with virtue gives it a foundational role in education.

Questions for Review and Discussion

1. Aretism asserts that cultivation of virtue is the highest social good that sports can achieve. What other goods might coaches seek through sports? Would you argue that any of these is more important than virtue?

2. In ancient times athleticism was associated with moral virtue and leadership ability. Would you say that this is true today? Why or why not?

3. Some ancient philosophers like Plato and Aristotle believed that virtue, like athletic ability, is more a matter of training than of birth. Do you think good athletic performance is more a product of birth or training? What about good moral behavior?

4. Drawing on your athletic experience, compare a hard-earned victory with an easy victory. Which was more meaningful and valuable to you? Have you ever had a meaningful athletic experience that ended in defeat?

5. Plato suggests that athletes who exhibit courage and hard work in sports will apply the same virtues in academic study—an idea that contradicts the stereotype of the modern student athlete. Do you think the problem is more with Plato's theory or with the modern stereotype? Why don't more student athletes show the same virtues in the classroom and on the field or court?

6. The chapter discusses five ancient virtues that might be cultivated through sport: respect, courage, moderation, justice, and wisdom. How have your coaches, or your experience in sports more generally, helped you to cultivate these virtues? Can you think of an experience in sports that worked against one of these virtues?

7. Try to name three specific actions that high schools and universities could take to better facilitate the cultivation of virtue through sports. Now name three things coaches could do.

Suggestions for Further Reading

Arnold, Peter. "Sport and Moral Education." *Journal of Moral Education* 23:1 (1994): 75–90.

Bäck, Allan. "The *Way* to Virtue in Sport." *Journal of the Philosophy of Sport* 36 (2009): 217–237.

Bradley, Bill. *Values of the Game*. New York: Broadway Books, 1998.

Dombrowski, Daniel. *Contemporary Athletics and Ancient Greek Ideals*. Chicago: University of Chicago Press, 2009.

Jones, Carwyn. "Character, Virtue, and Physical Education." *European Physical Education Review* 11:2 (2005): 140–142.

Kennell, Nigel M. *The Gymnasium of Virtue: Education and Culture in Ancient Sparta*. Chapel Hill: University of North Carolina Press, 1995.

McNamee, Mike. *Sports, Virtues, and Vices: Morality Plays*. London: Routledge, 2008.

Reid, Heather L. "Athletic Virtue: Between East and West." In *The Ethics of Sports: A Reader*, 340–347. Edited by M. McNamee. London: Routledge, 2010.

Four

The Ethical Coach:
An Interpretive Account of
the Ethics of Coaching

ROBERT L. SIMON

I certainly wanted to have great field hockey players, but I wanted them to have character, to be responsible, mature and successful women in whatever they choose.

> —Vernon-Verona-Sherill High School coach
> Wendy Seifried upon her retirement

I never wanted to do anything that would disappoint you.

> —Former VVS field hockey player referring to
> Coach Seifried[1]

A number of years ago, I attended a symposium on college athletics and its problems. One of the speakers coached a highly successful men's program at an athletically elite university. He started his remarks by claiming, "My job is to make money for university X."

While some may regard that as an accurate description of his major responsibility, others may doubt that it captures all the issues, even at the level of big-time college sports. After all, his team wouldn't make money if it didn't win consistently. And to achieve that, the coach would have to be good at tasks that lead to winning, such as recruiting, teaching, motivating, selecting strategies, and persuading players to buy into them. These tasks may conflict with one another, necessitating difficult choices. For example, should a star player who violates the team's code of conduct be benched or suspended even if that means losing games that otherwise would be won? Should the coach berate competent game officials in order to arouse the home crowd and give his team an emotional lift?

These examples suggest that there is a normative or ethical side of coaching. Perhaps a big-time college coach is expected to generate revenues for the institution and hence has a strong imperative to win. Such coaches might resolve conflicts between competing goals simply by estimating which choice will most likely lead to winning. But is winning to be achieved at all costs? Are there constraints on the pursuit of victory, such as good sportsmanship? Aren't there other important goals, such as developing players' skills, ensuring they get a good education, protecting their safety, and perhaps even helping them grow as persons of good character?

Coaches, then, often face ethical choices. The decision to override ethics in pursuit of victory may trigger extensive criticism of the coach, as in 2012, when some New Orleans Saints coaches were found complicit in the team's bounty system that in effect rewarded defensive players for making hard hits intended to injure rival players and remove them from the game. What ethical requirements apply to them? How should coaches be evaluated ethically? How might coaches ethically evaluate their own behavior? In what follows, we will explore three different approaches to understanding the ethical requirements that might apply to coaching. First, however, we need to clarify some issues that might affect our inquiry.

The preceding examples suggest that coaching involves far more than teaching techniques and strategies closely related to the sport. Indeed, even apparently strategic choices may have a subtle evaluational dimension, as, for example, when a basketball coach decides to play a man-to-man defense rather than a zone in part because he thinks it teaches players to show great intensity, concentration, and commitment.

What ethical requirements apply to coaches? The requirements that apply to any competent adult? Or are there special requirements or exemptions for coaches, based on special rights and duties arising from the coaching role? For example, may coaches lie to their players to motivate them to achieve? May a coach exaggerate the extent of injuries to a star player in the hope that opponents will become overconfident and fail to prepare for the challenge of keeping the fully recovered star from dominating the game? May a coach intimidate or even bully players, an issue discussed by Mark Hamilton later in this volume, if the coach believes that is the best way to get them to play harder? What about more subtle forms of manipulation?

Suppose a college coach tells a freshman player that she has a chance to start on the soccer team but does this to get her to play hard enough to challenge the veteran starters in her position to also work hard in practice. If the coach actually has no intention of playing the newcomer over the veterans, is that technique good coaching, even if dishonest?[2]

Suppose we conclude that being an ethical coach is "a many splendored thing," with a variety of factors contributing to our evaluation that must be weighed but without any clear scale on which to do the weighing. How should these factors be weighed? How should a winning coach who uses techniques that are morally questionable but not egregiously so be evaluated? If there is no formula for balancing one factor against another, doesn't this make our evaluation of coaches subjective? Is one person's good coach another's coaching disaster?

Objectivity and Relativism in the Evaluation of Coaching

What does it mean to say a judgment, claim, principle, or even process is objective? There are many ways of distinguishing between the objective and the subjective. I suggest that there is a common concept of objectivity that applies at least to the paradigm cases where the concept of objectivity of judgment applies—there are rationally defensible constraints that we must satisfy in order to be warranted in our beliefs. These include the constraint of not being swayed by prejudice and the constraint of using logically sound methods for evaluating evidence. A judgment or conclusion is not justified just because everyone agrees to it but rather a consensus on a conclusion is justified because of the soundness of the reasons that support it.[3]

In our inquiry, we will consider criteria for the moral evaluation of coaches. The conclusions we arrive at, while tentative and fallible, will claim to be objective in the sense that they can be defended by sound reasoning and survive criticism in extended discussion and debate. Alternately, if further inquiry shows they are incorrect or at least questionable, such a conclusion will be the result of reasoning that, if sound, also makes a claim to be objective. Thus, if we have good reasons for believing Coach X is an unethical coach, we can be correct—Coach X really is unethical—and someone who believes Coach X is ethical can be wrong or in error. Therefore, because we are dealing with subject matter that allows of correct and incorrect evaluations, we are in the realm of objectivity and not mere personal opinion, let alone bias and prejudice.[4] Sometimes it may be difficult to arrive at well-grounded conclusions, as when we debate hard cases in sport such as whether pitchers in baseball ought to retaliate for brush back pitches thrown at their teammates or whether a hard foul from behind to prevent a layup in a basketball game is simply good strategy or unfairly deprives an opponent of an advantage gained by superior play. (See William J. Morgan's discussion of different views of strategic fouling in Chapter 5.)

What counts as an ethical coach may vary with context. That is, the ethical requirements that apply to coaches at one level, such as professional sports, may vary in significant ways from those that apply at another, such as high school or children's sports. This does not make judgments subjective, as we can still have good reasons for judgments such as "Jones is a great college coach but doesn't have the patience to be a good coach with young children."

Keeping these points in mind, let us turn to substantive issues about the moral evaluation of coaches.

Winning as the Only Thing

According to what might be called the instrumental view, a good coach is someone who achieves the goals of coaching. Similarly, a good knife is one that cuts. However, as simple as this formula sounds, it raises at least two significant questions. First, what are the goals of coaching? Second, are there requirements that set moral limits or constraints on what the coach may do while attempting to achieve those goals?

One way of answering the first question is to reply that a good coach is one who wins. Winning is the goal of athletic competition. A coach who consistently loses is a failure as a coach. And indeed, there is something to this proposal. As writers such as Scott Kretchmar have pointed out, winning requires that players learn skills such as how to hold a lead, how to maintain poise when the opposition is making a run, how to mount a run from behind when the opponents take the lead, and how to excel under pressure, especially when a tight game comes down to the wire.[5]

Consider the extreme view, one not held by Kretchmar, that the only ethical obligation of the coach is to win. Coaches and players develop skills, select strategies, and make decisions in game situations that are designed to help them win; as winning is the common instrumental goal of sports, the job of the coach is and only is to promote victory.

However, cursory critical scrutiny suggests that winning is not the only ethical obligation of the coach. At many levels of sport it may not even be a primary one. For example, when coaching young children, it surely is more important to teach fundamental physical skills, teach age-appropriate strategies and game awareness (how to react appropriately to game situations), and arouse enthusiasm and a love of the game that might carry over for a lifetime. (However, as Torres and Hager argue later in this volume, competition still may be a valuable part of youth sports.) Winning may take on increased significance at the levels of professional and elite amateur sports. But don't those coaches also have a responsibility to protect the health of athletes, treat them with respect, and, at schools and colleges, promote their academic success?

A coach may have a winning record but not be a very good coach or satisfy the ethical requirements applicable to coaching. Winning records can be achieved by scheduling weak opponents, for example, or by employing hidden techniques that tilt the playing field. For example, when Bill Belichick's New England Patriots were accused of gaining illegal access to the play calling of rival coaches, critics charged that his teams won, not necessarily because they were better but because of "insider information" that gave them an advantage having nothing to do with their athletic or strategic skills. Or suppose a coach wins because he rewards his players for injuring opponents, as was alleged of the NFL New Orleans Saints in March 2012?

Winning, then, is not the sole criterion by which coaches should be evaluated. Winning does not exhaust the ethical responsibilities of the coach and, indeed, is to the coach's ethical credit only if achieved by ethically justifiable means. But what criteria should be applied to the moral evaluation of coaching?

A Kantian Approach: Athletes Should Not be Used as Mere Means to a Goal

The distinguished eighteenth-century philosopher Immanuel Kant defended an approach to ethics that is generally understood to lay down rationally defensible restraints on the pursuit of our goals, even our personal happiness, based on the intrinsic values of persons. Kant called what he regarded as the fundamental ethical principle the Categorical Imperative, which he expressed in several ways that he apparently regarded as equivalent. Perhaps the most morally influential formulation maintains that we should never treat others only as means to attaining a goal but as ends; as persons rather than as things. A related and perhaps equally influential formulation, which Kant himself might have thought equivalent, requires that it be possible or logically coherent for the point or motive of our act to be made a universal rule. Thus it would be logically incoherent for everyone to cheat in a golf tournament since there would be no golf tournament if the rules of golf were not followed. Also, cheating another reduces the victim to a thing or means to our own success rather than a person who is trying to compete with us under an agreed upon set of conditions for contesting the golf tournament. Thus cheating opponents in a golf tournament violates both versions of the Categorical Imperative.

The central basis for Kant's claim goes something like this. None of us does or even can regard ourselves as mere things. None of us want or even can want to simply be used to achieve the goals of others that we do not share. And so if we are to be consistent we must regard all others who also function as persons as ends in themselves as well. As philosopher and legal theorist Ronald Dworkin suggests, "We cannot consistently treat our own lives as objectively important unless we accept that everyone's life has the same objective importance."[6]

What does it mean to be treated a mere means? On one view, the key implication is that we should not be treated in ways we do not or would not (if reasonable and fully informed) consent to be treated. On a related view, we should not be exploited or taken advantage of. On a third view, which draws on Kant's emphasis on our status as rational choosing beings, we should be valued or cherished as persons (as intrinsically valuable beings) and not just units who might be traded off against other units in a cost-benefit analysis to achiever the greatest overall good or profit.

How does this abstract discussion apply to coaching? The most obvious application is that there is a Kantian requirement on coaches—coaches are not to use others, particularly the athletes they coach, as mere means.

In a consideration of coaching ethics, Jeffrey Fry provides several examples of how Kant's Categorical Imperative might apply. We already have considered two illustrations based on Fry's scenarios. In the first, a coach during preseason tells a promising rookie and a veteran that they are competing for a starting position on the team even though he already has decided to go with the rookie. The coach's motive is to get both players to work harder in practice, thus better preparing them for the season ahead. In the second case, the coach orders a player to make an especially hard hit on the opponent's key player in order to get the opposing star out of the game. The coach brushes off his player's moral qualms by telling him, "It's all part of the game."[7]

Fry goes on to give a very plausible Kantian analysis of why the coach's behavior in the first case probably is unethical and why it is clearly unethical in the second. In the first case, the coach is deceiving the veteran, especially if he had indicated earlier that the veteran would get a chance to start. Moreover, as Fry points out, if told the truth, the veteran might select another sport to play, decide to play at the professional level, or ask to be traded or, if in college, transfer to another school. The coach, in Fry's view, is reducing the athlete to a mere means to the team's success.[8]

Moreover, the coach's behavior violates the universality version of the Categorical Imperative: it is doubtful the coach's behavior can be made into a universal law of a public code of conduct for coaches. For if it was publicly known that coaches deceive in this sort of situation, no one would believe them in the first place and their deception wouldn't work.[9]

If the coach's behavior is dubious in the first case, it is clearly unethical in the second. By instructing his player to injure an opponent, the opposing player is not viewed as a person to be valued and respected, but as an obstacle standing in the way of victory. Indeed, as Fry notes, the coach's own player is also being used as a mere means since the coach disregards the player's moral qualms about carrying out the instruction.[10]

Should we conclude, then, that the coach's whole range of ethical responsibilities is captured by Kantian ethics, suitably interpreted and applied? A major difficulty with regarding the Kantian approach as the whole story of coaching ethics is illustrated by a third example of Fry's. In this case, a basketball team is nearing the end of a mediocre season, and a high school coach is faced with the decision of benching her seniors, who have all played for years in the program, in order to develop the potential of currently less skilled younger players so the team will be more competitive the following year. Should the coach show loyalty to the veterans who have worked hard for the program and continue to play them or focus on building a championship contender in the future? Fry comments,

> Even though her actions may promote the greatest overall utility, she has not taken the seniors' ends—i.e. goals for the season—seriously enough. . . . Instead, . . . coach is only committed to the players as long as they fulfill a narrowly defined role. Given that, she has lost sight of their humanity.[11]

While Fry's analysis seems correct as applied to his description of the case, the coach, as Fry might agree, has a number of options in slightly altered versions of this scenario. For example, the coach can be open with her players, tell them that she has a responsibility to build for the future as well as work as hard as possible for success this season, and inform the team that for the remaining games, she will try to give the younger athletes more playing time than previously. She can enlist the help of her seniors in building for the future. In this approach, the seniors are not totally ignored, but their playing time is reduced so that younger players can be prepared to replace them next season. However, this is done in an open way, with, one would hope, the cooperation of the seniors. Indeed, the coach arguably has responsibilities to future teams as well as to the present one.[12]

The point is not identifying one best solution to this coach's dilemma but rather achieving ethically acceptable results. What's needed is good judgment in balancing a variety of factors rather than simply applying an abstract injunction not to treat players as mere means to someone else's end. The Kantian injunction against treating others as mere means may set a moral baseline below which the coach must not fall, and perhaps may even be a necessary condition of moral acceptability. But above that baseline, good judgment might lead to a variety of solutions, some of which balance the competing values at stake.

We can think of a great many coaching situations that have ethical dimensions and call for good judgment in balancing a number of competing values in ways not easily captured by rules or formulas. How should a coach distribute playing time among team members? (Scott Kretchmar considers this question in Chapter 8.) Is it permissible for a coach to "work" the officials and, if so, how far may a coach go? (Mark Hamilton considers the ethics of intimidation in Chapter 9.) May a coach lay down rules for player conduct off the field and, if so, how far may the coach go? How much of a voice should players have in framing team rules or even in helping formulate team strategies?

To take a final example, how a coach addresses her team may call for good judgment that is sensitive to moral factors that are hard to codify under a rule. Thus a coach who encourages players to make suggestions about strategy, use of practice time, and decision making during games is making a different moral choice than a more directive coach who does not involve players in decision making. Both may avoid treating their players as mere means but surely there are different moral values involved in their approaches.

Clearly coaching is a complex activity that involves a network of strategic, technical, personal, and moral dimensions, all of which may be interrelated in particular cases. While I agree with Fry that there are important moral side constraints, perhaps Kantian in character, that may prohibit certain coaching decisions, such as telling a team member to deliberately injure an opponent, these side constraints are not always determinative in the complex situations that arise in coaching. These complexities may lead many to conclude that the ethical coach is not primarily a person who follows well defined moral rules or avoids violating Kantian prohibitions. Rather, the ethical coach is a person who makes good judgments in particular sporting contexts. Similarly, in evaluating coaches, the evaluators are not bound by a rule book but must look at the variety of virtues the coach exhibits and the judgment the coach makes in a variety of contexts.

The Ethical Coach as a Person of Practical Wisdom

In a high school basketball game I witnessed many years ago, two strong teams were taking each other down to the wire in a hotly contested game. Most of the starters on one team fouled out, and as the clock wound down, the outcome depended on foul shots by a rarely used substitute. In a time-out called by the opponents to "ice" the foul shooter, his coach looked him in the eye and, according to reports, said, "These are the most important shots you will ever have in your life!" In retrospect, this was probably not the best thing to have said, as the nervous substitute didn't even hit the rim in two attempts.

While the coach may not have said anything unethical, he may have used poor judgment in how he addressed the player. Perhaps the shooter would have done better if the coach had simply told him to take deep breaths and relax and reassured him about his value to the team regardless of the outcome.

Similarly, good judgment might be called for in other sorts of cases more directly involving ethics. For example, a high school golf coach sees that an inexperienced player on an opposing team inadvertently teed her last shot a few inches in front of the tee markers, a rule violation that calls for a penalty. Should the coach call for a penalty to be assessed? Or in light of the player's inexperience, the fact that her playing partners failed to notice and hence warn her in advance of the possible infraction, and that virtually no advantage was gained, should the coach simply advise the violator to check where she teed her ball more carefully in the future? Should the coach remind the other players of their obligation, recognized by golfers, to warn their competitors in advance of possible rules infractions? Clearly a lot will depend on contextual factors such as how inexperienced the player actually was (was it her first competitive match?), the type of match (a scrimmage versus a state championship), the attitude of the other players in the group (did they deliberately fail to warn the violator or were they simply inattentive)? If no precise rule or formula covers this case, the coach must simply exercise good judgment.[13]

Proponents of the view just articulated rightly point out that the coach must be a master of "spontaneous response."[14] Making just the right substitution, for example, at just the right time, or changing the defense just at the moment when the opponent is least likely to adjust to the change, call for good judgment in response to complex situations, not automatic application of strategic rules. Similarly, when the ethical dimension of decision making is paramount, good judgment rather than mastery of the rules is key. For example, knowing how to motivate a player whose play has been halfhearted may involve walking a fine line between intense criticism and verbal abuse. To take another example, consider a high school coach trying to choose between (or perhaps blend) two offensive strategies, one that emphasizes the talents of a star player and another that emphasizes cohesive team play that will develop the talents of all the players but perhaps result in less competitive success. This coach may need to strike a balance between two extremes that is not dictated by a rule book but requires sensitivity to the particular characteristics of the team.

Advocates of such a view maintain that the good coach is a person of practical wisdom; one who is adept at making the right judgment in particular contexts. Such a coach applies a variety of virtues, such as sensitivity, passion, and fairness, as dictated by the situation. Aristotle called such a quality *phronesis*, emphasizing that it, rather than rules, is fundamental in ethics. The ethical coach, then, is not simply a Kantian who avoids treating players as mere means but has the practical wisdom to make the decision most appropriate to the case at hand. On this view, the good coach does not need a philosophy in the sense of a general rule book for how to make decisions. Rather, a good philosophy of coaching may just summarize how wise and virtuous coaches decide. (See also the chapters by Reid and Hochstetler for discussion of the importance of good judgment in specific contexts.)

This account may well be perspicuous in describing what good coaches actually do, but questions can be raised about whether it is a complete account of the ethics of coaching. Although no manual of rules could be complete or fine-tuned enough to allow coaches to deduce good decisions from its pages, it does not follow that making good intuitive judgments is all there is to good coaching. Consider three criticisms of this approach.

First, coaches may be called on to *justify* their decisions in public forums (or to themselves when they second-guess their own actions). If the decision is questionable, people will want to know more about the reasons for the decision other than it just seemed right to the coach in the situation. Coaches may need to provide reasons, not just to themselves or to fans, but to their own players, to parents, to the press, and in educational institutions to the athletic director and other administrators, such as a principal or dean. Just as judges in higher courts need to defend their decisions in written opinions available for public scrutiny, coaches also may need to defend their decisions by presenting justifications for them and answering criticism in various forums.

Second, coaches need to assess not just single decisions but also whether the set of their decisions over time is internally consistent and coherent. Coaches who decide in one way at one time but then handle a relevantly similar case differently need to either explain why the cases are relevantly different or else acknowledge that they were inconsistent, and thus made a mistake or were unfair. (Perhaps they learned from experience and corrected an earlier error, but they cannot be correct in treating two cases that do not differ in any relevant respect differently.)

Finally, coaches are not infallible. They are most likely to avoid mistakes in complex cases if they test their judgments about specific cases by seeing if they cohere with a larger framework, including rules and principles, that might help justify them. For example, a coach is torn between suspending a star player for missing a practice without a good excuse but also needing that player in the next game that might decide the league championship. The coach leans toward allowing the player to participate because a loss would harm the other players on the team, who have done no wrong, but also questions whether she is placing too much importance on winning and whether it is unfair to exempt the star from team rules that apply to everyone else.

In cases where intuition is not determinative, appealing to a more general theory about the purposes of competitive sport and the role of the coach in achieving such goals might be helpful. Ideally, we should try to reflect over time so as to harmonize our judgments about particular cases with an overall theory that explains and justifies them, a state philosophers call "reflective equilibrium."[15]

Of course, such criticisms are not decisive. For one thing, advocates of the coach as a person of practical wisdom might emphasize that on their view, the best coaching decisions, especially ethical ones, are not based on hunches or intuitions but on deep-seated traits of character that enable the coach to act virtuously. Moreover, they would argue, if a situation is so complex that even a person of practical wisdom has difficulty deciding what to do, it is unlikely a more general philosophical theory will help either. Let me suggest, however, that before assessing the role of *phronesis* or practical wisdom in coaching, we consider one more alternative.[16]

Broad Internalism: An Interpretive Approach to Coaching

Consider the following example. You are playing in an important soccer game and the opposing team, through clever passing and dribbling, is in position to have a breakaway attempt at the goal. A rival player inadvertently bumps you. If you pretend to be injured and writhe on the ground as if in pain, the opposition, known for its sportsmanlike conduct, will follow the convention of soccer and kick the ball out of bounds, thereby losing its opportunity to score, so that your "injury" can be treated. Should you pretend to be injured?

Surely you should not. Faking an injury is not a fundamental skill in soccer. (Thus it would be absurd to claim that A is a better player than B because even though B is more skilled at passing, dribbling, shooting, and defense, A is much better at faking injuries.) The point of competitive athletics is to see whether your team is more skilled than its opponents. Negating the other team's skills through trickery changes the contest from one where the skills of soccer are being tested to one where deception irrelevant to soccer skills may become decisive.

Surely a major point of competitive sports is to test our relative abilities against worthy opponents and to learn from meeting challenges. Arguably, a good competitor should want to meet the challenge presented by the rules of the sport, not avoid the challenge by turning the contest into something other than a test of soccer skills.

This analysis rests on a broad theory about the purpose and value of competitive sport. I have elsewhere described this account as "a mutual quest for excellence," the idea being that in a sports contest, opponents voluntarily challenge each other so as to bring out the best in each participant.[17] On this view, competitive sports are an educational activity in which competitors are tested by the challenges of the sport and the play of opponents, and learn from the experience of competing. Winning a game, especially against a worthy opponent, is a sign of success. However, as noted earlier, one can meet the challenge of the sport without winning, as when one pushes a vastly superior opponent to the limit or plays an excellent game only to lose to a nearly equal opponent.

This approach to understanding and evaluating sports has been called broad internalism because it suggests that a broad interpretation of sport that makes sense of its internal features is crucial both to understanding and ethically assessing competitive athletics. Interpretations are to be assessed by their ability to explain the different key features of sports, such as explaining which primary skills the rules are designed to test, by their coherence or internal consistency, and by their ability to present sports in their morally best light.[18] Thus the crude theory that winning is everything fails to explain why winning is cheapened or lacks significance when it is achieved in spite of sloppy play against a vastly overmatched opponent.

Broad internalists, following legal theorist Ronald Dworkin, emphasize the role of principles as well as rules in interpreting sport. Unlike a rule such as "three strikes and you are out," principles have weight and need to be balanced against other considerations. How they apply to a situation requires seeing how they fit in an overall theory of the sport at issue, and perhaps the point of athletic competition itself (the mutual quest for excellence) in which the principle is embedded.

How does this apply to the ethics of coaching? First, the coach should apply a defensible interpretation of sports in making hard coaching decisions, especially those with an ethical dimension. Not only should the coach have a philosophy (as Doug Hochstetler argues in Chapter 6), but it should be interpretive or broad internalist in character.

This theory may (and in my view does) include the sort of Kantian side constraints discussed by Fry but goes beyond them in applying to complex cases that require the use of a broad set of principles of interpretation. For example, the judgment that the soccer player should not fake the injury might be based on a principle that enjoins players to seek out competitive challenges based on skill rather than avoid them through trickery.[19]

Second, I also suggest that a broad internalist theory is needed in order to *evaluate* the performance of coaches. Such a theory would provide an account of the role of the coach and how it is embedded in a broader account of the point and value of athletic competition. For example, if a coach achieves a winning record by avoiding worthy opponents, the behavior normally would be open to criticism on the grounds that under the theory of the mutual quest for excellence, athletes should welcome competitive challenges and be prepared to learn from their successes and failures in attempting to meet them.

Thus if we interpret sport as a mutual quest for excellence in meeting challenges for their own sake, we explain and justify major features of sport relevant to coaching. Winning, as we have seen, is important, since it often is a sign that the challenge of the contest has been met, but it is not everything since the challenge sometimes can be met without winning. This explains why coaches at most levels of sport should not act as if winning is everything and also justifies their emphasizing other values, such as playing one's best, trying to improve, and respecting opponents. Indeed, since opponents are not mere obstacles to be overcome but rather facilitators who freely enter into a mutually acceptable activity (the contest) in order to create a challenge, the coach should emphasize respect for the opponent and not teach viewing opponents as mortal enemies.

In hard cases, however, theories or broad interpretations of sports may only issue debatable guidelines for coaches rather than decisive answers. For example, let us consider the case discussed earlier where a high school coach seems forced to choose between showing loyalty to senior players who most likely will lose as many games as they win or bench the seniors and play currently less experienced and somewhat less talented younger players in order to give them experience and build a top team for the following season.

In this sort of case, coaches may need to use practical judgment in deciding how to deal with the team, but also need a rationale to justify their response should it be questioned. My own view is the situation calls for compromising competing values. I suggested earlier that the coach should be open with the team and point out the variety of challenges involved. Thus the team has an obligation to challenge opponents to the best of its abilities, but the coach also has a duty to help all the players develop their capacities to meet the challenges of the sport. Moreover, the coach arguably has a duty, although perhaps a less weighty one than others, to think not only about the next contest or even the present season alone but also to consider the players who will be on the team in later seasons.

As I suggested earlier, in view of the complexity of the situation the coach might explain the situation to the team, challenge the seniors to help develop the abilities of the younger ones during practice, and gradually move the younger players into the lineup through judicious substitution and variation in the starting lineup so that the younger players can gain experience by being in the game at the same time as the more experienced older players. Such a strategy might involve compromising, say, loyalty to the seniors by adding playing time for the others. But the seniors would not be relegated to the bench and would be involved as "assistant coaches," helping the less experienced athletes to improve. In this way, the coach would be acting as an educator by involving all members of the team in a quest to improve but still seeking to put a lineup in the game that vigorously challenges opponents. Although all these values may not be maximally implemented, none are disregarded either.

However, some may well dissent from the compromise proposed above, perhaps with good reason. But this is where the beauty of the interpretivist (broad internalist) approach shines through. Coaches and other members of the sporting community can engage each other in reasoned discourse to evaluate the soundness of different approaches in an attempt to reach reflective equilibrium. Such discourse may show that a number of approaches are equally defensible, although one resolution may emerge as correct or at least as more justifiable than others. What surely will not be the case is that any approach will turn out to be as reasonable as any other. Thus a coach who angrily tells the seniors that they lack ability, that he will no longer help them improve, and that their only future role on the team will be as practice players not only is cruel to the older players but is unfair to opponents by not giving any weight to the duty to create a meaningful challenge in actual contests.

What I have suggested, then, is that the ethical evaluation of coaching decisions and behavior is best understood as requiring a broad interpretation of the point of competitive sport and its moral justification. Such an interpretation is debatable and revisable but also is objective in that the arguments in its favor may or may not stand up to critical scrutiny. In hard cases, sometimes a plurality of approaches may be equally reasonable, but all should be subject to critical scrutiny. I have proposed that one broad internalist theory—the idea of sport as a mutual quest for excellence through challenge—is a strong candidate for the ethical and explanatory framework required by the internalist approach.

The exact form such a theory should take might vary according to the level and type of sport. Winning may play a much weightier role at the professional or Olympic level than in youth sports, for example. Thus in professional sports, the coach may be more justified in benching or even cutting a veteran player in favor of promising rookies than would a high school coach in cutting seniors who are not quite as good as younger players. But according to the idea of the mutual quest for excellence, even the professional coach would not be justified in acting as if winning was the only goal, overriding such other legitimate objectives as the safety of players and respect for the deepest values of the game.

To summarize, a broad theory can be useful not only to the coach in decision making, for after all the coach sometimes may need to make quick decisions and rely on practical wisdom as suggested by those who emphasize the role of *phronesis*, but also in the practice of justifying decisions once they are made, and in the critical scrutiny of sports by administrators and supervisors, as well as commentators and fans.

Evaluating Coaches in Educational Institutions

Let us conclude with a brief examination of the implications of this discussion for assessing the performance of coaches in educational institutions, particularly secondary schools and colleges and universities. When competitive sports are viewed as a mutual quest for excellence through challenge, sports clearly have an educational component. Athletes need to learn to meet the challenges of competition, to improve, to overcome failure, to value the ideas of a contest with a worthy opponent, and to respect the fundamental values of their sport. This requires critical scrutiny of one's own performance and that of others, willingness to learn from criticism and to work hard to perfect skills, ability to analyze decisions made in the heat of competition, and respect for truth in evaluating one's own performance and that of fellow competitors.

These values have a clear affinity with many values presupposed in academic pursuits such as the importance of critical scrutiny, respect for evidence and truth, and willingness to test one's ideas by exposing them to critiques in such contexts as classes, papers, artistic exhibitions and performances, and published books and articles. Seen in this light, academics and athletics not only can be compatible but actually might be mutually reinforcing in the right circumstances.[20]

This suggests that a crucial role of coaches in educational institutions is to educate. While they have many responsibilities, such as scheduling, recruiting, and representing their programs to alumni and the broader community, they are primarily teachers. If they are thought of in this way, their work helps to harmonize athletics and academics and affirms the view that athletics contribute to the academic enterprise rather than constitute an alien intrusion on the life of the mind.[21]

Critics might reply that perhaps such a model applies best to many secondary schools, colleges and universities in Division III of the NCAA (who explicitly endorse the integration of athletics and academics in the Division III mission statement), and NAIA institutions, as well as the Ivy League in Division I but add that the model has no application to high visibility sports at the athletically elite levels of Division I. Coaches at that level enjoy national prestige and often make more than the presidents of their institutions. Surely the major function of big-time collegiate athletic programs is providing entertainment and raising money for their institutions.[22]

However, the pursuit of revenue and the national publicity that goes with winning is a root cause of the scandals, low graduation rates in some programs, and charges of exploitation of athletes that have plagued big-time college sports and have led critics to call for their radical reform and even abolition. Perhaps a greater emphasis on evaluating coaches as educators would be part of a multifaceted program that emphasizes the educational benefits of competitive athletics, for both participants and spectators.

While the way to best achieve such a goal will vary with the kind of institution and the level at which it competes, I suggest that a major component of reform should require colleges and universities to include a formal recommendation by a faculty committee, independent of the athletic department, that evaluates coaches on how they contribute to the educational mission of the university. This already is the case in many colleges in Division III, including Hamilton College, where I teach. Here coaches normally hold faculty appointments. Also requiring a formal faculty review, Division I institutions would promote greater oversight of athletics by educators and take a step toward implementing respect for athletics as a legitimate program within academic institutions, over and above whatever entertainment value they provide. A coach who wins but runs a program that undermines the educational values of the institution may be successful in one sense. But it is doubtful at best if such a program can be defended on ethical grounds. In other words, coaches at educational institutions should be evaluated, in part, in ways parallel to the evaluation of faculty and other educators at their school.

Moreover, institutional oversight of big-time college athletic programs is crucial. The 2012 report on the Jerry Sandusky scandal at Penn State by former FBI director Louis Freeh claims to have found "total and consistent disregard by the most senior leaders at Penn State for the safety and welfare of Sandusky's child victims."[23] If true, this finding may indicate that the prestige and influence of top coaches and the natural desire to protect elite programs can overwhelm important values and overriding moral concerns.

Indeed, the Freeh report alleges that the desire to protect the prestige (and the financial benefits that accrued from it) of Penn State football kept high Penn State officials from reporting what they knew of Sandusky's crimes to the police. Less powerful employees allegedly felt powerless to challenge what amounted to a cover-up of Sandusky's activities. As a result of the Freeh report, the NCAA imposed unprecedented penalties on Penn State, including a $60 million fine (to be used to help the victims of child abuse), loss of football scholarships, and a four-year ban on Penn State participation in postseason bowl appearances.[24]

On the other hand, if we accept the twin ideas that athletics should be integrated with academics and that a primary task of coaches is to function as educators, a strong case can be made for my proposal for the academic evaluation of coaches and their programs.[25] A fuller examination of coaching at athletically elite colleges and universities would also examine the compensation of powerful coaches and perhaps, most important, their influence over other areas of the university. Fuller institutional and faulty oversight of athletics should be considered a primary goal of reform of big-time college sports.

Conclusion

Coaching has a major ethical component. An unethical coach, or one who coaches in an unethical way, normally is not a good coach. The major argument for this view is that the goals of competitive sports should not be understood only in terms of winning but more broadly in a way involving important moral norms.

These norms are partially captured by Kantian, contextualist, and virtue oriented accounts of sports. However, I have suggested that an interpretive or broad internalist approach, especially one that regards competitive sport as a mutual quest for excellence through challenge, provides a defensible overall account of the value of athletic competition. It brings out the educational aspects of competitive sport as an activity that values overcoming challenge for its own sake but also helps promote and illustrate the values and the self-knowledge that enable us to succeed in such a mission.

On such a view, the role of the coach is interpretive; on the broad internalist view, the best theory of the coach's role is the one we ought to adopt. The best theory is the one that makes the most sense of paradigmatic coaching practices and presents them in their morally best light. Consequently I have suggested that the coach is primarily an educator in the context of viewing athletic competition as a mutual quest for excellence. Coaches, especially in educational institutions, should be treated and evaluated under such a heading.

The test of such proposals is continuing critical examination, which contributes not only to a better understanding of coaching, one of the significant social roles in our culture, but also to appreciating the crucial role ethics should play in this important area of our sporting life.

Questions for Review and Discussion

1. What significance should be attached to winning in athletic competition? Even if winning isn't everything, what degree of importance should be attached to it?

2. Explain the difference between the Kantian and the virtue contextualist oriented approach (based on *phronesis*) to coaching ethics.

3. What is broad internalism (interpretivism) and how does the author think it applies to coaching ethics? Do you agree that the coach needs a theory of the broad internalist kind to make good ethical decisions? Do others need such a theory in evaluating coaching performance?

4. What is the author's argument that coaches primarily are educators? Is the author's argument sound? Does it apply outside educational institutions—e.g. in youth sports, on one hand, and at the level of elite or professional sports on the other?

Suggestions for Further Reading

Dixon, Nicholas. "On Winning and Athletic Superiority." *Journal of the Philosophy of Sport* 26 (1999): 10–26.
French, Peter. *Ethics and College Sports: Ethics, Sports, and the University*. Lanham, MD: Rowman & Littlefield, 2004.
Fry, Jeffrey. "Coaching a Kingdom of Ends." *Journal of the Philosophy of Sport* 27 (2000): 51–62.

Hardman, Alun R., and Carwyn Jones. "Sports Coaching and Virtue Ethics." In *The Ethics of Sports Coaching*, 72–84. London: Routledge, 2011.

Kretchmar, Scott. "In Defense of Winning." In *Sports Ethics: An Anthology*, 130–135. Edited by Jan Boxill. Malden, MA: Blackwell, 2003.

Russell, J. S. "Are Rules All an Umpire Has to Work With?" *Journal of the Philosophy of Sport* 26 (1999): 27–49.

Simon, Robert L. "Does Athletics Undermine Academics? Examining Some Issues." *Journal of Intercollegiate Sport* 1:1 (2008): 40–58.

———. *Fair Play: The Ethics of Sport*. 3rd ed. Boulder, CO: Westview, 2010. See especially chapters 2–3.

———. "Internalism and the Internal Values of Sport." *Journal of the Philosophy of Sport* 27 (2000): 1–16.

Five

Interpretivism, Conventionalism, and the Ethical Coach*

WILLIAM J. MORGAN

T he chapters in Part 2 make a persuasive case that coaches at all levels have significant ethical concerns, responsibilities, and duties. But what ethical resources can they draw on not only to arrive at morally acceptable, or even morally required, judgments, but also to justify the decisions they make? Should coaches act intuitively relying on their practical wisdom and experience, appeal to ethical theories, or just solve problems that crop up on the playing field?

In Chapter 4, Robert Simon forcefully argues that ethical decision making is a central dimension of coaching, and that the theory of sports he dubs "broad internalism" or simply "interpretivism" offers the best account of how ethical coaches should form their ethical judgments and justify them to others. According to interpretivism, coaches should base their ethical decisions on a consideration of the basic purpose(s) and value(s) of sports, on an interpretation that puts the athletic challenges central to competitive sports in

---

*I want to thank Robert Simon for his incisive comments and helpful revisions on a previous draft of this chapter.

their best light. By interpretively training our eyes on the point of athletic enterprise, Simon claims, we can divine appropriate normative standards of athletic conduct and subject them to critical inquiry. The kind of critical inquiry he has in mind is a rationally based discourse oriented to justification, in which proposed norms are subjected to various challenges and objections by the relevant discourse parties. Only norms that survive such scrutiny and prove their intellectual mettle by defeating all comers meet with our normative approval. Simon has developed this position more fully in several essays cited in later notes, but the main lines of his position are discernible from his discussion in this volume.

In what follows, I will focus on his account of broad internalism (interpretivism) because it is an important approach that has received considerable attention in the philosophy of sports literature. I will question whether coaches faced with important ethical decisions need to rely on a philosophically expansive and ultimately ahistorical account of moral reasoning, as Simon suggests is necessary, and offer an alternative approach, which while culturally and historically based retains critical force nonetheless.

Simon thinks that by focusing on the purpose of competitive sports and by insisting that the normative standards we generate in this interpretive manner pass reflective muster, we will help coaches make ethical decisions that are both relevant to what competitive sports is all about, and rationally justifiable to those who might object to them. Rival ethical takes on sports and coaching, Simon argues, fall short—either because they give short shrift to the proper aim of athletic enterprise or to the justificatory discourse necessary to validate principles of athletic conduct, or to both of these pillars of normative inquiry. An example of the former kind of failure, according to Simon, are Kantian-based ethical theories that bypass the question "What is the purpose of competitive sports?" in favor of universal rules that, for example, enjoin persons qua players to treat each other as ends rather than means, which make their relevance to sports strained at best. Examples of the latter sort of failure are virtue-based ethical theories that bypass the reflective testing of norms in favor of the practical judgments (wisdom) of knowledgeable and experienced coaches in particular situations, which weaken considerably their justificatory force. Simon thus thinks he can avoid both horns of this "dilemma of excessive abstraction from our actual situation, on the one hand, and too uncritical an immersion in it, on the other," by keeping his interpretive eyes fixed on the point of athletic enterprise and his reflective gaze fixed on the intellectual warrant of the normative principles generated in this manner.[1]

There is much to like in Simon's impressively argued account of the ethical coach, and I find myself in substantial agreement with what he has to say. But there is an important part of his argument that I do not find fully persuasive and leads me to believe that he has not solved the above dilemma by steering a middle course between "excessive abstraction" and "uncritical immersion." I am troubled by his strong claim that the intellectual force of the arguments required to justify athletic normative principles must be independent of all social or cultural features of actual athletic practices. In his admirably clear words, the "arguments and reasons" that ground these principles must have "justificatory force independent of particular historical or social contexts."[2] The problem with this claim, as I see it, is that the only principles that could clear this extraordinarily high rational bar would be too abstract, too general, too detached from our present sports practices to do the kind of substantive normative work that Simon claims they alone (or mostly alone) are capable of doing. Insisting, as Simon does, that the intellectual warrant of our normative principles of sports rises or falls on the basis of such reflective generality would not only weaken their capacity to serve as determinative guides as to how coaches and players should ethically comport themselves, but considerably weaken their motivational appeal as well, their ability to inspire the relevant parties to live up to the demands they place on them.

That aiming for principles this far removed from the social and historical contexts of sports comes at the severe cost of making them largely irrelevant to athletic practice in the above two senses is a lesson that the so-called hard cases in sports teach us. For it is these hard cases, which stretch to the breaking point the interpretive judgments and intuitions of coaches and players alike, that Simon himself concedes would likely require that we supplement his favored principles of sports with the practical judgment of wise and experienced coaches and players to determine what is or is not the normatively appropriate way to act. Simon is right that practical judgment is often needed in these tough ethical cases. But I want to argue that what is most needed when our normative predicaments require fine-grained normative judgments and responses from us is not so much the personal counsel of wise individuals but the collective counsel of the battle-tested social conventions of sports that shape, or so I will argue, so much of our understanding and appreciation of the purpose and value of competitive sports, to include the so-called practical judgment of coaches and players. It is because these kinds of conventional principles are embedded in our actual athletic practice, which, as we shall see, does not mean they are immune either from misinterpretation or willful violation, that they are able to speak to us more clearly and more forcefully than any set of abstract principles ever could.

However, it is just such conventional counsel that Simon rules out *tout court*, since on his account social conventions, whatever the kind, always bottom out in some sort of social agreement. They are no substitute, as he sees it, for moral evaluation that is based in theory, that is grounded in general principles that best explain the main features of sports and present them ethically in their best light. Conventions, it is implied, are to be evaluated in terms of such a theory and principles, and have no moral standing of their own. In short, conventions need rational support because they are not self-justifying. So from the fact that they are accepted it does not follow that they warrant our intellectual support.

The main focus of my criticism of Simon will thus take issue with this implication, more explicitly stated in his other publications, that conventions are nothing more than social agreements. I contend that Simon is simply mistaken in thinking that social conventions can be reduced to such agreements, that they simply register whatever the prevailing social consensus happens to regard as the purpose of competitive sports. On the contrary, I will argue that social conventions are what make possible rational discourse about the aim of athletic enterprise and reflective assessments of its value. That is because what counts as a good reason, a compelling intellectual consideration, in favor of conceiving competitive sports in one way rather than another, is itself a conventional matter that requires appeal to the relevant conventions without which we would be clueless as to what is the point of athletic engagement.

Interpretivism and the Ethical Coach

I want to begin, however, by considering why Simon's interpretivist rendering of competitive sports takes the abstract route that it does in seeking to validate its key normative principles. It is useful here to cite philosopher and legal theorist Ronald Dworkin's views on this matter since Simon makes it clear that his own normative approach to sports is indebted to Dworkin's normative approach to law. Dworkin thinks that normative inquiry has to reflectively distance itself from our actual social practices because, as he pithily puts it, the principles it yields are supposed to be "our critic, not our mirror." That is to say, normative principles of conduct are supposed to constrain the ways we may desire to act in law and sports to ensure our actions are indeed ethically justified, that they are in keeping with the central aims and values of these valued endeavors. They can't do this if they merely mirror what we are presently doing, if they simply endorse whatever actions we undertake regardless of their effect on the goods that law and sports trade in and the moral respect owed to the people we interact with in these social circles. As Dworkin sees it, then, normative principles "can make no contribution to how we govern ourselves except by struggling against all the impulses that drag us back into our own culture." This requires, he continues, that we make a rational move "toward generality and [therefore] some reflective basis for deciding which of our traditional distinctions [and justifications] . . . are genuine and which spurious, which contribute to the flourishing of the ideals we want." This reflective nod to generality to vindicate our normative principles, he makes abundantly clear, enjoins that we not let our interpretive judgments be influenced by social "convention[s]," since it is these very features of our cultural situation we need to struggle against with all our rational might.[3]

Simon's approach to normative inquiry differs from Dworkin's in one important respect: it claims to start on an historical note. Simon's concession to history, developed fully in his article on realism and discourse,[4] is a provisional and carefully delimited one that has mainly to do with his claim that rational discourse is a historically and culturally bound argumentative practice. Any claim then that giving and asking for reasons requires we repair to an abstract, entirely neutral vantage point is a nonstarter for Simon. Rather, we can begin the deliberative process, he insists, from where we presently find ourselves, from our current historical and social perspective, and argue our way toward a more coherent rationally defensible perspective from which to normatively assess social practices like sports. But such an historical beginning can only get us to where we need to end up, with universally valid normative principles, if and only if the deliberation that occurs in such an historical context is an impartial one through and through. By impartial deliberation Simon means both that all contributions to the discussion be viewed solely according to their intellectual merits rather than whether they support or undermine our own personal views, and that it be open to all comers. These two features of impartial inquiry go together, since if the only thing that matters in our rational deliberations is "the cogency of the argument or pertinence of the point being made," then who is making the argument is beside the point.[5] That means no one can be excluded from the conversation for any reason other than their contributions are either not cogent, or irrelevant, or, of course, both. The basic point of Simon's discourse approach to normative inquiry, therefore, is that conceptions of the point of athletic enterprise and the normative principles that can be divined from them can be considered universally valid ones if they survive this back and forth reflective testing.

On closer inspection, however, Simon's concession to history turns out not to be much of a concession at all. For the very moment conceptions of the purpose and value of sports and the corresponding reasons for favoring or disfavoring certain principles to ensure that purpose and value is realized are offered up for reflective scrutiny, all parties to the deliberations that follow, Simon holds, are supposed to evaluate them by appealing to standards that are, to reiterate, "independent of particular historical or social contexts." That means we can make quick work of the historical context in which such principles are first proposed and proceed apace to argue ourselves out of our culturally bound interpretations of athletic endeavor simply by making them answer to argumentative norms that transcend these cultural boundaries. The normative force of such back and forth discourse, therefore, rises or falls, Simon avers, on whether "it is based on principles and leads to conclusions that purport to be *something more* than a mere historical consensus."[6]

Simon's rendering of interpretivism suggests, then, that reasons or interpretations that are good and intellectually compelling presuppose some neutral, ahistorical perspective that begins with but ultimately transcends cultural practices in specific historical contexts.

On the view I will develop, however, what counts as a good interpretation of sports and a good argument to conceive and treat it in one way rather than another depends on the cultural context, on the social norms shared by particular communities of inquiry that they use to judge such things at particular times. That means that a justification as to how sports should be conceived and how coaches should ethically comport themselves in the athletic arena that works for one audience may not work, indeed may fall on deaf ears, for another audience.

Let me illustrate what I mean by contrasting two different approaches to the appropriate role of strategy in sports that found favor in two different athletic audiences. The first interpretation originated in England and spread quickly to most of Western Europe as well as the United States roughly from the latter half of the nineteenth century to the first few decades of the twentieth, when it started to lose favor. What has come to be called the gentleman-amateur conception of sports rooted the nobility of athletic competition squarely in trying to win but not too vigorously lest it taint our pursuit of athletic excellence by poisoning our social interactions with our fellow competitors. That meant that coaches of the day were obliged, among other things, to maintain a studied nonchalance toward victory merely for the sake of victory and to exhort their athletic charges to be generous toward their opponents, gallant in defeat, and humble in victory. It also meant, most importantly for our purposes, that coaches were obliged to temper their strategic designs so as not to upset the gentlemanly manner in which, at least on this particular interpretation of the point of competitive sports, it was supposed to be conducted.

This amateur-inspired constraint on the use of strategic means to achieve athletic excellence applied especially to the rules of sports, which coaches were to uphold in both letter and spirit. Coaches were supposed to dissuade players from intentionally breaking the rules and even from strategically bending the rules to gain a competitive edge. The sacrosanct regard for the rules characteristic of this amateur rendering of sports presumed that no self-respecting coach or player would ever deliberately contravene them. And what went for deliberately breaking or tinkering with the rules went as well for protesting how officials interpreted and applied them, which according to the amateur credo was strictly forbidden even if the officials were clearly mistaken in their calls. So the tactic of badgering officials for supposed bad calls in order to get a more favorable call later in the game was ethically taboo for coaches of this era.

The amateur censure of strategic manipulation of the rules extended as well to competitive tactics in the game. So strategies that involved, for example, team members setting the pace for their teammates or boxing in opponents in relay foot races and cycling to aid their fellow players were considered ethically unseemly and were criticized as a kind of "collusion" that no ethical coach rightly so called would, or should, stoop so low to employ. Similarly, efforts to "rattle one's opponents," to put them off their game, were also considered normatively out of bounds, as was exploiting vulnerable opponents even when their vulnerability was due to their own infelicitous actions, for example, running their scull aground in a race or dropping their tennis racket in a match. In such cases, players were supposed to wait for their opponents to recover before the competition resumed full-stop, and coaches were supposed to instruct them to act just so.[7] This scanting of strategy by coaches was not owed to a lack of intelligence or imagination on their part, but rather to an ethical conviction they shared that one and all such tactics were vulgar tricks. And while such tricks might have a legitimate place in the "slick" dealings of the marketplace, it was commonly surmised at the time, they ought to have no place in competitive sports, and no place, of course, in the normative repertoire of coaches.[8]

The second take on the proper role of strategy in sports played to a largely American audience, at first at least, and a very different audience at that thanks, among other things, to its growing concern that capitalism's encouragement of a life of ease and sloth was sapping the vitality of the nation, which depended, it supposed, on an active, strenuous life rather than a passive, comfortable one.[9] Social practices like competitive sports, unsurprisingly, were thought to be the right antidote for such capitalist-induced malaise, but only if pursued with utmost vigor and a committed sense of purpose. In this case, then, the uneasiness capitalist markets induced in the American sporting public regarding their cherished athletic practices, its fear it would turn them into halfhearted, lifeless endeavors, prompted it to reinterpret sports in its own distinctive image, one that directly opposed its amateur predecessors' gentlemanly take, borne of the very different worry that the mercenary motive unleashed by the market would destroy the nobility of sports. So instead of honoring the amateur precept that athletes should hold themselves back in their pursuit of athletic excellence, the devotees of this hybrid, modern conception of sports insisted such excellence should be pursued wholeheartedly, with as much effort, commitment, and passion as they could muster. As a consequence, coaches and players alike were given normative dispensation to spare no effort in their quest for athletic glory. That meant, most importantly again for our present purpose, that the amateur prohibition of strategizing lost whatever normative grip it had on this new American sporting audience, and not long after much of the Western sporting audience as well. Spurred on by this refashioned, modern conception of the aim of competitive sports, coaches began to treat sports as a kind of practical problem, indeed a recurring series of such problems, that are best, in the sense of most efficiently, resolved by exercising whatever strategic acumen they possessed.[10] In relatively short order, therefore, the reliance on strategy to win athletic contests, and the view that coaches are to be judged and compensated, in significant part, by their strategic expertise, went from being a much despised vice and a normatively loathsome way to regard sports to a much admired virtue and normatively respectable way to regard it.

This newfound respect for strenuous engagement in sports thus opened the floodgate for all manner of tactical thinking beginning with the rules themselves. Rules, of course, were not to be summarily violated under this new normative athletic regime, not just because such indiscriminate rule breaking and rule bending is hardly strategic, but because complying with the rules still enjoyed substantial normative support. But the rules were no longer regarded as sacrosanct, as directives to be strictly followed no matter the circumstance. Rather, they became fair game for strategic exploitation at certain points in an athletic contest. The strategic foul in basketball is a case in point, in which the point of breaking the rules, for example, deliberately fouling an opponent who is about to make an easy layup, is to gain a competitive advantage precisely by being penalized, by putting one's opponent at the foul line to attempt to make free throws that are, comparatively speaking, more challenging.

The normative license given strategic fouling on this modern take on sports, of course, was only part of the general normative license extended to other similar tactics in the game. For starters, the old, ethically frowned upon strategy of teammates collaborating with one another to improve their chances of winning by setting the pace in a footrace or thwarting one's opponents from gaining the lead in a cycling competition by boxing them in was no longer considered an example of illicit "collusion." On the contrary, it came to be seen as good athletic form rather than bad sportsmanship, as an example of precisely the sort of rational—in the sense of instrumentally rational that informs all such strategic thinking (divining the most efficient means to achieve predetermined ends)—winning play expected of the contemporary coach and athlete. The same rational compliment was to be paid as well, on this interpretation, to athletes who take tactical advantage of their opponents when they find themselves in vulnerable positions by virtue of their own, however unintentional, maladroit actions (recall my previous example of the sculler who inadvertently runs his scull aground). Being generous to one's competitors in such cases so that they can regain their competitive footing now seemed an offense against, rather than an example of, good athletic play, since such self-inflicted athletic misfortunes were reinterpreted as basic strategic lapses—actions that had the athletes adequately planned for they might well have anticipated and avoided. Letting opponents recover when they fall prey to such strategic gaffs on this new, strategy-friendly conception of sports no longer made any sense, rationally or normatively speaking.

What are we take away from these two strikingly different understandings of the normative status of strategy in sports from these two strikingly different athletic audiences? Well, several things, I think. The first is that there are apparently no super purposes when it comes to cultural practices like sports: there are no fixed purposes of athletic endeavor that remain unchanged across history just waiting to be discovered by those with the fortitude to push rational inquiry to the limit. Rather, as our brief foray into sports history shows, the purpose of competitive sports changes as we human agents ourselves change for many varying and complicated reasons and causes. Although both athletic audiences were motivated by the same desire to prevent sports from being overtaken by the market, because they ascribed markedly different purposes to their respective conceptions of sports, and, therefore, to their accounts of the ethical coach, their worries about the corrosive effects of the market were markedly different as well. The differing ways they construed the aim of competitive sports further changed the way they valued sports, to include, importantly, what specific mix of skills they considered integral to genuine athletic achievement. To say that sports serves a specific purpose is to say that certain ways of engaging in it better serve that purpose than others, and thus warrant our normative seal of approval, and other ways of engaging in it either serve it poorly, or not at all, and thus warrant our normative condemnation. This is, of course, why the amateur athletic community reproached coaches who dared to indulge their strategic fancies, since tactical skills were neither recognized nor valued as bona fide athletic skills, and why the modern athletic community that eventually replaced it lauded these very same coaching strategies, since these tactical skills were now recognized and valued as an important feature of true athletic excellence.

A second important moral to be drawn from these two cases is that changes in the conception of the point of athletic enterprise signal a corresponding change in the relevant community's normative vocabulary, specifically, in the evaluative standards, reasons, and thick moral and nonmoral concepts they employ to justify their normative judgments to one another by arguing for their rational cogency. The argumentative process of giving and asking for reasons presupposes that everyone so engaged is on the same page as to what qualifies as a reason in the first place, that, in other words, all parties to the discourse are of one mind regarding the relevant norms that govern such rational exchanges. It would, of course, be ideal if such a normative accord could be somehow stretched to encompass all past and present communities of inquiry and all future communities to come, but as our two examples show, I think, aiming for such universality in our rational judgments about sports, or anything else for that matter, is wishful thinking at best.[11] The reason why is, as Simon himself noted and I approvingly cited, that rational discourse is a culturally and historically bound affair, which means we can only profitably argue about our normative views of sports if we concur on what makes for a good as opposed to a bad argument. What history tells us is that such concurrence is attainable only within a community of inquiry, only within its operative normative vocabulary, which validates certain rational moves and invalidates others regarding proper coaching and player conduct.

But that rational discourse can do its appointed critical work only if it is moved to the interior of normative vocabularies is no reason to despair. For once this move is made we can argue with one another at length and in the requisite impartial manner regarding our reasons for favoring certain views of sports and disfavoring others. Impartiality of this intramural sort means just what Simon claimed it meant: that all contributions to the discourse be considered exclusively on their intellectual merits rather than whether they accord or not with our own considered views, and that it be open to all comers. But the notions of "intellectual merit" and "all comers" need to be suitably qualified to cover only those who share the social norms of rational inquiry of the particular athletic audience in question. Those who don't share these social norms can hardly expect their contributions to the discourse to achieve their intended rational purpose, since the reasons they put on offer will not be recognized as such by members of the relevant community because they have no place in their normative vocabulary. That is, their contributions will be appropriately dismissed not on the illegitimate grounds of who they are, but on the perfectly legitimate grounds that their contributions are not rationally cogent by present lights. So if we were to imagine a debate between devotees of amateur sports, who stoutly maintain that strategy has no legitimate standing in sports rightly so called because it undermines the kind of gentlemanly social interactions that should obtain there, and members of a modern athletic audience of a different cast of mind, who regard strategy to be pivotal to athletic excellence, what we would witness is not, I think, a fruitful give-and-take of reasons but, at best, rival disputants unprofitably talking past one another rather than profitably to one another.[12] Asking for a rational resolution to encounters of this kind, as I see it, is asking far too much because there doesn't seem to be any inferential path that leads from an amateur conception of sports to the modern one here discussed. That is, there is no apparent way rationally to get from an amateur conception of sports as a gentlemanly, strategic-averse pursuit to a modern, pedal-to-the-metal, strategic-receptive one if the argument begins with premises formulated in the old amateur vocabulary, nor, of course, is there a way to rationally pull this off the other way around. Indeed, the only way a debate of this kind could lead to a rationally persuasive outcome is if all the deliberative parties could repair to a third, neutral normative vocabulary in which to adjudicate their conflicting claims. But, of course, it is just such a leap from what I earlier called intramural impartiality to what I now want to call extramural impartiality, to the infamous view from nowhere, that I believe Simon and perhaps other interpretivists would rightly to my mind dismiss as little more than a rational fantasy.

The third, and for my purposes, last moral to be drawn from these historically contrasting interpretations of the aim of athletic endeavor is, in fact, a corollary of the other two. And that is that the principles that serve as the presuppositions of our normative inquiry into sports, as the basic premises of the arguments we formulate to justify our normative judgments to one another, are social conventions that do their justificatory work in a context-dependent manner as opposed to abstract principles that supposedly do their work in a context-independent manner.

What this means is that the idea that sports is best thought of as a gentlemanly engagement is itself a conventional idea, that is, an interpretation of the purpose of competitive sports that, again for various complicated reasons and causes, originated in and found favor with members of the amateur athletic community, and from which they derived their central normative principles regarding appropriate ethical conduct for coaches and players alike. As we have seen in the case of the ethical coach, that conventional take on sports led to the normative directive that coaches refrain from any tactical attempt to manipulate the rules or their opponents. So the key arguments amateurs of the time mounted to defend their claim that strategizing of this sort was not a legitimate part of the game, that it fell outside the relevant skills that are supposed to be tested in athletic competition, can be traced back directly to their reigning convention that sports warrants our normative approval if, and only if, pursued in moderation. Of course, the contrasting modern idea that sports is best thought of as a strenuous engagement through and through, one that calls for our full commitment and unsparing effort, which as we noted opened the door and gave wide berth to coaches and players alike to exercise their strategic wiles, is also a conventional idea, as are the main arguments its proponents mounted to defend the robust role they thought strategy should play in competitive sports.

The notion that our best interpretations of sports and the normative principles and arguments we formulate on their behalf are conventions is what makes interpretivists like Simon nervous because they view the social agreements that underwrite such conventions as a threat to rational argument itself. If our normative standards amount to nothing more than conventions, then claims such as the cited amateur one that coaches should shun strategizing because it corrupts sports, or its modern successor that coaches should welcome strategizing because it enriches sports, have nothing going for them save that different athletic audiences find them variously attractive or unattractive. What goes importantly missing in such cases is whether or not the claims made are rationally defensible, that is, to paraphrase Simon, whether we agree to them because we find them intellectually meritorious or find them intellectually meritorious because we agree to them. If the former, then our normative principles, to recall Dworkin's point, rightly serve as our "critic"; however, if the latter, then our normative principles wrongly serve as our "mirror." This is no minor point since everything turns on whether or not they maintain their critical edge. For if our normative principles simply rubber-stamp whatever it is we do in the athletic arena, then they have not just served us poorly but have utterly failed us. It is easy to see why because in that event "the status quo [would be] right . . . just [because] it is the status quo, not [because] it is supported by defensible reasons."[13] In other words, it would mean that an athletic audience could never be wrong about its normative judgments as to what is or is not appropriate athletic conduct, because what counts as a correct normative judgment on this conventional rendering is whatever the relevant athletic audience says it is.[14]

Simon's concern that normative inquiry not be coopted by the status quo is a legitimate worry. But his claim that a conventional take on normative inquiry of the kind I am endorsing here cannot but lead to such an uncritical result is, I think, mistaken. For as I have already noted rational discourse is itself a social practice, one that can only do its intellectual bidding if the deliberative parties are of one mind regarding what are the relevant rules of argument. And what I have been arguing is that the sort of social agreements that underlie our conventional interpretations of what is the purpose and value of competitive sports, and that ground the rational standards by which we assess their cogency as applied, for instance, to ethical coaching, are what allow argument and the crucial self-correcting role it plays to do its critical work.[15] So conventions rightly understood are not an excuse for us to take leave of giving and asking for reasons in favor of crudely tallying people's preferences, but what makes possible such giving and asking for reasons in the first place.

Implications for Coaches

If we give up on the idea that we can somehow turn conventional normative principles into unconventional, universal ones by waiving our rational wand, are we not conceding, just as critics of conventionalism like Simon have re-peatedly pointed out, that they lack any critical force? For if rational delibera-tion is powerless to effect such a change in our conventions, then, as noted, whatever an athletic community says is the aim of athletic enterprise must be right, can't be corrected, because all we have to go on, apparently, is its collec-tive word.

Not so, I counter, with one important qualification: while conventional-ism, at least the kind I am peddling, doesn't nullify the all-important self-correcting role that rational discourse alone can play, it does nullify what I take to be the more radical and untenable version of this claim that would have us believe that an *entire* athletic audience could be mistaken, and ration-ally shown to be so, about its conventional understanding of sports. For my conventionalist account does entail, unlike Simon's ahistorical alternative, that we can't meaningfully distinguish between what such a community thinks is the purpose of competitive sports and the ethical conduct that com-ports with it, and what it *really* is. That might seem like a knock against it, but I think otherwise because the claim that a whole community might be wrong about the point of its athletic enterprises strikes me as implausible on its face given that cultural practices like sports are social rather than natural kinds. That is, the purpose of sports is not something we discover but something we create, and since we, the relevant athletic community, are the creators, it's hard to see how we could be wholly wrong about what we have created. However, we can be, and often are, wrong about what inferences we draw from the premises formulated in our conventional normative vocabulary. For instance, we might come to see by the arguments we trade back and forth with the aid of that vocabulary that the premises of our arguments commit us to conclu-sions we have not previously drawn, in other words, that we have erred in our inferential judgments and are thereby compelled to accept these new conclu-sions and drop the old ones. This is quite enough, to my mind, to vouch for the critical credentials of conventionalist accounts like mine, in which the force of the better argument, rather than the sum of the audience members' preferences, serves as the final arbiter of their considered views.

I only have space to offer one example of such an inferential error to buttress my claim that conventional normative principles are not lacking in critical potency. That example has to do with the mix of tactics that fall under the umbrella of so-called gamesmanship, which has been gaining traction of late in certain athletic quarters, and in which its defenders seem to think that its normative legitimacy derives from that accorded to strategizing in general on the modern interpretation of sports. Gamesmanship can take many different forms, but the particular form I want to discuss involves what Howe aptly calls the "artful manipulation of the rules," in which coaches attempt to exploit the technicalities of the rules in order to gain a competitive advantage.[16] Perhaps the most famous (or infamous) case of such gamesmanship was the so-called pine tar incident in which Kansas City Royals baseball player George Brett's winning home run was disallowed because the pine tar on his bat exceeded that allowed by the rules.[17] What distinguished this case from other familiar examples of called rule violations is that Brett's indiscretion would have gone unnoticed, and so uncalled, were it not for the fact that Billy Martin, manager of the opposing New York Yankees, brought it to the head umpire's attention the moment Brett crossed home plate. Now, that Martin acted as he did by informing the chief umpire of the rule violation is, in itself, of no moment, since knowing the rules of baseball inside and out and pointing out when they are broken to game authorities is something we rightly expect of good coaches. What is of moment, however, and what makes this a case of gamesmanship rather than simple managerial acumen, is that Martin had noticed much earlier in the season that Brett's bat had an excess of pine tar on it but decided to wait for the most advantageous opportunity to disclose this information to the umpires. The ruse worked at first, since after being so informed, and after a brief deliberation, the umpires called Brett out for using an illegal bat. But it ultimately failed because when the Royals appealed the ruling to the president of the American League, Lee MacPhail, he overturned the umpires' decision.

MacPhail reasoned that although Brett was technically in violation of the rules, he gained no competitive advantage by his overuse of pine tar, as he clearly would have, for instance, if he had resorted instead to using a corked bat. In other words, MacPhail was saying that strictly applying the rule in this instance interfered with, rather than abetted, the purpose of competitive sports. By implication, he was also saying that Martin's exercise of managerial cunning in choosing at that opportune moment to inform the umpires of Brett's doctored bat also interfered with the aim of sports, because it was that tactical decision that provoked the umpires to rule in the wrong way, and thus to deprive Brett of his rightful athletic accomplishment. MacPhail's reasoning here is crucial to seeing why Martin and his defenders erred in thinking that the normative pass given managerial tactics like the strategic foul on this modern rendering of sports warrants giving the same normative pass to managerial tactics like the artful manipulation of the rules specific to gamesmanship.

That the umpires in the Brett case, in my view, got this wrong and MacPhail got it right, and that other members of the modern athletic community might be similarly divided in their judgments about this and like cases, shows, I argue, that conventional normative principles do indeed have critical force, that they not only make possible but require that we argue about what inferences properly follow from the premises they lay down, that like any other norms they can only do their work if the self-correcting role of rational argument is given its just due.

I'd like to think that if the umpires had the time to reflectively reconsider their initial judgments after the fact, and that if members of the modern athletic audience who were initially inclined to lump Martin's gamesmanship together with tactics like the strategic foul were to do the same, that MacPhail's argument would carry the day.[18] Of course, I may be wrong about this, and, in any event, have no way of knowing what the outcome of such an argument might be without joining in the argument itself—something I have been taking an initial stab at here. But trying to predict how this argument might turn out is beside the point. The moral of this story is that, contrary to critics of conventionalism, like all good normative theories, this theory not only sets us to arguing about what is the appropriate aim of competitive sports but, by spelling out what are the relevant rules of argument in this regard, makes it further possible for us to give a rationally persuasive answer to this all-important question. Thus, one can argue, on the basis of the reflective form of conventionalism that I have defended, that there are important limits to the kind of gamesmanship that coaches can employ that are morally defensible without being ahistorical, and that are rationally supportable without the sort of context-independent philosophical theory required by interpretivism.

Conclusion

To sum up, then, I think Simon is entirely right that ethical decision making is an indispensable dimension of "good" coaching, and that the normative theory he calls interpretivism is, if tweaked in the conventionalist way I suggest here, the best account of how ethical coaches should form their ethical judgments and justify them to others. My only disagreement with Simon, therefore, is his insistence that normative inquiry be carried out until we can certify that the principles that ground coaches' ethical determinations of how they should comport themselves are universally valid ones, which requires, of course, that the conventional starting points of such inquiry be somehow reflectively circumvented. I remain unconvinced that any normative probing of sports or for that matter any other kindred cultural practice can pull off this seemingly magical transition from the historical and contingent to the universal and necessary. That is why I maintain that trying to turn what are essentially conventional athletic normative principles into nonconventional ones is not a surefire way to establish their validity, but rather a surefire way to undermine their critical force and relevance. Coaches, then, should develop their ethical views by critically understanding, probing, and reflecting on the cultural traditions and practices in which they are embedded, which is not an argument for the status quo but for reforming it when such critical examination reveals that the status quo itself violates the conventions that underpin these traditions and practices.

Questions for Review and Discussion

1. Distinguish between Simon's version of broad internalism (interpretivism) and the author's conventionalist version. Now, contrast the author's conventionalist rendering of interpretivism with Kantian and virtue approaches to coaching ethics.

2. Explain why conventionalism of the kind the author develops here still qualifies as a critical theory, that is, as a theory that can be used to criticize dominant views of sports. Do you agree it is a critical theory, or do you think it is far more supportive of the status quo than it intimates?

3. The author distinguishes between intramural and extramural notions of impartiality. Explain the importance of this distinction in justifying coaches' ethical views. Is the distinction valid in your view?

4. Is the author's argument persuasive that the modern view of strategy does not justify tactics like gamesmanship? Or can you think of a way to justify gamesmanship based on the modern understanding of the strategic foul?

5. Is the author correct to argue that proponents of the amateur model of competition and proponents of the contemporary strategic/competitive model must inevitably talk past each other and never engage intellectually because they speak from different cultural and historical contexts? (See note 12 as well as discussion in the text.) Could Simon reply that we can't

know in advance of trying whether they could reach a rationally defensible consensus and cite a sport such as professional golf that blends competitive intensity with courtesy and even generosity toward opponents as an example of a reasonable compromise between both ideals?

Suggestions for Further Reading

Berman, Michael. "On Interpretivism and Formalism in Sports Officiating: From General to Particular Jurisprudence." *Journal of the Philosophy of Sport* 38 (2011).

Dixon, Nicholas. "Canadian Figure Skaters, French Judges, and Realism in Sport." *Journal of the Philosophy of Sport* 8 (2003).

Rader, Benjamin. *American Sports: From the Age of Folk Games to the Age of Televised Sports.* Upper Saddle River, NJ: Prentice-Hall, 2004.

Simon, Robert. "From Ethnocentrism to Realism: Can Discourse Ethics Bridge the Gap?" *Journal of the Philosophy of Sport* 31 (2004): 122–141.

Weatherby, W. J. *Chariots of Fire.* New York: Dell, 1981.

Six

Why the Coach Needs a Philosophy: A Pragmatist's Suggestions

DOUG HOCHSTETLER

You never arrive.
Take care of the little things.

More than twenty years removed from my intercollegiate football playing days, these words continue to resonate. I remember these comments and, more importantly, have attempted to embody these bits of wisdom in my life as I teach, write, and raise a family. These words are connected with a specific location, specific individual, and specific team. I heard them in Orange City, Iowa, as a member of a Northwestern College football team coached by Larry Korver. It is possible that I would have learned these lessons in a different setting (through music, the arts, or some other extracurricular activity), but this experience occurred because of my commitment to *this particular* football team. As a result, and coupled with my own attitude of openness, I grew as an athlete, scholar, and individual. I learned a great deal during this formative time of my life, playing wide receiver—how to explode from the line of scrimmage, run crisp pass patterns, and catch the football with my hands rather than my chest. I also learned lessons that extended past the football field, lessons about preparation, dedication, selflessness, and more. My experience occurred, in part, as a result of an individual philosophy of coaching—the ideas and beliefs embodied in Coach Korver's approach to his profession.

Developing a personalized set of beliefs and values is an important task for coaches, a step acknowledged by those in the sport-related professions.[1] Some recommend formalizing a personal coaching philosophy.[2] David Parsh, for example, outlines "Eight Steps to a Coaching Philosophy," posing questions[3] for coaches that prompt critical thinking and reflection. Helpful as these attempts are, the process of developing a coaching philosophy does not guarantee that the coach will actually live out the identified beliefs in practice. A coach may preach team discipline, for example, while failing personally to live in a disciplined manner. An additional concern, one more central to this chapter, is the tendency for coaches to develop a philosophy with an overly rigid approach—what Dweck terms a fixed mind-set—a belief system that is dogmatic and unyielding to change.[4]

These concerns point toward themes that American philosopher Henry Bugbee examined regarding the idea of certainty.[5] In addition to the technical decision making that coaches face regarding substitution patterns, styles of play, and training methods, coaching involves complex interpersonal relationships. As Hardman and Jones explain, "Coaches work with persons, not machines."[6] Given the difficulty and uncertainty characteristic of coaching, and the tenuous process of developing and living out an examined philosophy, how do coaches know the ideals they have chosen are the right ones, or are effective? Is certainty a state that coaches should necessarily strive for or attain? This certainty extends from the abstract, theoretical commitments to the day-to-day ways coaches live out these ideals as well. For example, to what extent does certainty relate to calling a play, inserting a particular player into the lineup, moving from man defense to zone, switching from primarily long-distance training to training with interval emphasis, and so forth?

In this chapter I will introduce Bugbee's writing and approach to philosophy, examine his notion of certainty, and describe the import for this reframed notion of certainty for coaching philosophies. I have in mind not merely any coaching philosophy and its implementation, but a normative sense of what it means for "good coaches" to develop and implement such a system. Here, following Loland, I am interested in how the good coach combines scientific or technical knowledge with the "practical search for reflective and good choices in the many dilemmas of his or her profession in split decision situations, [which requires] morally sound intuitions and reaction patterns."[7] The capability to negotiate these decisions requires a type of practical wisdom developed through what Standal and Hemmestad describe as the "right experience . . . [through becoming] good by doing good deeds . . . and this in turn is dependent on being in the presence of good role models."[8] Here

Bugbee provides assistance for developing a personal philosophy based on both personal experience and practical wisdom.

Coaching and Philosophy

The relationship between coaching and philosophy may not be readily apparent. Yet, as Walton explains, "To coach is to believe in something: the game, the athlete, the quest for excellence, the process of challenging one's self and striving to overcome."[9] Coaches, like philosophers, intentionally work toward clarifying ideas and beliefs. Although they do not engage in formal philosophical study, coaches deal with theoretical concepts such as justice, equality, and benevolence every day. For example, how might a coach distribute playing time between two athletes, one (a starter with stellar ability) who does not practice during the week because of a chronic hamstring injury and another athlete (one with limited talent) who remains committed to daily practices and workouts? How might a youth sport coach address this situation versus a high school or college coach? Additionally, how might the coach deal with a slumping player? Does the athlete's performance (or lack of it) justify an immediate reduction in playing time? Or does the coach stick with the slumping player in order to demonstrate confidence in a player who has a history of performing well?

When I refer to a coaching philosophy, I mean, borrowing from Lyle, "a comprehensive statement about the beliefs and behaviors that will characterize the coach's practice."[10] This collection of ideals may have philosophical underpinnings, such as a commitment to humanism, equality, fair play, or cooperation. Coaching philosophies have value in that they guide coaching actions and relationships, provide focus and clarity, and enable coaches to communicate their ideas and rationale to athletes, parents, and alumni. In many ways constructing and implementing a coaching philosophy involves the classical notion of *technē*.[11] Individual coaches identify a set of beliefs, guidelines, and practices that they believe will work. They are confident of these methods but not absolutely sure they will be successful. Many coaches copy philosophies from other coaches or modify them to mesh with a particular group of student athletes. At times they are representative of the broader coaching culture, while on other occasions they may be more idiosyncratic.[12]

As an example of specific coaching principles, former college basketball coach and athletic director Harry Sheehy[13] detailed the value he placed on work ethic. More than an abstract notion, this idea guided his approach to coaching basketball and included team selection. Sheehy described a potential team member, a player with limited ability who worked "endlessly" and "had a ball with him all the time." Because of the value Sheehy placed on work ethic, he took a risk and selected the student athlete for his team. This player eventually captained an NCAA Division III Sweet Sixteen team, confirming Sheehy's decision and underscoring the value of work ethic in his coaching philosophy.

All coaches employ a coaching philosophy, even though some may not articulate what ideals drive their decision making. Coaches demonstrate an implicit set of values even if their beliefs are not made explicit. A coach who contends that he does not rely on any general principles—for example, choosing to "wing it"—demonstrates a tendency toward contextualism. This coach makes decisions on a case-by-case basis, which is a particular kind of philosophical approach. Alternatively, deciding to shun the use of general principles may reflect skepticism, another type of philosophical position. The more central concern in these cases is, then, how to evaluate the type of philosophical approaches coaches construct and employ.

Developing this philosophical method—toward the sport, the athletes, and other individuals—requires the approach of a scientist and an artist. Coaches learn about the technical side of coaching in formal settings (through coaching education programs, through apprentice-like positions as assistants), acquiring the wisdom of the coaching community. This might include acquiring coaching education research related to pedagogy, training principles, or athlete-coach relationships. Yet coaches must find a way to integrate these conceptual notions as they work with and mold specific teams and individuals This process involves using theoretical knowledge in an applied manner—using pedagogical principles, for example, to teach budding basketball players how to shoot or defend; or leadership concepts to guide team captains toward ideals such as courage or selflessness. Following the development process, the coach must fully implement the philosophy, not simply stating the ideas and beliefs but actually translating these ideals into how one interacts with athletes, other coaches, officials, fans, and the media.

Coaches face tension over telling athletes how to live or letting them learn how to live on their own. Working with eighteen- to twenty-two-year-olds, for example, college coaches arguably should try to prepare athletes to make decisions autonomously, using critical thinking skills to bring this about. The athletes are growing toward adulthood, and the coach will not always be present to hand out praise or punishment. Even at the youth sport level, coaches should allow athletes to help in the decision-making process, guiding them along the way toward a developing personal agency. Part of the creative nature of incorporating a coaching philosophy is determining how to apply the theoretical concepts in practice.

Additionally, the construction of a coaching philosophy is both an individual and a communal process. An individual coach must own the beliefs and has ultimate authority in its authoring, even as the coach may consult other more experienced coaches for ideas, or glean from other coaching philosophies. The coach develops his own belief system, often drawing heavily from personal experience, for good and, at times, for ill. If, as an athlete, the coach played for a disciplinarian, then the younger coach may be more inclined to implement a similar coaching style. Likewise, a coach who spent time as a benchwarmer may develop ways to help all team members feel empowered and valued.

While coaches construct their philosophical ideals individually, this process often occurs against a communal backdrop such as an athletic department, institution, and athletic conference. For example, institutions may hire coaches with philosophical ideals consistent with an overall athletic department belief system. The coach develops these beliefs within the context of a particular sport ethos and practice. A youth soccer coach may construct a philosophy different from a collegiate soccer coach whose philosophy may be different yet from one constructed by a Premier League coach. Yet all three philosophies may contain common threads, given the nature of soccer and the wisdom found in literature of the coaching profession.

Coaches are not interested in merely theoretical ideas. They may love to discuss the intricacies of the triangle offense or particular motivational strategies, but they are much more concerned with how these ideas work. Division I coaches, for example, do not receive contract extensions based on their philosophical ideals but on how their teams perform, meaning how many wins or championships they attain; or, more recently, how many student athletes graduate from their programs. Coaches generally only philosophize in terms of the cash value. They want to see results and effectiveness, regardless of how this is quantified or valued.

Coaches strive for certainty and being absolutely confident in team selection, play calling, practice planning, and goal creation. Yes, there may be times of doubt or regret, times when they wish they had made different decisions. But when the moment of decision making appears, any hint of indecision appears, generally speaking, as weakness. Proceeding with certainty provides direction and projects confidence. Athletes do not want to follow or listen to coaches who project uncertainty. Granted, there may be occasions when a coach's uncertainty is viewed with respect, for example, in regard to situational play-calling. The coach may solicit input and place the ultimate decision-making responsibility with the athletes, in other words placing certainty in soliciting player input. Former Los Angeles Lakers coach Phil Jackson was especially noted for allowing his players to make decisions in particular situations. While this may have worked for Jackson, on occasion, it, like so many coaching decisions, depends on the relationship between coach and athletes. In these situations the coach becomes vulnerable and has to trust the players.

What kind of balance should coaches seek with regard to certainty? How does a conviction to act impact coaches, their philosophies, and ultimately how they interact with their athletes? Part of this depends on what we mean by certainty and how this concept is applied. Bugbee wrote at length about certainty, the import of which impacts sport and coaching in meaningful ways.

Bugbee and Certainty

Henry Bugbee (1915–1999) is an important part of the American philosophical tradition, following on the heels of Ralph Waldo Emerson, Henry David Thoreau, William James, and John Dewey. Bugbee's work is not intentionally instrumental and yet his writings contain themes at the heart of this philosophical creation process for coaches. To understand Bugbee, it is important to examine the philosophical conversation to which he belongs. As an American pragmatist, Bugbee reacted to themes found in earlier theories of knowledge known as rationalism and pragmatism. Rationalist philosophers such as René Descartes argued that knowledge grew out of foundational beliefs that were certain, impossible to doubt, and grounded in reason. Empiricists such as John Locke and David Hume argued instead that knowledge was founded on the senses, but viewed basic sense experience as foundational and certain. Rationalists and empiricists alike, then, maintained that knowledge was established on a foundation and regarded proof based on the foundation as the source of knowledge. Some later foundationalists relinquished the requirement of certainty but still maintained that knowledge rests on base beliefs that are fundamental compared to those derived from them.

Pragmatists developed an alternative approach that rejects foundationalism but also attempts to avoid skepticism and relativism. What they hoped to move toward instead is warranted assertibility, evidential support that is less than certain. In other words, the pragmatists emphasized that a specific position is or at least should be regarded as correct and true until something better is found. Closely related to pragmatism, writers such as Thoreau and Emerson represented transcendentalism, which advocated for a sense of self-reliance and self-awakening. These writers believed that some form of the "good life" (including knowledge) was available to those who remained alert to both self and nature.

Bugbee drew heavily from both pragmatists and transcendentalists, but refused to be defined by either philosophical tradition. He describes his mode of inquiry as "experiential," carving out a position for philosophical discovery that is not "a disclosure of the nature of objects."[14] Rather, Bugbee places more emphasis on the transactional relationships between humans and their environments. For example, both Bugbee and John Dewey emphasize the importance of aesthetic experiences—moments when our senses become heightened and are etched in memory. While Bugbee advocates for this meaning-seeking kind of life, he did not believe Dewey's scientific method or technical explanations generated this meaning by itself. The meaningful life, Bugbee argues, is not derived at entirely through scientific deduction or method, but also through direct contact with things and built on relationships. Bugbee advocates for a "felt clarity" rather than a strict reliance on "analytical clarity."[15] In this sense Bugbee runs alongside the transcendentalism of Thoreau with a premium placed on attentiveness.

Bugbee's approach toward philosophy related directly to personal experience, sifting through streams of consciousness as they appeared to him beside the Schuylkill River or Canadian Rockies. He advocates for attention to these wilderness experiences, especially noting their aesthetic qualities. His experiential approach began not with formal hypotheses or rigid formulas, nor did it necessarily entail any logical schema. Rather, Bugbee's method involves the very situation at hand and the themes that develop through the course of his immersion experiences. He then develops these ideas through the course of his journals and other academic writing.

Certainty became a prominent topic for Bugbee and runs throughout his writings. Rather than seeking a foundational version of ultimate certainty, however, Bugbee aimed to reclaim the concept in another manner. He writes that "certainty lies at the root of action that makes sense . . . a basis for action rather than arrival at a terminus of endeavor."[16] Certainty, for Bugbee, is the starting point, a place to begin, a place that acknowledges an aspect of fallibilism yet proceeds with hope. In this sense the theme of certainty aligned with a pragmatic notion of warranted assertability. Anderson describes Bugbee's certainty as a "working certainty" rather than a final and closed version.[17] Again, Bugbee writes that "certainty is profoundly resolute, but I would mark it out in diametrical contrast with complacency or being of a closed mind."[18] This notion of certainty helps inform our understanding of coaching and decision making, especially the point about open-mindedness.

In the same way, a coach's philosophy does not need to be dogmatic and may be written in pencil, so to speak. The coach must start somewhere, a particular point in time and space with a particular experience as a backdrop. With this working certainty the coach takes into consideration past experience and the present circumstances in order to reach the felt clarity. To do so the coach must listen to "things [or in our case, players] saying themselves" as Bugbee notes.[19] Coaches, then, are certain to the extent that this mind-set enables them to make decisions, identify beliefs, plan practices, recognize recruits, discern plays, and so forth. This type of certainty does not restrict reflection or dialogue. At times coaches may realize they have made a poor decision but use this as an opportunity for growth. In this way certainty becomes a continual testing ground, placing the felt clarity alongside personal experience to see what works in the real world. Bugbee continually verified his experiential intimations, and good coaching requires a similar confirmation of sport-related intuition.

Finally, this working certainty does not entail any "having" or "possessing." Bugbee writes, "I seriously doubt if the notion of 'certainty of,' or 'certainty that' will take us accurately to the heart of the matter. It seems to me that certainty is at least very much akin to hope and faith."[20] In this way, Bugbee reframes the concept in a surprising way, aligning certainty with the seemingly uncertain concepts of hope and faith. His point is that in order to act—for the philosopher, theologian, or coach—one must have a starting point and belief that the actions are pointing somewhere and make a difference. Bugbee continues that certainty is "not a matter of knowledge we can be said to *possess*" and instead is "a mode of being rather than of having."[21] He places great emphasis on relationships and the interchanges between people, between individuals and nature. As coaches relate to and with their athletes, for example, they learn about themselves, lessons of patience, dedication, love, and sacrifice through their commitment to the coaching profession.

Bugbee, Knowledge, and Truth

Bugbee's theory of knowledge and truth draws from both transcendental and pragmatic veins of thought. He argues for attention to both self and others, an alertness to intimations through reflection and commitment. Bugbee also recognizes that these intimations potentially lead toward growth: "That which illuminates our labors, in reflection as in other channels of endeavor, that which decisively empowers us in the deed, comes as an unanticipated precipitation of meaning."[22] By acting in concert with nature we acquire meaning and understanding in ways that we would not be able to fully predict, rationalize, or explain. Yet Bugbee wants us to trust these intimations, even as we test them out in the course of our lives. Arriving at meaning or knowledge does not mean avoiding rational thought but is rather an extension, enhancing how we interpret nature and understand our place in the world.

The attentive coach develops an awareness that provides knowledge and guidance in many ways. This awareness enables coaches to develop a feel for how their athletes are performing, which can inform substitution patterns and tactical methods. In terms of decision making, this alertness enables the coach to call a particular play as it comes to mind, one that fits the particulars of the situation, or mindfulness that impacts how one deals with disciplinary or relational issues. In addition, an attentiveness to team dynamics provides the coach with necessary information to develop team rules of conduct. At times the coach may decide to take more leadership in determining these guidelines, while on other occasions he may solicit more team input. For example, a team with seasoned veterans could benefit from this athlete wisdom, while a younger team, with unproven leadership, may benefit from the coach providing more of the input.

Bugbee goes on to write that philosophy is not "set up like the solution of a puzzle, worked out with all the pieces lying there before the eye. It will be more like the clarification of what we know in our bones."[23] Constructing a belief system, in other words, is not a predetermined, totally logical method of attaining certainty but rather an ongoing confirmation through experience. In this sense, experience impacts knowledge. From experiences interacting with others, coaches know, if they are attentive, how people act and react. Coaches understand how individual athletes respond to discipline, to encouragement, to direction—and that each athlete may respond in different ways throughout their respective career. In addition, coaches also recognize their own particular style, forming judgments about the methods and goals that seem to fit. Hopefully, coaches have the individual athletes' and team's best interests in mind, although at times the coach's ego may get in the way.[24]

The knowledge Bugbee has in mind, while challenging to describe, is not ineffable. Bugbee hopes to describe the everyday places and experiences that give rise to this kind of meaning. In this sense Bugbee is democratic in his appreciation for human experience to shape knowledge. He uses narratives as a method to understand the process of acquiring knowledge and meaning, detailing his experiences swamping, building a dam, and rowing. In the same way, we need to recognize and acknowledge the ordinary experiences that coaches undergo, experiences that have a bearing on the way these individuals develop, interpret, change, and understand their coaching philosophies. As an example of the import for coaches, Bugbee writes of his time spent rowing under the tutelage of Coach John Schultz. In Bugbee's words, Schultz was "interested in rowing wherever it was being done. . . . There was never any doubt about John's absorption in any rowing."[25] Bugbee's experience rowing for Schultz impacted Bugbee in terms of knowledge—not only in a physiological manner but also as a means to grow in his writing and philosophical thinking.

Bugbee is not renouncing deductive logic, critical thinking, or the scientific method. Trained as a philosopher, he realizes the value of the philosophic method and the analytical approach. His point is that the analytical approach is not the only method at our disposal, nor is it necessarily the best one. Bug-bee points toward other means: "I want the truth, marrow-bone truth, and I find the intimations of it whenever I am alive to things, even the most familiar and commonplace things, for the wilderness I take them to comprise."[26] Knowledge, then, requires getting close to, or immersed in, our everyday milieu as opposed to merely observing our surroundings from some theoretical and detached point of view. For coaches this means through attentiveness to practice and game settings, with athletes, colleagues, parents, and alumni, an immersion and commitment to the coaching profession.

Anderson, writing of Bugbee's sense of knowledge, says we "live in wilderness with things, and their residual wildness both demands our respect and attention and resists any complete 'knowing' on our part."[27] In a similar way coaches live in and with their athletes, their assistants, and the public. To coach well demands an attentiveness to and respect for these various groups and individuals. However, the coach cannot, now matter how much she tries, know her athletes in totality regardless of this attentiveness. As Bugbee clarifies, "Things exist in their own right; it is a lesson that escapes us except as they hold us in awe."[28] In other words, coaches can accept athletes for who they are, acknowledging that through a sustained commitment to the practice community, both coach and athlete will grow.

A coaching philosophy begins with various commitments (e.g., to humanistic coaching, to treating athletes as individuals, man-to-man defense, nationwide recruiting), and yet the coach may find that some, or all, of these judgments need to change over time—with a different team, against a different schedule, in a certain economic situation. Experience breeds confidence with decision making and developing this quality of certainty. Novice coaches make decisions that provide information for future decisions. This process helps develop a sense of certainty, fostering clarity of focus and direction. Throughout the course of his professional life, the coach with this working certainty remains firm in day-to-day decisions, yet open to ongoing interactions with the world and others. Despite the tension that exists between firm commitments and openness to change, the coach must move forward. On this note, Anderson writes that "it is precisely because of the precariousness of our situation that we require faith and working certainties to act, to live."[29] We need at least a working certainty in order to live out our humanity. We may never have a final sense of certainty, may never know *for sure* of our athletes' devotion to the team, or our own job security, but we need at least a modicum of these qualities in order to act and live. This working certainty develops through promises and trust, between individuals who interact with each other over time.

Implications for Coaches

If Bugbee is right about this working certainty, what does it mean for coaches with regard to their philosophies and the way this impacts their coaching? In this final section I want to briefly suggest three aspects crucial to these tasks—risk, humility, and alertness—and the extent to which they relate to both coaching philosophies and also their application to ethical issues. First, Bugbee's working certainty involves a degree of risk, a willingness to commit and become immersed in projects without absolute clarity. By its very nature, coaching necessitates taking calculated risks, developing and living out beliefs and ideals. Attempting to construct or even modify one's coaching philosophy is a daunting task and often is scrutinized by a public audience. Should the coach emphasize trust or integrity or excellence or perhaps another theoretical ideal?

In an ethical sense, our human projects and relationships inevitably contain both complexity and risk. Perhaps the safest route is to forgo coaching altogether—whether this is on a volunteer basis or as a profession. Some individuals actually come to this conclusion, determining that overinvolved parents, spoiled athletes, or unreasonable administrators and alumni create too much stress. In many ways highly pressurized sport settings are not about learning and growing through risk. Rather, coaches often seek to control as much as possible, from pregame meal selection to curfew hours to warm-up drills and more.[30] Yet the decisions coaches make require risk on a daily basis—which athletes to recruit, which drills to employ, or which motivational strategies to use and to what degree.

However, the very uncertainty and degree of risk in sport can be viewed through an appreciative lens. Anderson contends that our human achievements occur because of our individual and corporate exertion. He writes that these efforts "require that both we and those who have a stake in our performances take a gamble. They require a risk, and we are all too often afraid."[31] Some coaches realize the inexact nature of their position and yet are willing to invest in their athletes. Bugbee's crew coach, John Schultz, provides an example in this respect. Because of his love for rowing and for people, he entered the coaching ranks and remained committed to his craft. Furthermore, the decisions Schultz made impacted Bugbee and other athletes as well—his choices (and risks) made a difference. Simply put, coaching philosophies matter a great deal. These beliefs impact how coaches interact with others, how they handle disappointment and success. Coaches stake themselves to their beliefs and, in the right situation, coaching philosophies lived out by men and women impact the lives of their players, some of whom become coaches as well.

This aspect of risk also comes into play with regard to how coaches treat their athletes. This means considering these individuals as ends in themselves rather than as means to another end, not placing the athletes in situations where the likelihood of harm may occur. For example, the coach should understand that pushing an athlete to return to the playing field too soon after a concussion, even with a championship on the line, may create long-term health hazards. Other areas of note may include measuring the risk inherent in training programs, practice drills, and techniques, in addition to the overall emotional climate of team activities. As a friend of mine, a highly successful college basketball coach, once noted, he tries to use his program to build up athletes, rather than using athletes to build up his program.

In addition to involving risk, Bugbee's work necessitates humility, a theme that permeates Bugbee's work and fittingly serves as his final entry in *The Inward Morning*: "I am not content with what I have worked out; but I have worked out enough, perhaps, to be content to consider more carefully as I move along, and to welcome all manner of thinking other than my own."[32] Similarly, as coaches make decisions they need to work out their philosophical ideals, moving forward as though they are correct—while accepting the fact that they could be mistaken or that these beliefs could change. Heie describes humility in a similar manner: "I will seek to express my *commitment* to certain 'truths' with clarity. At the same time, I must be characterized by *openness* to the possibility that I am all wrongheaded about some of my present beliefs and need correction."[33] Coaches find themselves living with this tension of commitment on the one hand and openness on the other. This quality of humility impacts the way they interact with other people and conduct their responsibilities.

While many coaches demonstrate humility, other coaches become chained to their beliefs with very little flexibility and may exhibit hubris rather than humility. These individuals may be reluctant to even consider other approaches because they have been successful with their methods and beliefs thus far. They may be successful in spite of these ideals, however, rather than because of them. For example, many point to accolades heaped on former college basketball coach Bobby Knight. His motivational strategies included harsh and even arguably abusive tactics. One could certainly ask whether he might have attained similar objective measures of success (i.e., wins and championships) with a style of coaching representative of humility and openness.

The coach who demonstrates humility remains open to growth and change. This openness involves listening, being considerate, pondering the benefits of various philosophical ideas, interacting with players and assistant coaches from a variety of backgrounds, entertaining notions of different regimens, and considering both criticism and praise. The coach does not remain receptive by keeping the office door closed, shunning other coaches in the department, or refusing to relate with parents or alumni. Despite the openness that this quality of humility entails, the coach still remains confident, and in this sense humility should not be confused with meekness or any aspect of timidity.[34]

Coaches need to deliberate about their individual philosophy, choosing the path by which they intend to coach, working out their beliefs in the process. This ongoing course of discernment and decision making is a crucial aspect of successful coaching. It provides the needed structure for program goal-setting and individual growth. Further, coaches need to carefully explain these beliefs and ideas to others so as to be understood and not misunderstood. Yet coaches cannot draft these documents in a narrow way that restricts growth, nor in any final, solidified version for eternity.

This aspect of humility deeply impacts how coaches treat others, and a lack of humility often results in unethical consequences. The recent case of Bobby Petrino, former football coach at the University of Arkansas, serves as an example. Despite his stellar record, Arkansas administrators fired Petrino in the spring of 2012 for a series of embarrassing unethical acts.[35] In this situation, Petrino failed to recognize Bugbee's sense of humility related to nature and one's surroundings. As Bugbee wrote of his singular place within the larger natural surroundings, exemplary coaches recognize their own place as one part of the coaching system or one member of the athletic department (or university). These individuals maintain a healthy sense of self-regard without allowing hubris to gain a foothold.

Finally, Bugbee's notion of certainty requires on ongoing attitude of alertness. I want to turn again to Bugbee's narrative of his rowing coach, John Schultz. Once Bugbee was riding with Schultz in a Model-A Ford, following the crew team along the Schuylkill River. Bugbee writes:

> At the half mile the boats were even. John shoved the gas clear to the floor, and as we began to move ahead of the procession, jerking past a scattering of cars, I just heard him over the violence of the engine: 'When they come out from under the bridge. . . . That's where they need me!'[36]

Bugbee uses this story to demonstrate the type of attentiveness or attitude he has in mind. Coach Schultz knew, by virtue of countless hours spent with his athletes, from his watchful presence, the precise instant when his athletes need his guidance. Schultz sensed this occasion, one that he "felt in his bones." Similarly, reading this passage prompts us to remember our own awakening moments and those individuals or places where we felt such interactions. Bugbee tries to prod others toward analogous frames of mind, providing encouragement to seek out relationships and locations where we become open to self and others as we seek clarity and ultimately our own working certainty.

Through human commitments, entered into with this spirit of attentiveness, coaches discover, identify, and reformulate their philosophical beliefs. Bugbee wants us to approach interactions with others, however, not solely "in terms of goal-oriented endeavor, nor in terms of acquisition or achievement, nor in terms of the fulfillment of explicit moral standard, nor in terms of the realization or satisfaction of the ego."[37] Yes, coaches form commitments, in large part, to work toward common goals. However, Bugbee desires that we also recognize and appreciate the experience itself and the relationships we form in the process.

This quality of alertness impacts the ethical attitudes and behaviors of coaches, the way they interact with others, especially their athletes. The attentive coach strives to understand the athletes, to gain a sense of their perspective. By taking this approach, the coach demonstrates a willingness to appreciate the team members not only as athletes but as unique people. These kinds of coaches carve out deliberate moments to interact with their athletes, seeking to understand the athletes' broader lives when it comes to school, relationships, athletic performance, and so forth.

Let me conclude with several specific issues related to coaching philosophies with respect to ethics. Too often coaches either wholly embrace the philosophy of a mentor coach, or rely on a template drawn up in coaching education programs. These approaches are helpful to a degree but can be problematic. In this vein, Anderson observes that "we try—mostly ineffectively—to *produce* teaching and learning. But these are not the sorts of things one produces—teaching [coaching too] and learning are found in life's transitions, in the agency of a fundamental alertness, awareness, and attentiveness."[38] Coaches too seek to address problems (e.g., how to win, how to recruit, how to manage, how to discipline, how to relate to parents) through finding technical solutions. They go to clinics, trying the next best idea on motivation or team building, training programs, or off-season workouts. But in their haste they may cease being alert to the needs of their athletes, to the overall principles of their university, or to the mission of their own family. Bugbee reminds us, through narrative and through his own careful reflection, of the importance of attention as we relate with others and develop coaching philosophies.

To further clarify this point, consider the following example from a team sport. A college basketball coach may, through experience and observation, believe in an unstructured offense (dribble-drive) that relies heavily on the athleticism of his players. However, since his school is no longer able to attract top athletes and he is unwilling to adapt his style to these fundamentally sound yet less athletic players, the coach and team struggle. A new coach comes in and does well with these same players using a structured offense that relies more on intelligent shot selection than athleticism. The first coach did not revise his theory of basketball offense in light of experience and hence was dogmatically rather than pragmatically certain.[39]

It may appear that Bugbee's acceptance of and confidence in experience as a valid philosophic approach potentially suffers from a lack of critical justification. As compared with Dewey's scientific method, Bugbee's transcendental claims seem speculative or even solipsistic. In reality, Bugbee realizes that his claims, and the backdrop from which they arose, still need to be validated. Like other American philosophers, he believes philosophical ideals need to hold a cash value—they need to solve real problems. So, while Bugbee does not oppose the rigor of the scientific method, neither did he want this approach to totally dominate our approach to doing philosophy, especially at the expense of experience and the discoveries this mode of thinking and writing holds.

At this point I want to address the potential tension between Bugbee's philosophical ideas and the demands of highly competitive big-time NCAA Division I sports. As presently structured, the incentives in Division I run counter to a coach developing a philosophy emphasizing the virtues of sport (e.g., developing player skills, respecting players, teaching the game) due to the pressures for instant success, achieving conference and national championships, and above all bringing in revenue streams. Given these conditions, to what extent is it possible for the qualities Bugbee emphasizes to fit with the elite sport culture? It may be difficult to conceptualize elite level coaching in the manner Bugbee's themes suggest. Popular opinion does not view elite coaches as individuals who embody humility or risk. Yet I would argue that these qualities are even more important for elite-level coaches because of the pressures involved.

Focusing on the concepts Bugbee mentions, when formulating and living out a coaching philosophy, does not guarantee additional wins or a more lucrative contract. Bugbee's concerns are clearly not instrumental in this sense. Rather, this kind of attention could encourage a greater appreciation for the craft of coaching and for sports in general. Furthermore, the sense of working certainty and the openness this concept involves could help encourage coaches at all levels to continue toward growth and development—positive character traits that are useful for youth sport coaches and those at the elite and hypercompetitive levels. Finally, the notion of a normative approach to coaching philosophies is a crucial aspect of coaching. As Standal and

Hemmestad rightly contend, "Top-level sport is not a domain where 'anything goes'. There are already ethical guidelines for sports, such as fair play principles. . . . Thus, ethical judgments are always being made . . . [and] the coach with [practical wisdom]is better suited to deal with such dilemmas in a good way."[40] With increased television exposure and lucrative contracts, elite coaches are tempted to skirt ethical responsibilities to reap financial rewards. Their unethical, selfish behavior ultimately has a bearing on their team, department, and university. Conversely, coaches such as Tony Dungy, Dean Smith, or Vivian Stringer provide examples that it is indeed possible to coach in ways representative of Bugbee's ideals, with manners that respect both the player and the game.

When I was playing football at Northwestern, Coach Korver exemplified the risk, humility, and alertness characteristic of the working certainty Bugbee describes. Through my time and commitment, I developed as a football player and individual. My own distinctive life experiences and self-identity provided the ground from which I responded to Korver's coaching philosophy. In Davis's words, Korver "lit up" his coaching philosophy in a way that captured my attention and prompted me toward growth.[41] Not only did Korver's attitudes influence me, but his ideals also impacted many others including two players who later would succeed him when he retired. To be fair, not every player embraced Korver's philosophy. Some continued playing but did not wholly agree with his ideals. A few left the team for other pursuits. This was a risk Korver accepted, however, as he realized that while he could not impact everyone on the team in a way that he would have liked, he could impact many—including me.

Questions for Review and Discussion

1. To what extent have your coaches and their philosophies impacted your view of sport?

2. To what extent did the coaches and their philosophies impact your experience as an athlete?

3. How do coaches develop a coaching philosophy and how should they do so?

4. What did Bugbee mean by "certainty" and how does this relate to a coaching philosophy?

5. To what extent is it possible for coaches to approach their task in a manner consistent with Bugbee's themes?

6. How would you evaluate the pragmatic approach to the philosophy and ethics of coaching developed in this chapter as compared to either Simon's version of broad internalism (interpretivism) or Morgan's more context-specific modification of it? Is pragmatism of the kind suggested compatible with either Simon's or Morgan's views? If not, which approach do you think is intellectually more satisfactory? Which might be more useful to coaches?

Suggestions for Further Reading

Anderson, Douglas. *Philosophy Americana: Making Philosophy at Home in American Culture.* New York: Fordham University Press, 2006.

Bugbee, Henry. *The Inward Morning: A Philosophical Exploration in Journal Form.* Athens: University of Georgia Press, 1999.

Davis, Paul. "Objectivity and Subjectivity in Coaching." In *The Ethics of Sports Coaching,* 56–71. Edited by A. Hardman and C. Jones. London: Routledge, 2011.

Descartes, René. *Meditations on First Philosophy.* Cambridge: Cambridge University Press, 1986.

Dweck, Carol. *Mindset: The New Psychology of Success.* New York: Random House, 2006.

Fry, Jeff. "On Playing with Emotion." *Journal of the Philosophy of Sport* 30:1 (2003): 26–36.

Hardman, Alun, and Carwyn Jones, eds. *The Ethics of Sports Coaching.* London: Routledge, 2011.

Heie, Harold. *Learning to Listen, Ready to Talk: A Pilgrimage Toward Peacemaking.* Lincoln, NE: iUniverse, 2007.

Kretchmar, R. Scott. *Practical Philosophy of Sport.* Champaign, IL: Human Kinetics, 2005.

Loland, Sigmund. "The Normative Aims of Coaching: The Good Coach as an Enlightened Generalist." In *The Ethics of Sports Coaching,* 15–22. Edited by A. Hardman and C. Jones. London: Routledge, 2011.

Lyle, John. "Coaching Philosophy and Coaching Behavior." In *The Coaching Process: Principles and Practice for Sport,* 25–46. Edited by N. Cross and J. Lyle. Oxford: Butterworth & Heinemann, 1999.

Sheehy, Harry. *Raising a Team Player: Teaching Kids Lasting Values on the Field, on the Court, and on the Bench.* North Adams, MA: Story, 2002.

Standal, Oyvind, and Liv Hemmestad. "Becoming a Good Coach: Coaching and *Phronesis*." In *The Ethics of Sports Coaching*, 45–55. Edited by A. Hardman and C. Jones. London: Routledge, 2011.

Walton, Gary. *Beyond Winning: The Timeless Wisdom of Great Philosopher Coaches*. Champaign, IL: Leisure, 1992.

Warren, William. *Coaching and Control: Controlling Your Team, Your Program, and Your Opponents*. Upper Saddle River, NJ: Prentice-Hall, 1997.

PART 3

Coaching and the Ethics of Competition

ROBERT L. SIMON

It is the next-to-last inning of a high school softball game—the semifinal game of a sectional championship—with the visiting team down by one run. The team has a runner in scoring position and a solid senior player is coming to bat. She has been injured a good part of her senior year and has worked hard to come back. In fact, she has dreamed about helping her team in just such a situation. It was her dream that motivated her to work so hard at rehabilitation; without it she might have worked less or even fallen into depression or given up. If the team loses, it will be the last game of her high school career.

Her coach is aware of all this and wants to let her bat. However, the coach also knows that a sophomore substitute on the bench who has filled in for the senior while she was out has hit well against this particular pitcher in the past and is probably a better hitter overall than the senior. Should the coach send the sophomore in to pinch-hit for the senior, ending the senior player's dream and possibly her career, or let the senior bat even though it may not be best for the team?

Although I'm sure you would like to know my answer, any response is debatable. In my view, this is a hard case where there may be reasonable arguments on both sides. But coaches face such situations all the time. If winning is everything, the coach will send in the pinch hitter. Moreover, the coach needs to consider the other players on the team who all want to win and advance in the play-offs, possibly to sectional play and a state championship. On the other hand, this at-bat is especially significant to a senior player who has helped the team for many seasons. What about loyalty to her in light of her work ethic, courage, and past contribution? Even if such considerations are outweighed by other factors and the coach decides to pinch-hit, I would argue that the reasons on the other side need to be considered and given due weight. Indeed, the chapters in Part 2 made a cumulative argument that coaching involves constant evaluation and moral decision making.

In Part 3, contributors turn to the activity of coaching itself. As the above example illustrates, coaches constantly face ethical issues in games and practices: decisions about who to play, who to schedule, how to react to unfavorable calls by officials, when and how to discipline players who misbehave, and a host of other kinds of cases every season. The chapters in Part 3 explore a number of such key decisions and the ethical issues raised by them.

Three of the chapters question a set of widely held assumptions that are not usually challenged. For example, many athletes, coaches, and fans would acknowledge that bad calls by officials often influence the outcome of contests but deny that the coaches who benefit from such calls and know the calls are incorrect have an obligation to do anything about it. Bad calls by officials are just "part of the game" and there is no moral duty on the part of the beneficiary to attempt to rectify the unearned advantage. As a former student once said when I asked her in class what she would do if a basketball referee made an outrageously bad call in her favor, she replied, "Refs have made so many bad calls against me, I would just figure he owed me one!"

However, in Chapter 7, J. S. Russell argues for a different perspective; namely, that coaches have an obligation to help officials get the call right and where appropriate to rectify bad calls, even bad calls in favor of the coach's own team. Russell considers objections to his view (e.g., that bad calls eventually "even out") and concludes these replies do not withstand critical scrutiny.

Similarly, in Chapter 8, Scott Kretchmar explores the coach's obligations to bench players, team members who see little playing time in actual contests except when the score is so lopsided that the outcome is settled, and concludes the case for their participation in meaningful moments of competitive games, even at higher levels of competitive athletics, is much stronger than often appreciated. In Chapter 11, Cesar Torres and Peter Hager call into question the widely held view that children's and youth sports should be noncompetitive. These authors explain that competition, when properly directed, can have benefits even for children and present principles, based on an explicitly broad internalist conception of sport, to guide coaches in this area.

Chapters 9 and 10 explore the ethics of the coach's relation to players, the dangers of abuse of that relationship, and the benefits that might develop when the relationship is an ethically appropriate one. In particular, Mark Hamilton, while recognizing that coaches often need to be tough and demanding, distinguishes intimidation and bullying from appropriate ways coaches might relate to their athletes. He explains the harms a bullying coach can cause and argues that bullying and related forms of intimidation have no legitimate place in coaching ethics.

In Chapter 10, Jeffrey Fry draws on recent findings in neuroscience to suggest that coaching behavior can affect the developing brain of young athletes and thus perhaps have deeper effects than previously thought. If so, positive behavior by coaches can have an even more significant effect than previously believed, and the kind of bullying described by Hamilton might have even more dire consequences than many have believed.

It is worth noting that the chapters in Part 2 of this book and those in Part 3 have a number of interconnections. In particular, the models of coaching and of ethical justification outlined in Chapters 1 through 4 may provide a framework for evaluating those in Part 2, while the latter may provide concrete examples of the implications of some of the ideas developed in Part 1. For example, Torres and Hager, as noted above, explicitly appeal to a broad internalist conception of sports while Russell and Kretchmar implicitly rely (or so I would suggest) on a broad theory of what is important about participation in sports. Hamilton and Fry, on the other hand, explore the virtues and vices that coaches may exhibit and what means may be properly employed as they pursue the goals of competitive athletics.

I hope these chapters encourage thoughtful discussion of the issues raised and illustrate why Douglas Hochstetler's thesis that the coach needs a philosophy is not just a theoretical point but clearly applies to the practice of coaching itself.

Seven

Coaching and
Undeserved Competitive Success

J. S. RUSSELL

I suspect that the central moral problem facing all coaches is the problem of distributive justice, or how to allocate scarce goods or resources fairly. At all levels of sports, key goods such as playing time, access to training, and instruction are almost always in short supply. Norms for distributing those resources fairly are therefore required. Since coaches generally control allocation decisions, they have special duties to ensure fairness. Coaches from the recreational level to elite athletic development programs will recognize this as a constant moral demand (encapsulated in the idea of "being fair" to their players). It is a problem even at elite levels of sports, including professional sports. Coaches at these levels also need to develop talent and have obligations to give competitors opportunities that are due them. Yet these demands will inevitably conflict with the legitimate demands of other competitors and the priority that is placed on competitive success. At the highest levels of competition, then, these problems of distributive justice may only be heightened.

However, problems of distributive justice run more deeply in sports than these familiar examples. Although they are worthy of systematic treatment, I will not address them here. Rather, I want to focus on an issue in sports that is barely recognized as a problem of distributive justice although it is at least as profound a problem as the ones just mentioned. This is the problem of accepting undeserved advantages in competition. The undeserved advantages I shall focus on are erroneous judgments made by umpires. I shall argue that there should be a greater role for coaches in rectifying these injustices. This is bound to have an air of paradox about it. Unlike the idea that playing time, training, and instruction should be allocated fairly, which is unlikely to be gainsaid by anyone, being the recipient of undeserved advantages may not readily appear to be a problem of distributive justice. And of course even if we recognize that it is, it does not follow that coaches should act to mitigate the injustice or that, under certain circumstances, they have a moral obligation to do so. There is some work to do here, then.

Are Umpiring Errors Matters of Distributive Justice?

Consider the following scenarios:

1. An umpire blows a call at first base, calling a player out who was clearly safe. The out is the final out in the bottom of the ninth inning of a one-run game with the tying run on third and winning run on second. If the proper call were made, the batter-runner would have been safe, the runner at third would have scored (thus assuring that the game would at least go to extra innings), and perhaps the runner at second would also have scored, meaning that the game had been won by the home team. The coach of the fielding (visiting) team turns to one of his co-coaches and, shaking his hand over a successful win, says "we got one there." His colleague nods. The pitcher and his teammates leave the field inwardly (or perhaps even outwardly) acknowledging their great good luck.

2. An umpire awards three bases to a runner who started the play at first base when an infielder, on the initial play after the ball is hit, throws the ball out of play. This adds the winning run to the contest. However, the umpire has misapplied the rule, which states that only two bases shall be awarded from the base the runner occupies at the beginning of the play. The coach who is the recipient of this benefit knows this is an error and says nothing when the other coach formally protests the call.

These two scenarios illustrate the range of errors an umpire can make in the course of competition. One is an error making a call, the other is an error applying the rules. To put this in legal terms, we have "errors in fact" and "errors in law." This identifies the two sorts of mistaken judgements that umpires, or judicial officials generally, can make.

What makes these sorts of umpiring errors undeserved advantages and issues of distributive justice?

The first thing to notice is that competitive athletic successes can properly be described as *necessarily* or *inherently* scarce goods. This is evident from the nature of competitive sports. The competitors each strive to win, but only one can do so. Athletic success in this sense is a scarce good, in a way that many goods or resources are not. Gold, for example, is contingently scarce. There might be a vast store of it in some unknown but easily accessible place on earth so that all could have as much of it as they wanted. There would then be no scarcity of gold, and no problem of distributive justice regarding it. Winning is different. It is not contingently scarce but necessarily scarce. It is what economists and theorists of justice refer to as a "positional" or "relational" good. Classic instances of positional goods are awards and honors, because one person's possession of them excludes others who may also desire them. Competitive sporting success reflects this type of scarcity— all the competitors strive to win or be the best among their peers, but only one can win a game or a championship. The possibility of ties extends the idea of scarcity, since each competitor would prefer to win outright rather than tie an opponent.

Seen in this light, competitive successes appear to pose special problems of distributive justice. However, the fact that they are necessarily scarce does not mean that the problem of distributive justice takes priority over settling other claims of distributive justice. That depends on the importance or value of the good or resource that is scarce. But it does mean that our options for responding to the scarcity are limited. In normal circumstances, we might address problems of distributive justice by attempting to add resources, say, more seats at universities, more jobs to the economy, or increased food production, and so on. These sorts of avenues are not open to us in competitive sports. We cannot try to address (or, in many cases, sidestep) the problems of distributive justice by reducing scarcity, because we do not have the option of adding resources to address the problem. We cannot make everyone a winner in a competitive contest because that would contradict the very idea of a competitive contest. Our options are limited. Indeed, we have only one further option in the examples just given, and that is to correct the mistaken call.[1]

An obvious response at this point is to say that, contrary to appearance, the advantages or successes that come from umpiring errors do not pose problems of distributive justice, nor are the advantages and successes undeserved. The argument might go that it is not a problem of distributive justice because these sorts of errors tend to even out, and this evening out is sufficient to address any problem of distributive justice. Call this the "evening out argument." Second, they are not undeserved because the recipients of the advantage did nothing wrong to obtain the advantage. Call this the "innocent advantage argument." There are other objections that could be given against the arguments just presented, but these are, I suspect, the two main lines of objection, and I will consider them first. They are each easily answered.

Conventional sporting wisdom notwithstanding, we have no reason to believe that umpiring errors always, or even commonly, even out. This is just a hopeful claim that we comfort ourselves with. Over an entire season, it is always possible that one team or competitor will be the victim of more bad calls than other teams, or ones at crucial times, and that this will disproportionately affect their competitive success. A team might well lose a regular season championship because of a small number of "extra" or "especially consequential" umpiring errors made to its disadvantage perhaps in combination with errors that redounded to the advantage of the "winner." In fact, from an empirical perspective, we simply do not know how many season-long league championships (or play-off spots, etc.) are won or lost under these circumstances. My guess is that it is not an exceptional occurrence. If we are talking about a championship game or series, then the period of competition will normally be too short for any evening out to occur. In this context, umpiring errors may well determine an outcome. (Suppose the error at first described above occurs in the ninth inning of the seventh game of the World Series.)

Furthermore, we should not measure competitive athletic success simply as a matter of winning and losing, for there are other necessarily scarce competitive athletic goods that need to be allocated fairly. Athletes are often competing for individual awards or records (in baseball, for example, gold gloves for defense, or batting or pitching titles, or MVP awards, etc.) or team records (most wins in a season, longest winning streak, etc.) or for personal bests, and so on. Suppose that in the first scenario described above the runner had rightly been called safe, and as a result the fielder who threw the ball to first was charged with an error because it was a routine ground ball that he bobbled before throwing it. Suppose further that the failure to charge him with an error meant that he won a gold glove that someone else should have won. And suppose that the earned run that was not charged against the pitcher's record meant he finished the season with the lowest earned run average among pitchers, rather than finishing second. These are also examples of necessarily scarce competitive goods that are affected by umpiring errors. Evening out arguments can be applied in this context too, but once more we do not know whether the evening out occurs. This is particularly true where the margins of superiority over rivals are small and can be affected by a difference of one or two mistaken calls for or against an individual. For example, a batting title may be won by a few thousandths of a point, which might result from one "extra" scorer's decision to award a hit on what should have been a defensive error and no hit.

Moreover, there are situations where the evening out argument does not apply and a competitor is denied a scarce and highly prized good. Take an example from the recent history of baseball. In the 2010 baseball season, veteran umpire Jim Joyce wrecked a perfect game for Detroit Tiger pitcher Armando Galarraga by mistakenly calling a Cleveland Indian runner safe who would otherwise have been the final out of the game. By all accounts, the call was an obvious error. Replays showed a clear error even without benefit of slow motion. Slow motion replay showed the call to be an exceptional lapse of umpiring judgment. In this case, however, the call cannot be evened out with another blown call that evens things up. Galarraga already no longer had a perfect game because of the blown call. And there is no plausible opportunity for any evening out to occur in another game. We can confidently assert that Galarraga will never be in a position where an umpire's blown call will produce a perfect game for him. (As of May 2012 there were only twenty-one perfect games in major league history.) And who would want to be recognized and remembered for such a "perfect" game? The only other option in this case, as in the scenarios described earlier, is to overturn the mistaken decision. These are all good reasons to want to reduce the number of umpiring errors and to try to find creative ways to do so that are consistent with the good conduct of competitive contests.

A further response to the above argument might be that the advantages or successes given to opposing teams or competitors from these errors are not undeserved, since those who benefit from the errors did nothing wrong. They did nothing to seek or (let us say) encourage the error. They just happened to benefit from being in the right place at the right time. But this is not convincing. Let us put the example in a different context involving distributive justice. Suppose through a mistake at my bank someone else's money is transferred into my account. This is an innocent advantage in that I did not seek it but happened to be in the right place at the right time. The argument that I am entitled to this money and have no duty to disclose the error will not work. I am morally required to report this and to try to return it. If I knowingly take advantage of the windfall and spend it, I will be legally liable to repay it (and may be criminally charged).[2] If this reasoning is correct, it suggests by analogy that a similar thing is true of advantages conferred from recognized umpiring errors on teams or competitors who did not seek those advantages. If this is true in the bank error case, it creates a similar presumption about disclosure and repayment in the competitive case. That presumption can be overturned with an argument that demonstrates some important disanalogy between these cases, but the arguments that I can think of do not seem convincing.

Perhaps it will be argued that what distinguishes the banking from the competitive example is that these sorts of umpiring errors represent adversities that teams should be prepared to work through as part of competition. This is another bad argument, for changing a blown call just replaces one type of adversity for another—the adversity of having to deal with a changed blown call that was wrongly to one's advantage. As well, it will never be possible to eliminate all umpiring errors, and so teams will have to test themselves against this more familiar type of adversity in any event. Thus, since there is no evident loss of sporting adversity to test oneself against, the way remains clear to eliminate umpiring errors wherever reasonable on the grounds that what is at stake are scarce, much sought-after goods. More important, there is good reason to regard such adversities as irrelevant to sporting competition per se. If we think that competitive sports is something like a "mutually acceptable quest for excellence through challenge,"[3] as Robert Simon has argued, then competitors have an implicit fundamental commitment to each other to distribute the scarce goods of athletic competition in a way that is determined by the skills that are displayed in competition and not by mistakes that corrupt this process. If so, we now have arguments grounded both in distributive justice and in the agreement of competitors to do what can reasonably be done to minimize these sorts of errors. As in other areas of life, we will never get perfect justice, but we should do our best to strive toward it and to obtain the fairest results possible. The results may remain imperfect, but hopefully they will at least tend to be better measures of competitive athletic success. Moreover, if we do what is reasonably possible to allocate fairly the scarce goods of competition, the results will be ones that everyone should be prepared to accept as the most just outcome that could be achieved (more on this later).

I imagine one other response. Call this the "it's only a game" argument. It claims that while there may be an undeserved advantage from umpires' errors, it does not matter because games are basically trivial or gratuitous affairs. But this seems to be false. Games are not merely trivial or gratuitous to anyone who is serious enough to want to compete against others. People also invest great time and effort into developing and exercising game skills. They will not associate trivial value to their skills or sporting outcomes. But even if games are trivial or gratuitous in some sense, the fact that the goods that are sought through them are scarce and highly prized is sufficient to demand that distributive justice be taken seriously and reasonable efforts be made to minimize errors in distributing those goods. Compare how standards of distributive and corrective justice are carefully applied to many things that are at least as trivial. Think of allocation of rare gemstones and baseball cards, for example. There is no reason, then, to fail to regard distribution of athletic advantages and success as a serious issue of distributive justice just because what is at stake is arguably trivial.

Should Coaches Help Umpires?

So far I have argued that certain sought-after competitive athletic goods are scarce and that we should take reasonable measures that are at our disposal to ensure that they are fairly distributed. This should not be controversial. What is likely to be controversial is my claim that coaches should be enlisted, at least from time to time, to assist umpires to correct errors. In these cases, game players might also be consulted, but I have special reasons for wanting to focus on coaches which will become apparent in the following discussion.

This is bound to seem like a provocative idea. However, we have seen evidence by analogy and grounded in ideas of distributive justice and competitive sports that coaches, or participants should accept this obligation. There are other arguments that can be given as well. To begin with, there are important precedents in sports that suggest we should be open-minded about this proposal. For there are sports like curling, golf, and ultimate that are essentially self-officiated. Each has a role for officials, but participants are expected "to call their own game." Each of these games works pretty well, so that should encourage us to take seriously the practicality of a proposal to enlist coaches to assist umpires from time to time.

Why coaches, though? Why not go straight to the players, who arguably are in the best position besides the umpires, to make the calls? My reasons for this require some extended discussion. To begin with, sometimes players are not in the best position to see what happened, and coaches can be in a better position. Although I think that players should be consulted by their coaches in cases where there is a reasonable concern that an error has been made, there are certain advantages, particularly in team sports, to making the decision to assist umpires a team or "corporate" one. The competitors are teams, and so it is a team responsibility to address the issue, not specifically a matter for an individual player. This takes a burden off the individual player. A player may understandably feel that his or her honesty is being pitted against the interests of the team. Thus, a player may worry about recriminations from fellow players. Other players may disagree with a teammate's perception but not be in as good a position to say what happened. Some players called on to assist umpires may be concerned about the accuracy of their own assessment but will be understandably concerned about how this will be perceived by the umpires and others. Coaches can assist players to be comfortable reporting their views honestly. These are some good reasons to make the decision a corporate one, involving coaches and players offering advice to umpires when requested to do so. The burden for everyone is mitigated if the decision is made, in effect, by the team through the coach.

There will also be a useful symmetry to enlisting coaches in this way. Since the review of a call is most likely to be initiated by an opposing coach's complaint to an umpire, the umpire could then ask the other coach if he believes his team has just received an undeserved advantage and/or whether he wishes to confer with any of his players or coaches about this. This will mean that the leaders on the field, the coaches and the umpires, will be seen to work together to ensure that the competition produces a just outcome. There is an important symbolism here that shows that those participants who have direct responsibility for overseeing the good conduct of games and ensuring that standards of fairness and sportsmanship are applied will work together to achieve these goals and not be pitted against each other on these issues, and indeed against these goals, as is often the case.

There are related moral advantages to having coaches participate in these decisions and speak for the team. For one thing, it imposes on coaches a responsibility of moral leadership that is consistent with their managerial and supervisory role. For another, it is a way of responding, at least partially, to the morally flawed aspects of sports. Most critiques of sports argue that the problems that we see in sports—the win-at-all costs attitude, in particular—are the product of corrupting elements from outside sports, in particular, the desire for recognition or money.[4] These would, I think, be combated to a substantial degree if the proposal outlined here were accepted. For if coaches either led the effort, or were required to take steps from time to time, to ensure that the scarce competitive goods were fairly allocated, this would do much to put competition in sports on a higher moral ground. A win-at-all-costs approach is, of course, prepared to accept undeserved advantages to the extent it facilitates winning. But it does this at the expense of corrupting the idea of sports as a mutually agreed upon quest for excellence, and it ignores the demand that we allocate the scarce goods of competition fairly.

I have argued elsewhere that the moral flaws of sports extend beyond the common criticism that sports is corrupted by the culture outside it. While I am sure there is truth to these latter arguments, I argued that sports, despite its actual and potential moral virtues, is also internally flawed like many, and perhaps all, human institutions.[5] The arguments advanced here also would help to address these flaws, even if they would not completely eliminate them. My arguments about the morally flawed nature of sports are twofold. First, competitive sports is not simply a mutual quest for excellence in the sense that Simon describes. It is also a ritualized form of conflict.[6]

More specifically, I claim that competitive sports is better described as a mutually acceptable quest for excellence through ritualized conflict. As a result, it naturally (if not necessarily) engages suspect human motivations, like desires to dominate others or to seek retribution or revenge or to have feelings of hatred, to sharpen competitive desires and promote the pursuit of excellence. Such emotions are familiar features of the psychology of competitive sportspersons at all levels and in all sports. Thus we have baseball manager and hall of famer Leo Durocher stating that he wanted "scratching, diving, hungry ball players who come to kill you" playing for him, and Tiger Woods asserting that for him competition in anything from cards to golf is always about "wanting to kick your [opponent's] butt."[7] I argued that competition marked by friendly behavior and good sportsmanship may not always, or perhaps even often, be conducive to the highest level of athletic achievements, and that certain morally suspect motivations may be necessary for many athletes to excel at the highest level. These motivations plausibly exist in part because of their ability to focus the mind and assist us to succeed in human conflicts. A second, deeper argument claimed that sports contains a morally flawed conception of value. The pursuit of winning is a pursuit of relative value as an end, not perfection for its own sake. The relative value of winning is superiority over others. Thus competitive sports conceptually requires us to see success in part as dominance over others rather than pursuing something that is valuable for its own sake, like human perfection. There is a tension in sports then between the pursuit of perfection (the mutual quest for excellence) and the desire to win or come out on top of others as an intrinsic end of competition. Here I was following an argument from Kant[8] that aiming to be better than others as an end is a corrupt form of value that will encourage us to fail to recognize the value of pursuing perfection for its own sake and, implicitly, the absolute value of all persons. Thus it will encourage exactly the sorts of suspect motivations just mentioned. Kant's views are perceptive and in fact predict the sort of behavior that we find commonly in sports and that are reflected in the remarks of sportspersons like Durocher and Woods.

It should be clear now how enlisting coaches in helping to ensure that scarce competitive goods are allocated fairly can also help to respond to morally problematic features that are internal to competitive sports. The simple fact is that having coaches take responsibility for assisting umpires in their roles will deemphasize winning as the ultimate goal of competition and bring the focus more closely on ensuring that the excellences that the contests are designed to test are duly recognized and the scarce competitive resources are fairly distributed. If a coach acknowledges that an umpire made an error that wrongly awarded his team a win, that has the obvious effect of downplaying the idea that winning is everything in favor of recognizing that successful execution of individual skills should determine competitive results. To put this in Kantian terms, we downplay (although we do not eliminate) the focus on relative value and redirect it toward things that are properly valued intrinsically, such as human perfection. And while competitive contests may remain imperfect in their distribution of scarce competitive goods, the results will be ones that all should be better prepared to accept, since the participants will themselves share responsibility for ensuring that they are shared fairly. All should be able to acknowledge, then, that this is the best that can be done to ensure that competitive successes are fairly distributed. This is an advance from the perspective of distributive justice and from the perspective of competition. More generally, I can think of no other proposal that would go so far to ameliorate many of the most troubling moral problems that have come to pervade contemporary competitive sports. Although it is needed at all levels of sports, it should be accepted most readily at recreational and amateur levels where there is a greater need to use sports as a tool for moral education and where practices need to be adopted that will allow these levels of sports to separate themselves from the example that is often set by professional sports and its embrace of the competitive flaws described earlier.

Can Justice Be Done in Sports?

"This is fine in theory, but it won't work in practice." This challenge deserves to be taken seriously. Answering the question, What is justice? is fundamental but of little consequence without also answering the question, How shall justice be done? There is always a burden, then, to show how justice can be practically implemented.

Let me start, however, by pointing out a limitation about practical objections. Admittedly, the position that is being defended has the weight of culture going against it. But this is not a good reason not to adopt it, and it is a very bad reason for saying that it cannot be done. Moral progress typically depends on responding to injustices that are entrenched culturally. We have often seen practical moral revolutions occur in response to seemingly insuperable cultural obstacles (e.g., securing the abolition of slavery, rights for women, religious freedom, and democratic government, to name a few). The obstacles in the current context do not appear so insuperable, since much less is at stake. We have also already seen that certain successful sports are self-officiated. Given that self-officiated sports appear to reflect better examples of sportsmanship and civility and produce fewer complaints about results, we can reasonably hope that adding a measure of self-officiating to competitive sports wherever this is possible would have similar results. This gives us some reason for optimism that involving participants in umpiring decisions can be practical. Also, if we look at the history of sports, there are precedents that should encourage us. For example, it used to be common in tennis for players to concede umpiring errors. This all but disappeared long before the institution of electronic aids to officiating. Similar sorts of examples of corrective justice appear to have been more common in the past in many sports. This shows that there is no reason that competitors cannot make decisions or take actions to rectify injustices. Moreover, it is interesting that these sorts of examples occurred under circumstances where there were no rules requiring the competitors to rectify umpires' errors. It was done out of a sense of fairness and honor between competitors that seems to have disappeared in recent times. The arguments I have presented indicate that we should seek to recover and try to formally institutionalize those lost virtues.

A more interesting objection is a problem that is familiar from implementing recognized standards of distributive justice. Suppose the above arguments are accepted and rules for implementing them are adopted. The proposal will only work if coaches can reasonably expect other coaches to participate honestly in this process. If coaches expect other coaches to violate standards of distributive justice to their advantage, say, by lying about what they believe were the right decisions when consulted by umpires, the process will break down and the rules will not achieve their goals. Even coaches who would like to participate in these practices will, then, have no reason to participate honestly in this process. They might even plausibly argue that they have duties to be dishonest.

This is a familiar problem of rationing scarce resources under conditions that are fair but nevertheless permit "free riders" to take advantage of other persons' compliance with the rules and obtain unjust advantages. If the problem of free riders goes unaddressed, there is no reason to be confident that a system of distributive justice will work at all.[9] Since we can never assure perfect compliance, the problem is to reduce the number of free riders so that it is rational for coaches to comply because they expect other coaches will reciprocate. The typical, albeit imperfect solution is to codify punishments and enforce them against individuals who fail to comply with their duties. Such punishments, for example, fines and suspensions, could and probably should be adopted, say, for failing to participate in good faith regarding a review of a call. Admittedly, they will be difficult to prosecute. A coach can always say he was not sure enough about a call to make a decision, and it will be difficult to prove that he is lying. However, there are bound to be some cases where it is evident enough that a coach has lied and that a prosecution is successful. That may be sufficient to encourage enough compliance that the process would be workable.

I doubt, however, that problems prosecuting the enforcement of rules should lead us to be pessimistic about addressing the problem of free riders. What is helpful about sporting competition is that the events under scrutiny are *public*, so any free riding takes place directly under the scrutiny of others. Free riding tends to be a more serious problem in contexts where the free riders can hide their cheating behavior out of public sight (e.g., claiming a tax write-off for a business lunch when the meal was purely for personal reasons, etc.). However, even in these cases we often get reasonable compliance so the system does not break down. For example, doctors could lie about or exaggerate a patient's medical symptoms to push him to the front of the line for a special test, but it is not clear that this is a systemic problem. So even where there is a low probability of detection for free riding, we often get reasonable compliance with stated norms of distributive justice. The case of competitive sports should be less conducive to free riding than these sorts of examples. First, requests to assist umpires will probably be limited to a narrow range of important calls to ensure that games are not bogged down by stoppages. And it would be important that the umpire have some reasonable belief that he or she has made an error. So these are likely to be a small number of cases, and they are likely to concern cases where the errors are pretty clear to everyone else, except perhaps the umpire, who may nevertheless strongly suspect he has made an error. Second, as already noted it will be difficult in these sorts of cases for participants to hide their free riding. For example, an umpire who was unable to see whether a ball was hit over a fence or bounced over a fence because he was blinded by the sun, but wrongly believed it bounced over and calls a ground rule double on what was a home run, will have many reliable reports to draw on. Indeed, probably all other players will know exactly what happened. (In a two-umpire system, the base umpire would be watching the base runners while the plate umpire is watching the ball, so there would be no other umpire in a position to correct the call.) A coach who denies that he knows what happened in that case is pretty obviously lying, and it is reasonable to consider that his reputation will suffer, and that he may suffer further social consequences from lying. There is no way to eliminate all free riders, of course, but it will become well known soon who the free riders are, and they will be regarded by their peers and others as "cheaters" and rightly so. Whether or not such a coach was prosecuted, these considerations may be a sufficient deterrent for most coaches to ride free.

Perhaps the opposite problem will now seem pressing, namely, that individuals will be falsely accused of free riding and suffer social and other consequences as a result. This is possible, and can undoubtedly occur from time to time. However, it is unlikely if the coach has a record of honesty and he consults with his players and umpires in good faith (who can then report how a decision was arrived at). To protect the reputation of individuals, we might have a standard that the coach be certain beyond a reasonable doubt, or on a preponderance of evidence, that the call was an error (rather than simply on the balance of probabilities). In any event, we can only speculate at this point about the potential for casualties. It is encouraging, however, that self-officiated sports seem to proceed without victimizing the innocent. That empirical fact and the arguments given here are sufficient grounds to implement and test the ideas being proposed.

As an aside, it is worth noting that the problem of free riders helps to explain why the practice being proposed has not arisen naturally. Unless there are accepted norms of cooperation that there is some reason to think will be enforced either with legal or social punishment, it is not rational for a coach to offer to assist an umpire to correct a call or to answer such a request in good faith, because he has no reason to believe such an offer will ever be reciprocated. The corrupt conception of value that is part of sports adds further resistance. Participants have the goal of winning over others, after all. As well, the arguments about the connection between competitive success and distributive justice are not well understood. Perhaps if all these issues were understood better by sports participants and umpires, a practice of umpires consulting coaches could emerge naturally at some point. But it is undoubtedly too hopeful to expect education to solve this problem in any broad and systematic way, particularly in the current climate in which sports operates, and given reasonable concerns about free riding. Rules that clearly define and enforce expectations will be needed.

It is reasonable to ask how this would work in a formal sense. What sorts of rules should be adopted? This will be partly a matter of experimentation and experience, but some suggestions can be made. Sports leagues should explicitly recognize in their rules that umpires may consult with coaches about official decisions and that coaches have duties to comply honestly and in good faith with those requests. The rules should also state that a coach may consult with his or her players as part of responding to such a request. To ensure the efficient conduct of games, umpires could be directed to use this discretion on what appear to be key plays, like the ones described in the scenarios outlined at the beginning of the paper. However, I am not sure this is necessary. Baseball has a rule that permits umpires to overturn their own calls. It states that "the first requisite is to get decisions correctly. If in doubt don't hesitate to consult your associate" (Rule 9.05, *Official Baseball Rules*, 2011). This rule is not often invoked, but when it is, it is reasonable to think that umpires would be assisted if they could also consult coaches. But, as in law, there is a virtue, even if it is not overriding, in making a decision and letting the parties get on with the rest of the game (or their lives). In this respect, the *Official Rules of Baseball* set an instructive precedent in advising that umpires should not allow themselves to be "stampeded" by appeals to consult "the other man." It is fair to say baseball umpires have not fallen victim to this. It also remains to be seen how often coaches will request that umpires seek help from other coaches. They will probably learn quickly that they cannot put other coaches on the spot for "bang bang" plays because an opposing coach can reasonably claim uncertainty about the correct call. It is even possible that an ethos might emerge that only clear errors that are unaddressed by the umpires themselves will be pursued. The suggestion that the standard of proof for changing calls be a preponderance of evidence or no reasonable doubt standard should limit both coaches' requests for changes and umpires' willingness to pursue those requests. Taken together, these considerations show that there is good reason to believe that umpires can manage this area of discretion without jeopardizing the good conduct of games. Having said this, giving general direction to umpires that they may consult with coaches on judgments in an effort to ensure that the right calls are made is something that can also be experimented with in a variety of ways. For example, proposals can be applied initially in preseason games or in certain leagues in order to generate evidence for putting this practice into effect. We may learn from these and other efforts what works and what does not, including whether appeals of decisions should be limited in certain ways. Proper education of coaches, sports officials, and players on these matters should also be vigorously pursued.

The application of this proposal is bound to be different for different sports. For example, fast-moving sports with continuous play may sometimes make it difficult to review calls, since the play may advance despite the error. But it is still possible at a break in play to go back and consult coaches and their players as to, say, whether a goal was scored or some other key event occurred. For example, Frank Lampard's unrecognized goal in the 2010 World Cup semifinal, which would have pulled England into a 2–2 tie with Germany, would have been allowed, since the German goaltender Manuel Neuer acknowledged that Lampard's kick landed a foot inside the goal line, as replays confirmed. The German side won 4–1, but the outcome might have been different if that crucial play had been acknowledged. The basic point is that umpires in all sports will miss key events from time to time. If coaches, speaking on behalf of their teams, can agree that those errors should not be allowed to contribute to the outcome of a game, the goals as well as the morality of competitive sports will be advanced.

The proposals I have been making would appear to be less relevant in professional sports now that video replay is becoming a common aid to umpiring. But most professional sports below the highest levels will probably never use video replay, and virtually all amateur sports will never have video replay. So the proposal has practical relevance to nearly all sports. Even where video replay is available, it would nevertheless be useful and instructive to players and fans to permit umpires to consult opposing coaches from time to time about disputed decisions. If these could be resolved without recourse to video replay, or perhaps while it was going on, it would help to address the moral problems found in sports that were mentioned earlier.[10]

Conclusion

For some, my proposal will sound too radical to be taken seriously. But it is not clear that it is radical in any way that counts against the proposal. The conclusion of the argument that has been presented is perhaps surprising. But that is just a feature of any original argument. Moreover, in this case, the argument just traces out the implications of some compelling, and for the most part, familiar ideas about the nature of sports and justice. It also responds to plausible objections. There is nothing about the arguments, then, that makes them particularly radical. The proposal may be radical in the sense that it asks us to overturn some well-entrenched cultural practices. But this is often what philosophy, particularly moral philosophy, does. John Locke's rejection of the divine right of kings to govern and his idea that all humans, regardless of social rank, are entitled to the same inalienable rights was once such a radical idea that its author could claim authorship only after he died for fear that he would be executed. Mary Wollstonecraft's eighteenth-century defense of the rights of women presented a similarly radical challenge to cultural practices. The current proposal cannot be compared to these in either the originality of the arguments or its radical rejection of cultural orthodoxy. These historical examples, and many others besides, show us that we should be prepared to follow the arguments where they give us solid grounds for improving our cultural practices. The culture of competitive sports is no exception. We should insist that sports, like any other human institution, live up to reasonable moral standards. This becomes more important as sports become a more central part of human culture, as they are bound to do as basic human needs are met for more people and they have more opportunities for recreation and leisure. As competitive sports become a focus of more and more people's lives, the claims of justice will become more pressing, as will the importance of using sports as an example for other areas of human activity. Since coaches will be at the center of the sort of changes being proposed, they should be prepared to take these arguments seriously and assume a leading role in their implementation.[11]

Questions for Review and Discussion

1. Why does Russell think that umpiring errors reflect failures of distributive justice?

2. What arguments does Russell think will be used to show that coaches whose teams have benefited from an umpiring error should not be expected to assist umpires overturn that error? How does he respond to those arguments?

3. In addition to an argument based on distributive justice, Russell uses an argument from Robert L. Simon's work to show the importance of doing what is reasonable to ensure that umpires make the right decisions. What is that argument? Is one argument more fundamental than the other?

4. Is Russell right that the culturally entrenched practice of not having umpires consult with coaches is not a good ground in itself for rejecting his proposal?

5. Would Russell's proposal undermine the authority of umpires and kill the flow of many fast-paced sports such as basketball?

Suggestions for Further Reading

Aristotle. "The Varieties of Justice." In *Justice: Alternative Political Perspectives*. Edited by James Sterba. Belmont, CA: Wadsworth, 1980.

Berman, Mitchell N. "Replay." *California Law Review* 99 (2011): 1683–1743.

Browne, Alister. "Violating Rules of Rationing." *Canadian Journal of General Internal Medicine* 3:3 (2008): 127–128.

Chun, Janean. "Bank Deposit Error in Your Favor? Give It Back." *Daily Finance,* December 9, 2009.

Collins, Harry. "The Philosophy of Umpiring and the Introduction of Decision-Aid Technology." *Journal of the Philosophy of Sport* 37:2 (2010): 135–146.

Jailler, Ben. "Can You Keep Money Accidentally Paid into Your Bank Account?" www.money.co.uk/article/1005023-can-you-keep-money-accidentally -paid-into-your-bank-account.htm.

Major League Baseball. *Official Baseball Rules.* http://mlb.mlb.com/mlb /downloads/y2011/Official_Baseball_Rules.pdf.

Midgley, Mary. "The Game Game." In *The Ethics of Sports: A Reader.* Edited by Mike McNamee. London: Routledge, 2010.

Morgan, William J. *Why Sports Morally Matter.* New York: Routledge, 2006.

Rawls, John. *A Theory of Justice.* Cambridge: Harvard University Press, 1971.

Royce, Richard. "Refereeing and Technology: Reflections on Collins' Proposals." *Journal of the Philosophy of Sport* 39:1 (2012).

Russell, J. S. "Are Rules All an Umpire Has to Work With?" *Journal of the Philosophy of Sport* 26 (1999): 27–49.

———. "Competitive Sport, Moral Development, and Peace: Skeptical Reflections." In *A Companion to Sport Philosophy.* Edited by Cesar Torres. Forthcoming.

———. "The Concept of a Call in Baseball." *Journal of the Philosophy of Sport* 24 (1997): 21–37.

———"The Moral Ambiguity of Coaching Youth Sport." In *The Ethics of Sports Coaching.* Edited by Alun R. Hardman and Carwyn Jones. London: Routledge, 2011.

"Scarcity." Wikipedia: The Free Encyclopedia. http://en.wikipedia.org/wiki/Scarcity.

Simon, Robert L. *Fair Play: The Ethics of Sport.* 2nd ed. Boulder, CO: Westview, 2010.

Eight

Bench Players:
Do Coaches Have a Moral Obligation
to Play Benchwarmers?

SCOTT KRETCHMAR

Anyone who has ever played on a team or coached one knows the high stakes involved in grouping athletes into starters and reserves. Undoubtedly the public nature of organized sport contributes to these dynamics. After all, it is in front of fans, friends, parents, and sometimes national television audiences that athletes play lead roles, secondary roles, or no role at all.

I know there is safety on the bench. I have spent time there. Athletes who do not get into the game will never make the mistake that turns a certain victory into an improbable defeat. Those who live at the end of the bench will not face the sometimes extreme pressure and so-called trait anxieties encountered by those who play regularly (Smith et al. 1995). But there is potential harm there too. Every athlete, from the fabled Rudy of Notre Dame to the youngster on the local sandlot team, wants to get into the game.[1] While simply belonging to a team has its rewards, that is usually not enough.

In this chapter, I do not present knock-down arguments in favor of more equitable methods for distributing playing time. Rather, I argue that concerns over winning and excellence should be toned down in favor of better meeting the rights and interests of the players to get on the court or field. My theoretical framework is informed by deontological sentiments. I believe that context matters in deciding appropriate amounts of playing time. Thus I generally favor act over rule approaches to this problem. The deontological side of my thinking privileges the rights of players over arguments for utility. I will not be arguing that spreading out playing time maximizes pleasure or any other benefit. Rather, I argue that it is the right thing to do for the players involved.

Others take different positions on this issue and have good reasons for doing so. Isn't it sufficient, they would ask, to be identified as a talented performer by virtue of one's team membership, to wear the jersey, to work under the watchful eye of a coach, to practice and improve, to go on team trips, to experience the friendships that grow between members of close-knit groups? Shouldn't players be able to gain satisfaction by helping the squad in ways other than making plays on the court or field? Furthermore, if coaches are forthright about playing time, if they tell athletes and parents up front that they will be making decisions based on maximizing chances for competitive success, where is the harm? Sport is egalitarian, but it is also a meritocracy. Nobody is guaranteed playing time. It must be earned.

These considerations are persuasive but not decisive. I say this because the issue of rights to playing time is complicated. First, it depends, at least in part, on context. Moral qualms about a lack of playing time are typically greater in youth sports than, say, Division I NCAA college athletics, and even less so in professional sports. In other words, from the fact that it is morally appropriate to keep a reserve on the bench at one level of sports, it does not necessarily follow that it is equally appropriate at other levels or in other athletic contexts. Many youth leagues have rules that require minimum levels of participation. Such rules, however, would be inappropriate or even laughable if applied to the Boston Celtics or New York Yankees.

The second complicating factor is related to the goods that are said to accrue to benchwarmers. They may or may not be sufficient. We cannot assume that reserve players are "getting a good deal" merely by being members of the team. Much would seem to hinge on how these individuals were treated and on such contingent issues as whether or not the athletes were on scholarship or were being paid. And much would depend on how we adjudicate individual rights against corporate goals and how much weight we give to such stakeholders as fans and those with business interests.

Third, while a coach's honesty about playing time is laudable and helpful, it is not sufficient. Telling players up front that they may be treated, in effect, more as means than ends does not necessarily mitigate or excuse harms befalling athletes from subsequent manipulations. Of course athletes, so informed, could choose not to play. But in sporting situations where many

players achieve elite status on the foundation of large financial and psychological investments, the choice not to participate or to participate only under unfavorable terms places them in a very difficult situation, to say the least.

These kinds of considerations suggest that the rights, goods, and harms
associated with access to playing time will not be easily determined. Before
launching into this matter, however, I will clarify precisely what the issue is.

Benchwarmers are athletes who rarely play in actual games or play only
for short periods when the game outcome has been decided. Typically, these
are the younger, less seasoned, and less skilled individuals. These are the players who sit at the proverbial end of the bench. I am not as concerned about reserves who play significant minutes, who come off the bench regularly as role
players, or who otherwise get into many contests when outcomes are still up
for grabs. While some arguments presented here apply to them as well, their
status as game contributors significantly reduces ethical concerns related to
playing time.

In addition, playing time does not necessarily mean equal playing
time. "Meaningful playing time," as I call it, has to do with when an athlete
plays as much as how long that individual is on the court or field. Allowing
subs in high school basketball to play the last twenty-two seconds of a
blowout victory would not count as meaningful playing time to my way of
thinking.

My analysis works better for team sports like basketball, football, soccer,
and baseball, for example, than individual sports like tennis, golf, swimming,
and track and field. Some of the sting of not getting to play seems less severe
in these activities if only because many of them do not typically take place in
front of large crowds. Yet even in these sports, there are individuals who get
into the game and others who do not. The question of the ethics of playing reserves is still relevant, even if at a lesser level.[2]

Finally, it is important to distinguish between ethical and prudential reasons for playing reserves. Coaches may have strategic reasons to use their entire bench, but these motives and decisions do not speak directly to moral
duties or responsibilities. To be sure, moral and prudential reasons can coin-
cide, and when they do so, we count it as fortunate. But this need not be the
case. Thus I will not be focusing on strategic reasons for playing benchwarmers, such as the following:

1. The importance of keeping starters fresh and ready for late-game surges

2. The importance of having starters get out of the game to watch and reflect,
   get instructions, improve their mind-set, or spend time on the bench for
   other reasons

3. The significance of preparing for injuries to starters, of having well-seasoned reserves ready to step in

4. The possibility that reserves may mature into better players than some current starters

5. The likelihood that disgruntled reserves will quit the team or, at the college level, transfer to another institution

6. The fact that team morale may be improved, that practices may go better if everyone can look forward to playing time

7. The importance of providing stability to a program, of protecting it from the ups and downs due to graduation or departures for other reasons

Clearly coaches have strategically sound reasons for playing reserves. Consequently it is both ethical *and* smart for coaches to give meaningful playing time to all or most of their bench players. But once again, for purposes of this analysis, I will focus on the ethical requirements for such a decision.

First Experiences: Playing Time, Learning, and Fun

Moral hackles about lack of playing time seem to be raised most often when young children do not get onto the field or court. If my seven-year-old were to remain on the bench because some coach is nervous about losing a game, I might justifiably conclude that things are not right. Youth sport, it is commonly thought, should afford participation opportunities for the talented and untalented alike. Winning, if it is to have any influence on coaching decisions, should be a secondary consideration at most.

Even Little League, an organization that has been criticized for placing financial objectives over educational values, has a mandatory play rule.[3] Rule 8.3 reads as follows:

> In all divisions except Senior and Big League, every player on the team roster must have at least one plate appearance and play three consecutive outs on defense in each game. The penalty for a manager violating the rule is a two-game suspension. This rule is waived if the game is completed prior to the usual duration of the game (six innings in Little League and below, seven innings in Junior League). http://en.wikipedia.org/wiki/Little_League_Baseball#Mandatory_Play _Rule

Virtually all youth sports coaching books include similar recommendations, and most town leagues around the country have mandatory play rules. A virtual consensus exists that all team members in what might be called early or first-experience sporting contexts should get to play in all the games.

This insight seems to rest on what Simon (2010) and others have identified as rights to basic benefits. In a nutshell, the argument runs as follows: in youth sport, the focus should be on learning the game, on developing personal skills, and on enjoying the activity. Every kid, it would seem, has a right to learn and improve. Every child has a right to play in a physically and psychologically safe environment. Because of this, playing time should be well distributed. Performance anxiety should be kept to a minimum. This is a time for development and fun.

The developmental or educational side of the argument is a powerful one. It relies on old physical education principles related to preparation for life. Everyone, physical educators would say, should have skills that allow them to engage in healthful and enjoyable recreational activities across the life span. With a so-called obesity epidemic facing American youth, it is important for kids to get away from their computer screens, develop some skills for negotiating outdoor activities successfully, and enjoy themselves.

The idea of playing time as a basic benefit and an educational experience also points to the future well-being of young athletes. It is very difficult to tell who will excel in different domains of learning. Some mature slowly but pick up the pace later. Particularly in anatomically and physiologically intensive activities like sports, it is sometimes difficult to predict later performance capabilities. Thus in a liberal democratic society like our own, we should err on the side of opportunity. We should provide a basic education to everyone and keep these doors of empowerment open as long as possible so that late bloomers, as well as those who face socioeconomic, racial, ethnic, or biological developmental barriers, will have a chance. In most youth sports settings, this means that children should have access to the full sporting experience . . . both the practicing and the playing.

Furthermore, positive affect is crucial to the educational agenda. Those who enjoy the sporting experience are more likely to persist. Those who persist will continue their activities into adulthood and even old age. Those who have the lifelong companionship of a favorite sport or outdoor activity will lead healthier, happier, and longer lives. Positive affect, on this line of thinking, is tethered to participation. And, all things being equal, it is far more fun for a seven-year-old to play than to watch.

Empirical studies support these speculations. In a landmark survey of 20,000 American youth, researchers found that the number one reason given by athletes for participation was "fun" (Seefeld et al. 1992). Fun was followed by "doing something I am good at," while "staying fit and healthy" ranked third. Winning did not even crack the top 10. Children want to play, and they enjoy doing things that show some degree of competence.

Nationally recognized youth coaches like Bob Bigelow take positions that are consistent with this research. He argues that "meaningful playing time for every player is job one." He goes on to suggest that if playing reserves "ends up costing the game, and if that hurts [coaches] too much, they should get out of coaching youth athletics and do something else" (Bigelow 2011, 1).

Youth Sports: Playing Time in a Period of Transition

The language of rights and benefits works well with young children, but it loses force at higher levels of competition. As already noted, it does not carry much weight in professional sports where athletes are elite performers, where imperatives of winning and market logic hold sway, and where even bench-warmers command handsome salaries. But what about college . . . high school . . . or even junior high? Where do the right to playing time and the commitment to education and play disappear or at least carry less weight?

Many years ago I learned that the cut-off point could be found at the middle school level. Our family had just moved from upstate New York to rural Pennsylvania. My daughter had successfully tried out for the seventh and eighth grade girl's basketball team. Prior to the start of the season, the coach called a meeting for the parents and players. We were told to sit on the bleachers in the gym.

The coach was all business. With a serious expression on his face he informed us that the team would be focused on winning and preparing select players for future membership on the JV and varsity teams! Regular practices would be demanding, voluntary practices were not really voluntary, and playing time would be limited or nonexistent for "those who are not ready." Before sending us off, he reminded us that he, and he alone, would decide who, when, and how much anyone played.

I have some sympathy for the message delivered by the coach. I can appreciate problems presented by basketball parents who expect the coach, as the old joke puts it, "to start their child and the next four best players." Furthermore, this coach's businesslike, competitive approach is probably not unusual, even at the middle school level. These kids are in the pipeline, as it were, for future athletic experiences where winning and losing will matter more and the public will take greater interest in game results.

However, it still makes sense to ask if this approach is appropriate, particularly for middle school athletes. After all, we do not usually cut students out of any significant learning opportunities at this level of education. We don't say to those who are less capable in math or English that "they do not get to play anymore." Should we not, therefore, keep the educational door open and the play spirit alive a little longer in the athletic domain? A heavy focus on winning and excellence can come later. The earnestness against which Johan Huizinga (1950) railed—that overly sober and serious attitude that replaces the play spirit—can come later too.

These concerns are not shared by everyone. Some might cite the fact that schools place gifted academic students into accelerated curriculums by the seventh grade. Less talented students simply "do not make the team" and are channeled into less demanding courses of study. Also, some schools participate in competitions sponsored by Knowledge Masters, National History Day, Mathcounts, spelling bees, or science fairs—events that are designed to pit the best intellects from one school against those from another. Critics might point out that nobody is guaranteed "playing time" in these activities either.

While this is true, and while playing time for athletes might be dealt with more judiciously in middle school than in children's sports settings, this argument does not settle the case. To be sure, caution about playing time for a low-end reserve is warranted both for the sake of the team and the potential embarrassment for that individual. On educational grounds alone, we would not want to put a youngster in a situation where high cost and publicly visible failure is likely. Similarly, we would probably not want a coach to sacrifice all team goals for any hard and fast commitments to equal playing time.

On the other hand, we have to remember that we are dealing with eleven-, twelve-, thirteen-, and fourteen-year-olds in this situation. And we have to remember that controversy often surrounds educational stratifications and the limitations they place on those who are deemed "unqualified." Many educational policies are based on the premise that individuals need time to develop . . . sometimes even through their college years and beyond.[4] For reasons that are often outside their control—reasons that range from biological and economic to cultural—some students arrive at desirable destinations earlier than others. While the promotion of excellence is culturally important and while the rights of the gifted are as important as the rights of others, some balance would seem to be in order, particularly at these earlier levels of education. Because of this need for balance, some weight should still be given to the basic benefits argument. How much weight is merited is, of course, open to question.

I don't see any slam-dunk answers to this question. Conclusions have to do with judgment, with how values are prioritized. Middle school athletes are, as my daughter's coach reminded us, preparing for varsity experiences several years hence. Such preparation places a priority on excellence, winning, individual rights, and ultimately on public or fan interests and so-called front porch values of athletics for a school or school system. These can be important considerations.

The basic benefits argument, on the other hand, prioritizes competence and learning rather than excellence, group rights and participation, personal educational benefit over fan interest, and sports as an educational laboratory more than a high-visibility vehicle for educational or noneducational ends. These too are, or can be, important values.[5]

My own judgment is that the junior high school level of sporting experience should privilege basic benefits over scarce benefits, educational values over public entertainment benefits and related emphases on winning. Perhaps the ratio should be something like 70:30 or 60:40. This would suggest that coaches still have an important moral obligation to play all their athletes. The moral obligation is tethered to the fact that middle school is still a time for development, fun, and protection from overspecialization and high doses of performance anxiety. While the winnowing process has begun, while victories take on increased importance, and while all individuals cannot expect or get equal playing time, the logic of education and play should still provide the dominant themes for the experience. The coach should still be far more the inclusive, duty-bound educator than the exclusive coaching technician or instrumentalist.[6]

High School Athletics: Playing Time and Reciprocity

If my argument is on track, it stands to reason that high school coaches are less obligated to give playing time to benchwarmers. In this setting the group works more exclusively toward common ends—a victory, a winning season, a championship. Sacrificing individual interests for corporate goals is expected. Coaches can lose their jobs if win-loss records are not favorable. Hardly anybody in this kind of competitive environment is guaranteed playing time. This is where a commitment to excellence makes sense—both individual and team excellence. And arguably, team excellence cannot be achieved when coaches have to worry about playing time for low-end reserves, individuals whose play will likely endanger team objectives.

Furthermore, reserves at the high school level enjoy any number of benefits, even if playing time is not one of them. Several of these goods or benefits appear at the beginning of the chapter. Given these realities and under these circumstances, shouldn't lesser players be happy with their lot . . . or at least appreciate the reasons for their spot on the bench? I am not sure that they should.

First, although the educational, basic benefits argument is less weighty in high school and high school age settings,[7] it does not follow that it should disappear altogether. After all, high school sports take place in an educational context. Extracurricular activities like varsity sports are compatible with core educational values and purposes espoused by school systems and contribute to those ends. If playing, in addition to watching and practicing, carries educational benefit, and if rights to educational benefit apply to all members of a team, then coaches have a prima facie obligation to allow kids to play. Coaches, in other words, have a moral obligation *as educators* to give lesser players meaningful playing time.

I say that there is a prima facie obligation because I admit that the *actual* obligation, as noted previously, is undoubtedly less than the ideal of equal playing time. Rights to educational benefit do not trump all other values or considerations. Equal respect accorded to starters and reserves, for instance, may well provide a rationale for meaningful but unequal playing time.

Second, the ethics of fair play in the form of reciprocity could be used to forge a more equitable arrangement between coach and bench player. Coaches need the services of reserves, even individuals who are not required for game contributions. Much team success can be attributed to how well reserves practice, how well they serve as "scout team" members, how much spirit and enthusiasm they show, and so on.

But reserves want to play. They hope against hope that they will improve enough to become starters. If not that, they picture themselves getting into a game when the outcome is still undecided, perhaps even doing something heroic. But for that story to have any chance of becoming reality, the coach needs to put the athlete in the game.

Ethics enters this scene of mutual need and potential benefit, as Singer (1995) noted, on the foundation of two virtues—trust and fidelity. The athlete has to trust the coach because the player has to meet his part of the bargain first. A coach could defect and not put the player into the game in spite of the player's previous goodwill actions. Thus the coach must show the second virtue—fidelity—in order to make good on his promise to the player.

Kohlberg (1981) argues that this kind of "I'll scratch your back if you scratch mine" ethic involves a relatively low level of moral thinking.[8] It would be better if the issue could be settled on principles of justice—on the idea that fairness requires the coach to provide at least a taste of what the benchwarmer really wants in light of that individual's hard work and contribution to the team. But in the absence of high-minded ethics, trust, fidelity, and reciprocity might provide a degree of protection for athletes who want to get into the game but find themselves blocked by coaches who have the final say.

Critics might insist that the reciprocity argument does not work. First, reserves may be expendable. To that extent, coaches have no incentive to enter into such agreements. In addition, some might point out, this is not a relationship among equals. The coach is in charge. Compliance on the part of the player can be required. Coercion can serve as a substitute for ethics by agreement. The coach does not need to promise playing time because the coach does not need to offer it in order to get what he wants.

I do not find these arguments persuasive because they seem more descriptive than normative. The unequal status of the coach and the players fuels many of the ethical dilemmas that occur in sports. While the coach may be able to replace a reserve who is audacious enough to bargain for playing time, and while the coach has most of the power, the coach is still mentor and educator. As an individual who should have concern for all athletes on the team, the logic of reciprocity should appear attractive both ethically and motivationally. The coach should be sympathetic to the fact that the hardworking reserve has at least some call on a benefit that all players desire—getting on the court or field in a real game when it still matters . . . and for more than a couple of seconds.

It stands to reason, then, that prima facie educational obligations and the ethics of reciprocity (if not principles of justice or loyalty) would suggest that high school coaches do have a moral obligation to find meaningful playing time for all reserves . . . at least those who are dedicated, hardworking, and committed to team success.

Collegiate Level:
Playing Time and Competitive Excellence

It's not unreasonable to hold that basic benefits arguments, educational obligations, the ethics of reciprocity, and even principles of loyalty and justice continue to be operative at the collegiate level. This is still an educational setting. A reasonable presumption is that sports in this environment should privilege players and their interests over business-related, front porch–driven, win-at-all-costs philosophies. Thus college athletes who sit at the far end of the bench should get a chance to play too.[9]

A number of utilitarian economic arguments might be offered in opposition to this perspective. Particularly at the NCAA Division I level, and most notably in football and basketball, it could be argued that economic imperatives do (and should) trump educational objectives. Winning is essential. The use of low-end reserves flies in the face of this reality. Even coaches who would like to play reserves regularly will not do so. Unilateral disarmament, in big-time sports, is a nonstarter.

But there is another, less controversial argument against using reserves in games: college sports require the prioritization of excellence over mediocrity.

College athletes are elite performers. They should focus on team and individual excellence. They should aim at perfection . . . even if they never achieve it.

Here is where the ethical rub comes in. Arguably, team excellence is promoted most efficiently and effectively by catering to the best players on the team or those with the greatest potential. Time and energy investments make more sense there than elsewhere. On this line of reasoning, reserves in general, and end-of-the-bench reserves in particular, should serve facilitating roles—not to foster each other's performance but to maximize better players and thus the team. For any low-end reserves, this facilitating role will perpetuate their lesser status. After all, time used to facilitate teammates' growth is, at least in part, time lost for one's own performance needs.

This claim could be verified empirically. How do reserves spend their time in practice? How many reps do they get? How often does a coach give them individual attention, especially in contrast to the starters? How often are they required to learn the next opponent's offense in order to facilitate the starting team's defensive preparations? How infrequently are the starters asked to return the favor and facilitate the reserves' readiness to play against the next opponent?

Answers to these questions, for anyone who has participated in or observed college practices, are clear. Lower-end reserves are asked to sacrifice their own quest for excellence for the sake of the team. To be sure, this can still be a gratifying experience, and college athletes enter into such agreements with their eyes wide open. But it still needs to be made clear that the quest for excellence (and the winning that goes with it) carries risks for those who show less promise of achieving high levels of expertise and whose services are needed to facilitate the excellence of others.

Many reserves who are used as means to team ends but are not compensated with opportunities for playing time still approach practice with determination and hope. Like Rudy, they may put forth twice the effort of some starters. Because they are part of the team, they have a chance to get on the court or field . . . even if the cards are stacked against them.

And the cards usually are stacked against them. They begin their team journey with lesser skills and less game experience. Without equal attention at practice, and without learning opportunities provided by playing time, the gap between the starters and reserves tends to increase. In corresponding fashion, the odds of the reserve earning much playing time before graduation grow longer.

However, excellence is a powerful value and worthy objective. Sacrifices by teammates in its pursuit may be warranted, particularly at elite college levels. Nevertheless, when the value of excellence is combined with the logic of instrumentalism, individual rights may be put at risk and a more balanced view of sporting values may be lost.

These are precisely the concerns raised by the NCAA Committee on Women's Athletics (CWA) in 2007 when it argued that male practice players should be barred from women's intercollegiate programs. They claimed that the use of men violated the spirit, if not also the letter, of Title IX legislation and cited two reasons. First, the availability of males for practice allowed coaches to carry fewer women on their rosters. This reduced opportunity. In addition, with males on the court or field at practice, women reserves were standing on the sidelines and thus receiving less practice time.

No less personages than Tennessee's Pat Summit and Rutgers's Vivian Stringer supported the use of male practice players, and their primary argument rested on an appeal to excellence. Stringer said, "It is the male practice players that allow us to get better. . . . Male practice players are the most important element to the continued growth of women's basketball players" (*USA Today* 2007).

Jim Foster, the Ohio State women's basketball coach, took an opposing view. When told of all the good the male practice players brought to the sport he replied, "I'd like to hear the stories of the [women] who didn't get to practice and had to stand and watch." He continued, "To take even more time and more reps from a segment of players almost dooms them to mediocrity" (*USA Today,* 2007).

Most women coaches and administrators sided with Summit and Stringer. They agreed that male practice players can expedite the development of good female players and women's teams in the direction of excellence. At this level excellence should trump opportunity. There should be no turning back on the commitment to enhancing the quality of play. If males proved more efficient and effective in producing excellence in women's basketball, they should stay.

Predictably, the legislation proposed by the CWA went nowhere. Thus in Division III, male practice players are still permitted with certain restrictions.[10] In Divisions I and II, males can serve as "practice guys" with few limitations.[11]

This nexus between excellence and instrumentalism has obvious and important implications for the rights of benchwarmers and for any moral obligations of coaches to let them play. If those last few seats on the game bench can be left vacant—for purposes of promoting excellence—any and all moral obligations about playing those individuals disappear. No one needs to worry about the rights and interests of players who no longer exist.

Some might argue that the last few positions on the bench, at least at the college level, are not playing positions anyhow. Normal rotations in football, basketball, soccer, and the like do not require the full complement of athletes carried on a team. The use of male practice players, therefore, merely formalizes a relationship that existed before their use. End of the bench positions are de facto practice positions, not playing positions. Whether they are males or females makes no difference. They are facilitators. If men function better than women as practice facilitators, why not use them? Either way, no *playing* positions are lost.

But this begs the very question at issue. Should end of the bench positions be strictly practice positions? And should individual and team excellence stand as sufficient warrant for the sacrifices required of those who would facilitate such excellence? Could the logic of excellence and facilitation be extended to male teams too?

Why not reduce men's collegiate basketball teams to ten or eleven players, just as many women's teams have done? Perhaps new NCAA legislation could be passed to allow recently retired NBA players or semipros who are not even students to serve as practice guys for the men's teams—all for purposes of promoting excellence.

Michael Sandel (2007) confronted similar logical possibilities when he examined issues of technology and interests in achieving perfection. He worried that an unbridled quest for perfection can rob us of crucial elements of our humanity—humility, responsibility, and solidarity.

The most relevant of these for current purposes is probably solidarity. Teams, it seems to me, pool both their resources and their risks. Because individuals cannot control all sporting variables, they join hands in hopes of flourishing on the back of combined talents but also in recognition that protection is needed from unforeseen problems. Not all will play starring roles, but all could play important roles. Humility and mutual dependency lead to strong feelings of community, of "us."

According to Sandel, Promethean hopes for total control work against an ethic of solidarity. Social and psychological engineering replaces the magical "chemistry of a team" that often surprises us and fills us with gratitude. Maximal developmental strategies, controlled environments, and ideally prepared practice players replace the nonlinear and unpredictable drama of learning. Efficiency substitutes for the uncertain dynamics of the benchwarmer who lives with hope of playing time while sacrificing for the good of a larger cause. These trade-offs move us to a place where we no longer depend, wonder, and support.

Sandel would prefer the messier situation in which individuals willingly and humbly choose to pool their assets in order to minimize their liabilities. This is a world in which choice is tempered with chance.

The coach should be part of this pooling of risks and resources. A team is a family of stronger and weaker members, of individuals who serve different roles but have common aspirations. The coach and superior team members should be rooting for the lesser players to improve and succeed—to get into a game and do something well.

Conclusion

Benchwarmers occupy the real estate for a variety of reasons. Some individuals deserve to be there . . . and perhaps some even deserve to *stay* there. There is no absolute right to playing time at the upper levels of sports. Correspondingly, coaches have no absolute moral obligations to play reserves.

However, I have argued that a prima facie obligation does exist. It is stronger at introductory and youth levels of sports and lesser at higher levels. In youth sports settings, education, development, opportunity, healthful exercise, and play are basic benefits that should trump any concerns over winning, excellence, financial gain, and the like. Everybody should play, and everybody should play for significant portions of the game.

I derided the overly serious attitudes of middle school coaches for quickly abandoning these values. Late bloomers deserve a chance. All kids are still learning the basics. The spirit of play should be kept alive. All players should be given a reasonable chance to get on the court or field.

I suggest that educational values should play a role in high school sports. The ethics of reciprocity might serve to mitigate potential harms of the unequal power relationship between coach and benchwarmer. A coach might feel that justice requires at least a degree of compensation (in the form of playing time) for the hardworking low-end reserve. I agree, however, that both for the sake of the lesser player and the team, decisions about how much playing time is provided need to be judicious.

At the college level, commitments to excellence provide arguments that justify the parsimonious use of low-end reserves or even their elimination . . . if and when practice functions can be assumed more efficiently and effectively by others. In such an instrumental sporting world, a coach would be blamed not so much for abusing reserves but for having them on the team in the first place.

I prefer to err on the side of opportunity. I like the moral ties that exist in large families where one person in encouraged to look out for the other. I think it is a sign of strength, not weakness, when a coach worries about providing meaningful playing time for the last person on the bench. It is when those concerns disappear, and even more so when the players who should be the objects of such concerns disappear, that I worry about the health of the entire sporting enterprise.

Questions for Review and Discussion

1. Why does Kretchmar argue that context is so important in deciding on the ethics of playing time? Can you identify ten contextual issues that might affect an athlete's right to play . . . and a coach's moral obligation to put him on the court or field?

2. How important is it for a coach to be honest with players and parents up front about playing time? Do you agree with Kretchmar that such "truth in advertising" does not remove moral obligations for playing benchwarmers?

3. Was it useful to organize the article chronologically—from youth sports through intercollegiate athletics? Can you imagine other ways in which this argument could have been formatted?

4. Kretchmar places great emphasis on education in order to support his arguments for more equitable playing time. If one removed this issue, what other kinds of arguments remain?

5. Where do you stand on the issue of promoting excellence? What kinds of trade-offs are justifiable in a society that honors fine performances? Can you rally an argument to the effect that excellence should trump learning and athlete's rights to playing time at elite levels?

Suggestions for Further Reading

Bigelow, B. Youth Coaches: Meaningful Playing Time for Every Player Is Job One. 2011. www.monsteam.com.

Huizinga, J. *Homo Ludens: A Study of the Play Element in Culture*. Boston: Beacon, 1950.

Kohlberg, L. *The Philosophy of Moral Development*. San Francisco: Harper & Row, 1981.

MacIntyre, A. *After Virtue: A Study in Moral Theory*. 2nd ed. Notre Dame, IN: Notre Dame Press, 1984.

NCAA Division III Manual: Constitution, Operating Bylaws, Administrative Bylaws. Indianapolis: NCAA, 2011.

Patrick, Dick. "Women Practicing versus Men: Yea or Nay?" *USA Today,* January 16, 2007.

Sandel, M. *The Case Against Perfection: Ethics in the Age of Genetic Engineering*. Cambridge: Harvard University Press, 2007.

Seefeldt, V., M. Ewing, and S. Walk. *Overview of Youth Sports Programs in the United States*. Washington, DC: Carnegie Council on Adolescent Development, 1992.

Simon, R. *Fair Play: The Ethics of Sport*. Boulder, CO: Westview, 2010.

Singer, P. *How Are We to Live? Ethics in an Age of Self-Interest*. Amherst, NY: Prometheus, 1995.

Smith, R., F. Smoll, and N. Barnett. "Reduction of Children's Sport Performance Anxiety Through Social Support and Stress-Reduction Training for Coaches." *Journal of Applied Developmental Psychology* 16 (1995.): 125–142.

Nine

Coaching, Gamesmanship, and Intimidation

MARK HAMILTON

Having lived in Ohio all my life and being an avid Ohio sports fan, I know about coaches who use intimidation. I grew up watching Woody Hayes coach Ohio State; Bobby Knight is a local hero who grew up less than an hour away (my high school basketball coach was one of his college teammates). Throughout junior and senior high school I watched basketball games coached by Bill Musselman at Ashland College. Known for creating intimidating, energy-charged pregame warm-up drills and for later coaching the University of Minnesota in college basketball's best known on-the-court fight against Ohio State in 1972, Musselman is quoted as saying, "Losing is worse than death because you have to live with defeat." The list of intimidating coaches from Ohio is extensive—coaches who know how to threaten officials, players, and reporters, who bully anyone else who gets in their way on or off the playing field. And they are praised as coaches who know how to motivate players and win games. This used to be an accepted practice among coaches. While it has waned, it is still overlooked in a coach who wins. Any serious evaluation or moral critique of coaching ethics must include a close inspection of intimidation and bullying by coaches as a means of gamesmanship.

Gamesmanship

Gamesmanship is a method used by coaches or athletes to gain an upper hand in a contest. The concept originates from Stephen Potter's 1947 book, *The Theory and Practice of Gamesmanship.* In this well-known satirical work Potter calls it "'The Art of Winning Games Without Actually Cheating'—that is my personal 'working definition.'"[1] Leslie Howe characterized it "as an attempt to win one game by playing another . . . [it] is a deliberate strategy of competition . . . designed for winning regardless of athletic excellence."[2] It is using numerous strategic tactics to better one's position in the game or using dubious methods to secure an unfair victory while remaining within the constitutive rules of the game.[3] Although some consider all gamesmanship cheating, it is not cheating narrowly understood as intentionally violating the constitutive rules of a contest. Gamesmanship ruthlessly pursues victory by all means short of apparent rule breaking. Most consider it a legal but not necessarily moral approach to playing games. Howe continues, "Violation of the rules is already [necessarily] prohibited by the rules; attempting to violate the rules is cheating [which nullifies the game], and gamesmanship [I am supposing] is not identical with cheating, though it might have much the same end, namely, winning with less strictly athletic effort."[4] So while it may not technically violate the written rules of the contest, gamesmanship uses maneuvers that threaten the spirit of the game and attains victory through skullduggery.

There are numerous species in the genus of gamesmanship. These include attempting to gain competitive advantage by (1) manipulating but not actually violating the rules,[5] (2) withholding information, (3) practicing outright deception, or (4) using intimidation in its various forms.[6] This chapter will focus on the use of intimidation as it intensifies into bullying, which includes nonphysical ploys primarily expressed as verbal intimidation and threats or actual physical violence.

Potter describes the lesser forms of intimidation as attempts to disrupt the opponent's play or "break the flow." This encompasses getting "inside one's opponent's head" by such things as intentionally disrupting an opponent's play, distracting him, getting him to "over think" his moves, or disrupting his concentration.[7] Potter provides an example of disrupting a rival's concentration by falsely and intentionally accusing him of cheating.[8] Using trick plays, stealing signs, or bantering with opponents are acceptable forms of psychological subterfuge. Other measures include growing a shadow beard to create a "menacing" appearance or wearing ominous-looking uniforms. These are amusing more than intimidating, though they are motivated by a desire to apply psychological intimidation. More serious intimidation attempts include calling timeouts to "ice" a shooter or kicker, taunting, throwing inside in baseball, or firing slap shots at a goalie's head or stacking the ice with thugs in hockey.[9] But if these practices do not actually violate the rules of the game, can they possibly be justified?

Intimidation is always negative and should never be used, but at advanced levels is disputably a part of the regulative nature of the game.[10] Howe argues that "the good of competitive sport is that it is a test of the whole athlete—not just his or her physical skills."[11] It is a misconception to think that advanced sports involve only physical participation, when in fact there are strong intellectual dimensions and players participate as whole beings. This is the justification, says Howe, for using intimidating methods: "The opponent who directs a strategy of gamesmanship against a competitor constructs an opportunity for the other to fail, but the decisive move, the failure, belongs to the target. If the gamer's behavior is within the rules, it cannot be unfair, and the competitive failure of the target is not the result of unfair advantage. It is because the target did not pass one of the fundamental aspects of competition: the test of psychological strength and preparedness."[12] This can only be defensible at higher echelons of competition. Can the receiver running a pattern over the middle who is legally popped by a linebacker mentally recover from the linebacker's intimidating hit to repeat the pattern? Does the field goal kicker waiting to attempt the game-winning kick on the last play of the game withstand the pressure of the defensive team calling a time-out to ice him? Can the visiting college free throw shooter weather the intimidating pressure of the screaming hometown crowd? These mental tests are part of the challenge, and to remove this form of gamesmanship could radically alter the contemporary challenges of these sports.

Howe also makes a moral distinction between different forms of gamesmanship and argues that some forms are necessary while others are impermissible: "We have to make a distinction between 'weak' and 'strong' forms of gamesmanship, the former designating the forms of gamesmanship that are compatible with an ideal of sport as a 'mutual challenge to achieve excellence' and the latter marking out those that are not. Actions such as throwing inside, the fast break, hard tens, and withholding line-up and injury information would fall into the weak category; deception with regard to line calls and fouls ('simulation'), gross acts of intimidation such as physical abuse (especially where this is above the norm expected in that sport), mobbing officials, and disrupting players' preparations would count in the strong category. The criterion we need to apply, then, in attempting to distinguish between appropriate and inappropriate forms of gamesmanship is whether the practice improves both participants or not."[13] Or whether it contributes to the merit of the challenge. Some forms of gamesmanship are valuable and possibly necessary to games if they do not degrade the participants and they contribute to the success of the challenge. Others are morally suspect, asserts Howe, since they are athletically self-defeating.[14]

However, even weak forms of intimidation are unacceptable in recreational games or where the participants are young. These additional mental challenges are a legitimate part of the game only among those who have a sophisticated level of understanding of the sport and are playing at a reasonably competitive level.[15] Forms of weak intimidation are acceptable in higher levels of sports that include psychological testing as part of the regulative aspect of the game. Bullying is always immoral.

Intimidation and Bullying as Gamesmanship

Intimidation is intended to elicit fear, to browbeat or to frighten someone into submission by inducing distress or a sense of inferiority.[16] Consequently intimidation excludes the mild or weak forms of intimidation. Coaches use intimidation as a form of gamesmanship to gain an advantage over their opponents by breaking the will of the officials, the opponents, or their own players so they can improve their positioning in sporting contests. When understood this way, intimidation is nearly synonymous to bullying.

Bullying is "a conscious, willful, deliberate and repeated hostile activity marked by an imbalance of power, intent to harm, and/or a threat to aggression. Severe bullying can lead to a feeling of terror on the part of the person being bullied."[17] Bullying employs deliberate and repeated antagonistic activity that includes swearing and uncontrollable screaming as its most common manifestation, lurid, offensive comments hurled at an athlete including insults and put-downs. There is constant negativity and criticism that is derogatory in nature and includes publicly ridiculing and humiliating players. "The bully-coach's repertoire includes shouting, cursing, personal denigration, and humiliation. So intimidating is the bully-coach that few young people dare to summon the courage to approach him, let alone challenge his technique or pronouncements."[18] Bobby Knight exemplifies this behavior. As one observer reports, Knight had been seen to "get in kids' faces, grab them by the arms, and spray his spit onto cheeks as he ranted at them. We had seen him show disrespect to referees. He used his body, his eyes, facial gestures, and words to intimidate in the hope of affecting performance or decisions. . . . But his public bullying not only damaged his players, it also set a public example that amateur coaches inevitably mimicked."[19] The most dreadful forms of sports bullying include acts of violence, threats of physical violence, or blaming athletes for failure. Knight once said to player Steve Risley, "The reason we lost the game was you, it was your fault."[20]

However, Knight is not a rarity. Consider the following example of bullying as public humiliation in a seventh grade gym class by a junior high school football coach, probably similar to what has gone on in gyms or on playing fields everywhere. "We would play some sort of group game where the winners could return to the locker room one by one, leaving the loser for the end. This last would be called the 'Green Weenie' and his name would be placed on a chalkboard for everyone to see. I remember how hard I would try to avoid being last. On one particular day, I tried as hard as I could and actually came in second to last. I wasn't last!!! The coach just looked at me and said, 'You are always the greenie weenie' and wrote my name on the board as he laughed."[21] Some coaches are just mean. They pump themselves up to feel good and self-important by acting this way. Former NFL star defensive lineman Joe Ehrmann says, "Bullies act tough in order to hide feelings of insecurity and self-loathing. Coach Bully has an incomprehensible need to dominate his players."[22] Despotic coaches find pleasure in breaking people down. They make players feel inferior and in the process make themselves feel superior. This coach could be reliving his own glory, whether real or imagined, by destroying others. This has to be stopped, yet we inexcusably look past the indiscretions of these coaches if they generate enough wins.

Clarifications on Bullying

Bullying, first, is an overused term describing anyone who is demanding or expects competence and results. Unfortunately, any negative corrective is now interpreted as bullying. A boss who expects workers to complete a task or a parent who disciplines a child appropriate to the misbehavior is not a bully. We should be careful not to include every authoritarian coach who believes in a vigorous sense of personal discipline and carries this over to the competitive arena as being a bully. Bullying is a very specific type of strong intimidation that is aggressive and antagonistic and uses humiliation from a position of authority. It is selfish and does not consider the ends of the victim, though the bully can deceive himself into thinking it is for the victim's benefit.

Second, we should distinguish intimidation from toughness. Modern sports are complex, arduous, and demanding. They require toughness as part of preparation and performance. Practices for these sports are hard and should be if they are to create excellence. Coaches can be demanding and need to teach both physical and mental toughness without turning to strong forms of intimidation and bullying. Teaching toughness is not equivalent to bullying.

Third, intimidation should not be confused with intensity. A coach can be intense without being a bully. Intensity involves strong depth of feeling and great coaches have exceptional concentration levels. Some coaching personalities are naturally forceful and competition can be intense. A vehement, intense coach may not intend to create fear, but fearful feelings may result and an athlete may feel threatened by this coach's personality. Not all intimidating actions are bullying or necessarily immoral, however. Intense coaches must be acutely self-conscious and aware of how they come across to their athletes, especially young ones. Intensity may be perceived as intimidating, though the intent to intimidate is absent. Coaches like John Wooden, Tom Landry, Tony Dungy, Pat Summit, Larry Brown, and Phil Jackson are intense, but they never threaten the personhood of their players and are never bullies. A coach must teach that the actions and performances of athletes have consequences but without attacking the person or without being a raving lunatic. I had a high school basketball coach who was intense and very competitive. He had a steely stare and stood 6 foot 5. If he seemed imposing to a 5 foot 7 point guard, it was certainly not his intent to be threatening. We knew he cared about us personally and that his corrective instruction, while it may have seemed harsh at times, was not understood as personal. On the other hand my ninth grade football coach and college JV basketball coach were intimidating and did not seem to care about me. I believe they acted this way because they thought they were supposed to (one had played for Woody Hayes at Ohio State) and felt insecure. Many erroneously believe that creating this atmosphere earns them respect. I did not respect either coach. They both confused fear with respect. Intimidation may elicit fear but never earns respect.

Targets of the Bully Coach

The bully coach uses intimidation to coerce officials not to make calls against his or her team, to remove or diminish the opponent's ability to be an athletic threat, [23] or to motivate and challenge his or her players. Some coaches browbeat officials to gain advantage by causing the official to hesitate when making a marginal call against their team. This coach virtually terrorizes officials through violent bursts of indignation accompanied by yelling, arm waving, and menacing glares. Coaches will even feign anger in order to exert pressure or "work"[24] the official to get the next call. Some coaches cultivate a reputation as putting fear in the hearts of adjudicators. Major League Baseball has a long history of managers like Billy Martin, Earl Weaver, Lou Piniella, and Bobby Cox who have excelled in this practice. They wanted officials to ask themselves, Why inconvenience myself to make this call and take this abuse? I won't call it because I don't need him screaming in my face again. Although coaches are not necessarily in a dominant power relationship with officials, some use intimidation as a strong form of gamesmanship for which there is no moral justification. Some coaches teach their athletes to be intimidators and may offer a bounty to harm an opposing player.[25] Weak forms include directing a pitcher to throw inside or emphasizing hard contact in full contact sports. Others might call an opponent a name not worth repeating to rile him up or use excessively aggressive players to intimidate opponents or even take out an opponent's best player by causing a malicious intentional injury. Joe Ehrmann tells the following story:

> I was 11 years old. It was during a youth league basketball game, and I was in-bounding the ball from under the basket. But the opposing player was all over me and I could not get the ball in. The coach called 2 consecutive timeouts to avoid a 5-second call that would have cost us possession of the ball. The jumping-bean kid guarding the in-bounds pass was too close to me and the he wasn't giving me room. Coach pulled me aside after the 2nd time-out, gripped my arm, and would not let go as the referee's whistle summoned us back on the court. He put his face very close to mine so no one would hear and looked me straight in the eyes without blinking. "Bring the ball back over your head with both hands and smash it into his face," he said. He put his right hand on my left shoulder and squeezed it so tightly that it hurt. "Smash the ball as hard as you can in his face. You will teach him a lesson about who he is playing against." I remember walking to the space below the basket and looking at the kid whose nose I was about to break. I remember knowing I was going to do it even though most of me didn't want to. . . . I looked at my coach as the ref blew the whistle and handed me the ball. The coach kept staring at me without blinking. I gripped the ball, slammed it into my hands as my teammates broke in zigzags, lifted it above my head, and brought it down with all my force right into the kid's face. Blood shot everywhere and the kid's mother came rushing from the stands screaming at me as her son lay crying on the court. The whole gym stared at me. . . . Coach praised me in the locker room, upholding that play as something positive, and "the way the game was to be played!" Shame engulfed me.[26]

Here is a youth team coach forcing a young boy to direct violence at an athletic adversary. Attempting to win through gamesmanship can include bullying as a means to enhance and motivate performance by using fear rather than pursuing excellence to perform at a higher level. This behavior is rationalized as a way to toughen up young athletes in order to advance their performance and prepare them for real life. People like Hayes, Knight, and Musselman used these strong types of intimidation and became clichés. Their actions have been self-perpetuating. A multitude of coaches model these harmful methods. Coaches emulate one another, and "bully-coaches in youth and interscholastic sports have plenty of institutionally accepted role models whose fame condones such behavior."[27] They are all around us at every level of sports. Recently I became acquainted with a female college coach who bullied her athletes by depriving them of meals, harshly berating them, and treating them as nonentities.

Bullying is wrong for a variety of reasons. A coach who tries to intimidate officials, team members, and opposing players is attempting to win in ways other than exhibiting the abilities the game was designed to test. The bullying coach, then, is undermining the challenge of the game. Bullying coaches who treat their own players in objectionable ways are violating their moral duty to care for the welfare, health, and safety of their players and to treat them with respect and dignity. (On this point, see Mitten's discussion of the legal duties of coaches with respect to the health and safety of their athletes in Chapter 13.)

Creating Fear

Bullying creates fear in its victims. There are different kinds of fear and some have utilitarian value. Fear can alert one to real danger or cause one to focus energy and attention where it is needed. A proper fear response can save a life. And there can be appropriate forms of fear in sports coaching. A tough coach may justifiably use a tempered realistic fear of losing, fear of failure, or fear of a loss of playing time in order to get a player's attention or to inspire a player who is underachieving or lazy. But this should be done while affirming the athlete's personhood so that the athlete knows the coach is appropriately evaluating her performance and not dismissing her personhood. Coaches who cared about me caused me to be appropriately afraid of losing playing time. This kind of fear is closer to disappointment than to terror and does not threaten the athlete's personhood or identity. It is not the same as the fear elicited by a bully. Coaches who cannot control their tempers, punish athletes by overpracticing, withholding rewards, screaming in their faces, grabbing them, and throwing objects may deteriorate to the point of irrationality and actually lash out physically.

Bullying generates different responses: outright fear and fearful anxiety; both include fear of humiliation. The philosopher Martin Heidegger sharply distinguishes fear from anxiety. "Fear is always fear of something, and for the sake of something, for example one fears for one's life, or one fears about some possibility."[28] Anxiety, on the other hand is more subtle. "Anxiety is precisely anxiety over nothing,"[29] because it is not due to a singular event but an atmosphere or mood of despair that is just there.

Outright fear includes an expectation of physical injury. It is a pragmatic response to a frightening entity or experience. An aggressive coach poses a direct threat. The coach may use threatening language expressed in an angry tone, possibly expressing uncontrolled anger where the recipient may even perceive physical danger. Many coaches erroneously equate athletics with the military and with manhood and prowess. Some team-training camps and practices have been modeled on military boot camps emphasizing toughness, discipline, and a rigid chain of command.[30] These bullying coaches often make bold analogies between sports, war, and manhood. Like marine drill sergeants, these autocratic coaches find pleasure in breaking people down. I remember a college coach once coming out to a local basketball court where I was playing with some high school friends and bringing with him several large men who enjoyed pounding on younger, smaller high school guys. We had several pickup games with them, and when we finished we were physically beaten and emotionally broken. These were not impressive basketball players but thugs who bullied us into submission on the court that night.

At their most extreme, these coaches use threats of violence to induce a kind of terror. Players then have a choice: fight or flight. Those who fight become more aggressive and may challenge the coach or direct their aggression toward the opponent. They may achieve a higher level of athletic performance, but at what cost? Longtime NFL star defensive lineman Joe Ehrmann, who has coached high school for many years, says, "I realized that anger had driven much of my athletic success. Coaches leveraged it—they fired me up and charged me up by angering me."[31] This can become a way of creating cult-like devotion in athletes who would mindlessly run through a wall for the coach. The end, however, cannot justify such degrading means.

The other common response is flight. Many parents refuse to allow their children to quit teams because they fear quitting will become a pattern that carries over into all the difficult challenges in life. But there are behaviors more detrimental than quitting a team. Sometimes it is better to quit than endure abuse. The young athlete flees the sport, realizing that a game is not worth the pain or abuse.

We homeschooled our daughter Tess through eighth grade. Along the way she participated in lots of soccer, softball, and dance. She was ready to enter high school and participate in softball but wanted to take a look at other sports, especially basketball. She spent much of the summer before ninth grade becoming a respectable shooter. We met the new coach of a weak program that most of the good athletes were avoiding. The coach invited Tess to an open gym. When I picked her up, she was uncharacteristically quiet and only said, "Dad, I'm never going back there." The next day she picked up a tennis racket, and by her junior year she was a starter on varsity tennis, later playing college tennis. She was so upset by one day of basketball that she never went back. Years later she described the verbal mistreatment she experienced from a female coach who intimidated her. Tess fled to maintain her dignity.

The second type of fear is anxiety. It is more covert but possibly more damaging. Here a perpetually negative coach creates a destructive mood. It usually includes critical, degrading remarks but could also include punishing the team through abusive workouts or withholding privilege such as meal money. The coach is self-deceived into thinking he or she knows how to inspire athletic performance when in reality it creates a crushing feeling of anxiety and self-annihilation.

When a coach targets an individual, the intimidation begins slowly and the athlete may be oblivious to the effect it is having on her. The coach may speak derisively or make false insinuations, such as "you look like you're gaining weight." "You are not putting forth the effort." "You don't care." This coach knows how to humiliate the athlete and create a sense of anxiety. The athlete feels anguish but may not know precisely why. Her life is not being threatened, but she feels like a nonentity. She feels ashamed but does not know the reason. Athletes in this state will lower their eyes, retreat to solitude, and experience a sense of dejection. But they likely will blame themselves and may be deceived into thinking if they stick with it they will eventually succeed or become better persons.

These menacing coaches thrive on creating an atmosphere of anxiety; their coaching identity is tied to their ability to vex or trouble the athlete. It is part of an unbounded vanity. Bullies get enjoyment from intimidating others. The bully coach calls male athletes "girls," pansies, or worse if they don't measure up and pushes them by demeaning them. Coaches devoid of moral courage become defensive and attack anyone who questions their methods or motives.

Bully coaches create feelings of worry, unease, and dread, like the main character in Dostoevsky's novel *Notes from Underground*, who is overlooked and abused by everyone and feels like "an object of contempt," "like an insect on the wall" and states of his experience, "I sat ignored by everyone, crushed and annihilated."[32] Young athletes are particularly vulnerable to anger experiences and the resulting anxiety. The athlete bullied this way is more liable to stick it out, become depressed, and blame herself. A sense of failure too early in life can create a fear of failing, and immature athletes do not know how to cope with this. They retreat into solitude to survive. "Anxiety leads us to drop the mask of our everyday familiarity with the world. Anxiety makes everything of such little significance that even our own sense of self is lost. Anxiety is the recognition of a certain nothingness, the groundlessness in our existence."[33] The athlete experiences a sense of personal betrayal and alienation though she may not know why. "Anxiety reveals to us a certain homelessness—we are not at home in the world, the world faces us as something weird or 'uncanny.'"[34] Bullied athletes feel estranged, no longer at home in the game they love. (Indeed as Jeffrey Fry points out Chapter 10, recent research in neuroscience strongly suggests that the behavior of influential individuals can change the brains of young athletes, for the better in the case of good coaches but for the worse in the case of bullying ones.) Coaches unfortunately rationalize these actions by a naive pragmatic argument that it works, but it is destructive and dehumanizing. In the past, some allowed coaches to berate, humiliate, and physically and emotionally punish athletes in order to shape and inspire them, but no longer.

Players never forget their coaches. One coach has stated, "I have coached hundreds of players by now and I am certain of this: 100 percent of them will remember my name, the words I spoke to them, and the emotions generated by our conversations and interactions. Forever! This is part of the awesome power and responsibility of coaching. You give your players memories, for better or for worse that stay with them until the day they die."[35] How true this is. Coaches who bully and intimidate seldom understand the ongoing effects they have on young athletes. These coaches naively and irresponsibly think they are helping their players prepare for life when in reality their misbehavior can create a long-lasting fear in the athlete and damage a person more seriously than we imagine. Sports can beat up people and break them down so that they barely recover as adults.[36] And coaches seldom realize that they will be remembered for it. "Would these coaches behave differently if they comprehended the long-term effect of their behavior?"[37] I wonder what my ninth grade football coach and junior varsity college basketball coach would say if they knew how I remember them. Authority is not intimidation; bullying should not be confused with an intense personality or with teaching toughness. Bullying does not inspire respect, and coaches should bear in mind that they will be remembered long after an athlete's sporting days have ended.

Conclusion

Coaches who use intimidation as a means of gamesmanship have been given a pass for far too long. Of course, many coaches, I hope most, avoid bullying tactics and are important role models for their athletes. Unfortunately the bullying style has been viewed as normal in some coaching circles, and some coaches credit their aggressive bullying approach as the source of their success. In these cases the means are justified by the results, and few ask whether there is something intrinsically wrong with treating persons as less than persons. If humans do not have intrinsic significance as persons, then it is perfectly fine to treat them as objects to be degraded and abused. But then sports will have no real value and will become nihilistic endeavors of futility. Coaches are never justified in resorting to berating, humiliating, or bullying their athletes. It is wrong regardless of the spin. "While coaches . . . once routinely yelled, cursed, embarrassed, humiliated, and even physically grabbed [their] players, the reality is that those techniques simply do not work if you want to motivate players and help them reach their full athletic potential. Unfortunately, a few loose cannons . . . have fooled fans into thinking that an authoritarian, dictatorship leadership style is a winning style."[38] This is a myth of the past.

There is no doubt that "the 'strong' sort of gamesmanship certainly can bring one profit, in terms of victories scored, but it closes off the participant to the other benefits of sport, specifically, those that concern personal growth and development, and conceivably athletic development, as well."[39] Though these coaching practices have a long and often successful history in terms of winning success, gamesmanship through strong intimidation has no valuable, useful, or moral role in our contemporary sporting practices, and tolerance for this type of practice among coaches should be eliminated.

First, it fails as a strategy because it disrespects sporting contests and alters the nature of the game's challenge. Instead of asking whether one is a better coach, player, or team it asks who the best intimidator is. The game becomes secondary to the skill of intimidating.

Second, it fails because many successful coaches, like Tony Dungy and Phil Jackson, have proven that it is not needed.

Third, it is absurd to believe that bullying is required to motivate. How strange it would look for a college professor or music instructor to scream in a student's face, grab a student by the shirt collar, or curse a student for not performing adequately. Yet many condone the coach who uses these methods. Good teachers and motivators do not need to be bullies to succeed. As one student asked in class when covering this issue, "Is intimidation covering for their shortcomings as coaches?"[40]

Finally, the inherent worth of humans should have a great effect on coaching philosophy. Sports should be a humanizing activity whereas gamesmanship through intimidation and bullying is dehumanizing. Many coaches use athletes as a means to an end. Sporting contests should be arenas of integrity, and the intimidating, bullying approach to coaching eliminates honor from what should be an honorable profession. People deserve to be treated with dignity and respect because they have intrinsic value. Good coaches evaluate performances, not persons.

The coaching profession has been in need of redemption, and redemptive coaching must include discussion of the humanizing elements of sport and the dehumanizing elements of gamesmanship. Coaches can implement the teaching of virtue as one of their goals, but it must be planned and modeled.[41]

Questions for Review and Discussion

1. How does the author analyze the relationship between gamesmanship and bullying? Explain in some detail.

2. Are there forms of intimidation that are not bullying? If so, when does intimidation cross the line into bullying? Is there an age-appropriate level at which intimidation should never be part of our games? At what age if any should it be acceptable?

3. Do you agree that there are acceptable forms of intimidation at higher levels of our sporting contests which are a part of the moral regulative psychological challenge of the game? Why or why not?

4. How does the use of intimidation and bullying alter the goal of allowing the game to be decided by the participants and their skills?

5. Have you ever been bullied by a coach? Which type of fear did you experience and how did you respond?

Suggestions for Further Reading

Ehrmann, Joe. *InSideOut Coaching.* New York: Simon & Schuster, 2011.

Fry, Jeffrey. "Coaching a Kingdom of Ends." *Journal of the Philosophy of Sport* 27 (2000): 51–62.

Howe, Leslie. "Gamesmanship." *Journal of the Philosophy of Sport* 31 (2004).

Potter, Stephen. *The Theory and Practice of Gamesmanship.* New York: Bantam, 1947.

Stankovich, Chris. "Coach-Player Intimidation, Humiliation, and Physical Aggression Is Never Warranted." http://blog.drstankovich.com/blog/2011/02/coaching/coach-coercion-intimidation-and–humiliation.

Ten

The Neuroethics of Coaching

JEFFREY P. FRY

According to neurologist V. S. Ramachandran, we stand at the threshold of another scientific revolution. As recounted by Ramachandran, prior scientific revolutions challenged received views of our standing in the universe. Copernicus removed the earth from the center of the cosmos.[1] Darwin situated humans squarely within the animal world. Freud raised significant questions about the degree to which we consciously control our actions.[2] But Ramachandran claims that we are now "poised for the greatest revolution of all—understanding the human brain." This revolution, he says, is "about ourselves, about the very organ that made those earlier revolutions possible."[3]

Given the widespread implications of this neurorevolution, what ramifications could it hold for the world of sports? The recent past witnessed reluctance among some individuals to confront the issue of how the brain might be affected by sports participation.[4] Now there is a dawning realization of the extent to which engaging in sports can change the athlete's brain, particularly in the case of brain trauma. This raises urgent ethical questions about the roles and responsibilities of those who render decisions about who participates in sports under what conditions.

Consider the case of American football. Clearly the problem of concussions and other head injuries in American football, as well as in soccer, boxing, and other sports, warrants preventative measures, therapeutic intervention, and ethical reflection. In this chapter, however, I want to focus on ways that the choices and actions of coaches may over time be *subtly* changing their players' brains. Do coaches in their everyday interactions with athletes influence the functioning of their brains in ways that could be considered either harmful or beneficial to the athletes? If so, what are the ethical implications of these practices?

The issue of concussions in American football and other sports has been obscured in part by the long shadow cast by the profit motive. But inattention to subtler changes to the brain that potentially result from participation in sports is likely due to a widespread assumption of mind-body dualism, famously articulated by René Descartes (1596–1650). It is the view that the mind is immaterial or spiritual in nature, as opposed to the material body. This view is pervasive in Western thought.

Against this background I want to argue that we should take the brain more seriously in the context of sports, particularly in the context of coaching and being coached. In their introduction to *The Ethics of Sports Coaching*, Alun R. Hardman and Carwyn Jones claim: "Most, if not all, coaching exchanges have a moral dimension to them."[5] I suggest that this claim is supported by consideration of what I will call *the neuroethics of coaching*.[6]

Our brains are *responsive* to our interactions with individuals—coaches and others alike. But if, as the neuroplasticity thesis suggests, our brains are *malleable*, might it be the case that when one changes one's coach, one also changes one's brain in significant, perhaps lasting ways? If so, what kinds of change would be desirable? Furthermore, if coaches do exert this kind of influence, should they adopt a paternalistic stance to their role as game changers who are also brain changers? Or should coaches merely seek to do no harm? These and numerous other questions might be relevant in an account of the neuroethics of coaching.

To sum up, in this chapter I consider how neuroscience may help illuminate how sports, and coaches in particular, help or hinder us in our quest for "the enlargement of life."[7] This chapter is about sports, neuroscience, and the good life.

This chapter has three main sections. In the first section, I look at recent exciting, but sobering, findings from neuroscience on the plasticity of the brain and the ethical significance of mirror neurons. In the following section, I examine the implications of the themes outlined in the first section for the neuroethics of coaching. Finally, in the third section, I reply briefly to some reservations about the significance of the revolution in neuroscience.

In response to criticisms examined in the third section, I will argue that the brain is not the whole story of the good life. Nevertheless, it is a significant part of this story. By drawing attention to this critical three-pound, jello-like organ, I bring into sharper relief the vulnerability of the coached athlete. In turn, this may help enlarge our understanding of "the fragility of goodness," in the words of Martha Nussbaum, and thereby create greater empathy for the athlete.[8]

The Plastic Brain

There is a joke that goes like this. How many psychoanalysts does it take to change a lightbulb? The answer: one, but the lightbulb must really want to change. Although this joke reflects an assumption that engrained habits of thought and action are difficult to change, it allows that change is possible. But what if changes in one's thoughts, feelings, and behavior are paralleled by, and even intimately connected with, subtle and not so subtle changes in one's brain? In the recent past, the received view was that the brain's malleability is lost early in a human being's development. This view has now been spectacularly challenged.

One of the exciting discoveries by neuroscience in recent years has been the extent to which the brain exhibits plasticity, or the capacity to change, adapt, and rewire. As you read these words, your dynamic brain is in flux. Neurons are firing. Chemicals are being secreted. Neural circuits are being activated. Among the looming important questions regarding the plastic brain are the following: What is causing these changes in the brain? How much and what kind of change is occurring? How durable are these changes? And what are the implications of the brain's plasticity for conscious experience? In order to begin to respond to these issues it will be helpful to engage in some neurophilosophical reflection.

The Mind-Brain Problem

What connections exist between our brains and our experiences? There is a correlation between reported experiences and brain states. For example, neuroimaging technology reveals that when various experiences are reported, activity occurs in certain areas of our brains. Correlation is a relatively weak form of connection, however, since correlation in and of itself does not establish a causal relationship, let alone an identity relation. If condition A and condition B occur in correlation with one another, A may be the cause of B, B may be the cause of A, both A and B may be caused by some third factor, or by unrelated factors, and in some cases, it might turn out that A and B are identical.[9]

A stronger logical connection between brain states and putative mental states is posited by the identity thesis, a version of materialism which holds that mental states just are states of the brain and nervous system. On some variants of this view, there are no subjective mental qualities like sensations of pain or color, but rather only physical states of the brain.[10]

The jury is still out on the nature of the relationship between brain states and mental states. In this chapter, I assume an intimate connection between brain states and experiences, without resolving the issue of whether or not mental states are material brain states. In particular, I look at possible implications that follow from the hypothesized view that brain states and putative mental states are causally connected in bidirectional fashion.[11] I will leave aside the question of the identity thesis. But if it, or some other reductionist account of mental states, turns out to be the correct view, then this would strengthen my argument for the relevance of a neuroethics of coaching. I will also look at how our social interactions influence our brains and conscious states. But first we will look at the surprising extent of the brain's plasticity.

The Gospel (and the Sobering News) of Neuroplasticity

Norman Doidge is a psychiatrist, psychoanalyst, and researcher who has served on the faculties of the Columbia University Center for Psychoanalytic Training and the University of Toronto's department of psychiatry. In his book *The Brain That Changes Itself: Stories of Personal Triumph from the Frontiers of Brain Science*, Doidge examines the phenomenon of neuroplasticity.[12] Doidge's book is filled with inspiring and hopeful stories of the rehabilitation of damaged, but still plastic, brains. Sometimes this capacity is shown in response to traumatic injury to the brain itself, such as damage caused by a stroke. The brains of stroke victims sometimes adapt in remarkable ways that lead to a significant recovery of abilities.[13]

Nevertheless, Doidge acknowledges that the phenomenon of neuroplasticity is double-edged:

> Neuroplasticity isn't all good news; it renders our brains not only more resourceful but also more vulnerable to outside influences. Neuroplasticity has the power to produce more flexible but also more rigid behaviors—a phenomenon I call the "plastic paradox." Ironically, some of our most stubborn habits and disorders are products of plasticity. Once a particular plastic change occurs in the brain and becomes well established, it can prevent other changes from occurring. It is by understanding both the positive and the negative effects of plasticity that we can truly understand the extent of human possibilities.[14]

Doidge claims that our brains can both change and solidify in certain respects. Both of these abilities are potentially connected to our everyday interactions with one another.

V. S. Ramachandran has also written about the plasticity of the brain as evidenced in its remarkable adaptability. Ramachandran specializes in the study of anomalous neurological conditions, for example, phantom limb syndrome, which is experienced after the loss of a limb.[15] In treating a patient who had his left arm amputated above the elbow, Ramachandran encountered something truly noteworthy. When he touched the patient's left cheek, the patient reported that he experienced the sensation of being touched on the thumb of his amputated left arm. Ramachandran's explanation for this phenomenon is that there is a representation of the body (the so-called Penfield homunculus) mapped onto a strip of the cerebral cortex known as the postcentral gyrus. On this strip the representation of the face is next to that of the hand. After the patient's left arm had been amputated, no signals went to the part of the cortex representing the left hand. But that part of the brain became, as Ramachandran puts it, "hungry for sensory input."[16] Ramachandran writes that "the sensory input from the facial skin now invades the adjacent territory corresponding to the missing hand. Signals from the face are then misinterpreted by higher centers in the brain as arising from the missing hand."[17] The claim is that the brain has undergone "remapping" or "rewiring"—a capacity in the adult brain not recognized by earlier neurological orthodoxy.[18]

The theme of neuroplasticity is highlighted in a burgeoning area of neuroscience known as social neuroscience. It suggests that brain plasticity is manifested not merely in responding to sudden traumatic injuries, whether in the brain or elsewhere in the body. Instead, our brains are highly social and are constantly responding to our social interactions. Psychologist Daniel Goleman writes:

> Neuroscience has discovered that our brain's very design makes it *sociable*, inexorably drawn into an intimate brain-to-brain linkup whenever we engage with another person. That neural bridge lets us affect the brain—and so the body—of everyone we interact with, just as they do us.[19]

According to Goleman, even routine encounters affect our brains and emotions. Especially significant are connections with people we spend time with and care about. Our interactions with one another are, says Goleman, "like interpersonal thermostats." By means of our interactions "we create one another," even at a biological level.[20]

Goleman asserts:

> Repeated experiences sculpt the shape, size, and number of neurons
> and their synaptic connections. By repeatedly driving our brain into a
> given register, our key relationships can gradually mold certain neural
> circuitry. In effect, being chronically hurt and angered, or being
> emotionally nourished, by someone we spend time with daily over the
> course of years can refashion your brain.
>
> These new discoveries reveal that our relationships have subtle, yet
> powerful, lifetime impacts on us.[21]

Consider the insight of behavioral psychologist Donald O. Hebb regarding what is referred to as "Hebbian learning." Hebb's insight is encapsulated by neuroscientist Carla Shatz in the words "neurons that fire together, wire together."[22]

When we view neuroplasticity in the context of human relationships we once again see the importance of what Doidge calls the "paradox of plasticity." Plasticity allows for both change and lasting effects. This fact takes on added significance when we consider that, as Goleman points out, the brain is responsive to both nurturing and toxic environments. Goleman claims that these findings suggest an aspect of a "life well lived"—we live in a way that will benefit others at this subtle level of neural circuitry.[23]

All this suggests that our encounters with others are shaping not just one another's experiences, but also one another's brains. This entails ethical responsibility on our part. In particular, it casts a spotlight on responsibility in the sense pointed out by H. Richard Niebuhr. How we respond to one another in given situations takes on an added ethical dimension.[24]

The Role of Mirror Neurons

Another important development in neuroscience that bears on our understanding of our plastic brains has been the discovery of mirror neurons by neuroscientists in Parma, Italy.[25] They are thought to help us internalize the emotions of others and may provide a foundation for empathy.[26] As Goleman writes, "By mimicking what another person does or feels, mirror neurons create a shared sensibility, bringing the outside into us: to understand another, we become like the other—at least a bit."[27] Again, as he puts it, "mirror neurons bridge brains."[28]

UCLA neurologist and neuroscientist Marco Icaboni ties mirror neurons to watching sports. According to Icaboni, due to mirror neurons, when the cameras pan the crowds at televised sporting events and capture the emotion of the fans, this creates "emotional contagion" in the viewers watching the game at home. When we see a player catch a ball during a game, some of the same mirror neurons are activated as when we catch a ball ourselves.[29] In fact we are moved in a variety of ways at a prereflective level when we observe sports.[30]

Perhaps coaches, teammates, and others we encounter through sports can leave lasting impressions on our neural circuitry. In light of the sheer number of hours coaches and athletes spend together, as well as the emotional impact of sports, this becomes important. As we know, sports often create lasting memories, possibly because they are laden with emotion, and experiences with intense emotional salience can create memories with great staying power. Perhaps perceiving oneself as the "goat" of an important game or as a loser, and having such perceptions buttressed with continuous negative reinforcement from a coach or teammate, have a lasting impact on a young athlete's brain.

Even as the outline of a rationale for a neuroethics of everyday life comes into focus, it is important to note that the philosopher Thomas Metzinger argues that neuroethics is not enough. Metzinger proposes that in addition to neuroethics we need to develop consciousness ethics, which would focus on "acts whose primary goal is the alteration of one's experiential states or those of other persons."[31] According to Metzinger, "a desirable state of consciousness" should meet three criteria:

It should minimize suffering, in humans and all other beings capable of suffering; it should ideally possess an epistemic potential (that is, it should have a component of insight and expanding knowledge); and it should have behavioral consequences that increase the probability of occurrence of future valuable types of experience.[32]

As I am employing the term "neuroethics," it fits hand in glove with Metzinger's "consciousness ethics." Indeed, Metzinger writes:

In the new era of neuropedagogy, now that we know more about the critical formative phases of the brain, shouldn't we make use of this knowledge to maximize the autonomy of future adults? In particular, shouldn't we introduce our children to those states of consciousness we believe to be valuable and teach them how to access and cultivate them at an early age.[33]

Whether in a particular situation the cultivation of states of consciousness deemed valuable by adults meshes with the promotion of autonomy is debatable, as we will see. Nevertheless, I think that what Metzinger is getting at in highlighting autonomy is that we should promote states of consciousness that will help individuals realize aspects of what I referred to earlier as the enlargement of life.

Critical Periods of Brain Development

Coaches who are aware of developmental psychology, at least intuitively, may have some understanding and empathy when young athletes seemingly on cue exhibit familiar patterns of behavior at various age levels. But how many coaches and administrators consider that the brains of young athletes are undergoing development, and that they may go through critical stages in the course of this development? Some awareness of brain development may help coaches exhibit patience in dealing with athletes during the sometimes turbulent period of adolescence. For example, when a teenager is not up to a learning task or exhibits risky behavior, this may not simply be merely willful obtuseness, but rather an indication of the developmental stage reached by the individual's brain.[34] It behooves us, then, to consider the findings of what science writer Barbara Strauch refers to as "a brand-new discipline of adolescent neuroscience."[35]

Strauch cites research which supports the view that "the adolescent brain undergoes a massive remodeling of its basic structure, in areas that affect everything from logic and language to impulses and intuition."[36] According to John Mazziotta of UCLA, it is with babies and teenagers that one finds the "greatest change in the brain's structure and function."[37] Research by Jay Giedd of the NIH supports the claim that during puberty and early adolescence the gray matter of the brain thickens, marking a period of exuberance, followed by a pruning process. Furthermore, Giedd has found evidence that the frontal lobes, the so-called chief executive of the brain, may be among the last areas of the brain to reach stability and maturity.[38] Again, to quote Strauch: "The teenage brain is not only incredibly interesting but appears to be still wildly exuberant and receptive."[39] But again, this plasticity of the brain does not entail good news only. Strauch writes: "In fact, as the teenage brain is reconfigured, it remains more exposed, more easily wounded, perhaps more susceptible to long-lasting damage than most parents and educators had thought."[40]

We have considered neuroplasticity, mirror neurons, neurocircuitry, and their possible effects on the quality of our conscious experiences, particularly in critical periods of the brain's development. As I have already indicated, there is evidence for plasticity in the adult brain as well.[41] The issue is not whether we affect each other's brains as adults, since this seems to be going on all the time, but rather the extent and durability of the effects of those interactions. How might these and other insights drawn from neuroscience inform a neuroethical analysis of sport and of coaching in particular?

Your Brain on Sports

Participation in physical activity may have various kinds of salutary affects on our brains. In his book *Spark: The Revolutionary New Science of Exercise and the Brain*, John Ratey of Harvard Medical School makes a case for a number of these effects, including contributions to learning and to subjective states of well-being.[42] But what happens when physical activity is linked with coaching?

Change Your Coach, Change Your Brain?

The prospect of the plasticity of the brain, coupled with its mirror neuron systems, presents us with some intriguing possibilities in connection with sports, especially the idea of critical periods of development. If we accept the notion of plasticity of the brain, and the claim from social neuroscience that our social interactions can, over time, shape our neural circuitry, then the case of the parent-coach who oversees a child's athletic development over a period of years is of particular relevance and import.

Consider what may have been taking place in the brain of a young tennis prodigy by the name of Andre Agassi. In his book *Open: An Autobiography*, Agassi recounts how he hated tennis in his youth.[43] He felt unrelenting pressure from his father to practice and improve. Agassi recounts his anguish after losing a match at a tennis tournament while participating in a ten-year-old and under bracket:

> After years of hearing my father rant at my flaws, one loss has caused me to take up his rant. I've internalized my father—his impatience, his perfectionism, his rage—until his voice doesn't just feel like my own, it is my own. I no longer need my father to torture me. From this day on, I can do it all by myself.[44]

Having mirrored his father's emotional life for so long, the neural pathways had become well established in his brain. Once again, neurons that fire together, wire together.

There is no easy formula for a life well lived. We cannot always predict the long-term effects of adversity. Adversity may arguably play a role in the good life. But clearly there were aspects of Agassi's experience with tennis that did not represent for him the enlargement of his life. On the contrary, at times he experienced his life in tennis as a prison from which he longed to escape. This interpretation is buttressed by an epigraph to Agassi's book from a letter that painter Vincent van Gogh wrote to his brother in July 1880:

> One cannot always tell what it is that keeps us shut in, confines us, seems to bury us, but still one feels certain barriers, certain gates, certain walls. Is all this imagination, fantasy? I do not think so. And then one asks: My God! Is it for long, is it forever, is it for eternity? Do you know what frees one from this captivity? It is very deep affection. Being friends, being brothers, love, that is what opens the prison by supreme power, by some magic force.[45]

What is it that confines us? What barriers, gates, and walls are there? We can respond to these questions at various levels of description.[46] Icaboni suggests that our social interactions can set limits on our autonomy by implicating our imitative mirror neurons.[47]

Brain Change and Game Change: Neuroethical Coaching

In keeping with neuroplasticity and social neuroscience, author and educator Robert Leamnson writes in his book *Thinking About Teaching and Learning: Developing Habits of Learning with First Year College and University Students:* "Learning as brain-change, rather than brain use, is an idea that can make people uneasy."[48] This idea is not new. As William James once noted: "Things which we are quite unable definitely to recall have nevertheless impressed themselves, in some way, upon the structure of our mind. *We are different for having learned them.* The resistance in our systems of brain-paths are altered."[49]

The idea that teaching and learning involve brain change has particular relevance in sport. Coaches at the university level in the United States frequently tout the notion that they are teachers. Surely this is true in some sense. If coaches are effective teachers, learning must be going on. If learning is occurring, then according to Leamnson and James, the brain is changing. This warrants paying serious attention to what coaches are teaching.

This consideration takes on further relevance when we consider the fact that coaches often work with young athletes who have developing brains. Coaches need to understand, and to exhibit patience in light of, the biologically based limitations of children with their immature, developing brains. In addition, recognition of the plasticity of the brains of children and young people suggests a special responsibility for coaches. If what affective and so-cial neuroscience suggest is correct, and the plastic brains of young people are developing in connection with the interactions that young people have with significant people in their lives, coaches may be contributing in important ways to how that development proceeds.

This potentiality takes on further significance when coaches spend a sig-nificant amount of time with athletes, in some cases years. Coaches and ath-letes often develop strong affective bonds, with coaches becoming something like surrogate parents. Coaches often place athletes under stress and demand heightened concentration in situations where athletes care deeply about their sport.

Even with more mature athletes, coaches may help shape the underlying neural circuitry for what psychologist Carolyn Dweck calls mind-sets. Dweck identifies two mind-sets: the fixed mind-set and the growth mind-set. According to Dweck, the fixed mind-set and growth mind-set were ex-emplified by Bob Knight and John Wooden, respectively.[50] Both were highly successful collegiate basketball coaches. Dweck believes Knight exemplified the fixed mind-set—losing defines someone as a loser. This perspective high-lights rigidity over plasticity. Dweck writes: "A loss made him a failure, oblit-erated his identity. So when he was your coach—when your wins and losses measured him—he was mercilessly judgmental."[51] Again, in Dweck's words:

> It's not that Knight had a fixed mindset about his players' ability. He firmly believed in their capacity to develop. But he had a fixed mindset about himself and his coaching ability. The team was his product, and they had to prove his ability every time out. They were not allowed to lose games, make mistakes, or question him in any way, because that would reflect on his competence.[52]

On the other hand, Dweck views John Wooden as someone who exhib-ited the growth mind-set. Wooden highlighted improvement over time, an emphasis that is in keeping with the notion of a plastic brain—one that can change—but not immediately. Wooden asked for effort, but he did not de-mand victory.[53] For our purposes, it is important to note that both Knight and Wooden may have been helping to create the supporting neural frameworks for mind-sets in the athletes they coached.

Consider this possibility in light of mirror neurons, which, among other things, lead us to mimic those with whom we interact. Goleman writes:

> Mirror neurons create a shared sensibility, bringing the outside into us: to understand another, we become like the other—at least a bit. That

virtual sense of what someone else experiences fits with an emerging notion in the philosophy of mind: that we understand others by translating their actions into the neural language that prepares us for the same actions and lets us experience alike.[54]

This raises a sobering question. *Whose* experiences do you wish to share?

Then there is Phil Jackson, former National Basketball Association coach, who at times has had athletes meditate. Jackson himself practiced meditation in the hope of becoming less dictatorial as a coach. He also utilized a psychologist and Zen practitioner to guide his NBA players through meditation with the goal of relieving stress and promoting relaxation.[55] These conditions have correlations in our brains. Imagine transitioning from the volatile coaching style of someone like Bob Knight to the Zen-like approach of Phil Jackson. Change your coach, change your cortisol level, change your brain!

With this is mind, how should we respond then to a book coauthored by Craig Clifford and Randolph Feezell, *Coaching for Character*?[56] Perhaps coaches are always coaching for character of some sort or another. But suppose that coaching for character entails shaping neural circuitry in the brains of youths. How should we feel about the role that coaches play in establishing neural dispositions that may have correlations with character? Further, how should we assess this potentiality given the fact that some people view sport as a realm unto itself, with its own special morality?[57] Are coaches qualified to coach "for character?"

To this point we have considered a few reasons to think about the applications of neuroplasticity and social neuroscience to sport, and specifically to a neuroethics of coaching. While some of this is conjectural, I think that there is sufficient cause to warrant interest and concern about one's brain on coaching.

The Neurorevolution: Reservations and Responses

Finally, I want to respond to three reservations about the looming neurorevolution and the applications of neuroscience, including applications to sport. One concern is that it may be premature to think that we know enough to make such applications. As touched on above, one might argue that my attempts to apply neuroscience to sports are speculative. Yet even if some of the issues raised in this chapter are speculative, it seems reasonable to consider what *could* be the case, given the significance of what is potentially at stake.[58]

A second concern is linked to the work of philosopher Peter Hacker and his collaborator, neuroscientist Michael Bennett. The two have together

investigated and challenged presuppositions of neuroscience and neurophi-
losophy. Hacker and Bennett strongly object to ascribing psychological predicates to the brain. Instead, they think that we are constrained by logic to focus
on the person as a whole. Hacker and Bennett warn against committing the
mereological fallacy, or taking the part for the whole.[59] This idea is further developed by those who contemplate the "extended mind," which does not stop
at the end of our bodies.[60]

Whatever validity this critique may have in particular cases, I do not
think that it necessarily affects the importance of an emphasis on the central
role of the brain in connection with conscious experiences, or with respect to
the subjective sense of well-being. It seems highly plausible that the brain
does play a central—if not exclusive—role in either promoting or inhibiting
the project of the enlargement of life.

A third objection to highlighting the brain in connection with sport and
the good life is that no particular gain accrues from doing so, beyond what is
available by restricting ourselves to psychological considerations.[61] For example, one might argue that we already know that psychological abuse of athletes
by coaches is wrong apart from any reference to the brain; hence, giving focused attention to the brain in this context is superfluous. But I think that this
view is mistaken. By understanding the central role of the brain in living the
good life we broaden and deepen our understanding of "the fragility of goodness," to borrow from Martha Nussbaum. We broaden our grasp of the vulnerability of the athlete. We may also be led to a more empathic understanding of
others as we consider the stages of brain development, the receptivity and vulnerability of the brain to social influences, and the vulnerability of the brain to
trauma. Psychologist Steven Pinker captures this broad sentiment in poignant
fashion.

> This power to deny that other people have feelings is not just an academic
> exercise but an all-too-common vice, as we see in the long history of
> human cruelty. Yet once we realize that our own consciousness is a
> product of our brains and that other people have brains like ours, a denial
> of other people's sentience becomes ludicrous. 'Hath not a Jew eyes?'
> asked Shylock. Today the question is more pointed: Hath not a Jew—or
> an Arab, or an African, or a baby, or a dog—a cerebral cortex and a
> thalamus?
>
> If that sounds mechanistic, if it makes us seem like transitory things,
> what of it? Think about why we sometimes remind ourselves that 'life is
> short.' It is an impetus to extend a gesture of affection to a loved one, to
> bury the hatchet in a pointless dispute, to use time productively rather
> than squander it. I would argue that nothing gives life more purpose

than the realization that every moment of consciousness is precious and a fragile gift.[62]

Is the brain the whole story? By no means. But the brain appears to be a critical part of the story of a good life, and of the role of sport in a good life.

Conclusion

If V. S. Ramachandran is correct, we are on the verge of a great scientific revolution—indeed the greatest revolution we have yet experienced. No doubt it will unfold with anxiety as well as excitement. If it fulfills its promise it is likely to have far-reaching implications, including implications fraught with ethical significance. Emerging social and affective neuroscience may broaden our conception of the ethics of neuroscience and of the neuroscience of ethics. Reflection on neuroethics and its connection to "consciousness ethics" may help us understand how the neuroscientific revolution can contribute to the project of "the enlargement of life."

How coaches interact with athletes has mattered ethically in the past. Ethical concerns about coach-athlete interactions did not surface for the first time in thinking about the potential for brain change that comes from these interactions. But in another sense much changes when we place the athlete's brain in the foreground. In the *Apology* Socrates intimated that real harm is moral harm. As a result he was less concerned about his body.[63] But this may have been a false dichotomy, or at least an exaggerated distinction. If we accept the claims of social neuroscience, then coaching surely involves teaching and learning that changes brains and, in turn, the quality of consciousness.

This suggests a neglected sense in which we are vulnerable human beings. Within our skulls lies a vital organ that is fragile, vulnerable, and responsive to others at its microscopic level of organization. This recognition of the social brain gives added meaning to the insights of Anthony Skillen.[64]

In an insightful and moving article, "Sport Is for Losers," Skillen writes that sport can teach us (and thus, as we have seen, change our brains) "to live within the limits of a human fellowship informed by awareness of common frailty."[65] Part of this frailty consists of our fragile brains and of our neural vulnerability to one another.[66]

Questions for Review and Discussion

1. What does it mean to say that the brain is "plastic," and what is some of the evidence for this plasticity? Why is this plasticity both good news and sobering news?

2. What roles do mirror neurons play? How do you feel about the fact that when you mirror others, you become like them to some extent?

3. Given that exposure to coaches may change your brain, what kinds of coaches would you want and not want to play for?

4. If coaches can or do have an impact on the brains of athletes, especially young developing athletes, what are the implications for the ethics of coaching, since it is already generally accepted that coaches can affect the character of their players?

Suggestions for Further Reading

Agassi, Andre. *Open: An Autobiography*. New York: Vintage, 2010.

Bennett, M. R., and P. M. S. Hacker. *Philosophical Foundations of Neuroscience*. Malden, MA: Blackwell, 2003.

Bennett, Maxwell, et al. *Neuroscience and Philosophy: Brain, Mind, and Language*. New York: Cambridge University Press, 2007.

Blackmore, Susan. *Consciousness: An Introduction*. 2nd ed. New York: Oxford University Press, 2011.

Clark, Andy, and David J. Chalmers. "The Extended Mind." In *Philosophy of Mind: Classical and Contemporary Readings*, 643–651. Edited by David J. Chalmers. New York: Oxford University Press, 2002.

Clifford, Craig, and Randolph Feezell. *Coaching for Character: Reclaiming the Principles of Sportsmanship*. Champaign, IL: Human Kinetics, 1997.

Doidge, Norman. *The Brain That Changes Itself: Stories of Personal Triumph from the Frontiers of Brain Science*. New York: Penguin, 2007.

Hardman, Alun R., and Carwyn Jones, eds. *The Ethics of Sports Coaching*. London: Routledge, 2011.

Lazenby, Roland. *Mindgames: Phil Jackson's Long, Strange Journey*. Chicago: Contemporary, 2002.

Leamnson, Robert. *Thinking About Teaching and Learning: Developing Habits of Learning with First Year College and University Students*. Sterling, VA: Stylus, 1999.

Nussbaum, Martha C. *The Fragility of Goodness: Luck and Ethics in Greek Tragedy and Philosophy*. Cambridge: Cambridge University Press, 1986.

Omalu, Bennett. *Play Hard, Die Young: Football, Dementia, Depression, and Death*. Lodi, CA: Neo-Forenxis, 2008.

Pinker, Steven. "The Riddle of Knowing You're Here." In *Your Brain: A User's Guide*, 12–19. New York: TIME Books, 2009.

Plantinga, Alvin. *Where the Conflict Really Lies: Science, Religion, and Naturalism.* New York: Oxford University Press, 2011.

Ramachandran, V. S. *A Brief Tour of Human Consciousness.* New York: PI Press, 2004.

Strauch, Barbara. *The Primal Teen: What the New Discoveries About the Teenage Brain Tell Us About Our Kids.* New York: Anchor, 2004.

Eleven

Competition, Ethics, and Coaching Youth

CESAR R. TORRES AND PETER F. HAGER

Although organized youth sports in the United States date back to the nineteenth century, it was in the last fifty years or so that the experience became prevalent in the life of youths and their families.[1] One indication that youth sport has become a significant phenomenon in society is the widespread use since the 1990s of the term "soccer mom," which designates those mothers who coordinate the sport schedules of their children. One study indicates that in the year 2000, the number of youths "who played on at least one organized sport team was found to be 54% of kids ages 6 and 17."[2] A 2005 study shows that "among a slightly older age group of 10- to 17-year-olds, participation had jumped to 59%."[3] According to Ronald B. Woods, "Participation in youth sport [is] at an all-time high."[4] Along these lines, Christina Theokas reported in 2009 that "frequency of engagement in sports is extremely high for children and youth" and that "for the 19th consecutive year (2007–2008), the number of students participating in high school athletics increased."[5] Participation in youth sports is so extensive in the United States that Mark Hyman believes the country is obsessed with it.[6]

Hyman's characterization is meant as an indictment of the problems besetting it, not a citation of its merits. Competition, which typically plays a prominent role in youth sports, is at the center of this indictment. The condemnation of competition in this setting is nothing new. For example, the New York State Public High School Athletic Association temporarily abolished its state championships in the early 1930s "due to charges of overemphasis and overspecialization."[7]

While some critics simply oppose participation in competitive youth sports programs, others have taken a reformist approach.[8] This chapter analyzes the role of competition in youth sports and the ethics of coaching in such programs. Our approach will not focus on the consequences, negative or positive, of sports competition, but on its intrinsic character. We begin with an exploration of the most common criticisms of youth sports and of some of the reforms proposed to improve it. We then present an interpretivist account of competitive sports and its central purpose, which establishes a framework through which (1) a case can be made for competition in organized youth sports, (2) proposed reforms can be analyzed, and (3) an ethics of coaching that respects competitive sports' central purpose while advancing youth's interests, needs, and welfare can be proposed. We intend to demonstrate that, understood from an interpretivist perspective, competition in youth sports is morally defensible and coaches have a pivotal role to play in promoting and designing morally beneficial competitive experiences.

Problems and Reform Within Organized Youth Sports in the United States

The landscape of youth sports in the United States is haunted by a variety of ethical problems, many of which are related to those manifesting themselves at the elite level. Examples of on-field and off-field cheating and poor sporting behavior can be found in both media reports and the discussions of coaches, administrators, parents, and young athletes. Recruiting and eligibility violations, deceptive on-field rule breaking, the use of illegal performance enhancing substances and methods, intimidating and threatening forms of trash talk, and disrespectful behaviors toward coaches and teammates, as well as opponents and officials, are just some of the issues challenging proponents of youth sports today.

Many of these problems are grounded in the attitudes and tendencies of individuals within sports and society in the United States. One such tendency is what R. Scott Kretchmar has referred to as runaway individualism—an extreme form of individualism in which "individual rights, interests, and activities dominate and overwhelm social duties and concerns."[9] Among other things, runaway individualism "can lead to an insensitivity regarding the rights of others" and "can cause a person to lose touch with his or her cultural roots and shared community values."[10] This tendency can be observed more generally in people's habits of seeking their own interests through activities of their choice, without consideration for others participating in the activities or for the activities themselves.

Runaway individualism is evident at all levels of sports in the United States, where the members of sporting communities often seek personal gain in the form of achievement, advancement, financial profit, and legacy, without much thought for their moral obligations to other community members or for their sport as a unique type of activity. In the words of Alasdair MacIntyre, the reasoning of these individuals is instrumental rather than practical in nature—focused on goods external to their sport (e.g., fame, fortune, status, recognition, etc.) rather than on its internal goods (i.e., the challenges, skills, and strategies that make sports unique social practices) or the virtues that should be cultivated and employed in determining and overseeing their sport's best interests and interpretations.[11]

Two subcategories of runaway individualism have been identified. The first, which Kretchmar seems to recognize,[12] is a tendency to overemphasize personal achievement and personality; the second[13] is what appears to be an escalating obsession with advantage seeking. These tendencies toward egregious self-aggrandizement and obsessive advantage seeking have become so habitual for many athletes, coaches, and administrators that they have formed cults to rationalize the tendencies and act as apologists for them and for the poor sporting conduct they encourage and facilitate.

While the cult of egregious self-aggrandizement operates most visibly at the professional level, it is clearly at work at the youth and amateur levels, where young athletes toil diligently to earn recognition for their talent and gain advancement. In youth sports and interscholastic and intercollegiate athletics, it is not uncommon for such athletes and their parents to lobby coaches for more playing time, for the chance to play a specific position, or for the opportunity to play a more substantial role on their team.

The cult of obsessive advantage seeking has also fastened its talons on each level of sports in the country. Because of the strong emphasis on winning and the belief in doing whatever it takes to win, athletes, coaches, and administrators feel the need to spend increasing amounts of time working to secure as great an advantage (or as small a disadvantage) as possible. The escalation in analysis of game films, in the advance scouting of opponents, and in coaches' expectations regarding the amount of time young athletes should spend on conditioning, strength training, and sport-specific skill development are just a few examples of how obsessive advantage seeking is reshaping the landscape of youth sports.

A further indicator of this cult's influence is the willingness of athletes, coaches, and administrators to ignore or intentionally violate the rules of their sport and/or the regulations established by that sport's governing body or bodies. Although the majority of rules and regulations have been set in place to maintain sports as unique social practices and/or maintain conditions of fairness within their contests and practice communities, many tend to view competitors simply as obstacles to be circumvented on the road to victory. The violation of recruiting and eligibility rules and the doctoring of equipment to illegally enhance performance are two examples of rule breaking practices that place strategic advantage ahead of fair play in athletic competition.

The tendencies toward obsessive advantage seeking and egregious self-aggrandizement and their respective cults have developed to the point that they have become resistant to simple reforms. This is why simple appeals to fair play and good sportsmanship have done little to stem the tide of negative consequences flowing from them. Several attempts to reform youth sports have been employed to counteract the effects of these cults and tendencies, as well as the inclination to overemphasize winning and outcomes. For instance, the typical approach to reform utilized at the initial levels of youth sports (ages 5–11) has deemphasized competition, eliminating such elements as scorekeeping, standings, play-off and championship tournaments, and even organized teams and leagues.[14] These kinds of reforms were crafted by well-meaning individuals who were concerned that youth sports had been corrupted by coaches, administrators, and even parents, whose win-first approach to sports had marginalized the more traditional values of youth sports participation, such as skill learning and mastery, moral and social character development, and fun.

The problem with reforms that deemphasize competition in youth sports is that they stifle attempts to teach youths how to compete in a good and decent manner. We believe that competitive youth sports, when well organized and well led, can play an important educational role by teaching youth how to compete strongly against one another in the spirit of cooperation and friendship, without animosity or jealousy. Reforms that remove competitive aspects of sports or strongly deemphasize them jeopardize sports' ability to actualize its educational potential. Such reforms do not provide youngsters with a view or account of competition and value-based habits of action that will help them compete ethically in sport. Without tools of this kind, young athletes will not be well prepared to be competent contestants in sports and beyond. In the section that follows, we will examine an account of sports (interpretivism) which offers a different type of youth sports reforms (mutualist reforms) that maintain the competitive aspects of youth sports while increasing the moral accountability of participants as members of sports practice communities.

Interpretivism and Competitive Sport's Central Purpose

Interpretivism is a theory of sports that falls under the larger conceptual umbrella that Robert L. Simon calls "broad internalism," which is "the view that in addition to the constitutive rules of sport, there are other resources connected closely—perhaps conceptually—to sports that are neither social conventions nor moral principles imported from the outside."[15] According to Simon, interpretivism "derives the principles and theories underlying sport . . . from an appeal to the best interpretation of the game or an inference to the best explanation of its key elements."[16] Furthermore, for him, interpretivism maintains that:

> Certain principles and theories must be *presupposed* if we are to make sense of key elements of sport, such as the rules, the skills that are tested, and possibly the history, traditions, and central elements of the ethos of particular sports. . . . The form of the argument [that an interpretivist might employ] is that a particular activity, competitive sport, would lack a point, be not fully intelligible, or make no sense (or at least less sense than otherwise) were not certain underlying principles taken as normative or as applying to the activity in question.[17]

At its core, interpretivism holds that moral deliberation and assessment in sports should be guided by rationally grounded interpretations of its central purpose and features. An interpretation here means the rational articulation of sports as a comprehensive, coherent, and principled activity, not just as an intelligible activity. What is at stake in an interpretation of sports in general, and of a specific one in particular, are its defining point and most prominent characteristics. An interpretation, then, is not based on preference, thoughtless agreement, or tradition, but rather on carefully constructed arguments that ultimately render it legitimate. As Nicholas Dixon argues, "Whether a position on a debate about sport—be it about a particular issue or about fundamental principles—is defensible depends on the quality of the supporting arguments, not on whether it has the assent of the relevant athletic community."[18]

Interpretivists have explained, following the work of Bernard Suits, that a sport is a game—or artificial problem—created by rules and governed by a "gratuitous logic" that puts a premium on the execution of physical skills. The gratuitous logic is a fundamental element of sports and all games because it refers to the restriction of the means available to accomplish the stipulated goal.[19] This restriction, as detailed by rules, requires the use of less efficient rather than more efficient means to pursue those goals (e.g., hitting golf balls with clubs rather than just carrying them to the target). It is the gratuitous logic of each sport that distinguishes one from the other, equipping each with its distinctive characteristics and charm. In the process, the rules that codify the gratuitous logic of each sport facilitate the emergence of a set of highly specialized skills that Cesar Torres has referred to as constitutive and restorative skills. The former are meant to be tested and are typically implemented during open play; the latter are those that are implemented to restore sports after an interruption.[20] For instance, in basketball, the jump shot, the layup, screening, and rebounding are examples of constitutive skills while the free throw and in-bounding of the ball are examples of restorative skills. From an intepretivist perspective, both constitutive and restorative skills and the strategies used in conjunction with them form the basis of a sport's overall standard of excellence.

J. S. Russell holds that interpretivism presupposes two related principles. The first requires that the rules are interpreted "to generate a coherent and principled account of the point and purpose that underline the game, attempting to show the game in its best light."[21] The second states that "rules should be interpreted in such a manner that the excellences embodied in achieving the lusory goal of the game are not undermined but are maintained and fostered."[22] What these two principles indicate is that for Russell intepretivism demands that sports (and different sports in particular) be articulated as comprehensive, coherent, and principled activities. For him, an interpretivist account of sports requires the virtue of integrity: intepretivism looks for the most coherent version of sports' defining point and most prominent characteristics.

In the philosophy of sports, interpretivism was developed as a theory meant to explain the relationship between sports and moral values.[23] For instance, "Simon's main thesis is that the moral evaluation of sports should be rooted in the best interpretation of its main point and purpose."[24] Thus scholars working within the tenets of interpretivism have emphasized its normative implications. In this sense, Russell notes that interpretivism, especially in light of its commitment to the virtue of integrity, is a theory of sports "informed by basic considerations of moral equality" and that it implies "duties to foster a context of competition."[25] Consequently, participants in competitive sports are entitled to equal concern and respect, and have the obligation, for example, to "pursue genuinely worthy adversaries" and to "take reasonable measures to promote conditions that would allow competitors to function as worthy adversaries."[26] Deliberately avoiding worthy adversaries or attempting to tamper with their training would represent moral failures in competitive sports. The notion that interpretivism demands moral equality and the fostering of genuine competition conforms to the principles expounded above: an integrated account of sports requires making the best sense of its point, purpose, and distinguishing features as much as a commitment to advance that best sense.

Although intepretivism has emphasized the moral dimension of sports, it has distinctive aesthetic connotations. Torres has recently argued that interpretivism takes a combined moral-aesthetical point of view.[27] Interpretivism's moral demands are grounded in a systematic characterization of the point, purpose, and defining features of sports, in an effort to display them at their best. Such a characterization requires making reference to the intrinsic properties of sports, from which aesthetic predicates emerge and to which they refer back, considered worthy of sustained attention. These properties are related to the constitutive and restorative skills and the strategies used in conjunction with them that constitute the basis of a sport's overall standard of excellence. This means that an interpretation of sports involves deliberation and the construction of defensible arguments about the standards of excellence worthy of repaid attention that portrays them in their best light. Sporting communities engage in this kind of exercise when specifying their sport's best version. Any such specification comprises making aesthetic judgments. For example, soccer has been described the world over as "the beautiful game," and actions that dishonor such a view are typically labeled as "ugly."[28]

"The most cogent version of a sport requires that contestants treat each other as moral equals, and that they honor and foster the intrinsic properties worthy of repaid attention that characterize it."[29] Contestants, then, have simultaneous moral and aesthetic obligations; moreover, these obligations appear to be intertwined. Moral equality in competition is coupled with the "duties to foster a context of competition" in a practice that is defined by its intrinsic properties and standards of excellence. All this suggests that interpretivism presupposes that the central purpose of competitive sports is not simply to beat one's opponent but rather to accurately measure and compare contestants' athletic excellence. Simon and Russell, among others, recognize that competitive sports are best thought of "as a mutual striving for excellence."[30] This does not deny the zero-sum quality of competition, but rather puts it in the context of the best interpretation of sport. As Russell argues,

The value of winning seems to lie, then, in its contribution to constructing certain competitive contexts that will foster the exercise and display of distinctive sporting excellences, particularly contexts that attempt to measure and record superior displays of excellence.[31]

Clearly the mutualist defense of the central purpose of competitive sports can be understood as relying on interpretivism's interdependence of the moral and the aesthetic. The moral dimension necessitates fairness, the aesthetic dimension necessitates embodying intrinsic properties, and together they signify a mutual effort as well as a commitment to promote and honor excellence and the integrity of sports' best interpretation. Competition does not disaggregate contestants but rather binds them together in a mutual striving for excellence with moral and aesthetic connotations.

An Interpretivist Case for Competition in Youth Sports

In order to make an interpretivist case for competition in youth sports, it is appropriate to note that the term "youth" refers to the period between childhood and adulthood. More generally, the term is often used as a synonym for "youngster." This varied usage makes it difficult to determine precisely who should be labeled youths. For instance, the World Health Organization defines young people as those between the ages of ten and twenty-four.[32] The United Nations includes only "those persons between the ages of 15 and 24 years."[33] Acknowledging the significant differences among the people encompassed in this large age bracket, the United Nations distinguishes between "teenagers" (those between the ages of 13 and 19) and "young adults" (those between 20 and 24).[34] It is important to note, however, that the United Nations also considers teenagers to be "children," a group that includes "persons up to the age of 18."[35]

Regardless of the legal parameters of the definition of youth, the differences in the social, cultural, and political undertones and understandings that the term takes in different countries, and its specific age delimitations, the term unmistakably refers to the relatively lengthy period of time immediately prior to adulthood. As mentioned above, the term "youth" also encompasses the early stages of adulthood. This implies that the period of youth ranges roughly from the age of twelve to the age of legal adulthood, and that it shares some of the attributes of childhood. However, as youths are closer to adulthood than younger children, the difference is not of kind but of degree. Some youths are children who are closer to adulthood but have not yet reached that stage of life. This is the conceptualization of youth referred to in this chapter.

What typifies the youth traversing the last part of the path to adulthood? In her influential article "What Is a Child?" Tamar Schapiro, inspired by Kantian ethics, argues that "the condition of childhood is one in which the agent is not yet in a position to speak in her own voice because there is no voice which counts as hers."[36] For Schapiro, childhood is a normative predicament in which persons are in a state of underdevelopment: "the undeveloped agent, unlike the developed agent, is unable to work out a plan of life 'all at once.'"[37] Schapiro is aware of the enormity of the normative predicament in which children find themselves and believes that such a condition excuses a paternalistic attitude toward children if their ability to work out a plan of life all at once is not yet developed. Thus she proposes that adults have a duty to help children overcome this normative predicament, but realizes that only they can do so. In other words, children have to develop a voice that counts as legitimately theirs that will assist them in conceiving a broad life plan. Schapiro supports a principle stating that adults should, to the best of their ability, help children become developed agents. To do so, she contends that adults must recognize both negative and positive obligations to children:

> Our negative obligation as adults must be to refrain from hindering them [children] in this effort [of developing a perspective they can endorse as their own]. We do this by not treating children as if they belonged to a distinct and permanent underclass. . . .
>
> The second part of the principle, which prohibits us from treating children as a permanent underclass, determines both positive and negative duties. Negatively, it implies that we must refrain from acting in ways which hinder children's development as deliberators. . . . Positively, the principle demands that we make it our end to help children overcome their dependent condition. In nurturing, disciplining, and educating children, we must strive as far as possible to make them aware of their natural authority and power over themselves and of its proper exercise.[38]

For Schapiro, the negative and positive obligations adults have to children, whose ultimate goal is to facilitate the latter's most exigent quest to become developed agents who can authoritatively rule over themselves, "all stem from the idea that in order not to abuse our privilege as adults, we must make children's dependence our enemy."[39] This view indicates that paternalistic attitudes toward children are only temporarily justified. It also recognizes that children develop a capacity to authoritatively rule over themselves as they grow. Finally, it suggests that adults should allow this developing capacity to be exercised in matters that children are capable of facing and handling, especially those that affect them directly. As youths' dependence shrinks, the domains over which they exercise and rely on their own authority expand.

The interpretivist account of the central purpose of competitive sports articulated above is compatible with and advances youths' interests and needs. Specifically, it assists youths on the last part of their journey to adulthood by respecting their emerging authority over themselves, which includes providing opportunities to exercise, consolidate, and expand this capacity. First, by arguing that competitive sports are best construed "as a mutual striving for excellence,"[40] interpretivism compels youths to ponder their place in this mutuality. Since competitive sports is never an individual endeavor, but rather, as Simon maintains, a cooperative one, it provides youths with valuable opportunities to carve out their own space among themselves, which demands deliberation to find their own voices and make them public.[41] In carving out their own space, youths situate themselves not only in relation to peers but also relative to coaches, administrators, and parents, among other social actors involved in competitive sport.

This point is driven home by Edwin J. Delattre, who maintains that "the testing of one's mettle in competitive athletics is a form of self-discovery, just as the preparation to compete is a form of self-creation."[42] He further argues that "the claim of competitive athletics to importance rests squarely on their providing for us opportunities for self-discovery which might otherwise have been missed."[43] Under this view, sports is a rich terrain for youths to practice in a rather intense fashion their ability to responsibly decide for themselves among peers.

The mutualist approach to competitive sports demands that youths recognize the value of opponents not just for self-development, but instead as moral equals who are also searching for, and affirming, themselves through the quest for excellence. This recognition is important because it implies the realization that treating opponents in this way means also recognizing that the latter "are capable of forming and acting on intelligent conceptions of how their lives should be lived."[44] And this realization, in turn, might prevent competitors from using others simply to satisfy personal sporting ends or advance their own self-development. In addition, this realization might prevent youths from instrumentalizing themselves to secure victory in a sporting contest by dubious means. Likewise, this realization might assist youths in resisting attempts by others (e.g., opponents or coaches) to instrumentalize them for their own benefit. By conceiving of contestants as partners in a cooperative effort toward excellence, competitive mutualism overcomes the notion that "opponents are at best means to one's own ends, and at worst obstacles to be surmounted."[45] Through mutualism in sports, youths might learn that respecting themselves necessitates respecting opponents.

Conceiving competitive sports from a mutualist perspective promotes another relevant benefit for youths. As seen above, youths who engage in competitive sports are introduced to a practice with a set of intertwined moral and aesthetic values. Broadly speaking, the former are related to issues of fairness while the latter are related to the intrinsic properties and standards of excellence definitive of any particular sport. To accurately measure their relative athletic merit, contestants are obliged not only to recognize each other as equals but also to foster a context of competition that is conducive to excellence. This requires, for example, finding worthy opponents, following the rules, and demonstrating concern for excellence and self-control, among other qualities. As Simon explains, "The practice of competitive sports and athletics is value laden in important ways. Some values . . . are traits that all competitive athletes have strong reason to commend and act upon themselves."[46] What can be labeled, paraphrasing him, as the inner moral-aesthetic compound of competitive sports comprises the normative features that are indispensable to the attainment of athletic excellence.[47] The inner moral-aesthetic component of competitive sports exemplifies a form of life worth aspiring to with undeniable educational characteristics and the potential to positively influence the development of character. When introduced to and maturing into competitive sports, youths are confronted with the decision to embrace this form of life and its ensuing inner values. Whether or not they decide to do so, the deliberation is beneficial in itself as it represents an opportunity to practice their emerging autonomy. This development of autonomy is essential to human flourishing; a mutual understanding of competitive sports offers youths a way to foster it.

There is at least one more reason why the interpretivist account of competitive sports' central purpose advanced here is significant to youth, which is related to the previous point: it demonstrates what a good life entails and at the same time offers a route to pursue it. By a good life we have in mind what William J. Morgan calls a life of wholehearted engagement, which is characterized by an "active, passionate engagement in some enterprise, of engagement that is more mindful and self-conscious than habitual and unreflective, and more touched by elan because of the higher sense of purpose and aspiration it embodies."[48] Wholehearted engagement stands in contrast to mundane engagement, which is epitomized by the taking up of different pursuits simply to be occupied and avoid being bored. Morgan claims that sports "is one form of life in which such full engagement is called for."[49] Indeed, he believes that it "is one of a select few human undertakings in which full-blown engagement is a characteristic rather than uncharacteristic feature of the actions of its participants."[50] This is the case because of sports' distinctive and attractive gratuitous logic, which inverts the instrumental rationality of ordinary living and its concern for excellence. To be whole-heartedly engaged in sports portends to value and commit to its defining point and standards of excellence. What this all means for youths is that competitive sports serve as a potent exemplar of not only the substance of a good life but also of what it takes to achieve it.

While the mutualism articulated by the interpretivist account of competitive sports attends to and serves the interests and needs of youths, it also helps in responding to the general problems in youth sports noted earlier in the chapter. Mutualism requires bestowing equal concern to all contestants and fostering a competitive context in which excellence flourishes. As already noted, these broad requirements take different normative form: contestants are obliged to follow the rules of the sport, seeks out worthy opponents, make their best efforts in competition, recognize their strengths and weaknesses as well as those of their opponents, train and perform to the best of their ability, respect opponents and referees, wish and honor excellence, and so on. Undoubtedly, if competitive sports is understood and experienced in its mutualist version, egregious self-aggrandizement and obsessive advantage seeking would have no place in youth sports. As subcategories of runaway individualism, they are in stark contrast to the tenets of mutualism in sports. By overly stressing the advancement of self-interest, even to the expense of the interests of others, egregious self-aggrandizement denies the cooperative aspect of competitive sports and its ensuing duties. On the other hand, obsessive advantage seeking typically implies a "do whatever it takes" or "win at all costs" attitude that often leads to dubious actions that instrumentalize opponents and rebuff excellence. Mutualism in sports does not accept self-aggrandizement but rather self-discovery and self-creation as well as its collective dimension. In competitive sports one needs others to fully know one's caliber and to create excellence. As for advantage seeking, mutualism does not disapprove it altogether but only when it is contrary to the quest for excellence and the virtues needed to foster a competitive context. Mutualism in sports responds to the general problems in youth sports and presents a direction for more sensitive reforms. In the final section we make suggestions to reform coaching youth sports consonant with this view.

Suggestions for Strengthening Youth Coaching

Given the discussion throughout this chapter, it seems reasonable to argue that the overarching goal of youth sports coaches should be, paraphrasing Schapiro, to make young athletes' dependence their enemy. Coaches are positively obligated to comport themselves in a manner that is conducive for the young athletes they are working with to develop their own voice. This implies a careful evaluation and respect of what the young athletes are capable of doing at any given moment and their interests as well as what they will need in adulthood to conceive and pursue a broad life plan. Youth sports coaches should match these elements with coaching practices that promote their athletes' authority to rule over themselves. This requirement will often demand the implementation of paternalistic attitudes. For instance, as Dennis Hemphill illustrates, "it is justifiable for coaches or parents to insist that young athletes wear protective equipment or sit out of competition due to an injury that, if left unattended, might result in a more serious injury."[51] However, paternalism is limited to circumstances in which youths are unable to decide for themselves. This is because coaches are also negatively obligated to refrain from practices that will hinder youths' development of their authority over themselves. That youth sports coaches should make young athletes' dependence their enemy means negative and positive duties. While asking young athletes to cheat exemplifies a breach of the former duties, neglecting to confront a young athlete who intentionally harms an opponent exemplifies a breach of the latter duties.

We find it reasonable to conceive of youth sports coaches as individuals who open a path to a good life. This is no trivial matter. The role of youth sports coaches is of paramount importance as they are not simply technicians who facilitate skill acquisition and mastery, but rather individuals who introduce and mentor young athletes into a social practice with internal goods and standards of excellence. As such, youth sports coaches are initiators and facilitators of "a life of wholehearted engagement."[52] While it is only a possibility that young athletes would embrace sports wholeheartedly, coaches should realize that, as Morgan states, sports is a social practice that calls for full engagement.[53] They should also realize that coaching calls for such engagement and that consequently they represent role models for their young athletes. Coaches have a chance to start and guide their young athletes along a road that not only leads to but constitutes a good life.

What follows is a series a of suggestions for youth sports coaches that stem from the two general responsibilities that coaches have as individuals assisting youths and the interpretivist framework discussed in this chapter. Far from recipes, these suggestions should be taken as broad guidelines to organize and reform youth sports in a way that respects both their protagonists and the mutualist approach to competitive sports and its central purpose defended here. There is, of course, much latitude for coaches and administrators to develop their own strategies. While there is some necessary overlap among the suggestions, each one stresses a distinctive and important element in coaching youth sport.

Youth Sports Coaches Should Adopt a Mutualist Perspective on Competition

By focusing youths on achieving excellence in sports rather than simply winning, the mutualist perspective can help coaches teach athletes appropriate ways to approach competition. By distinguishing between excellence and winning and emphasizing the former rather than the latter, coaches can help their young charges learn to view the competitive process as one in which it is imperative to respect the internal goods of the sporting practice (i.e., the highly specialized skills and strategies that make their sport the unique type of activity it is), the standards of excellence of that practice, the opponents who provide them with opportunities to test themselves and quest for excellence in the sporting context, and others (e.g., officials, coaches, athletic trainers, administrators, and parents) who provide them with support within that context. Once learned, the mutualist view of sports competition will help young athletes develop an awareness of their moral obligations as athletes collectively striving for excellence within a particular sport, and, in turn, will help them to learn to compete in a good and decent manner within that sport.

The mutualist coach is able to impart to youth the moral duties that they owe to their opponents. Since mutualism recognizes opponents as partners in the competitive process rather than obstacles or enemies to be overcome or dominated, coaches can help young athletes understand why their opponents are worthy of respect, even when unsporting or aggressive behavior may make it seem otherwise. The mutualist coach will also be well positioned to explain to young athletes why they should respect and adhere to the rules of their sport, especially the constitutive rules that establish the means through which excellence in the sport is to be achieved.

Youth Sports Coaches Should Focus Young Athletes on the Goods Internal to Their Sports, Their Standards of Excellence, and the Virtues That Foster Their Attainment

Coaches should teach their young athletes to be strong and vigilant stewards of their sport by encouraging them to consistently strive for excellence in ways that respect and honor their sports' internal goods and standards of excellence, the constitutive rules, the means that are supported by these rules, and the gratuitous logic in which they are grounded. In MacIntyrean terms, coaches should instruct their athletes on how to be caretakers of the internal goods and standards of excellence of their sports and dissuade them from focusing on the subsidiary external goods, such as fame and advancement, that can accompany successful youth sports participation. By emphasizing the goods internal to the sport, its standards of excellence, and the virtues that facilitate their achievement, coaches emphasize the inner moral-aesthetic compound that makes excellence in each sport a unique entity and help their athletes to realize that athletic excellence cannot be achieved without moral responsibility. Such emphasis on these fundamental elements also points to the reason why sports invites a wholehearted engagement. That is, these fundamental elements are related to "the good of a certain kind of life"[54] that is realized when they are embraced. Coaches working in this spirit, then, open up possibilities for their young athletes to exercise and be inspired by that good.

Youth Sports Coaches Should Seek to Develop Resolution Seekers, Not Outcome Seekers

If coaches adhere to the first two recommendations above, they will help young athletes develop a view of competition that clearly places the pursuit of excellence through the moral and aesthetic process of sports competition ahead of the outcome of winning or competitive sport's external goods. In doing so, they should, in the words of Cesar R. Torres and Douglas W. McLaughlin, help athletes develop as resolution seekers rather than outcome seekers.[55] Coaches and athletes who place too much emphasis on winning are often outcome seekers who "are not ultimately interested in *how* they solve athletic challenges or in establishing valid differences in performances."[56] These individuals often find themselves mired in the practice of obsessive advantage seeking as they go to great lengths to pursue victory within their sports.

While the lure of winning can be strong, it should not override the moral and aesthetic obligations athletes have within their sports if those athletes learn to adopt a mutualist perspective that will, in turn, help them to prioritize the internal goods and the standards of excellence of their sports and their supporting values over the external goods that can come with winning. Young athletes accomplishing these two objectives stand out as resolution seekers, who are further characterized by Torres and McLaughlin as contestants who "do not merely hunt for favorable results regardless of athletic merit. Rather, they consider sporting contests as the sites in which athletic superiority is determined through testing excellences."[57]

To emphasize resolution seeking over outcome seeking, mutualist coaches will focus more on constitutive and restorative skill mastery as a means to athletic excellence, and less on it simply as a means to winning and its subsidiary rewards. While coaches typically stress the importance of skill execution in the pursuit of victory, many competitive foibles are forgiven and forgotten by outcome seeking coaches in winning's afterglow. Those same mistakes remain visible to vigilant mutualist coaches, who focus athletes on correcting them out of a sense of duty to the sporting practice and its standards of excellence rather than a base appetitive desire to win. It is this sense of obligation to sporting practice that mutualist coaches should strive to pass on to their young athletes, thus helping them to develop as both resolution seekers and as wholeheartedly engaged athletes.

Youth Sports Coaches Should Seek to Provide Young Athletes with Opportunities to Develop Their Authority over Themselves

Coaches often fail to give youths the opportunities they need to develop as autonomous individuals. Many coaches hesitate to share power with their young athletes or turn leadership roles or decision-making responsibilities over to their charges because they are afraid the young athletes will make significant mistakes that may lead to losses in competition. As are result, they are frequently stingy when it comes to providing such opportunities to young athletes. However, if competitive youth sports are to help young athletes move out of their state of dependence as both athletes and human beings, coaches must begin to allow their athletes to make more of their own decisions on the playing surface and during training sessions. Such a shift in responsibility will help the athletes develop their abilities to think critically and imaginatively, and to take greater ownership in their decisions and the consequences that stem from them. This does not mean that youth sports coaches should relinquish their authority; rather, they should change their outlook on how they exercise it in order to "contribute to the development of personhood by gradually expanding and supporting opportunities for athletes to develop decision-making abilities and commitments to meaningful engagement."[58] This does not mean that young athletes should be left in the lurch either. Again, the provision of opportunities for youths to develop their own authority demands that youth sports coaches gradually withdraw their authority. But they should remain available, supportive, and even protective of their young athletes as required by the situation.

Mutualist coaches who take this recommendation seriously will give their athletes more decision-making responsibilities and leadership roles to assist them in achieving greater autonomy and overcoming dependence. These roles and responsibilities might include play calling responsibilities in sports like soccer, football, and basketball, pitch calling duties in baseball and softball, or game and even practice planning opportunities in a variety of sports. Such opportunities will help young athletes develop as athletes and as human beings, and will allow them to take greater ownership of the decisions and consequences that help shape their sports experiences. Youth sports coaches should be wary of demanding that their young athletes blindly follow their orders.

Conclusion

In this chapter we have defended competition in youth sports and argued that coaches in this setting should be seen as individuals whose main role is to introduce and guide their young athletes in a social practice that, given its structure, leads to a fully engaged form of life while providing them opportunities to develop their own authority over themselves. Based on these general responsibilities, we have provided a number of suggestions to organize and reform coaching youth sports that also respect competitive sport's central purpose as mutualistically conceived. We believe our analysis shows how competition in youth sports and youth sports coaching can be carried out as ethically sound pursuits. While it does not escape us that, when understood in this way, youth coaching is a remarkably difficult pursuit, we would argue that it is extremely important and could also be a gratifying experience. Contributing to the moral growth of young athletes through meaningful engagement in sports would unavoidably test coaches in more than one way. This should make the sporting community more tolerant and respectful of coaches involved in youth sports, but should also make coaches more tolerant, understanding, and respectful of their young charges, together with their abilities, interests, potential, and future.

Questions for Review and Discussion

1. Describe the reforms proposed to improve youth sports in the United States.

2. What are major criticisms of and problems with the reforms proposed to improve youth sports in the United States?

3. How does interpretivism (also called broad internalism) explain competitive sports and its central purpose?

4. How does interpretivism's account of competitive sports and its central purpose help advance youth's interests, needs, and welfare?

5. Given the tenets of interpretivism and the interests, needs, and welfare of youth, articulate a defensible ethics of coaching youth sport.

Suggestions for Further Reading

Dixon, Nicholas. "Sport, Parental Autonomy, and Children's Right to an Open Future." *Journal of the Philosophy of Sport* 34:2 (2007): 147–159.

McNamee, Mike. "Beyond Consent? Paternalism and Pediatric Doping." *Journal of the Philosophy of Sport* 36:2 (2009): 111–126.

Russell, J. S. "Children and Dangerous Sport and Recreation." *Journal of the Philosophy of Sport* 34:2 (2007): 176–193.

Shields, David L., and Brenda L. Bredemier. *True Competition: A Guide to Pursuing Excellence in Sport and Society.* Champaign, IL: Human Kinetics, 2009.

Simon, Robert L. *Fair Play: The Ethics of Sport.* 3rd ed. Boulder, CO: Westview, 2010.

Torres, Cesar R. "The Danger of Selectively Changing the Rules in Youth Sport: The Case of the Strike Zone." *Journal of Physical Education, Recreation and Dance* 81:5 (2010): 29–34.

Torres, Cesar R., ed. *Niñez, deporte y actividad física: Reflexiones filosóficas sobre una relación compleja.* Buenos Aires: Miño y Dávila Editores, 2008.

Torres, Cesar R., and Peter F. Hager. "De-emphasizing Competition in Organized Youth Sport: Misdirected Reforms and Misled Children." *Journal of the Philosophy of Sport* 34:2 (2007): 194–210.

Tymowski, Gabriela. "Rights and Wrongs: Children's Participation in High Performance Sport." In *Cross Cultural Perspectives in Child Advocacy*, 55–94. Edited by Ilene R. Berson, Michael J. Berson, and Bárbara C. Cruz. Greenwich, CT: Information Age, 2001.

PART 4

Coaching, Compliance, and the Law

ROBERT L. SIMON

While the discussion so far has focused on ethical issues in coaching, remember that coaches have legal responsibilities as well. What are a coach's legal responsibilities in regard to the health and safety of players? How far are coaches legally required to go to prevent injury to their athletes, particularly in contact sports where the players apply physical force to each other's bodies? Does a coach have legal as well as moral responsibilities with regard to gender equity? What contractual obligations does a college coach incur when recruiting athletes for his or her institution? Perhaps most vexing of all, what is the relationship, if any, between a coach's legal responsibilities on the one hand and moral ones on the other?

Here I offer an overview of each chapter and then make a few remarks about the relationship between legal and moral responsibilities. That issue is complex and has generated an extensive literature of its own, in both jurisprudence and philosophy of law, but perhaps I can provide a brief guide that will help readers understand the broader intellectual context of these chapters.

In Chapter 12, Nancy Hogshead-Makar explains and defends Title IX, which prohibits gender discrimination in federally funded educational programs. Title IX is widely credited with ending the era in which women were basically excluded from most areas of organized competitive athletics, leading to an enormous expansion of women's participation in sports.

However, as Hogshead-Makar points out, there are also criticisms of Title IX, especially relating to the manner in which it has been interpreted by the government agencies charged with enforcement. Hogshead-Makar explains and examines these criticisms and finds them seriously flawed. She concludes her chapter by discussing the responsibility of coaches not to exploit, abuse, or discriminate against individual players. She argues that sexual relationships between coaches and players are unethical because they are exploitative, especially in view of the differences in power relationships between coaches and the athletes under their responsibility.

The question of what the law requires of coaches may be controversial. Individuals, including judges and lawyers, often disagree about what the law on a particular matter is, especially in hard cases where apparently reasonable arguments can be presented by opposing sides. In Chapter 13, Matthew Mitten presents a number of fascinating, controversial cases where courts have adjudicated issues involving the coach's responsibilities for the players' health and safety.

Clearly coaches have both legal and moral responsibilities to protect the health and safety of their athletes. But how far do these responsibilities extend? In particular, what does *the law* require of coaches? Can such requirements be morally justified?

Mitten suggests that the law in this area is not completely settled since courts in different jurisdictions have imposed different standards of care that yield contrary results when applied to the same case.

The first standard, roughly stated, is that coaches are bound by ordinary standards of negligence and due care and must take reasonable steps to protect the health and safety of their players. However, some courts worry that this negligence–reasonable care approach imposes too strict a standard on coaches, especially those who coach at very competitive levels. Coaches may become so afraid of violating the standard that they coddle their teams and are inhibited from requiring the kind of tough conditioning that prepares players for demanding competition. Even worse, fear of liability may prompt institutions such as high schools to limit participation to reduce the possibility of lawsuits. These courts recommend a looser standard, requiring only that coaches not have malicious intent to promote injury and not be reckless in their behavior.

Mitten, however, argues that the first standard is ethically superior and that the kind of consequences or utilitarian considerations proponents of the second standard are concerned about are neither sufficiently weighty nor sufficiently probable as to override protecting players from serious harm. Mitten is making in part a moral point that the first, stricter standard is more morally defensible than the second.

In Chapter 14, Timothy Davis explores the legal and moral conundrums that may arise during the recruitment of college athletes. How binding are the commitments coaches make to recruited athletes? For example, what if a coach promises more scholarships than are actually available, anticipating that some athletes will drop out? But what if they don't drop out? Do all prospective players have a right to a scholarship? If not, what legal recourse, if any, is available? Davis explores these and other related issues that may arise in the recruiting process and suggests how it might be carried out in an ethically acceptable fashion.

Morality and Law

The chapters in Part 4 explore important and often controversial legal cases bearing on the duties, rights, and responsibilities of coaches. They also examine the reasoning behind these decisions and argue for a conclusion about what standards courts should employ in deciding cases in the areas under discussion. But isn't it the job of judges to enforce the *law as it is* rather than impose their own moral standards about *what the law should be*?

Philosophers, jurists, and other theorists, as well as practicing lawyers and judges, have long debated the relationship between law and morality. Their discussions and debates are far too complex for me to fully cover here. What follows is a guide to the discussion that I hope lays a framework for evaluating the theses advanced in this section. Although some important positions are not covered in this discussion, the views considered have been influential in the theory of jurisprudence. Readers uninterested in exploring these complexities can simply take the chapters in this section as offering a moral critique of the law or recommendations about what the law should be.

The conclusions found in these chapters may be viewed as *recommendations,* either to legislators who draft statutes or to judges who interpret and apply them, as to the morally best way of deciding cases in this area. Court decisions, of course, are not always ethically sound. Thus in *Plessy v. Ferguson* (1896), the Supreme Court of the United States upheld racially segregated facilities under the infamous idea that they could be "separate but equal." That decision, reversed in *Brown v. Board of Education* (1954), upheld the immoral practice of racial segregation and was rightly criticized on moral grounds.

An intuitively justifiable view is that what the law is, is one thing; what it should be is another, a view known as legal positivism. It asserts that there are no significant moral tests for law. The most influential version of positivism, advanced by the distinguished twentieth-century legal theorist H. L. A. Hart, views sophisticated legal systems as bodies of rules of different kinds (criminal law, law of wills, and tax law are all derived from a supreme rule, called the rule of recognition).[1] Perhaps the rule of recognition in the United States is the US Constitution, although some have argued that (1) it is the original intent of the founders, and (2) the Constitution must be read as a flexible document that can be applied pragmatically to resolve contemporary issues. Hart's version of legal positivism resembles the idea that a game is defined by its constitutive rules, which emanate from a supreme rule—the official rule book applying to the game or sport in question.

On Hart's version of legal positivism, the judge applies the rules. But what about hard cases where rules require interpretation? Or were not anticipated by the rule makers? Suppose, to borrow a kind of example used by Hart himself, that a college administration passes a rule prohibiting the use of "vehicles" in the college quad, presumably in order to encourage pedestrian traffic. What should the campus safety officers do about students who skateboard in the restricted area? Is a skateboard a "vehicle" in the meaning of the statute? Some would say that we need to follow the original intent of the rule makers. But they may never have considered such a case or, if they had, might have different views of it. Similarly, the plain words of the rule may provide insufficient guidance, since "vehicle" may be a term with fuzzy edges. In such cases, Hart suggested that judges are forced to use their discretion. But in my view just which factors should legitimately influence their judgment is left unclear. In any case, readers sympathetic to positivism's separation of law and morality can view the recommendations in these chapters as arguments for how judges should use their discretion in hard cases involving coaching.

But perhaps there is a closer connection between law and morality than legal positivists acknowledge. An alternate view is often called the natural law approach because a major version of natural law theory arises from Aristotelean accounts, often mediated through Christian and particularly Catholic theology. It postulates that there are natural conditions necessary for human flourishing. Law is an instrument for promoting and protecting these conditions. On this view, as thinkers ranging from Thomas Aquinas to Martin Luther King have argued, an "unjust law" is not a genuine law and imposes no legal or moral duty to obey. Although the idea that "an unjust law is not a law" is puzzling, even sounding contradictory to many, it may be rendered more plausible by considering whether a game with arbitrary or changing rules is a genuine game.[2] In such a case, we can say plausibly that arbitrary or ever-changing rules are not true rules; similarly, an arbitrary or unjust law would not be a true law. This reasoning suggests that the immorality of a statute or judicial ruling counts against it being legally valid.

A different version of natural law, especially relevant to this book, has been proposed by legal theorist Ronald Dworkin and has had a major influence on the development of broad internalist or interpretive views of sport, as discussed in several chapters in this book and in the philosophy of sport literature generally.[3] On Dworkin's view, when a judge must apply such abstract legal requirements as that of equal protection of the laws (guaranteed by the Fourteenth Amendment to the US Constitution) or a requirement to avoid negligence, the judge must develop and rationally defend a theory of equal protection or negligence as the case may be. Interpretations are justified by their "fit" or ability to explain existing law in the form of statutes and significant judicial decisions (precedents) and also must be the morally most defensible interpretation available. Thus *Plessey v. Ferguson*, which upheld racial segregation in southern states, was later rightly rejected by the Supreme Court because it did not fit the language of equality in the US Constitution, Declaration of Independence, and other court decisions about equal protection, and because it surely is not a morally acceptable interpretation of equal protection. Dworkin's interpretivist approach has been criticized on a variety of grounds, for example, that it gives too much power to judges to come up with philosophical interpretations of legal terms that in reality only reflect their political leanings. Similarly, according to broad internalism, making moral judgments in sports requires a theory that makes sense of a sport's key features, such as provisions of the rules and interpretations of principles presupposed by the rules that present the sport in its morally best light.

Although the versions of legal positivism and natural law roughly described above do not exhaust all the alternative theories of the relation of law to morality, they do provide a framework for understanding the chapters in Part 4. Those sympathetic to positivism can simply view the recommendations of Mitten and Davis largely as theses about what the law ought to be, although both authors also describe existing law as it has evolved in court decisions. Those more inclined to agree with the natural law approach can take their arguments as establishing moral criteria for determining what the law is. For example, on a reading of Mitten's article that is sympathetic to the natural law approach, one might argue that a test for the legality of laws in the area of a coach's responsibility for the health and safety of athletes is whether the law reflects a *moral* standard of reasonable care and avoidance of negligence in treating players. On a view like Dworkin's, this does not involve judges imposing their own personal morality on the rest of us but rather searching for the best interpretation or theory of evaluative concepts already in the law such as "negligence" and "reasonable care."

Interested readers can explore the issue of the relationship of law to morality in the works cited in the endnotes. In any case, the chapters in Part 4 should acquaint readers, especially athletes and coaches, with some of the controversies involving their legal rights, duties, and responsibilities and, in addition, raise important questions about how the relevant law is best formulated and understood.

Twelve

The Ethics of Title IX and Gender Equity for Coaches: Selected Topics

NANCY HOGSHEAD-MAKAR

Title IX of the Education Amendments of 1972 expresses the nation's collective aspirational belief that girls and boys, women and men, deserve equality in educational experiences and opportunities. Our country has been shaped by ethical guidelines of equality, tolerance, freedom, and rule of law. By contemporary standards, it seems almost peculiar that equality for males and females in federally supported education was ever considered a radical idea.

Despite the progress of the past forty years, athletic departments remain an area of ongoing resistance to equity for men and women in higher education. The battle for gender equality in athletics is befuddling; athletic participation is characterized by ennobling ideals that transmit values of fair play, teamwork, sportsmanship, and compliance with the rules.[1] Yet full compliance with these values cannot be said to have been widely embraced where women seek parity of athletic opportunities in their individual schools.[2] Although athletic gains have been sweeping, women continue to lag behind men by every measurable criterion, including participation opportunities, scholarships, budgets, facilities, and recruiting.

The statutes, case law, and regulations interpreting Title IX may seem daunting, but they all arise from a simple ethical point that is relevant to every question raised today: whether girls and boys, men and women, are receiving equal educational opportunities in athletics.[3] The NCAA put it this way when it adopted Operating Principle 3.1: "An athletics program can be considered gender equitable when the participants in both the men's and the women's programs would accept as fair and equitable the overall program of the other gender."[4] Reflecting this view is that treating female athletic programs as second-class sends a visible message to everyone, on-campus and off-campus, that formal discrimination is acceptable. This chapter explores the responsibilities of coaches and athletic administrators to view gender equity in athletics not just as a matter of legal or technical compliance, but as a matter of ethical responsibility. In doing so, this chapter shares the goal of other feminist ethicists to eliminate or at least ameliorate oppression, particularly of women.[5]

Beyond basic concepts of fairness, Title IX can be defended on utilitarian principles. A large body of research tends to show that, despite the dumb jock myth, interscholastic sports participation provides boys and girls (from diverse socioeconomic, racial, and ethnic backgrounds) measurable positive educational impacts, including improvements in self-concept, higher educational aspirations in their senior year, improved school attendance, increased math and science enrollment, more time spent on homework, and higher enrollment in honors courses.[6] A sports experience provides a positive health trajectory for girls, including reducing the risk for obesity, heart disease, breast cancer, osteoporosis, tobacco and drug use, unwanted teen pregnancy, sexually transmitted diseases, depression, and suicide.[7]

Similarly, research by Professor Betsey Stevenson at the Wharton School of the University of Pennsylvania found that Title IX was responsible for one-fifth of the rise of female educational attainment for the generation that followed the new policy, as well as a 10 percent increase in women working full-time and a 12 percent spike in women in traditionally male-dominated occupations, such as accounting, law, and veterinary medicine.[8] While her research focused on girls, and comparisons just before and after the legislation passed, there is no reason to think that these benefits wouldn't be just as applicable for boys. In short, from a utilitarian perspective, sports make both boys and girls more productive members of society, thereby providing a justifiable investment of public tax dollars.

Coaches are uniquely positioned to advocate for the women and men in their programs, which includes providing gender equitable sports programming, setting ethical boundaries for sexual and romantic relationships, and ensuring ethical treatment for gender equity advocates complaining about sex discrimination in their departments. The coaching profession has been described as a "moral enterprise" that involves the transmission of values and ethics.[9] Yet when professors Ellen Staurowsky and Erianne Weight polled over one thousand coaches about their knowledge of Title IX requirements, they found that most college coaches lack the basic knowledge of the law and its application; coaches simply have not been educated about Title IX through reliable educational mediums.[10] The mainstay of Title IX advocacy and compliance should be coaches.

Ethical Underpinnings of Title IX

Congress passed Title IX on June 23, 1972.[11] Other than the constitutional right to vote, possibly no other piece of legislation has had a greater effect on women's lives than Title IX. Education has been this country's primary method to improve income potential and social class mobility. Yet for most of American history, women were formally excluded or limited in higher education opportunities, thereby blocked from improving themselves economically and socially. It was Title IX that cracked the barriers to women's ability to have equal opportunity to pursue education. As Senator Birch Bayh, one of the drafters of the legislation, stated:

> What we were really looking for was . . . equal opportunity for young women and for girls in the educational system of the United States of America. Equality of opportunity. Equality. That shouldn't really be a controversial subject in a nation [that] now for 200 years has prided itself in equal justice.[12]

Since its adoption, Title IX has become an iconic symbol. The statute is widely recognized as the source of a vast expansion of athletic opportunities for women in the nation's schools and universities. For example, in 1970–71, only 300,000 girls (compared to 3.7 million boys) participated in interscholastic sports. After the passage of Title IX, 2 million girls were participating by 1978–79, and the number of participating girls passed the 3 million mark in 2007.[13] Some laws have an expressive or transformational quality that transcends their remedial purposes; Title IX is one of those laws.[14] Indeed, Title IX's commercial panache has resulted in a company that sells women's athletic apparel marketing itself under the same name: www.titlenine.com.[15]

Four statutes require equality based on receipt of federal funds. Title IX was premised on the first statute passed, Title VI of the Civil Rights Act of

1964, which bars race discrimination in schools receiving federal funds. Title VI reads, "No person in the United States shall, on the ground of race, color, or national origin, be excluded from participation in, be denied the benefits of, or be subjected to discrimination under any program or activity receiving Federal financial assistance." Note that Title IX merely substituted the word "sex" in place of "race, color and national origin." The two other are Section 504 of the Rehabilitation Act of 1973, which banned discrimination against qualified handicapped persons in federally assisted programs or activities; and the Age Discrimination Act of 1975, which banned age discrimination in federally assisted programs or activities. These four statutes are almost identical, but it is Title IX alone that garners any significant pushback.

Other sources provide excellent overviews of the law, the legislative history, and its technical requirements as well as the uniform judicial rejection of legal attacks on Title IX.[16] This chapter discusses some of the ethical underpinnings of Title IX and gender equity that complement the laws.

Sports Are Uniquely Sex Segregated

After Title IX was passed, legal compliance in classrooms, membership in the marching band, and other school-sponsored activities were relatively straightforward. Schools could seek to comply with gender-neutral standards of merit—whether students had specified SAT scores or grade point averages, whether students could play instruments proficiently while marching, and so on.[17] What makes sports programs unique is that they are one of the few activities left in American college life that are formally sex segregated. After puberty, male and female physical differences warrant sex segregation in athletics in order to give girls and women equal educational opportunities to participate.

Interestingly, early discussions of Title IX compliance favored equal budget allocation between men's and women's programming. There are many attractive features in this proposal, not the least of which is its simplicity. Under an "equal budgets" regime, men and women could have adopted their own model of sport, rather than providing women and men with the right to a sports experience similar to each other. In other words, men and women could have chosen independently which model of sport to adopt: a high school–type broad-based participation at a relatively low cost, or the Division I model of a small number of participants with very large budgets. This equal budget option was scuttled by the passage of the Javits amendment that was approved by Congress in 1974 and remains in effect. The Javits amendment required the administrative agency to prepare and publish regulations covering intercollegiate athletics, and those implementing regulations "shall include with respect to intercollegiate athletics . . . reasonable provisions considering the nature of particular sports."[18] The published regulations ultimately became the 1975 Regulations.[19] These regulations allow different amounts of money to be spent on different sports, depending on the distinct needs of the sport. It recognizes that some sports, such as football and equestrian, are inherently more expensive than other sports, requiring costlier equipment or larger budgets for big spectator events. Other sports are relatively inexpensive to operate, such as cross-country. But if both genders are being provided the best equipment or if both genders are being provided barely functional equipment, it is not a violation of Title IX despite large discrepancies in spending, because both genders are considered to be receiving the same educational experience. Ultimately the Javits amendment preserved the ability of schools to fund men's football and basketball budgets because administrators can choose to retain sports that inherently require larger budgets.

Title IX, as applied to athletics, could not be accomplished by merely integrating existing programs, like the classroom or the band. Instead, schools had to create entirely new sports programs. It is the sex segregation that determines equality measurements; athletics require a comparison to men's sports programs with those made available to women. This comparison necessitates reviewing the equality of opportunities, facilities provided, the number of scholarships, and many other indicia, such as equipment, uniforms, access to tutors and medical treatment, coaching, scheduling, publicity, locker rooms, and competitions.[20] It's why courts hold that comparing men's and women's athletic programs is an "unavoidably gender-conscious comparison [that] merely provides for the allocation of athletics resources and participation opportunities between the sexes in a non-discriminatory manner."[21] And determining whether women are being discriminated against in athletics requires a comparison of the new and existing women's programs with the men's program. It was the first part of the 1975 Regulations that gave schools the most trouble—whether the school was providing girls with the proper number of sports opportunities. This led to the creation of the three-part test in the 1979 Clarification.[22]

The Ethics of the Three-Prong Test

A 1979 Policy Interpretation of the Department of Education created three independent ways for schools to demonstrate that students of both genders have equal opportunities to participate in sports. I've paraphrased for simplicity:

- Under prong 1, a school can show that the percentage of male and female athletes is about the same as the percentage of male and female students enrolled in the school (the proportionality test); *OR*

- Under prong 2, the school can show it has a history and a continuing practice of expanding opportunities for female students; *OR*

- Under prong 3, the school can show it is fully and effectively meeting its female students' interests and abilities to participate in sports.[23]

If a school meets any one of these tests, it will be found to be providing equal athletic participation. This three-part test has been in effect for more than three decades. It has been heavily litigated and has been upheld by the eight federal appeals courts that have considered it.[24]

Legality aside, why is the three-prong test ethical? Prong 1 is premised on the principle that a school should provide athletic opportunities so that students, regardless of gender, have an equal opportunity to play sports. If a school has 1,000 students, evenly split between males and females, but offers only 500 participation opportunities, that school should offer 250 of those opportunities to males and 250 to females. Each male and female would have an equal opportunity of playing in a sports program. Creating 300 sports participation opportunities for males versus 200 for females disproportionately favors men, and it is thereby unfair, without some justification.[25] So long as female students have the same chance of participating in athletics as male students, prong 1 is satisfied and the ethic of equality is met. Prong 1 also allows for administrative efficiency by adopting a strict numerical standard, thereby avoiding competing advocacy from men (or women) about whose programs are more important and worthy of scarce athletic department dollars. This is particularly true at larger schools with small percentages of the student body participating in athletics, like schools in the BCS. In 2010 just 1.7 percent of the student body at the University of Florida could participate in college athletics, just 1.6 percent at the University of Texas, and just 2.5 percent at Ohio State.[26] The ease of prong 1 compliance keeps the men's and women's programs from having to justify which sports are inherently more deserving of a team.

The ethics underlying prong 1, though powerful in vision and application, are not compelled. An alternative ethic is permitted under prong 3. Even if a school cannot meet the proportionality requirement of prong 1, it can provide fewer athletic opportunities to girls if the school can show it meets the "interests and abilities" of its female students. In other words, schools do not have to provide sports opportunities to females if they can show that their students are not interested in playing sports. This prong can, in application, effectively require girls to prove their interest in sports, whereas boys are presumed to be interested.[27] Prong 3 thereby presupposes that females are not as interested in sports, exactly the sort of gender stereotype that equality laws were designed to combat. In practice, however, prong 3 has not proven to be the brake on girls' participation that its promoters thought it would be. The reason is simple: the more sports that females are provided, the more sports participation has become normalized, and the less hesitant girls have become to ask for even more. As schools have made opportunities available, girls have rushed to fill them.

This leads to the ethics reflected in prong 2, which is the notion of continuous improvement for women's sports opportunities. The idea is although a school has not met the equality required by law, it can show significant strides toward doing so. Thus if a school has a history and continuing practice of program expansion, it can provide fewer than numerically equal opportunities, yet still be in compliance. This prong raises serious ethical questions. While it might make sense in the short term to allow compliance under prong 2, it makes little sense in the longer term. Forty years have passed since the passage of the law. The 1975 regulations required compliance in high schools and colleges within three years,[28] placing every institution on notice of what is required since at least 1975. Yet a school can deny willing and able females sports participation opportunities simply by making slow, incremental progress. No other area of civil rights law allows for this sort of dilatory practice on an ongoing basis; instead, they require equality in the here and now.

The three-prong test has been subject to steady vilification for over thirty years, typically by those who erroneously claim that strict proportionality (prong 1) is required under Title IX. They typically make no mention of the other two ways of achieving compliance, both of which can, in practice, work to reduce the level of sports opportunities for girls and women.[29] Thereby, the three ways of achieving compliance are not in ethical unison. Indeed, it can be argued that prongs 2 and 3 can undermine the basic ethic of equality depending on the manner by which schools, colleges, and universities implement the legal test.

Ethics of Sex Segregated Athletics:
Why Title IX Is Not a Quota Law or Affirmative Action

Ongoing data collection concludes that high schools and higher education institutions have responded to Title IX by increasing overall the level of female participation rather than by decreasing male participation.[30] Opportunities for sports participation by girls and boys, men and women, are increasing.[31] (See Figure 12.5 at the end of the chapter.) This expansion might not always prove to be true in the future. What if men's sports were losing at the expense of women; would Title IX become a quota system? In a true quota system, the law gives some type of preference to certain group members. Quotas are legally permissible (and fair) only for the purpose of correcting historical practices engaged in by the entity now wishing to provide the preference. Courts regularly identify quotas and quickly prohibit practices that don't meet remedial legal standards. For example, if a city were to be found to have intentionally discriminated against minorities in its contracting, a legal remedy to counteract such discrimination is a quota of contracts that are earmarked specifically for the excluded minority. It is not enough that the subcontractors have engaged in systemic discrimination, or that the overall environment for minorities in the field is fraught with discriminatory practices that work to prevent full economic participation by the minority; it must be the city itself that has engaged in discrimination, or the court will strike it down as unconstitutional.

Athletic departments, by contrast, are not providing females with sports in order to overcome past discrimination but to allocate scarce resources fairly. Because athletics are sex segregated, "determining whether discrimination exists in athletic programs requires gender-conscious, group-wide comparisons."[32] In other words, sex segregated athletics aren't about quotas so much as about comparing resources and sharing them. The only standard to determine whether there has been discrimination is to review what resources are provided to the opposite gender as a comparison.

When Congress was considering limiting the scope of Title IX and weakening regulations interpreting the law, it considered those arguing that requiring equal opportunity in athletics would impose quotas and result in reverse discrimination against men. Yet Congress specifically rejected these arguments.[33] The quota and affirmative action arguments fail for the same reason that equitable sharing of scarce resources does not equate to a quota or reverse discrimination within a family.

The ethics of sharing scarce resources plays out daily in families across the country, which struggle to fairly allocate financial and other resources to their children's education. For example, our son was born five years ahead of our twin daughters. Prior to their arrival, he was the center of our universe and, naturally, received a high level of family resources. When his sisters were born, he got less of the shared family resources, particularly the most valuable commodity every child covets: his parents' time. His portion of the family time and budget would now be shared with his sisters. He did not receive the same level of family resources as he did before his sisters were born, but that is not reverse discrimination or affirmative action. It is the natural and expected result of limited family budgets. While we increased our family budget to accommodate having three children, it still was not enough proportionally to ensure our son the same levels of programs and activities he previously enjoyed. Similarly, schools cannot necessarily increase the size of their athletic department budgets to maintain preexisting levels of spending pro rata. When a school decides that it will not increase its athletic budget but will share the overall resources equally among men's and women's sports, it is not discrimination against men or engaging in quota fulfilling activities. Instead, it is simply assuring that everyone in the family is treated equally.

This ethic is reflected in the Department of Education's 2003 clarification letter, which confirmed that "nothing in Title IX requires the cutting or reduction of teams in order to demonstrate compliance with Title IX, and . . . the elimination of teams is a disfavored practice."[34] Cutting teams will not help a team comply with prongs 2 or 3. Moreover, there is no economic defense to discrimination.[35] "A school may not skirt the requirement of providing both sexes equal opportunity in athletic programs by providing one sex more than substantially proportionate opportunity through the guise of 'outside funding.'"[36]

In short, schools face the same ethical conundrum that millions of families face: what to fund and what to cut to balance the family budget? Ideally, resources would be available to increase, at least incrementally, the school's athletic budget so that no sports opportunities need to be cut.[37] Sharing resources presents difficult choices that are not unlike ones that the parents of the student athletes have already had to make in raising their families.

Another illustration comes from a similar civil rights context from the 1960s, when new desegregation laws required cities to integrate public parks and swimming pools. Some communities closed these facilities rather than integrate them, akin to "cutting off the nose to spite the face." In *Palmer v. Thompson*[38] the Supreme Court upheld the city's racially motivated choice to close public pools, holding it was permissible because the closure placed whites and blacks in the same access to public facilities, or no access.[39] The analogy isn't completely accurate; *Palmer* is much more egregious. When schools close men's sports teams, they are not doing so in order to spite females or to express hostility toward either males or females. Rather, they are doing so to rectify a budget imbalance, replace it with another men's sport, or to shift resources elsewhere within the institution.

While this discussion has assumed a static or limited budget, most NCAA institutions are not cutting their budgets; they have been growing at a robust 7 percent over the past ten years. Over the same time period, academic budgets have not risen appreciably. Most of the new growth in athletics budgets has gone to other men. Between the 2005–06 and 2009–10 academic years, men's budgets increased by $5.2 million, while women's budgets increased by just $1.8 million.[40] Interestingly, two men's sports, football and basketball, make up 78 percent of the entire men's budget, leaving 22 percent for all other men's sports.[41] Title IX does not protect a sport, does not distinguish between sports, and does not favor or disfavor any particular sport. It protects men and women from discrimination, regardless of what uniform the athlete is wearing or the size of the team that the school has decided to offer.[42] Football is allowed eighty-four scholarships according to NCAA rules, which is typically far more than half of all scholarships offered to men.[43] Title IX allows schools to decide what sport model to adopt and which sports they choose to emphasize, and merely requires an equitable allocation between these educational opportunities.

Coaches and athletic administrators can be advocates for gender equity within their departments from both equality and utilitarian perspectives. When doing so, coaches could either tell athletes and department officials that their decisions are required by Title IX, or they could assume responsibility for creating a gender equitable environment within their department. If a school funds football for men and lacrosse for women, the school cannot ethically blame Title IX for the decision not to fund a male lacrosse team. They should instead explain how they've assumed the responsibility to distribute resources equitably between males and females within the athletics department.

The Ethics of Romantic or Sexual Relationships Between Coaches and Athletes

Athletics creates opportunities for sexual harassment due to the close relationship of team members with their coaches and the physical nature of sports. The Supreme Court has noted that different standards of behavior exist for classroom and athletics. If the coach smacks a professional football player on the buttocks as he heads onto the field, it is not sexual harassment, even if the same behavior would reasonably be experienced as abusive by the coach's secretary (male or female) back at the office.[44] Title IX also prohibits sexual harassment in education as a form of sex discrimination, including athletics. Four features of athletics that affect sexual harassment and assault include the coach-student relationship, the increased opportunity for harassment, the physical nature of sports, and the focus on the athlete's body.[45]

A coach's authority over athletes cannot be overestimated. They decide playing time, playing positions and possibly scholarship amounts. They exert power through praise, criticism, or withholding either; they grant or deny leadership opportunities. They exert a special power over an ambitious athlete by holding out the prospect of greater athletic accomplishments. They frequently impose restrictions on the athlete's personal life such as curfew, dress code, or membership in a sorority or fraternity.[46] Yet a coach may reach the elite coaching ranks without knowing about power: how it can be used and abused, and may have never had a course on ethics.

In a typical academic setting, students often have limited opportunity for one-on-one contact with professors. In the athletic context, by contrast, opportunities for such contact are common, and often arise in places conducive to sexual behavior. Most athletic teams travel overnight with their coaches to attend away games. Even without travel, coaches and athletes can spend over a third of all waking hours together. Coaches and trainers commonly work on and off the field to massage athletes' sore muscles and rehabilitate common sports injuries. In addition, sports are inherently physical, and many coaches apply a hands-on approach to demonstrate athletic moves. Coaches and athletes regularly use physical contact, such as a pat on the back or a hug, to convey praise and acknowledge success. Some coaches help athletes stretch before a workout or rub stiff muscles. Athletes and coaches regularly discuss the body as a tool; the status of injuries, the effect of prior workouts on specific body parts, and weight as it relates to performance. Such behavior can be entirely proper in the context of athletics, but would be inappropriate in the classroom. These special circumstances, including the authority of the coach, together with the coach's one-on-one contact, amplify the potential for harassment.

Title IX also protects lesbian, gay, bisexual, and transgender (LGBT) students from discrimination, particularly when the abuse and bullying centers around the athlete's sexuality, or the athlete's failure to conform to sex stereotypes. Typical forms of harassment involve epithets or abuse that would not be used if the athlete were of the opposite gender.

The culture of athletics has not protected athletes from sexual harassment from their coach in the way employees are protected from similar conduct from their manager. The boundaries of workplace harassment have normalized the impermissibility of quid pro quo sexual harassment and hostile environment harassment,[47] but many still view sexual and romantic relationships as permissible, so long as both parties are above the legal age of consent, and there is no overt coercion. In recognition of this permissive culture, many sports organizations have developed ethical policies that explicitly prohibit romantic and sexual relationships between coaches and athletes, re-gardless of the age of the athlete and coach, or whether the athlete consents to the attention. Like other professional settings marked by an imbalance in power and a duty of care, the ethical standards governing coaches should be designed to safeguard the well-being of persons for whom they are responsi-ble, rather than for the benefit of those in power.

The United States Olympic Committee's (USOC) policy is a model for its breadth and clarity.[48] It leaves no scenario unaddressed. Romantic and sexual relationships are addressed under the heading "exploitative relationships," and the ethics policy flatly prohibits them. "(b) Coaches do not engage in sexual/romantic relationships with athletes or other participants over whom the coach has evaluative, direct, or indirect authority, because such relation-ships are likely to impair judgment or be exploitative." The USOC policy goes on to prohibit sexual intimacy with current athletes, sexual intimacies with former sexual partners, as well as reviewing boundaries for starting a sexual relationship with a former athlete.

Unfortunately the USOC ethics policy for coaches does not apply to the national governing body (NGBs) of each sport unless the coaching associa-tion adopts it. Consequently many NGBs do not ban these types of relation-ships, or have no mechanism to remove coaches for having a romantic or sexual relationship with someone of age.[49] The Ted Stevens Olympic and Am-ateur Sports Act does have a nondiscrimination clause,[50] but because these disputes go through AAA arbitration rather than through the court system, they have not provided as effective protection as has Title IX. The USOC re-cently released materials that deal with misconduct directed toward athletes, including emotional, physical, sexual, bullying, harassing, and hazing.[51] It similarly prohibits relationships between coaches and athletes.[52]

The NCAA policy "Staying in Bounds: A Model Policy to Prevent Inap-propriate Relationships Between Student-Athletes and Athletic Department Personnel" is similarly thorough. It addresses the fact that romantic relation-ships are still common between coaches and athletes and pulls no punches.

> Some will argue that coach-athlete liaisons are not "abusive." Some will maintain that (as many coaches have told us) "you can't control the heart," or "you can't legislate against love," or "as long as the two people are adults, no one can stop them from dating." These comments are self-justifying and, frankly, self-delusional. When coaches enter into sexual relationships with student-athletes, they almost always try to keep these liaisons secret—even if both parties are unmarried—because coaches are well aware that such relationships are inappropriate and unethical. They know deep down that infatuation, sexual attraction,

and loving feelings do not, in fact, justify an authority figure in a sports program becoming sexually involved with a young adult who plays sports in that program. This is a violation of professional boundaries, and a violation of trust.[53]

In higher education, a typical amorous relationship policy will remove the supervisory capacity between consenting adults.[54] Other professional and ethical standards of conduct also prohibit sexual and romantic relationships between those in a power differential, such as doctors, lawyers, judges, and clergy. All regard it as unethical to have sexual relationships with those they treat, counsel, and appear before. In this way, middle-aged employees are better protected by cultural norms and formal ethical standards than are young athletes participating in club sports.

Retaliation, Commercialism, and Ethical Considerations

Coaches advocating for gender equity in their departments have never had the legal support they are currently enjoying. In 2005 the Supreme Court held that coaches who suffered retaliation for speaking up about gender inequity in their athletics department could sue under Title IX.[55] This makes sense; otherwise institutions could continue discrimination merely by firing or demoting people working to eliminate discrimination. Since that time, numerous women and men working in collegiate athletics have successfully sued their athletic department, alleging they were retaliated against for their advocacy for the women athletes. Juries continue to send decisive verdicts to women and men shown unfair treatment. Listed below are a few of the more recent cases.

- Fresno State lost three retaliation claims by former athletic department employees. Lindy Vivas, a onetime Fresno State women's volleyball coach, was awarded $5.85 million by a jury, later reduced to $4.52 million plus $660,000 in legal fees. Stacy Johnson-Klein, a former women's basketball coach, was awarded $19.1 million; her verdict later was reduced to $6.6 million, plus $2.5 million in legal fees. Fresno State settled with Diane Milutinovich, Fresno's former associate athletic director, for $3.5 million.[56]

- California-Berkley paid $3.5 million to its former women's swimming coach and athletics administrator, Karen Moe Humphreys. She filed a discrimination and retaliation suit alleging she was fired because she complained about treatment of women in the athletics department.[57]

- Florida Gulf Coast University paid $3.4 million in 2008 to two former women's coaches, Jayne Flood and Holly Vaughn, to settle their lawsuit alleging retaliating against the women after they voiced concerns about gender inequity in the school's athletic programs, and were fired shortly thereafter.[58]

- San Diego State University announced it would pay $1.45 million to former swimming and diving head coach Deena Deardurff Schmidt, in a settlement of her Title IX retaliation case. Schmidt's lawsuit alleged that the university had unrealistic expectations for her performance, as her team had lacked a swimming facility since 1999.

- Iowa State awarded $287,000 to former softball coach Ruth Crowe. In her Title IX retaliation suit against the university, Crowe had alleged that after nine years in the head coach position, the university dismissed her before her contract expired because she had complained about salary discrimination and the university's failure to allocate comparable money for recruiting female athletes.

In the past I have put this jury hostility into context by comparing a death from a medical malpractice case that averages just over $1 million in final verdicts.[59] Jury verdicts in Title IX retaliation claims, by contrast, involve a multiple of that amount in part because of the intentional and overt conduct on the part of the defendants.

These cases are also valuable in revealing obstacles to women's leadership in athletics. As a broad generalization, it's fair to say that athletic departments do not value the power of dissent. This can make it hard for advocates of gender equity. They have become a touch-point on the conflict between the educational mission of athletics and the commercial enterprise, particularly in Division I athletics.

Despite large television contracts, sponsorships, and ticket sales at the highest levels of sports, high school and collegiate sports are not for-profit businesses. Taxes are not imposed on revenues from corporate sponsorships, ticket sales, or donor contributions, and athletic facilities are built with tax-free bonds. Students are often forced to pay for athletics as part of their student fees, even for the few sports programs whose income exceeds expenses. The public forgoes taxes on the NCAA multibillion-dollar-basketball championship television contract with CBS and Turner Sports, as well as on billions more in guaranteed payouts from current media football contracts to the top five major conferences.[60] Even the tiny minority of schools actually operating at a profit[61] cannot deny their heavy reliance on public tax dollars that flow from their educational enterprise.

In addition, collegiate athletics receive direct subsidies from their institutions. The latest report from the Knight Commission on Intercollegiate Athletics found that roughly 80 percent of the football bowl subdivision programs averaged a net operating deficit of nearly $10 million. That's money coming from academics to athletics, not the other way around.[62] For public schools in particular, it is another source of tax dollars for athletics. Finally, businesses must pay their employees, while educational institutions do not pay student athletes. Schools are relieved of this obligation because of the athlete's status as a student. If the economic model of high school and intercollegiate sports is founded on utilitarian concepts, forgoing tax revenue as an investment in education for future health benefits and economic productivity for the country, women have an equal right to a fair share of the benefits arising from participation in sports.

The successes of the retaliation cases give advocates of gender equality grounds for cautious optimism. In the battles between the educational mission of athletics and the commercial enterprise, retaliation cases give men and women in athletics more reason to act ethically and champion women within the department; championing women's athletics provides job security. The momentum of multimillion-dollar verdicts and settlements on their side, coaches are better situated now than ever before to seek remedies that will help ensure that college athletic department values include equal opportunity for women's athletics, including its leadership.

Conclusion

Implicit in this chapter has been the notion that the conduct of coaches raises ethical as well as legal issues. Coaches are uniquely positioned to advocate for women and men in the athletic department. They can be forceful advocates for providing men and women with equitable sports programming, including participation, treatment, and scholarships. Coaches, through their coaching associations, must collectively decide to enforce ethical boundaries for sexual and romantic relationships between coaches and athletes. The athletic department may be sex segregated, requiring a different type of thinking than that applied to the classroom, but they collectively comprise one family of athletes, and all need to be provided for equitably. As transmitters of values and ethics, their unwillingness to tolerate inequity speaks loudly to their athletes and to the athletic community.

THE UNITED STATES OLYMPIC COMMITTEE
COACHING ETHICS CODE

Readers interested in the discussion issues of harassment and romantic and sexual relationships between coaches and athletes may consult the Coaching Ethics Code, which follows.

1.08 Sexual Harassment

(a) Coaches do not engage in sexual harassment. Sexual harassment is sexual solicitation, physical advances, or verbal or nonverbal conduct that is sexual in nature, and that either:

1. is unwelcome, is offensive, or creates a hostile environment, and the coach knows or is told this;

2. is sufficiently severe or intense to be abusive to a reasonable person in the context.

Sexual harassment can consist of a single intense or severe act or of multiple persistent or pervasive acts.

(b) Coaches accord sexual-harassment complainants and respondents dignity and respect. Coaches do not participate in denying an athlete the right to participate based upon their having made, or their being the subject of, sexual harassment charges.

1.13 Multiple Relationships

(a) In many communities and situations, it may not be feasible or reasonable for coaches to avoid social or other nonprofessional contacts with athletes and other participants. Coaches must always be sensitive to the potential harmful effects of other contacts on their work and on those persons with whom they deal. A coach refrains from entering into or promising another personal, professional, financial, or other relationship with such persons if it appears likely that such a relationship reasonably might impair the coach's objectivity or otherwise interfere with the coach's effectively performing his or her functions as a coach, or might harm or exploit the other party.

1.14 Exploitative Relationships

(a) Coaches do not exploit athletes or other participants over whom they have supervisory, evaluative, or other authority.

(b) Coaches do not engage in sexual/romantic relationships with athletes or other participants over whom the coach has evaluative, direct, or indirect authority, because such relationships are likely to impair judgment or be exploitative.

3.04 Sexual Intimacies with Current Athletes

Coaches do not engage in sexual intimacies with current athletes.

3.05 Coaching Former Sexual Partners

Coaches do not coach athletes with whom they have engaged in sexual intimacies.

3.06 Sexual Intimacies with Former Athletes

(a) Coaches should not engage in sexual intimacies with a former athlete for at least two years after cessation or termination of professional services.

(b) Because sexual intimacies with a former athlete are so frequently harmful to the athlete, and because such intimacies undermine public confidence in the coaching profession and thereby deter the public's use of needed services, coaches do not engage in sexual intimacies with former athletes even after a two-year interval except in the most unusual circumstances. The coach who engages in such activity after the two years following cessation or termination of the coach-athlete relationship bears the burden of demonstrating that there has been no exploitation, in light of all relevant factors, including:

(1) the amount of time that has passed since the coach-athlete relationship terminated,

(2) the circumstances of termination,

(3) the athlete's personal history,

(4) the athlete's current mental status,

(5) the likelihood of adverse impact on the athlete and others, and

(6) any statements or actions made by the coach during the course of the athlete-coach relationship suggesting or inviting the possibility of a post-termination sexual or romantic relationship with the athlete or coach.

Source: USACoaching.org. www.usacoaching.org/resources /Coaching%20Ethics%20Code_new.pdf

Data on Gender Equity in Sports

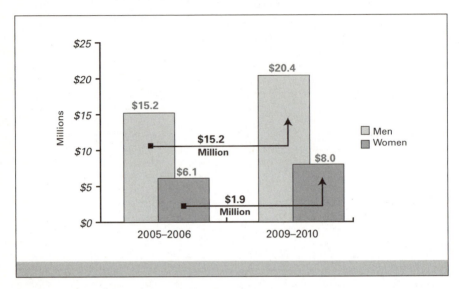

Figure 12.1. Median Total Expenses in Women's and Men's Athletic Programs: Football Bowl Subdivision

Source: NCAA Gender Equity Report, 2004–2010, p. 37

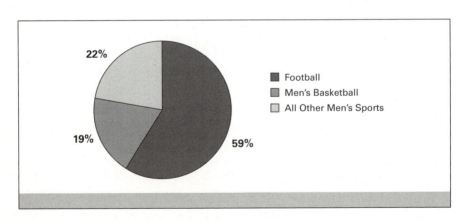

Figure 12.2. Percent of Expenses for FBS Men's Sports, 2009–2010

Source: NCAA Gender Equity Report, 2009–2010, p. 35

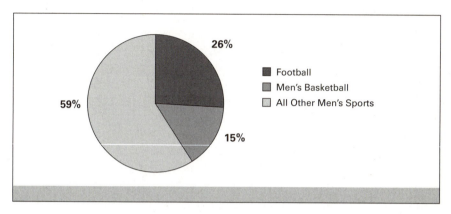

Figure 12.3. Percent of Expenses for Division III Men's Sports, 2009–2010

Source: NCAA Gender Equity Report, 2009–2010, p. 35

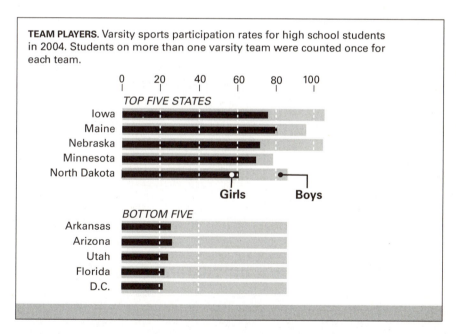

Figure 12.4. Interest in Sports Is Dictated by Opportunities

Source: Professor Betsy Stevenson, http://well.blogs.nytimes.com/2010/02/15 /as-girls-become-women-sports-pay-dividends/

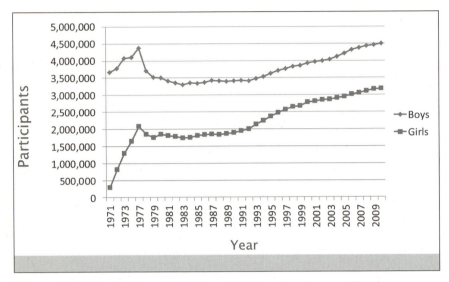

Figure 12.5. High School Athletics Participation Survey Totals, 1971–2012 (Boys' High School Sports Participation, 2010–2011 = 4,494,406, the Highest in History)

Source: National Federation of State High School Associations, 2010–2011 Athletics Participation Summary

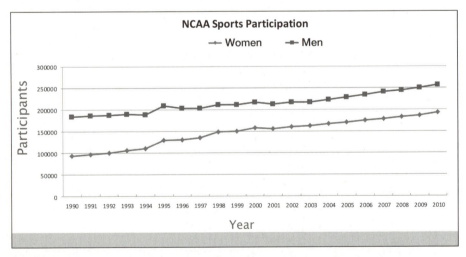

Figure 12.6. Sponsorship Levels: Total Participants, 1990–1991 and 2010–2011 (Includes Emerging Sports and Nonchampionship Sports)

Source: NCAA Sponsorship and Participation Rates Report, 1981–1982 and 2010–2011

Questions for Review and Discussion

1. Explain the three-part test for participation compliance with Title IX in athletics.

2. Why did some critics of Title IX argue that it implemented a quota?

3. What according to the author distinguishes a quota from Title IX and athletics?

4. Does Title IX protect men?

5. Look up your school's data on the Equity in Athletics Disclosure Act website: http://ope.ed.gov/athletics. Does your school satisfy any prongs of the three-part test? If so, which ones?

6. What utilitarian principles justify providing males and females with equal educational opportunities?

7. In addition to legal entanglements, what ethical problems are raised when coaches have sexual or romantic relationships with athletes? Do you agree that such relationships always are improper? How would you defend your view?

8. Why is a cause of action for retaliation an important right for advocates for gender equity? What would happen if advocates were unprotected?

Suggestions for Further Reading

Anderson, Elizabeth S., and Richard H. Pildes. "Expressive Theories of Law: A General Restatement." 148 *U. Pa. L. Rev.* 1503 (2000).

Brake, Deborah L. *Getting in the Game: Title IX and the Women's Sports Revolution.* New York: New York University Press, 2010.

———. "The Struggle for Sex Equality in Sport and the Theory Behind Title IX." 34 *U. Mich. J.L. Reform* 13, 16–18 (2001).

Buzuvis, Erin. "Sidelined: Title IX Retaliation Cases and Women's Leadership on College Athletics." 17 *Duke J. Gender L. & Pol'y* 1 (2010).

Chalenor v. Univ. of N.D., 292 F.3d 1042 (8th Cir. 2002).

Cohen v. Brown Univ., 101 F.3d 155 (1st Cir. 1996), cert. denied, 520 U.S. 1186 (1997).

Geisinger, Alex. "A Belief Change Theory of Expressive Law." 88 *Iowa L. Rev.* 35, 37 (2002).

Hogshead-Makar, Nancy. "Attitudes, Platitudes, and the Collegiate Sports Arms Race: Unsustainable Spending and Its Consequences for Olympic and Women's Sports." *Journal on Intercollegiate Sports.*

McAdams, Richard H. "An Attitudinal Theory of Expressive Law." 79 *Or. L. Rev.* 339 (2000).

Neal v. Bd. of Trs., 198 F.3d 763 (9th Cir. 1999).

Sabo, Don, and Phil Veliz. "Go Out and Play: Youth Sports in America." East Meadow, NY: Women's Sports Foundation, 2008. www.womenssports foundation.org/home/research/articles-and-reports/mental-and-physical -health/go-out-and-play.

Thirteen

The Coach and the Safety of Athletes: Ethical and Legal Issues

MATTHEW J. MITTEN

Regardless of the level of athletic competition, a coach is not at fault or legally responsible for an athlete's injury simply because it happens. By voluntarily choosing to participate in a sport, student athletes assume the inherent risk of injury during training, conditioning drills, practices, and athletic competitions, which coaches do not have a legal duty to eliminate or reduce. An inherent risk is one that is "part of the game," and it is an obvious or known risk that is among the potential consequences of normal competition in a sport. Suffering an eye injury from an elbow to the face while rebounding during a basketball game, receiving a knee injury when kicked by an opponent while playing soccer, or suffering a broken arm while being tackled during a football game are all inherent risks of playing these sports.

Although coaches generally are not liable for athlete injuries that are part of the game, there is potential legal liability if a coach's action or inaction increases the inherent risks of injury in a sport. To recover damages for an injury, an athlete is required to prove tortious (i.e., wrongful) action or inaction by a coach caused his injury. Negligence, which is the failure to use reasonable care to protect against foreseeable harm under the circumstances, is the legal theory generally relied on by athletes who have sued coaches for sports-related injuries. The reasonable care standard requires that coaches take appropriate measures to prevent or minimize the risk of injuries (particularly serious or permanent ones) or death during athletic competition. Consistent with the legal duty of reasonable care established by the negligence standard, a coach has an ethical obligation to not create an unsafe environment by enhancing a sport's inherent risk of injury and to take affirmative steps to protect their athletes from suffering serious injuries or death.

In some instances, the coach's legitimate objectives of maximizing athletic performance, maintaining discipline, and winning games or competitions conflict with the legal and ethical duty to protect the health and safety of athletes under his or her supervision and control. Some recent deaths and serious injuries suffered by young athletes during athletic competition or training illustrate this inherent tension and raise red flags. In August 2008 Max Gilpin, a fifteen-year-old Kentucky high school football player, died of complications from heatstroke during a practice at which David Stinson, the head football coach at Pleasure Park High School, required players to continue running in helmets and pads in 94 degree weather, although some were gasping for breath and/or vomiting. Stinson had decided he would not stop this conditioning drill until someone quit the team. Olivia Kahn, a fourteen-year-old novice member of the junior varsity swim team at East Union High School in California, broke her neck during an unsupervised practice dive into a shallow pool without adequate safety instruction, allegedly after her coach told her minutes before a swim meet that she would be required for the first time to dive into the pool rather than starting a relay race in the water. In February 2011 thirteen University of Iowa football players were hospitalized after suffering a muscle disorder known as exertional rhabdomyolysis, which can cause kidney failure in serious cases, as a result of grueling off-season conditioning workouts.

In this chapter I provide an overview of developing law regarding the nature and scope of a coach's duty to protect the health and safety of athletes participating in youth and high school sports (who generally are minors entrusted to coaches' custodial care) or college sports (who generally are adults not having a custodial relationship with their coaches) and illustrate a coach's ethical obligation to do so. State statutes and judicial decisions may immunize coaches at public educational institutions from liability for negligence that causes injury to athletes, and preinjury releases and waivers may protect both private and public school coaches from liability for their negligence.

This discussion is based on the premise that coaches have an ethical obligation to protect their athletes' health and safety, regardless of the level of athletic competition. Rather than being uniform nationwide, the governing law regarding a coach's legal obligation to protect athletes' health and safety varies from state to state. However, consistent with their ethical obligation, the law generally requires (or should require) coaches to exercise reasonable care to protect athletes' health and safety with liability for negligence if this duty is breached and they are injured.

Youth and High School Sports

One of a coach's primary responsibilities is to provide players with appropriate instruction regarding how to properly play and safely participate in a sport, which requires a coach to use reasonable care to protect athletes from foreseeable harm while playing the particular sport to avoid potential liability for negligence. In *Vendrell v. School District No. 26C, Malheur County*,[1] the plaintiff, a fifteen-year-old freshman who suffered a broken neck when tackled during a high school football game, claimed that his coaches' negligent instruction and training caused his injury. The Oregon Supreme Court ruled that a "coach or physical education instructor is required to exercise reasonable care for the protection of the students under his supervision," but determined that the coaches were not liable for his injury because they provided "adequate, standard instruction and practice" to their football team:

> No one expects a football coach to extract from the game the body clashes that cause bruises, jolts and hard falls. To remove them would end the sport. The coach's function is to minimize the possibility that the body contacts may result in something more than slight injury. The extensive calisthenics, running and other forms of muscular exercise to which the defendant's coaches subjected the defendant's squad were intended to place the players in sound physical condition so that they could withstand the shocks, blows and other rough treatment with which they would meet in actual play. As a further safeguard for the players' protection the defendant provided all of the players with protective equipment. Each player was taught and shown how to handle himself while in play so that a blow would fall upon his protective equipment and not directly upon his body. We have also noticed the fact that every player was instructed in the manner of (1) running while carrying the ball, (2) tackling an opposing player, and (3) handling himself properly when about to be tackled.

Based on different facts, a coach may be liable for negligently failing to provide adequate instruction necessary to protect players' health and safety. In *Thompson v. Seattle Public School District 47*, a Washington high school football player was awarded damages for injuries caused by his coach's negligent failure to warn him of the risks of lowering his head to ward off tacklers while carrying the football, which increased the risk of serious neck injuries.[2]

Courts also have held that a coach's legal duty to properly instruct and supervise young athletes in connection with a sport includes the obligation to provide them with appropriate protective equipment and to ensure its usage during athletic competition or to adequately warn them about the health and safety risks of not using it. For example, in *Baker v. Briarcliff School District*,[3] a New York court held that a coach's failure to properly warn students about the risks of not wearing a mouthpiece during a girls' high school field hockey practice "unreasonably increased [their] risks of injury" and created possible liability for a mouth injury suffered by a girl who was not wearing her mouthpiece as a result.

Although coaches do not ensure the health and safety of students entrusted to their care, they have a legal duty to adequately supervise them and to provide a reasonably safe practice environment. In *Stirgis v. St. John the Baptist Parish School Board*,[4] a Louisiana appellate court explained that a coach should provide "reasonable, competent supervision appropriate to the age of the children and the attendant circumstances," which includes "protecting against unreasonable risk of injury from dangerous or hazardous objects in the school buildings and on the grounds." The court ruled that conducting football throwing drills requiring players to make quick pivots and turns on a wet gymnasium floor may constitute negligent conduct by a football coach.

A coach also breaches the negligence standard of care by pushing an athlete beyond his or her endurance level and creating exposure to an unreasonably enhanced risk of injury above the sport's inherent risks. In *Vargo v. Svitchan*[5] a Michigan appellate court held that urging a high school football player to push "himself to and beyond his limits" with resulting injury may establish negligence liability. During the first of a scheduled series of weight lifting sessions to prepare him for high school football team tryouts, while being urged by the football coach "to perform to the utmost," a fifteen-year-old high school student fell while lifting a 250- to 300-pound weight and suffered injuries resulting in paraplegia.

Although Coach David Stinson did not acknowledge any liability for Max Gilpin's August 2008 death from heatstroke and was acquitted of criminally reckless homicide and wanton endangerment charges, Stinson's deposition testimony in a wrongful death suit filed by the boy's parents (settled for $1.75 million) evidences his negligence. Stinson testified he would not have stopped a grueling series of sprints by his players in football helmets and full pads in 94 degree weather even if players were vomiting, passing out, and calling for water. During this running drill Stinson apparently was more concerned with instilling discipline in his players than preventing them from overheating.

Another area in which coaches have a legal duty is the provision of emergency care. Coaches should promptly obtain emergency medical care for an injured athlete. In *Mogabgab v. Orleans Parish School Board*[6] two high school football coaches were found negligent for failing to obtain medical care for a student for almost two hours after he exhibited symptoms of heatstroke during practice, which caused his death. Although coaches are not required to have the same degree of knowledge as medical experts, they must recognize a medical emergency and act reasonably under the circumstances (e.g., by seeking prompt medical treatment for an ill or injured student).

Courts also have found coaches liable for improperly providing first aid that worsens an injured athlete's condition by, for example, moving the athlete before medical personnel arrive to provide treatment.[7] In *Halper v. Vayo*[8] an Illinois appellate court ruled that a coach may be liable for aggravating a high school wrestler's knee injury by attempting to treat the injury by manipulating his knee. The court explained: "Because of the substantial risks involved, we believe it can be reckless for an individual with no medical training to pull on the leg of a person with a knee injury and attempt to manipulate the knee assuming no exigency exists which necessitates such treatment."

Although coaches are not required or expected to be able to diagnose the nature and extent of a player's injury, in *Jarreau v. Orleans Parish School Board*[9] a Louisiana court observed "they should recognize their limitations in this regard and seek expert medical advice" before permitting an injured athlete to return to play. The failure to do so gives rise to potential liability for aggravated injuries. The court upheld a jury's finding that a coach negligently allowed a highschool student to continue playing football with an injured wrist despite his persistent complaints of pain and swelling.

On the other hand, a coach is not liable for an aggravated injury from continued play if it is not foreseeable under the circumstances or if reasonable care was used in determining its severity. In *Zemke v. Arreola*[10] a California appellate court ruled that a coach is not liable for a high school football player's severe and debilitating brain injury caused by second impact syndrome when he was permitted to return to a game after suffering a dislocated finger. His brain injury was not foreseeable because the player apparently suffered only an injury to his finger, and he did not appear to have or report any symptoms of an initial head injury. Similarly, in *Cerny v. Cedar Bluffs Junior/Senior Public School*[11] a coach exercised reasonable care by properly evaluating a high school football player for symptoms of a concussion before allowing him to resume play and was not liable for a subsequent injury causing severe brain injury.

An Alternative Liability Standard:
Intentional or Reckless Conduct

The foregoing cases adopt a negligence standard of legal liability and require coaches to exercise reasonable care to protect youth and high school athletes under their custody and control from foreseeable harm while participating in a sport. However, some courts recently have refused to impose a legal duty on coaches to use reasonable care when instructing and supervising athletes participating in youth and high school sports. In other words, a coach is not liable for negligent instruction or supervision that causes injury to athletes. Rather, injured athletes must prove the coach's conduct was more culpable than a mere failure to use reasonable care to protect them against foreseeable harm under the circumstances. These courts require proof that a coach intentionally or recklessly injured an athlete. This alternative standard makes it more difficult to hold coaches legally liable for injuries.

In *Kahn v. East Side Union High School District*[12] a fourteen-year-old freshman girl broke her neck during an unsupervised practice dive from a starting block into three and a half feet of water in the racing pool at her high school. She alleged that her coach negligently directed her to practice shallow water diving for the first time shortly before a competitive swim race without giving her adequate training or supervision. Because of her fear of suffering a traumatic head injury from diving into shallow water, the coach had allowed her to start two prior meets in the water rather than by diving into the pool, but he told her she would not be permitted to start her relay in the pool this time.

While recognizing that a coach has a legal duty not to increase the risks inherent in the process by which a young athlete learns a sport, the California Supreme Court expressed concern about imposing "a duty to mitigate the inherent risks of learning a sport by refraining from challenging a student" because it "could have a chilling effect on the enterprise of teaching and learning skills that are necessary to the sport." The court stated that "pushing an athlete to compete, excel, or move to the next level of competence ordinarily does not form a basis for liability on the part of athletic instructors and coaches." Rather than requiring that coaches use reasonable care when doing so, a majority of the court's judges adopted a much lower legal standard of care:

> [I]n cases in which it is alleged that a sports instructor has required a student to perform beyond the student's capacity or without providing adequate instruction, it must be alleged and proved that the instructor acted with intent to cause a student's injury or that the instructor acted recklessly in the sense that the instructor's conduct was 'totally outside

the range of the ordinary activity' involved in teaching or coaching the sport.

All of the *Kahn* judges concluded that the coach may be liable for reckless conduct causing the girl's injury:

If a jury were to find that defendant coach directed plaintiff (a novice on the swim team) to perform a shallow racing dive in competition without providing any instruction, that he ignored her overwhelming fears and made a last-minute demand that she dive during competition, in breach of a previous promise that she would not be required to dive, we believe the trier of fact properly could determine that such conduct was reckless in that it was totally outside the range of the ordinary activity involved in teaching or coaching the sport of competitive swimming.

Expressing concern that this legal standard places greater emphasis on enhancing athletic performance than on protecting young athletes' safety, Justice Werdegar asserted that a coach should be subject to liability if his conduct "constitutes a gross or extreme departure" from "the range of ordinary instructional activities, increasing the risks of injury beyond those inherent in teaching a sport." Advocating that this standard "will provide sufficient protection against unfair second-guessing of the instructor's judgment and, therefore, will not unduly chill participation in sports instruction," he explained that "society expects—legitimately, in my view—more from instructors and coaches than merely that they will refrain from harming a student intentionally or with wanton disregard for safety. An instructor's gross or extreme lack of care for student safety is not an inherent risk of school athletics programs."

Justice Kennard, another *Kahn* case judge, would require high school coaches to conform to the negligence standard of ordinary care:

Coaches of student athletes teach them the skills necessary to perform their sport of choice safely and effectively. Because student athletes, particularly minors, often consider their coach a mentor or role model, they trust the coach not to carelessly and needlessly expose them to injury. The majority's decision puts an end to that trust. . . .

Applying the negligence standard here would leave coaches free to challenge or push their students to advance their skills level as long as they do so without exposing the student athletes to an unreasonable risk of harm.

High school shop instructors who teach students how to operate a power saw or repair a car, and chemistry teachers in their laboratories, are held to a standard of ordinary negligence. Why should a different standard apply to an instructor who teaches students competitive swimming?

At this point, it is uncertain whether the *Kahn* majority's ruling that a coach is not liable for negligent instruction or supervision that causes injury is representative of a developing national judicial trend. South Dakota,[13] New York,[14] and Connecticut[15] courts have rejected it. However, in *Karas v. Strevell*[16] the Illinois Supreme Court followed *Kahn* in ruling that a coach is liable for an injury to a young athlete participating in an organized contact sport only if he intended to cause the injury or engaged in conduct "totally outside the range of the ordinary activity" involved with coaching the sport. The court expressed concern that applying an ordinary negligence standard to the numerous subjective decisions coaches make during a fast-paced game would open the door to litigation and unfairly burden them with potential liability. However, Justice Kilbride cautioned: "We cannot legitimately ignore younger athletes' greater physical vulnerability or their limited autonomy from their coaches and sporting organizations in assessing the propriety of their conduct toward their young athletes." This judge stated that coaches should be liable for player injuries if their action "was totally outside of the range of the ordinary coaching, instruction, supervision, or organization of *players of a certain age and experience level in a particular sport.*"

The danger of permitting "the range of the ordinary activity" involved in teaching or coaching the sport to establish a coach's legal duty of care is that it conclusively establishes customary practices in the coaching profession as the appropriate standard for protecting athletes' health and safety. In most instances, this standard probably achieves the desired level of safety and provides an adequate level of protection to youth and high school athletes. It is, however, an inappropriate legal and ethical standard of care when customary coaching practices unduly emphasize winning or athletic performance and expose young athletes to the risk of serious injuries. Surely we do not want to characterize a practice as ethically permissible just because everyone does it, which is what the customary practices standard in effect does. On the other hand, the negligence standard, which requires coaches to use reasonable care to protect against foreseeable harm *under the circumstances*, is a flexible and better means of ensuring that coaches adequately protect the health and safety of athletes under their supervision and control. It also ensures that they do not increase a sport's inherent risks of injury.

In some instances, federal or state laws may immunize coaches from negligence liability for policy reasons. Congress enacted the Volunteer Protection Act of 1997[17] to encourage the provision of voluntary service on behalf of nonprofit organizations and governmental entities by limiting the tort liability of volunteers. This federal statute generally provides that a volunteer is not liable for harm caused by negligence. In *Avenoso v. Mangan*[18] a Connecticut court held that the Volunteer Protection Act immunized a volunteer coach for a local nonprofit soccer club who has never received compensation for any of his activities from negligence liability for an injury suffered by one of his players during a soccer practice. Similar to the Volunteer Protection Act, some states immunize volunteer coaches for nonprofit organizations from negligence liability.[19] Other states (e.g., Massachusetts)[20] have statutes specifically immunizing volunteer coaches who provide services to nonprofit associations that operate sports programs primarily for children under eighteen years of age from liability for negligence.

In some jurisdictions, the doctrine of qualified immunity, which may be established by a state statute[21] or by the state's courts, protects public school employees, including coaches, from negligence liability when they are engaged in *discretionary acts*. For example, in *Gasper v. Freidel*[22] a student was injured while training in a public high school's weight facilities and sued his coaches. The South Dakota Supreme Court ruled that coaches are immune from liability for negligence:

> [C]oaches were carrying out the important function of conditioning student/athletes for all sports. For this court to second-guess Freidel's and Meyer's judgment on how to supervise and train athletes would infringe on the executive branch of the government. Most importantly, imposition of liability would impair the free exercise of discretion. No person will want to be a coach if his or her judgment in supervising athletic training is continually open to lawsuits. . . . No matter how well a coach trains an athlete, there are always unexpected events which may produce an injury. This court does not want to position itself to continually decide whether the string of athletic injuries that occur every year are the result of coaching negligence. . . . [S]tudent athletes who go out for sports know there are attendant dangers. Injury is one of those risks and athletes accept that as part of the price of participating in sporting events.

Mississippi courts also have ruled broadly that coaches act in a discretionary capacity when conducting practices, including making decisions about health-related matters involving student athletes entrusted to their care, and are immune from negligence liability. In *Prince v. Louisville Municipal School District*[23] a high school football player suffered heatstroke during practice requiring hospitalization and causing permanent injuries, allegedly because of two coaches' negligence. He alleged they negligently failed to keep a proper monitor on his health and condition, failed to provide necessary liquids, and failed to provide necessary medical care in a timely manner. The Mississippi Supreme Court held:

> [H]igh school football coaches Bowman and Chambliss were responsible for coordinating and supervising the football program at NanihWaiya High School. . . . In a typical practice there are strains, sprains and complaints from a coach's players. A coach must consider the good order and discipline of the team when confronted with situational complaints by the players. A coach must use his discretion in judging whether or not an individual player is injured and then, whether the player should report to a trainer or seek other medical aid. There was no evidence presented in the lower court to show that either Bowman or Chambliss did anything beyond exercising ordinary discretion in supervising the NanihWaiya football practice on August 29, 1991. Prince produced no facts that evidenced any disregard for his health or any other outrageous action on the part of Bowman or Chambliss that might have warranted a departure from our previous holdings.[24]

In *Harris v. McCray*[25] the Mississippi Supreme Court explained the adverse consequences that would result if public school coaches are not immune from negligence:

> High school football coaches around the state would lose their ability to control their football teams. Discipline of a football team would become non-existent. If a coach refused a player's request to have a water break—to see a trainer—to not have to run any more wind sprints—to not have to do any more one-on-one blocking drills, because of that player's complaint of "feeling weak" or "not feeling good" or simply "not feeling like it," that coach would be very much aware of the fact that he/she would be running the risk of being successfully sued . . . should that player later suffer physical/medical problems related to the coach's failure to cow to the player's every whim and wish. On the other hand, if the coach, in fear of a successful lawsuit, should cow to the player's every whim, wish and demand, then the coach would lose the respect of the players, and discipline and morale would be lost.

Mississippi law is troubling because it gives coaches broad latitude to maintain team discipline and eliminates any legal duty to use reasonable care to protect their players' health and safety. It permits utilitarian or instrumental concerns about interfering with coaches' autonomy to outweigh legitimate concerns about the protection of the health and safety of players entrusted to their supervision and control. In my view, it is legally and ethically better to require a standard of care that minimizes the likelihood of deaths or serious injuries during athletic competition or training, even if doing so may limit a coach's disciplinary authority.

Observing that qualified immunity's primary objective is to prevent governmental legislative, judicial, and executive policy decisions from being legally challenged and judicially second-guessed, other courts have recognized that coaching decisions generally do not involve the exercise of "policy-making, planning, or enforcement powers" involving "the exercise of a high degree of official judgment or discretion."[26] In *Hacking v. Town of Belmont*[27] the New Hampshire Supreme Court ruled that the decisions of coaches during the course of games are not entitled to immunity against negligence claims because they do not concern municipal planning and public policy that "involve the weighing of competing social, economic, or political factors." This judicial view, which refuses to apply the doctrine of qualified immunity to coaching decisions, would align the law consistent with a coach's ethical duty to protect student athletes' health and safety.

It also is important to understand that a coach's negligent *ministerial acts* (i.e., failing to comply with or to ensure players comply with the applicable sports-governing body or school rules) are not immunized from tort liability. In *Yanero v. Davis*[28] a high school baseball player who was not wearing a batting helmet was injured after being struck in the head by a ball thrown by a teammate. The Kentucky Supreme Court ruled that the doctrine of qualified immunity does not shield a coach from the negligent failure to require that players wear a batting helmet. They concluded: "The performance of that duty in this instance was a ministerial, rather than a discretionary, function in that it involved only the enforcement of a known rule requiring that student athletes wear batting helmets during baseball batting practice. The promulgation of such a rule is a discretionary function; the enforcement of it is a ministerial function."

Similarly, in *Felix v. Spaulding High School Union District*[29] a Vermont trial court determined that a high school football coach's decision to permit a student to play in an interscholastic game before attending ten practices as required by the Vermont Principals' Association bylaws and policies concerning athletics was a ministerial act. The student suffered a catastrophic spinal injury because he tackled an opposing player with his head down, allegedly because of his coach's negligent failure to provide him with proper instruction regarding how to tackle.

The doctrine of qualified immunity also does not protect coaches from liability for intentional, reckless, willful and wanton, or grossly negligent conduct, which is more culpable than simply failing to exercise reasonable care. In *Koffman v. Garnett*[30] the Virginia Supreme Court held that the following allegations, if proven, constitute gross negligence: "[Coach] Garnett ordered Andy to hold a football and 'stand upright and motionless' so that Garnett could explain the proper tackling technique to the defensive players. Then Garnett, without further warning, thrust his arms around Andy's body, lifted him 'off his feet by two feet or more,' and 'slam[ed]' him to the ground. Andy weighed 144 pounds, while Garnett weighed approximately 260 pounds. The force of the tackle broke the humerus bone in Andy's left arm. During prior practices, no coach had used physical force to instruct players on rules or techniques of playing football."

In some jurisdictions, courts have enforced preinjury liability waivers absolving educational institutions from negligence liability for a minor student's injuries while participating in extracurricular activities, which effectively also immunize coaches from negligence liability for injuries to student athletes. For example, in *Sharon v. City of Newton*[31] the Massachusetts Supreme Court rejected the argument that enforcement of a preinjury liability waiver would violate Massachusetts public policy by, among other things, undermining the legal duty of reasonable care that public high schools owe to their students. It explained:

> Our views with respect to the permissibility of requiring releases as a condition of voluntary participation in extracurricular sports activities, and the enforceability of releases signed by parents on behalf of their children for those purposes, are also consistent with and further the public policy of encouraging athletic programs for the Commonwealth's youth. This policy is most clearly embodied in statutes that exempt from liability for negligence: nonprofit organizations and volunteer managers and coaches who offer and run sports programs for children under eighteen years of age (G. L. c. 231, § 85V). . . .
>
> To hold that releases of the type in question here are unenforceable would expose public schools, who offer many of the extracurricular sports opportunities available to children, to financial costs and risks that will inevitably lead to the reduction of those programs. . . .
>
> [The student athlete] contends that to enforce the release would convey the message that public school programs can be run negligently, in contravention of the well-established responsibility of schools to

protect their students. We disagree. There are many reasons aside from potential tort liability why public schools will continue to take steps to ensure well-run and safe extracurricular programs—not the least of which is their ownership by, and accountability to, the citizens of the cities and towns they serve.

In contrast to *Sharon*, the Washington Supreme Court held that requiring a student and his parents or guardian to sign a standard form releasing a public school district from liability for negligence in connection with the student's participation in interscholastic athletics violates the state's public policy. In *Wagenblast v. Odessa School District*[32] the court ruled that the existence of the following factors invalidated the waiver: interscholastic sports were extensively regulated in Washington; interscholastic sports were "a matter of public importance"; participation in interscholastic sports was open to all students with the requisite skills and eligibility; there was "no alternative program of organized competition" for interscholastic sports; no sports participation was allowed unless the waiver was signed; and the student was under the coach's "considerable" control and subject to the risk that reasonable care would not be used to protect him from harm.

A Brief Defense of the Negligence Standard of Reasonable Care

Although the avoidance of both litigation and potential loss of athletic participation opportunities are legitimate concerns justifying judicial enforcement of preinjury liability waivers, it is questionable whether these policy objectives outweigh the need for application of a negligence standard of care. The negligence standard would encourage coaches to appropriately safeguard the health and safety of student athletes participating in interscholastic athletics. These three objectives are not necessarily mutually exclusive. A coach's exercise of reasonable care will reduce the number of student athlete injuries, thereby also reducing lawsuits and avoiding the loss of interscholastic sports participation opportunities caused by the costs of tort judgments and liability insurance.

Because the important goals identified by courts are not necessarily incompatible and dangerous customary coaching practices that cause injury should not be legally excused, there is strong justification for generally requiring coaches to adhere to the negligence standard of exercise reasonable care in carrying out their duties. Moreover, if we take into consideration the argument of other contributors to this volume, such as Simon and Boxill, that coaches are educators, the view that coaches should be held to the same legal and ethical standards as other teachers appears even stronger. Holding coaches legally liable only for intentionally or recklessly caused injury does not further other important goals of sport and eliminates a necessary level of protection for the health and safety of young athletes.

College Sports

In contrast to youth and interscholastic athletes, intercollegiate athletes generally are adults eighteen years of age or older who are not entrusted to the custodial care of their coaches. Like athletes competing at other levels of competition, college athletes assume the inherent risks of injury from participating in a sport. Similar to youth and high school sports coaches, those coaching intercollegiate sports have a legal duty not to increase a sport's inherent risks of injury to participating players; for example, by supplying defective equipment causing injury to intercollegiate student athletes, which may create negligence liability.[33] Like public high school coaches, public university and college coaches may have qualified immunity from negligence liability.[34] Unlike some youth sports organizations and high schools, universities and colleges generally do not require student athletes to sign preinjury waivers absolving the educational institution or its coaches from negligence causing injury while participating in intercollegiate athletics.[35]

There are relatively few cases in which college coaches have been sued for negligent instruction or supervision that causes injury to their own players, but coaches at this level of competition should use reasonable care to minimize the risks of injury, particularly death or serious harm. In *Moose v. Massachusetts Institute of Technology*[36] a Massachusetts appellate court ruled that two university track and field coaches were liable for negligently supervising and instructing a pole vaulter during practice, which contributed to his suffering a skull fracture and brain contusions when he fell into an improperly padded vaulting pit after a vault. However, *Crace v. Kent State University*,[37] a recent case involving serious injury to a college cheerleader, suggests that some courts may follow the *Kahn* majority and refuse to hold a coach liable for negligent instruction or supervision that causes injury to an intercollegiate athlete. Because injuries from falls while performing mounted stunts are an inherent risk of cheerleading that a coach has no legal duty to protect against, an Ohio appellate court ruled that a coach is liable only for intentionally or recklessly caused injuries to cheerleaders, which effectively means that injuries caused by a coach's negligence are inherent risks that must be assumed by cheerleaders. The *Moose* court's negligence standard requiring coaches to use reasonable care to protect against foreseeable harm under the circumstances is a better means of protecting the health and safety of intercollegiate athletes under his or her supervision and control.

Courts also have ruled that college coaches owe a legal duty not to increase the inherent risks of injury in a sport to opposing players as well as their players. But courts have narrowly construed the scope of this duty by holding that coaches are liable for injuries to opposing players caused by their own players' aggressive play only in limited circumstances. In *Avila v. Citrus Community College District*[38] the California Supreme Court ruled that a coach has no legal duty to prevent a pitcher on his team from intentionally throwing at the head of an opposing team's batter because "being intentionally thrown at is a fundamental part and inherent risk" of baseball. Similarly, in *Kavanagh v. Trustees of Boston University*[39] the Massachusetts Supreme Court held that a coach is liable for injury to an opposing player only if he expressly instructed or encouraged his players to intentionally or recklessly harm their opponents, not merely for encouraging their aggressive play. It reasoned, "With respect to any reasonable expectations as to who will protect competitors from excessively rough play or violence during a game, one would ordinarily expect that the referees would perform that function, not the opposing coach, team, or school."

Even if a college coach is not responsible for an intercollegiate athlete's original injury, there is potential liability for an aggravated injury that a coach could have prevented or reduced by using reasonable care. In *Kleinknecht v. Gettysburg College*,[40] the United States Court of Appeals for the Third Circuit held that a university, including its coaches, has a legal duty to use reasonable care to protect its recruited athletes from foreseeable harm and may be liable for negligent action or inaction in connection with the operation of its intercollegiate athletics program. This case involved allegations of negligent emergency medical assistance procedures, which delayed the administration of first aid care to an athlete who collapsed and died from cardiac arrest during an off-season varsity lacrosse practice in which players participated only in "skills and drills." The decedent had no medical history of heart problems and had been medically cleared to play lacrosse by both a team physician and his family physician. An autopsy failed to discover any heart abnormality, and it was uncertain what caused his cardiac arrest. The team's coaches were present during the practice, but they were not certified in cardiopulmonary resuscitation (CPR) and had never discussed how to respond to an emergency during off-season practices. No athletic trainer attended practice, and the nearest telephone was approximately 200 to 250 yards away from the practice field.

Although the victim's heart attack was unforeseeable under the circumstances, the court held that the possibility of severe and life-threatening injury is foreseeable during intercollegiate contact sports and there is a legal duty to have an appropriate university medical emergency response plan and to provide reasonable emergency care to injured athletes.

Consistent with *Kleinknecht*, courts have held that a coach has a legal duty to require an intercollegiate athlete to seek medical treatment for an injury. Courts have held that a coach has a legal duty not to pressure or permit an injured athlete to return to play without medical clearance. In *Lamorie v. Warner Pacific College*[41] a college basketball player asserted that his coach negligently required him to play with a nose and eye injury in violation of a physician's orders. Because the plaintiff feared losing his scholarship if he did not play, he participated in a team scrimmage and reinjured his eye. An Oregon appellate court ruled that the university could be held liable for the coach's negligence because the player's reinjury was a foreseeable risk of being directed to resume playing basketball without physician medical clearance.

However, in *Orr v. Brigham Young University*[42] a federal appellate court narrowly construed the legal duty of care that a university (and by implication, its coaches) owes to an injured college football player. Although the court held that a university is liable for negligent medical care provided by its sports medicine personnel, it refused to rule that coaches have a legal duty not to establish a win-at-all-costs mentality, to pressure student athletes to increase their performance at the risk of their health, and to create disincentives to report injuries or seek medical attention. It characterized the legal relationship between a university and its student athletes as contractual rather than custodial in nature and declined to find that its coaches "assumed the responsibility for his safety and deprived him of the normal opportunity for self protection" by recruiting him to play football.

Orr holds that a coach's legal duty of reasonable care to prevent an intercollegiate student athlete from aggravating an injury or potentially exposing himself to a risk of serious injury does not extend beyond simply following the recommendations of sports medicine care providers. It creates a questionable legal precedent that is inconsistent with our proposed ethical obligation of coaches: to avoid creating or facilitating harm to student athletes by discouraging them from disclosing injuries or encouraging them to sacrifice their health in the pursuit of individual athletic performance and/or the team's on-field success. Even adult student athletes may not have the maturity and judgment necessary to make sound athletic participation decisions consistent with their long-term health interests and place intercollegiate sports, which are an amateur, extracurricular activity that is a part of their college education (at least in theory), in proper perspective.

In 1990 Hank Gathers, Loyola Marymount University's star forward and a prospective National Basketball Association player, collapsed and died from cardiac arrest while playing in an intercollegiate basketball game in California. Before his death, Gathers had been diagnosed as having a potentially life-threatening heart rhythm disorder known as cardiomyopathy, but chose to continue playing college basketball. Gathers's death spawned the filing of multimillion dollar lawsuits by his mother, minor son, and other heirs against Loyola Marymount, its coach, and athletics trainer as well as several physicians participating in Gathers's care and treatment. Plaintiffs alleged Gathers was not fully informed of the seriousness of his heart condition, should not have been medically cleared to continue playing college basketball, and was given a nontherapeutic dosage of heart medication to enable him to perform at a higher level. The lawsuits further contended that defendants conspired and fraudulently failed to inform Gathers of the seriousness of his heart condition and the danger of continuing to play competitive basketball. Plaintiffs also alleged that, at the urging of Loyola Marymount's coach, Gathers's heart medication was reduced below therapeutic levels to enable him to play better. In sum, plaintiffs contended that Gathers was "sacrificed on the altar of basketball" in Loyola Marymount's quest for basketball success, notoriety, and economic gain.[43] These lawsuits ultimately were settled without any finding or admission of liability on the part of any defendants.

Marc Buoniconti, a former linebacker for The Citadel, sued the university along with its team physician and athletic trainer, seeking damages for permanent paralysis suffered while making a tackle during a 1985 college football game. Buoniconti had injured his neck during three prior games. Daily heat packs and whirlpool treatments did not improve the condition of his neck. In the game before he was paralyzed, Buoniconti suffered a sprained neck that prevented him from practicing, inhibited his sleeping, and required him to wear a soft collar for neck support. Believing that Buoniconti had suffered an extension injury to his neck, the team's athletic trainer fixed a ten-inch elastic strap to the face guard of Buoniconti's helmet and connected it to the front of his shoulder pads. The device prevented Buoniconti's head from going back and was approved by the team physician. The athletic trainer tightened the strap downward, causing Buoniconti to walk "like a robot . . . with his head down." While making a tackle with his head constrained by this device, Buoniconti broke his neck and was rendered a quadriplegic. Buoniconti asserted that the team trainer and physician were negligent for permitting him to play with a serious neck injury and with equipment that placed his neck in a position making it vulnerable to being broken. Before trial, Buoniconti settled his claims against The Citadel and its trainer for $800,000.

The *Larmorie* and *Orr* cases suggest that a coach has no legal duty to protect intercollegiate athletes' health and safety beyond acting in accordance with recommendations made by sports medicine personnel. Intercollegiate athletes often feel invincible, have a strong desire to play a sport for psychological or economic reasons, narrowly focus on their athletic objectives, and are willing to sacrifice their bodies and risk long-term adverse health consequences. A coach's ethical obligations to student athletes, which are broader than the legal standard of care, require more than simply following medical clearance recommendations. Although both of them were medically cleared to participate, perhaps the tragedies suffered by two former intercollegiate athletes, Hank Gathers and Nick Bouniconti, could have been prevented if their long-term health interests had been the coaches' top priority rather than the team's need for their services or their strong desire to play with a serious medical condition or significant injury that was not fully healed.

A coach has broad autonomy regarding playing decisions and the authority to refuse to permit an injured or otherwise physically impaired student athlete to play in a game or participate in an athletic event (even if he or she has been medically cleared) to prevent exposure to potentially serious harm. Surely one of a coach's primary ethical responsibilities is to protect the health and safety of his or her players. Our review of the foregoing cases suggests that the flexible negligence standard of reasonable care best furthers this important moral duty of the coach.

Questions for Review and Discussion

1. What factors justify holding coaches legally responsible for injuries to youth and high school athletes caused by their negligence?

2. Why do some courts refuse to hold coaches liable for negligent instruction or supervision injuring youth or high school athletes?

3. What legal standard provides the best means of ensuring that coaches conform to their ethical obligation to protect the health and safety of youth and high school athletes?

4. Should coaches have the same legal duty to protect the health and safety of intercollegiate athletes as they do for youth and high school athletes?

5. Should coaches have the same ethical obligation to protect the health and safety of intercollegiate athletes as they do for youth and high school athletes?

Suggestions for Further Reading

In addition to the works listed below, the author suggests that those interested in exploring the issues raised in this chapter consult the cases cited in the notes.

Benard, Howard P. "Little League Fun, Big League Liability." *Marquette Sports Law Review* 8 (1997): 93.

Brown, Jamie. "Legislators Strike Out: Volunteer Little League Coaches Should Not Be Immune from Tort Liability." *Seton Hall Journal of Sport Law* 7 (1997): 559.

Davis, Timothy. "*Avila v. Citrus Community College District:* Shaping the Contours of Immunity and Primary Assumption of the Risk." *Marquette Sports Law Review* 17 (2006): 259.

Doleschal, Janice K. "Managing Care in Interscholastic Athletic Programs: 14 Duties of Care." *Marquette Sports Law Review* 17 (2006): 295.

Fitzgerald, Timothy B. "The 'Inherent Risk' Doctrine, Amateur Coaching Negligence, and the Goal of Loss Avoidance." *Northwestern University Law Review* 99 (2005): 889.

Hurst, Thomas R., and James N. Knight. "Coaches' Liability for Athletes' Injuries and Deaths." *Seton Hall Journal of Sport Law* 13 (2003): 27.

Lake, Thomas. "The Boy Who Died of Football." *Sports Illustrated*, December 6, 2010, 131.

McCaskey, Anthony S., and Kenneth W. Biedzynski. "A Guide to the Legal Liability of Coaches for a Sports Participant's Injuries." *Seton Hall Journal of Sport Law* 6 (1996): 7.

Mitten, Matthew J. "Emerging Legal Issues in Sports Medicine: A Synthesis, Summary, and Analysis." *St. John's Law Review* 76 (2002): 5.

Fourteen

The Coach and Athlete Recruitment: Ethical and Legal Dimensions

TIMOTHY DAVIS

The real and perceived benefits that are derived from successful intercollegiate programs contribute substantially to the intense recruitment of high school athletes to participate in intercollegiate athletics. As colleges increase their athletic expenditures and search for new revenue streams, the competition among institutions for the best athletes is likely to intensify. At the center of college recruitment efforts are head and assistant coaches who are principally responsible for persuading high school students to attend their institutions. Coaches resort to various strategies in selling their athletic programs and institutions to recruits. In this chapter we will examine three aspects of coaching behavior during the recruitment process: conduct by coaches that violates National Collegiate Athletics Association (NCAA) rules and regulations, withdrawing scholarship offers that coaches make to student athletes, and coaches extending scholarship offers to student athletes that exceed what NCAA regulations permit them to honor.

We will consider standards of accountability that potentially govern these recruitment-related activities. I describe and assess legal norms and regulatory processes, both internal and external to intercollegiate athletics, which either regulate or potentially regulate coaches' recruitment behavior.

I conclude that some of these behaviors violate NCAA regulations and expose coaches, athletes, and their institutions to NCAA sanctions. There is considerable uncertainty, however, as to whether specific conduct in which coaches engage during recruiting will expose coaches or institutions to legal liability.

Apart from legal liability, however, we will examine the ethical dimensions of coaches' recruitment activities, with a focus on whether the coach-athlete relationship imposes ethical responsibilities on coaches to refrain from certain conduct during the recruitment process. I propose that the sports culture in which student athletes become inculcated prior to enrolling (and continuing into college) renders athletes vulnerable to false representations and other recruitment devices that coaches employ during the recruitment process. We will also consider whether the multiple roles that coaches may play in athletes' lives, such as teacher and transmitter of moral values, support imposing obligations on institutions to protect the interests of student athletes, even in the absence of legal liability requiring that they do so.

The Coach-Athlete Relationship

As is true for coaching, which is a multifaceted and complex endeavor,[1] complexity resides in the coach-athlete relationship. Given this complexity, the following discussion is intended only to provide limited insight into this relationship. Its focus is on the salient features of the coach-athlete relationship that lend context to the legal and ethical issues that resound in the recruiting process.

A principal role of a coach is to provide the instruction that enables athletes to maximize their athletic abilities.[2] In their role as educator, coaches impart technical expertise for improved individual performance and strategies for maximizing opportunities for competitive success.[3] Yet the role of the coach extends beyond merely conveying to athletes practical skills to improve athletic proficiency.[4] As explained below, their interpersonal interaction with athletes positions coaches to exert influence over matters ranging from athletes' values to their decision making.

Because it involves interpersonal interaction, coaching has been described as "fundamentally a moral practice."[5] As a "moral enterprise,"[6] coaching involves the transmission of values and ethics.[7] In fact, the ethical dimension of the coach-athlete relationship has been defined as pervasive.[8] As transmitters of values, coaches play an important role in identifying the "values, aims and objectives [that] ought to be pursued by athletes."[9] Thus coaches seek to instill values that may lead to athletic success, such as loyalty, hard work, enthusiasm, and confidence.[10]

There exists, however, another dimension to the coach as a transmitter of values. One scholar noted the attribute of practical wisdom—the ability to act in consonance with "virtues such as justice and fairness, temperance and enthusiasm, empathy and understanding."[11] Others have stated that "morally praiseworthy coach-athlete relationships that aim to be honest and sincere and to promote autonomy should be the gold standard."[12]

The extent to which coaches achieve the "gold standard," particularly as it relates to contributing to athletes' development of personal autonomy, may be inhibited by the power dynamic of the coach-athlete relationship. Coaches exert varying degrees of power over athletes.[13] However, athletes are not without power in their relationships with coaches.[14] Nevertheless, the coach-athlete relationship tends principally to be an asymmetrical relationship[15] in which coaches exert control over athletes.[16]

This power dynamic is exacerbated by the emotional bonds and trust that are critical aspects of the coach-athlete relationship.[17] The emotional bond, often manifested in a youth's admiration for the coach, can become a principal reason why athletes remain involved in sports.[18] As for trust, by the time most elite athletes play sport at the collegiate level, they would have developed relationships with coaches premised on the expectation that a coach would act to protect and promote the interests of the athlete.[19] Consequently athletes, particularly youngsters, are vulnerable to the influence of their coaches.[20] Therefore, the coach-athlete relationship is a quasi-fiduciary one in which athletes are particularly susceptible to the influence of coaches.

In varying contexts, courts have recognized the numerous roles coaches play in the lives of athletes.[21] In some instances, the influence wielded by coaches enhances their ability to exploit an athlete's vulnerability. For example, certain rules promulgated by interscholastic athletic associations seek to prohibit the exercise by coaches of undue influence in the high school recruiting process. These rules recognize the extent of the influence that coaches may exercise over athletes.[22]

A 2010 NCAA survey of approximately 20,000 collegiate student athletes provides some evidence of the influence coaches exert over student athletes during the recruitment process. Many of the athletes surveyed stated that they probably would not have chosen the college at which they matriculated if a different coach had been in place. For example, close to 60 percent of Division I men's basketball players responded that they would more than likely not have attended their institution had another individual been the coach.[23] Many athletes also reported that coaches had been overly aggressive—contacting them too often—during the recruiting process.[24]

The multiple roles assumed by coaches contribute to their ability to exert influence over athletes. Consequently, no matter how savvy athletes may believe themselves to be, by the time they become active participants in the college recruitment process, they are likely to have spent years in a system in which they have been inculcated with the multiple dynamics of the coach-athlete relationship. This alone renders athletes vulnerable to the conduct in which coaches may engage during the recruiting process.

Coaches, Athletes, and Recruiting

The emergence of highly commercialized college athletics over the past century and the concomitant pressure on college coaches to field successful sports programs have created an intense pursuit by colleges of high school athletes.[25] The factors that propel recruiting have been adroitly described by one commentator as follows:

> The pressure to produce winning teams increases efforts to recruit for athletic purposes. "Recruiting is the name of the game" is the cliché reflecting the necessity to have a team of superior athletic ability to win. The important variable is likely to be the ability of team members rather than the quality of the coaching or the desire to win. The coach's desire to excel, to do a superior job in training, to have players who achieve distinction, all can incline him to recruit. Yet, the primary pressure is usually external, from the institution or its alumni or supporters, in a "job-on-the-line manner."[26]

Although this opinion was expressed several decades ago, it is just as relevant today. Indeed, during this period the process by which colleges procure the services of these athletes has become more sophisticated and costly, devouring substantial amounts of athletic department resources.[27] Recruiting often becomes a college coach's number one priority, eclipsing leading and teaching.

Given these dynamics, encouraging high school athletes to attend his or her college is one, if not the most critical, function of the college coach. Indeed, coaches have been described as salesmen whose job is to convince high school seniors to sign the Letter of Intent signifying the prospective student-athlete will compete for their college.[28] As expressed by a sports journalist: "Coaches, after all, are salesmen. Their jobs depend mainly on convincing high school seniors to sign on the dotted line the first Wednesday in February."[29]

The recruitment efforts of athletic departments are also influenced by the student athlete's professional aspirations. High school recruits are interested in attending a school that will enable them to enhance their opportunity to compete professionally. These professional aspirations play a significant role in the athletes' school selection decision. For instance, because of professional aspirations, the amount of playing time likely to be afforded becomes a key consideration in a high school athlete's selection of a college sports program.[30] In addition, many high school athletes believe that starting as freshmen on a winning team will afford the maximum amount of playing time and television exposure. All of this will presumably improve their preparation and chances for the illusive yet coveted professional career. Coaches will exploit this goal by emphasizing the number of athletes from their program who have signed professional contracts. In short, the pressure on institutions to field winning teams and professional aspirations among student athletes serve as important elements of the context for the discussion that follows.

There are several problematic aspects of the process whereby promising high school student athletes are recruited to attend and participate in intercollegiate athletics at colleges and universities. These include the risky behaviors (e.g., drinking, going to bars and off-campus parties) in which many prospective student athletes engage during recruiting visits,[31] the use of female hostesses in the recruiting of male athletes, and the lack of adult supervision of recruits during their visits. In the following discussion we will focus on three specific aspects of the recruiting process in which coaches are intimately involved: the commission of NCAA rules violations during recruiting, revocation of scholarship offers, and oversigning.

NCAA Rules Violations

All too frequently, coaches commit recruiting violations as they seek to sign the most promising student athletes and thus gain an advantage over their competitors. This problem is illustrated by a celebrated example of rules violation. In 1987 the NCAA's enforcement arm imposed a one-year prohibition on Southern Methodist University's (SMU) football program from engaging in games against outside competition. The SMU case constitutes the only instance in which the NCAA has imposed the "death penalty" against a Division I intercollegiate athletics program. The conduct that led to the imposition of this sanction included the involvement of football coaches in facilitating cash payments to football recruits. Some of these payments continued after players matriculated at the university. In its report on the matter, the NCAA's Division I Committee on Infractions stated: "Past efforts at the university to design a program to gain a competitive advantage over the university's competitors by cheating did achieve its apparent goal—a winning record and national prominence for its football program."[32]

College coaches have engaged in a range of improper recruiting activities in violation of NCAA rules. At one end of the continuum is conduct not viewed as serious but nevertheless inappropriate, for example, a coach giving a recruit an item of clothing during recruitment, unknowingly making impermissible contact with a recruit, and engaging in limited but impermissible off-campus conduct with a recruit.[33]

At the other end of the spectrum are major violations.[34] These include, for example, offering or giving a student athlete money as an inducement to matriculate at the coach's institution, providing free lodging and airline tickets to a recruit or family and friends, making tuition payments at a junior college on behalf of a recruit, allowing a student athlete to use a vehicle, and arranging for someone to take a standardized college admissions test on behalf of an athlete. In a typical case involving a major violation of NCAA recruiting rules, some combination of the foregoing conduct and other impermissible inducements is present.[35]

Major violations of NCAA recruiting rules, specifically those involving improper offers and inducements,[36] typically result in colleges and universities self-imposing penalties and the NCAA imposing additional penalties. Both types of penalties have ramifications not only for culpable coaches but also for student athletes and their institutions. The following cases illustrate serious recruitment-related violations committed by coaches, with implications for coaches, student athletes, and their colleges or universities.

In a 2005 NCAA infractions case involving Baylor University,[37] a former head coach and assistant coaches of Baylor's men's basketball violated several NCAA rules, including those relating to impermissible inducements to prospective student athletes and attempts to cover up those violations. The coaches provided cash, clothing, tuition payments at a community college, meals, cost-free travel arrangements (e.g., airline tickets and lodging), and transportation (e.g., use of vehicles) to student athletes and their families. To explain their involvement in these violations, the assistant coaches cited, in part, loyalty to the head coach.

In addition, the NCAA Committee on Infractions (COI) found that the head coach engaged in unethical conduct. He did not act with high standards of honesty, attempted to conceal his violations and encouraged student athletes to engage in deceptive behavior, and provided false and misleading information to Baylor and to NCAA enforcement staff. In its report the COI stated, "In the end, the former head coach and his assistants' blatant disregard for NCAA rules brought incalculable disgrace to themselves, the university and intercollegiate athletics as a whole."[38]

The repercussions of this conduct were substantial. The head coach and his entire staff were replaced. In addition, the NCAA issued a show cause order that effectively prohibited the head coach from coaching at another NCAA member institution for ten years. Other penalties included a five-year probationary period, a one-year prohibition on postseason play by the men's basketball team, a reduction in the number of scholarships that could be awarded to basketball players, and restrictions on recruiting by the men's basketball coaches.

Recruitment violations by coaches can also result in vacating wins and revenues generated from conference and NCAA-wide championship events. This will occur if the coach's impermissible activities render an athlete ineligible to participate in intercollegiate competition. When an ineligible student athlete participates in intercollegiate contests, the NCAA's rule of restitution is triggered, which can lead to the vacation of wins and the records an athlete compiles while ineligible.[39] An athlete ruled ineligible may also be required to seek reinstatement before being permitted to participate in intercollegiate athletics.[40]

This is what transpired in an NCAA infractions decision involving violations of NCAA recruitment rules at Boise State University.[41] In 2011, the NCAA launched an investigation revealing that coaches of Boise State's women's tennis and women's and men's track programs had provided impermissible inducements, including cash and free lodging and meals, to prospective student athletes. In addition, the NCAA found that the coaches' intentional violation of its prohibitions against improper inducements and, in some instances, providing false information to the NCAA and Boise State, constituted unethical conduct. The COI wrote that the extensiveness of the violations in the women's tennis program resulted in a competitive advantage that warranted penalties in addition to those that Boise State had self-imposed.[42] Ultimately, the penalties included a postseason ban on the women's tennis team, restrictions on the number of available athletic scholarships, a vacation of the wins in which participating athletes were ineligible due to having taken impermissible inducements, vacation of those athletes' records, and a four-year show cause order for the head women's tennis coach.

As was true of its findings in the Baylor decision, the NCAA determined that the coaches not only violated NCAA inducement rules but engaged in unethical conduct. NCAA Bylaw 10.01.1, Honesty and Sportsmanship, imposes a positive duty on coaches and other individuals employed at its member institutions to act with "honesty and sportsmanship at all times so that intercollegiate athletics as a whole, their institutions and they, as individuals, shall represent the honor and dignity of fair play."[43] NCAA regulations also define what constitutes unethical conduct: the "knowing involvement in offering or providing a prospective" with an improper inducement.[44]

Coaches who commit recruiting violations breach their quasi-fiduciary obligations to not engage in conduct harmful to their athletes. This is seen most poignantly when a coach's violations result in penalties that harm athletes who did not behave improperly, such as being banned from postseason play. A coach who violates NCAA recruitment rules also fails to teach and model values such as fair play.

Revocation of Scholarship Offers and Oversigning

Two additional types of misconduct during recruitment present both legal and ethical issues: (1) a coach withdraws an oral scholarship offer made to a student athlete under circumstances that prevent the recruit from obtaining an offer from another college or university; (2) a coach signs more national letters of intent (NLI) or scholarship offers than the coach's college or university can accommodate under NCAA-imposed limitations. A discussion of the legal relationship between student-athletes and their colleges or universities provides a necessary predicate to consideration of revocation of scholarship offers and oversigning.

The Contractual Relationship

The express contractual relationship between a student athlete and a college or university arises out of the NLI, the statement of financial assistance, and various other university publications such as bulletins and catalogs. Several implications flow from a prospective student athlete signing an NLI. By signing an NLI, a prospective student-athlete agrees, for a period of one year, to attend the college or university named in the NLI. Thereafter, other institutions must cease all recruiting contacts with the student athlete. The named institution may freely contact the student athlete and publicly announce the signing. The NLI is not effective unless the student athlete has received a promise in writing from the named institution to provide athletic financial aid for a minimum of one year. In other words, without an accompanying promise of financial aid from the institution that signed the letter of intent, the NLI does not bind a student athlete to attend a particular institution, and the athlete may be recruited by another institution.

As it relates to the statement of financial aid, in exchange for the student athlete's commitment to attend, the college or university promises to provide financial assistance in the form of an athletic scholarship. A statement of financial assistance confirms that the college or university will extend financial aid to the extent of tuition, fees, room, board, and books. Statements of financial aid provide that the purpose of financial aid is to assist and enable student athletes to pursue a program of study and to participate in the educational process of the institution.

Through legislation adopted in 1973, the NCAA restricted schools to awarding one-year athletic scholarships renewable for each year for a period of four years.[45] In an important recent development, heralded by some as shifting the balance of power between coaches and players, NCAA legislation adopted in 2012 jettisoned the one-year limitation on the duration of athletic scholarships. The newly enacted legislation permits, but does not require, conferences and their institutions to award multiyear athletic scholarships.[46]

Revocation of Scholarship Offers

NCAA rules designate specific periods, based on the sport involved, during which a prospective student athlete can sign an NLI and accept a scholarship offer from a college or university. As noted above, the NLI, when combined with an offer of financial assistance, creates a binding contractual commitment between the athlete and the institution. During recruitment, it is common for coaches and athletes to make verbal commitments to each other. The recruit will orally commit to attend a particular college and a coach will orally promise a scholarship to the recruit. Given that a binding express contractual relationship does not arise until the student athlete and an institution's representative sign an NLI and offer of financial assistance, it is not uncommon for either or both parties to fail to honor a verbal commitment. Legal and ethical concerns emerge when the coach withdraws an oral offer previously extended to a prospective student athlete.

Consider the following scenario. Several weeks before they formalize their contractual relationship with a recruit, football coaches at four universities extend scholarship offers to a high school student athlete. Each coach states that his oral offer is contingent on the recruit not entertaining offers or exploring athletic programs at other schools. Nine months before he can sign an NLI, the recruit orally accepts the offer to play football at Big-Time University, one of the four colleges. The recruit discontinues exploring options at the other three universities that had orally extended scholarship offers. As expected, the other three universities withdraw their scholarship offers.

Over the next eight months, Big-Time's football coaches periodically call the recruit to determine if he remains interested its program and to express their interest in him. Three weeks before the date on which the recruit and Big-Time can formalize their agreement, Big-Time's head football coach accepts the head football coach position at another university. Big-Time's assistant football coaches reassure the recruit that the football program will stand by its oral commitment to him and that he has no reason to be concerned. The university promptly hires a new head football coach. A few days before the recruit and Big-Time can sign an NLI with a scholarship offer, Big-Time's newly appointed head football coach informs the recruit that the university has withdrawn its scholarship offer. The recruit requests reconsideration, but the coach informs him that the decision is final. Subsequently the recruit approaches the three other universities that made oral offers but is informed that they no longer have any scholarships to offer. Given how late it is in the season, the recruit receives no scholarship offers from other colleges.

Both student athletes and coaches must anticipate the possibility that one or the other will not abide by their oral commitment. This possibility encourages some student athletes to visit other schools even after making a verbal commitment to attend another institution. Similarly, a coach will continue to recruit for a position even after making a scholarship offer to other recruits who might potentially play at that position.

Several factors prompt coaches to revoke oral scholarship offers. Perhaps the coach receives an oral commitment from an athlete who seems to have greater athletic potential. In such a case, the coach may have viewed the recruit whose offer he canceled as a backup who could be called if the coach did not secure the player he really wanted. Or a coach might revoke a promised scholarship if he discovers that a recruit has expressed an interest in another program even though the athlete did so as a hedge against the possibility that his scholarship offer might be withdrawn. Here the coach likely views the recruit's expression of interest in another program as reflecting a lack of commitment to honor his oral promise.[47]

The same realities do not constrain the conduct of coaches who recruit multiple players for the same position after making an oral promise to other athletes who would also play at that position. Moreover, the consequences for a university when a recruit backs away from an oral commitment are not as severe as when an institution fails to honor an oral promise to a prospective athlete. As stated by one scholar:

A school that loses a recruit can usually replace him or her with another recruit, someone from the existing roster, or even a recruit from a future year. . . . In short, to use the jargon of risk aversion, recruits suffer more than schools from the possibility of broken yearly commitments because recruits cannot effectively manage the risk of disappointment through diversification. Recruits are one-time players in the early commitment game, and those who try to court multiple prospects actually damage their chances of keeping commitments they have. By contrast, schools are repeat players who easily diversify risk over multiple recruits and multiple recruiting years. Accordingly, coaches may worry that early recruits will break their commitments, but they know that they will not suffer catastrophic consequences because alternate plans will have been made. Recruits have no such luxury.[48]

Coaches defend their revocation of oral offers by arguing that prospective student athletes understand how the recruiting game is played, and a part of the game is the reality that no binding deal has been consummated until the required documents are signed. They argue that because both recruits and institutions live in a world in which commitments are often broken, they engage in the process as equals.[49]

These justifications are less than satisfying. No matter how savvy they may consider themselves, recruits are minors and lack the experience and sophistication to fully comprehend the process in which they are engaged.[50] Their youth and inexperience combine to render recruits overly trusting. In addition, recruits often have parents who are unable to protect the recruits' interests. Moreover, most recruits are not blue-chip athletes. Consequently they lack the depth of scholarship options to which coaches point in attempting to justify their revocation of scholarship offers.[51]

Legal Recourse

The substantial harm that prospective student athletes may suffer when scholarship offers are revoked gives rise to the possibility of legal recourse against institutions. To date, the question of institutional legal liability is murky due, in part, to the paucity of lawsuits that have been filed by athletes against colleges and universities. Although coaches frequently revoke scholarship offers, few athletes complain publicly. Most reports of scholarship revocations appear anecdotally in the popular press.[52] The few lawsuits that have been initiated have resulted in settlements.[53]

A recruit alleging that a scholarship was wrongfully revoked would likely assert a variety of legal claims, including breach of contract, a violation of the duty of good faith, and promissory estoppel.[54] Of these claims, promissory estoppel holds the most promise. It provides for the enforceability of a promise based on the promisee's (the person to whom the promise is made) justifiable reliance on that promise. Therefore, if a person makes a promise with reason to know that the promisee is likely to rely on that promise and the promisee does justifiably rely (changes his or her position), the promise is binding based on the promisee's reliance if injustice can only be avoided by enforcing the promise.

In the sporting context, courts have adhered to the conceptualization of promissory estoppel set forth above, which was largely adopted by the court in *Hall v. NCAA.*[55] There, the court stated that the elements for promissory estoppel include (1) a clear and unambiguous promise, (2) reliance on the promise, (3) the promisee's reliance was reasonable and foreseeable by the party who made the promise, and (4) detrimental reliance (an injury sustained by the party asserting the estoppel by reason of his reliance).[56] Other courts, in sports-related cases, expressly add the requirement that the doctrine can only be used when "injustice can only be avoided by the enforcement of the promise."[57]

To date, no court has ruled on whether promissory estoppel provides a basis for imposing liability on an institution where a coach revoked an offer of a scholarship to a recruit. A recent case involves an appropriate vehicle for assessing the viability of the doctrine. Daniel Smith asserted that the University of Hawaii improperly revoked a scholarship offer after the university's head football coach accepted a position at SMU.[58] As it relates to promissory estoppel, Smith alleged:

> On April 26, 2007, UH, through its agent Coach Reinebold, made a promise to provide Daniel a full athletic scholarship to play football at UH beginning in the fall of 2008. . . . Contemporaneously with the promise, UH instructed Daniel to refrain from speaking with any other colleges and universities about football and scholarship opportunities. He was explicitly instructed to inform any and all other colleges and universities who contacted him that he was committed to UH and would be attending UH on an athletic scholarship. . . . UH should have reasonably expected its promise would induce action on Daniel's part. . . . Based solely, on UH's promise, Daniel turned down an athletic scholarship offer from Portland State University. . . . Based solely on UH's promise, Daniel refused numerous offers to visit colleges and universities who were attempting to recruit him for their respective football programs. . . . Because UH abandoned Daniel at the eleventh hour of the recruiting process, just weeks before National Letter of Intent Day, Daniel was unable to secure an athletic scholarship at another college or university.[59]

The case was settled before a court adjudication of the merits of Smith's promissory estoppel claim.[60] The University of Hawaii paid Smith $41,500 and expended over $150,000 in legal fees defending the action.[61]

When student athletes have invoked promissory estoppel, courts have impliedly recognized the viability of the theory but have ruled against athletes on evidentiary grounds. An Illinois court, in *Hall v. NCAA,*[62] dismissed an incoming student athlete's promissory estoppel claim against the NCAA after he claimed that the NCAA promised to give him information that would help make him eligible for his freshman season, yet he still remained ineligible. In granting summary judgment in favor of the defendant university, the court did not reject the viability of promissory estoppel in the university-athlete context. Rather, it concluded that the athlete had failed to offer evidence sufficient to establish the elements of promissory estoppel.

Similarly, an Ohio court dismissed the promissory estoppel claims of a former basketball player at the University of Cincinnati after evidence indicated that he was ruled ineligible "because of his own failures, not because of any . . . unfulfilled promises."[63] The player challenged the decision to rule him ineligible on the basis of the fact that he signed a national letter of intent to play, but was later declared academically ineligible.

The facts as alleged by Daniel Smith could present a viable promissory estoppel claim based on an application of the traditional elements courts employ in assessing such a claim. A university would likely assert that a recruit's reliance was unreasonable given the realities of recruiting, in which both coaches and recruits fail to honor verbal commitments. Once again, the nature of the dynamic athlete-coach relationship lends support for judicial recognition of promissory estoppel if an athlete can establish facts akin to those asserted in the Smith case.

Oversigning of Student Athletes

Oversigning is a recruiting practice connected principally with college football that also raises legal and ethical concerns. It occurs when a college or university signs more student athletes to letters of intent or offers of financial assistance than the institution can honor and remain in compliance with NCAA rules. For example, NCAA rules restrict the number of football scholarships awarded to incoming freshman student athletes to twenty-five per year. This limitation operates in concert with the NCAA limitation on the total number of football scholarships, eighty-five, that can be awarded to football student athletes per year.[64]

Coaches willingly run the risk of signing prospective student athletes to more NLIs or offers of financial aid than a college can offer for several reasons. The practice of oversigning (1) provides coaches with a safeguard against a recruited prospect who cannot sign an NLI because he is academically ineligible to receive an athletic scholarship under NCAA rules; (2) allows coaches to hedge against the possibility that a recruited athlete will forfeit his amateur status; (3) affords coaches a supply of incoming student athletes who can replace athletes whose athletic scholarship a coach will not renew based on a coach's assessment that the athlete has underperformed athletically; and (4) facilitates a coach's ability to have players in reserve if a highly desired recruit elects, late in the recruiting season, to attend another college. The desire to gain a competitive advantage also prompts oversigning. "Coaches love over-signing because it gives them more talent to choose from, keeps it out of the hands of competitors."[65] In short, coaches oversign in order to have backup student athletes available if one of the above scenarios occurs.

If the anticipated attrition fails to occur, oversigned recruits as well as student athletes already on the roster from the previous football season are placed in a precarious position. The reality of oversigning is that the coach may have to get rid of players. One way this can be accomplished is for a team to release a recruit from his NLI. A more likely scenario includes a practice known as gray-shirting, which occurs when a coach requests that a recruit delay his enrollment with the hope that a scholarship will become available. Similarly, a coach may request that a recruit matriculate at the college or university and absorb the costs of attendance in anticipation that a scholarship will be awarded in the future. This often occurs in conjunction with a coach asking players to walk on the team without receiving the scholarship the coach promised while recruiting the athlete. Another tactic is to encourage athletes already on the team to take a medical red shirt; this frees up the injured athlete's scholarship while allowing the school to grant him a medical scholarship, which does not count against the NCAA scholarship limits.[66] Finally, the coach can refuse to renew the scholarship of a player on the roster or encourage him to transfer to another institution.

Oversigning has been criticized as being immoral and possibly violating athletes' legal rights.[67] Critics argue that typically a student-athlete is unaware that he is the athlete that may not make the team if one of the scenarios that bring the number of signees within NCAA limits does not occur.[68] As is true when scholarship offers are revoked, a recruit is placed in a particularly precarious position when he is told at the last minute that he will not make a team due to roster limitations. There is often a knowledge gap. In the past, "when top high-school seniors [made] their college commitments, dozens of signees head[ed] to some to the nation's most chronically over-signed schools were either unconcerned, or unaware, that these schools may have to cut some players to balance books."[69] At this point, opportunities for an athlete to visit other schools are extremely limited. Oversigning also jeopardizes the interest of student athletes who are cut to make room for a new recruit.

University of Florida president Bernard Machen has condemned the practice:

> The universities, with full knowledge of what they are doing, extend more athletic scholarships than they have. These schools play roulette

with the lives of talented young people. If they run out of scholarships, too bad. The letter-of-intent signed by the university the previous February is voided. Technically, it's legal to do this. Morally, it is reprehensible.[70]

It has also been argued that the practice is particularly egregious if a roster athlete is cut after his coach persuaded him not to take a scholarship from a different school the previous year.[71]

Oversigning also fails to comport with good coaching practices. Coaches take advantage of the power and influence that they wield over athletes and exploit the trust the athletes tend to repose in them. It also represents a failure of coaches to act with honesty and integrity and to model such virtues. Particularly as it relates to roster athletes who are cut but have done what was asked of them, oversigning violates the notion that coaches will not act contrary to the interest of athletes.

Legal recourse is a rather dubious option for student athletes to pursue. If an institution and athlete have only signed a national letter of intent, the athlete would have no legal cause of action, such as a breach of contract claim against his institution. On the other hand, if an athlete signed an offer of financial aid and the school refused to honor it because of oversigning, the athlete would have a breach of contract action.[72]

Several factors, however, reduce the likelihood that an athlete would pursue his or her legal rights. First, many athletes may not be aware of their legal options. In addition, the time it would take to pursue an action would inhibit some student athletes. Moreover, under former NCAA rules, the most an athlete would likely recover in damages in a successful breach of contract action would be a monetary judgment equal to the value of a one-year scholarship. (This could change for some athletes with the advent of the possibility of multiyear contracts.) Student athletes would no doubt balance the value of the legal judgment against the stigma that would likely attach to an athlete who challenged the system. Thus from an athlete's perspective, it might be wiser to either accept an offer from another school or simply wait and hope to get a scholarship with the team that subjected him to oversigning.[73]

To address concerns relating to oversigning, the NCAA modified its rules. Effective August 2010 and applicable to bowl subdivision football, the NCAA initially adopted a rule that imposed a yearly limit of twenty-eight on the number of prospective student athletes with whom an institution can enter into a national letter of intent or an offer of financial aid.[74] Realizing that this rule did not completely resolve the problems associated with oversigning, the NCAA subsequently adopted legislation that reduces the number from twenty-eight to twenty-five. In 2012 the NCAA approved legislation intended to curb the practice that is more restrictive. The proposed amendment provides as follows (federated provision, FBS only):

> 13.9.2.3 Limitation on Number of National Letter of Intent/Offer of Financial Aid Signings—Bowl Subdivision Football. [FBS] In bowl subdivision football, there shall be an annual limit of 25 on the number of prospective student-athletes who may sign a National Letter of Intent or an institutional offer of financial aid from December 1 through May 31. [D]

> 13.9.2.3.1 Exception—Counter During Same Academic Year. A prospective student-athlete who signs a National Letter of Intent or an institutional offer of financial aid and becomes an initial counter for the same academic year in which the signing occurred (e.g., midyear enrollee) shall not count toward the annual limit on signings.

In articulating the rationale for the rule, the NCAA stated:

> This proposal seeks to address concerns regarding the practice of "over-signing" football prospective student-athletes to National Letters of Intent or financial aid agreements. Reducing the signing limit from 28 to 25 is an appropriate step to focus recruitment and signing of prospective student-athletes to the Football Bowl Subdivision limit on initial counters. By limiting the number of signees, institutions will be encouraged to focus their recruiting efforts on prospective student-athletes with the necessary academic and athletic credentials to succeed at the certifying institution.[75]

The new rule took effect on August 1, 2012.

Conclusion

The coaches' conduct described in the three scenarios presented above raises ethical and legal issues. This assertion is derived from the multiple roles and functions assigned to college coaches that shape their relationships with student athletes and prospective student athletes (as detailed in the chapters in Part 1 of this book). Indeed, attributes of coaching that allow coaches to exert pressure on prospective student athletes during the recruiting process begin during the athletes' initial interaction with coaches. The long-standing nature of these interactions strengthens the influence coaches may wield over student athletes given that an athlete's beliefs, as they relate to the coach-athlete relationship, develop over a period of time extending to and through a coach's recruitment of him or her to play at the collegiate level. Consequently judicial decisions relative to conduct between student athletes and coaches should be considered against the backdrop of the ethical dimensions that arise from the relationships athletes develop with their coaches. Thus judicial consideration of issues, such as the viability of promissory estoppel to the revocation of oral scholarship offers, should not be made without consideration of the social dynamic of the coach-student relationships and how it impacts athletes' decision making. More importantly, institutions should consider the nature of the coach-athlete relationship when impliedly validating conduct by coaches during the recruiting process that harms the interests of student athletes.

Questions for Review and Discussion

1. Explain how the interests of college coaches and those of prospective athletes who are being recruited might conflict.

2. What rationale might coaches offer for offering more athletic scholarships to recruits than are actually available? What criticism(s) can be made of that rationale? In light of the criticisms, is the rationale sound or ethically acceptable?

3. Is it ethically permissible for a recruited high school student athlete to visit a university (in order to attract an offer of an athletic scholarship) after having made a verbal commitment to attend another? Why or why not?

4. What is the doctrine of promissory estoppel and what is its significance for the ethics of athletic recruiting?

5. Do recruited student athletes who lose their athletic scholarships because of oversigning have adequate legal recourse? Are there any nonlegal or moral incentives that might limit oversigning of athletic recruits by Division I colleges and universities?

Suggestions for Further Reading

Bateman, Jonathan D. "When the Numbers Don't Add Up: Oversigning in College Football." *Marquette Sports Law Review* 22 (2011): 7.

Cross, Harry M. "The College Athlete and the Institution." *Law and Contemporary Problems* 38 (1973): 151, 155.

Davis, Timothy. "Student-Athlete Prospective Economic Interests: Contractual Dimensions." *Thurgood Marshall Law Review* 19 (1994): 585, 599.

Doyle, Gregg. "Bad Guys Utilize Over-signing, and It Has to Stop." CBSSports.com, April 8, 2010.

Eitzen, D. Stanley. "Social Control and Sport." In *Handbook of Sports Studies,* 376–377. Edited by Jay Coakley and Eric Dunning. London: Sage, 2000.

Karp, Hannah, and Darren Everson. "Alabama's Unhappy Castoffs." *Wall Street Journal,* September 24, 2010.

———. "SEC Coaches Defend Oversigning." *Wall Street Journal,* March 1, 2011.

Nomura, Jamie U. "Refereeing the Recruiting Game: Applying Contract Law to Make the Inter-Collegiate Recruiting Process Fair." *University of Hawaii Law Review* 32 (2009): 275.

Yen, Alfred C. "Early Scholarship Offers and the NCAA." *Boston College Law Review* 52 (2011): 585.

Notes

Part One: Introduction

Chapter 1

1. This TV series, loosely based on the book and movie of the same name, aired from 2006 to 2011.

2. *Report of the Special Investigative Counsel Regarding the Actions of the Pennsylvania State University Related to the Child Sexual Abuse Committed by Gerald A. Sandusky,* 14, www.thefreehreportonpsu.com/REPORT_FINAL _071212.pdf.

3. For details of the investigation of the University of Minnesota men's basketball program, see *NCAA Infractions Report on the University of Minnesota,* October 24, 2000, http://news.mpre.org/features/199903 /11_newsroomcheating/infractionsreport.shtml. For a useful discussion of alleged bounty payments for injuring rival players, see Peter King, "Way Out of Bounds," *Sports Illustrated,* March 12, 2012, 34–41.

4. The figures cited are from the article "When Coaches Cross the Line," *USA Today,* December 29, 2011, 3C.

5. Sometimes we can identify egregiously wrong or unjust actions without having a clear positive theory of what is morally right or of the nature of social justice. However, ethical principles and ethical and political theories come into play when we are asked to justify or support our moral judgments or are challenged by whether our judgments concerning some cases are consistent with our judgments on other cases. Moreover, moral intuitions that may serve us well when confronted with clear cases might falter in regard to new or complicated cases. Thus we may all agree that it is wrong for a player to deliberately injure an opponent. But is it also wrong to try to distract an opponent through trash talk? Why or why not?

6. Just because people have a belief, even if firmly held, it does not follow that their belief is correct or that it is supported by good reasons.

Chapter 2

1. Jan Boxill, "Moral Significance of Sport," *in Sports Ethics: An Anthology* (Malden, MA: Blackwell, 2003), 1–12.

2. USADA, *What Sport Means in America: A Study of Sport's Role in Society* (Colorado Springs: U.S. Anti-Doping Agency, Outreach Education Research, 2010).

3. Ibid., 3.

4. Joe Ehrmann, *Inside Out Coaching* (New York: Simon & Shuster, 2011), 9.

5. Ibid., 10.

6. Steve Wieberg, "NCAA Survey Delves into Practice Time, Coaches Trust," *USA Today,* January 15, 2011. http://www.usatoday.com/sports/college/2011–01–14-ncaa-survey_N.htm.

7. Boxill, "Moral Significance of Sport," 1–7.

8. See Robert Simon, *Fair Play: The Ethics of Sports*, 3rd ed. (Boulder, CO: Westview, 2010), 24.

9. Kim Strom-Gottfried, "Ethical Action in Challenging Times," lecture on receiving the Smith P. Thiemann Jr. Distinguished Professor for Ethics and Professional Practice, October 12, 2006, 6–7, http://74.52.28.120/~jdn1754/nbr-content/EthicsLectureBooklet.pdf.

10. Ibid., 8–12.

11. Ibid., 13–14.

12. Robert Simon, "Sports, Relativism, and Moral Education," in *Sports Ethics,* 26.

Part Two: The Coach's Role

1. Some would argue, with justice I think, that such an individual is not really a coach at all but more of an instructor or technical adviser.

2. Readers interested in Dworkin's legal theory might start with Chapters 2 to 4 of his book *Taking Rights Seriously* (Cambridge: Harvard University Press, 1978). His most recent views on ethics and interpretivism are developed in *Justice for Hedgehogs* (Cambridge: Harvard University Press, 2011). My own views on broad internalism were first formulated in "Internalism and Internal Values in Sport," *Journal of the Philosophy of Sport* 27 (2000): 1–16, and were influenced by a number of earlier papers cited in my article. One such influential paper is J. S. Russell, "Are Rules All an Umpire Has to Work With?" *Journal of the Philosophy of Sport* 26 (1999): 27–49. Here Russell explicitly draws on Dworkin's work in legal theory.

3. Of course, professional athletes may engage in sports to make a living, but they do so through accepting and meeting the challenge of their sports;

in that sense meeting the challenge of the sport is fundamental to understanding and developing an ethic of sports.

4. Russell, "Are Rules All an Umpire Has to Work With?" 35.

5. Thus most members of the current basketball community would find nothing morally questionable about a losing team deliberately fouling at the end of a close contest in order to stop the clock and force opponents to hold their lead by making foul shots under pressure. However, a number of writers have raised serious questions about this practice of strategic fouling. For example, some have argued that strategic fouling breaks a tacit contract among competitors to abide by the rules, while others have argued it undermines the game by making less important rote skills, such as foul shooting, more important than primary creative skills like dribbling, shooting over defenders, and passing. While I have doubts about whether these arguments are sound, the critics of strategic fouling have succeeded in showing the prevailing view about strategic fouling is not necessarily acceptable just because it is widely accepted. For a summary of this debate and my own defense of strategic fouling under some circumstances, see Robert Simon, "The Ethics of Strategic Fouling: A Reply to Fraleigh," *Journal of the Philosophy of Sport* 32:1 (2005): 87–95.

6. Indeed, a topic of further discussion is whether the different approaches to the ethics of coaching suggested in this chapter are compatible with one another, at least in an adjusted form, or whether we must choose among them. For example, is the virtue approach suggested by Reid in Chapter 3 compatible with the broad internalism developed in Chapter 4? In other words, does viewing the role of the coach the way that Reid suggests—and taking the main function of sports to be the development of virtue among sports participants—the theory that makes the best sense of sporting practices and presents them in their morally best light? Or do we need a broader conception of sporting practice involving the ideas of challenge, fairness toward, and respect for other competitors, and conceptions of the rights and duties of participants in addition to virtue theory? Are these other values really distinct from virtue or are they examples of virtues themselves? These are complex questions that remain subjects of philosophical debate. For a helpful and quite accessible discussion of different theoretical approaches to ethics, including virtue theory, see James Rachels and Stuart Rachels, *The Elements of Moral Philosophy,* 7th ed. (New York: McGraw-Hill, 2011).

Chapter 3

1. The Greek term *aretē* is difficult to translate. In short, it refers to excellence—a disposition and ability to do great things that includes a moral

dimension. In the language of ethical theory it is usually translated "virtue," although "virtuosity" may better capture the sense in which morality and skill combine to yield exemplary action.

2. For a review, see Sharon K. Stoll and Jennifer M. Beller, "Do Sports Build Character?" in *Sports in School: The Future of an Institution,* ed. John Gerdy (New York: Columbia University Press, 2000), 18–30. Note that the definitions and measurements of "good moral character" used in this social science research are often questioned—and sometimes rejected—by philosophers.

3. For a complete explanation of this approach, see M. Andrew Holowchak and Heather L. Reid, *Aretism: An Ancient Sports Philosophy for the Modern Sports World* (Lanham, MD: Lexington, 2011).

4. Gilgamesh's feat is recounted in *The Epic of Gilgamesh,* trans. N. K. Sandars (London: Penguin, 1960), 69; Shulgi's comes from the "Hymn of Praise to Shulgi," in S. K. Kramer, *History Begins at Sumer* (Philadelphia: University of Pennsylvania Press, 1981), 285–288.

5. This is the argument made by Heather L. Reid, *Athletics and Philosophy in the Ancient World: Contests of Virtue* (New York: Routledge, 2011), 11–21.

6. For a philosophical exploration of the value of Heracles' strength, see H. Reid, "Hercules' Dilemma: Is Strength Really a Virtue?" in *Strength and Philosophy,* ed. M. Holowchak (New York: Mellen, 2010).

7. Homer, *The Odyssey,* trans. Robert Fagles (New York: Penguin, 1990), 8.130–233.

8. Ibid. Books 18–21.

9. For a more complete argument on this point, see Reid, *Athletics and Philosophy,* chaps. 1–3.

10. Nigel James Nicholson, *Aristocracy and Athletics in Archaic and Classical Greece* (Cambridge: Cambridge University Press, 2005), 21, explains that "what motivated anxiety about professional trainers was that, by appearing to add new abilities such as skill to their pupils, they threatened the idea that the qualities on which victory depended were inherited, and, second, that, while the training was traded as a commodity, the relationship between trainer and patron was sufficiently complex that to represent it in other terms was convincing."

11. In contrast to the more liberal and individualistic philosophies of modern times, ancient Greek conceptions of *aretē* always encompass civic responsibility. As Aristotle says, human beings are understood as political animals; human excellence must therefore include political virtues.

12. Kathleen Freeman, trans., *Ancilla to the Pre-Socratic Philosophers: A Complete Translation of Diels, Fragmente der Vorsokratiker* (Cambridge: Harvard University Press, 1948), DK 23 b33, p. 53.

13. The story is told in Iamblichus, *The Pythagorean Life,* trans. Thomas Taylor (London: Watkins, 1818), chap. 5. After watching the student play a complex ball game, Pythagoras concluded that he must also have the ability to learn complex ideas. This student eventually accompanied Pythagoras to the colony of Kroton in southern Italy, where he again recruited students at the gymnasium and founded a community of scholars and athletes renowned in the ancient world, not least for their success at the Olympic Games. Kroton was so dominant in the Olympic Games that the top seven finishers in the sprint race of 576 BCE all hailed from that single city—a phenomenon that gave birth to the proverb that "he who finishes last of the Krotonites is first among the rest of the Greeks" (Strabo 6.1.12).

14. For a fuller discussion, see Heather L. Reid, "Sport as Moral Education in Plato's *Republic,*" *Journal of the Philosophy of Sport* 34:2 (2007): 160–175; and "Plato's Gymnasium," in *Athletics and Philosophy,* 56–68.

15. Plato, Seventh Letter, in *Plato in Twelve Volumes,* trans. R. G. Bury (Cambridge: Harvard University Press, 1966), 7:335d-336b.

16. For a complete argument, see Nicholas Dixon, "On Winning and Athletic Superiority," *Journal of the Philosophy of Sport* 26:1 (1999): 10–26.

17. This argument is made repeatedly by Holowchak and Reid in *Aretism,* for example, page 166. It may also be the case that the beauty we see in athletic movements and perhaps even artistic movements, such as dance, depends ultimately on moral criteria. For a discussion, see Heather Reid, *The Philosophy of Sport* (Lanham, MD: Rowman & Littlefield, 2012), chap. 11.

18. I am not making a consequentialist claim here that the moral value of athletic virtue depends strictly on its beneficial outcomes; rather, I am distinguishing the athletic skill associated with victory from virtue—the latter of which can (and should) be exercised for human benefit beyond sports.

19. Plato *Hippias Minor* 364c–370e.

20. For a comparison of Socratic and Sophistic approaches to argument, see Reid, *Athletics and Philosophy,* chap. 4, especially pp. 46–48.

21. Plato *Apology* 30b. All Plato quotations are taken from the following volume, unless otherwise noted: Plato, *Complete Works,* ed. John M. Cooper (Indianapolis: Hackett, 1997).

22. According to NCAA statistics, the percentage of college athletes who go on to play professionally in the major men's sports of basketball, football, and soccer ranges from 1.0 to 1.7 percent. Since college athletics does not market itself as a preprofessional program, that placement rate is not seen as a failure. National Collegiate Athletic Association, "Estimated Probability of Competing in Athletics Beyond the High School Interscholastic Level," 2011, http://www.ncaa.org/wps/wcm/connect/public/test/issues/recruiting/probability+of+going+pro.

23. Plato *Republic* 413cd.

24. In *Republic,* Socrates' brief discussion of the guardians' dedicated gymnastic period includes the cryptic comment that their performance there "is itself an important test" (537b). In what follows he suggests that the best potential philosophers will be selected, at least partly, on the basis of this test (537c), and, presumably, the also-rans will be weeded out.

25. Plato *Republic* 410b.

26. Plato *Apology* 21d. Socrates is sometimes quoted as saying that the only thing he knows is that he knows nothing, but this exact phrase does not occur in the Platonic dialogues.

27. More precisely, the oracle said no one was wiser than Socrates.

28. Walter Burkert, *Greek Religion*, trans. J. Raffan (Cambridge: Harvard University Press, 1985), 56. For a complete argument about the connection between sports and sacrifice, see David Sansone, *Greek Athletics and the Genesis of Sport* (Berkeley: University of California Press, 1988).

29. Plato *Republic* 424e.

30. At *Gorgias* 463b ff., Socrates calls rhetoric a form of flattery that makes the soul seem healthy when in fact it is not.

31. For more on the role of respect in sports, see Heather Reid, *The Philosophical Athlete* (Durham, NC: Carolina Academic Press, 2002), chaps. 7–9.

32. Plato *Republic* 535bc.

33. The similar proverb, "You can learn more about someone in an hour of play than a year of conversation," is sometimes attributed to Plato, but it does not appear in the extant written texts.

34. Plato *Republic* 535b.

35. Ibid., 504cd.

36. Ibid., 537b.

37. Ibid., 524d ff.

38. The implications of this principle are diverse. One may be a decoupling of athletics and academics during specific time periods—for example, young athletes may devote four years to sporting excellence and another four years to academic excellence. It may also imply a lowering of athletic expectations during times of higher education, or a lowering of academic expectations during times of athletic striving. (I know many athletes who take lower course loads during their competitive season.) It does not imply, however, that individuals should abandon one type of activity in order to pursue excellence in the other. The student who never goes to the gym is just as imbalanced as the athlete who never goes to the library.

39. Coaches should also think of creative ways to align athletic and academic rewards. A student of mine once suggested that college basketball

players receive a score equivalent to their grade point average (instead of the standard 2 or 3 points) for each basket. A radical suggestion, perhaps, but it would motivate students to pay equal attention to athletics and academics.

40. Plato *Republic* 411e: "It seems, then, that a god has given music and physical training to human beings not, except incidentally, for the body and the soul, but for the spirited and wisdom-loving parts of the soul itself, in order that these may be in harmony with one another, each being stretched and relaxed to an appropriate degree."

41. Plato *Republic* 403d.

42. Ibid., 411e.

43. Ibid.,591c.

44. Plato *Phaedrus* 247b.

45. Plato *Republic* 442a.

46. Ibid., 424e.

47. Ibid., 416d.

48. Ibid., 502d–503a.

49. Ibid., 519e.

50. Ibid., 465d.

51. Aristotle, *Nicomachean Ethics*, trans. Terence Irwin, 2nd ed. (Indianapolis: Hackett, 1999), 1098a.

Chapter 4

1. Quoted from "Champions with Character," Utica *Observer-Dispatch*, January 19, 2012, 8A.

2. I borrow this kind of example from Jeffrey Fry, "Coaching a Kingdom of Ends," *Journal of the Philosophy of Sport* 27 (2000): 56.

3. I have argued more fully for such a view in Robert L. Simon, "From Ethnocentrism to Realism: Does Discourse Ethics Bridge the Gap?" *Journal of the Philosophy of Sport* 31:2 (2004). William J. Morgan questions this view in Chapter 5 of the present volume.

4. Of course, when evaluating any group of people, we will find shades of gray. Most coaches, like other people, will be less than perfect without having serious or significant moral flaws.

5. See Scott Kretchmar, "In Defense of Winning," in *Sports Ethics: An Anthology*, ed. Jan Boxill (Malden, MA: Blackwell, 2003), 130–135.

6. Ronald Dworkin, *Justice for Hedgehogs* (Cambridge: Harvard University Press, 2011), 112.

7. See Fry, "Coaching," 59.

8. Someone who reviewed this chapter has suggested, however, that players at elite levels may have implicitly consented to competition for

playing time, and even to coaches using tactics such as those described by Fry if needed to promote competitive success. If the players can be presumed to have consented, perhaps they are not being used as means or exploited after all. However, it is hardly clear that players have consented to the behavior described by Fry or that it would even be rational for them to do so.

9. Here I follow Bernard Gert, who argues that justifiable moral codes must be public or known to all to whom they apply. See Gert, *Morality: Its Nature and Justification* (New York: Oxford University Press, 1998), 191–195.

10. Fry, "Coaching," 59–60.

11. Ibid., 58.

12. A lot hinges on the sport at issue. For example, in cross-country, everyone on the team normally competes so there is no issue of replacing one runner with another.

13. Golf purists might insist on penalizing the offending player, and I would agree if the match in question was a formal, highly competitive one. But what if it is a preseason scrimmage or takes place in a developmental event for inexperienced players? The common courtesies widely recognized by golfers call on them to warn fellow competitors in advance of possible rule violations, so the player who teed the ball ahead of the markers is not the only player at fault in this case.

14. A. Launder, "Coach Education for the Twenty-First Century," *Sports Coach* 16:1 (1993): 1–2; quoted by Oyvind F. Standal and Liv B. Hemmestad, "Becoming a Good Coach: Coaching as Phronesis," in *The Ethics of Sports Coaching*, ed. Alun R. Hardman and Carwyn Jones (London: Routledge, 2011), 50.

15. Reflective equilibrium, following the work of John Rawls, might be thought of as the end result of a process of deliberation—our principles yield results that seem acceptable when applied to particular cases and our judgments about particular cases harmonize with our general principles. Perhaps such a state is an ideal to be aimed at rather than actually achieved, but the attempt to achieve it can, by eliminating incoherencies in our moral perspective, lead to defensible ethical judgments and arguably, if our system stands the test of critical scrutiny, justified moral belief. See John Rawls, *A Theory of Justice* (Cambridge: Harvard University Press, 1971), esp. 46–53, for an influential discussion of reflective equilibrium and its role in moral reasoning.

16. For fuller development of virtue-centered approaches to coaching, see Standal and Hemmestad, "Becoming a Good Coach"; and Alun R. Hardman and Carwyn Jones, "Sports Coaching and Virtue Ethics," in *The Ethics of Sports Coaching*, 45–55; 72–84.

17. For a fuller discussion of "the mutual quest for excellence," see Robert Simon, *Fair Play* (Boulder: Westview, 2010), chaps. 2–3.

18. For a fuller discussion of broad internalism, see Robert Simon, "Internalism and the Internal Values of Sport," *Journal of the Philosophy of Sport* 27 (2000): 1–16, as well as Chapter 5 in this volume. John Russell, "Are Rules All an Umpire Has to Work With?" *Journal of the Philosophy of Sport* 26 (1999): 27–49, has strongly influenced the development of interpretive (broad internalist) positions.

19. This is a principle rather than a rule because in some situations its force may have to be weighed against competing factors. For example, a football coach might not want the challenge of playing a stronger and bigger team because his players might be injured.

20. I have argued for the mutual reinforcement thesis in "Does Athletics Undermine Academics? Examining Some Issues," *Journal of Intercollegiate Sport* 1:1 (2008): 40–58. Critical comments by Drew Hyland and William J. Morgan also appear in that issue, pp. 59–71.

21. Following a different sort of argument to a similar conclusion, based on affinities between athletic and artistic performances in music and dance, is Myles Brand, "The Role and Value of Intercollegiate Athletics in Universities," *Journal of the Philosophy of Sport* 33 (2007): 9–20.

22. For a defense of the view that providing entertainment to large audiences through athletics is a defensible function of big-time intercollegiate sports, see Peter French, *Ethics and College Sports: Ethics, Sports, the University* (Lanham, MD: Rowman & Littlefield, 2004).

23. *Report of the Special Investigative Counsel Regarding the Actions of the Pennsylvania State University Related to the Child Sexual Abuse Committed by Gerald A. Sandusky*, July 12, 2012, p. 14, thefreeh reportonpsu.com.

24. The NCAA vacated the victories of Penn State football from 1998 to 2011, roughly the period when Sandusky committed his crimes and no one reported them to the criminal justice system. Critics of this penalty argue, with some justice in my view, that those victories were earned through the hard work of players who were uninvolved in the scandal and were innocent of any wrongdoing. See Gary Alan Fine, "George Orwell and the NCAA," *New York Times,* July 24, 2012, www.nytimes.com/2012/07/25/opinion/penn-states-vacated-victories.html?_r=1.

25. Other reforms that might help integrate athletics and academics more fully in Division I include restrictions on extended travel that conflicts with class attendance and restrictions on the level of training expected of athletes in the off-season.

Chapter 5

1. Robert Simon, "From Ethnocentrism to Realism: Can Discourse Ethics Bridge the Gap?" *Journal of the Philosophy of Sport* 31 (2004): 122–141.

2. Ibid. 125.

3. Ronald Dworkin, "To Each His Own," *New York Review of Books*, April 14, 1983, 4–6.

4. Simon, "From Ethnocentrism to Realism." Dworkin's normative theory of law is more complicated than I have so far indicated. For while he clearly thinks that a normative theory of law "must be abstract because [it] aim[s] to interpret the main point and structure of legal practice, not some particular part . . . of it," he also holds that "a practical imperative" of any interpretation of the law requires "there is enough initial agreement about what practices are legal practices" in a particular culture if that interpretation is to be successful. See Dworkin, *Law's Empire* (Cambridge: Harvard University Press, 1986), 90–91. That would put his position closer to Simon's normative theory of sport. In the same book, published after the article I cite in the text, he makes it clear that the full-throated abstract position he took in the article is best suited to "justice and other higher-order moral concepts" rather than law because of the former's "global reach" (pp. 424–425). Interestingly, Jürgen Habermas's well-known discourse on ethics, which differs from Simon's by claiming to be ahistorical at both front and back end, also thinks that discourse normative theory is best suited to moral concepts like justice rather than law for the same reason. See Habermas, *Moral Consciousness and Communicative Action* (Cambridge: MIT Press, 1990), 103.

5. Simon, "From Ethnocentrism to Realism," 128.

6. Ibid.

7. As one commentator of the time put it, "What sportsmanlike opponent cares to make his point against a helpless antagonist?" Price Collier, "Sport's Place in the Nation's Well Being," *Outing* 32 (1898): 886.

8. Caspar Whitney, "The View-Point," *Outing* 52 (1908): 766.

9. Benjamin Rader, *American Sports: From the Age of Folk Games to the Age of Televised Sports* (Upper Saddle River, NJ: Prentice-Hall, 2004), 130–131. The seeds of this new, strenuous life were sown at the turn of the twentieth century. Once it attained normative preeminence, however, it held sway until the waning decades of the twentieth century. By that time the market had managed to insinuate itself into the internal affairs of sport, much as it had in just about every organized human enterprise.

10. It is no coincidence that coaches at this time began both literally and metaphorically to sell themselves to the sporting public not as educators, or as stewards of the health of their players, but as "efficient manag[ers] of the

body" whose strategic expertise, they loudly proclaimed, is what separates winners from losers. Donald J. Mrozek, *Sport and the American Mentality* (Knoxville: University of Tennessee Press, 1983), 67.

11. That is not to say that on certain occasions we can't come up with universal negative injunctions against murder, torture, arbitrary imprisonment, and the like. See Michael Walzer's fine book on this point, *Thick and Thin: Moral Argument at Home and Abroad* (Notre Dame, IN: University of Notre Dame Press, 1994). Rather, it is only to say that such wide-ranging agreement, if history is our teacher, is beyond reach when it comes to our own homegrown cultural practices, no matter how much others may seek to emulate our local ways. The most we can expect to derive from such thinning out in this latter sense are abstract platitudes that have little if any normative substance, and thus offer little in the way of ethical guidance or motivation.

12. The sort of argumentative impasse I have in mind here is captured in the book *Chariots of Fire*, later made into a movie, in which Cambridge dons upbraid one of their student athletes, the runner Harold Abrahams, for adopting a professional approach to his sport "concentrated wholly on developing [his] own technique" and for hiring a professional coach to aid his efforts, which, they argued, betrayed the amateur code of sports favored at Cambridge. Abrahams responded with an angry outburst that ended the conversation: "You know, gentleman, you yearn for victory just as I do. But achieved with the apparent ease of gods. Yours are the archaic values of the prep school playground. . . . I believe in the relentless pursuit of excellence—and I'll carry the future with me!" W. J. Weatherby, *Chariots of Fire* (New York: Dell, 1981), 91–92.

13. Nicholas Dixon, "Canadian Figure Skaters, French Judges, and Realism in Sport," *Journal of the Philosophy of Sport* 30:2 (2003): 108.

14. Members of the relevant athletic community could be mistaken regarding the status quo view on, for example, ethical coaching. But that would be a descriptive failure. So it turns out that this version of conventionalism has an error theory after all, but hardly a very useful one.

15. Strictly speaking, however, most social conventions, to include those of sports, are not products of simple agreement. David Lewis's classic book, *Convention*, which spurred serious philosophical interest in this topic, was based on his attempt to disarm Quine's claim that language can't be conventional because, in Lewis's words, it "could not have possibly originated by agreement, since some [language] would have been needed to provide the rudimentary language in which the first agreement was made." *Convention* (Oxford: Blackwell, 2002), 2. So conventions of this wide-ranging kind can't be reduced to social agreements either owing to special features of the

practices they are supposed to govern, as in the case of language above, or because of the large numbers of people that, *per impossible*, would have to sign on to them in order for them to function as conventional norms. Theorists of conventions, instead, attempt to explain the emergence of conventions by appealing to forms of common practical reasoning that allow people to identify, for instance, "salient" features of the situations they find themselves in that make it possible to coordinate their behavior. For an insightful account of such common practical reasoning, see Gerald Postema, "Salience Reasoning," *Topoi* 27 (2008).

16. Leslie Howe, "Gamesmanship," *Journal of the Philosophy of Sport* 31 (2004): 212–225.

17. Pine tar is a sticky substance applied to baseball bats for better gripping purposes.

18. I think MacPhail is on the right side of this issue—gamesmanship looks more like a vulgar trick than a legitimate strategic skill. Had the officials been privy to Martin's calculated decision to call the pine tar violation to their attention at that precise moment, it might well have provoked them to deliberate more carefully about how to rule. That's not to say, however, as Berman has astutely pointed out, that there are only two possible ways this argument could turn out: either MacPhail was right and the umpires wrong, or the other way around. There are two other possible outcomes as well, that both MacPhail and the umpires were wrong, or that they were both right, that MacPhail was right to prevent an injustice given his executive oversight role and the umpires were right to limit their officiating to the rule rather than its underlying principles given their adjudicative role. Mitchell Berman, "On Interpretivism and Formalism in Sports Officiating: From General to Particular Jurisprudence," *Journal of the Philosophy of Sport* 38 (2011): 190.

Chapter 6

1. See, for example, R. Scott Kretchmar, *Practical Philosophy of Sport* (Champaign, IL: Human Kinetics, 2005).

2. Frank Reynolds, "Developing a Formal Coaching Philosophy," *Coaches Report* 12:2 (2005): 10–12; David Parsh, "Eight Steps to a Coaching Philosophy," *Coach and Athletic Director* 76:9 (2007): 56–57.

3. Parsh outlines the following questions: What do you want to accomplish? What are your priorities? What are the responsibilities? What are your teaching methods? How do you define success? How will practices and games be organized? What are your team rules and consequences? How will you communicate your philosophy?

4. Carol Dweck, *Mindset: The New Psychology of Success* (New York: Random House, 2006).

5. Henry Bugbee, *The Inward Morning: A Philosophical Exploration in Journal Form* (Athens: University of Georgia Press, 1999).

6. Alun R. Hardman and Carwyn Jones, eds., *The Ethics of Sports Coaching* (London: Routledge, 2011), 2.

7. Sigmund Loland, "The Normative Aims of Coaching: The Good Coach as an Enlightened Generalist," in *Ethics of Sports Coaching*, 15–22.

8. Oyvind Standal and Liv Hemmestad, "Becoming a Good Coach: Coaching and *Phronesis*," in *Ethics of Sports Coaching*, 45–55.

9. Gary Walton, *Beyond Winning: The Timeless Wisdom of Great Philosopher Coaches* (Champaign, IL: Leisure, 1992), xi.

10. John Lyle, "Coaching Philosophy and Coaching Behavior," in *The Coaching Process: Principles and Practice for Sport,* ed. N. Cross and J. Lyle (Oxford: Butterworth & Heinemann, 1999), 25–46.

11. This concept of *technē* comes from the Greek tradition and is understood as a particular skill or craft. The fulfillment of *technē* requires both *episteme* (theoretical knowledge) and *phronesis* (practical wisdom). Coaches need to acquire and develop the capacity for both aspects of *technē*.

12. Legendary college football coach John Gagliardi provides an unusual example in this regard by using coaching methods that have been described as "winning with no's," as in no tackling in practices, no wind sprints, no whistles, and more. Despite the seemingly odd methods, Gagliardi and his St. John's University team have consistently reached the national playoffs in NCAA Division III. See Austin Murphy, *The Sweet Season* (New York: HarperCollins, 2001), for more on Gagliardi and St. John's football.

13. Harry Sheehy, the author of *Raising a Team Player: Teaching Kids Lasting Values on the Field, on the Court, and on the Bench* (North Adams, MA: Story, 2002), coached men's basketball at Williams College for seventeen years before serving as athletic director. While coaching, he compiled a record of 324–104 (.757), and while he was lead administrator the Ephs won the NCAA Division III Directors' Cup every year. Most recently, Sheehy became director of athletics and recreation at Dartmouth College.

14. Bugbee, *Inward Morning,* 77.

15. Noted in Douglas Anderson, *Philosophy Americana: Making Philosophy at Home in American Culture* (New York: Fordham University Press, 2006).

16. Bugbee, *Inward Morning,* 36–37.

17. Anderson, *Philosophy Americana,* 67.

18. Bugbee, *Inward Morning,* 37.

19. Ibid., 141.

20. Ibid., 36.

21. Ibid., 37, 22.

22. Ibid., 170.

23. Ibid., 35.

24. For example, see Jeff Fry, "On Playing with Emotion," *Journal of the Philosophy of Sport* 30 (2003): 26–36.

25. Bugbee, *Inward Morning,* 49.

26. Ibid., 129.

27. Anderson, *Philosophy Americana,* 54.

28. Bugbee, *Inward Morning,* 164.

29. Anderson, *Philosophy Americana,* 71.

30. William Warren, *Coaching and Control: Controlling Your Team, Your Program, and Your Opponents* (Upper Saddle River, NJ: Prentice-Hall, 1997).

31. Anderson, *Philosophy Americana,* 173.

32. Bugbee, *Inward Morning,* 232.

33. Harold Heie, *Learning to Listen, Ready to Talk: A Pilgrimage Toward Peacemaking* (Lincoln, NE: iUniverse, 2007), 91.

34. As an example, while ranked the number one golfer in the world, Tiger Woods changed his swing coach and, perhaps more surprisingly, his swing. While many criticized his decisions, the changes also illustrated an openness to change and a humble recognition that his game could be improved.

35. Petrino achieved notoriety and success at Arkansas, attaining an 11–2 record in the 2011 season, including a 2012 Cotton Bowl victory. In the spring of 2012 the university dismissed Petrino, however, following an embarrassing series of events. Petrino sustained injuries from a motorcycle crash, carrying a rider (Jessica Dorrell) who was an athletic department employee. After some time, Petrino admitted having an extramarital relationship with Dorrell and providing Dorrell with an undisclosed $20,000 gift. In addition, Dorrell had received preferential treatment in the hiring process for her university job. Arkansas athletic administrators went on to fire Petrino.

36. Bugbee, *Inward Morning,* 49.

37. Ibid., 53.

38. Anderson, *Philosophy Americana,* 62–63.

39. I am grateful to Robert Simon for providing this very astute and fitting example. Those who follow college basketball remember the tremendous success Princeton coach Pete Carril had with his patented "backdoor" cutting offensive system, one that matched well with the type of student athletes at Princeton.

40. Standal and Hemmestad, "Becoming a Good Coach," 53.

41. Paul Davis, "Objectivity and Subjectivity in Coaching," in *Ethics of Sports Coaching*, 56–71.

Part Three: Coaching and the Ethics of Competition
Chapter 7

1. On the general relationship between distributive justice and scarcity, see John Rawls, *A Theory of Justice* (Cambridge: Harvard University Press, 1971), 127–129. On scarcity and inherently or necessarily scarce goods, see "Scarcity," *Wikipedia,* http://en.wikipedia.org/wiki/Scarcity. On the varieties of justice, see Aristotle, "The Varieties of Justice," in *Justice: Alternative Political Perspectives*, ed. James Sterba (Belmont, CA: Wadsworth, 1980).

2. See Janean Chun, "Bank Deposit Error in Your Favor? Give It Back," *Daily Finance,* December 9, 2009; and Ben Jailler, "Can You Keep Money Accidentally Paid into Your Bank Account?" www.money.co.uk/article /1005023-can-you-keep-money-accidentally-paid-into-your-bank -account.htm, for reviews of the law in the United States and the United Kingdom respectively. See also the US Treasury Department, "Answers and Solutions for Customers of National Banks," http://www.mymoney.gov /content/answers-and-solutions-customers-national-banks.html.

3. Robert L. Simon, *Fair Play: The Ethics of Sport*, 2nd ed. (Boulder, CO: Westview, 2004), 27.

4. William J. Morgan, *Why Sports Morally Matter* (New York: Routledge, 2006).

5. J. S. Russell, "Competitive Sport, Moral Development, and Peace: Skeptical Reflections," in *A Companion to Sport Philosophy*, ed. Cesar Torres (forthcoming). See also John Russell, "The Moral Ambiguity of Coaching Youth Sport," in *The Ethics of Sports Coaching,* ed. Alun R. Hardman and Carwyn Jones (London: Routledge, 2011).

6. I am applying Midgley's suggestion that games are ritualized conflicts. Mary Midgley, "The Game Game," in *The Ethics of Sports: A Reader,* ed. Mike McNamee (London: Routledge, 2010).

7. Quoted in Russell, "Competitive Sport."

8. Immanuel Kant, *Lectures on Ethics* (New York: Harper Torchbooks, 1963), 215–217.

9. See Alister Browne, "Violating Rules of Rationing," *Canadian Journal of General Internal Medicine* 3:3 (2008): 127–128, for a succinct review of these issues.

10. See Mitchell N. Berman, "Replay," *California Law Review* 99 (2011): 1683–1743; Harry Collins, "The Philosophy of Umpiring and the Introduction of Decision-Aid Technology," *Journal of the Philosophy*

of Sport 37:2 (2010): 135–146; and Richard Royce, "Refereeing and Technology: Reflections on Collins' Proposals," *Journal of the Philosophy of Sport* 39:1 (2012), for discussions of the role of replay and other decision aids in sport. For a discussion of umpire discretion regarding calls and rules in some other contexts, see J. S. Russell, "The Concept of a Call in Baseball," *Journal of the Philosophy of Sport* 24 (1997): 21–37; Russell, "Are Rules All an Umpire Has to Work With?" *Journal of the Philosophy of Sport* 26 (1999): 27–49. None of these discuss the role coaches or participants may have in overturning erroneous decisions.

11. I am indebted to Alister Browne for years of discussion on this topic and for comments on an earlier draft of this chapter.

Chapter 8

1. I mention Rudy because it was the fact of his being on the field in a real game that validated his project and served as the dramatic climax in the movie version of his story. Had Rudy just made the team, it would have produced a feel-good narrative. But getting into an actual game was the epiphany event— what the fans wanted . . . and of course, what Rudy wanted as well.

2. Sports like cross-country running effectively acknowledge rights of substitutes to play by allowing some of them to compete. Even though only a subset of runners' scores will count, nobody knows for sure who that will be when the race begins. So, one could say that cross-country is an example of a benchwarmer-friendly sport.

3. See, for example, concerns raised about ESPN television and the potential exploitation of young athletes, http://itsaboutthemoney.net/archives/2011/08/16/does-espn-exploit-little-leaguers. Also, I realize that one can read such must-play regulations with cynical or supportive eyes. In the former case, these rules are seen as hypocritical covers for underlying business motives or adult agendas. In the latter case, such rules would indicate that competition in these contexts is truly about the athletes and transcendent values like education and fun.

4 These concerns about premature judgments or decisions are elevated when one considers the fact that some coaches may not be good judges of talent. Because many junior high school coaches are young and inexperienced, the chances for these kinds of mistakes are increased.

5. When I cluster these values or emphases into two categories, I do not see that elements of each one necessarily entail one another. Rather, these are rough-and-ready groupings. Excellence, for example, does not entail public performance and even less, commercialization. But excellence is something

that typically attracts public interest. And public interest is one factor in commercial viability.

6. I use the terms "technician" and "instrumentalist" advisedly. They connote expertise but also a kind of value-free approach to problem solving. MacIntyre (1984), for example, roundly criticizes such an approach when he introduces the stock character of the manager. The worry is that many coaches operate too frequently in the amoral atmosphere of seeking maximal efficacy.

7. These nonschool settings I have in mind would include organizations like American Legion Baseball, AAU competitions, sport camp experiences, and the like.

8. This is stage 2 moral reasoning, according to Kohlberg. It is based on high degrees of self-interest (What is in it for me?) and fails to tap into universal principles that might govern human relationships—principles like loyalty and justice.

9. It is interesting that a nod is given in the direction of the importance of playing time at both high school and college levels by traditional "senior night" games. This is when all seniors get a chance to start and play for a short time. One wonders if this gesture is taken by some graduating players as more an insult than an honor.

10. In Division III, Bylaw 14.1.11.1 (NCAA 2011) limits the use of male practice players to one day a week, to the traditional playing season for the team in question, and to half the number of starters for that sport.

11. Limitations in Divisions I and II have more to do with normal eligibility requirements than practice restrictions. Practice guys have to be bona fide students.

Chapter 9

1. Stephen Potter, *The Theory and Practice of Gamesmanship* (New York: Bantam, 1947), 4.

2. Leslie Howe, "Gamesmanship," *Journal of the Philosophy of Sport* 31 (2004): 212.

3. The constitutive rules are considered the written rules that define a game.

4. Howe, "Gamesmanship," 213.

5. Included in this understanding of the manipulation of rules are questionable forms of performance enhancement that may not be cheating but could test the rules. This could include such examples as equipment advances that are unavailable to others or nontherapeutic surgical enhancement.

6. Howe, "Gamesmanship," 213.

7. Potter, *Theory and Practice of Gamesmanship*.

8. Ibid, 70.

9. Howe, "Gamesmanship," 214.

10. The regulative nature of the game is defined as the rules that regulate the activity, including "supporting the constitutive rules by explaining behaviors that aid in successful occurrences of the games . . . . [T]hey specify strategies, techniques, procedures and natural facts," as described in Chad Carlson and John Gleaves, "Categorical Shortcomings: Application, Adjudication, and Contextual Descriptions of Game Rules," *Journal of the Philosophy of Sport* 38:2 (2011): 199. They are the way the game should be played beyond its constitutive rules.

11. Howe, "Gamesmanship," 219.

12. Ibid., 214.

13. Ibid., 221.

14. Ibid., 215.

15. As to when this age appropriateness occurs there is room for debate, but for argument's sake this author will suggest at least the early teenage years. By then the young athlete may be sophisticated enough to deal with the weak forms of gamesmanship. There is no place for "icing" a ten-year-old.

16. Merriam-Webster dictionary, http://www.merriam-webster.com /dictionary/intimidate.

17. "Bullying Prevention," http://education.alberta.ca/teachers/safeschools /bullying-prevention.aspx.

18. Reprinted with the permission of Simon and Schuster, Inc., from *InSideOut Coaching: How Sports Can Transform Lives*, by Joe Ehrmann, with Paula Ehrmann and Gregory Jordan. Copyright © 2011 by Building Men and Women for Others, Inc. All rights reserved.

19. Ibid., 80.

20. Knight quotes: http://www.therxforum.com/archive/index.php /t-19832.html.

21. http://www.bullyingonline.org/cases/case97.htm.

22. Ehrmann, *InSide Out Coaching*, 77.

23. Howe, "Gamesmanship," 215.

24. To "work" an official is a colloquial term for "work over" or irritate an official so the referee will feel intimidated and thus be less eager to call a foul or penalty on the team making the complaint.

25. Some of the most outrageous examples of horrific sportsmanship occur when coaches direct players to harm opponents, even offering bounties for hits. Two such examples are provided in the article "Zeal Can Cloud Judgment," http://www.usatoday.com/sports/college/mensbasketball/2005 –02–28-chaney-sportsmanship_x.htm.

26. Ehrmann, *InSideOut Coaching,* 18.

27. Ibid.

28. Dermot Moran, *Introduction to Phenomenology* (New York: Routledge, 2000), 241.

29. Ibid.

30. Ehrmann, *InSideOut Coaching,* 76.

31. Ibid., 64.

32. Fyodor Dostoevsky, *Notes from Underground* (New York: Bantam, 1974), 88.

33. Moran, *Introduction to Phenomenology,* 241.

34. Ibid.

35. Ehrmann, *InSideOut Coaching,* 47.

36. Ibid., 12.

37. Ibid., 81.

38. Chris Stankovich, "Coach-Player Intimidation, Humiliation, and Physical Aggression Is Never Warranted," http://blog.drstankovich.com/blog /2011/02/coaching/coach-coercion-intimidation-and–humiliation.

39. Howe, "Gamesmanship," 221.

40. A comment made in my college sports ethics class by Elizabeth Patrick, February 2012.

41. I have written of this in the chapter "Hardwood Dojos," in *Basketball and Philosophy* (Lexington: University Press of Kentucky, 2007).

Chapter 10

1. The idea that the Copernican revolution lowered the standing of human beings has been called into question. See Alvin Plantinga, *Where the Conflict Really Lies: Science, Religion, and Naturalism* (New York: Oxford University Press, 2011), p. 6 n. 4.

2. Ramachandran discusses the first three revolutions in *A Brief Tour of Human Consciousness* (New York: Pearson, 2004), 1–2. Lone Frank attributes a discussion of four prior revolutions (the fourth being the discovery of DNA and the attendant possibilities of genetic engineering) to Ramachandran in *Mindfield: How Brain Science Is Changing Our World* (New York: Oxford University Press, 2009), 12–13.

3. Ramachandran, *Brief Tour,* 2.

4. For suggestions of the prior inertia of the National Football League in this regard, see Bennett Omalu, *Play Hard, Die Young: Football, Dementia, and Death* (Lodi, CA: Neo-Forenxis, 2008), chap. 4.

5. Alun R. Hardman and Carwyn Jones, eds., *The Ethics of Sports Coaching* (London: Routledge, 2011), 2.

6. The word "neuroethics" predates my usage. Neil Levy explains that neuroethics "has two main branches." He writes: "The *ethics of neuroscience* refers to the branch of neuroethics that seeks to develop an ethical framework for regulating the conduct of neuroscientific inquiry and the application of neuroscientific knowledge to human beings; *the neuroscience of ethics* refers to the impact of neuroscientific knowledge upon our understanding of ethics itself." Neil Levy, *Neuroethics: Challenges for the 21st Century* (Cambridge: Cambridge University Press), 2007, 1.

My topic is related to *the ethics of neuroscience*. I extend this notion by drawing on the newly developing fields of social and affective neuroscience to illuminate how we affect one another's brains and thereby the quality of one another's life experiences, in everyday life and in sporting contexts. In addition, what I say is also related to *the neuroscience of ethics*. This is particularly the case insofar as this discussion bears on the nature of human agency and its development through social interactions. Thus in the way that I approach the topic of neuroethics and sport, the two branches of neuroethics are two sides of a coin.

7. I have borrowed this phrase from John Kekes, *The Enlargement of Life: Moral Imagination at Work* (Ithaca, NY: Cornell University Press), 2006.

8. Martha C. Nussbaum, *The Fragility of Goodness: Luck and Ethics in Greek Tragedy and Philosophy* (Cambridge: Cambridge University Press, 1986).

9. I am indebted here to Susan Blackmore, *Consciousness: An Introduction,* 2nd ed. (New York: Oxford University Press, 2011), 156.

Some philosophers of mind and neuroscientists are confident of a causal relationship between brain states and putative mental states, even if the causal influence is unidirectional and mental states turn out to be epiphenomenal in nature, or lacking in causal efficacy. This confidence is due in part to the capability of neuroscientists to stimulate areas of the brain in laboratory settings and to record the accompanying bodily sensations and other experiences reported by subjects. Thus a somato-sensory area of the brain is stimulated and a person reports a sensation in a hand, or a motor area of the brain is stimulated and a body part moves. Stimulation of the brain can even produce movements without an accompanying sense of conscious willing of the movement. See a recounting of the well-known Wilder Penfield experiments in Sandra Blakeslee and Matthew Blakeslee, *The Body Has a Mind of Its Own: How Body Maps in Your Brain Help You Do (Almost) Everything Better* (New York: Random House, 2008), chap. 2.

10. For a discussion and attempted refutation of what he takes to be ontologically reductionistic, materialist views of mind, including

functionalism, see John R. Searle, *Mind: A Brief Introduction*, Fundamentals of Philosophy Series (New York: Oxford University Press, 2004), especially chaps. 2–4. Searle's own view, which he calls "biological naturalism," attempts to avoid both reductive materialism and dualism.

11. For an argument as to how conscious states might be causal in nature without presupposing dualism, see Searle (above), especially chap. 7.

12. Norman Doidge, *The Brain That Changes Itself: Stories of Personal Triumph from the Frontiers of Brain Science* (New York: Penguin, 2007).

13. Ibid., 132–163.

14. Ibid., xx.

15. See Ramachandran, *Brief Tour,* 10–18.

16. Ibid., 13.

17. Ibid.

18. Ibid.

19. Daniel Goleman, *Social Intelligence: The New Science of Human Relationships* (New York: Bantam, 2007), 4.

20. Ibid., 5.

21. Ibid., 11.

22. Cited in Doidge, *Brain,* 63.

23. Goleman, *Social Intelligence,* 12.

24. H. Richard Niebuhr, *The Responsible Self: An Essay in Christian Moral Philosophy*, Library of Theological Ethics (Louisville, KY: Westminster John Knox, 1999).

25. See Giacomo Rizzolatti and Corrado Sinigaglia, *Mirrors in the Brain: How Our Minds Share Actions and Emotions*, trans. Frances Anderson (Oxford: Oxford University Press, 2008). A group led by Rizzolatti discovered mirror neurons in the 1990s.

26. Goleman, *Social Intelligence,* 57–59.

27. Ibid., 42.

28. Ibid., 43.

29. Marco Icaboni, *Mirroring People: The Science of Empathy and How We Connect with Others* (New York: Picador, 2009), 5.

30. Ibid., 270–271.

31. Thomas Metzinger, *The Ego Tunnel: The Science of the Mind and the Myth of the Self* (New York: Basic, 2009), 233.

32. Ibid.

33. Ibid., 236.

34. See Barbara Strauch, *The Primal Teen: What the New Discoveries About the Teenage Brain Tell Us About Our Kids* (New York: Anchor, 2004).

35. Ibid., 14.

36. Ibid., 13.

37. Quoted in Ibid., 13.

38. See Ibid., 15–18.

39. Ibid., 17.

40. Ibid., 21.

41. See also Barbara Strauch, *The Secret Life of the Grown-Up Brain: The Surprising Talent of the Middle-Aged Mind* (New York: Viking, 2010).

42. John J. Ratey with Eric Hagerman, *Spark: The Revolutionary New Science of Exercise and the Brain* (New York: Little, Brown, 2008).

43. Andre Agassi, *Open: An Autobiography* (New York: Vintage, 2010).

44. Ibid., 38.

45. Ibid., epigraph.

46. On the significance of different "levels of description" see Searle, *Mind*, 49.

47. See Icaboni, *Mirroring People*, 268–272.

48. Robert Leamnson, *Thinking About Teaching and Learning: Developing Habits of Learning with First Year College and University Students* (Sterling, VA: Stylus, 1999), 14.

49. Quoted by Leamnson, *Thinking*, 14.

50. Carol S. Dweck, *Mindset: The New Psychology of Success* (New York: Ballantine, 2006), 202–211. Whether Dweck's characterizations of Knight and Wooden are accurate or not, the general point that coaches exemplify mindsets may still be salient.

51. Ibid., 203.

52. Ibid., 205.

53. Ibid., 207.

54. Goleman, *Social Intelligence*, 42–43.

55. Roland Lazenby, *Mindgames: Phil Jackson's Long, Strange Journey* (Chicago: Contemporary, 2002), 11, 32–33.

56. Clifford Craig and Randolph Feezell, *Coaching for Character: Reclaiming the Principles of Sportsmanship* (Champaign, IL: Human Kinetics, 1997).

57. See the notion of "bracketed morality" in David Lyle Light Shields and Brenda Jo Light Bredemeier, *Character Development and Physical Activity* (Champaign, IL: Human Kinetics, 1995), 120, 122.

58. I am indebted to an anonymous reviewer who raised the concern, and to Robert Simon, who suggested a response along the lines that I have offered. Note also that if one acknowledges that learning and the memory formation involve changes in one's brain, then it seems reasonable to suggest that coaches at least to some extent contribute to brain change in athletes.

59. See M. R. Bennett and P. M. S. Hacker, *Philosophical Foundations of Neuroscience* (Malden, MA: Blackwell, 2003), and the contributions of Bennett and Hacker in Maxwell Bennett et al., *Neuroscience and Philosophy: Brain, Mind, and Language* (New York: Columbia University Press, 2007). I am indebted to Leon Culbertson, who called my attention to Bennett's and Hacker's critique.

60. See Andy Clark and David J. Chalmers, "The Extended Mind," in *Philosophy of Mind: Classical and Contemporary Readings*, ed. David J. Chalmers (New York: Oxford University Press, 2002), 643–651.

61. Again I am indebted to Leon Culbertson, who called my attention to a version of this critique.

62. Steven Pinker, "The Riddle of Knowing You're Here," in *Your Brain: A User's Guide* (New York: TIME Books, 2009), 12–19.

63. See Plato's *Apology* in *The Last Days of Socrates: Euthyphro, The Apology, Crito, Phaedo,* rev. ed., trans. Hugh Tredennick (New York: Penguin, 1969).

64. I have borrowed the term "social brain" from Goleman, *Social Intelligence.*

65. Anthony Skillen, "Sport Is for Losers," in *Ethics and Sport*, ed. M. J. McNamee and S. J. Parry (London: Routledge, 1998), 181.

66. I would like to thank Elizabeth Agnew and Robert Simon for their helpful comments as I was writing this chapter. Material from this chapter was presented at the 38th annual meeting of the International Association for the Philosophy of Sport, Rome, Italy, September 2010, and at the 7th annual conference of the British Philosophy of Sport Association, Cardiff, Wales, March 2010. I am grateful for the feedback I received at those presentations.

Chapter 11

1. See David K. Wiggins, "A History of Organized Play and Highly Competitive Sport for American Children," in *Advances in Pediatric Sport Sciences*, 2 vols., ed. Daniel Gould and Maureen R. Weiss (Champaign, IL: Human Kinetics, 1987), 1:1–24; Wiggins, "A History of Highly Competitive Sport for American Children," in *Children and Youth in Sport: A Biopsychosocial Perspective*, ed. Frank L. Smoll and Ronald E. Smith (Madison, WI: Brown & Benchmark, 1996), 15–30; and Ronald B. Woods, *Social Issues in Sport*, 2nd ed. (Champaign, IL: Human Kinetics, 2011), 97–98. For simplicity's sake, throughout the chapter we refer to organized youth sports simply as youth sports.

2. Woods, *Social Issues in Sport*, 101. All statistics in this chapter refer to the United States.

3. Ibid.

4. Ibid.

5. Christina Theokas, "Youth Sport Participation: A View of the Issues: Introduction to the Special Section," *Developmental Psychology* 45:2 (2009): 303.

6. See Mark Hyman, *Until It Hurts: America's Obsession with Youth Sports and How It Harms Our Kids* (Beacon: Boston, 2009).

7. New York State Public High School Athletic Association, *2010–2012 Handbook* (Latham, NY: New York State Public High School Athletic Association, n.d.), 25. The handbook is available at http://www.nysphsaa.org.

8. See, for example, Wiggins, "History of Organized Play"; Wiggins, "History of Highly Competitive Sport"; and B. M. Sayre, "The Need to Ban Competitive Sports Involving Preadolescent Children," letter, *Pediatrics* 55:4 (1975): 564–565. Recent condemnations of competition in organized youth sport could be seen as part of a larger condemnation of competition in society. Alfie Kohn is among the most ardent opponents of competition. See Kohn, *No Contest: The Case Against Competition*, rev. ed. (Boston: Houghton Mifflin, 1992). For a summary of the reforms, see Cesar R. Torres and Peter F. Hager, "De-emphasizing Competition in Organized Youth Sport: Misdirected Reforms and Misled Children," *Journal of the Philosophy of Sport* 34:2 (2007): 194–210.

9. R. Scott Kretchmar, *Practical Philosophy of Sport* (Champaign, IL: Human Kinetics, 1994), 99.

10. Ibid.

11. See Alasdair MacIntyre, *After Virtue*, 2nd ed. (Notre Dame, IN: University of Notre Dame Press, 1984), 187–196, for an in-depth discussion of social practices and the distinction between internal and external goods.

12. Kretchmar, *Practical Philosophy of Sport*, 100.

13. Ibid., 101–102.

14. For a discussion of these reforms, see Torres and Hager, "De-emphasizing Competition."

15. Robert L. Simon, "Internalism and Internal Values in Sport," *Journal of the Philosophy of Sport* 27 (2000): 7. See Simon's chapter in this volume for more on broad internalism.

16. Simon, "Internalism," 8.

17. Ibid., 8–9.

18. Nicholas Dixon, "Canadian Figure Skaters, French Judges, and Realism in Sport," *Journal of the Philosophy of Sport* 30:2 (2003): 110.

19. See Bernard Suits, *The Grasshopper: Games, Life, and Utopia* (Toronto: University of Toronto Press, 1978), 22–41; and William J. Morgan, *Leftist*

Theories of Sport: A Critique and Reconstruction (Chicago: University of Illinois Press, 1994), 210–234.

20. Cesar R. Torres, "What Counts as Part of a Game? A Look at Skills," *Journal of the Philosophy of Sport* 27 (2000): 84–90.

21. J. S. Russell, "Broad Internalism and the Moral Foundations of Sport," in *Ethics in Sport*, ed. William J. Morgan, 2nd ed. (Champaign, IL: Human Kinetics, 2007), 55.

22. Ibid.

23. See, for example, Dixon, "Canadian Figure Skaters"; William J. Morgan, "Moral Anti-Realism, Internalism, and Sport," *Journal of the Philosophy of Sport* 31:2 (2004): 161–183; Russell, "Broad Internalism"; Russell, "Are Rules All an Umpire Has to Work With?" *Journal of the Philosophy of Sport* 26 (1999): 27–49; Simon, "Internalism and Internal Values in Sport"; Cesar R. Torres, "What Is Wrong with Playing High?" *Journal of the Philosophy of Sport* 36:1 (2009): 1–21; and Cesar R. Torres and Peter F. Hager, "The Desirability of the Season Long Tournament: A Response to Finn," *Journal of the Philosophy of Sport* 38:1 (2011): 39–54.

24. William J. Morgan, "Metaethical Considerations of Sport," in *Ethics in Sport*, ed. William J. Morgan, 2nd ed. (Champaign, IL: Human Kinetics, 2007), 4.

25. Russell, "Broad Internalism," 56.

26. Ibid.

27. See Cesar R. Torres, "Furthering Interpretivism's Integrity: Bringing Together Ethics and Aesthetics," address delivered at the 39th annual congress of the International Association for the Philosophy of Sport, Rochester, NY, September 8–11, 2011.

28. See Jesús Ilundáin-Agurruza and Cesar R. Torres, "Embellishing the Ugly Side of the Beautiful Game," in *Soccer and Philosophy: Beautiful Thoughts on the Beautiful Game*, ed. Ted Richards (Chicago: Open Court, 2010), 185–196.

29. Torres, "Furthering Interpretivism's Integrity."

30. Russell, "Broad Internalism," 57. See also Nicholas Dixon, "On Winning and Athletic Superiority," *Journal of the Philosophy of Sport* 26 (1999): 10–26; Warren P. Fraleigh, *Right Actions in Sport* (Champaign, IL: Human Kinetics, 1984); R. S. Kretchmar, "From Test to Contest: An Analysis of Two Kinds of Counterpoint in Sport," *Journal of the Philosophy of Sport* 2 (1975): 23–30; Kathleen M. Pearson, "Deception, Sportsmanship, and Ethics," in *Philosophic Inquiry in Sport*, ed. William J. Morgan and Klaus V. Meier, 2nd ed. (Champaign, IL: Human Kinetics, 1995), 183–184; Robert L. Simon, *Fair Play: The Ethics of Sport*, 3rd ed. (Boulder, CO: Westview, 2010), 24–37; and

Cesar R. Torres and Douglas W. McLaughlin, "Indigestion? An Apology for Ties," *Journal of the Philosophy of Sport* 30:2 (2003): 144–158.

31. Russell, "Broad Internalism," 58.

32. See, for example, the World Health Assembly resolution WHA64.78, May 24, 2011, "Youth and Health Risks," http://www.who.int/mediacentre/factsheets/fs345/en/index.html.

33. United Nations, Youth: Frequently Asked Questions, http://social.un.org/index/Youth/FAQs.aspx.

34. Ibid.

35. Ibid. This is the conventional view on children. See also Tamar Schapiro, "What Is a Child?" *Ethics* 109:4 (1999): 734.

36. Schapiro, "What Is a Child?" 729.

37. Ibid., 730.

38. Ibid., 735–736.

39. Ibid., 737.

40. Russell, "Broad Internalism," 57.

41. Simon, *Fair Play*, 27.

42. Edwin J. Delattre, "Some Reflections on Success and Failure in Competitive Athletics," *Journal of the Philosophy of Sport*, 2 (1975), 135.

43. Ibid.

44. Ronald Dworkin, *Taking Rights Seriously* (Cambridge: Harvard University Press, 1977), 272.

45. Torres and Hager, "De-emphasizing Competition," 198.

46. Simon, *Fair Play*, 196.

47. Ibid., 195–197.

48. William J. Morgan, "Sport, Wholehearted Engagement, and the Good Life," *Sport, Ethics, and Philosophy* 4:3 (2010): 241.

49. Ibid., 242.

50. Ibid., 251.

51. Dennis Hemphill, "Sport-Smart Persons: A Practical Ethics for Coaching Young Athletes," in *The Ethics of Sport Coaching*, ed. Alun R. Hardman and Carwyn Jones (New York: Routledge, 2011), 107.

52. Morgan, "Sport, Wholehearted Engagement, and the Good Life," 241.

53. Ibid., 242.

54. MacIntyre, *After Virtue*, 190.

55. See Torres and McLaughlin, "Indigestion?" 148–150.

56. Ibid., 148.

57. Ibid.

58. Hemphill, "Sport-Smart Persons," 104.

Part Four: Coaching, Compliance, and the Law

1. Hart's own influential views as well as his critiques of earlier versions of positivism are most famously developed in his book, *The Concept of Law* (New York: Oxford University Press, 1997).

2. An example of a purported game that collapses under its own arbitrariness is "Calvinball" from the cartoon strip *Calvin and Hobbes.* In Calvinball, each player can change the rules simply by declaring them changed in some particular way. Consequently there are no rules and therefore no game.

3. As noted in the introduction to Part 1, readers interested in Dworkin's legal theory might start with chapters 2 to 4 of his book *Taking Rights Seriously* (Cambridge: Harvard University Press, 1978). A fuller treatment is provided in his book *Law's Empire* (Cambridge: Harvard University Press, 1988). His most recent views on ethics and interpretivism are developed in *Justice for Hedgehogs* (Cambridge: Harvard University Press, 2011). For an excellent overview and critical discussion of these positions in legal philosophy, see Jules Coleman and Jeffrie G. Murphy, *Philosophy of Law: An Introduction to Jurisprudence* (Boulder, CO: Westview, 1989).

Chapter 12

1. "The Olympic movement does its greatest work by instilling values of sport into the hearts and minds of young people everywhere. Sport is a universal language. It teaches us how to strive for excellence in all that we do. How to live in friendship and peace. How to respect ourselves, each other and the rules. Excellence, friendship and respect are the fundamental Olympic values. They anchor all our activities." Jacques Rogge, speech before the Chicago Council on Global Affairs and Economic Club of Chicago, 2007.

2. For a thorough discussion of the hurdles to asserting the right to a sports opportunity, see Welch Suggs, *A Place on the Team: The Triumph and Tragedy of Title IX* (Princeton: Princeton University Press, 2006); Susan K. Cahn, *Coming on Strong: Gender and Sexuality in Twentieth-Century Women's Sport* (Cambridge: Harvard University Press, 1995); Kristen Galles and Jocelyn Samuels, "In Defense of Title IX: Why Current Policies Are Required to Ensure Equality of Opportunity," 14 *Marq. L. Rev.* 11 (2003); and Nancy Hogshead-Makar and Andrew Zimbalist*, Equal Play: Title IX and Social Policy* (Philadelphia: Temple University Press, 2007).

3. The NCAA embraced the concept of sports as education when Walter Byers coined the term "student athlete." Walter Byers, *Unsportsmanlike Conduct: Exploiting College Athletes* (Ann Arbor: University of Michigan Press, 1995), 69.

4. Some have debated whether this equity principle may mean different things to different people and urge the following definition: that gender equity would make no unjustified distinctions based on gender. Robert Simon, "Gender Equity in Athletics," in *Sports Ethics: An Anthology*, ed. Jan Boxill (Malden, MA: Blackwell, 2003).

5. A. M. Jaggar, "Feminist Ethics," in *Encyclopedia of Ethics*, ed. L. Becker and C. Becker (New York: Garland, 1992).

6. Ellen Staurowsky et al., *Her Life Depends on It II: Sport, Physical Activity, and the Health and Well-Being of American Girls and Women* (2009), 13–15, 28, 32–33, 37, http://www.womenssportsfoundation.org/home/research /articles-and-reports/mental-and-physical-health/her-life-depends-on-it.

7. Ibid.

8. As reported by Tara Parker Pope, "As Girls Become Women, Sports Pay Dividends," *New York Times*, February 15, 2010, http://well.blogs.nytimes .com/2010/02/15/as-girls-become-women-sports-pay-dividends.

9. Alun R. Hardman and Carwyn Jones, eds., introduction to *The Ethics of Sports Coaching* (London: Routledge, 2011), 2.

10. Ellen Staurowsky and Erianne Weight, "Title IX Literacy: What Coaches Don't Know and Need to Find Out," *Journal of Intercollegiate Sport* (December 2011): 190–209.

11. 20 U.S.C. Sections 1681–1688. The law was renamed as Patsy T. Mink Equal Opportunity in Education in 2002, after the death of Representative Patsy Mink, one of the authors of the law. The law is still referred to as Title IX.

12. Senator Birch Bayh, address to the Secretary's Commission on Opportunity in Athletics, August 27, 2002, www.ed.gov/about/bdscomm /list/athletics/transcript-082702.pdf.

13. "More Hurdles to Clear: Women and Girls in Competitive Athletics," Clearinghouse Publication no. 63 (Washington, DC: U.S. Commission on Civil Rights, 1980), 3. The data from 2007 can be found at www.nfhs.org/custom/participation_figures/default.aspx.

14. Richard H. McAdams, "An Attitudinal Theory of Expressive Law," 79 *Or. L. Rev.* 339 (2000).

15. The company has numerous sites throughout the western and midwestern states of the US.

16. See, for example, Title IX Legal Manual, http://www.justice.gov/crt /about/cor/coord/ixlegal.php; *Breaking Down Barriers: A Legal Guide to Title IX and Athletic Opportunities*; and Kristen Galles and Jocelyn Samuels, "In Defense of Title IX: Why Current Policies Are Required to Ensure Equality of Opportunity," 14 *Marq. L. Rev.* 11 (Fall 2003).

17. The initial adoption of gender-neutral admission standards resulted in some men (who otherwise might have been admitted) being denied entry to

some institutions. For example, the 1964 *Report of the Virginia Commission for the Study of Educational Facilities* found that 21,000 women were denied admission to that state's higher education system—versus not one male applicant being rejected. When men had to compete for admission to institutions of higher education with a larger group of applicants, which included more women, many were denied admission. In contrast, Title IX does not reduce or eliminate athletic opportunities for men; it simply requires equality between the men's and women's programs, which can be done by expanding men's and women's opportunities.

18. S. Conf. Rec. No. 1026, 93d Cong., 2d sess. 421 (1974).

19. See 34 C.F.R. §§ 106.41 Athletic scholarships regulation: 34 CFR 106.37(c).

20. Ibid.

21. *Cohen v. Brown Univ.* (1997).

22. 44 Fed. Reg. at 71413 (1979). Interestingly, the three-part test was created, proposed, and promoted by the NCAA. At the time, males were the majority of students in higher education. They knew it would give schools a long time to add sports gradually, and it was presumed that females were less interested in playing sports than males were.

23. 44 Fed. Reg. at 71413 (1979). For ease of reading, I have substituted "female athletes" instead of the verbiage in the regulations that refer to protecting the "underrepresented gender." While a few women's colleges apply the test to men, the overwhelming majority of schools apply the test to women.

24. See *Chalenor v. University of North Dakota*, No. 00–3379ND (8th Cir. May 30, 2002); *Pederson v. Louisiana State University*, 213 F.3d 858, 879 (5th Cir. 2000); *Neal v. Board of Trustees of the California State Universities*, 198 F.3d 763, 770 (9th Cir. 1999); *Horner v. Kentucky High School Athletic Association*, 43 F.3d 265, 274–75 (6th Cir. 1994); *Kelley v. Board of Trustees, University of Illinois*, 35 F.3d 265, 270 (7th Cir. 1994), *cert. denied*, 513 U.S. 1128 (1995); *Cohen v. Brown University*, 991 F. 2d 888 (1st Cir. 1993) [*Cohen I*], and 101 F.3d 155, 170 (1st Cir. 1996), *cert. denied*, 520 U.S. 1186 (1997) (this case was before the 1st Circuit twice, first on Brown University's appeal of a preliminary injunction granted by the district court (*Cohen I*), and the second time after a trial on the merits [*Cohen II*]); *Roberts v. Colorado State Board of Agriculture*, 998 F.2d 824, 828 (10th Cir. 1993), *cert. denied*, 510 U.S. 1004 (1993); and *Williams v. School District of Bethlehem*, 998 F.2d 168, 171 (3d Cir. 1993).

25. Galles and Samuels, "In Defense of Title IX."

26. Nancy Hogshead-Makar, "Hurricane Warning Flags for All Olympic Sports: Biedieger v. Quinnipiac," *Boston Coll. L. R.*, Spring 2011. (Given these

small percentages of spots to play sports, it would be almost impossible for these schools to prove that they were meeting the interests and abilities of either men or women students.)

27. It is easy to presume that girls are uninterested in sports, particularly when women's athletic achievements are practically ignored by the mainstream media. See Michael A. Messner and Cheryl Cooky, "Gender in Televised Sports; News and Highlights Shows, 1989–2009," Center for Feminist Research, University of Southern California, June 2010. Researchers found that women's sports accounted for less than 2 percent of network news and ESPN Sportscenter. Although more women than ever participate in all levels of sports, coverage of their gender is drastically declining. In 2004 network affiliates dedicated 6.3 percent to women's sports. Last year it dropped to 1.6 percent.

28. See 34 C.F.R. §§ 106.

29. Galles and Samuels, "In Defense of Title IX."

30. John Cheslock, "Who's Playing College Sports? Trends in Participation," 2007, www.womenssportsfoundation.org/~/media/Files /Research%20Reports/Whos%20Playing%20College%20Sports/fullreport .pdf; "Intercollegiate Athletics: Recent Trends in Teams and Participants in National Collegiate Athletic Association Sports," www.gao.gov/new.items /d07535.pdf.

31. *Sports Sponsorship and Participation Rates Report,* 1981–82–2008–09 NCAA, www.ncaapublications.com/productdownloads/PR2010.pdf National Federation of State High School Federations, "High School Sports Participation Tops 7.6 Million, Sets Record," www.nfhs.org/content.aspx?id=4208&terms=sports+participation. NCAA sports sponsorship and participation rates: www.ncaapublications.com /Uploads/PDF/ParticipationRates2009c2f40573–60aa–4a08–874d–1aff 4192c5e4.pdf.

32. *Neal v. Bd. of Trs.* (1999).

33. Sex Discrimination Regulations: Hearings Before the Subcomm. on Postsecondary Educ. of the House Comm. on Educ. and Labor, 94th Cong. 1 (1975). Statement by Representative O'Hara, chair of the subcommittee.

34. 2003 clarification letter, paragraph 11.

35. *Chalenor v. Univ. of N.D.* (2002).

36. Ibid. An outside funder that contributes to a particular team is giving to either men or women, due to the sex-segregated nature of athletics. A funder could no more give microscopes to only the men in a classroom while the school gives women magnifying glasses.

37. Budgets are increasing at a feverish pace, particularly in Division I athletics, where growth has been over 7 percent per year over the last ten

years. Knight Commission on Intercollegiate Athletics, *College Sports 101*, www.collegesports101.knightcommission.org.

38. *Palmer v. Thompson*, 403 U.S. 217 (1971).

39. *Clark v. Thompson*, 206 F. Supp. 539 (S.D. Miss. 1962), aff'd per curiam, 313 F.2d 637 (5th Cir.).

40. *NCAA Gender Equity Report,* 2004–10, 37.

41. *NCAA Gender Equity Report,* 2009–10, 35.

42. Theoretically schools could offer one sport to men, football, with one hundred athletes, and seven sports to women, with soccer at twenty-five athletes, golf at five athletes, tennis at ten athletes, swimming at twenty athletes, cross-country at ten athletes, basketball at fifteen athletes, and lacrosse at fifteen athletes. Thereby the school would be choosing to offer one hundred athletics opportunities to males and one hundred to females.

43. Peter Keating, "The Silent Enemy of Men's Sports," http://espn.go.com /espnw/title-ix/7959799/the-silent-enemy-men-sports

44. *Oncale v. Sundowner Offshore Servs., Inc.,* 523 U.S. 75, 81 (1998). "A professional football player's working environment is not severely or pervasively abusive . . . if the coach smacks him on the buttocks as he heads onto the field, even if the same behavior would reasonably be experienced as abusive by the coach's secretary (male or female) back at the office."

45. Nancy Hogshead-Makar and Shelden E. Steinbach, "Intercollegiate Athletics' Unique Environments for Sexual Harassment Claims: Balancing the Realities of Athletics with Preventing Potential Claims," 13 *Marq. Sports L.J.* 173 (2003). Sexual harassment can, of course, occur in athletics in ways that are similar to other contexts. See, for example, *Norris v. Norwalk Pub. Schs.,* 124 F. Supp. 2d 791, 792–93 (D. Conn. 2000). A coach pinched a student athlete, grabbed her ponytail, and hit her legs and head.

46. Hogshead-Makar and Steinbach, "Intercollegiate Athletics' Unique Environments."

47. "Quid pro quo" sexual harassment occurs when a position, raise, continued employment, or promotion is conditioned on the receipt of sexual favors. "Hostile environment" sexual harassment occurs when a worker is subject to a pattern of exposure to unwanted sexual behavior from persons other than an employee's direct supervisor, and supervisors or managers do not take steps to stop such behavior. The objectionable actions must be frequent, severe, or pervasive.

48. See pages 210–211 for the United States Olympic Committee coaching ethics policy.

49. 36 U.S.C. 220501 *et seq.*

50. 36 U.S.C. 220522 (8) provides an equal opportunity to amateur athletes, coaches, trainers, managers, administrators, and officials to participate in

amateur athletic competition, without discrimination on the basis of race, color, religion, sex, age, or national origin, and with fair notice and opportunity for a hearing to any amateur athlete, coach, trainer, manager, administrator, or official before declaring the individual ineligible to participate.

51. "Recognizing, Reducing, and Responding to Misconduct in Sport: Creating Your Strategy," *USOC Safe Sport Handbook*. http://pressbox .teamusa.org.

52. Ibid. Sexual Misconduct:

(1) Any touching or nontouching sexual interaction that is (a) non-consensual or forced, (b) coerced or manipulated, or (c) perpetrated in an aggressive, harassing, exploitative or threatening manner;

(2) Any sexual interaction between an athlete and an individual with evaluative, direct or indirect authority. Such relationships involve an imbalance of power and are likely to impair judgment or be exploitative.

(3) Any act or conduct described as sexual abuse or misconduct under federal or state law (e.g. sexual abuse, sexual exploitation, rape).

Note: An imbalance of power is always assumed between a coach and an athlete.

Safe4Athletes.org was founded to address the need for a stronger response to the issue. Organizers noted that little punishment was meted out to coaches who violate ethical policies, and there was rarely a designated person to whom abused athletes could address their concerns, without fear of an all-powerful coach.

53. Mariah Burton Nelson and Deborah Brake, "Staying in Bounds," http://www.nacwaa.org/sites/default/files/images/Staying%20in%20 Bounds.pdf; see also the Women's Sports Foundation's policy: www.womenssportsfoundation.org/Content/Articles/Issues/Coaching /S/Sexual-Harassment—Sexual-Harassment-and-Sexual-Relationships -Between-Coaches-Other-Athletic-Personn.aspx.

54. See, e.g., University of Colorado at Boulder, https://www.cu.edu /policies/policies/HR_COI-Amorous.html.

55. *Jackson v. Birmingham* (2005).

56. *USA Today,* May 12, 2008, www.usatoday.com/sports/college /2008–05–12-titleix-cover_N.htm.

57. *USA Today,* May 12, 2008, www.usatoday.com/sports/college /2008–05–12-title-ix-qanda_N._htm.

58. Public Justice Foundation, 2008.

59. Nancy Hogshead-Makar, "Attitudes, Platitudes, and the Collegiate Sports Arms Race: Unsustainable Spending and Its Consequences for Olympic and Women's Sports," *Journal on Intercollegiate Sports* (2010).

60. When efforts were under way in Congress to exempt football and men's basketball from Title IX, the arguments were rebuffed. The implication was that sex discrimination is acceptable when someone profits from it and that money-making propositions should be given congressional absolution from Title IX. Sex Discrimination Regulation Hearings Before the House Subcommittee. on Post-Secondary Education of the Commitee on Education and Labor, 94th Cong. 166 (1975). Statement by Representative Mink.

61. Twenty-two school athletic departments in the country are operating at a profit. Knight Commission on Intercollegiate Athletics, *Restoring the Balance: Dollars, Values, and the Future of College Sports* (Miami, FL: John S. and James L. Knight Foundation, 2010), www.knightcommissionmedia.org/images/restoring_the_balance_2010.pdf.

62. Ibid.

Chapter 13

1. 1376 P.2d 406 (Ore. 1962).

2. Glenn M. Wong, *Essentials of Sports Law,* 4th ed. (Santa Barbara, CA: Praeger, 2010).

3. 613 N.Y.S.2d 660 (N.Y. App. Div. 1994). See also *Larson v. Cuba Rushford Central School District,* 912 N.Y.S.2d 827 (N.Y. App. 2010) (coach's failure to provide proper supervision of cheerleading activities unreasonably increases risks of injury to participants and creates potential negligence liability to cheerleader injured during practice session).

4. 2011WL2329216 (La. App. 2011).

5. 301 N.W.2d 1 (Mich. Ct. App. 1980).

6. 239 So.2d 456 (La. Ct. App. 1970).

7. *Gahan v. Mineola Union Free Sch. Dist.,* 660 N.Y.S.2d 144 (N.Y. App. Div. 1997).

8. 568 N.E.2d 914 (Ill. App. Ct. 1991).

9. 600 So. 2d 1389 (La. Ct. App. 1992).

10. 2006 WL 1587101 (Cal. Ct. App. 2006).

11. 679 N.W.2d 198 (Neb. 2004).

12. 75 P.3d 30 (Cal. 2003).

13. *Wilson v. O'Gorman High School,* 2008 WL 2571833 (D. S.D. 2008) (concluding that "the South Dakota Supreme Court would not adopt the Kahn standard, but rather would apply the general negligence standard" in connection with coach's alleged negligent instruction and supervision of high school gymnast during practice).

14. *Morales v. Beacon City Sch. Dist.*, 44 A.D.3d 724, 726 (N.Y. Sup. Ct. 2007) (holding that "plaintiff raised a triable issue of fact as to whether the coach failed to properly train and supervise the plaintiff, and whether this failure unreasonably increased the plaintiff's risk of injury").

15. *Avenoso v. Mangan*, 2006 WL 490340 at *6 (Conn. Super.) ("[T]he normal expectation of young children and their parents is that adult coaches will conduct themselves in such a way as to avoid injury to the children. . . . In short, the normal expectations of those involved, in the coaching of young children, including the children and their parents, are more consistent with a standard of care that would require coaches to avoid acting negligently.")

16. 884 N.E.2d 122 (Ill. 2008).

17. 42 U.S.C. § 14501, et seq.

18. 2006 WL 490340 (Conn. Super.)

19. N.H. Rev. Stat. §508:17.

20. M.G. L. A. 231, § 85V.

21. *Welch v. Young*, 950 N.E.2d 1283 (Ind. App. 2011) (coach who is an employee of Indiana public high school is immune from negligence liability while acting within the scope of his employment pursuant to Indiana Code § 34–13–3–5[b]).

22. 450 N.W.2d 226 (S.D.1990). See also *Schnarrs v. Girard Bd. of Education*, 858 N.E.2d 1258, 1265 (Ohio App. 2006) (coach's "determination to use male players during girls' basketball practices demonstrated a positive exercise of judgment and a considered adoption of a particular course of conduct to achieve an object, viz., improving skills for upcoming games. Thus, the school district cannot be held liable, because [the coach], by virtue of his position, had the discretion to plan and conduct practices."); *Starkey v Hartzler*, 1997 WL 197202 (Ohio App.) (coach immune from negligence in connection with discretionary discipline that injures eighth grade football player).

23. 741 So. 2d 207 (Miss. 1999).

24. In a dissenting opinion, Justice Banks argued: "In *Womble v. Singing River Hosp.*, 618 So.2d 1252 (Miss.1993), this Court removed a then relatively recently discovered blanket immunity for 'discretionary' medical decisions. We concluded that medical treatment decisions, however discretionary, were not governmental policy decisions and, therefore, no immunity attached. Womble put medical personnel back on an even footing with all other governmental personnel, where they had always been and where they belonged. Today's decision elevates athletic coaches to the same perch from which we removed medical personnel. . . . In my view the football coach and trainer in the instant case owed a duty of reasonable care to the player, the

breach of which should incur liability from which there is no immunity. That is not to say that they were, in fact, negligent in breach of their duty. Perhaps what they did was fully in keeping with reasonable care under the circumstances. All I say is that there should be no immunity."

25. 867 So.2d 188, 193 (2003). See also *Covington County Sch. Dist. V. Magee,* 29 So.3d 1 (Miss. 2010) (public school district immunized from negligence liability relating to the heatstroke death of a high school football player during practice because the coach's decision to hold practice under the weather conditions is a discretionary act).

26. *Elston v. Howland Local Schools,* 865 N.E.2d 845, 852 (Ohio 2007).

27. 736 A.2d 1229 (N.H. 1999).

28. 65 S.W.3d 510 (2002).

29. 2010Vt. Super. Ct. LEXIS 1.

30. 574 S.E.2d 258 (2003).

31. 769 N.E.2d 738 (2002).

32. 758 P.2d 968 (Wash. 1988).

33. *Zides v. Quinnipiac Univ.,* 2006 WL 463182 (Conn. Super.) (coach negligently provides defective L-screen that did not adequately protect pitcher from risk of severe head injury during batting practice).

34. *Sorey v. Kellet,* 849 F.2d 960 (5th Cir. 1988) (a college head football coach's general authority over the football program provides qualified immunity under Mississippi law from negligence liability in exercising discretionary functions); *Lennon v. Petersen,* 624 So. 2d 171 (Ala. 1993) (a college head football coach has qualified immunity under Alabama law).

35. *Zides v. Quinnipiac Univ.,* 2006 WL 463182 (Conn. Super.) (refusing to enforce liability waiver which does not expressly state that college baseball assumes risk of injury caused by university or its coaches' negligence).

36. 683 N.E.2d 706 (Mass. App. 1997).

37. 924 N.E.2d 906 (Ohio App. 2009).

38. 131 P.3d 383 (Cal. 2006).

39. 795 N.E.2d 1170 (2003).

40. 989 F.2d 1360 (3d Cir. 1993).

41. 850 P.2d 401 (Or. Ct. App. 1993). See also *Searles v. Trustees of St. Joseph's College,* 695 A.2d 1206 (Me. 1997) (coach may be liable for insisting that a student athlete with knee problems play basketball contrary to the medical advice of the college's athletic trainer).

42. 108 F.3d 1388 (10th Cir. 1997).

43. Complaint, *Gathers v. Loyola Marymount Univ.* (Los Angeles Cal. Super. Ct., filed April 20, 1990) (No. C759027). In defense of these claims, issues were raised regarding whether Gathers was taking his medication in

the prescribed dosage and/or engaging in pregame running on his own initiative to reduce its side effects of making him feel sluggish and preventing him from playing to his full potential.

Chapter 14

1. Robyn L. Jones, "How Can Educational Concepts Inform Sports Coaching?" in *The Sports Coach as Educator,* ed. Robyn L. Jones (London: Routledge, 2006), 1–3.

2. Felicity Wikeley and Kate Bullock, "Coaching as an Educational Relationship," *in Sports Coach as Educator,* 14. "Coaches are educators in that their role is to work with one or more athletes in order to move the latter's performance to an improved level." Stanley D. Eitzen, "Social Control and Sport," in *Handbook of Sports Studies,* ed. Jay Coakley and Eric Dunning (London: Sage, 2000), 376.

3. Eitzen, "Social Control and Sport," 376.

4. Sigmund Loland, "The Normative Aims of Coaching," *in Sports Coach as Educator,* 19.

5. Alun R. Hardman and Carwyn Jones, eds., introduction to *The Ethics of Sports Coaching* (London: Routledge, 2011), 2.

6. Ibid.

7. Loland, "Normative Aims of Coaching," 19. Coaching "affects the attitudes, values and behaviours of athletes towards each other how they play sport. Most, if not all, coaching exchanges have a moral dimension to them."

8. Hardman and Jones, introduction, 2.

9. Alun R. Hardman and Carwyn Jones, "Sports Coaching and Virtue Ethics," in *Ethics of Sports Coaching,* 2.

10. Stanley D. Eitzen and George H. Sage, *Sociology of North American Sport,* 8th ed. (Boulder, CO: Paradigm, 2009), 53.

11. Loland, "Normative Aims of Coaching," 19.

12. Hardman and Jones, introduction, 2.

13. Robyn L. Jones and Mike Wallace, "The Coach as 'Orchestrator,'" in *Sports Coach as Educator*, 55.

14. Ibid.

15. Ibid., 71 (noting calls for shared leadership).

16. Eitzen, "Social Control and Sport," 376–377 ("with few exceptions, coaches impose their will over athletes").

17. Mike McNamee, "Celebrating Trust: Virtues and Rules," in *Ethics of Sports Coaching,* 35.

18. Eitzen and Sage, *Sociology of North American Sport*, 58.

19. McNamee, "Celebrating Trust," 35.

20. Ibid.

21. See, for example, *Kavanagh v. Trustees of Boston Univ.*, 795 N.E.2d 1170, 1179 (Mass. 2003) (stating that "a coach's ability to inspire players to compete aggressively is one of a coach's important attributes"); *Kahn v. East Side Union High Sch. Dist.*, 75 P.3d 30, 43 (Cal. 2003) (finding that in his or her role as an instructor, a coach must challenge students to achieve their athletic potential, even if this may involve pushing them beyond their existing capacities).

22. See, for example, *Tennessee Secondary Sch. Athletic Assoc. v. Brentwood Academy,* 127 S.Ct. 2489, 2495 (2007) (noting the influence that coaches exert over middle school students can negatively affect "informed and reliable decision making").

23. National Collegiate Athletic Association, *Examining the Student-Athlete Experience Through the NCAA GOALS and SCORE Studies,* January 13, 2011, 12.

24. Ibid., 10.

25. Timothy Davis, "Student-Athlete Prospective Economic Interests: Contractual Dimensions," *Thurgood Marshall Law Review* 19 (1994): 585, 599.

26. Harry M. Cross, "The College Athlete and the Institution," *Law and Contemporary Problems* 38 (1973): 151, 155.

27. Davis, "Student-Athlete Prospective Economic Interests," 599.

28. Barry Temkin, "Suit Could Chill Recruiters' Pledges," *Chicago Tribune,* September 5, 1993, 20C.

29. Ibid.

30. Davis, "Student-Athlete Prospective Economic Interests," 601.

31. Heather J. Lawrence, Anastasios Kaburakis, and Christina Merckx, "NCAA Division I Recruiting, Identifying, and Mitigating Institutional Risk Associated with the Official Visit," 18 *J. Legal Aspects Sport* 18 (2008): 89, 92–93.

32. *Southern Methodist University, NCAA Public Infractions Report,* February 24, 1987, 3.

33. See University of Kansas, *NCAA Public Infractions Report,* October 12, 2006; Millersville University of Pennsylvania, *NCAA Public Infractions Report,* January 19, 2006.

34. The NCAA Division I manual defines a secondary violation as a "violation that is isolated or inadvertent in nature, provides or is intended to provide only minimal recruiting, competitive or other advantage and does not include any significant impermissible benefit." National Collegiate Athletic Association, Article 19.02.2.1, *2011–12 NCAA Division I Manual* (hereafter NCAA Manual), 319. All other violations are considered major violations. Article 19.02.2.2, NCAA Manual.

35. For an example of such an infractions case, see NCAA Division I Committee on Infractions, *California State Polytechnic University, Pomona, Public Infractions Report,* December 16, 2011.

36. NCAA rules prohibit a coach and other institutional representatives from directly or indirectly giving or offering to give financial or other benefits to a prospective student athlete and his or her relatives and friends unless the NCAA specifically permits the offering or giving of such benefits. Article 13.2.1, NCAA Manual.

37. NCAA Division I Committee on Infractions, *Baylor University, Public Infractions Report,* June 23, 2005.

38. Ibid., 2–3.

39. Article 19.7 Restitution, NCAA Manual.

40. For an example of a case involving the negative implications for student athletes of a coach's violations of NCAA recruiting rules, see NCAA Division I Infractions Appeals Committee, *University of Memphis, Public Infractions Report,* March 22, 2010. There the NCAA deemed a student athlete recipient of the improper recruiting-related inducements as ineligible to participate in intercollegiate competition. The NCAA required the student athlete rendered ineligible to participate in intercollegiate athletics to apply for reinstatement in order to have her eligibility restored.

41. NCAA Division I Committee on Infractions, *Boise State University, Public Infractions Report,* September 13, 2011.

42. Ibid., 60.

43. NCAA Manual, 45.

44. Article 10.1 Unethical Conduct, NCAA Manual, 45.

45. Articles 15.3.3.1 and 15.3.3.1.2, NCAA Manual; see also Doug Segrest, "The One-Year Itch: Some Athletes Lose Their Single-Year Grants to Better Players," *Birmingham News,* October 23, 2011.

46. Michelle B. Hosick, "Multiyear Scholarship Rule Narrowly Upheld," www.ncaa.org/wps/wcm/connect/public/NCAA/Resources/Latest+News/2012/February/Multiyear+scholarship+rule+narrowly+upheld.

47. Alfred C. Yen, "Early Scholarship Offers and the NCAA," *Boston College Law Review* 52 (2011): 585.

48. Ibid., 606.

49. Ibid., 606–607.

50. Ibid., 607.

51. See Jamie U. Nomura, "Refereeing the Recruiting Game: Applying Contract Law to Make the Inter-Collegiate Recruiting Process Fair," *University Hawaii Law Review* 32 (2009): 275.

52. See, for example, Bruce Pascoe, "UA Rescinds Scholarship Offer," *Arizona Daily Star,* September 30, 2008 (examining allegations that the

University of Arizona revoked a scholarship offer to a recruit); Jeff Call, "BYU Football: Cougars Rescind Scholarship Offer to Hawaiian Prep Star," *Desert News,* January 29, 2010 (one week prior to the date when an NLI could be signed, BYU allegedly revoked a scholarship offer to football recruit Kona Schwenke, because he visited Notre Dame).

53. See Mike McGeeney, "Freshman Sues Davidson over Retracted Scholarship," *Amherst Student News,* http://amherststudent-archive.amherst .edu/current/news/view.php?year=2002–2003&issue=12&section=news &article=04.

54. See Nomura, "Refereeing the Recruiting Game," 275 (providing a detailed discussion of the claims an athlete would likely assert and how a court would like rule).

55. 985 F.Supp. 782, 796 (N.D. Ill. 1997).

56. *Accord, Federation Internationale Du Sport Universitaire v. Greater Buffalo Athletic Corporation,* 1994 WL 411908 at *2 (W.D.N.Y. 1994).

57. See *Weaverton Transport Leasing, Inc. v. Moran,* 834 A.2d 1169, 1174 (Pa. Super. Ct. 2003).

58. *Smith v. University of Hawaii,* Circuit Court of the First Circuit, Hawaii, Civil No. 08–1–0250–02 (Feb. 5, 2008).

59. Ibid., 10–11.

60. Fred Lewis, "Football Player's Case Costs Thousands," *Star Advertiser,* June 12, 2011.

61. Ibid.

62. 985 F.Supp. 782, 796 (N.D. Ill. 1997). Although it did not involve a promissory estoppel claim, the court in *Fortay v. University of Miami,* 1994 WL 62319 (D. N.J. Feb. 17, 1994) lends support for such a claim. There the court held that oral promises made by a coach during his recruitment of a student-athlete could provide a basis for imposing liability on an institution. Fortay alleged the coaches promised to provide guidance that would enable the athlete to develop his football skills, not to recruit other quarterbacks, and that Fortay would be the starting quarterback by his third year.

63. *Williams v. University of Cincinnati,* 752 N.E.2d 367, 377 (Ohio Ct. Cl. 2001).

64. See Jonathan D. Bateman, "When the Numbers Don't Add Up: Oversigning in College Football," *Marquette Sports Law Review* 22 (2011): 7 (discussing oversigning in detail).

65. Hannah Karp and Darren Everson, "SEC Coaches Defend Oversigning," *Wall Street Journal,* March 1, 2011.

66. Hannah Karp and Darren Everson, "Alabama's Unhappy Castoffs," *Wall Street Journal,* September 24, 2010 (reporting that some athletes have

complained that they were forced to take medical red shirts even though the athletes were not so incapacitated that they could not compete).

67. John Infante, "Ovesigning and NCAA Federalism," www.ncaa.org/blog /2011/06/oversigning-and-ncaa-federalism (describing the practice of oversigning as unethical in part because a coach is making a promise that he can't keep).

68. Bateman, "When the Numbers Don't Add Up," 7.

69. Karp and Everson, "Alabama's Unhappy Castoffs."

70. J. Bernard Machen, "Florida President: Grayshirting Is Morally Reprehensible Practice," SI.com, February 1, 2011.

71. Gregg Doyle, "Bad Guys Utilize Over-signing, and It Has to Stop," CBSSports.com, April 8, 2010.

72. Bateman, "When the Numbers Don't Add Up," 7.

73. Ibid.

74. Article 13.9.2.3, 2012–13, NCAA Manual.

75. NCAA Division I Proposed Bylaw Amendments 13.9.2.3; 15.5.1.10.1 (2011).

About the Contributors

Robert L. Simon (editor) is Bartlett Professor of Philosophy at Hamilton College in Clinton, New York. He is the author (with Norman E. Bowie) of *The Individual and the Political Order*, and sole author of *Neutrality and the Academic Ethics* and *Fair Play*. He is editor of the *Blackwell Guide to Social and Political Philosophy* and the author of numerous articles in political philosophy and ethical issues in sports. He is a past president of the International Association for the Philosophy of Sport and received its Distinguished Scholar Award in 2004. Simon coached men's golf at Hamilton College from 1987 to 2001; several of his teams were nationally ranked in Division III of the NCAA.

———

Jan Boxill is senior lecturer and director of the Parr Center for Ethics at UNC–Chapel Hill. She is editor of *Sports Ethics* and *Issues in Race and Gender*, and has written articles on ethics in sports, Title IX, and affirmative action. Currently, she is working on a book, *Front Porch Ethics: The Moral Significance of Sport*. Jan played basketball at UCLA and coached at both the high school and the collegiate level, serving as the head women's basketball coach at the University of Tampa. She has served as the public address announcer for women's basketball and field hockey, and now serves as the radio color analyst for women's basketball at UNC.

Timothy Davis, John W. and Ruth H. Turnage Professor of Law at Wake Forest, is one the country's best known sports law scholars. He has coauthored a casebook on sports law, *Sports Law and Regulation*, and coauthored *The Business of Sports Agents*. Tim serves on the review board for the U.S. Anti-Doping Agency and is a member of the advisory board for the National Sports Law Institute.

Jeffrey P. Fry is an associate professor in the Department of Philosophy and Religious Studies at Ball State University, Muncie, Indiana. Jeff has served as associate editor and book review editor of the *Journal of the Philosophy of*

Sport and has been a member of the editorial board of *Sport, Ethics, and Philosophy: Official Journal of the British Philosophy of Sport Association.*

Peter F. Hager is currently an associate professor of sports studies at the College at Brockport, State University of New York, where he has taught since 2000. Peter has coauthored articles in the *Journal of the Philosophy of Sport* and *Journal of Physical Education, Recreation, and Dance* with Cesar Torres.

Mark Hamilton is a graduate of Wittenberg University, where he studied philosophy and religion and was captain of the baseball team. He has been teaching philosophy at Ashland University since 1981 and has also served as the assistant baseball coach. Hamilton teaches courses in ethics, philosophy of religion, and general philosophy, as well as a popular course in sports ethics. He is also a teaching pastor/elder in Providence Church, near Ashland, Ohio. He has published numerous journal and magazine articles as well as chapters in books, including *Baseball and Philosophy, Poker and Philosophy, Basketball and Philosophy,* and *Theology, Ethics, and Transcendence in Sport.*

Doug Hochstetler, associate professor of kinesiology, teaches at Penn State University, Lehigh Valley. His research interests include sports ethics, meaning, and physical activity, as well as historical aspects of sportsmanship and fair play. He has published in a variety of disciplinary journals, both theoretical and applied.

Nancy Hogshead-Makar, a former Olympian and Gold Medal winner, is one of the nation's foremost exponents of Title IX of the Education Amendments of 1972, particularly in the context of intercollegiate sports. She has testified before Congress numerous times on the topic of gender equity in athletics, has written numerous scholarly and lay articles, and has been a frequent guest on national news programs, including *60 Minutes, Good Morning America,* CNN, and ESPN. In 2007 *Sports Illustrated* magazine listed her as one of the most influential people in the thirty-five-year history of Title IX. She is the coauthor of *Equal Play, Title IX, and Social Change.*

Scott Kretchmar is professor of exercise and sports science at Penn State University. He has been editor of the *Journal of the Philosophy of Sport* and has authored a popular text in the philosophy of sport: *Practical Philosophy of Sport and Physical Activity.* He has written numerous articles on ethics, the nature of sports, and the operation of human intelligence in physical activity. He is founding editor of the *Journal of Intercollegiate Sport.*

Matthew J. Mitten is a professor of law and the director of the National Sports Law Institute and the LL.M. (Masters in Law) in sports law program for foreign lawyers at Marquette University Law School (Milwaukee). He teaches courses in amateur sports law, professional sports law, and torts as well as a sports sponsorship workshop. He has authored *Sports Law in the United States*, coauthored *Sports Law and Regulation: Cases, Materials, and Problems*, and has published several articles in leading law reviews and medical journals. He has presented at more than one hundred law or medical conferences throughout the United States and in Australia, Canada, China, England, Korea, and Turkey.

William J. Morgan is a professor in the Division of Occupational Science at USC. He has served as editor and published extensively in the *Journal of the Philosophy of Sport*. He has authored two books, *Why Sports Morally Matter* and *Leftist Theories of Sport: A Critique and Reconstruction*, and edited several anthologies focusing on the philosophy of sports and sports ethics.

Heather Reid is professor and chair of the Philosophy Department at Morningside College in Sioux City, Iowa. Reid's first book, *The Philosophical Athlete*, was published in 2002. In 2010, while a visiting scholar at the University of Rome, she completed her new book, *Athletics and Philosophy in Ancient Greece and Rome: Contests of Virtue*.

J. S. Russell chairs the Department of Philosophy at Langara College in Vancouver, British Columbia. He has published extensively in philosophy of sports, philosophy of law, social and political philosophy, and applied ethics. He has been editor of the *Journal of the Philosophy of Sport* since 2006.

Cesar R. Torres is a professor in the Department of Kinesiology, Sport Studies, and Physical Education at the College at Brockport, State University of New York. A philosopher and historian of sports, he has published over forty pieces in peer-reviewed journals and edited collections and another forty-plus pieces in newspapers and magazines. With an interest in the diffusion of sports philosophy in the Spanish-speaking world, he authored *Gol de media cancha: Conversaciones para disfrutar el deporte plenamente*, edited *Niñez, deporte y actividad física: Reflexiones filosóficas sobre una relación compleja*, and coedited *¿La pelota no dobla? Ensayos filosóficos en torno al fútbol*. He is associate editor of the *Journal of the Philosophy of Sport* and reviews editor of *Soccer and Society*.

Index